ECONOMIC DEVELOPMENT FINANCE

In memory of Abe, Janet, and Amy

ECONOMIC DEVELOPMENT FINANCE

KARL F. SEIDMAN
MASSACHUSETTS INSTITUTE OF TECHNOLOGY

SAGE Publications
Thousand Oaks ■ London ■ New Delhi

For information:

Sage Publications, Inc.
2455 Teller Road
Thousand Oaks, California 91320
E-mail: order@sagepub.com

Sage Publications Ltd.
1 Oliver's Yard
55 City Road
London EC1Y 1SP
United Kingdom

Sage Publications India Pvt. Ltd.
B-42, Panchsheel Enclave
Post Box 4109
New Delhi 110 017 India

Printed in the United States of America

Library of Congress Cataloging-in-Publication Data

Seidman, Karl F.
Economic development finance / Karl F. Seidman.
        p. cm.
Includes bibliographical references and index.
ISBN 0-7619-2709-3 (cloth)
    1. Economic development—Finance. 2. Business enterprises—United States—Finance. 3. Real property—United States—Finance. I. Title.
HD75.S43 2004
338.4′3—dc22   2004007120

This book is printed on acid-free paper.

04   05   06   07   10   9   8   7   6   5   4   3   2   1

Acquisitions Editor:	Al Bruckner
Editorial Assistant:	MaryAnn Vail
Production Editor:	Diane S. Foster
Copy Editor:	Robert Holm
Typesetter:	C&M Digitals (P) Ltd.
Proofreader:	Eileen Delaney
Indexer:	Will Ragsdale
Cover Designer:	Edgar Abarca

Contents

List of Tables   xiii

List of Exhibits   xvii

List of Boxes   xix

List of Figures   xxi

Preface   xxiii

Part I: Introduction   1

1. Capital Availability and Economic Development   3
    The Growing Field of Economic Development Finance   3
    The Purpose and Design of This Book   4
    The Role of Finance in the
        Economic Development Process   5
    Capital Availability and Capital Market Imperfections   7
        Market Imperfections and
            Capital Supply Gaps in Practice   9
        Implications of Market Imperfections
            for Economic Development Finance   15
    A Framework for Expanding Capital Availability   17

Part II: The Basics of Business Finance   21

2. Financing Business Enterprises
    The Role of Equity and Debt   23
        Equity Financing   24
            Terms and Issues in Equity Financing   24
            Advantages and Disadvantages of Equity   26
        Debt Financing   27
            Terms and Issues in Debt Financing   27
            Advantages and Disadvantages of Debt   32
        Hybrid Financing   33
        Financing and the Stages of Firm Development   33
            Data on Small Business Capital Sources   34
        The Use of Equity and Debt in Hypothetical Firms   37
        Looking Ahead   39

3. An Introduction to Business Financial Statements 41
    Accounting Concepts and Accrual Accounting 41
    Financial Statements: The Balance Sheet 44
    Financial Statements: The Income Statement 50
    Connecting the Balance Sheet and Income Statement 53
    Financial Statements: The Cash Flow Statement 54
        Constructing a Cash Flow Statement 55
    Using Financial Statements 58

4. Analyzing Business Financial Statements 60
    A Framework for Firm Evaluation 60
        Assessing Economic Development Benefits 61
        Business Plan Evaluation 63
        Analyzing Financial Condition and Performance 65
        Financial Projections 65
    Analysis of Individual Financial Statements 65
        Insights From the Balance Sheet 65
        Knowledge From the Income Statement 69
        Analyzing the Cash Flow Statement 72
    Ratio Analysis 74
        Profitability and Operating Results 74
        Short-Term Liquidity and Cash Needs 76
        Capital Structure and Debt Capacity 77
        Common Size Financial Statements 78
    Beyond Ratio Analysis 81
    The Final Test: Preparing and
        Evaluating Financial Projections 82
    Analyzing Crystal Clear Window Company 84
        Preparing a Cash Flow Statement 84
        Determining Debt Service Coverage 87
        Ratio Analysis 87
        Implications of the Analysis 89

5. Working Capital Finance 91
    The Importance of Working Capital Finance 91
        Three Meanings of Working Capital 91
        Business Uses of Working Capital 92
        Permanent and Cyclical Working Capital 94
    Forms of Working Capital Financing 95
        Line of Credit 95
        Accounts Receivable Financing 97
        Factoring 98
        Inventory Financing 99
        Term Loan 100
    Sources of Working Capital for Small Businesses 101
    Underwriting Issues in Working Capital Financing 102

Case Study: Crystal Clear Window Company 103
   Introduction 103
   Firm History 105
   Operations 106
   The Use of Aluminum Windows 106
   Financial Status 107
   Recommendation 108
   Assignment 108

6. Fixed Asset Financing 111
   Fixed Assets and Business Operations 111
   Differences Between Fixed Asset and
      Working Capital Finance 112
      Implications for Firms 113
      Implications for Lenders 113
   Fixed Asset Debt Instruments 115
      Term Loans 115
      Mortgage Loans 116
      Leasehold Improvement Loans 117
      Bonds 118
      Leasing 118
   Sources of Fixed Asset Financing 120
      Fixed Asset Financing Gaps 122
   Case Study: Phoenix Forge 123
      Introduction 123
      Economic Conditions in the Youngstown Region 123
      Summary of Phoenix Forge Business Plan 124
      Phoenix Forge Financial Plan 129
      Financial Projections 130
      Assignment 130

7. Real Estate Finance 133
   The Real Estate Development and Finance Process 134
      Predevelopment Phase 134
      Construction and Development Phase 136
      Occupancy and Management Phase 137
      Financing Process 138
   Real Estate Financial Statements 138
      Development Budget 139
      Operating Pro Forma 142
      Determining Supportable Debt and Equity 144
   Real Estate Debt Instruments 146
      Predevelopment Financing 146
      Construction Loans 148
      Permanent Mortgage Loans 148
      Mini-Perm Loans 149

	Bridge Loans	149
	Underwriting Real Estate Debt	149
Sources of Real Estate Financing		
	and Capital Availability Problems	151
	Financing Gaps for Development Projects	152
Case Study: City Plaza		153
	Introduction	153
	Development Plan and Budget	154
	Financing Plan	155

Part III: Policies to Perfect Private Capital Markets   **159**

8.	Loan Guarantee Programs	161
	Loan Guarantees and Capital Availability	162
	The Myriad Forms of Guarantees	162
	Advantages and Disadvantages of Guarantees	164
	Valuing Loan Guarantees	165
	Small Business Administration 7(a) Program	166
	State Loan Guarantee Programs	170
	Capital Access Programs	172
	Issues in the Design and Management	
	of Guarantee Programs	174
	Guarantee Program Policy Levers	175
	Program Challenges and Best Practices	177
	Case Study: Massachusetts Emerging Technology Fund	178
	Background	179
	The ETF Legislation	180
	Designing the New Program	181

9.	Bank Regulations and Development Banks	184
	The Critical Role of Banks in	
	Economic Development Finance	184
	The Community Reinvestment Act	185
	History and Overview of the	
	Community Reinvestment Act	185
	Using CRA to Expand Capital Availability	189
	CRA's Impact on Bank Lending	193
	Critiques of CRA	197
	New Challenges for the Community Reinvestment Act	198
	Community Reinvestment and the Insurance Industry	200
	Bank Community Development Corporations	201
	Bank CDC Regulations	201
	Bank CDC Experience	202
	Commercial Banks as Development Finance Institutions	205
	Challenges to Creating and Operating	
	a Commercial Bank	209
	Special Operating Requirements	210

Part IV: Institutional Models for Economic Development Finance   **215**

10.	Revolving Loan Funds	217
	The Revolving Loan Fund Model	217
	Revolving Loan Funds' Characteristics and Performance	221
	RLF Characteristics	221
	RLF Performance	224
	Design Issues for Revolving Loan Funds	227
	Targeting Policy	227
	Financial Policies	228
	Capital Policies	230
	Underwriting Criteria	230
	Development Services	231
	Relationship Building	233
	Management Challenges and Best Practices	235
	Best Practices in RLF Management	236
11.	Venture Capital and Equity Investment Funds	240
	The Private Venture Capital Industry	241
	Fund-raising	242
	Investing	243
	Exiting Investments	246
	Implications for Development Finance	247
	The SBIC and SSBIC Programs	248
	State Government Venture Capital Policy	250
	Community Development Venture Capital	256
	Industry Profile	257
	Industry Trends and Challenges	257
	Addressing Venture Capital Challenges	259
	Strategy Challenges	260
	Operating Challenges	261
	Capitalization Challenges	263
12.	Community-Based Financial Institutions	267
	Community Development Loan Funds	268
	CDLF Characteristics	269
	CDLF Financing Roles	271
	CDLF Operating Challenges and Needs	273
	Community Development Credit Unions	277
	CDCU Characteristics	279
	CDCU Lending and Development Roles	281
	Banking Services for the Poor	282
	Small Business Lending	285
	CDCU Operating Challenges and Needs	287
13.	Microenterprise Finance	292
	Three Models of Microenterprise Finance	293

Peer Group Lending 293
Individual Lending Model 294
Training-Led Model 295
An Overview of the U.S. Industry and Its Performance 297
Program Performance 299
Program Outcomes 301
The Economic Development
Role of Microenterprise Development 303
Design Issues and Management Challenges 304
Best Practices in Microenterprise
Finance and Development 307
Marketing 307
Training 308
Technical Assistance Services 309
Case Study: Lawrence Working Capital 310
Background 310
Lawrence Working Capital Program 311
Lawrence Hispanic Business Community 312
New Business Development Programs 313
Assignment 313

Part V: Federal and Municipal Government Finance Tools 317

14. Federal Economic Development Programs 319
The Uses of Federal Economic Development Programs 319
Small Business Administration 321
Programs Delivered by Banks and
Financial Institutions 321
Programs Delivered Through
SBA-Approved Intermediaries 323
Department of Housing and Urban Development 324
Community Development Block Grants 324
Section 108 Program 326
Economic Development Initiative 326
Community Development Financial
Institution (CDFI) Fund 328
CDFI Certification 328
Core/Intermediary Program 328
Small and Emerging CDFI Assistance (SECA) Program 330
Native American CDFI Technical Assistance Program 330
New Market Tax Credit Program 331
Economic Development Administration 331
Planning Grants 332
Local Technical Assistance Grants 332
Public Works and Economic Development Program 333

Economic Adjustment Assistance Program 333
Funding Process 333
Health and Human Services 334
Case Study: Financing an Inner-City Supermarket 334
Northside 335
Supermarket Project 335
Financing Plan 339

15. Municipal Finance Tools 341
An Overview of Municipal Debt 341
Economic Development Uses of Municipal Debt 343
Industrial Development Bonds 343
IDB Case Study: New Boston Seafood Center 346
Tax-Increment Financing 348
The Tax-Increment Financing Process 349
Economic Development Uses of TIF 351
Issues in TIF Debt Financing 352
Assessment District Financing and
Business Improvement Districts 354
Business Improvement Districts 356
Case Study: Downtown Orlando TIF District 358

Part VI: Managing Development Finance Institutions 363

16. Program Planning and Design 365
Defining Development Goals and Targeting Strategy 367
Growth Fund Example 369
Assessing Demand 370
Growth Fund Example 372
Analyzing Capital Market Supply
and Identifying Financing Gaps 372
Growth Fund Supply Analysis 376
Implementation Needs and Resources 377
Implementation Needs for the Growth Fund 379
Finalizing Program Strategy and Design 380
Case Study: Expanding an Urban Microloan Program 382
Loan Fund Background 383
Dorchester Business Base 384
The Assignment 384

17. Managing the Lending and Investment Process 386
The Investment Process and Key Management Principles 386
Principles for Sound Investment Management 387
Marketing and Project Identification 391
Marketing Approaches and Audiences 392
Effective Marketing Practices 393

Project Screening 394
    Best Practices for Investment Screening 394
The Underwriting and Commitment Process 396
    Best Practices in Investment Decision Making 396
Investment Servicing and Monitoring 402
    Servicing and Monitoring Options 403
    Best Practices for Servicing and Monitoring 404
Case Study: Portland Development
    Commission Industrial Site Loan Fund 406
    Financial Products 407
    Organization and Staffing 407
    Operations and the Lending Process 408
    Lending Activities and Outcomes 409
    Assignment 410

18.   Raising and Managing Capital 412
Capital Management and Development Finance 412
Pricing Loans and Investments 413
Managing and Funding Losses 417
Raising New Capital 418
    Grants and Equity Capital 419
    Debt Sources 421
    Managing Capital 423
    Asset Sales and Securitization 424
Financial Modeling of Development Finance Institutions 427
    Components of the Financial Model 427
    Creating the Model 430
Case Study: Raising New Capital for
    the Manufacturer's Fund 433
    Loan Products and Portfolio 433
    Capitalization and Financial Position 434
    New Funding Options 434
    Goals and Constraints 436
    Recommendation 436

Part VII: Conclusions 441

19.   Economic Development Finance Practice and Its Future 443
Ten Principles for Economic Development Finance Practice 444
An Agenda for the Future 446

Glossary 451

References 461

Index 471

About the Author 493

List of Tables

Table 1.1	Summary of Market Imperfections by Capital Market Type	16
Table 2.1	Estimated Distribution of Capital Sources for U.S. Small Businesses	35
Table 2.2	Sources of Small Firm Financing by Firm Age	36
Table 4.1	Summary of Financial Ratios	79
Table 4.2	Common Size Balance Sheet Ratios for ABC and Comparable Pharmaceutical Firms	80
Table 4.3	Financial Ratios for Crystal Clear Window Company in 1968	88
Table 5.1	Summary of Working Capital Finance Instruments	96
Table 6.1	Summary of Fixed Asset Finance Instruments	115
Table 7.1	Summary of Real Estate Debt Instruments	147
Table 7.2	Lithgow Block Commercial Project Financing Sources	154
Table 7.3	City Plaza Lease Summary and Rent Roll	156
Table 8.1	Different Forms of Guarantees	163
Table 8.2	Comparison of Guarantee Payments Under Different Order of Loss Terms	164
Table 8.3	Summary of Selected State Guarantee Programs	171
Table 9.1	Performance Measures Used in CRA Ratings for Large Banks	188
Table 9.2	Economic Development Commitments in Bank CRA Agreements	190
Table 9.3	Relative Profits and Performance of CRA-Related and Non-CRA Small Business and Housing Loans	196
Table 9.4	Comparison of OCC and BOGFRS CDC Regulations	203
Table 9.5	Distribution of ShoreBank Corporation Development Investment by Unit, 1974 to 1995	207
Table 10.1	Federally Funded RLFs by Agency	220
Table 10.2	Summary Statistics for RLFs Funded by Five Federal Agencies	221
Table 10.3	Comparison of Findings From Four RLF Studies	222
Table 10.4	Comparison RLF Characteristics by State	224
Table 10.5	Performance Data From State RLF Profiles	226
Table 10.6	Impact of Financial Policies on RLF Lending Capacity and Financial Position	229

Table 11.1 Sources of Investment Into Venture
Capital Funds for Selected Years, 1981 to 2001   243

Table 11.2 Venture Capital
Investment by Industry, 1997 to 2000   244

Table 11.3 Venture Capital
Investment by State, 1980 to 1996 and 2001   245

Table 11.4 Average Size of Venture
Capital Investments, 1970 to 2000   245

Table 11.5 Investments by SBICs, SSBICs, and
All Venture Capital Partnerships, 1990 to 1996   249

Table 11.6 State Government Venture Capital Programs   251

Table 11.7 Examples of State Venture Capital Programs   254

Table 12.1 Average CDLF Ratios by Fund Type   270

Table 12.2 Average CDLF Ratios for
Business Loan Funds by Asset Size   272

Table 12.3 Comparison of CDCU Financial Ratios   279

Table 13.1 Summary Data for U.S.
Microenterprise Programs in FY2000   298

Table 13.2 Distribution of U.S.
Microenterprise Programs by Type in 1999   298

Table 13.3 FY2000 Performance Measures
for MicroTest Microenterprise Programs   299

Table 13.4 Self-Reported Outcomes
From Six Microenterprise Programs   302

Table 14.1 Four Uses of Federal
Economic Development Programs   320

Table 14.2 CDFI Certification Criteria   329

Table 14.3 FY2002 Appropriations From EDA Programs   332

Table 14.4 Summary of Potential Debt and Equity Sources   339

Table 15.1 Projected Assessed Values for
Projects by Probability, FY1983 to FY1992   360

Table 15.2 Projected Tax Assessment
and Tax Increment Revenue   360

Table 16.1 Secondary Data
Sources Used to Plan Targeting Strategies   368

Table 16.2 Secondary Data Analysis Results
From Massachusetts Growth Fund Study   369

Table 16.3 Secondary Data Sources for Capital Supply Analysis   374

Table 16.4 Distribution of Dorchester
Small Businesses by Neighborhood   384

Table 16.5 Largest Business Types
Among Dorchester Small Businesses   385

Table 17.1 Marketing Tools   393

Table 17.2 Application Standard
for Permanent Real Estate Loan   395

Table 17.3   Sample Underwriting Standards for Business Debt,
             Business Equity, and Real Estate Debt Financing   397
Table 17.4   Loan Servicing and
             Monitoring Functions and Activities   403
Table 18.1   Loan Pricing and Risk
             Management Policies to Preserve Capital   417
Table 18.2   Options for Raising New Capital   419
Table 18.3   Assumptions Used in Financial Model   431
Table 18.4   Securitization Transaction   436

List of Exhibits

Exhibit 2.1	Firms' Growth Stages and Financial Characteristics	34
Exhibit 3.1	Cash and Accrual September Income Statements for College Books	44
Exhibit 3.2	American Biotechnology Company Balance Sheet—June 30, 2002	45
Exhibit 3.3	American Biotechnology Company Income Statement for the 12 Months Ending June 30, 2002	51
Exhibit 3.4	Steps to Prepare a Three-Part Cash Flow Statement	56
Exhibit 4.1	Evaluation Framework for Economic Development Financing	62
Exhibit 4.2	American Biotechnology Company Balance Sheet—June 30, 2002	67
Exhibit 4.3	American Biotechnology Company Income Statement for the 12 Months Ending June 30, 2002	70
Exhibit 4.4	American Biotechnology Company Statement of Cash Flows for the 12 Months Ending June 30, 2002	73
Exhibit 4.5	Crystal Clear Window Company Income Statement for 12 Months Ending 12/31/68	85
Exhibit 4.6	Crystal Clear Window Company Balance Sheets as of 12/31/67 and 12/31/68	86
Exhibit 4.7	Cash Flow Analysis for Crystal Clear Window Company	86
Exhibit 5.1	Crystal Clear Window Company Comparative Income Statements	104
Exhibit 5. 2	Crystal Clear Window Company Comparative Balance Sheet	105
Exhibit 5.3	Crystal Clear Window Company Sales Projection, 1970	109
Exhibit 6.1	Phoenix Forge Projected Income Statements Years 1 Through 3	130
Exhibit 6.2	Phoenix Forge Projected Balance Sheet Years 1 Through 3	131
Exhibit 7.1	Real Estate Development Phases and Financing Issues	135

Exhibit 7.2   Downtown Building Reuse Development Budget   140
Exhibit 7.3   Operating Pro Forma for Downtown Building Reuse   143
Exhibit 7.4   City Plaza Development Budget   155
Exhibit 7.5   City Plaza 5-Year Operating Pro Forma   156
Exhibit 9.1   Organization of ShoreBank Corporation   206
Exhibit 12.1   Chicago Community Loan Fund Financing Products   274
Exhibit 12.2   Cascadia Revolving Fund Financing Products   275
Exhibit 14.1   Supermarket Development Budget   337
Exhibit 14.2   Nolton Supermarket\Retail
               Center 10-Year Operating Pro Forma   338
Exhibit 15.1   New Boston Seafood
               Bond Offering Memorandum   347
Exhibit 18.1   Projected 5-Year Cash Flow Statement   428
Exhibit 18.2   Projected 5-Year Balance
               Sheet and Income Statement   429
Exhibit 18.3   Manufacturers' Fund FY2000 Cash Flow Projection   437
Exhibit 18.4   Projected Balance Sheet, June 30, 2000   438

List of Boxes

Box 4.1   Projecting Cash Receipts From Sales   83
Box 4.2   Projecting Cash Outlays From Expenses   84
Box 6.1   Legal Documents Used in Fixed Asset Financing   117
Box 7.1   Calculating the Loan
           Principal for a Real Estate Project   145
Box 10.1   RLF Management Challenges   235
Box 11.1   Venture Capital Management Challenges   260
Box 12.1   CDLF Management Challenges   276
Box 12.2   CDCU Management Challenges   288
Box 13.1   Microenterprise Program Challenges   305
Box 14.1   Grove Hall Mall Section 108 Project Summary   327
Box 14.2   Worcester Biotechnology
           Park Section 108 Project Summary   327
Box 15.1   Summary of Inland Valley Development
           Agency Tax Allocation Bond, Series 1997   354
Box 16.1   Outline for Massachusetts Growth Fund Prospectus   381

List of Figures

Figure 2.1	Comparison of Principal Balance Over Time for Interest Only and Amortizing Loans	30
Figure 5.1	Cash Flow and the Working Capital Cycle	93
Figure 5.2	Positive Net Working Capital Requires Long-Term Financing	95
Figure 10.1	Mechanics of a Revolving Loan Fund	218
Figure 10.2	Integrating RLF Policies	234
Figure 15.1	TIF Financing Process	350
Figure 16.1	Components of a Development Finance Strategy	366
Figure 17.1	Stages and Decisions in the Investment Process	388
Figure 17.2	Options for the Investment Decision Process	401
Figure 18.1	Diagram of a Loan-Backed Securitization	426

Preface

This book grew out of a graduate course, Financing Economic Development, which I first taught in 1994. My goals for the class were threefold: (1) providing a foundation in the technical skills involved in financing firms and projects; (2) fostering an understanding of the full range of finance policies, program models, and tools used by economic development practitioners; and (3) exposing students to the issues and challenges involved in managing development finance institutions. This vision for the course reflected my view of the field gained from broad professional experience that included running a local small business finance program, formulating policy in the state legislature, consulting on program design, management, and evaluation, and managing a state quasi-public real estate lending corporation. The course agenda proved ambitious, and no existing book fit the bill. After assembling materials from many sources, I found it was still necessary to develop new materials in several areas, including instruction on key financial analysis skills and case studies that challenged students to apply new skills and concepts in confronting issues faced by development finance practitioners. After 8 years, I decided to consolidate my work and write a comprehensive treatment of economic development finance.

Although my primary goal is to create a complete textbook, there is also a growing need among practitioners for a better treatment of the field. As economic development finance practice has grown more varied and complex over the last 20 years, practitioners need to understand more program models and finance tools and have access to best practices and lessons learned from accumulated experience.

Thus, the purpose of this volume is to provide a comprehensive treatment of economic development finance practice for both students and professionals who are new to the field and seasoned practitioners who want to broaden their knowledge and skills. It provides a foundation in the technical aspects of business and real estate finance needed by professionals who oversee transactions and manage programs, while surveying the full range of policies, program models, and financing tools used in economic development practice within the United States. For the latter focus, the book summarizes the scholarly and practitioner literature on each policy or institution on four issues: its content and characteristics, the extent of its use and impact, unique program design and management issues, and best practices. Three chapters are devoted to crosscutting management issues for development finance programs: program and product design, the lending and investment process, and capital management.

Although the book's subject matter is technical and often involves financial calculations, readers do not need a financial background or special math skills. An introduction to key financial terms, concepts, and accounting knowledge is provided in the early chapters. Basic arithmetic and algebra skills are sufficient to handle the calculations, formulas, financial analysis, and case assignments.

Most chapters conclude with a case study and assignment designed to help readers apply the methods, information, and ideas introduced in the text. These cases provide practice in analyzing information and formulating recommendations for real-world situations and problems. Virtually all the cases are based on actual projects and organizations, although the facts or details in some cases were altered for teaching purposes or to provide confidentiality. The learning that occurs in tackling and discussing these cases helps students improve their financial skills and sharpen their capacity to analyze problems and exercise judgment on important practice issues.

An explanation of one formatting feature is needed. Throughout the book, some phrases are printed in italic type. These are important terms, concepts, or practices that are highlighted for emphasis and to draw the reader to their initial definition or explanation. Most of these italic terms are also defined in the glossary.

Many people contributed directly and indirectly to this book. Because it's an outgrowth of my teaching, I am indebted to my colleagues at MIT's Department of Urban Studies and Planning, both for providing the opportunity to develop the Financing Economic Development course and for their support over the years. Lang Keyes has been a source of guidance, advice, and support for many years, both during my years in state government and at MIT. Bish Sanyal was a source of inspiration and encouragement during his tenure as department chair and helped secure MIT financial support for the project. Larry Vale has continued this precedent in the past 2 years, as the book was written. Theo Selzer first planted the idea for the book, as a teaching assistant for the course. He also authored a case study and helped prepare some of the teaching materials that are included in the book. Michelle Caulfield and Martha Tai provided research assistance on Chapter 12 and Chapter 8, respectively. I also benefited from the practitioners and organizations that sponsored student projects for the class, some of which formed the basis for case studies. My wife, Deborah Becker, deserves special recognition for her patience during the 2 years that I worked on the book and for her endurance in proofreading the first draft—a true labor of love.

PART I

Introduction

1 Capital Availability and Economic Development

The Growing Field of Economic Development Finance

In recent decades, finance has emerged as a large and increasingly complex field within American economic development practice. State governments were early innovators in development finance, creating new programs in the 1980s to help restructure their economies.[1] Many local governments used federal grants to create revolving funds to advance their economic development agendas, while applying their taxing and bonding powers to facilitate new development projects or revitalize downtown districts. Grassroots community organizations built their unique brand of economic development finance with nonprofit loan funds and community development credit unions that raise capital from socially oriented investors. Meanwhile, banks and other private financial institutions expanded partnerships with government and community-based organizations to better address economic development needs. While there is no census of economic development finance programs, several thousand exist across state and local governments, the nonprofit sector, and for-profit financial institutions. As their numbers grow, these programs are expanding their organizational diversity and employing new finance tools.

The prominence of finance programs in economic development strategies is evident among the Empowerment Zones (EZ) and Enterprise Communities (EC) designated by the U.S. Department of Housing and Urban Development (HUD) in 1994 (Hebert et al., 2001). Sixteen of eighteen sites studied in HUD's 5-year evaluation established programs to improve access to capital as part of their job creation and business development initiatives.[2]

With the expansion of economic development finance programs, a growing need exists for skilled professionals to staff and manage these programs. Economic development finance practitioners require specialized knowledge and skills that cut across several fields. In addition to analyzing financial statements and understanding how firms and development projects are financed, they need to comprehend key areas of public policy and how municipal finance relates to economic development. A solid grounding in how capital markets operate must be combined with knowledge on how to link finance programs to broader economic and community development goals. Development finance practitioners also need diverse management skills that encompass market analysis and program design, overseeing investment transactions, building partnerships to advance development outcomes, managing assets, and raising new capital.

Practitioners who do not manage finance programs also are affected by the growing innovation and diversity in the development finance field. They need to understand which program models and finance tools are best suited to their economic development goals and capital markets. Over a dozen program models exist to expand capital availability. Consequently, it no longer suffices for local professionals to select a federal grant source and set up a revolving loan fund. Instead, they must know which models will advance their goals, how to attract private funding to their program and projects, and how to fit programs and tools together into a comprehensive development finance tool kit. While each community differs, practitioners can benefit from the lessons and experience of the many existing finance programs to effectively adapt program models to their situation. Furthermore, existing programs within a region and the tools available under federal and state laws are assets that economic developers can deploy to enhance their effectiveness. With a deeper understanding of business and project finance, available finance tools, and the capabilities of different finance models, practitioners will be better equipped to help finance growing firms, implement projects, and build stronger collaborations between finance programs and other services.

The Purpose and Design of This Book

The bottom line is that all economic development practitioners need to be well versed in the basics of development finance and the state-of-the-art application of program models, policies, and tools. *Economic Development Finance* is written to provide a comprehensive treatment of the field geared to both students studying the subject for the first time and practitioners seeking to expand and update their knowledge. Scholars will also benefit from the extensive information on economic development practice collected in this volume. It covers the technical skills needed by professionals who oversee transactions and manage programs and surveys the current breadth of economic development practice in the United States, covering key concepts, tools, and program models. To address practitioner, student, and academic needs, this book covers the following topics:

- Foundation skills in accounting, business, and real estate finance, and financial statement analysis (Chapters 2 through 7)
- Policies to expand capital availability by private financial institutions (Chapters 8 and 9)

- Program and institutional models for economic development finance (Chapters 10 through 13)
- Federal and municipal economic development programs and tools (Chapters 14 and 15)
- Management of development finance institutions (Chapters 16 through 18)

The Role of Finance in the
Economic Development Process

Before delving into the technical aspects of economic development finance, a working definition of economic development is needed along with an understanding of how finance contributes to the economic development process. Economic development is often viewed as the process of generating new jobs and economic activity within a defined area. However, there are two limitations to this definition. First, the outcome of economic development transcends jobs, income, and wealth. It includes an area's quality of life. Although less tangible than jobs or income, quality-of-life goals are part of many economic development strategies. Examples include a safe and healthy environment, access to rewarding leisure activities, and opportunities for community celebration and civic engagement. Postwar economic revitalization in Pittsburgh demonstrates the role of quality-of-life issues in economic development. One of the city's priorities was reducing air pollution and implementing comprehensive air pollution control as a first step in making the city attractive for new investment.[3] Second, economic development is a process that must be sustained over time for regions to reproduce positive economic and social results. Albert Shapero makes this point when discussing Jane Jacobs's comparison of Birmingham and Manchester, England. Birmingham remained a dynamic city into the mid-twentieth century not because of static economic results but rather due to its successful adaptation to new economic conditions.[4] Thus, the economic development process creates assets that enable a region to sustain and recreate its desired economic and community outcomes over time. Incorporating these two broader considerations, our definition of economic development is

A process of creating and utilizing physical, human, financial, and social assets to generate improved and broadly shared economic well-being and quality of life for a community or region.

Within this definition, finance has two explicit roles. First, it is one input into the process that generates the desired outcomes of jobs, income, and quality of life. As one input into this process, it is a necessary but insufficient factor for successful economic activity. Businesses, the primary units of economic activity, require many conditions and inputs to be viable:

- A market for their goods and services
- Transportation access to get their goods or services to customers and receive inputs

- Information and technology to efficiently design, produce, deliver, and service products
- Labor and its embedded skills for production, administration, management, and service aspects of the business
- Management and entrepreneurial capacity to design and coordinate the process
- Materials and energy used in production
- Facilities and equipment needed to operate all aspects of the business
- Financial capital to purchase these inputs and bridge the time gap between when cash is spent and revenue is received

This list shows that financing is not only one of many factors in an enterprise, but it comes relatively late in the business development process. In other words, financing becomes a constraint to business formation and growth when the other production factors are in place but appropriate financial capital is not available.[5] Nonetheless, when financial capital is not available to firms or projects that can use it productively, economic activity slows as new firms are not started, existing firms postpone investments, and existing enterprises contract or fail. Sustained capital availability problems, as redlined urban neighborhoods have experienced, can undermine an area's desirability and well-being as businesses fail and leave, the housing stock deteriorates, and community infrastructure and facilities are not maintained and upgraded.

A second implication of this list is that capital availability not only concerns the funding of enterprises, it also affects the quality and supply of other inputs into the economic development process. Since businesses are the primary generators of economic activity, economic development finance practice focuses on the direct financing of firms. However, regions also need to finance the infrastructure that supports business activity, the land and real estate facilities to house firms, and the education and training for a highly productive and innovative workforce. Consequently, this book addresses tools and programs used in real estate and infrastructure finance. These two areas overlap with business finance in economic development practice since several tools and programs that finance firms can be applied to real estate and infrastructure projects. The basics of real estate finance and its capital availability issues are covered in Chapter 7; later chapters on tools and program models address their application to both real estate projects and businesses. Chapter 15 covers municipal finance—the primary means for funding infrastructure projects.

Beyond funding specific enterprises and projects, economic development finance concerns the creation of institutional capacity to ensure sustained capital availability for communitywide economic development needs. This challenge transcends the use of specific tools and programs to encompass broader issues of practice, program design, and management. It requires a view of practice that embraces building bridges and active collaboration with private financial institutions, ongoing program innovation and adaptation, and identifying new investment sources to meet evolving regional capital needs. The treatment of program management in Chapters 16 to 18 also incorporates this view of economic development finance as regional asset and institutional capacity-building.

Capital Availability and Capital Market Imperfections

Economic development finance practice is inherently intertwined with the operation of private capital markets. In simple terms, development finance interventions fill private capital market gaps; their goal is to ensure capital availability when private financial markets fail to supply capital to firms and projects that can productively use it. *This conception of economic development practice is reflected in the two-part theory of development finance intervention elaborated in this chapter. The first form of intervention is working with private financial institutions to reduce market imperfections, eliminate regulatory barriers, and remove other obstacles that prevent private markets from supplying development capital. The second type of intervention is creating alternative institutions to directly supply capital to markets, projects, and firms that private institutions cannot serve due to their risk level, transaction size, social benefits, or other reasons.* When such interventions succeed in filling capital gaps, new economic activity results, as financing is provided to start, grow, or maintain a business, or to develop a real estate project, that would not otherwise receive the requisite capital. When a program delivers financing that can be secured from private markets, it *substitutes its capital* for what private market institutions will supply and no new economic activity results. As the primary pitfall of development finance, avoiding capital substitution is the practitioner's North Star to true economic development impact.

Since economic development finance is about filling private capital market gaps, sound practice requires a theory of capital market gaps: what they are, what causes them, and how to address them. The balance of this chapter is devoted to these issues. First, *capital market gap* is more fully defined. Second, the theory of competitive markets is considered to identify the conditions under which capital markets may fail to supply capital to projects or firms. Next, the structure and operation of private capital markets is examined to uncover the actual sources and occurrence of capital supply gaps. A final discussion addresses how the nature of capital market gaps shapes economic development finance practice and elaborates the two-pronged theory of intervention: (1) expanding capital availability by addressing the causes of market imperfections within private financial institutions and markets; and (2) creating new programs or institutions to fill gaps that can't be addressed through market-perfecting policies.

The theory of competitive markets argues that when competitive market conditions exist, capital is efficiently allocated to investments that offer the highest return to capital, adjusted for investment risk. Thus, a capital market gap exists when capital markets fail to allocate capital to firms and projects, or entire classes of firms or projects, that offer a rate of return equal to that offered by other investments with the same level of risk. In other words, when market imperfections exist, capital is not allocated to firms and projects that can use capital most productively. When systematic conditions in market structure or operations cause market imperfections, the resulting capital gap will be systematic, affecting an entire class of financial transactions, firms, or projects. Capital market imperfections, therefore, create supply gaps that generate a need for interventions to ensure capital availability for community economic development.

Microeconomics provides a theory of perfect competition to identify the potential sources of capital market imperfections.[6] The efficient allocation of capital in perfectly competitive capital markets rests on the following assumptions about the structure and operation of capital markets:

- There are many suppliers and users of capital in the market.
- Suppliers and users have perfect information about the transaction or there are no significant costs to secure such information.
- The costs to complete a transaction are insignificant relative to the size of the transaction.
- The transaction has no externalities (all costs and benefits associated with the transaction are reflected in prices).
- Participants are rational benefit maximizers who make decisions to maximize their economic returns consistent with their risk preferences.

Market imperfections occur when these underlying assumptions do not exist for actual capital markets. When there is a lack of competition and a monopoly or oligopoly exists in the supply of capital, then the suppliers of capital may set terms or allocate capital in ways that prevent firms that offer a competitive rate of return from receiving capital. A lack of information, high costs to gain information, or high transaction costs for certain firms or transactions can reduce the net return on these investments and limit capital availability. Suppliers of capital will avoid these investments, even if they use capital as productively as other firms, and instead seek out investments with more available information and lower information and transactions costs. Nonrational or benefit-maximizing investment behavior might also lead to capital market gaps. If investors are risk averse, then capital will not be available for higher-risk firms, projects, or investments, even when such investments provide a return that compensates for the higher risk. Investors who supply capital for nonrational reasons, such as discrimination, fads, or beliefs other than expected risk-adjusted returns, may oversupply capital to certain investments and prevent the flow of capital to other projects that can use the funds more productively. A final potential source of capital market failure is the existence of externalities in which all costs or benefits associated with an investment are not reflected in private returns. In other words, the social return from an investment may be very different than the financial return earned by private investors. For example, a firm that produces a highly efficient and low-emission engine will generate social benefits from reduced air pollution, but the resulting health care and other cost savings are not captured in the engine's prices and return to investors. If the financial return to financing this firm is not competitive with similar investment alternatives, then the firm will not be supplied with capital by the private market, even if the social returns are great. For this reason, it may be socially desirable to intervene in capital markets to expand financing for firms or projects that generate significant public or social returns, even when other market imperfections do not exist.

This discussion suggests two benefits that result from addressing capital market imperfections.[7] First, increased economic efficiency and productivity should occur as firms that can use capital most productively are supplied funds. Second, economic development or social benefits are generated from supplying capital to firms or projects which yield desirable outcomes that private markets don't adequately value (e.g., lower unemployment or reduced pollution). These economic benefits provide a public policy rationale for economic development finance interventions and, when measurable, offer a way to test whether the returns from a specific program or policy outweigh its costs (Bartik, 1990).

Market Imperfections and Capital Supply Gaps in Practice

While the theory of perfect competition provides insight into potential capital supply gaps, the institutional structure and operation of capital markets determines what capital market imperfections actually exist and how they influence capital availability. Capital markets are the collective set of institutions through which savings and the economy's surplus financial resources are accumulated and channeled to households, businesses, governments, and other entities that demand capital to support their consumption and investment. Capital markets have two organizational forms that operate differently with distinct consequences for market imperfections: public capital markets and private capital markets. Both are private sector markets in which the public-versus-private distinction refers to the nature of and access to information within each type of market rather than their governmental status. *Public capital markets* are characterized by extensive publicly available information on investments, standardized investment instruments, liquid investments that are easily bought and sold, and federal and state government regulation. It is the first characteristic, the large amount of publicly disclosed information, that accounts for the label, "public" capital markets. Another aspect of public markets is that individual investors can directly purchase the financial assets sold in these markets. An individual can evaluate the range of investment options and directly purchase shares of stock in Intel Corporation or buy notes (a form of debt) of the United States government or DuPont Corporation. As indicated below, this is an important difference between private and public capital markets.

Public capital markets include the stock markets that provide equity or ownership investments in businesses, the bond markets[8] that supply debt financing to governments, businesses, and other entities (e.g., nonprofit organizations such as universities), and the money markets, which supply short-term debt (i.e., less than 1 year in duration) for businesses, governments, and nonprofit entities.

Three kinds of financial institutions handle transactions in these markets: investment banks, securities brokers, and securities dealers. Investment banks bring new stock and debt sales to market, either by buying the securities from a firm and then reselling them to the public (underwriting) or by locating and selling the securities directly to specific buyers (placement). Investment banks also package financial assets, such as home mortgage loans, into securities and bring these derivative securities to market. Securities brokers arrange the sale of existing securities between buyers and sellers while security dealers buy and sell securities themselves to earn a profit and to ensure the existence of an active market in which to buy and sell securities.

An important factor in assessing capital market imperfections is the process by which a firm raises capital in a public market. To raise debt or equity capital in public capital markets, a firm must undertake the following steps:

- Prepare legal documents that define the security and its terms
- Complete detailed disclosure information on the firm, the investment being offered, and its risks
- File the disclosure and offering documents with the federal Securities and Exchange Commission (SEC) and, in many cases, with state government security divisions
- Secure a credit rating (for debt securities)
- Offer and sell the securities to investors

The sale of stock or debt in a public market costs at least several hundred thousand dollars, when an investment bank is not used. An investment bank's fee adds several hundred thousand to several million dollars, depending on the size of the security offering. According to a U.S. General Accounting Office study, the average cost for completing an initial public offering (IPO) of stock in 2000 was 14.4% of total proceeds, or $720,000 for a $5 million IPO, and 9.4% of total proceeds, or $920,000 for a $10 million IPO.[9]

While offering securities to the public without an investment bank reduces transaction costs, this is quite difficult to accomplish and likely to raise less capital when it is feasible. Moreover, investment banks, seeking to increase their profits, are selective about which securities they bring to market. The major investment banks prefer large offerings that generate large fees and offerings by firms that can be readily sold to investors. Many observers feel that this behavior limits access to the public equity and debt markets to offerings of at least several million dollars and limits stock IPOs to either firms with minimum annual profits of $1 million and high growth rates or early-stage firms without profits that are in industries with very high expected growth (i.e., Internet-related or biotechnology firms) (GAO, 2000).[10]

Public capital markets approximate perfect competition in some ways, but other characteristics generate market imperfections. On the one hand, public markets are highly competitive with many buyers and sellers participating in the market to set fair prices, and investors have access to extensive information at little or no cost. On the other hand, the high transaction costs required to access these markets and the profit requirements of investment banks make them infeasible for most firms or projects that need less than several million dollars in capital. Moreover, investment fads and cyclical factors affect supply and can generate excess capital for some firms and industries while preventing others from raising capital in public markets. The Internet stock boom of the late 1990s exemplifies this phenomenon. Many young Internet-related firms were able to sell stock to the public even with minimal sales, no profits, and very uncertain prospects for future profitability. Extreme optimism about the "new" Internet economy generated a large supply of capital for firms in this industry, many of which quickly failed (Sohl, 2003).[11] As capital flowed to Internet firms, some firms in profitable industries with good growth prospects reported difficulties accessing public credit markets.[12] These investing patterns do not fit the expected behavior of rational benefit maximizers posited in microeconomic theory.

Private capital markets are organized differently and provide an alternative source of capital to firms and projects that cannot access the public markets. In private capital markets, an intermediary organization holds and manages funds for investors, with financing transactions negotiated between the intermediary and the capital user. While investors in the public markets can directly buy and sell securities, the suppliers of capital in private markets place their funds in a financial institution, which decides where to lend and invest these funds. For example, when a household deposits savings in a bank or purchases an insurance policy, it relies on the bank or insurance company's staff to invest these funds and provide the expected return. Consequently, suppliers and users of capital are matched on the financial institution's balance sheet, not through the direct sale and holding of securities by investors. A second aspect of private capital markets is that financing transactions are negotiated between the firm and the financial institution and are not based on publicly available information and standardized securities. The financial institution conducts its own investigation (called due diligence) of the firm's potential to provide the expected return on investment and negotiates specific terms and conditions with the firm seeking capital.

Five primary financial institutions comprise the private capital markets:

Commercial banks are government chartered financial institutions with broad lending powers that have access to government deposit insurance.

Thrift institutions are government chartered financial institutions with more limited lending powers and access to government deposit insurance. They often focus on home mortgage and real estate lending. Savings banks and savings and loan institutions are in this category.

Commercial finance companies are financial institutions that are not government chartered and do not raise capital through deposits. They have more flexibility in the type of loans and investment that they can make and often provide higher-risk debt to both households and firms.

Insurance companies manage the financial assets and liabilities associated with insurance products. They invest premiums received from life and other insurance obligations to cover the financial obligations of their insurance policies. Life insurance companies, with long-term liabilities, are an important source of long-term financing for firms and real estate projects.

Venture capital funds are private investment entities that primarily supply equity to firms with the potential for very high returns.

While private financial markets are not formally organized into separate equity and debt markets, as are public markets, direct equity investments are largely made through venture capital firms. The other institutions are primarily suppliers of debt financing. Although some banks, finance companies, and insurers make their own direct equity investments, they typically invest equity through participation in venture capital funds.

In addition to these formal institutions, private capital markets include informal noninstitutional sources, such as family members, friends, and angel investors. While the size and extent of informal financing is not well documented, it is believed to be an important capital source for start-up businesses and for raising small amounts of equity. A firm's access to informal capital, however, is tied to the owner's social and professional network and the wealth of family and friends.

National banking and the growth of electronic banking have reduced geographic variations in capital availability, but competition and supply in private capital markets still depends on the type and number of private institutions serving a region. Regional differences are most evident in the venture capital industry, with investments highly concentrated in California, Massachusetts, New York, and Texas.[13] While this pattern reflects the greater investment opportunities in these states, the concentration of venture capital funds and angel investors in these states is also a factor. Consequently, a firm's ability to access private equity partly depends on its location. Debt availability is widespread since there are many sources of debt and most areas have several financial institutions competing to make business loans. Nonetheless, areas with a concentrated banking market may face a monopoly or oligopoly situation that affects capital supply. Rural areas are most likely to experience this problem since they typically have fewer banks. Researchers found that limited competition in banking markets reduces the availability of moderate or higher-risk debt since financial institutions without competition earn above average profits on lower-risk lending.[14] Business strategy decisions among the financial intermediaries servicing a region also shape capital availability, especially in more concentrated markets. These decisions define which markets financial institutions serve, the debt products they offer, and the financing terms and criteria they employ. For example, if lenders decide that interest rate conditions make it too risky to offer fixed rate financing, then firms may be limited to variable rate debt. Similarly, some banks may decide that larger or more predictable profits will be earned by investing in the bond market compared to small business lending, which will limit the funds available for small business loans.

The process to secure financing differs in private capital markets and yields separate market imperfections from those in public markets. The process to secure financing in private capital markets involves the following steps:

- Determining the type and size of financing needed
- Identifying the specific intermediaries that provide this type of financing
- Preparing a proposal or request for financing
- Contacting the intermediary to discuss the requested financing
- Participating in the lender's due diligence process and decision-making process
- Negotiating the financing terms and legal documents
- Completing the legal documentation and loan closing to obtain funds

Note that the financial costs that firms face to complete transactions in private capital markets are much lower than for public markets. No filing, registration, or underwriting fees are needed to gain financing from a private financial intermediary. The primary transaction expenses in private capital markets are legal fees to prepare loan or investment documents, but these are far less than legal costs for an IPO or public debt sale. Consequently, monetary transaction costs are not a significant obstacle to financing in private markets. However, intermediaries in private capital market often impose other costs on firms as they seek to manage risks from more limited information and their illiquid investment via the terms of loan and investment agreements. Investment or loan agreements may add reporting costs, place limits on the firm's actions, or set financial standards that constrain its business and financial flexibility.

Information availability and costs are addressed differently in private capital markets and pose a greater obstacle to financing. In public markets, the firm seeking capital bears the responsibility for, and incurs the legal, accounting, printing, and other costs associated with preparing disclosure documents to issue securities. In private markets, on the other hand, the financial intermediary supplying capital conducts it own research and due diligence to evaluate the risks associated with potential financing transactions. While firms compile and prepare some information, the financial intermediary must verify this information, collect additional information, and adjust its financing based on its risk analysis. Unlike the public markets, where information disclosure is legally regulated and subject to both well developed standards and third party review, much critical information about a firm or project is known within the firm and opaque to the capital supplier in private markets.[15] Moreover, the information costs associated with making a loan or equity investment have a large fixed component that is not proportional to the loan or investment size. As bankers often comment, it costs them as much to make a small loan as a large one. These fixed information costs often make it unprofitable to extend small loans or make small equity investments. Therefore, financial institutions often do not consider business or commercial real estate loans below $50,000 to $100,000. Thresholds for venture capital investments are far higher with many funds unwilling to consider transactions under $5 million.[16]

Government regulation also influences capital supply in private financial markets since many intermediaries, especially government insured depository institutions, are subject to government oversight and regulation. One goal of government regulation of financial institutions is ensuring the safety and soundness of depositors' funds. Regulations create financial incentives for institutions to hold less risky assets, which can lead to risk-averse lending policies among some banks. Moreover, when financial or economic conditions increase the potential for bank losses and failures, regulators may directly seek to change bank lending practices. For example, when the Massachusetts economy entered a recession in the early 1990s, bank regulators feared a repeat of the wave of bank failures that occurred in Texas and strictly examined the loan portfolios of many banks. In some cases, they placed banks under orders to cease and desist from making certain types of loans. These regulatory actions contributed to a large reduction in bank lending and a credit availability crunch. Regulators were subtler as the risk of a recession rose in the late 1990s. Concerned about liberal lending practices, the Federal Reserve Bank sent out a letter to banks in June 1998 warning them to tighten business lending standards because a recession could leave them with many bad loans.[17]

Finally, private financial institutions can also be subject to investment fads, nonprofit-maximizing decisions, and discriminatory biases that contribute to capital supply gaps. Venture capitalists often follow investment fads and biases in the stock markets since they depend on IPOs to earn their investment returns. Consequently, venture capitalists had the same predilection to overinvest in Internet-related firms during the 1990s as did stock market investors. Banks and private market intermediaries also can be influenced by biases. Some lenders practice statistical discrimination in which they classify an entire group of businesses, such as restaurants or start-ups, as too risky without evaluating the merits and risk of specific transactions.[18] Several studies document racial disparities in home mortgage lending in several cities during the 1980s and 1990s, even after controlling for borrower credit, property condition, and market factors.[19]

Implications of Market Imperfections for Economic Development Finance

As the prior section shows, the operation of capital markets does not match the assumptions underlying perfect competition but instead is characterized by market imperfections that can create capital availability gaps. Table 1 summarizes the market imperfections identified from the analysis of market structure and operations for both private and public markets. Despite the United States' well-developed capital markets, a firm's ability to secure capital is not simply a function of its capacity to provide lenders and investors a competitive rate of return. Rather, the firm's location, industry, amount and form of capital needed, and the number and type of financial institutions serving its area can all affect its access to capital. Nonetheless, some common capital supply gaps emerge from the analysis of capital market imperfections. First, equity capital in amounts below several million dollars is not available from public markets and institutional sources. Moreover, for small and early-stage firms, equity capital is largely limited to firms in "hot" industries with perceived high growth potential. Second, debt capital for small firms and in amounts below several million dollars is largely available from private financial institutions. Thus, debt availability is dependent on competition and lending policies within the local banking and commercial finance market. Small business and real estate loans below $50,000 are not available from private financial institutions in most markets, and in some cases the threshold may be higher. Furthermore, regulatory policies, cyclical economic conditions, and limited competition all affect the cost and availability of debt.

Several implications for economic development finance practice emerge from this analysis. First, local economic and financial market conditions shape capital supply gaps. Therefore, to design effective intervention strategies, practitioners need to understand local capital market conditions, the private financial institutions active in their region, and how their business strategies and lending policies affect capital supply. The formal aspects of capital market analysis and its application to program design are discussed in Chapter 16. Since capital markets are dynamic, with conditions changing

Table 1.1   Summary of Market Imperfections by Capital Market Type

Potential Imperfection	Public Equity Market	Public Debt Market	Private Equity Market	Private Debt Market
Competition (Supply side)	Extensive	Extensive	Limited, depends on location, investment, and sector	Moderate, depends on location, investment, and sector
Information Access	Extensive publicly available information provided by firms. Firms followed by analysts	Extensive publicly available information provided by firms. Credit ratings available	Must be collected and analyzed by investor; may not be feasible for small transactions	Must be collected and analyzed by lender; may not be feasible for small transactions
Transaction Costs	High costs to firm for legal, disclosure, printing, and underwriters' fees	High costs to firm for legal, disclosure, printing, and underwriters' fees	Low to moderate costs, primarily for legal work	Low to moderate costs, primarily for legal work
Rational Profit-Maximizing Behavior	Cyclical factors and fads affect investor demand; may be discrimination for or against certain industries	Cyclical factors and fads affect investor demand; may be discrimination for or against certain industries	Cyclical factors and fads affect investor demand; may be discrimination for or against certain industries	Regulations affect type of loans. Discrimination for or against certain industries, type of firms, locations, etc., may occur
Regulatory Factors	Impose high transaction costs	Impose high transaction costs	Nonregulated	Limits types and level of risk; banks are required to meet community credit needs
Conclusions	Not viable for raising small amounts of equity below several million dollars	Not viable for raising small amounts of debt below several million dollars	Hard to raise small amounts of equity. Available largely for firms with very high growth potential and capacity for IPO or acquisition	Most important capital source for small firms and development projects; limited supply of long-term debt, small loans, and riskier financing

from year to year, practitioners also gain critical knowledge through their ongoing engagement in financing transactions and dialogue with private financial institutions, firms, and industry associations. Second, development finance professionals are in the business of expanding the supply of small amounts of capital and higher-risk capital. These are the most ubiquitous capital supply gaps to address. Finally, the private capital markets are the most important financing source for small businesses and small-scale or unconventional development projects, both of which will have little access to the public markets. Developing relationships with and designing programs that work in tandem with key private capital market institutions, especially commercial banks and venture capital firms, is central to the work of economic development finance.

_____ A Framework for Expanding Capital Availability

Expanding capital availability for economic development entails two types of market interventions: (1) perfecting the operation of existing capital markets and (2) creating alternative development finance institutions. The first form of intervention changes the operation of private capital market institutions either by eliminating the sources of market imperfections that create capital gaps or changing the behaviors, perceptions, and risk preferences of private financial institutions. Practitioners produce the greatest impact by changing the performance of existing capital markets since they are the primary means for financing economic activity and allocate hundreds of billions of dollars of capital. This critical area of economic development finance practice involves three interventions:

- *Risk-sharing tools and policies* that encourage private sector institutions to bear greater risks and extend higher-risk debt financing. Loan guarantees are the most common example of risk sharing. Other approaches include portfolio-based loan insurance and financial incentives. Chapter 8 focuses on these interventions.

- *Bank regulatory policies* can reduce barriers to economic development investments by financial intermediaries and create incentives and standards to expand services, lending, and investment for economic development purposes. Banks also provide an institutional platform that development finance practitioners can use to address disinvestment and capital market failure. The use of banking regulations and banking institutions to expand capital availability is the focus of Chapter 9.

- *Absorbing information and other transaction costs* for private lenders and investors by collecting and generating information, preparing financing applications, analyzing potential investments, or servicing loans. This is a crosscutting approach that is discussed under program models in Chapters 10 through 13.

Despite the importance of expanding capital availability through private sector financial markets, there are limits to the first intervention strategy. When the institutional structure of capital markets does not support the channeling of sufficient capital to regional economic development needs or when private financial intermediaries are too risk averse, it becomes necessary to establish alternative financial institutions to ensure capital availability. New public sector, nonprofit, and community-based financial institutions can redirect the region's own savings and attract external funds to expand the supply of capital to business enterprises and development projects. Five alternative development finance institutions are covered in this book:

- *Revolving loan funds,* a common and easily adaptable finance program model that emerged from local economic development practice, are discussed in Chapter 10.
- *Venture capital* models for expanding the availability of equity and high-risk investment capital are the subject of Chapter 11.
- *Two community-based financial institutions*—community development loan funds and community development credit unions (grass roots institutions that typically serve low-income areas and populations)—are covered in Chapter 12.
- *Microenterprise funds,* a fast-growing form of U.S. development finance inspired by practices in developing countries and focused on very small enterprises and the self-employed, are addressed in Chapter 13.

These two modes of intervention, perfecting existing capital markets and creating alternative institutions, are not mutually exclusive. Economic development finance involves using both strategies, often in complementary and synergistic ways. For example, a region might create loan guarantee programs to expand bank financing for higher-risk small business debt of $100,000 or more while also creating a new revolving loan fund or microenterprise fund to supply debt in smaller amounts. Similarly, state regulations might be altered to allow increased bank, insurance company, and pension fund investment in venture capital while new quasi-public intermediaries are created to manage this new source of private equity capital. These are only two examples of the many ways in which both intervention strategies can be combined. Each community will create its own examples based on local economic development goals and opportunities, and in accordance with its capital market environment.

As an entry point into economic development finance, this chapter has focused on the supply side of capital markets to develop the concept of capital market perfections and how it shapes intervention strategies. However, this presents an incomplete picture of financial markets, ignoring the demand side of the marketplace. Economic development finance practice also requires an understanding of the financing needs of small businesses and development projects and what forms of capital should be supplied to address these needs. Additionally, practitioners need skills to manage individual financing transactions, such as evaluating whether a business or development project can productively use capital and defining the appropriate type and terms of financing to offer.

The next section addresses these demand side issues. It begins with an overview of how businesses are financed and explains the roles and language of equity and debt capital. Following this introduction, the text takes a detour in Chapters 3 and 4 to explain how businesses report financial information and how this information is used to evaluate a firm's financing needs and its capacity to productively use and repay new capital. With this foundation in place, the next three chapters provide a detailed look at the most common uses of economic development finance: business working capital, business fixed assets, and real estate development projects.

Endnotes

1. David Osborne (1999) discusses the role of governors and state governments in economic development finance in *Laboratories of Democracy*, especially in chapters on Massachusetts, Michigan, and Pennsylvania.

2. Hebert et al. (2001), *Interim Assessment of the Empowerment Zone and Enterprise Communities Program: A Progress Report*, pp. 5-2–5-3.

3. Frey Foundation (1993), *Taking Care of Civic Business*, p. 51.

4. Shapero (1984), pp. 12–14.

5. By implication, financing is only one part of a region's economic development strategy that must be linked to other initiatives that address the quality and supply of the other economic assets.

6. A definition of perfect competition can be found in Nicholson (2002), *Microeconomic Theory: Basic Principles and Extensions*, pp. 422–423. A discussion of "imperfect competition" when these assumptions do not hold is found on pp. 469–481.

7. Timothy Bartik (1990) provides a more complete economic development argument for addressing market imperfections that extends beyond capital markets in *The Market Failure Approach to Regional Economic Development Policy*.

8. The bond market is the primary supplier of capital for the municipal debt tools discussed in Chapter 15.

9. U.S. General Accounting Office (GAO) (2000), *Efforts to Facilitate Equity Capital Formation*, p. 24.

10. These points, and other obstacles that small businesses face in raising equity from public stock markets, are discussed in the U.S. GAO (2000) report *Efforts to Facilitate Equity Capital Formation*.

11. Sohl details a number of these failures in his 2003 article and cites a statistic from Webmergers.com that 516 Internet firms shut down during the first 11 months of 2001.

12. In my consulting work, I discovered that firms in the medical device industry, which grew faster than most manufacturing industries in the 1990s and had favorable long-term growth trends, reported far greater difficulty completing IPOs during this period than Internet firms.

13. U.S. GAO (2000), p. 17–18; From 1990 to 1996, these four states accounted for 55% of the total number and dollar amount of venture capital investments made, according to Table 1.3 in Gompers and Lerner (1999), *The Venture Capital Cycle*.

14. See Lawrence Litvak and Belden Daniels (1979), *Innovations in Development Finance*, pp. 49–50.

15. A good discussion of this issue is found in Allen E. Berger and Gregory F. Udell (1998), "The Economics of Small Business Finance: The Roles of Private Equity and Debt Markets in the Financial Growth Cycle," *Journal of Banking and Finance, 22,* 1998.

16. From the author's research and a survey of venture capital firms summarized in Weaver (1998), *Venture Capital Investment Patterns: Implications for Regional Economic Development.* This large minimum investment size partly reflects growth in the size of venture capital partnerships during the 1990s, which pressured managers to seek larger transactions and increase their minimum investment size.

17. *Boston Globe,* July 1, 1998, "Fed Warns Banks to Maintain Lending Discipline for Businesses."

18. Litvak and Daniels (1979) point out that such discrimination may be a way to address high information costs (p. 22).

19. See Gregory Squires (1993), *From Redlining and Reinvestment,* pp. 12–13.

PART II

The Basics of Business Finance

2

Financing Business
Enterprises

The Role of Equity and Debt

W hile business finance appears quite complex with its arcane language and dizzying array of financial instruments, at its core, finance boils down to a choice between two forms of investment: equity and debt. Decisions, both at the transaction level (i.e., financing a specific firm or project) and the policy level (i.e., designing effective interventions to achieve economic development goals), emanate from the differences between equity and debt. This chapter introduces these two principal ways to finance economic activity, explains the key issues associated with their use, and relates them to firms' capital needs. It also defines key terms, calculations, and ratios used in business and development finance. By explaining the language, variations, and uses of equity and debt financing, its apparent complexity will be simplified and the mystery associated with its jargon reduced. Thus, this chapter has three goals:

- Explaining equity and debt, their differences and the implications of these differences for financing businesses
- Defining the technical aspects of equity and debt instruments, including how to calculate payment amounts and key ratios used in debt financing
- Relating the use of equity and debt financing to a firm's growth stages

This background prepares the reader for later chapters that address how firms and development projects are financed and detail the financial analysis used to evaluate a firm's capacity to repay debt investments. Moreover, an understanding of equity and debt financing informs the effective design of development finance interventions, which must deliver the appropriate form of financing to accomplish economic development goals. Since firms use equity and debt differently and these uses can vary with a firm's industry and growth stage, economic development goals are closely linked to financing instruments. Practitioners must know when equity financing is needed and when debt is the right tool.

Equity Financing

Thus far, the terms "equity" and "debt" have been used without any explanation or definition. But the buck stops here; these terms will now be defined. As with most business enterprises, we begin with equity.

Equity is the owners' investment in a business. Equity is the ownership share that is received in exchange for a financial or other contribution to a business. As a business owner, the equity investor participates in the business's financial return like a sole business proprietor. Consider a small bookstore owned by one person named Smith. Smith has a right to the cash flow generated by the bookstore, after all other claims are paid. Smith must pay her landlord for rent, the publishers for the store's inventory of books, wages to her employees, and so on. Once all these expenses are paid, she is entitled to what is left over. She might take this cash out directly as a dividend to herself as the store's owner, or she may reinvest it in the bookstore, perhaps to expand inventory or hire more employees to stay open later. Finally, Smith may sell the bookstore to a new owner. In this case, she would receive cash equal to the net proceeds (i.e., the cash received from selling the business less any expenses involved in selling it). Her investment return from the sale would be the net proceeds less the cash that she had previously invested in the business. This example demonstrates the two forms of return that equity investors receive: (1) dividends—payments from the earnings of a business over a specific period (note that owners only receive dividends to the extent that these earnings are not retained and reinvested in the business); and (2) gains (or losses) from the sale of an ownership stake. A gain occurs if the value of the business increases between purchase and sale. When the business's value decreases, the owner incurs a loss from the sale.

The residual and contingent nature of returns on equity financing is also evident from the bookstore example. An equity investor gets what is left over after all other expenses and claims have been paid. Equity returns also are not fixed. The business is not obligated to make any payments to its owners, and they may receive nothing if the business fails to earn profits (or chooses to reinvest all profits). On the other hand, owners can earn a very large return with a sharp rise in a company's earnings and value. These conditions make the returns to equity investors more uncertain and variable than the returns to debt holders. As compensation for bearing this greater risk, equity investors expect a higher return on their investment in a business than lenders receive.

Terms and Issues in Equity Financing

Equity has specific legal terms and presents particular issues that shape its use and structure in financing transactions. Since most businesses are organized as a corporation,[1] the discussion focuses on corporate stock, which is the most common type of equity financing. Corporate stock has two forms: common stock and preferred stock.[2] Common stock is, by far, the most widespread form of equity and accounts for the vast majority of stock sold in public capital markets. Common stockholders, as owners of the corporation, have both financial and governance rights. *Financial rights* are a claim to dividends distributed by the firm and proceeds from the sale of the company. *Governance rights* are set by the firm's bylaws and typically include election of the board of directors and approval of major business decisions, such as mergers and new stock authorizations beyond those established during incorporation. Preferred stockholders, as the name implies, have a preferred claim to the firm's dividend payments, typically at a defined fixed rate. This first, or senior, right to dividends is usually a cumulative right whereby common stockholders cannot be paid dividends until the cumulative dividends owed to preferred stockholders are paid. If a firm issued preferred stock with a 5% dividend rate and paid no dividends to preferred stockholders for 5 years, it must pay preferred stockholders the full 5 years of dividends before any dividends are paid to common shareholders. Preferred stockholders typically have fewer governance rights, usually limited to when a corporation fails to make dividend payments. While public market sales of preferred stock occur infrequently, many venture capitalists acquire preferred stock since it gives them a superior claim on the earnings of a firm before a public stock sale occurs.

Equity financing issues largely relate to firm ownership and the definition and protection of the associated financial and governance rights. These terms are typically negotiated as part of private market equity investments made by venture capitalists and angel investors. The single most important issue in equity financing is *company valuation.* It is the value placed on the company that determines what share of the company new investors receive for a given amount of financing. For example, assume a medical device manufacturer is valued at $10 million before an equity investment is made. If a venture capitalist invests $10 million in new equity in the company, then the postinvestment value will be $20 million. The venture capitalist will expect a 50% ownership share in exchange for the investment. If the company's preinvestment valuation is $5 million, then the venture capitalist will require two thirds of the firm's stock for the $10 million investment since it represents two thirds of the postinvestment value. Company valuation is an art rather than a science and is based on assumptions about the company's future earnings growth and the present value of these earnings to investors based on their expected rate of return.[3]

Private equity investors also set investment terms to protect their financial and governance rights. Governance rights are safeguarded by obtaining voting rights even as holders of preferred stock, requiring the right to directly hold or elect one or more seats on the board of directors and the right to elect a majority of directors if the company defaults on key conditions of its investment agreement. Other investment terms allow investors to control their potential financial returns. First, equity funds are often invested in stages based on the firm's achievement of set milestones, which controls the amount of capital put at risk. Second, antidilution provisions require firms to provide additional stock so that investors maintain their ownership share when stock splits, dividend payments, or other actions would effectively reduce their percentage of the firm's equity. Another common term is the granting of conversion and registration rights to private investors; these rights ensure that their stock can be converted to liquid public stock shares when the company makes a public stock offering. Private equity investors also retain approval rights over any sale of the company. Since a company sale fixes the value of their stock and the resulting financial return, investors need this right either to prevent a private company sale when they believe a public stock sale will provide higher returns or to prevent the sale for too low a price.

Advantages and Disadvantages of Equity

Equity financing offers four primary advantages to firms. First, it has no fixed payment requirements and, thus, does not add to a firm's fixed costs. When a firm's cash flow is lower than expected, equity does not impose any fixed payment burdens. Dividends can be deferred and cash can be utilized to address business needs and opportunities. Second, equity is a long-term and "patient" source of funding. Equity investors, as firm owners, are concerned about building the future earnings and value of the firm rather than receiving the next interest and principal payment. For this reason, equity is appropriate to finance investment needs when earnings and returns may not occur for several years and high-risk projects in which future returns are very uncertain. A third benefit of equity is that it leaves a firm's assets available for other financing needs. Unlike lenders, equity investors do not claim a firm's assets as collateral to be sold, if necessary, to return their investment. Thus, the assets that a firm acquires with equity capital can be used to raise debt capital. For this reason, equity financing helps leverage debt financing by funding the acquisition of assets that provide collateral and a financial cushion to absorb unexpected financial losses. Finally, equity places fewer restrictions on the use of funds and the financial status of a business than debt. Since equity investors have some control over the business via their governance rights and are less concerned with short-term collateral and repayment, they place fewer restrictions on firm finances. Lenders, on the other hand, want to ensure that their financing increases a firm's assets and generates cash flow to regularly repay their investment. Consequently, they usually set financial standards for their borrowers (called financial covenants) and may restrict how loan proceeds are used.

Despite these advantages, equity has some disadvantages for firms. Most importantly, raising new equity capital dilutes the ownership and control of the firm. In return for new equity, existing owners must give up a portion of their ownership and open up the election of board members, key business decisions, and potentially the appointment of management to outside investors. This trade-off can be difficult for an entrepreneur who is used to exercising control over the business and has a strong vision for the enterprise. Ownership dilution also requires the original owners to share any increase in the firm's value with the new equity investors. A second disadvantage to equity financing is its limited availability. While many sources of debt exist, equity investors are few and far between. Few firms either fit the investment criteria of venture capitalists or are ready for an initial public offering of stock. Most businesses, therefore, must appeal to family and friends or locate angel investors to raise informal equity capital. This is a difficult prospect, especially for people with modest means and few social and business contacts with potential angel investors. Finally, equity is an expensive form of capital. Investors expect a high rate of return to compensate them for the uncertainty and large risks associated with equity investing; it is common for investors in the informal and private equity markets to seek an annual rate of return in the 30% to 50% range. To earn this high return, investors require a large share of the firm's stock for a modest infusion of capital, particularly when the firm's market and growth potential is not extremely high.

Debt Financing

Debt is a contract between a lender and a borrower by which funds are provided to the borrower and then repaid to the lender (debt holder) according to a defined interest rate and principal repayment schedule. Debt differs from equity in two important ways. First, there are specific terms for how the investor (lender) is to be repaid. Unlike equity, in which the investor's return depends on the future earnings and value of the company, the debt holder's return is set by the contract terms. Moreover, debt is a fixed obligation of the firm that must be paid independently of the firm's earnings. When a firm fails to make debt payments, lenders usually have the right to sell specific firm assets to obtain repayment. Financial returns are limited to those specified in the debt contract, even if the firm becomes extremely profitable. Second, debt does not confer any governance rights to debt holders, who cannot exercise any control over the firm's governance and management. Although debt contracts may establish financial requirements for borrowers, they do not give lenders the power to elect board members, approve mergers, or influence major business decisions.

Terms and Issues in Debt Financing

With more complex and varied features, debt contracts address financing terms (i.e., the size and timing of interest and principal payments), the lender's rights to collateral, and myriad requirements to minimize the risk of nonpayment. Despite its many legal forms and names,[4] debt is defined by a common set of financial terms that determine the stream of payments required to repay the borrowed funds. These key financial features include loan principal, interest rate, loan term (sometimes called maturity period), and amortization period. *Principal* refers to the amount of funds borrowed. When ABC Construction Company borrows $1 million from Community Bank the loan principal is $1 million. *Interest rate* refers to the price charged to the firm for the use of borrowed funds and is usually indicated and calculated by an annual percentage rate. For example, if the interest rate on Community Bank's loan is 10%, ABC Construction Company must pay interest at the rate of 10% per year on its $1 million loan. For one year, interest payments would equal 10% of $1 million or $100,000 ($1,000,000 * .10 = $100,000). Interest is calculated on the outstanding principal amount at the beginning of the period covered by the interest payment. If ABC Construction Company had repaid $200,000 of principal in the first year of its loan, then interest payments for the second year are calculated by applying the 10% interest rate to the $800,000 of outstanding principal (the $1 million of original principal less the $200,000 in principal payments during the first year). Thus, interest payments for the second year would be $80,000 ($800,000 * .10 = $80,000). Interest rates are either fixed or variable. Under a fixed interest rate loan, the borrower pays the same interest rate over the entire loan term. Variable rate loans have an interest rate that is changed (reset) at set time intervals based on a specified formula. Variable interest rate loans are also called floating rate loans. A common formula for variable rate business loans is an interest rate of "prime" plus a specified margin (e.g., prime plus 2%). When the bank's prime rate changes from one reset date to the next, the interest rate charged to the borrower is altered to reflect the new prime rate. Reset periods range from daily to one year or longer. Three- or five-year variable rate home mortgage loans are quite common. *Loan term* or *maturity period* refers to the amount of time from the original date of the loan (i.e., the day when the borrower signed the debt contract and received the loan proceeds) to when the loan must be fully repaid. The date of the loan term when principal must be fully repaid is called the maturity date. *Amortization period* is the time period for which the regular repayment of loan principal is determined. The distinction between amortization period and loan term exists because principal payment amounts can be based on a different time period, or schedule, than the loan term. For example, a loan may have a 5-year term, but with payments based on a 15-year amortization period. This means that regular loan payments are calculated as though principal was being repaid over 15 years, but the loan must be fully repaid at the end of 5 years. In this case, there will be a large unpaid principal balance at the end of year five, as payments were made on a longer 15-year repayment schedule. This final principal payment amount is called a "balloon payment" and loans of this type are sometimes called "balloon" loans due to the large final principal payment.

The following three examples show how different amortization periods affect both regular loan payments and balloon payments. Each example assumes that ABC Construction Company borrows $1 million from Community Bank with a 3-year loan term and 10% interest rate. Regular payments of interest and principal are made every month.

Interest Only Loan. ABC Construction Company is only paying interest on the principal amount. Monthly payments are equal to one twelfth of the annual interest or $8,333.33 ($1,000,000 * .10/12 = $8,333.33). Payments for months 1 through 35 are $8,333.33. The final payment in month 36 equals this interest payment plus the full loan principal amount. Thus, the final payment is $1,008,333.33.

Fully Amortizing Loan. Here the loan term and amortization period are the same so that the loan principal is fully amortized (or repaid) over the loan term. Loan payments are based on a 3-year or 36-month amortization period. Payments for all 36 periods are $32,267.19.[5] There is no balloon payment.

Partially Amortizing Loan. In this case, the amortization period is 5 years so loan payments are calculated based on this 5-year or 60-month repayment period. Payments for the first 35 months equal $21,247.04.[6] There is a final balloon payment of $481,688.56 that includes the regular monthly payment of $21,247.03 plus the remaining unpaid principal of $460,441.52.

Note how the amortization period influences the monthly loan payment amount and the principal balance over time. Figure 2.1 shows how the principal balance changes over the loan term for the three debt types. Without any principal amortization, interest only loan payments are very modest. Since there is no reduction of principal over the loan term, the firm must make a very large balloon payment. A lender would be hesitant to make such a loan since it risks losing the full principal amount if something goes wrong and ABC Construction is unable to make the final balloon payment. Payments under the fully amortizing loan are much higher and the loan principal is fully reduced over time so that the firm avoids a balloon payment. However, if these payments are too high for ABC Construction, such that it cannot afford the loan, the partially amortizing loan provides an alternative. A 2-year extension of the payment schedule has a large impact on loan payments, reducing the company's annual payments by over $132,000 (or 34%). This substantial saving might make an investment that is not affordable with 3-year amortization financially feasible. ABC Construction Company will face a large balloon payment in 3 years, but it may be willing to incur this risk if it expects cash flow to increase enough over the 3 years to make the balloon payment. A second option would be to obtain another loan to pay off the balloon payment and repay this second loan over another few years.

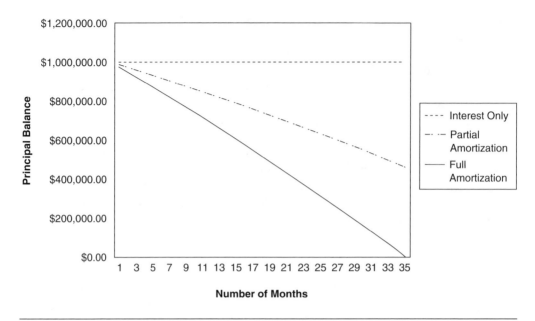

Figure 2.1   Comparison of Principal Balance Over Time for Interest Only and Amortizing Loans

Loan collateral is a second critical aspect of debt transactions. In return for providing debt, lenders typically require the borrower to make available, or pledge, specific assets as collateral that provide an additional source of loan repayment if the borrower's cash flow is insufficient. When assets are pledged as loan collateral, also referred to as security for the loan, the debt holder has a legal right to sell the collateral and apply the sale proceeds to unpaid interest, principal, and collection costs. A lender's priority in receiving the proceeds from the sale of collateral is determined by the seniority of the lender's claim, or security interest, in the collateral. Senior, or first position, lenders have a first priority claim on the collateral. Senior lenders must be paid in full before any sale proceeds are available to repay lenders with a lower priority claim. A lender with the second priority claim is said to have a second position with respect to the collateral. Other lenders might have a third or fourth position security interest. Collectively, lenders with security interests below the senior lender are referred to as subordinate or junior lenders. Loans also vary by the type of collateral used to secure a loan. Loans secured by real estate are called mortgage loans, after the legal instrument used to establish the lender's security interest in the collateral. Equipment loans refer to loans with equipment as collateral. An accounts receivable loan is secured by a firm's unpaid invoices to its customers.

Some lenders also require a *guarantee* to provide still further assurance that a loan will be repaid, especially if the firm's financial performance is not strong and/or the value of the collateral is insufficient to fully cover the loan. A guarantee's value depends on the financial strength of the guarantor (the party making the guarantee). As discussed above, personal guarantees are provided by a firm's owner(s) and their quality depends on the wealth of these individuals. However, even when the business owner does not have substantial wealth, lenders may seek a personal guarantee as evidence of the owner's personal stake and commitment toward repaying the debt. Corporate guarantees are made by the business entity that receives the loan or a related entity. A general corporate guarantee in effect extends the collateral standing behind the loan to all of the corporation's assets. When a borrower is a subsidiary of a larger corporation, a lender may seek a guarantee from the parent corporation both to ensure that the greater financial strength of the parent corporation stands behind loan payment and to prevent the parent corporation from draining assets and earnings from the subsidiary that weaken it financially and render it unable to repay the loan. A guarantee can also be provided by a third party with stronger credit than the borrower. Government programs (e.g., U.S. Small Business Administration loan guarantees) are one type of third-party guarantee, but insurance companies and banks also provide them. Mortgage insurance is a common type of third-party guarantee that compensates for low collateral coverage in home mortgage loans. Third-party guarantees also are used in public debt sold by governmental entities.

To complete this tour of debt-related terms, we discuss two terms that lenders use to evaluate the capacity of a firm or project to repay debt. *Debt service coverage ratio* measures how a firm's cash flow compares to the required principal and interest payments (also called debt service payments). This ratio is calculated for annual figures as follows:

$$\text{Debt Service Coverage Ratio} = \frac{\text{Annual Cash Flow Available to Pay Debt Service}}{\text{Annual Principal and Interest Payments}}$$

Consider the third ABC Construction Company loan example discussed earlier with monthly payments of \$21,247.03. Total annual principal and interest payments for this loan are \$254,964.36 (12 * \$21,247.03). If ABC's total annual cash flow available for debt payments is \$325,000, then the debt service coverage ratio is \$325,000/\$254,964.36, which equals 1.27. Private sector lenders typically require a minimum coverage ratio of 1.20 to 1.25, but this varies with the type of business and the perceived risk of the project. All else being equal, lenders like a higher ratio since it provides a larger cash flow cushion for loan payments if the business experiences unforeseen problems. The second lending ratio is the *loan-to-value ratio*, which compares the total loan principal to the market or appraised value of the pledged collateral. This ratio is calculated as follows:

$$\text{Loan-to-Value Ratio} = \frac{\text{Total Loan Principal Amount}}{\text{Value of Pledged Loan Collateral}}$$

Using the ABC Construction Company loan to illustrate this ratio, assume that the company pledges four construction vehicles and real estate (a 2-acre site with two large garages and a small office building) as collateral for this loan. Community Bank commissioned an appraisal that valued this property at $1.2 million. The loan-to-value ratio for the loan is $1,000,000/$1,200,000 or .83. Lenders typically seek a loan-to-value ratio of .80 or lower.

Advantages and Disadvantages of Debt

The advantages of debt financing largely mirror the disadvantages of equity. First, there is no dilution of ownership with debt financing. A business need only repay the amount borrowed plus the specified interest; any growth in the firm's value over the loan period fully accrues to the owners. Second, debt is less costly than equity since lenders bear less risk through receiving regular principal and interest payments and collateral, which provides a second avenue for repayment beyond the firm's cash flow. Consequently, small business and commercial real estate debt is usually available at interest rates in the 8% to 12% range, depending on prevailing interest rates. Finally, there is greater availability of debt financing than equity. Beyond the many conventional sources, such as banks and finance companies, firms can also receive credit from suppliers (known as trade credit) and borrow through corporate credit cards. Furthermore, the owner's personal credit and assets offer another potential source of debt, as when personal credit cards or a second mortgage are used to raise funds to start and grow a business.

Four major disadvantages exist with debt financing. First, unlike equity, debt must be repaid even when a firm's revenue declines or costs rise unexpectedly. These fixed payments reduce monies available to reinvest in the business to improve earnings and can generate financial hardship when earnings decline. Debt payments that exceed a firm's cash flow and cash reserves can lead to bankruptcy or, in the worst case, liquidation of the firm's assets to repay debt holders. The consequences of failing to repay a lender (closure and liquidation of the firm) are far graver than those from failing to satisfy the expected returns of equity investors (an inability to raise new equity). A second closely related disadvantage is that debt usually requires a firm to pledge its assets as collateral. This limits the business' ability to borrow in the future, for example in a financial emergency, and can lead to the loss of the pledged asset, or to firm bankruptcy or liquidation when debt is not repaid from cash flow. Third, lenders may establish financial or other restrictions that reduce the firm's operating flexibility. Lenders may require a borrower to hold a minimum cash balance, maintain certain financial ratios, or restrict the use of assets that serve as loan collateral. These requirements place constraints on the business that may either prevent expansion or add costs. To achieve the required cash balance or financial ratios, a company may need to reduce inventory, which might result in lower sales if it runs out of some products. Finally, lenders may require a personal guarantee from the firm's owner to ensure debt repayment. Loans of this nature are known as *recourse loans,* since the debt holder has recourse to the personal assets of the borrower to satisfy repayment. Recourse loans are quite common in small business lending and reflect the close interrelationship between the business owner's personal assets and business assets.[7]

Hybrid Financing

Thus far, we have considered financing instruments as either purely debt or purely equity. Firms, investors, and financial institutions, however, have found ways to create hybrid financial products that combine elements of equity and debt. While hybrid instruments are not ubiquitous, both conventional financiers and economic development lenders use them. The two most common hybrid financial instruments are convertible debt and debt with warrants. *Convertible debt,* as the name implies, is a type of debt in which the debt holder has the option to convert the debt into firm equity, usually common stock. *Debt with warrants* is a loan provided to a firm partly in exchange for the right to purchase some amount of stock at a preset price for a specified period of time.

Financing and the Stages of Firm Development[8]

Firm growth occurs in distinct development stages in which both the availability and use of debt and equity financing varies. A common view of the major business development stages are seed, start-up, growth, and maturity, as presented in Exhibit 2.1. In the earliest seed and start-up stages, businesses are characterized by limited information and high uncertainty of future earnings. Moreover, firms in these stages are investing to create and build their businesses but are not yet generating significant revenue and profits. Firms in these early stages are expected to rely heavily on informal sources of capital, since information on them is limited and costly to obtain, and their earnings prospects and future value is highly unpredictable. Equity is the primary capital source since they do not generate the cash flow needed to make fixed debt payments. One exception is trade credit in which vendors extend very short-term credit to their customers. As firms reach the growth stage, they generate a sales and profit history to inform investors about their business skills, cash flow, and value, their cash flow grows and becomes more predictable, and

Exhibit 2.1   Firms' Growth Stages and Financial Characteristics

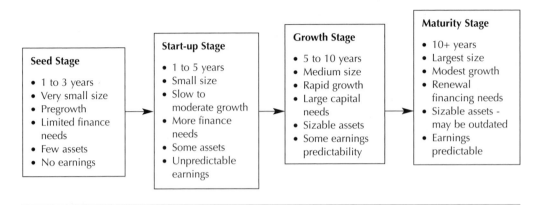

they acquire assets that provide security to lenders. Firms in this stage can utilize more debt and have greater access to institutional capital sources on both the equity and debt side. When firms reach the maturity stage or grow in size and profits, they have still greater access to debt capital with predictable cash flow and substantial assets. Finally, some firms face special financing problems in the mature stage when a declining market or new sources of competition sharply reduce sales and profits. While these firms need to invest to modernize production and/or introduce new products to restore sales or generate new growth, their poor past performance and uncertain future makes it difficult to secure debt from banks and other financial institutions. Without a strong market or earnings growth potential, they are also poor prospects for equity investment. Such firms are more likely to depend on owner financing, informal investors, and nontraditional capital sources, such as government and nonprofit economic development finance programs.

Data on Small Business Capital Sources

After reviewing the characteristics and relative merits of debt and equity, it is important to consider what empirical data indicate about the use of these two types of capital. Since large firms are less affected by capital market imperfections and are not targeted for development finance interventions, this discussion concentrates on small businesses. Allen N. Berger and Gregory F. Udell summarized existing data and research on this issue in their 1998 article in the *Journal of Banking and Finance*. Their compiled data on the distribution of equity and debt financing for U.S. small businesses[9] is presented in Table 2.1. Berger and Udell emphasize that the data represent rough estimates rather than a complete and accurate picture of small business financing sources. Overall, this data indicate that small businesses rely almost equally on equity and debt, with each supplying half of total business

Table 2.1   Estimated Distribution of Capital Sources for U.S. Small Businesses

Capital Source	All Small Businesses (except farm, financial, and real estate)	Small Businesses with < 20 employees and < $1 million in sales	Small Businesses with ≥ 20 employees and ≥ $1 million in sales
Principal Owner Equity	31.33%	44.53%	27.22%
Angel Finance	3.59%	n.a.	n.a.
Venture Capital	1.85%	n.a.	n.a.
Other Equity	12.86%	n.a.	n.a.
Total Equity	49.63%	56.00%	47.67%
Commercial Banks	18.75%	14.88%	19.94%
Finance Companies	4.91%	3.08%	5.47%
Other Financial Institution	3.00%	3.53%	2.83%
Trade Credit	15.78%	11.81%	17.01%
Principal Owner Debt	4.10%	5.59%	3.63%
Other Sources	3.83%	5.11%	3.45%
Total Debt	50.37%	44.00%	52.33%

SOURCE: Berger & Udell (1998, pp. 613–673, Table 1)

financing. Principal owners are the largest single source of financing at 35.43%, almost all of which is invested as equity.

Commercial banks and trade credit[10] are the next most important sources, supplying 18.75% and 15.78% of funds, respectively. Collectively, these three sources provide 69.96% of the financing for small businesses. Commercial banks are by far the most important institutional source of small business financing, accounting for almost 19% of total capital and over one third of all debt; they supply ten times more capital than venture capital firms and over three times the amount provided by finance companies. On the debt side, finance companies and other financial institutions supplied slightly less than 8% of total debt and equity. On the equity side, venture capital accounted for 1.85% of all small business funding, suggesting that only a small minority of firms utilize this capital source. Some important differences exist between the smallest small firms, those with fewer than 20 employees and sales of less than $1 million, and the larger ones. The smallest firms rely more heavily on equity and principal owner investment while larger firms use more commercial bank debt and supplier credit.

Equity accounts for 56% of total financing for the smallest businesses, compared to 48% for the larger firms. Principal owner equity is especially important for the smaller businesses, contributing 44.5% of their total funding compared to 27.2% for the larger firms. When debt is included, principal owners provided half of all financing to firms with less than 20 employees versus 30.85% for the larger ones. Since larger firms use more debt than equity, it is not surprising that commercial banks and trade credit supply more capital to these businesses. These two sources account for 36.9% of larger firms' financing versus 26.7% for the smallest enterprises.

Empirical studies reveal far greater use of both debt and external financing by firms than suggested by the growth stage theory of firms. One study of Wisconsin businesses found that external financing far exceeded the financing provided by owners. Moreover, the study found that external financing declines over a firm's first 7 to 8 years, and then increases.[11] This contradicts the accepted view that firms have limited access to external debt and equity at start-up and increase their reliance on outside financing as they age. Data compiled by Berger and Udell, summarized in Table 2.2, also indicates extensive use of debt financing by small firms during the start-up stage. Infant firms, 2 years old or younger, received 47.9% of their financing from debt, almost the same percentage as for firms between 5 and 24 years old. Moreover, banks and finance companies were the sources of this debt financing. This surprisingly large proportion of debt financing might result from the start-up firm's use of the owner's personal assets to guarantee loans.[12]

A second counterintuitive pattern is the declining share of debt and the increasing proportion of owner equity for firms over 4 years old. Berger and Udell cite two causes of this trend.[13] First, as firms grow and become more profitable, their retained earnings rise, increasing owner's equity and reducing reliance on external financing. Second, owners may use their increased equity to buy out other equity investors and lenders, especially informal angels, family, and friends. This interpretation is consistent with the decline in other sources of debt over the same period.

Since these figures are averages across all small firms, they likely mask considerable variation in financing patterns across different industries, business types, and owners. Businesses with large up front research and development expenses probably rely heavily on equity during the infant and adolescent years whereas retail and service businesses that generate revenue more quickly can use more debt in their early years. Similarly, high-income owners with more savings can make larger equity investments than low- and moderate-income business owners, who may be forced to primarily rely on debt.

Table 2.2   Sources of Small Firm Financing by Firm Age

Capital	0–2 Years	3 to 4 Years	5 to 24 Years	25 Years or Older
Principal Owner	19.61%	17.37%	31.94%	35.42%
Total Equity	47.90%	39.37%	48.00%	56.50%
Commercial Banks	15.66%	30.84%	17.86%	17.25%
Finance Companies	8.33%	2.51%	5.85%	3.28%
Other Fin. Institutions	3.84%	2.36%	2.87%	3.38%
Trade Credit	13.40%	13.42%	17.10%	13.86%
Principal Owner	6.02%	6.19%	3.91%	3.68%
Other Sources	4.85%	5.31%	4.41%	2.05%
Total Debt	52.10%	60.63%	52.00%	33.50%

SOURCE: Berger and Udell (1998, pp. 613–673, Table 2)

The Use of Equity and
Debt in Hypothetical Firms

To conclude this chapter, we consider the financing needs for three hypothetical businesses to assess the suitability and the role of debt and equity in addressing each firm's needs. This exercise provides tangible examples of how the abstract aspects of equity and debt discussed in this chapter relate to authentic business situations. It is also intended to foster stronger intuition about when each type of financing is appropriate. For each example, two issues are discussed: What is the firm's capacity to support equity or debt financing? What mixture of debt and equity is appropriate to use, and what are the likely sources?

Recycling, Inc. is a start-up corporation that has licensed a new technology that allows it to combine an unsorted stream of plastic waste into molded products. Recycling, Inc. has preliminary agreements to receive recycled waste from several communities. It also is negotiating a contract to supply a major retailer with plastic storage bins made from this recycled plastic. The company is seeking financing to lease space and set up a manufacturing facility to produce the bins.

As a start-up business using a new technology, Recycling, Inc.'s future cash flow is very uncertain, and it has few hard assets to collateralize loans. Consequently, the firm will have to rely heavily on equity financing to cover its start-up manufacturing costs and cumulative losses until it is profitable. In raising equity, a key issue is the company's capacity to secure investment from venture capital funds in addition to relying on the principal owners and other informal sources. Its ability to raise venture capital will depend on the potential market size and earnings growth of the business. On the positive side, Recycling, Inc. has the potential to produce a large variety of products that, in total, represent a large market. On the negative side, it is producing commodity products in which sales are often cost-driven and profit margins are low. An investor would carefully consider Recycling, Inc.'s ability to either achieve a sustainable cost advantage over other producers or identify a large and growing market for recycled products that would accept a price premium. Once the firm secured sufficient equity capital to start up and sustain its operations for a few years, it should be able to raise debt for equipment (the equipment is high-quality collateral), trade credit from its suppliers, and perhaps a short-term loan from a bank or finance company.

Talking Systems is a 20-year-old supplier of electronic components for defense systems and wireless communications devices. It has a contract to supply Motorola with a new product that requires increasing its output by 30%. It needs financing to acquire the equipment to set up a new production line and for the materials and labor to produce the component.

Talking Systems is a well-established firm with both an earnings history and, presumably, substantial assets. Moreover, the new contract will generate a predictable income stream from a large corporate customer. Therefore, it should be able to use primarily debt to finance its expansion. Talking Systems can pledge the equipment installed for the line and its inventory as collateral to raise this debt. Since lenders will finance only a portion of these assets' value (they will require a loan to value ratio of 80% or lower), Talking Systems will need to supplement this debt with other funds.[14] Equity is one way to fill this gap, either with cash from Talking Systems's retained earnings or by raising new equity through a stock sale. However, Talking Systems may be able to raise these additional funds by pledging other business assets to raise more debt. Its capacity to fully fund the expansion with debt depends on the availability of the firm's assets as collateral (i.e., whether they secure other loans), the value of its assets, and the firm's overall profitability and cash flow. If the amount of new debt is large (tens of millions of dollars) and Talking Systems is financially strong, then a public sale of debt in the bond markets might be used. Otherwise, Talking Systems will borrow from an institutional lender (a bank, finance company, or insurance company) that provides the best financing terms.

Town Market is a locally owned business that has successfully operated a 15,000-square foot grocery store in an urban neighborhood for the past 10 years. It plans to open a second 10,000-square foot store on the ground floor of a newly renovated low-income housing development in another neighborhood. It has signed a 10-year lease for the space and needs financing to make improvements to the unfinished retail space, acquire equipment and inventory, and cover other operating expenses until the store generates positive cash flow.

Town Market's new store has elements of both a start-up and an existing business expansion. The second store is a new location where a customer base must be established in a different competitive environment. Thus, its future sales and cash flow are somewhat uncertain. On the other hand, Town Market has a successful track record, a financial history that informs its expected cash flow and profits at the new store, and its cash flow and assets from the first store can be used to finance the new one. Its ability to raise debt solely from the cash flow and collateral at the second store will depend on competition at this location. If there is limited competition, lenders are more likely to overlook the start-up nature of the new store. Limited assets at the new store pose a second obstacle to raising debt. Since Town Market does not own the real estate or store improvements, it cannot pledge them as collateral. Its collateral at the new store is limited to equipment and inventory. Assuming limited competition, Town Market should be able to raise debt for equipment and inventory (probably relying on trade credit from grocery wholesalers). It would need to supplement this debt with equity to fund store improvement costs and other operating expenses. Given the firm's small size and prosaic business, it is unlikely to raise equity from venture capitalists or angel investors. Instead, it would rely on the owners' personal funds, retained earnings from the first store, or, perhaps, funds from family and friends. Town Market might be able to raise more debt and reduce its equity investment by pledging available assets and cash flow from its first store. A second option is having the new store's landlord fund the store improvements in exchange for higher lease payments, in effect borrowing from the landlord. The landlord has an incentive to fund such improvements to secure a long-term lease. Moreover, unlike a third-party lender, the landlord can recoup this investment if Town Market fails by re-leasing the space to another grocery store.

Looking Ahead

This introduction to how businesses use debt and equity and the key terms and issues associated with these financial instruments provides a necessary foundation for studying the primary business uses of capital: working capital and fixed assets. However, a slight detour is required before we can effectively address these topics and present the issues involved in extending credit to firms. We need to explain how businesses report financial information and how this information is used to evaluate a firm's financing needs and capacity to repay new debt. The next chapter introduces key accounting concepts and business financial statements, and Chapter 4 provides an economic development framework and methods to evaluate a business that is seeking new capital. Chapters 5 and 6 then return to business finance needs and tools by looking at the financing of working capital and fixed assets, respectively.

Endnotes

1. Businesses can be organized under three legal forms: a sole proprietorship, a partnership, and a corporation. A sole proprietorship occurs when a single individual owns the businesses without a separate legal entity and the business is a personal asset. A partnership exists when multiple parties jointly own an enterprise, and equity takes the form of a partnership interest rather than a share of stock. Real estate projects are often organized as partnerships with a limited partnership structure in which investors are "limited partners" who receive a defined share of the partnership earnings and assets but have no responsibility for business operations. A general partner is responsible for management of the business. Limited partners' liability in the business or development project is restricted to their financial investment, as is the case for corporate shareholder. Limited partnerships also are used to finance venture capital funds, oil and gas exploration, and research and development activities.

2. The discussion of common and preferred stock draws on Brealey and Myers (2002), *Principles of Corporate Finance*, pp. 383–389. Chapters 14 and 15 provide an overview of the corporate debt and equity.

3. See Coopers and Lybrand, *Venture Capital: The Price of Growth*, 1993 Update, for a more detailed discussion of company valuation and its role in venture capital investing.

4. Common names include loan, note, bond, debenture, and line of credit.

5. The payment amount was calculated using the Excel spreadsheet payment formula, = pmt(interest rate for payment period, number or payment periods, loan principal). For this loan the formula is pmt(.10/12,36,1000000). Note that the interest rate and number-of-payment period are based on months, not years, since monthly loan payments will be made. Financial tables or an electronic calculator can also be used to calculate the monthly payment.

6. In this case, the Excel monthly payment formula is: "= payment (.10/12,60,1000000)" since the amortization is over 60 months.

7. Berger and Udell (1998), p. 626, make this point in their excellent analysis of small business finance.

8. This discussion draws on Berger and Udell (1998), pp. 7–8; Litvak and Daniels (1979), *Innovations in Development Finance,* pp. 36–37; and Richards (1983), *Fundamentals of Development Finance,* pp. 15–23.

9. Berger and Udell (1998) define small businesses as firms with fewer than 500 full-time equivalent employees.

10. Trade credit is financing provided by vendors who supply goods and services on credit.

11. This 1997 study by Fluck, Holtz-Eaton, and Rosen entitled, *Where Does the Money Come From?* is cited in Berger and Udell (1998), pp. 624–625.

12. Berger and Udell (1998), p. 626.

13. Berger and Udell (1998), p. 625.

14. Talking Systems also needs cash for its labor costs and to extend trade credit to its customers (i.e., to receive payments after it ships products to its customers).

3

An Introduction to Business Financial Statements

In this chapter, we build on the basic knowledge of how businesses are financed by looking at how firms organize and report financial information. This understanding of financial statements relates to economic development finance in several ways. First, it is critical for assisting individual businesses to secure financing. A careful reading of a firm's financial statements reveals how it has financed its activities and helps identify the appropriate financing to address its fiscal needs. Second, financial statement analysis is central to evaluating a firm's capacity to repay debt or generate the return required by equity investors. Third, financial statements provide insight into common financing issues faced by similar firms, such as those in the same industry, at the same stage of development, with similar ownership, or in the same size class. For all these reasons, development finance practitioners need to be literate with financial statements.

To develop this literacy, this chapter covers three topics. It begins by introducing several important concepts that underlie accounting and financial statements and explains the difference between accrual and cash accounting. Next, it explains the three major financial statements used to summarize businesses, the balance sheet, the income statement, and the cash flow statement and defines the major categories of financial information included on these reports. Future chapters build on this knowledge of financial statements to develop skills in evaluating a business's capacity to support new capital and in structuring appropriate financing.

Accounting Concepts and Accrual Accounting

Robert N. Anthony, David F. Hawkins, and Kenneth A. Merchant in their classic introduction to accounting, *Accounting: Text and Cases,* identify 11 basic concepts that guide accounting practice.[1] While all eleven concepts are important, three concepts are especially helpful in highlighting how financial statements are prepared and clarifying the nature of accrual accounting. The first principal is called the *dual aspect concept,* which is summarized by a simple equation that is the foundation for the balance sheet. This equation, assets = equities, indicates that everything that is owned by a firm (its assets) is claimed by someone, either its creditors (whose claims are called liabilities) or its owners (whose claims are called owner's equity). This concept is common sense; all of a firm's possessions must belong to someone. As discussed in the previous chapters, creditors have a first claim on a firm's assets while the owners have a residual claim.

An important corollary to the dual aspect concept is that every financial transaction of a business must impact at least two accounts of the firm. For the dual aspect equation to remain true, when a transaction increases an asset account, then either another asset account must decrease or an equity account must increase. Accountants use a system of debits and credits to keep the asset and equity aspects of a firm's financial accounts in balance.[2] For every transaction, the total of debit entries must equal the total of credit entries to ensure that assets will equal equities after the transaction is recorded. Accounting is referred to as a dual entry record-keeping system due to the balancing of debits and credits for each transaction.

Two additional concepts, the realization concept and matching concept, are used to determine when revenue and expenses[3] are recognized (i.e., recorded as such in the firm's accounts). Under the *realization concept,* revenue is recognized and credited to a firm's accounts when goods are shipped or services are rendered. Note that revenue is not recognized when payment is made for the goods or services. This is central to accrual accounting in which revenue is recorded when it is earned (i.e., when goods or services are provided), not when payment is received. Under the *matching concept,* which governs how expenses are allocated, expenses are recognized in the same period when the revenues associated with those costs are recorded. By matching expenses with the recognized revenue for a given period, financial statements provide an accurate representation of the economic results of the sales occurring during the period. Note, as with revenue, that expenses are not recorded based on when payment is made. Since some costs are not directly related to producing goods or services but are general costs of the firm (e.g., insurance or salaries for the accounting staff), these expenses are recognized in the period for which they are associated. Insurance costs and accounting department salaries for October would be recorded as an expense in the October accounting records.

The realization and matching concepts are central to accrual basis accounting, which is required under generally accepted accounting principals (GAAP), the standards for all private sector financial statements. To understand accrual accounting, it is helpful to compare it to cash basis financial reporting. Under cash basis reporting, transactions are recorded based on the receipt and expenditure of cash. Cash basis revenue is recorded when the payment for goods and services is received and expenses are recognized when cash payments are made. Cash basis reporting presents the impact of business activities on a firm's cash flow and cash position, but it has a serious pitfall. With cash basis financial reports, the income received during a period is not linked with the associated costs, and there is no determination of whether the business was profitable during a given time period. Accrual accounting, on the other hand, does not follow the cash. Instead, it seeks to accurately present a firm's "earned income," the actual economic results of its activities over a period. Accrual accounting statements answer the question: What were a business's financial results for a period based on the revenue generated and the associated costs in that period, independent of when payment is received and bills are paid.

In differentiating accrual from cash accounting, it is useful to distinguish between *revenue,* the accrual concept, and *receipt,* the cash activity. Revenue refers to income generated by the provision of goods or services to a customer. Revenue is a function of the delivery of goods and services in a period, and its financial reporting is unrelated to the timing of any payment. Receipt refers to the collection of cash: it records when a customer makes a payment, which may differ from when the customer actually receives goods or services. A similar distinction exists between *expense,* the accrual concept, and *expenditure,* the cash transaction. Expenses refer to the costs incurred during a period that are related to either the generation of revenue in that period or a general business cost for the period. Expenses are recorded in financial statements independent of any cash outlays for the period. Expenditure, on the other hand, refers to the outlay of cash, whether or not that outlay is tied to revenue-generating activities during that period.

To see the difference in financial reports based on cash and accrual accounting, consider the following activities of College Books, a mail order bookstore during the month of September 2002. During this month, College Books shipped $2,000 in books to customers. These customers paid for the books in October, after their receipt. College Books acquired the inventory of books sold in September during the months of June, July, and August, paying $1,200 over these 3 months. General business costs for College Books are monthly rent payments of $200 paid on the first day of each month and monthly salaries of $500, paid on the last day of each month.

Both a cash basis and accrual basis income statement for College Books are presented in Exhibit 3.1. In the cash basis statement, no revenue is recorded in September since College Books did not receive any payment in this month. Similarly, no deduction is made for the cost of the books shipped in September since the firm paid for these books in the prior 3 months. The only cash payments in September were $700 for its rent and salaries. Consequently, the cash basis statement for College Books shows a loss of $700. The accrual income statement reports income of $2,000 corresponding to the sales price for the books shipped that month. The cost of these books is matched to the revenue and reported as a $1,200 expense. The other $700 in monthly costs also are deducted as September expenses, showing a final net income of $100. Although the cash statement shows that College Books's bank account declined by $700 during September, it does

Exhibit 3.1   Cash and Accrual September Income Statements for College Books

	Cash Statement	Accrual Statement
Revenue	$0	$2,000
Cost of Goods Sold	$0	($1,200)
Rent	($200)[a]	($200)
Salaries	($500)	($500)
Net Income	($700)	$ 100

NOTE:

a. A figure shown in parentheses in financial statements represents a negative number, either a deduction or a loss.

not show the economic results of College Books's activities for the month (i.e., whether or not the firm earned a profit from its September sales). The accrual statement provides a more complete and accurate picture of the store's financial results.

Financial Statements: The Balance Sheet

Accounting systems function to generate reports that provide an accurate picture of a business's financial condition and performance. There are two standard financial reports prepared by businesses: the balance sheet and the income statement (also called a profit and loss statement or a statement of revenues and expenses). For the firm's owners and managers, these reports inform decisions about the firm's management, operations, and capital spending. Economic development professionals use this information to make decisions about whether to provide debt or equity financing to a firm. Practitioners also use financial statement analysis in their technical assistance work, to identify weaknesses and management issues that firms need to address to improve their performance and access financing. Although the balance sheet and income statement are separate reports, they are closely linked and should be analyzed together to understand a firm's finances. A third financial report, the cash flow statement, details how the firm's activities affect cash flow. While a cash flow statement is included in audited financial statements prepared by independent accounting firms, firms without audited statements often do not prepare this key financial statement themselves. Thus, the steps to construct a cash flow statement from the balance sheet and income statement are detailed below.

The *balance sheet* is a snapshot of a business's financial position at a single point in time. It organizes financial information about the firm's assets (things of value that it owns), liabilities (its financial obligations), and shareholder's equity on a specific date. Exhibit 3.2 presents the balance sheet for a fictional firm, American Biotechnology Company (ABC). Note that the balance sheet includes a date, June 30, 2002, which is the date for which the report applies. The asset and liability values listed in the report are for that specific date. Since ABC may undertake transactions that significantly change its financial position on the next day, this static picture is an important limitation of the financial information in a balance sheet. As the name implies, the balance sheet must balance; that is, the total assets must equal the total liabilities and shareholders' equities, per the dual aspect principle and the dual entry accounting method. ABC's total assets and total liabilities and shareholders' equity both equal $81.8 million.

Exhibit 3.2 American Biotechnology Company Balance Sheet—June 30, 2002

ASSETS

Current Assets

Cash and Cash Equivalents	$410,000
Marketable Securities	3,000,000
Accounts Receivable, net of allowance	16,065,000
Inventory	16,178,000
Prepaid Expenses	779,000
Total Current Assets	36,432,000
Investments	3,343,000
Property Plant and Equipment, less accumulated depreciation	21,905,000
Purchased Technology and Goodwill	19,310,000
Other Assets	810,000
TOTAL ASSETS	$81,800,000

LIABILITIES AND SHAREHOLDERS' EQUITY

Current Liabilities

Accounts Payable	$7,148,000
Income Taxes Payable	12,000
Accrued Expenses	3,973,000
Deferred Income	985,000
Current Portion of Long-Term Debt	1,367,000
Total Current Liabilities	13,485,000
Deferred Income	361,000
Long-Term Debt, less current portion	5,022,000
Total Liabilities	18,868,000
Shareholders' Equity	
Common Stock Issue, par value $.01 per share	
Authorized 40,000,000 shares,	
Issued 23,305,000 shares	233,305
Additional Paid-in Capital	110,198,695
Accumulated Deficit	(47,500,000)
Total Equity	62,932,000
TOTAL LIABILITIES AND SHAREHOLDERS' EQUITY	$81,800,000

There are two common interpretations of the balance sheet.[4] The first interpretation is a statement of the firm's resources and the claims against those resources. Assets correspond to the resources owned by the firm while the liabilities and shareholders' equity are the claims against those assets. Liabilities are the claims of suppliers, lenders, and other outside parties while shareholders' equity represents the claims of the firm's owners. Thus, one immediate piece of information that the balance sheet provides is the relative size of the claims of outside creditors versus those of the firm's owners. In ABC's case, owner's claims, at $62.9 million, are over three times those of outsiders, at $18.9 million. A second interpretation of the balance sheet is a statement of the firm's sources and uses of funds. The liabilities and shareholders' equity represent the sources of funds while the assets show how the firm used these funds. This view is very useful since it tells us how the firm has financed itself and what assets it has acquired with this financing. For ABC, shareholders' equity provided the primary source of funds, and the largest uses of these funds have been for property, plant, and equipment ($21.3 million) and purchased technology and goodwill ($19.3 million).

Financial information in the balance sheets is reported under specific categories. While the categories in each firm's balance sheet can vary somewhat,[5] Figure 3.2 includes the major categories listed on most balance sheets. Figures on the balance sheet reflect the original cost paid for items, not their current market value.[6] "Book value" is often used to refer to this cost valuation of a firm's assets on its financial statements. Assets are grouped into two types: current assets and noncurrent assets. Current assets are those assets that are normally converted into cash within 1 year or, in some cases, within the normal operating cycle of the business. For example, since large aircraft take longer than 1 year to manufacture, the inventory of an aircraft manufacturer represents the materials that would be converted to cash under their normal production and sales cycle, rather than over 1 year. Assets are listed in a specific order, with those most easily converted into cash (referred to as more "liquid" assets) listed first followed by less liquid assets. Thus, current assets are listed before noncurrent assets, and cash is the first item listed.

The current asset categories on ABC's balance sheet are cash, marketable securities, accounts receivable, inventory, and prepaid expenses. *Cash* refers to both cash that is in the firm's direct possession and funds held in ABC's bank accounts that are immediately available for its use. *Marketable securities* are investment securities with maturities of 1 year or less that can be readily redeemed or sold. Firms often have more cash than they need for near term expenditures, and they invest these funds in certificates of deposit, commercial paper, treasury bills, or other short-term investment instruments to increase interest income earned on these funds. *Accounts receivables* are the uncollected bills for goods and services that ABC has shipped or rendered. Since most businesses do not operate on a cash sales basis, accounts receivable are usually a large and important part of a firm's current assets.

ABC's accounts receivables total $16 million, almost one fifth of its total assets. *Inventory* refers to goods held by the firm in one of three forms: (1) raw materials and supplies that are used in the firm's business; (2) unfinished goods-in-progress that the firm is still in the process of manufacturing; and (3) finished products. Some firms list inventory under these three separate categories on their balance, but others, like ABC, consolidate all three types of inventory into one figure. Inventory is a major asset for some business, such as manufacturers, retailers, and wholesalers, but is of little significance to service businesses. *Prepaid expenses,* the final current asset category, are costs that the business has paid for but that are not yet treated as expenses based on the matching concept. Businesses often pay in advance for expenses recognized in future periods. For example, a firm may pay for an annual insurance policy in advance of the policy period. This advance payment is an asset, something of value that the firm acquired that will be used in the future course of its business. The prepaid expense amount will be reduced each month of the period covered by the policy, as the business "uses" its insurance policy. An accounting entry will be made to record a business expense equal to the reduction in the prepaid expense asset.[7]

ABC's noncurrent assets, those with a life longer than 1 year, include property, plant, and equipment; purchased technology and goodwill; and other assets. *Property, plant, and equipment* represent the land, buildings, and equipment owned by the business. These items are often listed under the term *fixed assets* since they are, with the exception of noninstalled equipment, immovable. Since property, plant, and equipment have a limited useful life, firms reduce the value of their fixed assets each year to account for the implicit costs associated with their wearing out and replacement over time. The term for this reduction in value of fixed assets is *depreciation.* Thus, ABC's $21.9 million of property, plant, and equipment is listed net of accumulated depreciation: the figure represents the original cost of these assets less the cumulative depreciation deductions taken. Other firms list the original cost, accumulated depreciation, and the net value as separate items on their balance sheet. When a business depreciates the value of its fixed assets, it enters a corresponding accounting entry as a depreciation expense on the income statement. Purchased technology and goodwill represents the value of other firms and technology acquired by ABC. When a firm acquires the assets of another firm, it may pay more than the stated book value of its assets. Accountants use *goodwill* to account for this excess of the acquisition price over the book value. Goodwill may relate to acquired assets that have real value to firms, such as brand names, customer lists, experience, and relationships, but that cannot be directly valued. Goodwill also can reflect the difference between a firm's book value and its market value at the time of acquisition. *Other assets* is a catchall category for other things owned by the firm that do not fit into other categories or do not warrant a separate listing.

The equities side of the balance sheet is divided into two sections, liabilities and shareholders' equity. As with assets, liabilities to be paid within either 1 year or the business's normal operating cycle are listed first under current liabilities. ABC's balance sheet includes the typical current liabilities categories: accounts payable, income taxes payable, accrued expenses, deferred income, and current portion of long-tem debt. *Accounts payable* are ABC's unpaid bills for goods and services that it received as of June 30, 2002. Accounts payable and accounts receivable are two sides of the same transaction. One firm's account receivable is another's account payable. An account receivable is the vendor's uncollected invoice for goods or services rendered; an account payable is the customer's unpaid bill for goods or services received. *Income taxes payable* are ABC's unpaid portion of its tax liability on its net income from the prior period. Depending on the applicable state and local taxes, a firm may have additional tax liabilities for property, excise, and other taxes. *Accrued expenses* is a concept similar to prepaid expenses. It refers to expenses that have been recognized for accounting purposes but have not yet been billed or paid. With the matching of revenue and expenses under accrual accounting, costs are recognized as expenses for a period if they are directly tied to goods or services delivered during that period or are general expenses for the period. When such a cost is recognized as expense in a period but has not yet been billed or paid, there is an associated liability for that expense item. Interest payments are a good example of accrued expenses. Some debt contracts require interest payments every quarter or 6 months, but the firm is incurring an interest payment obligation each month. The interest obligation will be deducted as an expense each month. This interest expense is not paid monthly but builds up, or accrues, as an obligation to be paid at a future date. Accrued expenses can also be viewed as the opposite of prepaid expenses. For prepaid expenses, a firm generates an asset by paying for expenses in advance of their "use." With accrued expenses, a firm creates a liability by "using" an expense before it has been billed or paid. *Deferred income* refers to an obligation to provide goods or service for which ABC received advance payment. For example, ABC may have entered into research and development contracts and received up front payment for some of these activities. If ABC needs to acquire facilities and equipment and hire scientists before it can begin the research, it might be paid for some costs in advance. Although ABC has received cash, it cannot recognize this payment as revenue, since under the realization concept it has not provided these services yet. Thus the advance payment is offset by a deferred income liability for the same amount. The deferred income liability will be reduced as the company completes the research and development services and recognizes the revenue for these activities. Note, in Figure 3.2, that ABC has a second deferred income liability that is not listed under current liabilities. This means that ABC received advance payment for obligations that extend beyond 1 year. The portion of the advance payment for research activities over the next year is listed under current liabilities while the balance is listed as a noncurrent liability. *Current portion of long-term debt,* the last current liability listed on ABC's balance sheet, is the portion of ABC's total outstanding debt that must be repaid over the next year. As with deferred income, the balance sheet divides debt liabilities into two portions: the amount payable over the next year and the amount payable beyond 1 year. Only the principal component of debt is listed on the balance sheet. Interest payments are an expense included on the income statement. To calculate ABC's total debt service for a given year from its financial statements, one needs to sum the interest expense from the income statement for that year (interest payments) and the current portion of long-term debt from the balance sheet for the end of the prior year (principal payments).

Shareholders' equity completes the equity side of the balance sheet. The presentation of shareholders' equity can be confusing since it includes three parts: (1) par value; (2) additional paid-in capital; and (3) accumulated retained earnings or deficit. *Par value* is a stated value for the stock that is legally required. It does not have any relationship to the stock's actual market value. Since the par value is the lowest value at which a share of stock can trade, it is usually set at one cent ($.01). Thus, the balance sheet lists the stock's par value as the number of issued shares of stock times the par value. The first line of shareholder's equity for ABC in Figure 3.2 reads as follows:

Common stock issue, par value $.01 per share

Authorized 40,000,000 shares,

Issued 23,305,000 shares   233,305

This line means that ABC is legally authorized to sell up to 40 million shares of common stock, but had issued only 23.305 million of these shares as of June 30, 2002. With a par value of $.01, the total par value of the issued shares is $233,305. However, firms do not sell their stock at par value. Instead, they receive a higher amount of money when their stock is sold to shareholders. This difference between the actual funds raised from stock sales and the listed par value is shown on the balance sheet as *additional paid-in capital*. For ABC, additional paid-in capital is $110,198,695. The total amount that ABC raised from its stock sales is $110,432,000, the sum of par value and additional paid-in capital. The final component of shareholder equity, *retained earnings*, represents the increase in equity value from the accumulated reinvestment of the company's profits (net income). When a business earns a profit, it can distribute some or all of these profits to its shareholders as dividends. The portion that is not paid out as dividends is reinvested in the company and called retained earnings. Since net income represents the firm's residual income after all expenses, it belongs to the firm's owners and any portion retained by the businesses represents an increase in shareholders' equity. Another way to think about this accounting relationship is that when net income is reinvested in a business, it increases the company's assets. Since no external party provided the funds to increase these assets, there is no increase in liabilities to external parties. Consequently, the owners must have a claim on the increased assets, and the owners' equity account increases to balance the increase in assets.

In ABC's case, the balance sheet shows an accumulated deficit of $47.5 million rather than accumulated retained earnings. This means that the company has generated more losses over its life than profits. Its accumulated losses, after deducting any accumulated net income, total $47.5 million. ABC invested its equity to fund research and development and other activities that have not yet generated sufficient revenues to earn sustained profits. Its up front investment to acquire technology and develop new products has exceeded its cumulative profits. This is a common situation for biotechnology companies, which have long lead times, often 10 years or longer, before a new product is developed, tested, and approved for use by regulators. These accumulated losses serve to reduce the book value of the shareholder equity in the same manner that retained earnings increase it. Accumulated losses diminish the firm's assets, which must be consumed to cover the excess of expenses over revenues.[8] Since assets have declined without any reduction in liabilities, the value of the shareholders' claim has been reduced. ABC's losses reduced the book value of shareholders' equity from $110.4 million to $62.9 million. It is important to recognize that this book value for shareholder equity is not the same as the market value of the firm's stock. ABC's stock price may have increased, despite the accumulated losses, if investors believe that the company has good future earning prospects.

Financial Statements: The Income Statement

The second major financial statement produced by firms is the *income statement,* also referred to as a *profit and loss statement* or a *statement of revenue and expenses.* While the balance sheet presents a firm's financial position at one point in time, the income statement shows the financial results from a business's activities over a period of time. It summarizes the two parts of a company's financial flows that determine its profits: revenues and expenses. By relating a firm's expenses to its revenue over a period of time, the income statement presents the economic results of the firm's activities for that period (i.e., its profits).

Exhibit 3.3 presents American Biotechnology Company's income statement for the year ending June 30, 2002. Note that the income statement specifies the time period that it covers. Revenue is listed on the top of the income statement with expenses listed below and net income (profit) presented at the bottom. Beyond this general format, firms use many different presentations of revenue and expenses for their income statement. The main variation occurs in how expenses are separated to present different subtotals before the final net income line. For ABC, income before interest and taxes (known as IBIT or

Exhibit 3.3   American Biotechnology Company Income Statement for the
12 Months Ending June 30, 2002

Revenue	
Product sales	5,013,000
Research and development revenue	7,675,000
Interest income	239,000
Total Revenues	12,927,000
Expenses	
Cost of goods sold	4,967,000
Research and development expenses	2,077,000
Sales, general and administrative expenses	2,908,000
Depreciation	1,000,000
Total Expenses	10,952,000
Income before interest and taxes	1,975,000
Interest expense	(119,000)
Provision for income taxes	(102,000)
Net income	1,754,000
Less cash dividends	0
Retained earnings	1,754,000
Accumulated deficit at beginning of year	(49,254,000)
Plus retained earnings for year	1,754,000
Accumulated deficit at end of year	(47,500,000)

EBIT—for earnings before interest and taxes) is presented as a separate item before the final net income figure is calculated. This allows the reader to see the firm's profits without financing and tax costs. Another common format calculates a gross margin before deducting selling, general, and administrative costs, which helps in understanding the firm's core profitability from operations before administrative, sales, and overhead costs are considered.

ABC lists three sources of income: product sales, research and development, and interest income. *Product sales* and *research and development revenue* account for the revenue realized during the 12 months from each respective activity. Interest income is revenue earned from the company's investment of surplus cash in marketable securities. Since the income statement presents separate expense figures for manufactured products and research and development activities, it is possible to determine a gross profit for each activity. *Gross profit* (also known as *gross margin*) is the difference between revenue and the direct costs involved in producing goods or delivering services. *Costs of goods sold* is the name used for the direct expenses incurred by ABC to make its products, including materials, labor, energy, and other items. The gross margin for ABC's product sales is calculated by subtracting the costs of goods sold from product sales:

Gross margin for products = 5,013,000 − 4,967,000 = 46,000

Gross margin for research and development is calculated in the same manner by subtracting research and development (R&D) expenses from R&D revenues:

$$\text{Gross margin for R\&D} = 7,675,000 - 2,077,000 = 5,598,000$$

From these figures, it is clear that ABC's R&D activities are more profitable than its manufacturing business, by a factor of over 100! Looking only at ABC's bottom line net income masks this difference. A useful way to present gross margin is as a percentage of sales. ABC's *gross margin percentage* for each activity is

$$\text{Gross margin percentage on product sales} = \frac{47,000}{5,013,000} = 0.9\%$$

$$\text{Gross margin percentage on R\&D} = \frac{5,598,000}{7,675,000} = 72.9\%$$

ABC's next expense item is *selling, general, and administrative costs,* or SGA expense. SGA includes all the indirect expense of the firm, including the salaries for executives, salespeople, the accounting department, and other general overhead such as insurance and real estate costs for administrative offices. The following expense item is depreciation, which we touched upon in the discussion of fixed assets. *Depreciation* is a noncash expense that accounts for the diminution in an asset's value over time. Depreciation is deducted as an expense to represent this economic cost to a business, but it has no impact on ABC's cash flow. ABC never writes a check or makes a payment for its depreciation expense.

After SGA and depreciation expenses, ABC reports its income before interest and taxes. This earnings amount is often referred to as *operating profits* since it measures a firm's earnings from all its operations before the impact of financing, taxes, or other nonoperating expenses are considered. Like gross margin, operating profit is more informative when expressed as a percentage of total revenue. ABC's operating profit percentage was 15.3% of revenue in fiscal year 2002.[9] The final net income figure is listed after deducting interest expenses on ABC's debt and a provision to cover expected tax payments. ABC's net income in FY2002 was $1,754,000, or 13.6% of sales. Thus, interest and taxes had only a small impact of ABC's net income, reducing it by less than 2 percentage points.

The final part of the income statement reports dividend payments to shareholders and retained earnings. In ABC's case, there were no dividend payments in this year. All of its $1,754,000 in net income was retained for reinvestment in the business. In the final lines of the income statement, retained earnings for the current year are added to the retained earnings at the beginning of the year to calculate ABC's final retained earnings as of June 30, 2002. Since ABC has generated cumulative losses during its lifetime, it has "negative retained earnings" which is called an *accumulated deficit.* The $1,754,000 in retained earnings for FY2002, therefore, reduced its accumulated deficit from $49,254,000 to $47,500,000. These last three lines of the income statement formally connect the income statement to the balance sheet. Referring back to ABC's June 30, 2002, balance sheet in Figure 3.1, note that the accumulated deficit under shareholders' equity is $47,500,000, matching the income statement's figure for accumulated deficit at year end.

Connecting the Balance Sheet and Income Statement

Thus far, we have only touched on the interrelationship between the balance sheet and income statement. However, these two financial statements are closely connected, with two ways to view their interaction. In the first view, two balance sheets and the intervening income statement provide a full picture of a firm's financial performance and change in financial condition for a given period. The beginning and ending balance sheets for a year show the changes in assets, liabilities, and owners' equity whereas the income statement shows how revenue and expense flows contribute to these balance sheet changes over that year. One direct connection is that retained earnings from net income on the income statement increases shareholders' equity on the balance sheet. Another direct connection occurs when an expense item on the income statement is coupled with a decrease in an asset account (e.g., when a depreciation expense on the income statement is matched with the depreciation of fixed assets). In this manner, decreases in an asset account, such as prepaid expenses, inventory, and fixed assets are often connected to an increase in expenses. On the other hand, sales generate an increase in accounts receivable, an asset account. The change in accounts receivable from one balance sheet to another is a function of two things: new accounts receivables created by sales and the conversion of accounts receivables into cash through their collection. Finally, the sale of an asset can result in revenue on the income statement. When the asset is sold for more than its book value, it yields income called capital gains. Conversely, when the firm sells an asset for less than its book value, it has a capital loss. By relating income statement items to the balance sheet, we gain a deeper understanding of what accounts for balance sheet changes.

A second way to view the interrelationship of the balance sheet and income statement is through the lens of cash flow (i.e., how both contribute to a firm's cash flow). The income statement generates cash flow through the excess of revenue over expenses. To the extent that revenue and expenses are fully converted into cash transactions, net income is a good proxy for cash flow. However, since financial statements are not based on cash transactions, they need to be adjusted to present their contribution to cash flow. One type of adjustment corrects for noncash expenses such as depreciation. A second type of adjustment captures the impact of balance sheet changes on cash flow. For example, the cash flow from sales is affected by the collection of accounts receivable. When accounts receivable increase over a year, this reduces the cash flow realized from sales. Net income must be reduced by this increase in accounts receivable to show actual cash flow for the period. An increase in other asset accounts, such as inventory or fixed assets, results from the firm converting cash into other assets. Thus, the general rule is that increases in asset accounts are a use of cash (i.e., decrease cash flow). Increases in liability accounts are a source of cash that increase cash flow. A clear example of this is when a firm secures new debt; it receives cash from the debt proceeds as the liability for outstanding debt increases. When accounts payable increase, this represents an increase in the firm's unpaid bills, which means that some of the expenses shown on the income statement were not converted into cash outlays. Thus, an addition to net income is made equal to the increase in accounts payable to show actual cash flow. These examples demonstrate that both the income statement and balance sheet must be analyzed to determine a firm's cash flow over a period.

Financial Statements: The Cash Flow Statement _____

As indicated above, *the cash flow statement* details how a firm's income statement and changes to its balance sheet accounts contribute to cash flow for a specific period. It may seem surprising that cash flow statements are prepared since earlier in this chapter it was argued that accrual financial statements provide a more accurate picture of a firm's economic performance than cash basis statements. If accrual statements are more accurate, why bother with cash flow analysis? The answer is twofold. First, a company needs cash flow to pay its bills and make debt service payments. Although accrual statements provide a better picture of a business's economic profits than a cash flow statement, a firm does not pay its bills with profits. We need to know the firm's actual cash flow to determine whether it can meet the payments for a proposed loan. Second, cash flow statements provide insight into how a firm generates and uses cash flow, which can indicate areas for improved management and operations. For example, if a profitable company experiences cash flow problems due to large increases in its accounts receivables, then it needs to change its credit policies and collection practices. Another argument against preparing a cash flow statement is that a business's net cash flow for a period is revealed by the change in the balance sheet cash account for that period. By definition, the change in cash from one period to another is the firm's net cash flow. Why undertake the tedious work of constructing a cash flow statement when net cash flow is already known? Although net cash flow is significant, it is more important to understand what contributed to this end result. A firm that loses money from its core business, but has positive cash flow from the one-time sale of assets, is quite different from one with positive cash flow from its core operations and after other costs. Moreover, we do not know how the firm's cash flow related to its level of debt payments. A firm with $40,000 in net cash flow and $30,000 in annual debt service is a better credit risk than a business with the same net cash flow but debt payments of $250,000.

Constructing a Cash Flow Statement

A statement of cash flows is included in the standard audited financial statements prepared by a firm's independent accountants. Since many privately held companies, and most small businesses, do not produce audited financial statements, practitioners need to know how to prepare a cash flow statement for a specific period. To prepare a cash flow statement, the balance sheets for the beginning and end of the period and the income statement for the period are necessary. Two types of adjustments are made to the income statement to determine cash flow: (1) noncash expense items (e.g., depreciation) are added back; and (2) cash flows from changes in balance sheet accounts are incorporated.

When preparing a cash flow statement, it is helpful to divide the statement into three sets of activities that affect cash flow: operations (purchasing, production, and sales activities); investment activities (purchase of plant and equipment to support operations); and financing activities (securing or retiring debt and equity). Beyond showing the relative impact of operations, investment, and financing on a firm's cash flow, this format simplifies the calculation of debt service coverage ratios. It highlights the cash flow available to make debt service payments (i.e., the cash flow prior to financing activities) and the principal and interest payments for the period. For these reasons, the following explanation and example organizes the cash flow statement into these three components: cash flow from operations, cash flow from investments, and cash flow from financing. This is not the only way to present a cash flow statement, but it is well suited to analyzing a business's borrowing capacity. Exhibit 3.4 summarizes the steps to prepare this cash flow statement format.

The first step in cash flow analysis is finding the correct starting point from the firm's income statement. Since we need to compare cash flow to debt payments, the starting figure should exclude the interest expense. Therefore, begin with *net income before interest and tax payments*, which many firms list as a separate line on the income statement as income (or

Exhibit 3.4   Steps to Prepare a Three-Part Cash Flow Statement

Part One: Cash Flow From Operations

Step   1:   Begin with income before interest and taxes from the income statement.
Step   2:   Subtract taxes.
Step   3:   Add back in noncash expenses from the income statement (e.g., depreciation and
             amortization).
Step   4:   Adjust cash flow for balance sheet changes from operations:
             calculate changes in asset accounts (accounts receivables, inventory, prepaid expenses,
             and other noninvestment or financing accounts). A decrease in an asset account
             produces a cash inflow (positive) and an increase in an asset account produces a cash
             outflow (negative).
             Calculate changes in liability accounts (accounts payables, accrued expenses, deferred
             income, and other noninvestment or financing liability accounts). An increase in a
             liability account produces a cash inflow (positive) and a decrease in a liability account
             produces a cash outflow (negative).
Step   5:   Calculate *net cash flow from operations* by summing these figures.

Part Two: Cash Flow After Investing Activities

Step   6:   Adjust cash flow for changes in balance sheet investment accounts (fixed assets,
             equipment, patents, goodwill, marketable securities, investments, etc.). An increase
             indicates a cash outflow (negative) while a decrease is a cash inflow (positive). Base
             calculations on gross amounts before any depreciation or amortization.
Step   7:   Calculate *net cash flow after investing activities* by summing and adding these changes
             to *net cash flow from operations*. This figure is used to calculate the debt service
             coverage ratio.

Part Three: Cash Flow After Financing Activities

Step   8:   Adjust cash flow for changes in balance sheet and income statement financing
             accounts (from the balance sheet: current and long-term portions of debt and changes
             in outstanding stock; from income statement: interest expense and dividend payments).
             A balance sheet increase indicates a cash inflow (positive) while a decrease is a cash
             outflow (negative). Income statement items are cash outflows.
Step   9:   Calculate *net cash flow after financing activities* by summing and adding these changes
             to the *net cash flow after investing activities*.
Step 10:   *Net cash flow after financing activities is the final net cash flow.* Check to see that it
             agrees with the change in balance sheet cash account.

earnings) before interest and taxes (IBIT). Next, subtract the tax payments
(or allowance for taxes) from the IBIT amount. When IBIT is not listed as a
separate line on the income statement, begin with the final figure for net
income after interest and taxes and add back the interest payment amount.
Once net income after taxes and before interest payments is determined, the
second step is adding back noncash expense items, which are accounting
items that were subtracted from revenues as an economic expense but do not
involve a real cash outflow. Depreciation is the most common noncash item,
but amortization of patents, goodwill, and other costs is a second example.
Third, incorporate the cash flow impact from balance sheet changes related

to operating activities, for both assets and liabilities/owners' equity. The relevant asset accounts are accounts receivable, inventory, prepaid expenses, and other noninvestment related accounts. Liability accounts for this portion of the cash flow analysis are accounts payable, accrued expenses, deferred income, other payable accounts, and other liability accounts that are not debt or equity financing items. An increase in an asset account is a cash outflow (use of cash) that is a negative entry on the cash flow statement. Conversely, a decrease in an asset account is a cash inflow (source of cash) treated as a positive entry on the cash flow statement. Consider accounts receivable to see the relationship between asset accounts and cash flow. An increase in accounts receivable means that uncollected sales are higher, which reduces the cash flow received from the sales revenue shown on the income statement. If accounts receivable decrease, cash collections from sales exceed the sales revenue on the income statement, generating a cash flow increase. Liability accounts have the opposite effect on cash flow: a decrease in a liability account is a cash outflow, whereas a liability account increase is a cash inflow. For example, when deferred income increases, the firm has received additional cash that is not included in the period's revenue on the income statement but needs to be added to represent true cash flow. If deferred income decreases, the business recognized some deferred income as revenue on its income statement in the period, although the associated cash inflow occurred in a prior period. Thus, a cash outflow deduction from net income is made to reflect the cash effect of the deferred income change. Once the cash flow impact of these balance sheet accounts is determined, they are summed up and added to the earlier figure for net income before interest payment plus noncash expenses. The resulting sum is *net cash flow from operations*. It indicates whether the firm is generating positive or negative cash flow from its core purchasing, production, and sales activities. A negative cash flow may indicate management problems, such as carrying too much inventory or slow accounts receivable collection. However, it may also indicate a well-managed firm that is expanding its inventory and accounts receivables as its sales grow, using internal cash flow to finance them.

In the second part of the cash flow analysis, the cash impact from investment activities is calculated. Investment activities include the purchase of long-term assets to support the firm's operations and expand sales. These investments are shown on the balance sheet as increases in fixed asset accounts (plant and equipment), patents or purchased technology, and goodwill (intangible assets from the purchase of other businesses). A second type of investment activity is using excess cash to acquire marketable securities or other financial investments. Changes in any of these asset accounts are included in the investment activity part of the cash flow analysis. As with the operating assets, increases in these accounts are a cash outflow while decreases represent a cash inflow. In this case, it is intuitive that when a business purchases new equipment, for example, it uses cash; and when a fixed asset account declines, the firm is selling the asset and generating cash. *These changes must be calculated based on the gross value asset accounts before any depreciation or amortization.* The change in gross value represents the actual cash transaction without the confusion of noncash deductions. Calculate the cash flow impact from changes in each investment-related account and then add these figures to the net cash flow from operations. The resulting figure is *net cash flow after investing activities.* This figure is used to determine the debt service coverage ratio, since it represents the firm's cash flow prior to its debt service payments and other financing activities.

The final step incorporates the impact of the firm's financing transactions (i.e., new borrowing and stock sales, the repayment of debt, interest payments, and dividend payments) on cash flow. For this analysis, include both balance sheet and income statement items. From the balance sheet, calculate changes in debt accounts and total proceeds from stock sales. Since debt is divided into two accounts, current portion of long-term debt and long-term debt, the change in the sum of these two accounts must be calculated to determine the change in total debt. When this sum increases, there is a cash inflow from additional borrowing. On the other hand, when the sum of the current and long-term portions of debt declines, it represents a cash outflow from the firm to pay-down of debt. Debt-related cash flow also includes interest payments, which are obtained from the interest expense item on the income statement. For equity financing, cash flow from stock issuance equals the change in the total shareholders' paid-in capital. Total paid-in capital is the sum of stock par value and additional paid-in capital from the shareholders' equity section of the balance sheet. Note that retained earnings are excluded since they were already counted within the firm's net income. If the change in retained earnings is added, it will double count this portion of net income. An increase in total paid-in equity capital represents cash inflow from additional stock sales. A decrease indicates the use of cash to buy back stock. The final item included in cash flow from financing activities is the deduction of dividend payments itemized on the income statement. For the final net cash flow calculation, sum the cash flow changes from all the financing accounts and add them to net cash from after investing activity. This final figure, cash flow after financing activities, is the firm's *net cash flow.* To check the accuracy of the cash flow analysis, compare this net cash flow figure to the change in the balance sheet cash account for the period. The two figures should be identical.

Using Financial Statements

This chapter provided an introduction to the language, presentation, and organization of business financial statements. With this knowledge, the reader is prepared to develop skills in analyzing business financial statements to inform economic development finance decisions. Although information in financial statements can be used for a variety of purposes, the primary goal of economic development practitioners is to evaluate the firm's financial health, its capacity to productively use new debt or equity, and the appropriate structure for any new financing. The next chapter provides a framework and financial tools to undertake this type of analysis.

Endnotes

1. These 11 principles are money measurement, entity, going concern, cost, dual aspect, conservatism, time period, realization, matching, consistency, and materiality. They are first introduced on page 26 and then further discussed in Chapters 2 and 3 of Anthony, Hawkins, and Merchant (1999), *Accounting: Text and Cases.*

2. Debit entries increase asset accounts and decrease liabilities and owners' equity while credit entries have the opposite effect—they increase a liability or owner's equity account while decreasing asset accounts.

3. Accountants distinguish between costs and expenses. Costs involve any use of resources by a business whereas expenses are costs that are deducted from revenue for a particular accounting period. Some costs, such as the purchase of equipment or inventory, are not expenses but rather add to business assets. See, Anthony, Hawkins, and Merchant, pp. 59–64, for a more detailed discussion of costs and expenses.

4. These two interpretations are drawn from Anthony, Hawkins, and Merchant (1999), pp. 32–35.

5. Different firms also use different names for the same category. For example, "marketable securities" is sometimes listed as "investments" or as "certificates of deposit."

6. One exception is financial assets, such as marketable securities, for which a market value is easily determined. These assets are listed at the lesser amount of their cost or market value.

7. In terms of credits and debits, the reduction in the prepaid asset account is a debit and the insurance expense is a credit.

8. This is the definition of a loss. Profit is when revenues exceed expenses.

9. This percentage was calculated by dividing the difference between total revenue and total expenses before interest, depreciation, and taxes (1,975,000) by total revenue (12,297,000).

4

Analyzing Business Financial Statements

With a basic understanding of the balance sheet and income statement in place, this chapter presents analytic tools used to evaluate a business's financial condition and performance and to assess its capacity to support new capital. Financial information can be analyzed from different perspectives and for different purposes. Firm managers use information to find ways to improve profitability and determine future investment and financing needs. Investment analysts may use financial statements to assess whether a company's share price appears undervalued or overvalued and, thus, its potential for investment returns from share price appreciation. Lenders focus on what the financial statements indicate about a firm's capacity to repay a loan. For development finance professionals, financial statement analysis has two dimensions. Financial analysis of a business should occur in the larger context of economic development goals. Detailed financial analysis is only warranted when the firm, its business plan, and expected investments promise to generate outcomes that are consistent with the local development strategy and objectives. Consequently, the chapter begins with a framework for evaluating a business for economic development financing within this broader context. Second, economic development finance is primarily concerned with debt financing. While some development finance programs provide equity financing, the vast majority supply debt. The discussion of financial statement analysis, therefore, concentrates on evaluating firms for debt financing. When venture capital programs are discussed in Chapter 11, several unique issues associated with evaluating equity investments will be covered.

A Framework for Firm Evaluation

An economic development assessment of a firm or project that is seeking financing needs to address four questions:

- What benefits will the firm or project provide and how do these benefits fit the local economic development goals and strategy?

- Is the business plan sound and does it provide the basis for success in the marketplace?
- What does the firm's financial condition and performance indicate about its capacity to support the proposed financing?
- Are financial projections realistic, and do they demonstrate the ability to repay the proposed financing?

These questions are listed sequentially based on their priority for economic development finance practitioners. The first concern is ensuring that financing the firm or project will advance the area's development goals. If this criterion is not satisfied, the firm is not suitable for financing and further business and financial analysis is unnecessary. Second, the firm and proposed investment must be viable from a market and management perspective—a critical test to realize both economic development and financial objectives. Economic development benefits will occur only if the firm succeeds in the marketplace. A sound business plan and competent management are key predictors of this success. Similarly, a development finance program is likely to incur losses when it finances firms with weak business plans. Once these critical thresholds of positive development impact and market viability are crossed, detailed financial analysis of the business becomes relevant. When the analyst turns to financial matters, the firm's historical information and its financial projections must be examined to gauge its financial health and capacity to repay the proposed financing. In the following paragraphs, the major issues for each component of this four-part evaluation framework are summarized (see Exhibit 4.1). The balance of the chapter details tools used in the later parts of the framework: analyzing historic financial performance and projected financial statements.

Assessing Economic Development Benefits

The analysis of financing proposals begins with an evaluation of how the firm and its project will advance local economic development goals and generate desired benefits. While the specific factors to consider depend on each community's goals and strategy, key issues are likely to include some combination of the following:

- *Business type and industry* (e.g., strategies focused on growing technology-based firms, retaining existing manufacturers, or diversifying goods and services in a neighborhood)
- *Firm size, stage, or ownership* (e.g., strategies aimed at growing micro and small businesses, minority or women-owned firms, or incubating start-ups)
- *Firm and investment location* (e.g., strategies to target development to specific areas or to encourage reuse of historic, vacant, or brownfield properties)
- *Job quality and employment practices* (e.g., strategies aimed at creating high-paying jobs or generating jobs and training for targeted groups)

Exhibit 4.1   Evaluation Framework for Economic Development Financing

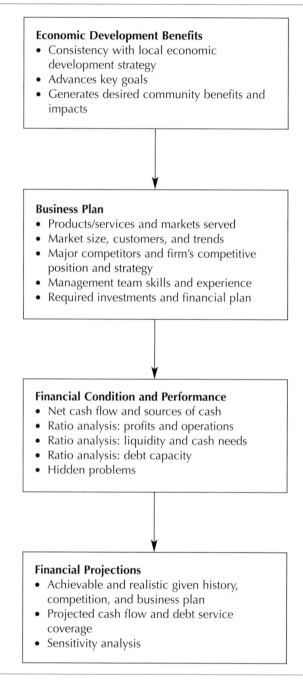

In addition to reviewing the strategic impact of a proposed project, it is important to consider the specific community benefits that will be generated. Many programs use quantitative targets for specific benefits (e.g., a maximum ratio of dollars lent per job created). While these ratios apply a simple benefit-cost test to potential loans or investments, a more complete assessment of the expected benefits from a proposed project entails reviewing information across the following indicators:

- The firm's current and projected employment and its commitment to hire local residents or targeted groups
- The type of expected jobs including their wage levels, employee benefits, skill requirements
- Projected new tax revenues
- The firm's ownership
- Environmental impacts on the community, both positive (reuse of contaminated sites, recycling of waste streams, etc.) and negative (hazardous wastes used, waste produced, traffic generated)
- Other community impacts (e.g., providing new goods or services, developing beneficial products or technologies, civic involvement, etc.)

Business Plan Evaluation

The business plan is at the core of a company's capacity to succeed, grow, and generate the expected economic development benefits. Therefore, it is a critical component of the evaluation. While many start-up businesses prepare an elaborate business plan, its length and detail should reflect the complexity of the business and the strategic issues that it faces. A restaurant requires a simpler business plan than a semiconductor manufacturer. Nonetheless, each business plan needs to cover the following key issues:

- Defining the company's products or services, customer markets, and competition
- Providing a persuasive case for how the company will achieve its sales targets in light of its competition
- Demonstrating the required management skills
- Explaining the financing plan and how it relates to the overall business plan

Small businesses often operate without a formal business plan and may need help either to translate their implicit business plan into a written form or to define a business plan for the first time. This assistance can be provided directly by finance program staff or by third-party technical assistance providers.

Once the business plan is prepared, several questions are central to its evaluation. A first consideration is whether the business plan is clear and consistent. Inconsistencies may reflect a poor business concept or insufficient focus on plan implementation, but they may also reflect omissions or miscommunication that can be readily resolved. Second, relate the company's projected sales level to the total size of its market to assess what market share it plans to achieve. Then, consider if the projected market share seems achievable given the firm's strengths and the nature of its competition. The third and most important part of the business plan analysis is assessing the firm's strategy to address its competition. Both current and potential competitors need to be considered. Potential competitors include both new firms that might enter the market and substitute products. For example, a local bookstore focused on competing with Internet-based booksellers might overlook a local newsstand's expansion into book sales or how a new café may erode the store's role as a gathering place. When analyzing a firm's competitive position, an important issue is the basis on which businesses compete in that market. These terms of competition can include cost, product or service quality, convenience, unique distribution channels, fast response time, seller financing, and proprietary technology.[1] The business plan should explain how the business expects to gain a competitive advantage or differentiate itself from its competitors, given its capacities, customers, and the market environment. For example, a local grocery store may plan to compete with large supermarkets by offering home delivery, but its customers must want this service and be willing to pay for it for the strategy to be feasible. The fourth part of the assessment considers the skills and experience of the company's management. The required management skills vary with the business type and complexity, but managers need to recognize their limitations and have a plan to address these weaknesses. For example, technology-based businesses founded by scientists and engineers should augment their expertise with marketing and financial managers. Since an essential ingredient for any business is good accounting and financial systems, the business plan also must address this key capacity issue. Finally, the firm's investment and financing plans should be evaluated. Planned investments should be consistent with and sufficient to implement the business plan. For example, the plan should anticipate expanded investments in working capital along with the new plant and equipment needed to produce and market a new product. Similarly, the proposed financing plan needs to reflect the type of assets being financed, the available cash flow to service debt, and the level of financial risk. A retail store with plans to expand its store size and inventory to serve a local market will not be able to completely finance the expansion with long-term debt. Its financing plan needs to include some new equity investment and short-term debt, supplier credit, or both to finance the inventory expansion.

When analyzing the business plan, development finance professionals should not limit their review to information and documents provided by the firm. They should speak with the firm's customers, suppliers, and lenders, check the entrepreneur's and key managers' references and prior business experience, and consult with industry experts. Recent reports or studies on the industry and articles from the business and industry trade press are also valuable information sources to understand market and industry trends that inform a plan's viability.

Analyzing Financial Condition and Performance

In this part of the review, a firm's financial statements are analyzed to determine what its current financial condition and historic performance indicate about its capacity to support new debt. A careful reading of the balance sheet provides considerable insight into a firm's financial health and the financial risks posed by the business's management of short-term liquidity and long-term financial obligations. Similarly, the income statement reveals important information about the firm's overall performance and profitability and how interest payments and noncash expenses influence earnings. Finally, the cash flow statement indicates whether the company has sufficient cash flow to cover required debt payments. The key questions and tools that guide this analysis of financial statements are discussed below. First, valuable information that can be gained from each individual financial statement is presented. Next, the use of ratio analysis to assess a firm's financial health and performance is discussed. This technique combines information from the balance sheet and income statement to calculate a variety of ratios and then compares them to industry averages and/or ratios for comparable companies in the same industry.

Financial Projections

After diagnosing the company's financial condition and performance, the last analytical step is forecasting future cash flow to determine projected debt service coverage and evaluate how well projected debt service coverage stands up to downside risks. This exercise translates the business and financing plan into a financial forecast to test whether the increased cash flow from new investment will support the capital needed to finance it. Moreover, it allows the analyst and the businesses to see how well the firm's cash flow and financing plan stands up to the likely deviations from projections due to lower than expected sales, unexpected cost increases for key inputs, interest rate changes, or other factors. When projections indicate that debt repayment depends on achieving overly optimistic sales goals or that small changes in input costs, receivables collections, or other factors will create financial problems, then the financial plan needs to be modified. In this case, utilizing less debt and more equity, debt with longer amortization, or staged borrowing can help lower repayment risk. Changes in the business plan or management practices also might be needed to reduce future financial risks.

Analysis of Individual Financial Statements

Insights From the Balance Sheet

Although the balance sheet is a snapshot of a business's financial situation, it provides valuable information on the firm's financial practices and health.

This section explains several important financial characteristics of a business that can be learned from analyzing the balance sheet. When the balance sheet was introduced, we explained that it can be viewed as a sources and uses of funds statement. From this vantage point, the balance sheet informs the reader about how the firm has financed its assets and what assets have been acquired with its financing and net income over time. The liability and equity side of ABC's balance sheet, in Exhibit 4.2, shows that the firm relies heavily on common stock equity. Shareholders' equity totaled $62.9 million on June 30, 2002, compared to total liabilities of $18.9 million. In other words, ABC had over $3 dollars in equity for every dollar in liabilities. Moreover, supplier credit (accounts payable) is the largest liability at $7.1 million. Formal debt, at $6.4 million,[2] constitutes only one third of all liabilities. The *debt-to-equity ratio* measures a firm's relative reliance on debt versus equity financing. It is the ratio of total liabilities to total shareholders' equity. ABC's debt-to-equity ratio as of June 30, 2002, is .30. In other words, ABC has 30 cents of liabilities for every dollar of equity. The debt-to-equity ratio also measures a firm's leverage. A business with a high debt-to-equity ratio, in which liabilities are several times its equity, is said to be highly leveraged—it has used one dollar of equity to leverage several dollars of debt. There are advantages to a high debt-to-equity ratio, but it does increase the financial risk for a firm. High reliance on debt creates high fixed payments and raises the level of sales and cash flow needed to make these payments. ABC's low debt-to-equity ratio indicates limited reliance on debt financing, small fixed debt payments, and a low level of financial risk.

The asset side of the balance sheet shows how the firm invested the funds generated from internal earnings and secured through credit and stock sales. ABC requires large investments in a mix of assets, with these investments almost equally divided between short-term and long-term assets. Long-term investments in both fixed assets (property, plant, and equipment) and the acquisition of other firms and their technology (purchased technology and goodwill) total $41.2 million, just over half of ABC's total assets. Two short-term assets, accounts receivables and inventory, account for the bulk of ABC's remaining assets, each equal to $16 million, or 20% of total assets. ABC also holds over $6.7 million in cash, marketable securities, and investments. This may represent cash that will be needed for upcoming costs or a reserve to cover unanticipated costs, or both. This static listing of business assets does not, by itself, reveal a lot about the company. More is revealed when these figures are related to past levels and through the ratio analysis discussed below. Perhaps the most important fact about ABC's use of funds is the accumulated deficit of $47.5 million. In effect, ABC has used $47.5 million of its financing to cover accumulated losses—more than the total amount invested in fixed assets, acquisitions, and technology. This figure raises questions about the source of these losses, how long they may continue, and whether additional equity will be needed to cover further losses.

Current asset and current liability accounts indicate a firm's capacity to meet short-term obligations—an important issue for several reasons. If a

Exhibit 4.2   American Biotechnology Company Balance Sheet—June 30, 2002

ASSETS

Current Assets	
Cash and Cash Equivalents	$410,000
Marketable Securities	3,000,000
Accounts Receivable, net of allowance	16,065,000
Inventory	16,178,000
Prepaid Expenses	779,000
Total Current Assets	36,432,000
Investments	3,343,000
Property Plant and Equipment, less accumulated depreciation	21,905,000
Purchased Technology and Goodwill	19,310,000
Other Assets	810,000
TOTAL ASSETS	$81,800,000

LIABILITIES AND SHAREHOLDERS' EQUITY

Current Liabilities	
Accounts Payable	$7,148,000
Income Taxes Payable	12,000
Accrued Expenses	3,973,000
Deferred Income	985,000
Current Portion of Long-Term Debt	1,367,000
Total Current Liabilities	13,485,000
Deferred Income	361,000
Long-Term Debt, less current portion	5,022,000
Total Liabilities	18,868,000
Shareholders' Equity	
Common Stock Issue, par value $.01 per share	
Authorized 40,000,000 shares,	
Issued 23,305,000 shares	233,305
Additional Paid-in Capital	110,198,695
Accumulated Deficit	(47,500,000)
Total Equity	62,932,000
TOTAL LIABILITIES AND SHAREHOLDERS' EQUITY	$81,800,000

business does not manage its balance sheet well and short-term liabilities exceed short-term assets and cash flow, then the business might be forced into bankruptcy even if it is profitable and successful in other respects. Second, many small firms rely heavily on credit to finance their businesses, especially when they have limited sources of equity. Heavy reliance on debt, especially short-term credit, increases a firm's need to generate cash flow to meet fixed debt payments and requires more careful scrutiny of its capacity to meet these obligations. Recall that the definition of current assets is assets that are expected to be converted into cash within a year. Current liabilities are obligations to be repaid within a year. Therefore, the ratio of current assets to current liabilities indicates how large a cushion the firm has to meets its financial obligations over the next year. The difference of current assets minus current liabilities is referred to as *net working capital.* Positive net working capital indicates that a firm has sufficient short-term assets to cover liabilities that will come due over the next year. A larger net working capital amount means the firm has a greater cushion to cover unexpected events, such as unsold inventory or uncollected accounts receivable. ABC's net working capital on June 30, 2002, totaled $22.9 million, equal to current assets of $36.4 million less current liabilities of $13.5 million. This is a good financial position that provides the firm with surplus current assets far beyond what is needed to pay the current liabilities. A convenient way to summarize the net working capital position is the *current ratio,* which is calculated by dividing current assets by current liabilities. For ABC, the current ratio for June 30, 2002 is calculated as follows:

$$\text{Current Ratio} = \text{Current Assets/Current Liabilities}$$

$$\text{Current Ratio} = \$36.4 \text{ million}/\$13.5 \text{ million} = 2.70$$

With a current ratio of 2.70, ABC has $2.70 of current assets available to convert into cash over the next year for every dollar of liabilities that it will need to pay during the next year.

The balance sheet also reveals cash flow management issues through the accounts receivable and accounts payable items. Accounts receivable indicates how well the business collects its unpaid bills and handles extending credit to its customers. The amount of accounts receivables can be related to a firm's sales by calculating how many days' worth of sales equal the total accounts receivable figure on its balance sheet. This ratio, called *days receivable,* is calculated as follows:

$$\text{Days Receivable} = \frac{\text{Accounts Receivable}}{\text{Sales}/365}$$

The denominator equals one day's worth of sales, so the ratio tells us how many days' worth of sales are uncollected as accounts receivable. Since this figure represents how long it takes the firm, on average, to collect invoices, it should be close to the firm's normal credit terms. When a firm ships goods on credit with a 30-day payment term, then we would expect its accounts receivable to be close to this amount, for example, in a 20- to 40-day range. If the days receivable ratio is much higher, this indicates that either the firm is not making sufficient efforts to track and collect its unpaid invoices or it is extending credit too liberally to customers who cannot pay promptly. When accounts receivable are not collected promptly, a firm is, in effect, using its potential cash flow to make loans to its customers. This use of its cash can be costly when it forces the firm to borrow funds or incur penalties for late payment of its own bills to replace the uncollected cash. A similar analysis can be made that relates a firm's accounts payable to its annual expenses. The average day's worth of expenses in accounts payable should reflect the payment terms on its bills from its vendors and not lead to costly late payment or interest charges.

Knowledge From the Income Statement

The income statement provides a more limited view of a business than the balance sheet. While the balance sheet captures the historical impact of a firm's activities on its financial condition, the income statement presents its financial results over one time period. Nonetheless, this information is important as it shows the company's financial performance in the recent past. Since the balance sheet is a composite of the company's history, it may show a good financial position even when a firm has performed poorly in recent years. Conversely, as in ABC's case, the balance sheet may hide recent improvements in financial results. Since ABC's balance sheet shows a cumulative loss of $45 million, one might conclude that the company is not profitable. However, the income statement (Exhibit 4.3) shows that ABC was profitable in FY2002. Thus, the first and most critical information provided by the income statement is whether a firm is profitable and how large those profits are, both in absolute terms and relative to sales. When a firm is profitable, its operations are covering all its expenses and providing a financial return to the company's owners. It is important to emphasize that net income reported on the income statement is an accrual accounting measure of profits and is not the same as a firm's cash flow for the period. Actual cash flow, revealed in the cash flow statement, may be higher or lower than net income.

A second insight from the income statement is the relationship of gross margin to the break-even sales level. The *break-even sales level* is the amount of sales that a firm must obtain to begin earning a profit. At the break-even sales level, a firm has covered its fixed costs so that each new dollar of sales contributes to profits. The gross margin percentage provides an easy way to calculate break-even sales level because it indicates what percentage of each dollar of sales is available to pay fixed costs. When a firm has a 25% gross margin, this means that 75% of its sales price is devoted to the direct cost of producing its goods with the remaining 25% available to cover the company's overhead and fixed costs. If this firm has $1 million in annual fixed costs, then it must reach $4 million in yearly sales to cover its fixed costs and reach a break-even sales level. Thus, to calculate the break-even sales level, fixed costs are divided by the gross margin percentage, as shown in the following formula:

$$\text{Break-even Sales} = \frac{\text{Fixed Costs}}{\text{Gross Margin Percentage}}$$

Exhibit 4.3   American Biotechnology Company Income Statement for the
12 Months Ending June 30, 2002

Revenue	
Product sales	5,013,000
Research and development revenue	7,675,000
Interest income	239,000
Total Revenues	12,927,000
Expenses	
Cost of goods sold	4,967,000
Research and development expenses	2,077,000
Sales, general and administrative expenses	2,908,000
Depreciation	1,000,000
Total Expenses	10,952,000
Income before interest and taxes	1,975,000
Interest expense	(119,000)
Provision for income taxes	(102,000)
Net Income	1,754,000
Less cash dividends	0
Retained earnings	1,754,000
Accumulated deficit at beginning of year	(49,254,000)
Plus retained earnings for year	1,754,000
Accumulated deficit at end of year	(47,500,000)

This formula demonstrates the relationship between gross margin and profits. A business with a low gross margin must achieve a high level of sales to be profitable whereas a high gross margin business needs far lower sales to earn profits. A high gross margin business is considered very forgiving since it can make many mistakes, such as market itself poorly, rent more space than it needs, or incur higher production waste, and still earn a profit. However, a low gross margin business is compelled to meet its sales targets and control its expenses to earn a profit. If it misreads the marketplace and sales decline by a few percentage points, then it is likely to have a loss.

Projecting break-even sales requires determining the firm's fixed costs. This is not an easy task since many costs are aggregated into general categories on the income statement and balance sheet. SGA expenses, for example, may include both fixed costs, such as rent and key managers' salaries along with variable costs, such as sales staff salaries or travel expenses that could be reduced if sales decline. More detailed information and discussions with a company are necessary to ferret out the true fixed costs, such as rent, insurance, critical management and administrative salaries, debt payments, and so forth. However, insights can be gained even with a rough estimate of breakeven sales. Take the example of ABC's manufacturing business, for which the gross margin is .9%. ABC's income statement reports a SGA expense of $2,908,000 and an interest expense of $119,000 while the balance sheet showed payments for the current portion of long-term debt as $1,367,000. The interest and principle payments are clearly fixed costs but some of the SGA expense may be avoidable. Let's assume that three quarters of these expenses, or $2,181,000, are fixed costs. Thus, ABC's total estimated fixed costs are $3,667,000; the sum of $2,181,000 in SGA expenses, $119,000 in interest payments, and $1,367,000 in principal payments. Since these fixed costs cover both ABC's manufacturing and research and development businesses, a further assumption is necessary to allocate these costs between the two businesses. Since the R&D business generates 60% of ABC's revenue, it is reasonable to assume that the manufacturing business represents a minority of these fixed costs. If the fixed costs for ABC's manufacturing businesses are conservatively estimated at one third of the total ($1,222,000), then by dividing $1,222,000 by the .9% gross margin for its manufacturing business, we find that ABC needs $135.7 million in sales to reach breakeven—a level 27 times its current annual sales. Even with these rough calculations, we have learned that ABC needs to greatly increase its sales and achieve far better manufacturing efficiency to be profitable in this business.

From a lender's perspective, the income statement relates a company's income to its debt payments and provides a first indication of debt service coverage. By comparing an adjusted EBIT figure that excludes depreciation (a noncash expense item) to total debt service, we gain an initial determination of how well earnings cover existing debt payments and the firm's capacity to take on new debt. To estimate debt payments, we must include both interest and principal payments. Interest payments are included as an expense on the income statement, but principal payments are detailed as the current portion of long-term debt under current liabilities on the balance sheet. Remember that the definition of the current portion of long-term debt is the principal payments for the next year. For ABC, the current portion of long-term debt on the June 30, 2002, balance sheet is $1,367,000, and the interest expense for the 12 months ended June 30, 2002, is $119,000. However, these two figures are not for the same year—the interest expense is for the 12 months prior to June 30, 2002, but the current portion of long-term debt is for the next 12 months. To get consistent figures that cover the same year, it is necessary to go back to ABC's balance sheet for June 30, 2001, and use the current portion of long-term debt from that report. This balance sheet reported $1,670,000 in principal payments for FY2002. Total debt service for that year is $1,789,000 ($1,670,000 in principal and $119,000 in interest). The estimated debt service coverage ratio from adjusted earnings is:

$$\frac{\text{Net income} + \text{depreciation} + \text{interest expense}}{\text{Total Debt Service}}$$

In ABC's case, the figures and resulting ratio are

$$\frac{\$1,754,000 + \$1,000,000 + \$119,000}{\$1,789,000} = \frac{\$2,873,000}{\$1,789,000} = 1.60$$

The 1.60 ratio indicates ABC's income is more than sufficient to cover debt service payments, with a healthy surplus of 60%. This healthy surplus suggests, at first glance, that ABC can afford to take on additional debt. A complete cash flow statement, as described in Chapter 3, is needed to confirm this "back of the envelope" assessment.

A final piece of information to gain from the income statement is uncovering important trends in a firm's financial performance. By comparing income statements over time, key trends in revenues, expenses, gross margin, and net income are revealed. These trends include how fast the firm's sales are growing, if it is becoming more or less efficient in its core production or service activities, and whether its profits are growing, both absolutely and relative to sales. Any significant deterioration in these financial results indicates a potential problem that warrants further investigation.

Analyzing the Cash Flow Statement

Cash flow statement analysis adds two critical pieces of information beyond what is learned from the balance sheet and income statement. First, it provides a true debt service coverage ratio that compares available cash flow to principal and interest payments. Since the cash flow statement details cash flow prior to any financing transactions and annual principal and interest payments, it makes the data needed for this key ratio more transparent. The formula for calculating debt service coverage from the cash flow statement is

$$\text{Debt Service Coverage Ratio} = \frac{\text{Cash Flow After Investing Activities}}{\text{Principal Payments} + \text{Interest Payments}}$$

Exhibit 4.4 is American Biotechnology Company's statement of cash flow for the year ending June 30, 2002. Applying the above formula, cash flow after investing activities of $1,722,000 is divided by total principal and interest payments of $1,627,000 ($1,525,000 plus $102,000) to yield a debt service coverage ratio of 1.06. Since this is a very tight coverage ratio, further analysis is needed to determine what conditions and balance sheet changes contributed to the firm's cash flow for the year and whether cash flow will improve in later years. The second value of the cash flow statement, revealing how a firm has generated and used cash flow, helps answer this question. Exhibit 4.4 shows that ABC's major uses of cash were to increase inventories by over $2 million and to make a $1.15 million investment in property, plant, and equipment and technology. The later use of cash is a long-term investment that should increase future cash flow. A $2 million increase in inventories, however, is a red flag. Did the large inventory expansion result from poor sales or excessive returns that indicate problems in the firm's market or management? On the other hand, the company may have new contracts that required an investment in inventories that will result in increased sales and cash flow for 2003. ABC's major cash inflow beyond $2.75 million in earnings (after adding back the $1 million depreciation expense) was $1.448 million from a decrease in investments and $750,000 from reduced marketable securities. In other words, ABC sold assets acquired to invest excess cash balances in order to generate cash needed to meet its business costs. ABC had a large cash flow deficit and tapped into cash-equivalent assets to address it. This may indicate a serious problem in which ABC's business operations do not generate sufficient cash flow to cover its costs, which will ultimately lead to bankruptcy. It may also represent investments under its business plan, and for which the firm raised equity, that will lead to positive cash flow in the coming years.

Exhibit 4.4   American Biotechnology Company Statement of Cash Flows for the 12 Months Ending June 30, 2002

Income before interest and taxes	$1,754,000
Less taxes	($102,000)
Plus depreciation	$1,000,000
Adjust for Balance Sheet Changes:	
Asset Accounts	
Change in marketable securities	$750,000
Change in accounts receivable	($206,000)
Change in inventories	($2,032,000)
Change in prepaid expenses	($25,000)
Liability Accounts	
Change in accounts payable	$318,000
Change in income taxes payable	($30,000)
Net Cash Flow From Operating Activities	$1,427,000
Changes in long-term asset accounts	
Change in investments	$1,448,000
Investment in property plant and equipment	($854,000)
Purchased technology and goodwill	($299,000)
Net Cash Flow After Investing Activities	$1,722,000
Changes for finance activities:	
Interest payments	($102,000)
Proceeds from new debt borrowed	$0
Principal payments	($1,525,000)
Net Cash Flow for the Period	$95,000

This example shows that the firm's stage and context is critical in interpreting the cash flow statement (and all financial statements). Early-stage and fast-growing firms often have large cash needs that exceed internally generated funds and require external financing. If the firm is executing a sound business plan under market conditions that promise future sales and cash flow and has an appropriate financial structure, then the tight debt service coverage ratio and cash flow changes in 2002 do not necessarily preclude new financing. For an established firm that is not experiencing rapid growth, the cash flow statement indicates serious business or management problems. A firm at this stage should generate positive cash flow from operations that are sufficient to cover its investment and financing needs. New financing would not be warranted unless the firm's problems were carefully diagnosed and an effective plan to reverse them was being implemented.

Ratio Analysis

Ratio analysis is another tool to evaluate the financial condition and performance of a business. By calculating financial ratios, comparing them to industry averages, and tracking trends in the ratios over time, practitioners can identify financial risks and gain more insight into the firm's strengths and weaknesses. While many financial ratios can be calculated and related in a variety of ways,[3] a useful framework for ratio analysis, especially from a lender's perspective, is to focus on three issues: (1) profitability and operating results; (2) short-term liquidity and cash needs; and (3) financial structure and capacity to support new debt.

Profitability and Operating Results

Overall profitability is a critical indicator of a firm's financial health and performance. Since firms must earn profits relative to both their overall revenue and owner's equity, several ratios are used to measure profits according to both standards. Two important measures of profit on sales are

$$\text{Gross Margin Percentage} = \frac{\text{Total Revenue-Cost of Goods Sold}}{\text{Total Revenue}}$$

$$\text{Net Profit on Sales} = \frac{\text{Net Income (Profits)}}{\text{Total Revenue}}$$

Gross margin indicates the firm's profit rate on its direct costs before general overhead, sales, and administration costs are considered. It indicates profit levels on core business activities and is used to determine the break-even sales revenue needed to support fixed overhead costs. Net profit on sales measures the firm's overall profit rate on sales after all expenses are considered. It shows the share of every dollar in sales that is returned to the firm as profits. These two ratios are closely connected. A firm's gross margin bounds its overall net profit on sales; a firm with a low gross margin will have a lower net profit on sales. Similarly, a high gross margin business should also have a relatively high net profit on sales. When this is not the case, a closer examination of its sales and administrative costs is warranted to determine whether excesses or inefficiencies exist. A firm may earn a good profit rate on sales but require a very large investment in assets to achieve this result. Profit and operating ratios based on investment are used to indicate how well the firm is utilizing its overall assets and whether it provides a good return on the owner's investment (which affects its ability to raise new equity capital). Three common ratios that measure return on investment include

$$\text{Investment Turnover} = \frac{\text{Total Sales (Revenue)}}{\text{Total Assets}}$$

$$\text{Return on Assets} = \frac{\text{Net Income (Profits)}}{\text{Total Assets}}$$

$$\text{Return on Equity} = \frac{\text{Net Income (Profits)}}{\text{Total Shareholders' Equity}}$$

The first two ratios measure the firm's efficiency in generating sales and profits from its investment in total assets, indicating its overall asset utilization. Return on equity investment is used to gauge how well the firm is performing for its owners by measuring its profits as a percentage of the owners' total investment.

Since profit rates and asset levels vary greatly across industries, no absolute standard applies in interpreting these ratios for a specific firm. Instead, the analysis should review trends in these ratios over time and compare them to averages ratios for the entire industry and comparable firms in the industry (i.e., those with an equivalent level of sales). These comparisons identify whether operating performance is improving or deteriorating over time and how the firm's performance compares to similar firms and potential competitors in its industry. Finally, consider how the firm's current environment affects the outlook for sustaining profitability. For example, new competitors entering the market may reduce sales and profit margins. On the other hand, economic or demographic factors that increase demand for the firm's products may expand sales faster than expenses and investment to improve profit ratios. Ratio analysis is often not conclusive but it provides insights and raises questions to pursue with the firm to better understand how it is addressing weaknesses in its business and financial performance.

Short-Term Liquidity and Cash Needs

This second focus for ratio analysis is a critical concern for small businesses, which often operate under short-term cash flow pressures due in part to their limited access to equity and long-term debt. A firm with a sound business strategy, growing sales, and good profits can still face financial problems or bankruptcy if its short-term cash flow is not managed to provide sufficient liquidity to address unexpected costs or deferred cash receipts. The following four ratios help assess a firm's liquidity and its management of key assets that affect near-term cash flow:

$$\text{Current Ratio} = \frac{\text{Current Assets}}{\text{Current Liabilities}}$$

$$\text{Quick Ratio} = \frac{\text{Current Assets} - \text{Inventory}}{\text{Current Liabilities}}$$

$$\text{Days Receivables} = \frac{\text{Accounts Receivables}}{\text{Annual Sales}/365}$$

$$\text{Inventory Turnover} = \frac{\text{Cost of Goods Sold}}{\text{Average Inventory for Period}}$$

The current and quick ratios compare short-term assets, which are converted into cash over the next year, to liabilities that must be paid in that year. The current ratio compares all current assets to all current liabilities whereas the quick ratio takes a more conservative approach. It omits inventory from the assets available to cover liabilities since the market value and potential cash flow from inventory is very uncertain. Since firms need a cushion of excess current assets over current liabilities to minimize the potential liquidity problems, lenders look for a current ratio well in excess of 1, usually in range of 1.5 to 2.0. A quick ratio of 1.0 is desirable but may be hard to achieve, especially for small firms in industries that require carrying substantial inventory. As with other ratios, one needs to judge them in the context of the specific industry, the firm's history, and the market environment.

Days receivable (also known as the average collection period) and inventory turnover indicate how well the firm manages key current assets. The days receivable ratio measures how quickly a business collects its accounts receivable and converts them to cash. The number of days' worth of sales carried as accounts receivable tells, on average, how long it takes the company to receive payment on its sales. While 30 days is a healthy standard for days receivable, this figure varies by industry and is related to the payment terms offered to customers. Thus, the days receivable ratio should be equal to or less than the standard payment terms that a firm offers to its customers. When calculating this ratio, remember that the accounts receivable amount is divided by daily sales for the period. While the formula assumes an annual income statement, the ratio may be calculated for sales over a different period (e.g., a quarter or six months). In this case, the sales revenue would be divided by the number of days in the period (90 for the first quarter, 182 for the first half of the year, etc.). Inventory turnover relates the average level of inventory carried in a period to the cost of materials used to produce the goods sold in that period. A high inventory turnover ratio is good since it means that the firm is not carrying excess inventory and is quickly trans-forming its investment in inventories into sales. Maintaining low inventories is beneficial since it reduces a business's required investment level and low-ers costs to store, handle, and account for inventory. However, a business must balance the financial benefits of minimizing inventory with its ability to produce goods and satisfy customer demand on a timely basis. Industry standards are particularly important for evaluating this ratio since inventory requirements vary greatly by product and business type.

Capital Structure and Debt Capacity

A third set of financial ratios reveals a firm's reliance on debt to finance its assets and how debt payments relate to its earnings and cash flow. Since debt payments are fixed obligations, heavy use of debt increases the risk that a firm may not meet these obligations if its sales and cash flow decline. Before extending new credit, a lender uses these ratios to test whether a business is overextended in its existing use of debt and has the financial flexibility to take on additional debt. These ratios include

$$\text{Debt/Total Assets Ratio} = \frac{\text{Total current and long-term debt}}{\text{Total assets}}$$

$$\text{Debt/Equity Ratio} = \frac{\text{Total current and long-term debt}}{\text{Total shareholders' equity}}$$

$$\text{Times Interest Earned} = \frac{\text{Earnings before interest and taxes}}{\text{Interest expense}}$$

$$\text{Debt Service Coverage Ratio} = \frac{\text{Annual cash flow before debt service}}{\text{Annual principal and interest expense}}$$

The first two ratios are closely related measures of a firm's reliance on debt. Debt to total assets directly shows the share of assets financed with debt. A ratio above .50 means that business relies more on debt than on equity whereas a ratio close to 1.0 indicates very little use of equity financing and a highly leveraged firm. The debt to equity ratio directly shows how many dollars of debt were issued for every dollar of equity capital secured. A debt-to-equity ratio of 4:1 means that the firm has borrowed $4 for every $1 of shareholder equity raised. With a high debt-to-equity ratio, a firm has high fixed debt payments and less capacity to absorb unexpected cash flow shortfalls. High financial leverage adds to the risk of financial distress and bankruptcy and necessitates a careful analysis of the company's capacity to add more debt. When calculating these two ratios, the definition of debt is not obvious. Do we mean any liability of the firm or only those liabilities evidenced by formal debt contracts? The answer depends on the purpose of the analysis and definitions used in comparative industry statistics. When debt is defined as total liabilities, the broadest view of debt obligations is being used. Such a broad measure is helpful in understanding the firm's overall capital structure and the risk of near- to medium-term financial distress. A more limited definition based on formal debt provides insight into how the firm is financing its long-term investment needs and the relative use of debt and equity in financing noncyclical assets. Whichever definition is used, be consistent in applying the chosen definition and ensure that it matches definitions used in comparison data.

Debt-to-equity and debt-to-total assets ratios vary by industry, according to the level of required asset, the nature of these assets, and the timing and certainty of future cash flow. Some industries (e.g., pharmaceuticals and biotechnology) need large up-front investments but have long delayed and very uncertain future cash flows. Consequently, they are financed primarily with equity. Other industries with lower investment levels and more pre-dictable cash flow (e.g., grocery stores) are highly leveraged and rely heavily on debt financing.

Times interest earned and debt service coverage ratio measure how well earnings and cash flow cover debt service costs. Times interest earned shows the ratio of earnings before interest and taxes to annual interest expenses. Since this ratio only addresses the interest component of debt service, it is an incomplete measure of debt burdens. Nonetheless, it provides a quick way to assess the significance of interest expenses. Moreover, interest is the most fixed of debt obligations. Lenders may allow some deferral or restructuring of principal payments when a firm faces financial problems, but they almost always require full payment of interest. The debt service coverage ratio (DSCR) is more comprehensive since it compares actual cash flow to total principal and interest payments. Lenders typically require a debt service cov-erage ratio of 1.25 or higher. However, when a business is seeking new debt, its existing DSCR must be higher to provide the capacity to increase debt payments and still achieve a final ratio of 1.25.

Table 4.1 summarizes the formulas and interpretation for all the ratios discussed in this section.

Common Size Financial Statements

Common size financial statements, which convert figures on a company's balance sheet and income statement into a percentage of the statement total,

Table 4.1   Summary of Financial Ratios

Ratio Name	Formula	Interpretation
Gross Margin	(Total Revenue—Costs of Goods Sold)/Total Revenue	Profit from direct production before overhead costs.
Net Profit on Sales	Net Income/Total Sales	Overall profit rate per unit of sales; share of each sale dollar going to profits.
Investment Turnover	Sales/Total Assets	Sales generated relative to total firm investment; dollar of sale for each dollar of investment.
Return on Assets	Net Income/Total Assets	Overall profit rate on assets; profit return on total firm investment.
Return on Equity	Net Income/Shareholders' Equity	Overall profit rate on the owners' investment in the firm.
Current Ratio	Current Assets/Current Liabilities	Ability of short-term assets to cover short-term liabilities. Indicator of firm's liquidity over next year.
Quick Ratio	(Current Assets—Inventory)/Current Liabilities	Strict measure of liquidity. Ability of most liquid short-term assets to cover short-term liabilities.
Days Receivable	Accounts Receivable/(Sales in Period/Days in Period)	Average collection period for accounts receivable. Indicator for how well a business manages its customer credit and collections.
Inventory Turnover	Costs of Goods Sold/Average Inventory	How many times a firm converts inventory into sales for a period. Indicates how well it manages its inventory investment.
Debt-to-Total Assets	Total Current and Long-Term Debt/Total Assets	Extent to which a firm used debt to finance its assets.
Debt-to-Equity	Total Current and Long-Term Debt/Shareholders' Equity	Measures firm's relative use of debt and equity. A high debt-to-equity ratio increases the risk of financial distress.
Times Interest Earned	Earnings Before Interest and Taxes/Interest Expense	Indicates the degree to which earnings cover interest costs. One factor in a firm's capacity to carry more debt.
Debt Service Coverage	Annual Cash Flow Before Financing/Total Principal and Interest Payments	Relates a firm's cash flow to total debt payments. Direct measure of a firm's ability to pay existing debt and to carry additional debt.

are another useful type of ratio analysis. For a common size balance sheet, asset accounts are expressed as a share of total assets while liability and equity accounts are presented as a percentage of total liabilities and shareholders' equity. A common size income statement shows all line items as a percentage of total revenue. Common size statements provide an easy way to compare a firm's operating results, financial position, and sources and uses of funds to other firms and industry averages. With figures shown as percentages, an analyst can readily identify variations and similarities between a subject firm's finances and its comparison group. It provides a quick assessment of whether the firm is performing better than industry averages or its peer group and uncovers unusual balance sheet accounts and/or expense items for further investigation.

A comparison of common size balance sheets for ABC and the average of 30 pharmaceutical firms in a comparable sales class ($2 to $10 million per year) reveals key differences between ABC and this peer group (see Table 4.2). First, current assets represent a much smaller share of ABC's assets whereas intangible investments in technology and goodwill are far larger. Second, ABC has a much different financial structure that is heavily weighted toward equity. Third, ABC has a lower share of current liabilities than other firms to match its lower investment in short-term assets. This comparison indicates that ABC is far less leveraged than similar firms in its industry, which lessens risk to lenders. It also raises questions about whether the firm's investment in current assets is sufficient and if it has overpaid or overinvested in intangible assets. These questions need to be explored with the firm's management before making a lending or investment decision.

Table 4.2   Common Size Balance Sheet Ratios for ABC and Comparable Pharmaceutical Firms

Balance Sheet Category	ABC	Pharmaceutical Firms ($2 to $10 million in sales)
Assets		
Cash & Marketable Securities	4.2%	9.9%
Accounts Receivable	19.6%	29.4%
Inventory	19.8%	23.1%
Other Current Assets	1.0%	1.9%
Total Current Assets	44.5%	64.4%
Fixed Assets	26.8%	25.4%
Intangible Assets	23.6%	1.9%
Other Assets	5.1%	8.3%
TOTAL ASSETS	100.0%	100.0%
Liabilities and Shareholders' Equity		
Accounts Payable	8.7%	17.2%
Income Taxes Payable	0.0%	0.5%
Current Debt	1.7%	7.9%
Other Current Liabilities	6.1%	9.3%
Total Current Liabilities	16.5%	34.9%
Long-Term Debt	6.1%	26.2%
Deferred Taxes	0.0%	0.3%
Other Liabilities	0.4%	7.2%
Net Worth/Shareholders' Equity	76.9%	31.4%
Total Liabilities and Shareholders' Equity	100.0%	100.0%

SOURCE: Robert Morris Associates (2002)

A second use of common size financial statements is to prepare financial projections. For existing firms, the common size ratios from a recent income statement are used to project income statements from the sales forecast for future years. Similarly, common size balance sheets can be used to estimate the impact of new financing and expected retained earnings on a firm's assets. Analysts also can use common size statements to compare financial projections to historic financial statements to test their plausibility and root out overly optimistic assumptions. For start-up firms, average common size statements for the entire industry or a comparable subgroup provide a starting point to forecast financial statements; they provide an industry history to inform financial planning.

A source of comparative financial data is necessary for ratio analysis. Four publications compile this data from firms across many industries and publish summary financial ratios and common size financial statements, usually on an annual basis: (1) Leo Troy's *Almanac of Business and Industrial Ratio*; (2) Robert Morris Associates' *RMA Annual Statement Studies*; (3) *Industry Norms and Key Business Ratios* published by Dun & Bradstreet Report; and (4) *Financial Studies of Small Business*. These publications can be purchased but are also available in business libraries and some general public libraries. Some publishers also provide data in a CD-ROM format or via online subscription services.

Beyond Ratio Analysis

Although ratio analysis helps to evaluate a firm's likelihood to fulfill economic development objectives and repay new debt, it is limited by its reliance on the historic figures included in financial statements. Additional financial issues should be analyzed to uncover "hidden" or potential problems that are not readily revealed on financial statements. A key issue to review is how a business's existing debt contracts affect its capacity to incur additional loans in three ways—through financial covenants, the availability of collateral, and future debt payments. As discussed in Chapter 2, debt contracts include financial covenants and collateral requirements to protect lenders from potential losses. These provisions affect the financial risk for new lenders and the conditions under which the firm can borrow additional funds. For example, new borrowing will change the firm's net worth and debt-to-equity ratio, which may violate financial covenants in existing loan agreements. Second, sufficient collateral must be available to secure new debt. In some cases, lenders take a blanket first lien on all assets so a new loan is only possible if the new lender will accept a subordinate position on collateral. This lender must be comfortable that a second lien on collateral offers sufficient security for the proposed debt. Third, required interest and principal payments under existing loan agreements must be understood. When existing debt is not fully amortizing with level payments over time, there may be step-ups in interest and principal payments over time or large balloon payments in future years. The repayment details of a firm's existing debt affects its capacity to repay new loans and influences decisions on the best way to structure these loans. A careful review of existing debt contracts, therefore, is necessary to determine if their covenants and security terms allow additional financing and to decide whether a firm's expected cash flow will be sufficient to repay both present and new loans.

Another concern is whether contingent or unfunded liabilities pose serious financial risks for the firm. Some liabilities may be uncertain or contingent, such as claims under lawsuits, but others are known and predictable. For example, pension and health insurance obligations to retired employees may not be adequately funded. Other examples include increasing rents under real estate leases, requirements to buy back stock from shareholders, and fixed employee compensation under employment contracts. Although these liabilities often are disclosed in the notes of audited financial statements, many firms do not prepare audited statements. Even audited statements may not reveal these obligations completely or transparently. Consequently, practitioners need to seek out this information and analyze its impact on future financial obligations.

The Final Test: Preparing and Evaluating Financial Projections

After diagnosing the company's financial condition, the next step is forecasting cash flow to assess its ability to support the financing plan and absorb downside risks from lower sales and higher expenses. Although a company seeking financing may prepare financial projections, practitioners should prepare their own projections to check the plausibility and accuracy of the firm's forecast and to test the financial risks of the proposed financing under alternative assumptions and scenarios.

Preparing cash flow projections involves four steps. First, create a baseline projection of future sales revenue, operating expenses, new investments, and debt service. These projections should reflect the firm's historic performance and the impact of new projects to be undertaken with the requested financing. The common size financial statements discussed earlier in the chapter provide a good starting point to project operating expenses from the sales forecast. They are especially helpful for new businesses since average financial ratios for comparable firms in the same industry can be used to prepare projections. Second, convert these projections into a cash flow pro forma. This step recognizes that cash flow will come from actual cash receipts and outlays rather than sales and expenses. Two primary adjustments are needed to convert the projected sales and expenses into a forecast of cash collections and expenditures. Boxes 4.1 and 4.2 show the calculations involved in making these adjustments. Cash receipts come from collecting accounts receivable, which include both the remaining uncollected receivables from prior year sales and collections on current year sales.

Consequently, cash receipts from sales equal accounts receivable when the year begins plus projected sales for the year less the expected accounts receivable at year end (see Box 4.1). Similarly, cash outlays for expenses include the accounts payable at the beginning of the year plus the projected costs of goods sold and other operating expenses for the year less the expected accounts payable at year-end (see Box 4.2). Other expected cash flow changes also need to be included in these projections, such as expenditure for new plant and equipment and projected debt service on existing and new loans. Other cash receipts might include funds for new debt and stock sales, proceeds from asset sales, for example, equipment replaced by new investments, and increased interest income from carrying larger cash balances. In the third step, the tax implications from expanded profits and new investment need to be incorporated. Tax impacts clearly include higher tax payments from increased profits, new property, and more employees, but also can involve tax savings from investment tax credits and increased depreciation expenses. Finally, evaluate how well the firm's projected cash flow and capacity to repay the proposed new financing stand up to less rosy circumstances. The best way to assess this downside risk is to pick two or three reasonable scenarios and then project their impact on the firm's cash flow. One scenario might be slightly lower sales. A second scenario could entail a large increase in energy prices or other key input costs. A third scenario would look at repayment risk if reduced sales and higher operating costs occur simultaneously.

Box 4.1 Projecting Cash Receipts From Sales

Cash Receipts = Collection of Beginning Period Accounts Receivable
              + Sales Revenue – End of Period Accounts Receivable

Example:
2003 Year-End Accounts Receivable = $75 million
Projected 2004 Net Sales = $2,400 million
Projected 2004 Year-End Accounts Receivable = 20 days' average sales
20 days' average sales = one day's sales times 20 = ($2,400 million/365)
  *20 = $132 million

Projected 2000 Cash Receipts (in millions):

Collection of 2003 Year-End Accounts Receivable =	$75
Plus 2004 Projected Sales	$2,400
Less 2004 Year-End Accounts Receivable	($132)
Projected 2004 Cash Receipts	$2,343

Box 4.2   Projecting Cash Outlays From Expenses

Cash Expenditures = Payment of Beginning Period Accounts Payable + Costs of
                   Goods Sold + Other Operating Expenses – End of Period
                   Accounts Payable

Example:
2003 Year End Accounts Payable = 100 million
Projected 2004 Cost of Goods Sales (COGS) = $1,600 million
Projected Other Expenses = $550 million
Expected 2004 Year-End Accounts Payable = 30 days of COGS and other expenses
30 days of COGS and Other Operating Expenses = One Day of COGS and Other
Operating Expenses Times 30
30 Days of COGS and Other Expense = [($1,600 + 550)/365]*30 = $177 million

Projected 2004 Cash Outlays (in millions):

Collection of 2003 Year-End Accounts Payable	$100
Plus 2004 Projected Expenses	$2,150
Less 2004 Year-End Accounts Payable	($177)
Projected 2004 Cash Receipts	$2,073

Analyzing Crystal Clear Window Company

The prior sections introduced tools for business financial analysis. In practice, development finance professionals combine these tools to understand a firm's capacity to support new debt. In this section, the case of Crystal Clear Window Company, a manufacturer of aluminum storm windows, is used to illustrate the mechanics of cash flow and ratio analysis and discuss their implications for the firm's credit worthiness. Although this analysis is not a complete evaluation, it demonstrates key financial aspects of business credit analysis.

Preparing a Cash Flow Statement

Using the company's income statement for 1968 (Exhibit 4.5) and balance sheets for year-end 1967 and 1968 (Exhibit 4.6), a cash flow statement was prepared and is presented in Exhibit 4.7. To begin the analysis, income before taxes and interest payments is identified on line 8 of the income statement ($14,511). The provision for taxes from line 11 is then subtracted and noncash expenses, in this case the depreciation expense on line 5, are added back in. Next, adjustments are made for the cash flow impact of changes in the balance sheet accounts. First, the cash flows from current asset accounts are listed, which include accounts receivable, inventory, and prepaid expenses. For Crystal Clear Window Company, all asset accounts increased,[4] which consumed cash and, thus, are subtracted from income to reduce cash flow. Changes in liability accounts (other than the debt accounts) are included next. Crystal Clear Window Company reduced one liability account (bank overdraft), which used cash and is subtracted from cash flow, but increased two accounts (accounts payable and accrued income taxes) that provided a source of cash and a positive change to cash flow. All these figures are then totaled to calculate cash flow from operating activities. Note that the company's cash flow from operations is positive ($4,034), but is less than half of net profit on the income statement. Cash flow after investing is calculated by adjusting for investments in property, plant, and equipment. Crystal Clear Window Company used cash to invest in both equipment ($2,126) and leasehold improvements ($254). After subtracting these figures, cash flow after investing activities is $1,654. Finally, the cash flow statement incorporates the firm's financing activities. Interest payments reduced cash flow by $1,444, but Crystal Clear received a cash inflow of $2,500 from additional borrowing. The end result is net positive cash flow of $2,780, which equals the change in the cash account on the balance sheet to confirm the accuracy of the calculations. From this analysis, we learned that the firm's core operations produced modest cash flow of $4,034, but its investments in plant and equipment consumed almost 60% of these funds. Moreover, the final positive cash flow was due in large part to increased debt.

Exhibit 4.5 Crystal Clear Window Company Income Statement for 12 Months Ending 12/31/68

Line 1	Net Sales	$472,788
Line 2	COGS	($364,309)
Line 3	Gross Profit	$108,479
Line 4	SGA	($92,764)
Line 5	Depreciation	($1,722)
Line 6	Profit From Operations	$13,993
Line 7	Discounts Earned	$518
Line 8	Profit Before Interest and Taxes	$14,511
Line 9	Interest Expense	($1,444)
Line 10	Net Profit Before Taxes	$13,067
Line 11	Provision for Taxes	($4,422)
Line 12	**Net Profit**	**$8,645**

Exhibit 4.6   Crystal Clear Window Company Balance Sheets as of 12/31/67 and 12/31/68

	ASSETS	12/31/67	12/31/68
Line 1	Cash	$0	$2,780
Line 2	Accounts receivable, net	$33,206	$40,826
Line 3	Inventory	$45,185	$52,433
Line 4	Prepaid expenses	$861	$1,323
Line 5	Total current assets	$79,252	$97,362
Line 6	Machinery and equipment	$36,345	$38,471
Line 7	Leasehold improvements	$7,964	$8,218
Line 8	Accumulated depreciation	($7,118)	($8,840)
Line 9	Total fixed assets	$37,191	$37,849
Line 10	Total assets	$116,443	$135,211
	LIABILITIES AND SHAREHOLDER EQUITY		
Line 11	Bank overdraft	$3,773	$0
Line 12	Accounts payable	$37,773	$44,287
Line 13	Accrued expenses	$9,440	$14,322
Line 14	Notes payable	$20,000	$22,500
Line 15	Other liabilities	$0	$0
Line 16	Total current liabilities	$70,986	$81,109
Line 17	Owner's capital	$27,000	$27,000
Line 18	Retained earnings	$18,457	$27,102
Line 19	Total equity	$45,457	$54,102
Line 20	Total liabilities and equity	$116,443	$135,211

Exhibit 4.7   Cash Flow Analysis for Crystal Clear Window Company

Income before interest and taxes from the income statement (line 8)	$14,511
Subtract provision for taxes on the income statement (line 11)	($4,422)
Add back noncash expenses, depreciation (line 5)	$1,722
Adjust for Balance Sheet Changes:	
Asset Accounts	
Subtract increase in accounts receivable (line 2) a use of cash	($7,620)
Subtract increase in inventories (line 3) a use of cash	($7,248)
Subtract increase in prepaid expenses ((line 4) a use of cash	($462)
Liability Accounts	
Subtract decrease in payoff of bank overdraft (line 11) a use of cash	($3,773)
Add increase in accounts payable (line 12) a source of cash	$ 6,514
Add increase in accrued income taxes (line 13) a source of cash	$4,822
Net Cash Flow From Operating Activities	**$4,034**
Changes in long-term asset accounts	
Subtract increase in machinery and equipment (line 6) a use of cash	($2,126)
Subtract increase in leasehold improvements (line 7) a use of cash	($254)
Net Cash Flow After Investing Activities	**$1,654**
Changes for finance activities:	
Subtract interest payments on income statement (line 9) a use of cash	($1,444)
Add increase in notes payable on balance sheet (line 14) a source of cash	$2,500
Net Cash Flow for the Period	**$2,780**

Determining Debt Service Coverage

With the completed cash flow analysis, the firm's debt service coverage ratio is readily calculated by comparing cash flow before financing activities to total principal and interest payments for the same period. Cash flow before financing activities is the numerator, since this figure is the business's cash flow before interest and principal costs, and avoids double counting these payments. Moreover, it allows us to see the firm's capacity to make debt payments without the use of new borrowing or equity sales. To determine debt service payments, the interest expense from the income statement is added to the figure for current portion of long-term debt from the ending balance sheet for the prior year—this represents the next year's principal payments. Thus, the current portion of long-term debt on the December 31, 1967, balance sheet is Crystal Clear Window Company's required principal payments for 1968. Since there is no current portion of long-term debt, the company has no principal payments for 1968. It is borrowing on an interest-only basis with principal due in later years. With only interest payments of $1,444 for 1968, debt service coverage is calculated as follows:

$$\text{Net Cash Flow After Investing Activities} = \$1,654 = 1.14$$
$$\text{Interest and Principal Payments} = \$1,444$$

This coverage ratio indicates that Crystal Clear Window Company had a small cash flow margin to cover its interest payments, but its cash flow was insufficient to repay any principal. Even with interest-only payments, the 1.14 coverage ratio is below the 1.25 standard of conventional lenders.

Ratio Analysis

A review of Crystal Clear Window Company's financial ratios provides further insight into the company's financial condition and performance. Key ratios for 1968 are shown in Table 4.3, based on the formulas in Table 4.1. The first five ratios, which indicate overall profitability and operating results, show that the company has tight profit margins but good utilization of and return on its assets.

With a 23% gross margin, Crystal Clear Window Company devotes most of its sales revenue to covering its direct production costs with only 23 cents of each dollar available to cover sales, overhead, and interest costs. Since net profits are just 2% of sales, small increases in material, labor, or overhead costs could eliminate its profits if these costs cannot be converted into higher prices. These ratios indicate that the company's continued profitability depends on keeping its overhead low and maintaining or improving its production efficiency. On the other hand, CCWC is earning a good return on its total assets and invested equity and has not invested too much capital in the business. A comparison of these ratios with industry averages would

Table 4.3   Financial Ratios for Crystal Clear Window Company in 1968

Ratio	Calculation	Ratio Value
Gross Margin	(472,788–364,309)/472,788	0.23
Net Profit on Sales	8,645/472,788	0.02
Investment Turnover	472,788/116,443	4.06
Return on Assets	8,645/116,443	0.07
Return on Equity	8,645/45,457	0.19
Current Ratio	97,362/81,109	1.20
Quick Ratio	97,362–52,433)/81,109	0.55
Days Receivable	40,826/(47,2788/365)	31.52
Inventory Turnover	36,4309/((52,433+45,185)/2)	7.46
Debt-to-Total Assets	81,109/135,211	0.60
Debt-to-Equity	81,109/54,102	1.50
Times Interest Earned	14,511/1,444	10.05

show if the firm's performance is typical of the entire industry and suggests areas for operating improvements if ratios are well below industry norms.

Some ratios for CCWC's liquidity and management of short-term assets and liabilities are positive, but others raise concerns. The days receivable ratio shows that the company collects its sales invoices within 31 days on average. Although this is considered a fine collection period, it should be compared to the company's own credit policies and industry averages to verify that it indicates good collection practices. The inventory turnover shows a good ratio of sales to inventory, but this is hard to evaluate without comparative industry data. On the other hand, the firm's liquidity is not good. With a current ratio of 1.2, CCWC only has a 20% margin of short-term assets available to cover its short-term liabilities. Most lenders prefer a larger cushion. Moreover, when inventory is subtracted, the most liquid assets only cover 55% of liabilities. This shows that almost half of CCWC's current assets are invested in inventory and that it is highly dependent on converting its inventory into cash to meet its short-term obligations. Inventory is also the company's largest asset category. Thus, the inventory's value as collateral is important for any decision to extend credit and will require further scrutiny. These ratios also raise concerns about how efficiently the firm is managing its inventory. More information on its inventory management practices and comparisons with industry ratios (e.g., the average common size balance sheet ratio for inventory) are needed to resolve this issue.

The final three ratios on the company's financial structure show considerable use of debt, measured as both short-term liabilities and loans. These obligations constitute 60% of its capital and exceed shareholders' equity by 50%. A closer examination of the balance sheet shows that all of the firm's liabilities are short-term with 55% of these constituting accounts payable. This situation is both a cause and result of the company's tight liquidity. The heavy reliance on short-term liabilities places CCWC under considerable pressure to generate cash flow to pay these obligations and may require it to delay payment of its bills, adding to its accounts payable balance. Additional use of longer term financing through expanded equity investment and some long-term debt would improve this situation. While the times interest earned figure suggests ample earnings to cover interest payments and some principal repayment, the cash flow analysis showed no capacity to repay principal in 1968. The expanded investment in accounts receivable and inventory needed to support the firm's sales growth absorbed much of the firm's cash flow.

Implications of the Analysis

The cash flow and ratio analysis reveals a growing company with some operating strengths but financial conditions that make new debt financing risky. It provided a yellow light—proceed with caution, a common financing situation faced by economic development practitioners. Since CCWC is profitable and appears to be utilizing and managing most assets well, there is a sound basis for trying to work out a viable financing plan, provided the company fits economic development goals and is following a viable business plan. Further analysis is needed to assess financial risks and forecast sales and cash flow over the next few years. A key issue to evaluate is the likelihood for continued sales growth and whether increased sales will result in production and overheard efficiencies that improve profit margins and cash flow. Analysis of the business plan, market, and competition will address the first question, and common size financial statements and a closer review of the firm's cost structure and operations can speak to the latter issue. A second question is whether cash flow can be improved through better accounts receivable collection and inventory management. An expanded ratio analysis with comparative industry data would shed light on this issue, but expertise from appropriate technical assistance providers may also be needed. Finally, the collateral value of accounts receivable and inventory will need to be determined to understand their potential contribution to debt repayments. If this analysis shows that cash flow will grow in subsequent years and reasonable collateral exists, then it is feasible to supply debt to finance the firm's growth. The ratio analysis suggests a key parameter for this debt (i.e., that it improves the firm's liquidity by limiting new short-term obligations and improving the balance between short-term and longer term financing). Consequently, a proposed loan would need to be repaid over several years and perhaps be matched with an additional equity investment. The specific loan size, amortization period, and term would be set based on the cash flow projections, collateral value, and the economic development lender's required debt service coverage and loan-to-value ratios.

With the introduction to financial statement analysis completed, it is time to consider the debt financing needs of firms in greater detail. The next two chapters focus on short-term working capital and long-term fixed asset financing, respectively. Each chapter defines the form of financing, explains special issues associated with it, summarizes the primary credit tools used, and reviews key considerations in extending financing. A case study of a representative loan request is included to help readers test their financial analysis skills and develop judgment in evaluating a firm's loan request and structuring appropriate debt terms.

Endnotes

1. For a good discussion of how the terms of competition affect competitive advantage, see Magaziner and Reich (1982), *Minding America's Business,* pp. 89–98.

2. This figure for debt is the sum of the current portion of long-term debt ($1.367 million) and long-term debt ($5.022 million).

3. Anthony, Hawkins, and Merchant (1999), Chapter 13, pp. 390–409, provides a more comprehensive overview of ratio analysis.

4. It is common for growing companies to increase all current asset accounts. These assets are directly tied to expanded sales since increased sales results in higher accounts receivable, larger inventory is often needed to supply more goods being sold, and more expenses are prepaid as overall expenses grow.

5

Working
Capital Finance

With a good foundation in how businesses are financed and how to interpret their financial statements, we are prepared to address specialized financing issues for enterprises. This chapter focuses on financing a firm's working capital needs while Chapter 6 discusses the financing of longer term fixed assets. To address working capital finance, the chapter begins by discussing the different definitions of working capital, and explaining its importance to a business, both for long-term operations and for managing the short-term cash flow cycle. In the next section, the different debt instruments used to finance working capital are described. Following the discussion of debt instruments, the most common working capital finance sources are reviewed. Firms face many working capital finance options, both in the debt instrument used and institutional sources. The development finance professional's job is to first understand the firm's financing needs and capacity and then to help it locate and structure appropriate working capital debt. To help develop these skills, the underwriting issues involved in structuring working capital debt are reviewed and a case study assignment, Crystal Clear Window Company, is provided to apply this knowledge to a specific and realistic working capital financing situation.

The Importance of Working Capital Finance

Three Meanings of Working Capital

The term working capital has several meanings in business and economic development finance. In accounting and financial statement analysis, working capital is defined as the firm's short-term or current assets and current liabilities. *Net working capital* represents the excess of current assets over current liabilities and is an indicator of the firm's ability to meet its short-term financial obligations (Brealey & Myers, 2002). From a financing perspective, working capital refers to the firm's investment in two types of assets. In one instance, working capital means a business's investment in short-term assets needed to operate over a normal business cycle. This meaning corresponds to the required investment in cash, accounts receivable, inventory, and other items listed as current assets on the firm's balance sheet. In this context, working capital financing concerns how a firm finances its current assets. A second broader meaning of working capital is the company's overall nonfixed asset investments. Businesses often need to finance activities that do not involve assets measured on the balance sheet. For example, a firm may need funds to redesign its products or formulate a new marketing strategy, activities that require funds to hire personnel rather than acquiring accounting assets. When the returns for these "soft costs" investments are not immediate but rather are reaped over time through increased sales or profits, then the company needs to finance them. Thus, *working capital* can represent a broader view of a firm's capital needs that includes both current assets and other nonfixed asset investments related to its operations. In this chapter, we use this last meaning of working capital and focus on the tools and issues involved in financing these business investments.

Business Uses of Working Capital

Just as working capital has several meanings, firms use it in many ways. Most fundamentally, working capital investment is the lifeblood of a company. Without it, a firm cannot stay in business. Thus, the first, and most critical, use of working capital is providing the ongoing investment in short-term assets that a company needs to operate. A business requires a minimum cash balance to meet basic day-to-day expenses and to provide a reserve for unexpected costs. It also needs working capital for prepaid business costs, such as licenses, insurance policies, or security deposits. Furthermore, all businesses invest in some amount of inventory, from a law firm's stock of office supplies to the large inventories needed by retail and wholesale enterprises. Without some amount of working capital finance, businesses could not open and operate. A second purpose of working capital is addressing seasonal or cyclical financing needs. Here, working capital finance supports the buildup of short-term assets needed to generate revenue, but which come before the receipt of cash. For example, a toy manufacturer must produce and ship its products for the holiday shopping season several months before it receives cash payment from stores. Since most businesses do not receive prepayment for goods and services, they need to finance these purchase, production, sales, and collection costs prior to receiving payment from customers. Figure 5.1 illustrates this short-term cash flow and financing cycle. Another way to view this function of working capital is providing liquidity. Adequate and appropriate working capital financing ensures that a firm has sufficient cash flow to pay its bills as it

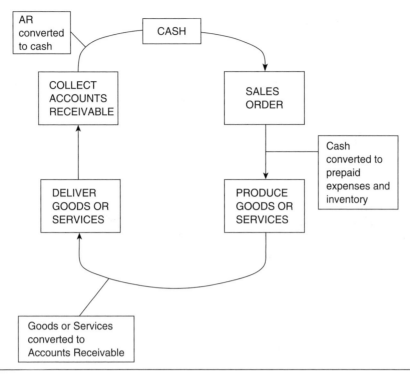

Figure 5.1   Cash Flow and the Working Capital Cycle

awaits the full collection of revenue. When working capital is not suffi-ciently or appropriately financed, a firm can run out of cash and face bank-ruptcy. A profitable firm with competitive goods or services can still be forced into bankruptcy if it has not adequately financed its working capital needs and runs out of cash. Working capital is also needed to sustain a firm's growth. As a business grows, it needs larger investments in inventory, accounts receivable, personnel, and other items to realize increased sales. New facilities and equipment are not the only assets required for growth; firms also must finance the working capital needed to support sales growth. A final use of working capital is to undertake activities to improve business operations and remain competitive, such as product development, ongoing product and process improvements, and cultivating new markets. With firms facing heightened competition, these improvements often need to be integrated into operations on a continuous basis. Consequently, they are more likely to be incurred as small repeated costs than as large infrequent investments. This is especially true for small firms that cannot afford the cost and risks of large fixed investments in research and development projects or new facilities. Ongoing investments in product and process improvement and market expansion, therefore, often must be addressed through working capital financing.

Permanent and Cyclical Working Capital

Firms need both a long-term (or permanent) investment in working capital and a short-term or cyclical one. The permanent working capital investment provides an ongoing positive net working capital position, that is, a level of current assets that exceeds current liabilities. This allows the firm to operate with a comfortable financial margin since short-term assets exceed short-term obligations and minimizes the risk of being unable to pay its employees, vendors, lenders, or the government (for taxes). To have positive net working capital, a company must finance part of its working capital on a long-term basis. Since total assets equal total liabilities and owner's equity, when current assets exceed current liabilities, this excess is financed by the long-term debt or equities (Brealey & Myers, 2002). Figure 5.2 demonstrates this point graphically. For current assets (area CA) to be greater than current liability (area CL), long-term debt and equity must finance part of area CA. Beyond this permanent working capital investment, firms need seasonal or cyclical working capital. Few firms have steady sales and production throughout the year. Since the demand for goods and services varies over the course of a year, firms need to finance both inventories and other costs to prepare for their peak sales period and accounts receivable until cash is collected. Cyclical working capital is best financed by short-term debt since the seasonal buildup of assets to address seasonal demand will be reduced and converted to cash to repay borrowed funds within a short predictable period. By matching the term of liabilities to the term of the underlying assets, short-term financing helps a firm manage inflation and other financial risks. Short-term financing is also preferable since it is usually easier to obtain and priced lower than long-term debt.

Working capital financing is a key financing need and challenge for small firms. As discussed in Chapter 2, small businesses have less access to long-term sources of capital than large businesses, including limited access to equity capital markets and fewer sources of long-term debt. Thus, many small firms are heavily dependent on short-term debt, much of which is tied to working capital.[1] However, limited equity and reliance on short-term debt increases the demand on a firm's cash flow, reduces liquidity, and increases financial leverage—all of which heighten the financial risks of extending credit. Consequently, small firms may have trouble raising short-term debt while at the same time facing obstacles to securing the longer-term debt necessary to improve their financial position and liquidity, and lessen their credit risk. Development finance has an important role in addressing this problem, either by offering working capital loans when private loans are not available or by providing debt terms that reduce a firm's financial risk and help it access private working capital financing. In particular, practitioners can help businesses finance permanent working capital to reduce their short-term financial pressures.

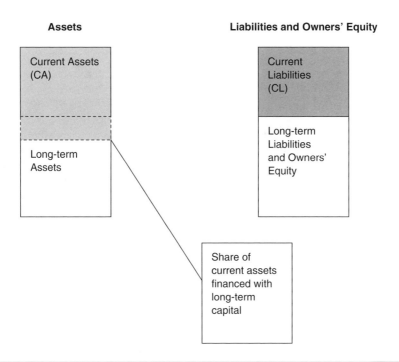

Figure 5.2   Positive Net Working Capital Requires Long-Term Financing

Forms of Working Capital Financing

Working capital financing comes in many forms, each of which has unique terms and offers certain advantages and disadvantages to the borrower. This section introduces the five major forms of debt used to finance working capital and discusses the relative advantages of each one.[2] The purpose of this information is to provide insight into the different ways in which debt can be structured and prepare practitioners to choose and structure a debt tool best suited to a firm's financial situation and needs. Table 5.1 summarizes the major features of the five working debt tools described below.

Line of Credit

A *line of credit* is an open-ended loan with a borrowing limit that the business can draw against or repay at any time during the loan period. This arrangement allows a company flexibility to borrow funds when the need arises for the exact amount required. Interest is paid only on the amount borrowed, typically on a monthly basis. A line of credit can be either

Table 5.1   Summary of Working Capital Finance Instruments

Finance Instrument	Description	Key Terms
Line of Credit	Maximum loan limit established. Firm draws on loan as needed up to limit.	Can be unsecured or secured. Annual repayment. Compensating balance may be required.
Accounts Receivable (AR) Loan	Loan secured by accounts receivable.	Loan amount based on a percentage of accounts receivable. Accounts receivable assigned to lender as sales occur. Loan balance paid down with AR collection.
Factoring	Sale of accounts receivable to a third party collector (factor). Factor bears collection risk.	Company paid based on average collection period less a collection fee. Collection amount can be advanced with an interest charge.
Inventory Loan	Loan secured by inventory.	Loan amount based on a percentage of inventory value. Lender receives security interest in inventory and may take physical control. Release of inventory with loan repayment.
Term Loan	Medium-term loan. Principal repaid over several years based on a fixed schedule.	Loan amount tied to collateral value. Can be fully amortized or a balloon loan. Typical term is three to seven years.

unsecured, if no specific collateral is pledged for repayment, or secured by specific assets such as accounts receivable or inventory. The standard term for a line of credit is 1 year with renewal subject to the lender's annual review and approval. Since a line of credit is designed to address cyclical working capital needs and not to finance long-term assets, lenders usually require full repayment of the line of credit during the annual loan period and prior to its renewal. This repayment is sometimes referred to as the annual cleanup.

Two other costs, beyond interest payments, are associated with borrowing through a line of credit. Lenders require a fee for providing the line of credit, based on the line's credit limit, which is paid whether or not the firm uses the line. This fee, usually in the range of 25 to 100 basis points, covers the bank's costs for underwriting and setting up the loan account in the event that a firm does not use the line and the bank earns no interest income. A second cost is the requirement for a borrower to maintain a compensating balance account with the bank. Under this arrangement, a borrower must have a deposit account with a minimum balance equal to a percentage of the line of credit, perhaps 10% to 20%. If a firm normally maintains this balance in its cash accounts, then no additional costs are imposed by this requirement. However, when a firm must increase its bank deposits to meet the compensating balance requirement, then it is incurring an additional cost. In effect, the compensating balance reduces the business's net loan proceeds and increases its effective interest rate. Consider a line of credit for $1 million at a 10% interest rate with a 20% compensating balance requirement. When the company fully draws on the line of credit, it will have borrowed $1 million but must leave $200,000 on deposit with the lender, resulting in net loan proceeds of $800,000. However, it pays interest on the full $1 million drawn. Thus, the effective annual interest rate is 12.5% rather than 10% (one year's interest is $100,000 or 12.5% of the $800,000 in net proceeds). Like most loans, the lending terms for a line of credit include financial covenants or minimal financial standards that the borrower must meet. Typical financial covenants include a minimum current ratio, a minimum net worth, and a maximum debt-to-equity ratio.

The advantages of a line of credit are twofold. First, it allows a company to minimize the principal borrowed and the resulting interest payments. Second, it is simpler to establish and entails fewer transaction and legal costs, particularly when it is unsecured. The disadvantages of a line of credit include the potential for higher borrowing costs when a large compensating balance is required and its limitation to financing cyclical working capital needs. With full repayment required each year and annual extensions subject to lender approval, a line of credit cannot finance medium-term or long-term working capital investments.

Accounts Receivable Financing

Some businesses lack the credit quality to borrow on an unsecured basis and must instead pledge collateral to obtain a loan. Loans secured by accounts receivable are a common form of debt used to finance working capital. Under *accounts receivable debt,* the maximum loan amount is tied to a percentage of the borrower's accounts receivable. When accounts receivable increase, the allowable loan principal also rises. However, the firm must use customer payments on these receivables to reduce the loan balance. The borrowing ratio depends on the credit quality of the firm's customers and the age of the accounts receivable. A firm with financially strong customers should be able to obtain a loan equal to 80% of its accounts receivable. With weaker credit customers, the loan may be limited to 50% to 60% of accounts receivable. Additionally, a lender may exclude receivables beyond a certain age (e.g., 60 or 90 days) in the base used to calculate the loan limit. Older receivables are considered indicative of a customer with financial problems and less likely to pay.[3] Since accounts receivable are pledged as collateral, when a firm does not repay the loan, the lender will collect the receivables directly from the customer and apply it to loan payments. The bank receives a copy of all invoices along with an assignment that gives it the legal right to collect payment and apply it to the loan. In some accounts receivable loans, customers make payments directly to a bank-controlled account (a lock box).

Firms gain several benefits with accounts receivable financing. With the loan limit tied to total accounts receivable, borrowing capacity grows automatically as sales grow. This automatic matching of credit increases to sales growth provides a ready means to finance expanded sales, which is especially valuable to fast-growing firms. It also provides a good borrowing alternative for businesses without the financial strength to obtain an unsecured line of credit. Accounts receivable financing allows small businesses with creditworthy customers to use the stronger credit of their customers to help borrow funds. One disadvantage of accounts receivable financing is the higher costs associated with managing the collateral, for which lenders may charge a higher interest rate or fees. Since accounts receivable financing requires pledging collateral, it limits a firm's ability to use this collateral for any other borrowing. This may be a concern if accounts receivable are the firm's primary asset.

Factoring

Factoring entails the sale of accounts receivable to another firm, called the factor, who then collects payment from the customer. Through factoring, a business can shift the costs of collection and the risk of nonpayment to a third party. In a factoring arrangement, a company and the factor work out a credit limit and average collection period for each customer. As the company makes new sales to a customer, it provides an invoice to the factor. The customer pays the factor directly, and the factor then pays the company based on the agreed upon average collection period, less a slight discount that covers the factor's collection costs and credit risk (Brealey & Myers, 2002). In addition to absorbing collection risk, a factor may advance payment for a large share of the invoice, typically 70% to 80%, providing the company with immediate cash flow from sales. In this case, the factor charges an interest rate on this advance and then deducts the advance amount from its final payment to the firm when an invoice is collected (Owen et al., 1986; Brealey & Myers, 2002).

Factoring has several advantages for a firm over straight accounts receivable financing. First, it saves the cost of establishing and administering its own collection system. Second, a factor can often collect accounts receivable at a lower cost than a small business, due to economies of scale, and transfer some of these savings to the company. Third, factoring is a form of collection insurance that provides an enterprise with more predictable cash flow from sales. On the other hand, factoring costs may be higher than a direct loan, especially when the firm's customers have poor credit that lead the factor to charge a high fee. Furthermore, once the collection function shifts to a third party, the business loses control over this part of the customer relationship, which may affect overall customer relations, especially when the factor's collection practices differ from those of the company.

Inventory Financing

As with accounts receivable loans, *inventory financing* is a secured loan, in this case with inventory as collateral. However, inventory financing is more difficult to secure since inventory is riskier collateral than accounts receivable. Some inventory becomes obsolete and loses value quickly, and other types of inventory, like partially manufactured goods, have little or no resale value. Firms with an inventory of standardized goods with predictable prices, such as automobiles or appliances, will be more successful at securing inventory financing than businesses with a large amount of work in process or highly seasonal or perishable goods. Loan amounts also vary with the quality of the inventory pledged as collateral, usually ranging from 50% to 80%. For most businesses, inventory loans yield loan proceeds at a lower share of pledged assets than accounts receivable financing. When inventory is a large share of a firm's current assets, however, inventory financing is a critical option to finance working capital.

Lenders need to control the inventory pledged as collateral to ensure that it is not sold before their loan is repaid. Two primary methods are used to obtain this control: (1) warehouse storage; and (2) direct assignment by product serial or identification numbers.[4] Under one warehouse arrangement, pledged inventory is stored in a public warehouse and controlled by an independent party (the warehouse operator). A warehouse receipt is issued when the inventory is stored, and the goods are released only upon the instructions of the receipt-holder. When the inventory is pledged, the lender has control of the receipt and can prevent release of the goods until the loan is repaid. Since public warehouse storage is inconvenient for firms that need on-site access to their inventory, an alternative arrangement, known as a field warehouse, can be established. Here, an independent public warehouse company assumes control over the pledged inventory at the firm's site. In effect, the firm leases space to the warehouse operator rather than transferring goods to an off-site location. As with a public warehouse, the lender controls the warehouse receipt and will not release the inventory until the loan is repaid. Direct assignment by serial number is a simpler method to control inventory used for manufactured goods that are tagged with a unique serial number. The lender receives an assignment or trust receipt for the pledged inventory that lists all serial numbers for the collateral. The company houses and controls its inventory and can arrange for product sales. However, a release of the assignment or return of the trust receipt is required before the collateral is delivered and ownership transferred to the buyer. This release occurs with partial or full loan repayment.

While inventory financing involves higher transaction and administrative costs than other loan instruments, it is an important financing tool for companies with large inventory assets. When a company has limited accounts receivable and lacks the financial position to obtain a line of credit, inventory financing may be the only available type of working capital debt.

Moreover, this form of financing can be cost effective when inventory quality is high and yields a good loan-to-value ratio and interest rate.

Term Loan

While the four prior debt instruments address cyclical working capital needs, term loans can finance medium-term noncyclical working capital. A *term loan* is a form of medium-term debt in which principal is repaid over several years, typically in 3 to 7 years. Since lenders prefer not to bear interest rate risk, term loans usually have a floating interest rate set between the prime rate and prime plus 300 basis points, depending on the borrower's credit risk. Sometimes, a bank will agree to an interest rate cap or fixed rate loan, but it usually charges a fee or higher interest rate for these features. Term loans have a fixed repayment schedule that can take several forms. Level principal payments over the loan term are most common. In this case, the company pays the same principal amount each month plus interest on the outstanding loan balance. A second option is a level loan payment in which the total payment amount is the same every month but the share allocated to interest and principle varies with each payment. Finally, some term loans are partially amortizing and have a balloon payment at maturity. Term loans can be either unsecured or secured; a business with a strong balance sheet and a good profit and cash flow history might obtain an unsecured term loan, but many small firms will be required to pledge assets. Moreover, since loan repayment extends over several years, lenders include financial covenants in their loan agreements to guard against deterioration in the firm's financial position over the loan term. Typical financial covenants include minimum net worth, minimum net working capital (or current ratio), and maximum debt-to-equity ratios. Finally, lenders often require the borrower to maintain a compensating balance account equal to 10% to 20% of the loan amount. (Brealey & Myers, 2002; Owen et al., 1986)

The major advantage of term loans is their ability to fund long-term working capital needs. As discussed at the beginning of the chapter, businesses benefit from having a comfortable positive net working capital margin, which lowers the pressure to meet all short-term obligations and reduces bankruptcy risk. Term loans provide the medium-term financing to invest in the cash, accounts receivable, and inventory balances needed to create excess working capital. They also are well suited to finance the expanded working capital needed for sales growth. Furthermore, a term loan is repaid over several years, which reduces the cash flow needed to service the debt. However, the benefits of longer term financing do not come without costs, most notably higher interest rates and less financial flexibility. Since a longer repayment period poses more risk to lenders, term loans carry a higher interest rate than short-term loans.[5] When provided with a floating interest rate, term loans expose firms to greater interest rate risk since the chances of a spike in interest rates increase for a longer repayment period. Due to restrictive covenants and collateral requirements, a term loan imposes considerable financial constraints on a business. Moreover, these financial constraints are in place for several years and cannot be quickly reversed, as with a 1-year line of credit. Despite these costs, term loans can be of great value to small firms, providing a way to supplement their limited supply of equity and long-term debt with medium-term capital.

Sources of Working Capital for Small Businesses

Commercial banks are the largest financing source for external business debt (Berger & Udell, 1998), including working capital loans, and they offer a large range of debt products. With banking consolidation, commercial banks are multistate institutions that increasingly focus on lending to small business with large borrowing needs that pose limited risks. Consequently, alternate sources of working capital debt become more important. *Savings banks* and thrift lenders are increasingly providing small business loans, and, in some regions, they are important small business and commercial real estate lenders.[6] Although savings banks offer fewer products and may be less familiar with unconventional economic development loans, they are more likely to provide smaller loans and more personalized service. *Commercial finance companies* are important working capital lenders since, as nonregulated financial institutions, they can make higher-risk loans. Some finance companies specialize in serving specific industries, which allows them to better assess risk and creditworthiness, and extend loans that more general lenders would not make. Another approach used by finance companies is *asset-based lending* in which a lender carefully evaluates and lends against asset collateral value, placing less emphasis on the firm's overall balance sheet and financial ratios. An asset-based lending approach can improve loan availability and terms for small firms with good quality assets but weaker overall credit. Commercial finance companies also are more likely to offer factoring than banks. Trade credit extended by vendors is a fourth alternative for small firms. While trade credit does not finance permanent or long-term working capital, it helps address short-term borrowing needs. Extending payment periods and increasing credit limits with major suppliers is a fast and cost-effective way to finance some working capital needs that can be part of a firm's overall plan to manage seasonal borrowing needs.

Other working capital finance options exist beyond these three conventional credit sources. First, loan guarantees provided through the U.S. *Small Business Administration (SBA) 7(a) program* can help early-stage small firms, and those with weaker credit and collateral, secure loans. Under its 7(a) authority, the SBA offers the Green Line Program, a specialized loan guarantee for line-of-credit financing. The SBA 7(a) program is discussed in greater detail in Chapter 8. Business development corporations (BDCs) are a second alternative source for working capital loans. BDCs are high-risk lending arms of the banking industry that exist in almost every state. They borrow funds from a large base of member banks and specialize in providing subordinate debt and lending to higher-risk businesses. While BDCs rely heavily on bank loan officers for referrals, economic development practitioners need to understand their debt products and build good working relationships with their staffs. Venture capital firms also finance working capital, especially permanent working capital to support rapid growth. While venture capitalists typically provide equity financing, some also provide debt capital. A growing set of mezzanine funds,[7] often managed by venture capitalists, supply medium-term subordinate debt and take warrants that increase their potential returns. This type of financing is appropriate to finance long-term working capital needs and is a lower-cost alternative to raising equity. However, the availability of venture capital and mezzanine debt is limited to fast-growing firms, often in industries and markets viewed as offering the potential for high returns. Government and nonprofit revolving loan funds also supply working capital loans. While small in total capital, these funds help firms access conventional bank debt by providing subordinate loans, offering smaller loans, and serving firms that do not qualify for conventional working capital credit.

Many entrepreneurs and small firms also rely on personal credit sources to finance working capital, especially credit cards and second mortgage loans on the business owner's home. These sources are easy to come by and involve few transaction costs, but they have certain limits. First, they provide only modest amounts of capital. Second, credit card debt is expensive with interest rates of 18% or higher, which reduces cash flow for other business purposes. Third, personal credit links the business owner's personal assets to the firm's success, putting important household assets, such as the owner's home, at risk. Finally, credit cards and second mortgage loans are not viable for entrepreneurs who do not own a home or lack a formal credit history. Immigrant or low-income business owners, in particular, are least able to use personal credit to finance a business. Given these many limitations, it is desirable to move entrepreneurs from informal and personal credit sources into formal business working capital loans that are structured to address the credit needs of their firms.

Underwriting Issues in Working Capital Financing

While underwriting working capital loans follows the broad framework presented in Chapter 4, several unique issues warrant discussion. Since repayment is closely linked to short-term cash flow, especially for cyclical working capital loans, finance practitioners need to scrutinize these projections in detail. Borrowers will need to provide monthly or quarterly cash flow projections for the next 1 to 2 years to facilitate this analysis. Moreover, this requirement helps assess how carefully the firm plans and monitors cash flow and helps identify weaknesses in this key management area. Detailed monthly projections can also uncover ways to improve cash flow that may reduce borrowing needs and improve the firm's capacity to repay and qualify for a loan. For example, a firm may be able to reduce its inventory, offer incentives for more rapid payment of invoices, or improve supplier credit terms. For working capital loans, lenders will pay special attention to liquidity ratios and the quality of current assets since these factors are most critical to loan repayment. Finally, the underwriting analysis needs to evaluate the applicant's need for permanent versus cyclical working capital debt. Small businesses with limited long-term capital are under heavy pressure to meet short-term cash flow needs. Adding short-term working capital loans does not address this problem and may make matters worse. Thus, it is important to analyze why the firm is seeking debt, what purpose the loan will serve, and how these relate to short-term cyclical needs versus long-term permanent working capital needs. In some cases, practitioners need to revise the borrower's loan request and structure debt that better reflects the firm's needs. This might entail proposing a term loan in place of a line of credit when the business needs permanent working capital or combining short-term and medium-term debt instruments to create a good balance between cyclical and permanent working capital debt. These alternatives can improve a firm's cash flow and liquidity to partially offset the greater repayment risk that results from extending loan repayment. Loan guarantees and subordinate debt can reduce this additional risk and help convince conventional lenders to both supply credit and provide it on terms that fit a borrower's financial needs.

Case Study: Crystal Clear Window Company[8]

Introduction

Mr. Robb, assistant vice president at Commercial National Bank, will present a loan request from Crystal Clear Window Company to the loan committee today. Mr. Robb has spent considerable time on the credit request. He made a thorough investigation of the principals involved, studied the business and evaluated its potentials, and made several plant visits to become familiar with the firm's operations. He also checked with both suppliers and purchasers of the finished product. Finally, he secured the necessary financial data (See Exhibits 5.1 and 5.2), evaluated the firm's sales projections, and secured an appraisal of the machinery and equipment. This and other pertinent information was passed on to the loan committee members so that each member could evaluate the request prior to today's meeting.

Exhibit 5.1 Crystal Clear Window Company Comparative Income Statements

	12/31/67 12 months	% of Sales	12/31/68 12 months	% of Sales	12/31/69 5 months	% of Sales	5/31/70 12 months	% of Sales
Sales	$390,273		$473,920		$597,441		$206,778	
Returns and Allowances	1,764		1,132		3,667		1,022	
Net Sales	388,509	100.0%	472,788	100.0%	593,774	100.0%	205,756	100.0%
Cost of Goods Sold								
Labor	72,560	118.7%	90,046	19.0%	108,505	18.3%	41,566	20.2%
Materials	211,983	554.6%	258,155	54.6%	330,966	55.7%	111,772	54.3%
Freight in	6,366	11.6%	7,844	1.7%	9,873	1.7%	3,490	1.7%
Maintenance	1,577	0.4%	864	0.2%	2,816	0.5%	1,233	0.6%
Rent	6,712	1.7%	7,400	1.6%	9,300	1.6%	4,100	2.0%
Depreciation	2,994	0.8%	1,542	0.3%	1,970	0.3%	368	0.2%
Total	$302,192	77.8%	$365,851	77.4%	$463,430	78.0%	$162,529	79.0%
Gross Profit	$86,317	22.2%	$106,937	22.6%	$130,344	22.0%	$43,227	21.0%
Selling and shipping								
Salaries	17,056	4.4%	18,920	4.0%	23,447	3.9%	12,500	6.1%
Freight out	6,417	1.7%	7,862	1.7%	10,867	1.8%	3,714	1.8%
Travel	6,775	1.7%	9,637	2.0%	12,033	2.0%	5,150	2.5%
Advertising	6,682	1.7%	6,947	1.5%	9,441	1.6%	2,037	1.0%
Total	$36,930	9.5%	$43,366	9.2%	$55,788	9.4%	$23,401	11.4%
Administrative expense								
Salaries	$33,973	8.7%	$38,667	8.2%	$38,960	6.6%	$16,218	7.9%
Utilities	3,580	0.9%	4,464	0.9%	4,896	0.8%	2,663	1.3%
Rent	960	0.2%	1,000	0.2%	1,000	0.2%	420	0.2%
Insurance	922	0.2%	1,123	0.2%	1,490	0.3%	580	0.3%
Depreciation	167	0.0%	180	0.0%	180	0.0%	90	0.0%
Taxes and license	916	0.2%	1,130	0.2%	1,442	0.2%	600	0.3%
Interest	1,188	0.3%	1,444	0.3%	1,668	0.3%	680	0.3%
Bad debts	1,166	0.3%	1,317	0.3%	1,580	0.3%	325	0.2%
Miscellaneous	1,445	0.4%	1,697	0.4%	2,227	0.4%	814	0.4%
Total	$44,317	11.4%	51,022	10.8%	$53,443	9.0%	$22,390	10.9%
Profit from operations	$5,070	1.3%	$12,549	2.7%	$21,113	3.6%	($2,564)	-1.2%
Discounts earned	766	0.2%	518	0.1%	220	00.0%	0	0.0%
Net profit before taxes	5,836	1.5%	13,067	2.8%	21,333	3.6%	(2,564)	-1.2%
Provision for taxes	1,473		4,422		7,880		0	
Net profit	$4,363		$8,645		$13,453		($2,564)	

Exhibit 5.2   Crystal Clear Window Company Comparative Balance Sheet

	12/31/67	12/31/68	12/31/69	5/31/70
ASSETS				
Cash	$0	$2,780	$1,244	$0
Accounts receivable	34,706	42,326	52,814	93,237
Allowance for doubtful	−1,500	−1,500	−1,500	−1,500
Inventory	45,185	52,433	74,479	79,109
Prepaid expenses	861	1,323	1,218	1,533
Total current assets	$79,252	$97,362	$128,255	$172,379
Machinery and equipment	$36,345	$38,471	$41,770	$44,298
Leasehold improvements	7,964	8,218	8,426	8,426
Accumulated depreciation	−7,118	−8,840	−10,990	−11,448
Total fixed assets	37,191	37,849	39,206	41,276
Total assets	$116,443	$135,211	$167,461	$213,655
LIABILITIES AND SHAREHOLDERS' EQUITY				
Bank overdraft	$3,773	$0	$0	$0
Accounts payable	37,773	44,287	51,848	77,220
Accrued expenses	9,440	14,322	18,058	13,410
Notes payable	20,000	22,500	30,000	40,000
Other liabilities	0	0	0	18,034
Total current liabilities	$70,986	$81,109	$99,906	$148,664
Capital	$27,000	$27,000	$27,000	$27,000
Retained earnings	18,457	27,102	40,555	37,991
Total equity	$45,457	$54,102	$67,555	$64,991
Total liabilities and equity	$116,443	$135,211	$167,461	$213,655

Firm History

Henry Rapp and Alan Keith organized Crystal Clear Window Company in 1960. Mr. Rapp is 42 years of age and had considerable experience with a large speculative builder of houses in an adjoining state. He is knowledgeable in the areas of construction, building materials, and real estate credit. Mr. Keith, 32, is a machinist who learned his trade from his father and was employed for several years in the production area of a national aluminum fabricating firm. Both men left their respective employers on good terms and were told that should they ever want to return the welcome mat would be out. Neither Mr. Rapp nor Mr. Keith is a man of means. Mr. Rapp put all of his savings, $16,000, in the business when it was formed, and Mr. Keith invested $11,000—$7,000 from his savings and $4,000 from the sale of his house. Both men live frugally, and there is no evidence that they are affected by "keeping up with the Joneses." Both Mr. Rapp and Mr. Keith are stockholders, and the latter serves as treasurer of the corporation. From a practical standpoint, the business operates as a partnership.

Operations

Crystal Clear Window Company operates in leased quarters and produces aluminum windows and sliding glass doors of standard sizes. The operation is primarily one of assembly. The firm purchases extruded window frames from a national aluminum manufacturer. These frames are then sawed and punched to size for assembly, and the prepared frames are assembled along with the necessary glass and screens, which are also purchased to size. Screens are purchased from the same firm that provides the aluminum frames. Glass, imported in sizable lots from concerns in Belgium and Australia on a letter of credit basis with draft terms at sight, comprises approximately 25% of the cost of materials. The cutting and punching machines are relatively simple and inexpensive. The firm maintains duplicate machines that can be substituted in the event of a breakdown. In the assembly process, a large amount of labor is used, although approximately 55% of the firm's total outlay is for materials. The workforce is relatively young and not unionized, and there appears to be a high degree of esprit de corps among the 20 employees.

Two salesmen are employed who call on building materials suppliers within a 300-mile radius of Jonesboro. The windows produced have consistently exceeded the specifications established by the American Aluminum Manufacturers Association, whose standards are acceptable to the Federal Housing Authority. The high quality increases the marketability of the windows, for few building supply dealers will handle a product that does not meet the standards required by the FHA in its appraisal program. This firm has emphasized an economical operation. Extruded frames, for example, are purchased in such lengths that the loss from sawing and cutting is kept to a minimum. The firm follows a policy of keeping its inventory of raw materials, supplies, and finished products as low as efficient operations will permit. They have restricted their sales to reputable building suppliers who are financially strong. The firm's returns and allowances for uncollected receivables have been very low.

The Use of Aluminum Windows

There has been fabulous growth in the use of aluminum windows in recent years. Although aluminum windows have been produced for quite some time, the aluminum window industry per se has been in existence only about 20 years. The use of aluminum windows varies throughout the country; nationally, however, about 80% of the single-family dwelling units and about 90% of the multiple units constructed at the present time use aluminum windows. Aluminum windows have several advantages over wooden windows. Aluminum windows are less expensive and their maintenance is considerably less. They can be manufactured in a shorter period of time. The time required to produce a wooden window varies depending on the type of wood used, but in general the manufacturing process requires about triple the time required for aluminum windows. Another significant advantage of aluminum windows is the on-site cost. Wooden windows are installed by carpenters whose hourly wage is much higher than that of workers who install aluminum windows. The installation time of a wooden window is much more than that of an aluminum window, since weights must be installed and slides must be manufactured on the site. Since holes for nails that support the aluminum windows are drilled at the factory, the aluminum window can be installed within a few minutes. For these reasons, the demand for aluminum windows appears likely to continue.

Financial Status

Sales of Crystal Clear Window Company have mushroomed since the firm began in 1960—from $2,050 for the first month of operations to $597,441 for all of 1969. The original capital and retained earnings of the company have not been sufficient to support this volume of business activity. A large part of the financing has come from (1) funds that have been made available due to the fact that the firm's accounts payable are due on a net 60-day basis and accounts receivable are due on a net 30-day basis;[9] and (2) loans from Mr. Mulder, who is Mr. Keith's father-in-law, that now total $40,000. Mr. Mulder would like these loans repaid because he retired a few months ago and needs the funds to purchase property in Florida where he and his wife plan to retire. Mr. Mulder has loaned the funds to the firm at the same rate of interest that he could have earned on a certificate of deposit at a local bank, which has varied from 3% to 5.5%. Both Mr. Rapp and Mr. Keith have been quite appreciative of this loan.

The firm had some difficult initial years, which resulted in meager profitability. However, through trial and error, costs were stabilized, the break-even point was established, and with greater market penetration greater profitability was achieved—as shown by the increasing profits and the percentage of profits to sales. As volume continued to expand, the working capital requirement expanded faster than the accumulated earnings. Consequently, the firm faced increasing demand for additional working capital support as disclosed by the increasing reliance on debt, the bank overdraft, and decreasing discounts earned on early invoice payments. The anticipated rate of sales expansion, the possibility of outgrowing the present quarters, and the need for additional equipment all suggest continued absorption of funds for the foreseeable future. For example, sales have practically doubled during the last 3 years, while equipment has shown only a modest increase.

Management's record for honesty and fair dealing is excellent as judged by the comments of employees, suppliers, and customers. Their ability to produce and market a product is attested to by increasing sales, nominal bad debt losses, and a relatively low level of returns and allowances. The economic outlook for this business is favorable. However, financial understanding on the part of management is an unknown factor since they have been shielded from financial reality by the availability of friendly debt.

Recommendation

Mr. Robb recommended to the loan committee that the bank finance Crystal Clear Window Company with a line of credit secured by accounts receivable. He proposed a $75,000 maximum line with an advance rate equal to 80% of outstanding accounts receivable and an 8.5% interest rate. The line of credit would have an annual cleanup, require an increase in deposit balances, and the principals would have to guarantee the loan. All three members of the loan committee had different ideas about the loan application. Mr. Edwards thought that the bank should not finance the firm under any conditions and pointed out the poor debt-to-worth and current ratios. He suggested that the bank advise the company owners to sell additional stock. Mr. Robb pointed out that it was difficult and very expensive for a firm of this size and financial strength to sell stock. Mr. Davis said that the firm needed a term loan of about $40,000 to replace the loan from Mr. Mulder that must be repaid. Mr. Robb felt that a term loan would not give the firm much financial relief since it would require monthly principal payments, and that the company would need more funds in the future. He felt Crystal Clear Window Company needed an open-ended amount of credit and that a term loan would be too restrictive. Mr. Edwards then interjected that the firm should attempt to reduce its need for funds by (1) offering selling terms of 1% 10 days net 30 in order to reduce the financial burden of carrying receivables,[10] and (2) purchasing glass locally rather than from abroad. Purchasing glass abroad has forced the firm to carry large inventories in order to have an adequate supply of glass on hand. Local purchases would reduce the required inventory, freeing up funds for other working capital needs. Mr. Conrad was concerned about the firm's financial ratios and suggested a short-term seasonal loan that the bank could review every 90 days and call should the firm be in financial trouble. Mr. Conrad pointed out that the bank was lending other people's money and needed to be cautious. He asked Mr. Robb how the bank could control lending against accounts receivable given the risk that the firm might offer false invoices as collateral.

Mr. Robb held his ground and argued that the firm's management had proven itself to be honest and successful in building the business from scratch. He also was confident that an adequate verification program could be established to reduce the risk of false invoices to a minimum.

Assignment

Commercial National Bank's vice president has asked you to resolve the differences between the views of Mr. Robb and the loan committee. Your assignment is to analyze the firm's financial condition, credit needs, and cash flow and recommend how the bank should proceed. As part of your financial analysis of Crystal Clear Window Company, complete the following calculations using the financial reports provided in Exhibits 5.1 to 5.3:

(1) net working capital, current ratio, quick ratio, and days receivable for year-end 1967, 1968, 1969, and 5/31/70

(2) net cash flow for 1969 after investment and financing activities

(3) projected net cash flow for 1970 before any payments on the proposed loan. This cash flow projection should assume 1970 sales of $750,000 and 1970 expenses at the same expense ratios as listed in the 1969 income statement. To project 1970 annual cash flow, estimate 1970 *cash receipts* by adding 1969 year-end accounts receivable (i.e., cash collected in 1970 from prior year sales) to 1970 sales and then subtracting 1970 year-end accounts receivable (i.e., uncollected cash from sales made in 1970). Assume that 1970 year-end accounts receivables equal 30 days' worth of 1970 annual sales. Next, estimate 1970 *cash expenditures for* both materials and nonmaterial expenses. For materials expenditures, adjust the 1970 materials expense by adding payment of 1969 year-end accounts payable and subtracting unpaid accounts payable at 1970 year-end. Assume that accounts payables at 1970 year-end equal 60 days' worth of annual material expenses. For *nonmaterial expenses, assume all expenses* are paid on a current cash basis within the year so that the cash expenditure and expense amounts are the same. Use the 1969 expense ratios to estimate the nonmaterial expenditures. Be sure to include a provision for taxes but omit depreciation since it is a noncash expense.

Prepare a recommendation to the vice president on what action the bank should take on the proposed $75,000 loan secured by accounts receivables.

Exhibit 5.3   Crystal Clear Window Company Sales Projection, 1970

Month	Projected Sales
January	$40,000
February	30,000
March	30,000
April	40,000
May	70,000
June	80,000
July	90,000
August	90,000
September	90,000
October	80,000
November	70,000
December	40,000
Total	$750,000
Estimated net profit	$19,000

Support your recommendation with the results of your financial analysis. Your recommendations can include approving the $75,000 line of credit as currently proposed, declining the loan, or proposing alternative loan terms. In preparing your recommendations, consider the following questions:

- What is the market outlook for the company's products?
- What is the experience and capacity of the management team?
- Will the company generate sufficient cash flow to repay the loan?
- What are the proposed uses of the loan proceeds and their role in financing Crystal Clear Window Company's working capital needs? Are the proposed financing terms consistent with these needs?

Endnotes

1. The evidence from small businesses financial data on this point is mixed. Berger and Udell (1998) found that equity accounted for 50% of small firm's capital— a fairly high share of long-term financing. U.S. Census Bureau aggregate balance sheets for manufacturers in 2001 show that small manufacturers had a level of short-term debt (11.7%), twice that of all manufacturers (5.9%). Small manufacturers also had a lower proportion of equity capital but a slightly larger share of long-term debt. See U. S. Census Bureau (2002). *Quarterly Financial Report for Manufacturing, Mining and Trade Corporations 2001*, Table 1.1

2. This section draws on discussions of short-term and working capital finance from Brealey and Myers (2002), pp. 622–626 and Owen et al. (1986), pp. 92–98.

3. Some older receivables reflect slow payment processes or policies by a strong credit customer, such as government agencies or large corporations.

4. The discussion of inventory control methods is based on Brealey and Myers (2002), pp. 624–626 and Owen et al. (1986), pp. 95–96.

5. Interest rates in capital markets usually increase as the term of debt increases. Thus, a lender's cost of funds for a longer term loan is higher, which adds to the interest rate charged to a borrower.

6. New England federally regulated thrift institutions, for example, held 9.1% of the outstanding small business loans among financial institutions in 1999 compared to 5% for the entire nation. Similarly, these New England thrifts had a far larger share of their assets in commercial real estate and small business loans, 25.3%, than all U.S. federally regulated thrift institutions, at 11.9%. See Gilligan (2000).

7. According to Venture Economics (2001), $6.2 billion in new capital was committed to mezzanine funds in 2000, and over $3.3 billion in new mezzanine fund investments were made that year. *Private Equity Market Update 2001* from www.ventureeconomics.com

8. This case study is adapted from Reed & Woodland (1970), *Cases in Commercial Banking*, and is used by permission of Don Woodland.

9. Net 60-day basis means payment is due in full within 60 days, and net 30–day basis means payment is due in 30 days.

10. This would provide customers a 1% discount if they paid within 10 days.

6

Fixed Asset Financing

This chapter extends the discussion of specific business finance needs from working capital to fixed assets. *Fixed assets* refers to the hard assets—real estate and equipment—that support a firm's activities and are often listed on the balance sheet as property, plant, and equipment. The chapter begins by explaining the importance of fixed assets for enterprises. Next, the differences between financing fixed assets and working capital are presented, including their implications for firms and lenders. In the third part of the chapter, the major debt instruments used to finance fixed assets are introduced, and key financing terms and issues involved in structuring these debt tools are elaborated. Key sources of fixed assets financing are then described, including two public sector programs created to expand firms' access to capital for fixed asset investments. This section concludes with a discussion of the typical capital gaps in financing fixed assets and options for development finance practitioners to address these gaps. Finally, a case study of an employee buyout of a company provides the reader an opportunity to apply financial analysis skills and information from this chapter to evaluate and structure financing for a complex transaction with a large fixed asset component.

Fixed Assets and Business Operations

While working capital fuels a firm's operations, fixed asset investments provide the core facilities needed to support a business, including real estate to house operations and equipment to undertake them. For most businesses, facilities are critically important, even as advanced telecommunications and the Internet provide greater flexibility in conducting business. Manufacturers need well-designed plants and state-of-the-art equipment to ensure their efficiency and productivity. The scale, location, and material-handling systems in distribution facilities are critical to wholesalers, and to large retailers, including Internet-based ones, such as Amazon.com. Real estate and equipment are critical to retailers, who need stores with an adequate size in accessible locations to serve their customers. Increasingly, retailers use specialized equipment, such as computerized inventory management systems, to improve their merchandising and keep their stores well stocked.[1]

Fixed asset investments serve other purposes beyond supplying core operating facilities. First, they support a firm's expansion to meet increased demand or to have a branch presence in new market areas. Thus, as a firm grows, it needs to finance expanded fixed assets along with increased working capital. Second, businesses regularly need to upgrade their facilities and introduce new technologies to address regulatory requirements, reduce costs, ensure product quality, and maintain their competitive position. With the increasing pace of technological change, the frequency and importance of these facility and equipment upgrades and their financing is growing, even for firms that are not expanding their real estate assets. Third, fixed assets provide important secondary business facilities, such as administrative offices, research and development laboratories, warehouse and distribution centers, and retail outlets. Financing these buildings is part of a firm's fixed asset investment strategy. Moreover, when secondary buildings are specialized or costly, they pose greater financing challenges than the property, plant, and equipment for core operations.

Differences Between Fixed Asset and Working Capital Finance

Fixed asset investments are usually larger in size, involve a longer time span, and have a greater impact on the firm than working capital investments. Although some firms own few fixed assets, they represent a significant share of total assets for most firms. Property, plant, and equipment accounted for 25% of total assets for manufacturing corporations and 39% for retail companies in 2001.[2] Moreover, fixed asset investments are more costly than working capital and are made in larger increments. Although inventory, accounts receivable, and other working capital assets are accumulated incrementally, a firm purchases real estate and equipment in large fixed amounts that can involve hundreds of thousands or millions of dollars. Fixed assets also have a long life, ranging from several years for some equipment to decades for buildings. Both the large size and long life of fixed assets lead firms to seek long-term financing to acquire them. Fixed asset debt maturities vary from several years for equipment loans to 20 years or longer for building—far longer than the short- and medium-term loans commonly used to finance working capital. Moreover, their long life and extended financing period make fixed asset investments irreversible actions that have a large impact on a firm's fixed costs. Working capital investments, on the other hand, are more easily reversed. If a firm purchases too much inventory, it will incur losses for this decision, but its impact will dissipate by the end of the year, if not sooner, as inventory levels are corrected. Any debt secured to finance the inventory will be repaid, the liability will be erased, and the company will be free to make new financing decisions. A mistake in building a new plant and financing it with long-term debt, on the other hand, has ongoing consequences. If a recession or market change renders the new facility unnecessary, the firm has fixed debt payments that may continue for one to two decades along with tax, insurance, and maintenance costs. Although the building could be sold (and the debt repaid), a large loss to the company would likely result. Moreover, the firm would have incurred significant transaction costs and wasted management resources in the process. Alternatively, fixed asset investments often are designed to generate a large increase in production, sales, and profits. When done correctly, they offer greater promise to increase a firm's value and to generate more jobs, taxes, and other economic development benefits than do working capital investments.

Implications for Firms

Given their irreversibility and large financial impact, businesses scrutinize fixed asset investments and their financing very carefully. They spend more time specifying their needs, designing the building, choosing a site, and selecting equipment, often considering multiple options in the process. Firms also analyze new fixed asset investments by preparing detailed multiyear projections of the investment's impact on future cash flow. With these projections, an enterprise can calculate whether the increased cash flows from a fixed asset investment, when discounted to reflect their cost of capital and the time value of money, exceed the initial investment cost. This is referred to as a *net present value analysis* and seeks to determine whether the net cash flow impact of the investment is positive, and thus increases the firm's overall profits and value.[3]

Firms also spend more time weighing financing options and deciding on a financial plan that minimizes their costs and risks. Economic development professionals can guide firms through this important decision by informing them of available financing options, advising them on structuring a sound financial plan and helping to prepare a strong application package, and accessing gap financing when it is needed.

Implications for Lenders

As with firms, lenders face greater risks from the longer term of fixed asset loans compared to working capital debt. While lenders can gain confidence in a firm's cash flow for the next 1 to 3 years needed to repay working capital credit, there is far greater likelihood that market, technology, or internal business changes may alter expected cash flow over the extended repayment periods that are common for fixed asset loans. Consequently, lenders carefully scrutinize fixed asset loans, set higher underwriting standards for these loans, and pay more attention to the collateral and guarantees that secure repayment.

Lenders first manage the greater risk of long-term fixed asset financing with a thorough due-diligence analysis of the business factors that will affect future cash flow. Thus, a loan officer will develop a good understanding of the firm's market environment and competition to determine trends, potential market changes, and competitive threats to the business's sales and cash flow. He or she will be particularly concerned with the management's experience and capacity to respond to these market and competitive threats, and the firm's financial wherewithal (i.e., balance sheet strength) to absorb adverse changes and still repay the loan. Finally, the lender's due diligence will carefully analyze the projected cash flow and their underlying assumptions to ensure that they are realistic and can repay the proposed debt with lower than expected sales and/or higher than anticipated costs.

In addition to more careful underwriting, lenders set higher standards for long-term fixed asset loans and seek ways to reduce their loss risk. Higher standards include a larger equity investment by the firm and a lower loan-to-value ratio. For example, a bank may prefer a 70% to 75% loan-to-value ratio versus 80% for a short-term loan, even for collateral of comparable quality. Stricter financial covenants may be set to manage risk and provide early warning of potential repayment problems. Through obtaining corporate and personal guarantees, lenders gain access to a larger asset base in the event that the firm's cash flow and the assets directly financed by the loan are insufficient to provide full repayment.

In some cases, even with these measures, lenders seek ways to further reduce the risk of making a large long-term fixed asset loan. One option is sharing risk with a co-lender, which is typically done by selling a participation in the loan to another lender. With a *loan participation*, one lender underwrites the loans, makes the loan commitment, and is responsible for collection and loan administration, but arranges for one or more additional lenders to share funding of the loan. For example, lender A may commit $5 million for a 10-year fixed asset loan to ABC Manufacturing and then get two other lenders to participate in the loan by each providing $1.5 million to fund it. In this manner, Lender A reduces its financial exposure to 40% of the loan and shares the risk of future losses with the two other lenders. A second risk reduction option is securing a third-party guarantee. The U.S. Small Business Administration (SBA) is the major provider of such guarantees, but many state governments and some local governments guarantee loans. Chapter 8 addresses the use of loan guarantees to expand capital availability in detail.

Table 6.1   Summary of Fixed Asset Finance Instruments

Finance Instrument	Description	Key Terms
Term Loan	Medium-term loan. Principal repaid over several years based on a fixed schedule.	Usually secured with loan amount tied to collateral value. Can be fully amortized or a balloon loan. Typical loan terms of 3 to 7 years.
Leasehold Improvement Loans	Loan used to make improvements to leased premises.	Loan term and amortization tied to lease period. Leasehold mortgage can provide some security to lender.
Real Estate Mortgage	Long-term loan secured by a mortgage on land and buildings. Used to acquire or construct property.	Loan terms of 10 to 20 years. Amortization period can be longer.
Corporate Bond	Debt sold publicly, or privately placed with institutional investors.	Trustee represents bondholders. Maturities range from 1 year to 30 years, and sometimes longer. Principal paid at maturity.
Equipment Leasing	Equipment use financed through rental agreement rather than ownership and a loan.	Term varies with equipment's value and useful life. May include option to buy at lease maturity.

Fixed Asset Debt Instruments

Several debt instruments are used to finance fixed assets with the choice of a financing tool partly shaped by the type of asset being financed. Since equipment and buildings have distinct collateral issues and require different loan terms, separate loan instruments are used to finance each asset type. Still another loan type is required to finance improvements to leased real estate. Firms also are increasingly using leases to finance fixed assets rather than securing capital to acquire them. Consequently, practitioners need to understand the basics of leasing and its potential advantages over borrowing. In this section, the five primarily debt financing tools are explained: term loans, equipment loans, mortgage loans, leasehold improvement loans, bonds, and leases. Table 6.1 provides a concise summary of each instrument.

Term Loans

Term loans are medium-term loans in which principal is repaid on a fixed schedule. Chapter 5 covered their role in funding working capital needs, but term loans also are commonly used to finance equipment. Term loans usually have a maturity date between 3 and 7 years and a floating interest rate. The interest rate is set relative to the prime lending rate, varying from prime for the strongest credit customers to prime plus 300 or 400 basis points for higher-risk loans. Principal amortization can either equal the loan term, in which case the loan is fully repaid at maturity, or have an amortization period that exceeds the long term, in which case a balloon payment is due at the loan maturity. When used to finance equipment, lenders seek full amortization of loan principal. This reduces the risk that equipment will decline in value below the outstanding loan balance—a situation that leaves the lender not fully collateralized and creates an incentive for the borrower to not repay the loan.[4] Despite this depreciation risk, equipment loans are one of the easiest types of debt for small firms to obtain; lenders view equipment as good collateral since it is easy to value and is readily retrieved and sold when a loan default occurs.

Mortgage Loans

When a business borrows to finance building acquisition or development, it typically uses a long-term *mortgage loan*. This type of loan is similar to the loans that finance home purchases and is named for the legal instrument that establishes the lender's security interest in the property being financed. To collateralize a loan, the lender places a mortgage on the property being financed that allows it to sell the property to recover its loan if the borrower fails to make loan payments, a process called foreclosure. Because there are collection costs involved in foreclosure and some risk that the property may decline in value over time, lenders limit their mortgage loan to 70% to 80% of the property's appraised value. Thus, to secure a senior mortgage loan, the firm needs to cover 20% to 30% of the property value[5] with either its own cash or subordinate loans, or both.

Terms and interest rates for mortgage loans vary depending on the lender, its source of funds, and its willingness to lend long-term. A typical mortgage loan will have a 10- to 20-year term, although amortization can be longer, especially for 10-year loans. However, some banks are uncomfortable with a 10-year loan and may instead provide only a mini-permanent loan for 5 to 7 years. Both floating and fixed rate mortgage loans are available, although lenders increasingly prefer floating rate loans to reduce their interest rate risk. When lenders provide a fixed rate loan, they often charge a prepayment penalty to address potential losses if they need to re-lend the repaid principal at a lower interest rate. In place of a fixed rate loan, some lenders provide a variable rate loan and then offer to sell an interest rate cap to the borrower. While the cap eliminates the borrower's exposure to large payment increases with higher interest rates, the costs of these caps are high and their benefit versus borrowing with a higher initial fixed interest rate should be carefully analyzed.

Since real estate loans are more complex lending transactions and subject to more regulations, extensive legal documentation accompanies these loans.

Box 6.1 Legal Documents Used in Fixed Asset Financing

Loan Note: loan contract detailing the amount borrowed and repayment terms.

Loan Agreement: defines additional terms and conditions of the loan, including representations of the borrower, loan covenants, and default provisions.

Security Agreement: instrument used to perfect the lender's collateral interest in property and its rights to take possession and sell property to collect amounts due under the loan note.

Mortgage and Security Agreement: same function as a security agreement when real estate is the collateral.

Collateral Assignment of Contracts: gives lender rights to assume company's interest in essential contracts or permits; it is an important document when financing building construction.

Environmental Indemnification: a promise by the borrower to protect or hold harmless the lender from any liability or costs from violation of environmental laws or property contamination from hazardous materials.

Although the work of writing and negotiating the fine points of these documents is usually left to the lender's and borrower's attorneys, economic development practitioners should be familiar with the type and purpose of the major legal documents used in mortgage loan transactions. A brief explanation of these documents is provided in Box 6.1.

Leasehold Improvement Loans

Thus far, fixed assets have been viewed as property owned by a firm. However, many businesses lease their space and need to finance improvements to these facilities. For example, a restaurant may need to install special gas lines and ventilation systems or a manufacturer may need to add structural reinforcements to support very heavy equipment or reduce vibrations for high-precision processes. A *leasehold improvement loan* is used to finance building improvements for rented building space. Since the lender cannot secure the loan with a mortgage on the building (the borrower does not own the property), leasehold improvement loans can be difficult to obtain. To overcome this collateral constraint, a business needs to provide alternative collateral or guarantees to secure the loan. When the improvements increase the rental value of the space, the tenant's lease can be a source of security. In this scenario, the lender obtains a leasehold mortgage that allows it to take over the borrower's lease and sublet the space to another user if the borrower fails to repay the loan. By subletting the space at a rent premium, due to the leasehold improvements, the lender can recoup losses from the borrower's failure to repay the loan. For example, a leasehold improvement loan to fit-out specialized laboratory space for a biotechnology firm creates a specialized and more valuable facility to sublet. If the original borrower defaulted on the loan, the lender could use its rights under a lease-hold mortgage to sublet the space at a higher rent, provided there was demand for such space from other firms in the area. Since the loan and the underlying investment value are tied to the business's tenancy, a leasehold loan is fully amortized over the business's lease term.

Bonds

Bonds are a common form of debt used in public capital markets and in private placements to institutional investors. Bonds entail a different legal and institutional arrangement than a direct loan. In a *bond financing,* a three-way legal arrangement exists between the borrower, the bondholders (the suppliers of capital), and a trust company. The trust company represents the bondholders to ensure that the borrower complies with the terms of the bond contract. (Brealey & Myers, 2002). Third-party representation allows a company to divide the financing into parts and sell each part to a different bondholder. This can expand the market for a company's debt and allow debt to be tailored to the needs of specific investors, potentially providing lower interest rates and better financing terms.

Although bonds are not widely used by small businesses, the federal tax code allows the sale of tax-exempt bonds for manufacturers, nonprofit organizations, and other businesses in certain targeted areas. Since these bonds are not subject to federal income taxes, they supply low-interest debt for eligible businesses and development projects. Industrial development bonds, a common tool used in economic development finance, are introduced later in this chapter and then discussed more fully in Chapter 15.

Leasing

A lease is an alternative way to finance fixed assets in which another party (the lessor) owns the assets and the firm (the lessee) rents it. Although leasing is commonly used to finance equipment, it can also be used to finance real estate assets. This section briefly explains how leasing works and its advantages and disadvantages as a fixed asset financing tool.[6]

A *lease* is a contract between the owner and user of some property in which the owner allows the lessee use of the property for a specified period of time, the term of the lease, under specific conditions in exchange for regular lease payments. At the end of the lease term, use and control of the asset reverts back to the lessor, although the lessee may have an option to buy the asset at a specified price. The financial aspects of the lease include (1) any required up front payment at lease signing; (2) the periodic, usually monthly, lease payment; and (3) the obligation to pay expenses for taxes, insurance, repair, and maintenance costs related to the property's use. Because a lease provides the exclusive use of desired property over a fixed period of time in exchange for a stream of payments, from the firm's perspective, a lease functions just like acquiring property and financing it with a cash down payment and a loan. To determine which financing option is preferable, a firm must compare the cash flow impact of a lease with the cash flow impact of an asset purchased with debt financing.

From an accounting viewpoint, leases are classified as either an operating lease or a capital lease. An *operating lease* is a short-term lease with a term far less than the leased asset's useful life and with the lessee operating more like a renter without the obligations of an owner. A *capital lease* is a long-term lease with a term close to the leased asset's useful life and with the lessee having obligations similar to an owner. While accounting standards allow operating lease payments to be treated as an expense, capital leases are accounted for much like property acquisition with debt. Under a capital lease, the leased equipment is recorded as an asset and the lease obligation is recorded as a liability with lease payments divided into two components: a lease interest expense and an amortization of the lease liability (Anthony, Hawkins, & Merchant, 1999). Some firms prefer to lease because operating leases can be treated as "off balance sheet financing" in which the lease obligation is not listed as a liability on the balance sheet, which can improve the firm's financial ratios. However, this rationale for leasing is not a sound economic one since the decision to lease should be based on the real financial costs and benefits rather than the form of its presentation. Moreover, since lease obligations are disclosed in the notes to a firm's financial statements and prospective lenders and investors will ask for disclosure of lease obligations from firms without audited financial statements, the "off balance sheet" treatment does not hide a lease's financial impact from an informed and careful analyst.

Although accounting treatment is not a real advantage, leasing can provide sound economic advantages to a business. First, the financial payments under a lease may be lower than through asset acquisition with debt financing. A lease may lower both up front costs and periodic payments, compared to the down payment, transaction, and debt service costs for a purchase with debt. Smaller lease payments are likely to occur when the leased asset has a sizable residual value at the end of the lease term. In this case, the lease payments will be based on the change in asset value over the lease term rather than the full cost of the asset. In effect, the lease allows the business to finance only the change in an asset's value rather than the full cost of the asset. This is particularly beneficial if the business expects to replace, or will no longer need, the asset at the end of the lease term. Second, a firm can avoid restrictive covenants required under a loan agreement by leasing an asset and not incurring any debt. A third advantage to leasing is that a firm may be able to obtain a cancellation option under a lease. These last two advantages, no restrictive covenants and a cancellation option, provide a business greater financial and operational flexibility than acquiring an asset with debt financing. Moreover, the cancellation option allows a firm to reverse a major financial investment, reducing a key risk associated with fixed asset investments. Because lease cancellations impose costs for the lessor, including finding a new lessee and bearing the interest rate risk associated with re-leasing, leases carry financial penalties for cancellation. Fourth, a lease may allow a firm to avoid some of the costs and obligations of ownership. When the lessor is responsible for maintaining the leased equipment, the lessee avoids this expense as well as the management time and effort related to planning for and overseeing maintenance. Although expected maintenance costs will be reflected in the lease rate, the lessor may operate on a larger scale and have efficiencies in this work that it can pass on to lessees. Finally, a lease may offer tax savings to a firm when the tax reduction from lease payments exceeds the sum of tax savings from tax credits, depreciation, and interest expenses via asset acquisition with debt financing.

Along with these benefits, leasing has some disadvantages that a firm must consider. First, the lessor retains title to the asset and can easily take back the asset upon default. Although a lender also can take possession of the asset when it secures a loan, the process for seizing and selling loan collateral is slower and usually offers more opportunity for the borrower to remedy a default than is the case with a lease. Moreover, when the firm owns the asset, it retains an equity interest in the property and is entitled to any sale proceeds in excess of the loan obligations when the bank sells the collateral. A second disadvantage of leasing is that the firm obtains no gain from appreciation in the asset's value. Although firms acquire assets to increase their business cash flow and value, not for investment gains, a business should not ignore this potential benefit, especially in real estate markets in which real potential for appreciation exists. Finally, a lease does not confer the tax benefits from investment tax credits and depreciation that go to the owner. Therefore, a firm needs to compare the financial impact of leasing an asset versus acquiring it with debt financing on after-tax cash flow basis to determine whether greater tax advantages reside with leasing or ownership.

Sources of Fixed Asset Financing

As with working capital loans, commercial banks, thrift institutions, and finance companies are the major fixed asset lenders for small businesses. According to a 1995 SBA study, banks were the largest supplier of business credit, accounting for 54%, and finance companies were the second largest source with 13%.[7] However, data has not been collected that documents the relative role of banks and financing companies in providing fixed asset versus working capital debt. Since finance companies focus on short- to medium-term asset-based lending, they are probably a larger supplier of working capital and equipment debt than real estate loans. For equipment financing, both specialized leasing companies and equipment manufacturers also are important capital sources. Some finance companies specialize in equipment leasing and are a key source to finance equipment needs. They may have a greater knowledge of specialized equipment and may be active in buying and selling certain equipment, which allows them to provide better financing terms than less specialized lenders. Equipment manufacturers, either directly or through an affiliate finance company, frequently finance equipment purchases or leases. Since financing is often offered as an incentive to generate sales, manufacturing may offer better terms than other lenders, including below-market interest rates, lower down payments, and longer lease or repayment terms.

Federal policies add two financing sources for fixed asset investments. Economic development practitioners need to understand these sources and use them, when appropriate, to expand capital supply for small firms. First, as previously mentioned, the federal tax code allows tax-exempt *industrial development bonds* (IDBs) to be used to finance buildings and equipment for manufacturing firms. Since the 1980s, Congress has increasingly restricted the use of IDBs in response to their widespread use by large businesses and for projects without real economic development benefits. They are now limited to modest-sized financing for manufacturers. A firm can only use $40 million in IDB financing over its lifetime and is limited to $10 million within any 6-year period. Moreover, each state operates under a total cap for the amount of tax-exempt bonds that can be issued for IDBs, multifamily housing bonds, and other uses. Despite these limitations, IDBs allow small manufacturers to access lower-cost debt and long-term fixed rate loans. Since IDBs involve additional legal and transaction costs, they are usually only cost effective for financing of at least $1 to $2 million dollars. For smaller loans, the added legal, transaction, and credit enhancement (insurance or guarantees needed to make the bonds marketable on public credit market) costs outstrip the interest savings from tax-exempt rates. Sometimes this problem can be overcome by pooling several small loans into one larger IDB, a practice elaborated in Chapter 15.

A second widely used tool is the SBA 504 program, which helps small businesses finance fixed asset investments. Under the 504 program, a private lender provides a senior loan for 50% of the project cost, a subordinate SBA loan (called a debenture) finances 40% of the project, and the business contributes 10% in cash equity. The SBA subordinate loans are originated by SBA-licensed organizations called certified development corporations and then approved by SBA regional offices. Since federal government debt funds the SBA subordinate loans, they carry a below market interest rate, which adds to the attractiveness of the program. However, its greatest benefit is not its lower interest rate but its ability to leverage private debt and provide 90% debt financing for equipment and/or real estate assets through the availability of a large subordinate loan.

Fixed Asset Financing Gaps

Two common problems create financing gaps related to the fixed asset investment needs of small firms. One gap is faced by businesses with limited access to equity capital and little free cash to supply the equity needed to meet lenders' loan-to-value requirements. This problem is most pressing for large real estate investments, which require at least several hundred thousand dollars to meet lenders' 70% to 75% loan-to-value requirement. Even when a firm's cash flow can support a loan at 80% to 90% loan to value, lenders typically will not accept the higher ratio and greater collateral risk. Another frequent problem in financing business real estate occurs when a building's development costs exceed its market or appraised value. Since lenders set the loan amount based on the property's appraised value rather than its costs, this situation leaves a funding gap that exceeds the standard 20% to 30% equity requirement. For example, an expanding manufacturer may need to move out of its leased space and build a new 20,000 square foot plant with the development costs totaling $2 million. If the bank's appraiser values the new building at $1.5 million, then the maximum loan with a 75% loan-to-value ratio is $1,125,000 (75% of the $1.5 million appraised value). The company now must raise $875,000 in equity—$375,000 more than if the appraised value equaled the $2 million cost.

A gap between an asset's actual cost and its appraised value occurs for several reasons. In weak market areas or during economic recessions, a large inventory of industrial or commercial space exists that keeps market rents and building values low. Despite the surplus real estate, the firm may need to build a new building to address its location or operating requirements. Even under strong market conditions, a firm may need special improvements or design features that increase the building's cost but not its rent and market value. Because conventional lenders do not consider these specialized features as adding to a building's value, the firm must finance their full cost with other funds. Third, areas with high or rapidly growing construction costs may see a gap between the costs of a plain vanilla building and appraised values when rents do not increase at the same pace as costs.

Two options exist to address the funding gaps that result when a building's cost exceeds its appraised value. One option is to provide a loan guarantee to reduce the lender's collateral risk and expand its acceptable loan amount. A guarantee provides additional repayment security to convince a lender to accept a higher loan-to-value ratio or to accept the guarantee as a substitute form of collateral. A second option is supplying a subordinate loan to fill the gap between the senior mortgage loan amount and the firm's available equity. The SBA 504 program uses this approach by providing a large subordinate loan to reduce the firm's equity investment to 10% of the project's cost. For both these options to work, the business must generate enough cash flow to repay debt at the higher loan-to-value level. When cash flow, rather than collateral value, constrains the debt amount that a business can borrow, the firm will need to increase its equity investment, reduce the development costs, or find other sources, such as a grant, to fill the funding gap. In this situation, flexible debt terms also can help overcome the problem. Longer principal amortization reduces annual debt service costs, which allows the available cash flow to support a larger loan amount. Creative debt structuring can also address financing gaps that occur when the cash flow from a new fixed asset investment accrues over several years and, thus, a gradual increase in debt service is needed. Deferred principal payments and interest rate step-ups are debt structure options to address this financing need. In return for the added risk of this loan structure, it is appropriate for a lender to earn a higher return through an interest rate premium, fees, or stock warrants.

Case Study: Phoenix Forge

Introduction

Phoenix Forge, a small forge located in Youngstown, Ohio, has operated for many years as a subsidiary of a large conglomerate. Phoenix Forge uses five hammers to make forged metal parts for cars, trucks, aircraft, off-highway equipment, the petrochemical industry, and the military. It is 1984 and the parent company, faced with declining sales and losses at Phoenix Forge, has offered to sell the company to its employees in lieu of closing the plant. The employees want to purchase Phoenix Forge and operate it as an employee-owned corporation. They recruited an ex-plant manager of Phoenix Forge, who successfully completed the turnaround of another small forge company (Atlantic Forge), as the new company president. The employees now need to raise $1.2 million to purchase the company and fund working capital and fixed asset investment needs during their first 3 years of operations.

Phoenix Forge employees have prepared a business plan and approached a local bank, the City of Youngstown, and the Community Loan Fund to secure the needed capital. The employees requested a $200,000 subordinate loan from the Community Loan Fund (CLF), a regional nonprofit economic development loan fund whose mission is to retain existing manufacturing jobs and stimulate new job creation by providing gap financing to small businesses. As the loan officer for CLF, your task is to review the business plan summary and financial projections presented in this document and prepare a recommendation to the CLF board of directors on the loan request.

Economic Conditions in the Youngstown Region

Youngstown is located in northeast Ohio within the Youngstown-Warren metropolitan area. The region's economy is heavily dependent on manufacturing, especially steel and metalworking. Foreign competition and economic recession hurt the region's manufacturers, leading to many plant closings and layoffs since the late 1970s. Nonfarm employment declined 11% from 1977 to 1983, shedding almost 30,000 jobs. Employment in manufacturing dropped 33% from almost 92,000 jobs in 1977 to 61,279 in 1983. These job losses have contributed to declining population and unemployment rates well above national and state levels.

Summary of Phoenix Forge Business Plan

The Market Outlook

The major markets for forged metal products are in transportation (including automotive, trucks, buses, and motorcycles), off-highway equipment, aircraft, ordnance, agriculture (farm implements), and petrochemical. Total sales of forged metal products increased by 4% in 1983 and are expected to grow by 8% to 10% in 1984. A synopsis of market demand for each market segment, comparing 1982 to 1983 (the last full year for which statistical data is available) follows.

Transportation. The combined automotive, truck, bus, and motorcycle producers showed an increase from 13.6% to 19.4% of total forging industry sales; 1984 is showing a strong increase that is projected to continue through 1986.

Off-Highway Equipment. Forgings for off-highway equipment remained the third largest market segment, but its market share dropped from 8.3% in 1982 to 6.7% in 1983. Thus far, 1984 shows a slight increase with year-end results expected to regain the 1982 level and possibly exceed it.

Aircraft. Aircraft, aircraft engines, and missiles were the leading segment of forging sales in 1983 with 38.3% of the total. This share was down from 41.9% in 1982, although dollar volume was the same in both years. The reduction in the aircraft market share corresponds to the increase in the transportation share.

Ordnance. This market segment increased from 5.8% in 1982 to 6.4% in 1983 and is continuing with a slight increase in 1984.

Agriculture. Forgings for agricultural uses remained unchanged at a 3% market share in 1983.

Petrochemical. The oil field machinery and equipment market decreased precipitously from 5.1% in 1982 to 2.2% market share in 1983 and is not expected to show any significant improvement until the second quarter of 1985.

Market demand for forgings is showing a substantial increase in 1984 with orders expected to grow in 1985 and beyond as original equipment manufacturers recover from the 1980 to 1982 recession, according to the Forging Industry Association. Strong advance bookings for automotive parts and gradually growing orders by off-highway equipment, agricultural equipment, and oil field users are the basis for such optimism. Phoenix Forge has major customers in the transportation, off-highway equipment, and petrochemical segments of the market. Its customers, confirming projections from the Forging Industry Association, increased their orders in 1984 and plan further increases for 1985.

Phoenix Forge Marketing Strategy

Phoenix Forge's marketing strategy includes the following components:

- *The primary target industries will be transportation, especially automotive, off-highway equipment, petrochemical, and ordnance.* Automotive represents a large portion of Phoenix Forge's customers and has the strongest market outlook. Although demand in the off-highway equipment and petrochemical segments declined in the past few years, Phoenix Forge has several important customers in these segments. It expects to secure 20% of its sales from these existing customers, based on its existing supplier relationships and its capacity to provide same-day or overnight delivery. Ordnance has been targeted as a second growth area since it is a growing segment where the new president has strong customer relationships to generate new orders.
- *The key to success will be to capture market share* because Phoenix Forge cannot achieve its projected sales by industry growth alone. Increased market share will be achieved by lowering prices, offering delivery within 24 hours, developing selected new products, and undertaking an aggressive marketing campaign.
- *An aggressive and expanded sales effort by the new management team will be undertaken* to strengthen relationships, build orders with existing customers, and secure new ones from the new president's relationships. Potential new customers have been targeted at several firms, including Rockwell Allegan, Dana, Goodyear, and Firestone.
- *Phoenix Forge will market a high-quality, cost-competitive product.* The firm already has a strong reputation for quality forgings but needs to reduce its costs to be profitable and meet price competition. Employee ownership will assure higher productivity with an increased commitment to quality than existed under the former owner. Costs will be lowered by decreasing material waste, reducing overhead, and increasing worker productivity.

- *Initial interest among prospective customers is high.* Phoenix Forge now
  has a contractual commitment from Harsco, a verbal commitment from
  Rockwell, and strong interest from five other firms. Orders from these
  seven customers would generate the projected first year sales level.

Competition

Competition in the forging industry comes from three sources:

- Large, sophisticated, high volume manufacturers
- Small family-owned businesses
- Imports

The large companies are highly sophisticated, very cost conscious, and
high-volume suppliers. The number of small family-owned businesses is
declining rapidly. Generally, they are unsophisticated, not quality conscious,
and survive by accepting a low return on their assets and little debt. Foreign
competitors are entering the market but, to date, have only been able to
penetrate the market for high-volume, relatively simple forgings.

Phoenix Forge believes it can be competitive by serving low- to medium-
volume customers that are quality conscious and customers who are sensi-
tive to fast delivery and turnaround. These customers allow the firm to
leverage its strong-quality position and location advantage for quick deliveries. Over time, Phoenix Forge plans to introduce more complex forgings to
strengthen its position as a quality producer and keep ahead of the growing
threat from foreign competitors.

Sales Forecast

The sales forecast for successive 12-month periods beginning on the date
of employee ownership (projected for January 1985) is

	1st Year (1985)	2nd Year (1986)	3rd Year (1987)
Sales	$3,365,000	$6,300,000	$9,990,000
Profit/(Loss)	$(169,000)	$201,000	$458,000

The sales forecast makes the following assumptions about the market
segments served by Phoenix Forge and growth in orders among existing and
new customers:

1. Forgings for the transportation market will grow gradually in
   demand over the next several years with sales among existing customers expected to increase by 10% to 15% annually. New customers will contribute another 40% to 50% annual sales increase
   within this segment.

2. The off-highway market will also grow gradually, with existing customers increasing sales by 5% to 10% each year and new customers generating another 30 to 40% in annual sales growth within the segment.

3. Demand in the petrochemical market will grow gradually beginning in mid-1985 but develop into vigorous growth in 1987 and beyond. Existing customers will increase orders 10% in 1986 and 25% in 1987 while new customers will add 20% in annual sales in 1986 and 50% in 1987.

4. Ordnance sales will grow modestly over the next several years. Phoenix Forge will gain $1 million in annual sales in 1986 and 1987 through gaining new customers in this segment.

When forging demand was strong in the petrochemical market (1981), Phoenix Forge recorded sales in excess of $10 million. Achieving this sales level again can be accomplished with proper market conditions and an active marketing effort. The firm's annual production capacity is $15 to $18 million. Phoenix Forge is well regarded by its customers for on time delivery and quality. However, poor management by its conglomerate owner resulted in high, noncompetitive pricing which, along with the steep recession, led to declining sales in the early 1980s. Furthermore, the prior management focused exclusively on serving existing customers. No marketing efforts were undertaken to secure new business. With competitive pricing, continued high-quality, fast delivery, and active marketing, Phoenix Forge will increase its market share among existing customers and capture new customers. Conversations to inform purchasing managers from existing customers about the employee acquisition and new president have, without exception, met with enthusiasm and the promise of increased business.

The new president's relationships with original equipment manufacturers, developed during his tenure at Phoenix and Atlantic Forge, is a valuable asset that will be used to secure new customers that stopped buying from Phoenix Forge as its prices became noncompetitive. He also knows several ordnance firms that have never purchased from Phoenix Forge. Based on his experience at Atlantic Forge and the initial response from several firms, the new president is confident that he can add one new customer each quarter over the next 2 years. These new customers should yield at least $4 to $5 million in new sales by 1987.

Operations

Phoenix Forge is in the heart of the transportation and off-highway equipment market. Overnight delivery can be made to almost all major customers in these markets and, in many cases, same-day delivery is routinely accomplished. This delivery advantage is becoming increasingly important as customers are reducing inventories and requiring "just-in-time" deliveries. It is possible, and planned, for Phoenix Forge to be profitable while operating at its present level of sales ($3 to $4 million), as demonstrated by the new president's experience at Atlantic Forge. There are similarities between Phoenix Forge and Atlantic Forge. Both companies have five forging hammers of similar size, similar labor rates (Phoenix at $10.50/hour and Atlantic at $11.04/hour), and similar fringe benefits. With all these similarities, the "cost of sales" should be similar for both firms.

Atlantic Forge has sales of $2,124,000 through the first half of 1984 (monthly average of $354,000) and shows a pre-tax profit of $151,200. Phoenix Forge, on the other hand, had 1983 sales of $4,140,000 and a pre-tax loss of $351,000.

Several differences between the companies contribute to their respective profit and loss situation:

1. Phoenix Forge has below average net weight yield in material used per forging resulting in a higher material cost per forging. At Atlantic Forge, the material yield per forging averages 82% versus 70% for Phoenix. Thus, Phoenix discards 12% more materials as scrap than Atlantic. Recognizing the difference in product mix between the two companies, it is feasible to improve Phoenix Forge's yield to 77%. Since material now accounts for 50% of total costs at Phoenix, a 7% improvement in scrap rates alone would allow Phoenix to drop its prices by 3.5% and increase its profit margin. A review by the new president and discussions among employees has identified three improvements needed to reduce scrap rates: (1) more frequent hammer maintenance to ensure better hammer performance and calibration; (2) improved die design to yield forgings with less scrap; and (3) training to increase workers' skills in hammer operation, die design, hammer maintenance, and quality control.

2. Phoenix Forge will operate with a smaller administrative staff than Atlantic and can do so because of the difference in product mix. Phoenix is expected to have total administrative salaries of $12,400 per month versus $24,000 per month for Atlantic Forging. The combined cost savings from higher material yield and lower administrative costs will allow Phoenix Forge to reduce its prices by 5% to 6%, bringing them in line with its major competitors.

3. Phoenix Forge has in the past made relatively simple forgings. To survive and grow, the firm must introduce new, more complex, forgings that allow it to accommodate more customer needs. This will require a new level of skill among hammer operators, quality control staff, and die designers. Additional staff training is budgeted to build these employee skills.

4. Phoenix Forge, under employee ownership, will employ five administrative/supervisory personnel, including a president, financial manager, plant superintendent, quality control manager, and office manager. Additions to

staff, including a sales manager, foreman, and clerical staff, will be made at appropriate times as dictated by manufacturing volumes, sales, and profits.

Initially, the president will assume the sales manager responsibility. Since he has good personal relationships with existing customers, strong relationships with potential customers, and is well known in the industry, he is best qualified to market the firm and build its sales base. Once sales growth is consolidated and increases to a level that will support additional staff, a new full-time sales manager will be hired.

The board of directors will include two employees, legal counsel, a banking representative, and the company president. Employees will own all of the firm's shares, have the right to approve the board of directors, and hold veto power over major corporate decisions (e.g., sale or merger of the firm).

The staffing plan at acquisition calls for 18 employees, 6 will be salaried and 12 hourly. As sales and production grow, the staff is projected to increase to 81 employees over 3 years as follows:

- End of Year 1 (1985): 38 employees, with 31 hourly and 7 salaried
- End of Year 2 (1986): 56 employees, with 45 hourly and 11 salaried
- End of Year 3 (1987): 81 employees, with 69 hourly and 12 salaried

Phoenix Forge Financial Plan

A $1.2 million financing plan is proposed to complete the employee buyout that includes $764,000 to acquire the firm and its assets and $436,000 to meet working capital requirements and cover first year operating losses. The proposed sources for the $1.2 million include

- $100,000 in equity invested by employees for their shares in the corporation
- $436,000 private bank loan, secured by a first lien on all fixed assets, with a 16% interest rate. Principal payments will be $36,000 at the end of year one and $100,000 at the end of each subsequent year
- $464,000 CDBG loan from the City of Youngstown, secured by a first position on accounts receivable and a second position on all fixed assets, with a 9% interest rate. Principal payments will be $64,000 at the end of year one and $100,000 at the end of each subsequent year
- $200,000 loan from Community Loan Fund, secured by a third position on all assets, with a 10% interest rate. Principal payments will be $100,000 at the end of year 1 and $100,000 at the end of year 2

The appraised "fire sale" value of the property, plant, and equipment is $900,000.

Existing employees have raised the required $100,000 equity from their savings and have deposited it in escrow, awaiting completion of the company purchase. Both the private lender and the City of Youngstown have indicated their willingness to provide their portion of the financing plan and are awaiting the CLF's decision before making a final commitment.

Financial Projections

The projected balance sheet and income statements for Phoenix Forge during its first 3 years as an employee-owned firm are attached as Exhibits 6.1 and 6.2. The assumptions used to prepare these projections include

- Raw material cost projected at 50% of net revenue, based on current experience without assuming savings from higher yield rates
- Hourly labor costs of $7 unskilled to $11 skilled. Salaried labor and fringe benefits projected at 5% below forging industry averages
- Taxes are not paid until year three when they total $150,000. Initial losses and investment tax credits shelter taxable income through the first 30 months of operations
- Operating levels: one shift during the first 15 months, two shifts during the second 15 months, and three shifts thereafter.

Exhibit 6.1   Phoenix Forge Projected Income Statements Years 1 Through 3 (figures in $ thousands)

	Year 1	Year 2	Year 3
Gross Sales	$3,365	6,260	9,900
Bad Debt Allowance	34	63	99
Net Sales	3,331	6,197	9,801
Cost of Goods Sold	2,924	5,366	8,347
Operating Costs			
Utilities	200	200	215
Other	120	114	116
Operating Profit/(Loss)	87	517	1,123
Interest Expense	132	136	163
Depreciation	124	180	352
Taxes	0	0	150
Net Income	$(169)	$201	$458

Assignment

As the loan officer for the Community Loan Fund, prepare an analysis and recommendation to the CLF board on the requested $200,000 loan. The analysis should address the following issues:

Exhibit 6.2   Phoenix Forge Projected Balance Sheet Years 1 Through 3 (figures in $ thousands)

	Startup	End of Year 1	End of Year 2	End of Year 3
ASSETS				
Current Assets				
Cash	$ 436	$ 56	$ 74	$ 95
Accounts Receivable	000	$ 277	$ 509	$ 805
Inventory	000	$ 178	$ 311	$ 476
Total Current Assets	$ 436	$ 511	$ 894	$1,376
Fixed Assets				
Land	$ 25	$ 25	$ 25	$ 25
Buildings	333	$ 333	$ 333	$ 333
Machinery and Equipment	406	$ 406	$ 622	$ 946
Less: Depreciation	(000)	$ (124)	$ (304)	$ (656)
Total Fixed Assets	$ 764	$ 640	$ 676	$ 648
TOTAL ASSETS	$1,200	$1,151	$1,570	$2,024
LIABILITIES AND EQUITY				
Current Liabilities				
Line of Credit	—	$ 161	$ 549	$ 583
Accrued Expenses	—	$ 20	$ 31	$ 43
Accounts Payable	—	$ 139	$ 258	$ 408
Current Portion of Long-Term Debt	$ 200	$ 300	$ 200	$ 200
Total Current Liabilities	$ 200	$ 620	$1,038	$1,234
Long-Term Debt				
Community Loan Fund	$ 100	—	—	—
CDBG	$ 400	$ 300	$ 200	$ 100
Bank Loan	$ 400	$ 300	$ 200	$ 100
Total Long-Term Debt	$ 900	$ 600	$ 400	$ 200
TOTAL LIABILITIES	$1,100	$ 1,220	$ 1,438	$ 1,434
EQUITY				
Employee Shares	$ 100	$ 100	$ 100	$ 100
Accumulated Profits	—	(169)	32	490
Total Equity	$ 100	$ (69)	$ 132	$ 590
TOTAL EQUITY & LIABILITIES	$1,200	$1,151	$1,570	$2,024

1. The expected economic development benefits that will result from the loan

2. The strength of the company's business plan, operations, and management

3. An analysis of the financial projections and the firm's capacity to meet required debt service payments

4. A recommendation on making the loan, including the appropriate loan terms and structure and any recommendations or conditions to strengthen the business and financial plan

To support your financial analysis and recommendation, complete the following calculations for each of the 3 years' financial projections:

- Current ratio, quick ratio, average collection period for receivables, inventory turnover, and the debt-to-equity ratio
- Gross profit margin percentage, operating profit margin, and net income margin, all as a percentage of sales
- Prepare a net cash flow schedule for each year and calculate the debt service coverage ratio provided by cash flow after investing activities. Treat the line of credit as a source of operating cash flow, not as a financing activity for the cash flow analysis.

Endnotes

1. Business analysts cite superior inventory management systems as one critical factor in Wal-Mart's success. See Moser and Moukanas (2002), "Finding the Right Drivers of Value Growth," *Mercer Management Journal,* p. 6.

2. Data is from U.S. Census Bureau (2002), *Quarterly Financial Report for Manufacturing, Mining and Trade Corporations 2001,* Tables 1.1 and 59.1. Among small manufacturers with assets of $25 million or less, fixed assets were higher, at 31%, than the percentage for all manufacturers.

3. Net present value analysis and investment decision making is a major issue in corporate finance. Brealey and Myers (2002) devote a third of their textbook to the mechanics and issues associated with net present value analysis.

4. When the equipment's value drops below the outstanding loan principal, the company is financially better off not repaying the loan and letting the lender reclaim the collateral.

5. Property value for loan collateral is established by a third-party appraisal that estimates an asset's value if acquired through a sale between two independent parties acting freely. Appraised value often differs from the actual acquisition or development cost.

6. For a more detailed treatment of leasing, the reader can consult a book on corporate or small business financing, such as Brealey and Myers (2002), *Principles of Corporate Finance,* Chapter 24, or Owen et al. (1986), *The Arthur Young Guide to Financing for Growth*, Chapter 6.

7. Cynthia E. Griffen (1998), "Breaking the Bank: Non-bank Lenders Are Pulling Ahead in Small-Business Financing."

7

Real Estate Finance

Real estate development follows business development as the second major economic development activity. Businesses are the primary engines for creating jobs and income for regions and communities, but real estate development supports business activity and enhances an area's quality of life by creating attractive commercial districts. Real estate development supplies the land and buildings needed to house enterprises. Without real estate to address firms' needs, communities are constrained in growing and attracting new enterprises and will lose existing business as they expand. Thus, an important economic development function is ensuring the ongoing real estate supply to support the desired forms of economic development and direct it to targeted investment areas. A second purpose of real estate development is creating and sustaining vital commercial districts that provide the amenities, services, and attractions to serve as strong community centers and regional destinations. Real estate projects attract the economic uses and shape the physical fabric that makes commercial districts attractive and vibrant. For many cities, large-scale real estate development has been central to their strategies to maintain downtown as a hub for growing service sector businesses and as a destination for regional shopping, entertainment, and tourism.[1] On a smaller scale, rural towns, small cities, and urban neighborhoods also use real estate development to revitalize their commercial districts.[2] Finally, development projects are critical to remove blight and reuse polluted, abandoned, and underutilized properties that contribute to crime, poor community image, and disinvestment. A growing area of economic development practice focuses on the redevelopment of brownfields as a means to achieve the cleanup of polluted sites, encourage compact "smart growth" to reduce the social and environmental costs of consuming more land for development, and attract economic activity to central cities and existing economic centers.[3]

Because real estate is a critical economic development focus, this chapter introduces practitioners to how real estate projects are financed and their unique issues, tools, and financing sources. This account begins with an overview of the development process and its associated financing stages.

In the second section, the financial statements used for real estate projects, the development budget, and the operating pro forma are explained along with how these financial statements interrelate to define the amount of debt and equity investment that a real estate project can support. As in the prior chapters, the next two sections review the financial instruments used in real estate finance and the major institutional sources for capital, concluding with a consideration of the resulting financing gaps and how they can be addressed. To help the reader apply these real estate finance skills, the chapter ends with a case study on structuring financing for a real estate project.

The Real Estate Development and Finance Process

Real estate projects, like businesses, have development phases with distinct financing needs. Exhibit 7.1 summarizes the financing issues and tools used in the three phases of real estate projects: predevelopment; development and construction; and occupancy and management. Financing forms match each development stage. Equity and equity-like sources fund predevelopment costs. Construction loans finance the construction phase. Long-term permanent financing replaces, or "takes out," construction loans for the occupancy and management phase. Within this general pattern, some crossover occurs because equity supplements debt financing during the last two phases and debt can fund some predevelopment costs. More importantly, debt constitutes a much larger capital source for real estate projects than for business enterprises. Although debt and equity each finance about half of small business assets, debt usually finances 70% to 80% of a real estate project. This greater use of debt reflects the more predictable nature of real estate cash flow and the use of capital to finance assets with substantial and enduring collateral value.

Predevelopment Phase

A real estate project begins with the predevelopment phase when, as the name suggests, the steps that precede actual development of the project occur. This is roughly analogous to the research and development stage for a business. The predevelopment process starts with formulating a development concept, identifying an appropriate site, and securing site control. In some cases, the site is identified first and a development concept suitable to the site is formulated (e.g., for the reuse of an abandoned building). Site control is critical to real estate development because a project cannot be undertaken unless a developer can secure the needed site. In addition to outright acquisition, site control can be secured by a purchase option, entering into a long-term lease, or obtaining a developer designation for a government-owned site. Once site

Exhibit 7.1   Real Estate Development Phases and Financing Issues

Phase One: Planning and Predevelopment

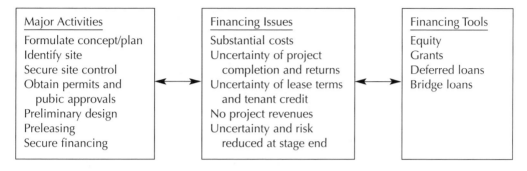

Phase Two: Construction and Development Phase

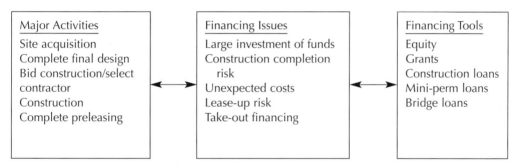

Phase Three: Occupancy and Property Management Phase

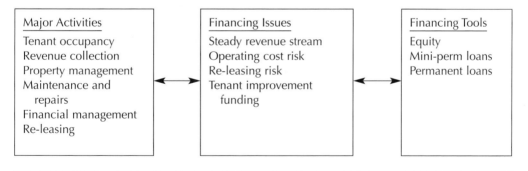

control is obtained, the predevelopment process continues with four primary activities: completing site planning and preliminary design; securing the government permits and approvals needed for the project; obtaining preleasing or presale agreements to demonstrate the market demand and revenue stream needed to support project financing; and securing the required project financing. It is important to note that the long-term, or permanent, financing for a real estate project is typically committed in this predevelopment phase. A permanent lender agrees up front to fund the project upon its completion, occupancy, and compliance with other funding requirements. Once the permanent debt is secured, the developer uses this take-out financing commitment to obtain a construction loan. Depending on the project's scale and complexity, the predevelopment stage can last from 1 year to several years. A large, complex project, such as redevelopment of a military base, which requires extensive planning with public participation, many public approvals, and raising large amounts of financing, can have a predevelopment stage as long as a decade.

The predevelopment stage poses several financing challenges to developers. A substantial outlay of funds is needed to complete this process, but considerable uncertainty exists about whether the project will proceed to development and the expected revenues and financial returns will be realized. A developer may invest hundreds of thousands or millions of dollars in this phase but fail to secure the required approvals and financing, or only secure them on terms that make the project infeasible. Moreover, these predevelopment investments are made several years before any revenue from the project will be generated, and long delays in securing cash flow will erode the expected rate of return. Finally, changes in economic or market conditions between predevelopment and project completion can result in lower rents or sales prices and slower than expected leasing or sales, which greatly reduce project revenues. Although developers and lenders reduce this risk through preleasing and presales agreements, major economic and market changes will lead to the cancellation or renegotiation of such agreements. For all these reasons, predevelopment costs are usually funded with developer and investor equity. For public and nonprofit developers, grants provide an important source of equity-like funds for predevelopment costs. In addition to equity and grant financing, two types of debt also can be used. Deferred loans, in which interest and principal payments are delayed until construction or permanent financing, help fund predevelopment costs.[4] In the late predevelopment stage when key development hurdles have been overcome, a bridge loan can fund the last pieces of predevelopment work until construction or later-stage financing is secured. For example, a developer may need a bridge loan to complete site acquisition if an option agreement will expire before the construction loan or another piece of required financing is secured.

Construction and Development Phase

After predevelopment, the project moves into the development and construction stage when site and building improvements occur. This stage entails site acquisition (if this did not occur in the predevelopment phase), preparing the final design specifications, selecting the construction team, and completing construction. Preleasing or presales efforts also continue during this period to achieve commitments for full occupancy before construction is completed. The construction and development phase can last from less than a year for small-scale projects to 2 years for large building projects. A very large project with multiple buildings to be constructed over many years is often financed and undertaken in separate stages to reduce financial risks.

Most development costs are invested in the project during the construction phase, but the financial risks in this phase are limited by preleasing/ prelease requirements and the commitment of permanent financing in the predevelopment phase. The main financial risk in this phase is completing construction within budget and in good quality. Building rehabilitation projects pose the greatest such risks because new conditions that add construction costs may be discovered during renovation. Developers and lenders manage this risk by including a construction contingency amount in the project budget. Lenders also closely monitor construction and pay out funds gradually to prevent the developer from fully drawing down the loan and running out of funds before the project is completed and can be occupied. A second risk to the construction lender is that either the developer will fail to meet the preleasing and other requirements needed to secure the "take-out," or permanent financing or the permanent lender will decide not to fund the loan for other reasons. A three-party agreement between the developer, construction lender, and permanent lender can reduce these risks by aligning key requirements between the construction and permanent loans and establishing a legal obligation between the permanent and construction lenders. Strong experience and capacity within the developer and construction team also reduce these risks.

Occupancy and Management Phase

Once the project is constructed and is certified to comply with the applicable zoning and building codes, it receives a certificate of occupancy and is occupied by its tenants or owners. At this stage, the real estate process moves from development to asset management. In the management phase, activities shift to maintaining the property in good condition, attending to tenant needs, financial management (including collecting rents and managing expenses), completing the building's lease-up, and releasing space as tenants leave. During the management phase, the construction loan is taken out by a permanent mortgage loan, and the project's financing cycle is complete. Over time, completed properties face two important financing needs: replacing building components as they wear out and completing interior improvements for new tenants. Reserves should be built into the original financial plan to address these needs. Both funds from the initial development budget and annual contributions from cash flow are used to fund these reserves.

Financing Process

Given the interrelationship of financing sources and phases, most real estate development projects follow a standard financing path and process. This process begins with identifying and securing the predevelopment financing to plan a feasible project and to gain site control. The availability of this early-stage money is critical because it allows the developer to control the site and to sufficiently advance the project design, market and financial analysis, and permitting process to convince other investors and lenders that the project is feasible. Next, the equity and permanent debt financing must be secured. This puts the project's long-term financing in place, which is required to gain financing commitments from construction and bridge lenders. Because equity financing is more difficult to obtain and is a requirement for permanent lenders, developers raise equity before securing a permanent loan. However, the sequence for securing permanent debt and equity depends on the project and its funding sources. In some cases, a permanent loan commitment is easier to obtain and adds momentum to attract equity investors or grant funds, or both. Although one lender may provide both the construction and permanent loans, most projects have separate construction and permanent lenders. Thus, once the permanent debt and equity is finalized, developers secure their short-term construction financing to complete the financing plan. Once all financing sources are committed, construction loan requirements have been met, and the project is ready to proceed with construction, the developer closes (i.e., completes and signs the required legal documents) the construction loan, along with any remaining equity investments and bridge financing, if needed. The construction loan is then used to fund the construction and other development costs through periodic loan requisitions and disbursements, supplemented by equity and bridge financing. When construction is complete, a certificate of occupancy is in place, and lease-up and other requirements are satisfied, the permanent loan closing occurs with the loan proceeds used to pay off the construction loan balance.

Real Estate Financial Statements

Two financial statements are used to present and analyze financial information for a real estate project: the development budget and the operating pro forma. A development budget presents the uses and sources of funds to develop the project and is similar to the balance sheet. An operating pro forma, also called a cash flow statement, summarizes the expected revenues, operating expenses, debt service, and net cash flow for the project over many years, typically covering the term of the permanent debt, and is equivalent to a business income statement. Examples of a development budget and operating pro forma are presented in Exhibits 7.2 and 7.3 for a downtown reuse project. Note that these financial statements are for a building construction project where funds are used to develop a building that is leased to tenant businesses to generate revenue. Although most real estate projects fit this model, some entail land development in which funds are invested to acquire, improve, and subdivide land into parcels that are sold to generate revenue. Still other projects involve the development and sale of buildings or condominium units, in which revenue is received from the sale of buildings or condominium units. The form of the financial statements presented in Exhibits 7.2 and 7.3 still applies to these other project types, but the cost and revenue line items must be altered to reflect the different development costs and revenue sources involved. Moreover, the operating pro forma for most land development or condominium projects will cover fewer years, due to the shorter period for property sales and debt repayment compared to a leased building project.

Development Budget

A *development budget* summarizes the planned uses and sources of funds for a real estate project. The uses of funds portion is typically listed above, or to the left of, the sources of funds. As with a business balance sheet, the total uses of funds must equal the total sources of funds. Exhibit 7.2 presents a development budget for a real estate project that involves the acquisition and total rehabilitation of a 15,500-square foot vacant historic building in the downtown area of a small city. Plans call for converting the building into a ground floor restaurant and small retail space with second and third floor office space above. In the uses of funds section, the specific costs needed to carry out the proposed development are detailed. These costs fall in three broad categories: property acquisition, construction (also called "hard costs"), and "soft costs." Soft costs include professional fees, insurance, taxes and interest during construction, the developer's costs and profit, and initial project reserves. Note that the property will be acquired for a nominal $1. This unusually low acquisition cost reflects the building's poor condition, which eliminates its value given market rents and the required investment for its development. For most projects, sizable acquisition costs will exist. Construction costs represent the largest expense at $1,322,000, or 78% of total development costs. For soft costs, the largest items are design fees, legal and financing fees, and the developer's overhead and profit. Design fees are paid to architects and engineers to analyze the property's condition and prepare the detailed plans that define the scope and form of the building improvements, including construction drawings that document the specific construction work to be done. Real estate projects typically have high legal fees to cover the many legal tasks involved in acquiring property, negotiating design and construction contracts, completing loan and other financing transactions, and completing tenant leases. Finance fees include fees paid to

Exhibit 7.2   Downtown Building Reuse Development Budget

Uses of Funds	Amount	Per Square Foot
Acquisition	$1	$0.00
Construction	$1,102,000	$71.56
Contractor's Overhead, Profit, and Contingency	$220,000	$14.29
Design and Engineering	$88,000	$5.71
Legal, Finance, and Insurance Fees	$93,750	$6.09
Construction Interest	$46,000	$2.99
Taxes During Construction	$2,250	$0.15
Developer's Overhead and Profit	$100,000	$6.49
Debt Service Reserve	$16,700	$1.08
Operating Reserve	$10,000	$0.65
Soft Cost Contingency @ 5%	$16,500	$1.07
Total Uses (Total Development Costs)	$1,695,201	$110.08

Sources of Funds	Amount
First National Bank Loan	$433,000
Net Syndication Proceeds	$270,000
Developer Equity	$100,000
State and Federal Grants	$892,201
Total Sources	$1,695,201

lenders for a loan, appraisals needed for financing, and the final accounting of all development costs. Developer's overhead and profit covers the developer's direct staff and other business costs entailed in developing the project and the up-front return for the time and investment made in the project. The $100,000 budgeted for developer overhead and profit is small and reflects a nonprofit developer that does not seek a profit and can subsidize its overhead costs with other funding. The $46,000 construction interest line item is for interest payments on the construction loan during the construction and development period. Construction loans require monthly interest payment, but because the project does not generate income to pay interest during construction, interest payments must be funded as a development cost. Two reserve accounts are also funded through the development budget: a $16,700 debt service reserve and a $10,000 operating reserve. These reserves provide financial support for the developer and the lender if operating costs are higher than expected or if delays occur in fully leasing the property. A final $16,500 line item provides a contingency to fund higher than budgeted amounts for any soft cost items.

Development cost items are often expressed on a square foot basis, as shown in the far right column of Exhibit 7.2. This is a convenient way to quantify unit costs, independent of the project's size, and facilitate comparisons with other development projects. A low per-square-foot item can indicate that the development budget has underestimated important items and may either fall short of funds or need to cut back on construction scope or quality to meet the budget. High per-square-foot costs can reveal when a project is budgeting or paying too much for certain items and it may be appropriate to renegotiate them. On the other hand, there may be unique conditions or complexities that justify these higher costs.

The sources of funds section lists the amount of money provided by each funding source. Debt sources are listed above equity investors, as with a business balance sheet. The hypothetical downtown project in Exhibit 7.2 has four funding sources: First National Bank loan, syndication proceeds, developer equity, and state and federal grants. The type of funding sources and the amount raised from each source depends on the project's cash flow and how this cash flow is divided between lenders and equity investors. Thus, the sources of funds section links the development budget to the operating cash flow. Just as a firm's cash flow is used to structure its financing, the cash flow from a real estate project determines the financing plan detailed under sources of funds. After defining the sources listed in Exhibit 7.2 and explaining the operating pro forma in Exhibit 7.3, the discussion will return to how financing is structured from the project's cash flow. The $433,000 loan from First National Bank is the private debt portion of the funding plan. It represents the amount of debt that First National Bank will provide based on its lending standards and underwriting of the project. In this case, First National Bank based its loan on a 1.25 debt service coverage ratio and 75% loan-to-value ratio and required the project to be 90% preleased before loan closing. Syndication proceeds denote the cash obtained from equity investors who invest to receive federal tax credits. Because the project involves rehabilitation of an historic building listed on the National Register of Historic Places, property owners receive tax credits equal to 20% of the development costs for a qualifying historic rehabilitation and these tax credits can be sold to private investors.[5] The third funding source is the equity invested by the developer, which is $100,000. Notice that this amount equals the developer's overhead and profit included as a use of funds. Therefore, the developer is not putting cash into the project but rather is agreeing to undertake the project without taking any compensation for its overhead costs and profit. This arrangement is only feasible if the developer has other funding sources to cover its staff and other costs needed to undertake the project. Finally, the development budget calls for $892,301 in state and federal grants, or 53% of the total development costs. These grants fill the gap between the project's revenue and actual development costs. In other words, market rents in this city only cover 47% of the costs to rehabilitate this vacant property, and a subsidy is needed to cover the other 53%. This subsidy may be warranted to preserve an important historic building, eliminate a source of blight (and perhaps crime), attract new investment and economic uses to the downtown, and catalyze additional investment and activity in surrounding properties.

Operating Pro Forma

An *operating pro forma* presents the forecasted revenue, expenses, and net cash flow for a real estate project. Because it is prepared prior to development, it details the expected, not actual, cash flow from the project. Exhibit 7.3 shows the revenue and expense categories for a typical leased building. Revenue is generated from three sources: rental payments; common area charges; and cost escalators. The last two items are common in commercial leases that require tenants to pay for the cost of maintaining common areas and increases in taxes and operating expenses. Annual rent amounts are usually calculated based on a square foot rental price multiplied by the amount of space leased. For example, the retail space is 800 square feet and is projected to rent for $8 per square foot. Thus, its annual rent is 8 times $800, or $6,400. Similar calculations are made for the restaurant and office space, which is projected to rent for $9 per square foot. In some retail leases, tenants also pay an additional rent based on their sales. For example, a grocery store may pay a fixed rent of $8 per square foot plus 5% of any sales above $3 million. Although this project will not collect this "percentage" rent, it is an important revenue source for large retail projects and projects in a strong retail location. A vacancy allowance is deducted from the projected rent to account for nonleased space and uncollected rent. Although the developer intends to fully lease the building, some space may take longer than expected to lease, and tenants, even in a fully leased building, may not make lease payments due to financial problems, failure, or bankruptcy. The vacancy allowance provides insurance that the projected cash flow expected by lenders and investors will materialize even with leasing or rental collection problems. Net rent is the rental income after subtracting the vacancy allowance.

After rent, the additional charges collected from tenants for common area expenses, tax increases, and operating cost increases are listed. Common area charges are determined by allocating the actual costs for cleaning, lighting, heating, and maintaining common areas to tenants based on their share of occupied space. Tax and operating cost escalators are more complicated. They are calculated based on an increase from their cost in the base, or first year, of the lease and then allocated to tenants according to their share of space. Therefore, tax and operating cost escalators are not paid until the second year of the lease and increase over the lease period. If a tenant leaves after 5 years and the space is leased to a new tenant in the sixth year, this new tenant will begin paying cost escalators in year seven. This explains the unusual pattern of tax and operating cost escalators shown in Exhibit 7.3. Notice that the operating cost escalator begins at zero in year one and then increases gradually for the next 4 years. In year six, it is projected to be zero again, based on the conservative assumption that all new leases are signed for the second 5 years. The tax escalator works in the same manner but has a different pattern for this project due to the lag in the tax assessment for the

Exhibit 7.3 Operating Pro Forma for Downtown Building Reuse

Revenue	2003	2004	2005	2006	2007	2008	2009	2010	2011	2012
Rent-Restaurant	$48,438	$48,438	$48,438	$48,438	$48,438	$58,126	$58,126	$58,126	$58,126	$58,126
Rent-Other Retail Space	$6,400	$6,400	$6,400	$6,400	$6,400	$7,680	$7,680	$7,680	$7,680	$7,680
Rent Office Space	$62,388	$62,388	$62,388	$62,388	$62,388	$74,866	$74,866	$74,866	$74,866	$74,866
Less Vacancy	($11,723)	($11,723)	($11,723)	($11,723)	($11,723)	($14,067)	($14,067)	($14,067)	($14,067)	($14,067)
Net Rent	$105,503	$105,503	$105,503	$105,503	$105,503	$126,604	$126,604	$126,604	$126,604	$126,604
Common Area Charges	$6,163	$6,409	$6,666	$6,932	$7,210	$7,498	$7,798	$8,110	$8,434	$8,772
Tax Escalator	$0	$0	$4,552	$4,714	$8,272	$0	$3,732	$4,080	$4,437	$4,802
Operating Cost Escalator	$0	$777	$1,585	$2,425	$3,299	$0	$945	$1,928	$2,951	$4,014
Total Revenue	$111,666	$112,690	$118,306	$119,575	$124,284	$134,102	$139,080	$140,722	$142,426	$144,192

Expenses	2003	2004	2005	2006	2007	2008	2009	2010	2011	2012
Management Expense	$6,500	$6,760	$7,030	$7,312	$7,604	$7,908	$8,225	$8,554	$8,896	$9,102
Maintenance and Repairs	$13,119	$13,644	$14,190	$14,757	$15,347	$15,961	$16,600	$17,264	$17,954	$18,272
Common Area Maintenance	$3,816	$3,969	$4,127	$4,292	$4,464	$4,643	$4,828	$5,022	$5,222	$5,431
Common Area Util./Heat	$3,434	$3,572	$3,715	$3,863	$4,018	$4,178	$4,346	$4,519	$4,700	$4,888
Heating Fuel	$3,805	$3,957	$4,115	$4,280	$4,451	$4,629	$4,814	$5,006	$5,207	$5,415
Insurance	$3,600	$3,744	$3,894	$4,050	$4,211	$4,380	$4,555	$4,737	$4,927	$5,124
Real Estate Taxes	$2,244	$0	$4,595	$7,599	$7,789	$11,976	$16,367	$16,776	$17,195	$17,425
Marketing and Brokerage	$500	$520	$541	$562	$585	$4,736	$633	$658	$684	$712
Legal and Accounting	$5,000	$5,200	$5,408	$5,624	$5,849	$6,083	$6,327	$6,580	$6,843	$7,017
Replacement Reserve	$9,500	$9,880	$10,275	$10,686	$11,114	$11,558	$12,021	$12,501	$13,001	$13,371
Operating Reserve	$2,000	$2,080	$2,163	$2,250	$2,340	$2,433	$2,531	$2,632	$2,737	$2,747
Total Expenses	$53,518	$53,325	$60,053	$65,275	$67,772	$78,486	$81,245	$84,249	$87,367	$89,504
Cash Flow Before Debt	$58,149	$59,365	$58,253	$54,299	$56,512	$55,617	$57,835	$56,473	$55,058	$54,305
Debt Service	$43,461	$43,461	$43,461	$43,461	$43,461	$43,461	$43,461	$43,461	$43,461	$43,461
Net Cash Flow	$14,687	$15,903	$14,792	$10,838	$13,051	$12,155	$14,374	$13,012	$11,597	$10,844
Debt Service Coverage	1.34	1.37	1.34	1.25	1.30	1.28	1.33	1.30	1.27	1.25

newly renovated building and a 5-year tax abatement that does not introduce full taxation until 2009. Taxes in 2003, the first year of occupancy, represent taxes on the prerenovation assessed value whereas the taxes in 2004 will be zero under the tax abatement agreement. Because no increase in taxes occurs until 2005, this is the first year in which tenants make tax escalator payments. Notice that total revenues increase from 2003 to 2007 even though net rent is constant due to the increases in common area charges and escalators. These charges help the building owner offset increasing operating expenses.

In the expense section of the pro forma, the expected operating costs for various items are detailed, including property management fees, maintenance and repairs, utilities, taxes, insurance, marketing, and legal and accounting. These figures can be prepared and evaluated based on operating costs from comparable properties. This data can be obtained from local developers and property managers and books prepared by the Institute of Real Estate Management (IREM) and the Urban Land Institute that compile operating costs for a variety of property types. The pro forma in Exhibit 7.3 also includes developer contributions to replacement and operating reserves. The replacement reserve sets aside funds for the expected replacement of building components over time. Lenders typically require this reserve and control it to ensure that funds are available to maintain the property's condition and value over time. Whereas some lenders use a per-square-foot figure to set annual replacement reserve contributions, a more thorough method is to undertake a separate analysis of the expected useful life of each major building component, the expected replacement cost when each component needs to be replaced, and how much money needs to be set aside each year, along with interest earned on the reserve account, to fully fund these replacement costs. Operating reserves provide a cushion to cover unexpected cost increases or higher than expected vacancy losses. Although not all lenders require them, it is a good practice to follow, especially in the early years of a project and for properties with modest net cash flow. Total operating expenses are subtracted from total revenues to calculate cash flow before debt service.

Determining Supportable Debt and Equity

Once net cash flow is established, it is possible to determine the level of debt and equity investment that the property will support and whether grants or other subsidies are needed to make the project financially feasible. To determine the amount of debt that the property can support, the cash flow before debt service is first divided by the lender's required coverage ratio (a 1.25 coverage ratio is used for this example). The resulting quotient provides the annual debt payments that can be made and still have sufficient net cash flow to meet this debt coverage ratio. Next, the net present value of

Box 7.1   Calculating the Loan Principal for a Real Estate Project

1. Use annual cash flow before debt service for the year with the lowest amount ($54,299 in 2006).

2. Divide this amount by the required debt service coverage ratio to determine the maximum acceptable debt service payment ($54,299/1.25, which equals $43,439).

3. Calculate the present value of this monthly cash flow stream at the expected monthly interest rate for the expected loan amortization period *in months*. Through this calculation you are answering the question: what present value amount is equal to a monthly stream of cash flows discounted over n months at an interest rate of i? This figure has the same value as the amount of principal that can be repaid at interest rate i over n months with the monthly cash flow. This is the amount of senior debt that the project can support. (Present value of $43,439/12, at $i = .08/12$, and $n = 240$ is $432,777. Round up to $433,000 and annual debt service of $43,461.

this stream of annual debt service payments is calculated based on the expected interest rate and amortization period for the loan; this present value is the loan principal that the project can borrow. A review of the figures in Exhibit 7.3 reveals that net cash flow varies each year, and after increasing in 2004, declines in years 2005 and 2006. If the first year (2003) cash flow is used to calculate the loan size, then the debt coverage ratio will drop below the required 1.25 level in these latter years. Thus, the lowest annual figure for cash flow before debt service should be used to determine the supportable debt amount for the project. For the downtown project in Exhibit 7.3, the lowest cash flow before debt is $54,299. When this figure is divided by the 1.25 coverage ratio, maximum annual debt payments total $43,439. The loan amount that this cash flow can repay is $432,777—the net present value of this payment with an assumed interest rate of 8% and 20-year amortization. In the final development budget (see Exhibit 7.2), the loan is rounded up to $433,000 and the annual debt service becomes $43,461 (the figure in the second-to-last line of Exhibit 7.3). Notice that the debt service coverage ratio remains at 1.25 or higher for all years in the operating pro forma. Box 7.1 details the steps and calculations used to determine the amount of supportable debt for a real estate project.

Cash flow after debt service payments is net cash flow, which provides a return to the project's equity investors. For the Downtown Building Reuse Project, the annual net cash flow is projected to vary between $10,800 to almost $15,900, depending on the year. The size of equity investment supported by this net cash flow depends on the investor's desired rate of return and expected cash flow from the property's sale at a future date.[6] Because private real estate investors often seek returns in the 15% to 25% range, especially for small high-risk projects outside the best locations and without high-quality tenants, the amount of private equity that could be raised from the expected cash flow is very small. Instead, the project relies on historic preservation tax credit to raise equity capital. Net cash flow compensates the developer for its direct costs, overhead, and effort to undertake the project. (Remember the developer did not receive any cash compensation for these expenses in the development budget but rather contributed them as developer equity.) Based on the $100,000 in developer equity invested in the project, the developer's annual rate of return from project cash ranges from 10% to 16% but will increase somewhat with any gain realized in a future property sale. Subordinate debt financing is a second alternative for using net cash to finance a project, especially if a nonprofit or public sector developer is undertaking the project for reasons other than direct investment returns. In this case, the net cash flow is used to borrow money from a subordinate, or second mortgage lender, instead of going to the developer and equity investors. With long-term principal amortization and an interest rate below the required return for equity investors, a subordinate loan raises more capital than equity. With its junior claim on property cash flow and collateral, subordinate debt is often treated like equity by the senior lender and does not deter the project's ability to secure a larger senior loan.

These calculations of the project's supportable debt and equity investment link the operating pro forma to the development budget via the sources of funds section. They also determine any "funding gap" for the project (i.e., the difference between the project's total development costs and the amount of debt and equity that can be raised from property cash flow, which must be filled with grants and/or other subsidy sources). As shown in Exhibit 7.2, the cash flow and tax credits from the Downtown Building Reuse Project only support $803,000 in debt and equity; $891,000 in grants is necessary for the development to be feasible.

Real Estate Debt Instruments

Although the prior sections introduced several types of debt used to finance real estate projects, this section provides a more complete overview of the major financing instruments. As suggested in the discussion of the development process, financing instruments closely match development stages and include predevelopment financing, construction financing, permanent mortgage loans, mini-perm debt, and bridge loans. Table 7.1 presents a description and summary of key terms for each type of debt.

Predevelopment Financing

Financing the large up-front costs for planning, site control, design, legal services, and other tasks is a significant challenge for real estate–based economic development projects. In addition to the limited number of grant

Table 7.1   Summary of Real Estate Debt Instruments

Finance Instrument	Description	Key Terms
Predevelopment Loan	Loan provided to cover project planning and predevelopment costs.	Repayment is often deferred until construction or permanent financing. Usually unsecured.
Construction Loan	Loan to finance building construction/rehabilitation or infrastructure improvements or both.	Funds drawn based on construction progress. Loan term matches construction and lease-up period. Interest-only paid monthly. Principal repaid with permanent loan.
Real Estate Mortgage	Permanent long-term financing that replaces construction or mini-perm loan. Secured by mortgage interest in real estate.	Loan terms of 10 to 30 years. Amortization period can be longer. Payments usually made monthly.
Mini-perm Loan	Medium-term loan in lieu of permanent financing. May be replaced by a permanent loan or repaid from property sale. Can either take out or be an extension of a construction loan.	Maturities usually range from 5 to 7 years with longer amortization period. Payments usually made monthly.
Bridge Loan	Short- to medium-term loan used to bridge grant reimbursement, equity investment, or permanent loan.	Maturities range from 1 to 5 years. No principal amortization. Interest usually paid monthly. Secured by subordinate mortgage.

sources for these activities,[7] government and nonprofit lenders provide flexible *loans for predevelopment purposes*. A key feature of these loans is deferred and flexible repayment terms, especially terms that link repayment to permanent and construction financing. Thus, predevelopment loans typically are balloon loans with no amortization of principal. Some lenders provide "forgivable" predevelopment loans that convert into a grant if the project does not proceed to development, recognizing that the capacity to repay a predevelopment loan often depends on securing financing to develop the project. Government agencies, foundations, and some nonprofit lenders make forgivable loans. Interest rates are typically below market and may be deferred until the loan maturity date. When predevelopment loans precede site acquisition, there is no collateral available to secure these loans, making them quite risky. For this reason, government programs and nonprofit entities make most predevelopment loans. These lenders manage the risk associated with such loans by dispersing them in small increments as certain development milestones are achieved. One exception is acquisition financing to acquire property in advance of development. In this case, the property serves as collateral, and when a low loan-to-value ratio exists, acquisition loans from banks and other private sector lenders are possible.

Construction Loans

Construction loans are short-term loans used to finance the construction and development phase of a real estate project. Commercial banks and thrift institutions are the usual sources for such loans, which are secured by a senior mortgage on the land and building improvements funded by the loan. Construction loans, like predevelopment loans, are balloon loans with no principal amortization during the loan term. Instead, they are repaid by permanent financing. However, interest is paid monthly and must be included in the overall development budget. To protect the collateral for their loan, construction lenders carefully monitor construction progress and funding in part to ensure that the developer does not run out of funds before the project is completed. Consequently, they hold back a portion of the loan until construction is complete and disburse loan proceeds periodically, typically monthly, based on construction progress. For these reasons, construction loans are costly to administer, with lenders often hiring a consulting architect or construction manager to monitor construction progress and review loan disbursement requests. Borrowers are charged fees to compensate the construction lender for these administrative and consulting costs. As part of their loan security, construction lenders take an assignment of all permits and contracts associated with the project. These assignments allow the lender to step in and complete the project if the developer defaults on the loan or is unable to complete the project. A completed project is critical to realizing the property's full collateral value because a partially completed project is likely to be discounted in value if the lender needs to foreclose.

Permanent Mortgage Loans

Mortgage loans provide the long-term permanent financing for real estate projects. In many ways, permanent mortgage loans are the financial cornerstone of real estate projects. They finance the largest portion of the project and leverage other financing by ensuring that long-term patient capital is in place (e.g., construction loans depend on having a permanent mortgage loan commitment). Permanent real estate mortgage loans have long maturity periods, often between 10 and 20 years. Principal amortization periods usually match the loan maturity but can be longer, as high as 25 or 30 years, especially for mortgage loans with a 10- or 15-year term.

For fixed rate loans, the interest rate is pegged to interest rates on U.S. Treasury securities with the same maturity. For example, a 20-year mortgage loan may be provided at 300 basis points above the rate on 20-year U.S. Treasury bonds. Interest rates on variable rate loans are tied to short-term indexes, such as the prime rate or the LIBOR (London Inter-bank Overnight Rate). In addition to taking a senior mortgage on the financed land and property, lenders usually require an assignment of all leases for the property. This assignment allows the direct collection of rent and property oversight if the borrower defaults and foreclosure is necessary. In addition to a senior mortgage loan, economic development projects often have additional mortgage loans secured by a second or even third mortgage. Although subordinate loans are riskier than senior ones and should carry a higher interest rate, government and nonprofit lenders may supply them at below-market interest rates and with deferred payments to enhance project feasibility.

Mini-Perm Loans

These loans are a medium-term alternative to permanent mortgage loans, often provided by banks that do not want to hold a long-term commercial real estate loan. *Mini-perm loans* have maturities of 5 to 7 years but with payments based on a longer principal amortization (e.g., 20 years). Interest rates can be either variable or fixed rate. They are secured with a senior mortgage on the financed property and an assignment of leases. Some mini-perm loans are simply extensions of the construction loan and allow the developer to finance the project without a long-term permanent loan. A developer may prefer this approach when it expects to sell the project in several years and can avoid the costs of securing a separate permanent loan. A mini-perm loan also is advantageous when medium-term interest rates are lower than long-term rates and the developer expects long-term rates to decline within a few years. A mini-perm loan allows the project to be financed initially at the lower interest rate and then to be locked in at a low long-term rate in the future.

Bridge Loans

A final debt tool used in real estate finance is the *bridge loan,* which, as the name indicates, provides temporary financing until the final source of financing is available. Bridge financing is often used to bridge the receipt of syndication proceeds from equity investors, which are paid in stages based on project milestones. Another common use of bridge financing is funding direct costs in advance of grants that are paid on a reimbursement basis. Bridge loan maturities must match the timing of the final investment, but they are usually 2 to 3 years or less. As with construction and predevelopment loans, loan payments are interest-only with no principal amortization. Bridge loans are secured by a junior mortgage on the financed property subordinated to the construction or permanent lender and, possibly, other subordinate lenders.

Underwriting Real Estate Debt

Real estate projects present unique underwriting and credit analysis issues, compared to businesses, that warrant a brief discussion. Three topics are central to underwriting real estate loans: (1) development team capacity; (2) project cash flow risk; and (3) collateral risk. Reviewing development team capacity is similar to analyzing firm management for business loans. Lenders want to be sure that the parties responsible for the project have the requisite skills and experience to successfully complete the development and manage it over time. Because real estate projects involve a development team with many participants, the experience of each team member must be reviewed, including the developer, architects and engineers, contractors, attorneys, and the management company. Beyond a paper review of team experience, visiting comparable projects and checking references are important to evaluate the capacity of development team members. Team members responsible for completing the initial project often receive the most careful review, yet a thorough assessment of the property management company is important, especially for permanent lenders, because the property manager's management and maintenance practices protect the lenders' collateral over the loan's entire repayment period. In assessing development team capacity, practitioners also should consider whether gaps exist for specialized tasks, such as tax credit syndication or tenant relocation.

Four issues are critical to underwriting the adequacy of project cash flow to repay debt over time. First, the property's ability to secure tenants to initially occupy the project at the projected rent must be evaluated. Although this lease-up risk is addressed by setting preleasing requirements as a loan condition, lenders also need to compare the property's location, construction quality, amenities, and rents to comparable properties and review regional market conditions for the planned property type. For development lenders, this review should strengthen the project by identifying weaknesses that can be addressed prior to development to maximize the property's capacity to achieve preleasing and income goals. Because a real estate project's ability to generate income depends on the tenants' ability to pay their rent, analyzing the credit of proposed tenants is a second focus in underwriting project cash flow. A property with financially weak tenants is riskier than one leased to strong-credit tenants. The importance of tenant credit to real estate projects leads most lenders to require the right to approve all tenants as a loan condition. However, economic development lenders need to balance concerns about tenant credit quality with their mission to foster new business creation and promote local business ownership. These goals are not advanced if only well-established businesses and national chain stores are deemed creditworthy tenants. A third concern is overall market risk and the project's ability to re-lease space with tenant turnover. This analysis is closely related to the questions of property location, quality, and competition considered in the analysis of initial lease-up risk, but it is also affected by the initial lease terms (long-term leases that match the loan maturity mitigate this risk) and the presence of reserves for marketing, brokerage fees, and tenant improvements to address future vacancies. Finally, the operating budget must be reviewed to ensure that sufficient funds will be available to address all expense items, inflation assumptions are realistic, and provisions exist to cover cost increases over time (e.g., lease escalator terms). Even when a project achieves its expected cash flow, it can incur financial problems if operating costs are higher than expected.

A third set of underwriting issues concerns the loan collateral. In real estate lending, appraisals are used to establish the value of the property securing the loan. A third-party professional appraiser is hired to establish this value. Appraisers use three methods to determine value: replacement cost (based on the cost to build the property new); comparable sales (based on recent arms-length sales of similar properties); and discounted cash flow (based on the present value of the cash flow that the property can generate). For multitenant lease properties, appraisers largely rely on the discounted cash flow method. Once the appraised value is established, lenders use this amount to determine a maximum loan amount based on their loan-to-value ratio. Even when the property's cash flow will support a larger loan, conventional lenders will cap the loan at their maximum loan-to-value ratio according to the appraised value.[8] Collateral value also is shaped by construction quality, property maintenance practices, and the adequacy of replacement funding. Construction quality can be assessed from the construction specifications, contractor experience, and careful oversight of the construction process. Both a careful review of the property manager's capacity and analysis of the operating budget are important to ensure that the value of the real estate collateral is maintained over time by sound management and regular replacements.

Sources of Real Estate Financing and Capital Availability Problems

Real estate finance has undergone significant changes over the past decade with public capital markets playing a greater role in providing both debt and equity capital.[9] Although these changes expanded and diversified the supply of capital for real estate development, they primarily benefited large and high-quality projects such as regional shopping centers and suburban and downtown office buildings. Economic development projects often involve greater risk and may be smaller than conventional real estate projects and, thus, are less able to access these new capital sources. Instead, they rely on traditional private capital markets and government and nonprofit financing sources.

Four institutional sources are most important in supplying debt to real estate–based economic development projects. Commercial and thrift banks are the primary sources of construction and mini-perm loans and, to a lesser extent, permanent mortgage loans. Thrift institutions, with a tradition in residential real estate lending, tend to be more active in commercial real estate lending than in small business credit. Moreover, an increasing number of banks now offer subordinate debt or equity investment for real estate projects through special lending units or products created to address the economic and community development needs of low- and moderate-income communities. (See Chapter 9 for more details on these bank development finance models.) Insurance companies and pension funds are the major sources of permanent debt because they hold long-term loan assets that match their long-term liabilities. Most insurance companies and pension funds do not directly invest their funds but rather use investment managers and other intermediaries to make and manage their real estate investments. Whereas most institutional investors target large and high-quality projects, some have alternative investment funds that finance projects with economic and community development goals. Examples include the AFL-CIO Real Estate Investment Trust, capitalized with union pension funds, and two investment pools established by life insurance and property and casualty insurance industries in Massachusetts.[10] Government lending programs are a third source of real estate financing, especially for supplementing private sector first mortgage lending. Several state governments have agencies that finance redevelopment projects and supply permanent loans for real estate developments. Examples include the New Jersey Economic Development Authority and the Massachusetts Development Finance Agency. Local governments are active lenders for real estate projects, often providing the subordinate debt and equity-like investment essential to project feasibility. They can also enhance project feasibility through below-market transfers of city-owned land, property tax reductions, and building parking, roads, or other infrastructure to support the project. Government leases also can supply a strong anchor tenant to help finance a project while attracting other users to the development. Finally, a growing number of nonprofit entities provide capital to economic development projects, especially in low- and moderate-income areas. The Local Initiative Support Corporation (LISC) retail initiative provides equity investment for retail development projects, primarily supermarket-anchored projects, in inner city neighborhoods. Local LISC offices also provide predevelopment loans and subordinate debt for real estate projects. Community development loan funds (discussed in Chapter 12) are another debt source for real estate projects, including acquisition, predevelopment, construction, and bridge loans.

Financing Gaps for Development Projects

Real estate projects face two major financing problems: limited sources of equity and weak market conditions with rents and property values that are insufficient to cover development costs. Although the limited supply of equity financing partially reflects weak market conditions, it also results from the small size and higher perceived risk of unconventional projects and those in second- and third-tier markets. Without access to equity capital, developers can neither fund the predevelopment work needed to gain site control and bring a project to fruition nor fund the 20% to 30% of total development costs required to meet lender loan-to-value standards, even with a feasible level of cash flow. This equity gap can be filled through public and nonprofit financing sources that provide predevelopment and subordinate loans. Historic and other investment tax credits also help generate equity financing to fill this gap. The second funding problem stems from historic disinvestment in many communities that reduced real estate demand and rents such that the economic conditions for feasible real estate projects no longer exist. Under these conditions, market rents will only cover a fraction of the development costs, and a direct capital subsidy is needed to make the project feasible. This type of subsidy is justified when the development project will lead to significant new investment and economic activity that provides economic and fiscal benefits that justify the subsidy. A combination of direct grants, long-term deferred loans, and reduced land transfer costs (for publicly owned or assembled land) help fill the funding gap between development costs and the amount of debt and equity supported by market rents.

The Lithgow Block illustrates how one community-based developer assembled financing sources to address these gaps and achieve a feasible financing plan. This project, located in Boston's Codman Square neighborhood, involved the renovation of a blighted and long vacant historic commercial building into 20,650 square feet of leased retail and office space. Table 7.2 summarizes the project's permanent financing sources. The senior mortgage debt from Bank Boston and the Massachusetts Government Land Bank covered only 39% of total development costs. Thus, a majority of the project's costs (61%) was financed by subordinate debt, grants, and equity. Two subordinate mortgage loans totaling $355,000 used the project's residual cash flow after senior debt service to fill part of this gap, but $1.4 million, or 42.5% of the budget, came from federal grants, historic tax credit syndication, and a deferred city loan that did not draw upon project income. Subsidies exceeding two fifths of total development costs were needed to make the project feasible. The complexity of assembling financing and filling the funding gap is evident in the seven separate sources used to finance the project.

Case Study: City Plaza

Introduction

City Plaza is a 60,000-square-foot shopping center located on an eight-acre site adjacent to the downtown area of a medium-size city. It is a neighborhood-oriented shopping center that caters to the convenience needs of residents in the surrounding neighborhoods. The plaza has a mixture of

Table 7.2   Lithgow Block Commercial Project Financing Sources[a]

Funding Source	Type of Financing	Security Position	Amount
Bank of Boston	Mini-perm loan	First mortgage	$418,750
Massachusetts Government Land Bank (state agency)	Mini-perm loan	First mortgage	$981,250
Local Initiatives Support Corporation	Mini-perm loan	Second mortgage	$75,000
Massachusetts Community Development Finance Corporation (state agency)	Mini-perm loan	Second mortgage	$280,000
City of Boston	Forgivable 30-year loan	Third mortgage	$600,000
National Equity Fund	Equity from historic tax credits	Not applicable	$309,624
U.S. Office of Community Services	Federal grant	Not applicable	$350,000
Total Development Costs			$3,014,624

NOTE:

a. Table 7.2 is based upon information from Chien et al. (1996), *From Despair to Development: An Evaluation of the Lithgow Block Residential and Commercial Projects*. Mini-perm loans had a 7-year term.

regional chains, national franchises, and locally owned businesses including a drugstore, donut shop, electronic shop, discount store, bank branch, medical office, and laundromat. After the closure of a 20,000-square-foot fitness center 1 year ago, the property ran into financial difficulties and showed signs of neglected maintenance and management. It also faces foreclosure from its current lender.

Neighborhood Housing and Development Corporation (NHDC), a nonprofit community development corporation serving the neighborhoods next to City Plaza, is interested in acquiring and stabilizing the shopping center. NHDC is concerned about City Plaza's recent deterioration, the loss of additional tenants, and the potential for the property to become a magnet for loitering, vandalism, and drug activities. Moreover, NHDC would like to attract a grocery store to the vacant health club space, addressing the neighborhood's lack of a local supermarket.

Development Plan and Budget

NHDC plans to acquire the property from the current owner, make deferred repairs to the property, and renovate the health club space for a grocery store to be operated by the retail division of a national grocery wholesaler. A development budget for the project has been prepared, which is presented in Exhibit 7.4. Based on discussions with City Plaza's owner,

Exhibit 7.4   City Plaza Development Budget

Budget Item	Amount
Property Acquisition	$1,000,000
Property Improvements	$330,000
Legal Expenses	$50,000
Development Consultant	$25,000
Financing Fees	$25,000
Appraisal	$10,000
Environmental Assessment	$10,000
Architectural	$30,000
Soft Costs Contingency	$10,000
Total	$1,490,000

and tax assessments on other shopping centers in the city, NHDC estimates a $1 million acquisition price.

Working with a local contractor and a development consultant, the costs to renovate the health club for a grocery store, make needed repairs, and cover other development expenses were estimated. Total development costs are projected at $1,490,000.

NHDC's development consultant prepared an operating pro forma for the property based on a careful review of City Plaza's existing leases and negotiations with the grocery wholesaler that plans to open a retail store at the center. Income from current leases and rent from the new grocery store at $8 per square foot will total $337,000 in the first year (see Table 7.3). As leases expire, rents are assumed to increase by 4% per year for lease renewals (or new tenants). Additional income will be received from common area maintenance charges, additional rent from tenant sales on two leases, and a lease for a portion of the site's parking lot. After deducting operating expenses, City Plaza's cash flow is projected at $156,585 in the first year, but declines to $144,550 in year four because expenses grow faster than income. Lease renewals in year five and six reverse this trend with net cash flow increasing slightly in year five before reaching $167,000 in year six.

Financing Plan

Based on the development budget and operating pro forma, NHDC needs to establish a financing plan for the project. Through initial discussions with lenders, foundations, and other sources, NHDC identified the following funding availability and terms:

- $150,00 in city and foundation grants
- Two local banks interested in providing a senior mortgage loan— based on an 80% loan-to-value ratio and 1.25 debt service coverage— at 8% with a 20-year term and amortization

Table 7.3   City Plaza Lease Summary and Rent Roll

Tenant	Square Feet	Base Rent	Lease Expiration
Donut Shop	2,010	$20,100	1 year
Discount Store	10,085	$31,000	2 years
Drugstore	8,680	$33,720	2 years
Bank Branch	5,375	$36,000	4 years
Electronics Store	3,500	$20,300	2 years
Laundromat	8,450	$22,750	6 years
Medical Office	1,900	$13,300	4 years
New Supermarket	20,000	$160,000	10 years
Total	60,000	$337,170	

Exhibit 7.5   City Plaza 5-Year Operating Pro Forma

Revenue	Year 1	Year 2	Year 3	Year 4	Year 5
Lease Income	$337,170	$337,974	$344,776	$344,776	$352,171
CAM	$27,822	$28,935	$30,093	$31,296	$32,548
Additional Rent	$8,038	$8,440	$8,862	$9,305	$9,770
Parking Income	$12,155	$12,155	$12,155	$12,155	$12,155
Total Gross Revenue	$385,185	$387,504	$395,885	$397,532	$406,644
Vacancy/Loss Allowance	($19,259)	($19,375)	($19,794)	($19,877)	($20,332)
Effective Gross Revenue	$365,926	$368,129	$376,091	$377,655	$386,312
Expenses					
Legal and Professional Fees	$17,500	$18,200	$18,928	$19,685	$20,473
Utilities	$22,750	$23,660	$24,606	$25,591	$26,614
Maintenance and Repairs	$19,142	$19,908	$20,704	$21,533	$22,394
Insurance	$37,100	$38,584	$40,127	$41,732	$43,402
Taxes	$49,500	$50,738	$52,006	$53,306	$54,639
Trash and Snow Removal	$12,000	$12,480	$12,979	$13,498	$14,038
Security	$20,349	$21,163	$22,009	$22,890	$23,805
Miscellaneous	$1,000	$1,040	$1,082	$1,125	$1,170
Replacement Reserve	$30,000	$31,200	$32,448	$33,746	$35,096
Total Expenses	$209,341	$216,973	$224,890	$233,106	$241,631
Income Before Debt	$156,585	$151,156	$151,201	$144,550	$144,681

With this information and the projected income before debt in the operating pro forma, answer the following questions to help NHDC formulate
its financing plan:

- What size senior mortgage loan can NHDC obtain for the City Plaza
  project?
- Will the senior mortgage loan and $150,000 in grant funds provide
  sufficient financing for NHDC to undertake the project?
- If not, what is the size of the remaining funding gap and what options
  could NHDC pursue to fill this gap?

Endnotes

1. Two good books on city downtown development efforts include Frieden and Sagalyn (1989), *Downtown, Inc*, and Michael Pagano and Ann Bowman (1997), *Cityscapes and Capital.*

2. Mt. Auburn Associates' (2002), *The Impact of CDC-Sponsored Commercial Redevelopment Projects on Commercial Revitalization in Four Boston Neighborhood Commercial Districts* documents the role of real estate development in neighborhood revitalization. Bruce Ferguson et al. (1996) discuss the importance of developing appropriate sites to attract supermarkets and retail activity in inner city neighborhoods.

3. A good overview of policy issues and practices in brownfield redevelopment is found in Collaton and Bartsch (1996), "Industrial Site Reuse and Urban Development—An Overview," pp. 17–61.

4. For example, the Massachusetts Community Economic Development Assistance Corporation provides deferred redevelopment loans to nonprofit developers for affordable housing and economic development projects. See CEDAC's Web site www.cedac.org for a fuller description of these programs. They are also described in Seidman (1987), "A New Role for Government: Supporting a Democratic Economy."

5. An expert in historic tax credit syndication is the best source for estimating the likely investment proceeds from the syndication. Alternatively, the developer may identify one investor, typically a corporation, that will purchase the tax credits and commit to a specific investment amount.

6. Tax benefits are a third potential return for investors, especially "active" real estate investors who are allowed under IRS rules to deduct property losses, generated in part by depreciation expenses, against net income from other properties.

7. For example, the U.S. Economic Development Administration provides technical assistance grants that can cover some of these costs. See Chapter 14 for a more detailed discussion of this and other grant programs.

8. Of course, the loan amount could be increased by pledging addition collateral, such as other properties, cash, or securities.

9. The two major trends are the rise of real estate investment trusts (REITs) to provide equity financing, primarily for large development companies, and the securitization of commercial property loans into mortgage-backed securities. See Lawrence Raiman (1999), *The New World Order of the REIT Business,* for a discussion of REITs. Lewis S. Ranieri (1996), "The Origins of Securitization, Its Sources of Growth and Its Future Potential"; and Steven Baum (1996), "The Securitization of Commercial Property Debt" address the emergence of commercial mortgage-backed securities.

10. These two funds, known respectively as the Massachusetts Life Initiative and the Massachusetts Property and Casualty Initiative, were created as part of a law to reform state taxation of insurance companies.

PART III

Policies to Perfect Private Capital Markets

8

Loan Guarantee Programs

Within development finance practice, loan guarantees, with the exception of a large federal program, are used far less than direct financing. Despite their limited use by practitioners, guarantees offer great potential to overcome market failures and expand capital availability through private intermediaries. Both a long-standing federal Small Business Administration (SBA) program and a recent innovation at the state level demonstrate the importance of guarantees in development finance practice. This chapter reviews the three principal models among loan guarantee programs: (1) the SBA's 7(a) program; (2) state government guarantee programs; and (3) the Capital Access Program. In contrast to other development finance actors, the federal government relies heavily on loan guarantees and the SBA 7(a) program is, by far, its largest small business credit program. As a widely studied program, it also provides evidence on how loan guarantees affect credit availability and insight into the sound design and management of guarantee programs. Consequently, after first reviewing key guarantee issues and discussing their advantages and disadvantages as a development finance tool, the second part of this chapter is devoted to understanding the 7(a) program and its impact on capital availability. State governments are a second major operator of loan guarantee programs, often using them to address targeted credit needs. Since few studies or analyses of state programs exist, the treatment of this topic is limited to presenting illustrative examples of how states use loan guarantees. One interesting and fast-growing innovation in loan guarantee tools is the Capital Access Program (CAP), which uses a portfolio-based guarantee to entice expanded bank lending to small businesses. Drawing upon a 1999 U.S. Treasury Department study, the fourth section explains the CAP model and summarizes the experience and lessons from its use in 20 states. Next, the critical issues and best practices in loan guarantee program design and management are presented building on the lessons and experience gained from these programs. A case study concludes the chapter and challenges the reader to tackle the issues involved in designing and implementing a new guarantee program for technology-based firms.

Loan Guarantees and Capital Availability

Loan guarantees are a primary tool to expand the supply of capital to small firms and higher-risk projects by private intermediaries. Since loan guarantees shift the risk of extending credit from the lender to the third party that issues the guarantee (the guarantor), they provide an incentive for lenders to offer loans that they would not otherwise make. Under a loan guarantee, the guarantor compensates the lender for uncollected loan payments when the borrower fails to pay. Compensation is set by an agreement between the guarantor and the lender. However, most guarantees are risk-sharing mechanisms by which the lender receives partial compensation for losses. With some funds at risk, lenders retain an incentive to underwrite and monitor guaranteed loans to limit their losses and reduce the "moral hazard" problem when a lender assumes excess risks because a third party bears the cost for losses. On the other hand, the guarantee must be large enough to convince lenders to supply credit to riskier transactions. Achieving the right balance between providing an insufficient guarantee to change lender behavior and offering too generous a guarantee that fosters imprudent lending is a central challenge for loan guarantee programs.

The Myriad Forms of Guarantees

Guarantees can be used to achieve varied economic development purposes. While this chapter focuses on loan guarantees as a tool to expand credit for small businesses, other guarantee forms exist that may be better suited to certain development finance needs. Table 8.1 summarizes several different types of guarantees and their uses. When factors related to a firm's market or performance are an obstacle to securing capital, a guarantee that addresses these underlying issues may be more effective. For example, small construction firms must secure performance bonds to bid on most public sector and large private construction projects. Thus, providing this type of guarantee may be more important than loan guarantees to support the expansion of these businesses. Similarly, guaranteeing demand for a new product may be more successful at generating investment in some new technologies than loan guarantees. Although evaluating the most effective use of each form of guarantee is beyond the scope of this chapter, it is important to consider how options beyond a standard loan guarantee can address business development obstacles.

Even within the narrow field of loan guarantees, however, many variations exist. Loan guarantees differ with respect to what losses are guaranteed, the percentage and order of loss paid, and the timing of payment. When a borrower defaults on a loan, the lender faces three types of losses: unpaid loan principal, unpaid interest, and the collection costs to sell collateral. Many loan guarantees cover all three losses, but they may limit

Table 8.1   Different Forms of Guarantees

Guarantee Type	Description	Use
Market Guarantee	Guarantees the level of sales when market demand is very uncertain.	Investment in new products or technologies.
Price Guarantee	Guarantees the purchase or contract price when prices are volatile.	Agriculture price supports to manage crop production.
Performance Guarantee	Guarantees a firm's successful completion of a contract.	Construction industry to address costs of replacing or repairing a contractor failure.
Cost Guarantee	Covers unexpected or excess costs.	Hazardous waste cleanup cost insurance.
Loan Guarantee	Guarantees payment of loan or other financial obligation.	Small business lending. Public debt markets.
Lease Guarantee	Guarantees lease payments to a landlord.	Supports investment in very costly or specialized buildings.

payments for interest and collection costs. Some guarantees only cover principal and interest losses with the guarantor responsible for collecting on the collateral. A second variation in guarantees is the level and order of loss coverage; the combination of these two factors determines how much loss risk is transferred from the lender to guarantor. The level of guarantee concerns what percentage of the loan is guaranteed whereas the order of loss determines the order in which losses are incurred between the lender and guarantor. A first loss guarantee pays for losses from the first dollar of loss incurred until the maximum guarantee amount is exhausted. In this case, the lender will only incur losses when the total loan loss exceeds the guarantee amount. A second loss guarantee only pays for losses that exceed the nonguaranteed portion of the loan. Payment on a pro rata loss basis shares the loss between the lender and guarantor based on the guarantee percentage. Table 8.2 shows how the order of loss affects guarantee payments for a 60% loan guarantee on a $500,000 loan with an actual loss of $200,000. Under a first loss guarantee, the lender would receive the full $200,000 loss because it is below the maximum guarantee amount of $300,000 (i.e., 60% of the $500,000 loan amount). With a second loss guarantee, the lender incurs the full loss and receives no guarantee payment because the total loss does not exceed the nonguaranteed portion. For the pro rata guarantee, the lender receives 60% of the loan loss or $120,000. A further variation in guarantee terms concerns when the guarantee is actually paid. Some guarantees issue payment only after all collateral is liquidated and the final loss is realized; other guarantees pay the lender at a specific late payment or default date and are reimbursed from collection proceeds. For example, direct-pay letters of credit, used to guarantee bond issues, pay bondholders when the borrower fails to make scheduled debt service payments.

Table 8.2   Comparison of Guarantee Payments Under Different Order of Loss Terms

	Guarantee A	Guarantee B	Guarantee C
Loan Amount	$500,000	$500,000	$500,000
Guarantee Percentage	60%	60%	60%
Order of Loss Paid	First	Second	Pro rata
Actual Loss	$200,000	$200,000	$200,000
Guarantee Paid	$200,000	$0	$120,000

Advantages and Disadvantages of Guarantees

Since they operate through private lenders, loan guarantees offer advantages over direct loan programs to increase capital availability. First, loan guarantee programs can function on a more efficient "wholesale" level without negotiating transactions on an individual basis with borrowers. By establishing eligibility and credit criteria and defining sound guarantee terms, programs can delegate the details of reviewing and structuring loans to lenders and limit their role to either a final review of the proposed loan or postloan audits to ensure compliance with the program and guarantee terms. This approach also uses private lenders' greater capacity to reach borrowers with more offices and larger lending staffs than government or nonprofit entities. Second, loan guarantees require interaction between borrowers and private lenders, which helps firms establish banking relationships and expand their future access to capital. Moreover, lenders may change their practices over time from the knowledge they acquire through participating in guarantee programs. For example, a bank may be reluctant to finance restaurants without loan guarantees due to their perceived high failure rates. However, after lending to restaurants using loan guarantees for several years, the bank may realize that failure rates are lower than expected and learn how to predict successful entrepreneurs. With this experience, the bank might target restaurants as a lending market and rely less on guarantees to make these loans. Finally, loan guarantee programs can increase credit availability with lower capital funding than direct loan programs. Under a guarantee program, capital is only expended when loan losses occur. Since most guaranteed loans do not incur losses and the guarantee does not cover the full loan amount, each dollar of loan guarantee capital generates a large multiple in private loans.

Despite their merits, guarantee programs have drawbacks in addressing development finance needs. First, guarantees are more complex to implement than direct loan programs. Since guarantees are three-party arrangements, programs must balance incentives among the borrower, lender, and guarantor to be effective. Transactions also require legal arrangements among all three parties that are more complicated to negotiate than direct loan transactions. A second disadvantage is that loan guarantee programs depend on lender acceptance and commitment to succeed. If lenders resist using a guarantee because they don't understand it, find it too cumbersome, or lack confidence in the guarantor, then the program will have little impact. A third obstacle is that the guarantor must have sufficient financial strength and credibility to be accepted by lenders, a factor that favors large government entities as guarantors. Nonprofit entities or small governments can overcome this hurdle by securing guarantees with cash reserves, but this approach lowers the leveraging benefits of guarantee programs. Lastly, loan guarantees create an incentive to use debt and thus may lead firms to substitute debt for equity capital or to borrow more funds than they need. This was the conclusion of Wenli Li (1998) who analyzed the relative impact of direct government lending, loan guarantees, and outright grants on firm investment, bankruptcy, and business entry under a theoretical model economy designed to replicate the asymmetric information conditions found in small business borrowing. Li found that grants were most effective at promoting entrepreneurship whereas loan guarantees attracted riskier business with few assets. Direct loans worked best at targeting cash-poor borrowers with good projects. Entrepreneurs also tended to overinvest under direct loans and loan guarantee programs.

Valuing Loan Guarantees

Since guarantees reduce the risk and increase the expected returns of a loan, they have real financial value to firms and lenders. Guarantee programs need to understand how to quantify this value and use it to set fair pricing for the guarantees that they supply. Sound pricing reduces the potential for capital substitution and provides an incentive for lenders to exercise care in underwriting and monitoring loans (Almeyda & Hinojosa, 2001). It also promotes a program's sustainability by providing a sufficient revenue stream to cover guarantee obligations without relying on ongoing government appropriations or infusions of new capital for loss reserves.

This section introduces three approaches to valuing and pricing loan guarantees, drawing on a review article written by Miguel Almeyda and Sergio Hinojosa for the World Bank.[1] Rather than detailing the complex methods and calculations involved in applying each technique, the discussion explains the theory behind each method and data issues involved in applying it. Readers can consult the Almeyda and Hinojosa article and their citations for details on how to apply each method. One way to price loan guarantees is to use historic loss data from comparable programs to determine the likelihood and distribution of future losses for a specific program and then to set the guarantee fees at an amount that will cover these expected costs. A major obstacle to applying this approach, however, is the limited availability of historic loss data for comparable programs and loans. This approach also assumes that loss rates will be stable over time, which may not be true if new trends or conditions will alter the market, cost structure, or competitive environment for firms served by a program. A second approach applies option pricing theory to value loan guarantees. The option pricing method is based on the recognition that a loan guarantee is equivalent to a put option. A put option allows its holder to sell an asset for a fixed price (the exercise price) over a defined period of time (put maturity). Since a loan guarantee allows the lender to exchange its rights to the scheduled loan payments and underlying collateral in exchange for the guaranteed payments (if the borrower defaults on the loan contract), it provides the lender with a put option with an exercise price equal to the present value of the guaranteed payments (Brealey & Myers, 2003). This equivalency between a put option and a guarantee allows the use of an option valuation tool, known as the Black-Scholes formula, to determine the price of loan guarantees.[2] An extension of this approach is used by the Office of Management and Budget to value some forms of federal government insurance and guarantees (Almeyda & Hinojosa, 2001). However, this method requires estimating the variability of income from the guaranteed loan or project, which, once again, requires historic data for comparable financial assets. An alternative method to value the put option, called binomial tree analysis, assigns probabilities to a range of cash flow outcomes for the guaranteed firm or project and the resulting guarantee cost. The price of the put (or guarantee) is then the weighted cost of the guarantee across these outcomes discounted by the applicable risk-free rate of return.[3] For the third method, a guarantee is treated as the difference between the value of a risk-free bond and a risky bond. It uses bond prices and historic data on bond default rates and recovery rates (i.e., the percentage of cash recovered from a defaulted bond) to value a guarantee. An advantage of this method is its reliance on data that is easier to obtain—U.S. Treasury bond prices represent the value of the risk-free bond, and bond rating agencies compile data on bond default and recovery rates. However, it is necessary to identify a risky bond that is a comparable credit risk to the firms or projects guaranteed under the subject program. This is a difficult task since the large firms and projects that use bond markets are very different from the small firms and development projects typically served by economic development guarantee programs. Despite the data and comparability problems faced in applying these valuation methods, they still provide practitioners a critical tool to estimate and recover the market value of their guarantee. Using the best available data and/or estimated parameters to price a guarantee, although imperfect, is still preferable to setting guarantee fees without a well-founded economic basis.

Small Business Administration 7(a) Program

This section reviews the mechanics of the major SBA loan guarantee program, and summarizes data on its activity levels, businesses served, and the characteristics of loans made with a 7(a) guarantee. The discussion draws on studies that compare loans made with 7(a) guarantees to those made without a guarantee, offering insight into how the 7(a) program alters the behavior of lending intermediaries. In the final part of this section, research findings on the impact of the 7(a) program on capital availability and small business performance are discussed.

The SBA 7(a) program guarantees loans of up to $2 million made by private banks or finance companies to small businesses for working capital, fixed asset acquisition, or both. A guarantee can be made for up to 85% of the loan principal for loans of $150,000 or less and 75% for loans above $150,000.[4] The maximum guarantee amount is $1 million.[5] Interest rates on loans made with a 7(a) guarantee are negotiated between the borrower and lender but are subject to SBA limits, which vary between prime plus 2.25% and prime plus 4.75%, based on loan size and maturity.[6] Guaranteed loans can have maturities of up to 10 years for working capital loans and 25 years for fixed asset loans. Lenders decide which loan requests are appropriate for a 7(a) guarantee and then originate the loan guarantee application for SBA approval. In 1983, the SBA established the Preferred Lender Program (PLP), which provides selected lenders with the authority to commit 7(a) guarantees and perform most actions involved in servicing and liquidating loans without SBA approval. PLP is a more efficient way to process 7(a) guarantees, and early studies found lower default rates for PLP loans compared to other 7(a) guaranteed loans.[7] Another innovation in the 7(a) program was the introduction of the LowDoc program in 1994, which uses a streamlined approval process for small loans. Under LowDoc, lenders submit a simplified application with a two-page form and the lender's loan analysis to secure guarantees for loans under $150,000. After introducing this program, SBA's average loan size declined, and loans under $100,000 became the largest size category for 7(a) loans in FY1995 (U.S. GAO, 1996b).

Over $9 billion in 7(a) loan guarantees were committed in federal FY2001, making it the largest federal economic development or business finance program.[8] Following a decade of rapid growth, the program's annual guarantee volume stabilized after 1995. From FY1986 to FY1995, the annual number of guaranteed loans increased 266% from 15,000 to 55,000, and the dollar value of these loans grew from $3.6 billion to $8.3 billion (U.S. GAO 1996b). However, total guarantees grew by only 8% from FY1995 to FY2001. In FY1995, the total SBA 7(a) portfolio accounted for 6.7% of all outstanding business loans by commercial and savings banks (U.S. GAO, 1996a), large enough to impact private credit availability. Although this share has undoubtedly declined since 1995, the 7(a) program still represents the largest and most widespread tool for expanding capital availability to small enterprises.

Two 1996 studies by the U.S. GAO supply detailed data on borrower and loan characteristics under the 7(A) program. The first study (U.S. GAO, 1996b) analyzed trends in 7(a) loans from 1986 to 1995. Although white males owned most businesses using the program, GAO found that a growing share of minority- and women-owned businesses received 7(a) guarantees over the 10 years. Minorities received 10.8% of the dollar value of guaranteed loans during FY1986, but their share grew to 18% in FY1995. Asian and Pacific Islander borrowers received a larger value of 7(a) guaranteed loans than other minority groups. Women also saw their share of the dollar amount of 7(a) loans increase from 10% in FY1986 to 24.4% for FY1995. Women-owned businesses particularly benefited from the LowDoc program, accounting for 26.5% of all loans. According to this study, the average size of SBA-guaranteed loans dropped from $233,000 in FY1986 to $150,900 in FY1995, reflecting the impact of the LowDoc program. Loan maturities under the 7(a) program averaged 10 to 12 years, with LowDoc loans averaging 7 years.

A second GAO report (U.S. GAO, 1996a) compared a sample of 7(a) loans to a comparable sample of nonguaranteed small business loans revealing that lenders use the 7(a) program to provide loans with longer term and lower equity requirements and to serve more start-up and minority-owned businesses. Loans made under the 7(a) program had an average maturity of 13 years, far longer than the 3.3-year average for nonguaranteed loans. One reason for the longer term is that most nonguaranteed loans (51.5%) were lines of credit, but only 2.1% of 7(a) loans were credit lines. Guaranteed loans also were relatively large, with 59% of the 7(a) loan sample above $100,000 compared to 18% for the conventional loans. Although only 0.4% of nonguaranteed loans went to start-up firms, 22.1%, or more than one in five of the 7(a) borrowers, were new enterprises. Minority-owned businesses also constituted a higher percentage of 7(a) borrowers (13.5%) than among recipients of nonguaranteed loans (8.2%). These last two findings are consistent with another study by George Haynes, which analyzed 7(a) loans using data from the 1988 National Survey of Small Business Finance.[9] Lenders surveyed by GAO also reported that the 7(a) program allowed them to lend to firms with less equity and to make loans with longer terms, confirming both the study's statistical findings and results from an earlier report. This 1983 GAO study surveyed 8% of the 8,900 lenders participating in the 7(a) program. These lenders reported that SBA guarantees led them to extend credit to firms that would not otherwise receive loans. A large majority of lenders (82%) indicated that the loans made with 7(a) guarantees either would not have been made or would otherwise have had more stringent terms. Almost half (43%) reported that the guarantee enabled them to make larger loans than were permitted by bank policy or federal regulations (U.S. GAO, 1983).

A final group of studies assessed the impact of the 7(a) program on bank lending practices, capital availability, and firm performance. Although each study uses different evaluation metrics and methods that preclude direct comparison, collectively they provide insight into the 7(a) program's overall impact and limitations. George Haynes conducted the most comprehensive analysis of the 7(a) program, assessing how it affected the allocation of credit both to high-risk borrowers and borrowers in financially concentrated markets. Haynes's hypothesis was that borrower risk levels and financial concentration have separate effects on credit availability. For the SBA 7(a) program to effectively address both capital gaps, it must expand the supply of capital to higher risk firms *and* change lending practices in highly concentrated financial markets where reduced competition limits credit availability and terms. Econometric analysis of borrowers with and without SBA loan guarantees was applied to determine if high-risk borrowers and those residing in highly concentrated financial markets have a higher probability of receiving an SBA loan guarantee than other borrowers. Haynes found that borrower risk mattered most in allocating SBA loan guarantees and that the program distinguished between high-risk borrowers in high concentration financial markets and low-risk borrowers in low concentration financial markets. Medium-risk borrowers in high concentration markets had the highest probability of receiving a SBA 7(a) guarantee (6.1%) while low-risk borrowers in low concentration markets have lowest probability (1.3%). He concluded that the SBA 7(a) program mitigated financial market failure by allocating more capital to high-risk businesses and by distinguishing between high-risk borrowers in markets dominated by a few lenders and low-risk borrowers in markets with many lenders. However, the probability of obtaining a SBA guarantee was not greater for borrowers in highly concentrated financial markets versus less concentrated ones, suggesting that the 7(a) program was not effective at addressing credit availability problems in banking markets with limited competition.

Price Waterhouse conducted the only formal 7(a) program evaluation in 1992. It compared the performance, from 1984 to 1989, of a sample of businesses that received SBA-guaranteed loans in 1985 with sample firms of similar size and industry composition that never received SBA-guaranteed loans. Firms with a SBA 7(a) loan had higher survival rates, faster revenue growth, and much higher job growth than firms without SBA-guaranteed loans. In 1989, over three quarters (77%) of the SBA 7(a) borrowers were still in business compared to 65% for the control group. Moreover, revenues grew by 123%, on average, among 7(a) borrowers versus 101% for non-7(a) firms, and job growth was almost three times faster (101% versus 36%) for the businesses that received 7(a) loans. Since Price Waterhouse did not control for other causal factors or analyze the extent to which the 7(a) guarantee itself (and improved access to capital) contributed to the results, it is difficult to attribute the differences in firm performance to the 7(a) program. It is possible that strong growth-oriented firms sought out the 7(a) guarantee and achieved higher growth and survival rates independent of receiving the SBA guarantee.

A final study raises questions about the appropriate SBA guarantee level. William Hunter (1984) analyzed factors that influenced both borrower default and bank and borrower care in ensuring loan repayment for a sample of SBA-guaranteed loans made from 1971 to 1980. He found empirical evidence that default probability is most directly influenced by the care exercised by lenders in ensuring loan repayment, and that the SBA guarantee level affects this care. Lower guarantee levels and higher bank exposure increases the probability of bank care with a $1,000 increase in the bank's exposure estimated to increase the probability of bank care by about 2.1%. Hunter's model of loan default also found that using SBA-guaranteed loans to repay existing debts increases the probability of default by 12%, a large impact. Hunter concluded that SBA loan guarantees distort incentives for increased bank care since the loan guarantee levels and premiums are not tied to risk. Since this study was completed in 1984, it may not reflect the current factors influencing defaults on SBA-guaranteed loans. Nonetheless, it points to the importance of providing incentives for strong lender care and suggests that loan guarantee programs could reduce their default rates and better target guarantee capacity by linking guarantee levels to indicators of default risk (e.g., debt-to-equity ratio) and not using loan guarantees to refinance existing debt.

Several implications for development finance practice emerge from this review of the SBA 7(a) program. First, the 7(a) program is a critical financing program that expands capital availability for small firms, especially start-up businesses, and allows lenders to offer medium- and long-term debt. Consequently, development finance practitioners need to understand whether and how lenders in their community are using the SBA 7(a) program and work to expand its use to fill critical capital gaps. When lenders are not actively utilizing the 7(a) program, development finance organizations can become 7(a) experts and help package applications for lenders. Second, program details matter. SBA's success with the Preferred Lender and LowDoc programs suggests that other loan guarantee programs can operate efficiently, particularly in guaranteeing small loans, by delegating authority to lenders and simplifying required documentation. However, guarantee levels and fees need to be closely aligned to program goals and provide strong incentives for lender care in overseeing loans. Although simplicity argues for standard guarantee levels and fees, some tailoring of these key incentives to borrower risk and market conditions is warranted.

State Loan Guarantee Programs

Beyond the SBA, state governments widely use loan guarantee programs as part of their array of small business finance tools. The credit strength and larger reserve needed to be a credible guarantor is one reason why states, rather than local governments or nonprofit entities, are more likely to establish guarantee programs. Since no comprehensive study of state guarantee programs exists, data is lacking on the number, size, purposes, and impacts of these programs. With SBA 7(a) guarantees widely available, one would expect state programs to target industries, areas, or borrowers that either are not well served by the 7(a) program or are especially important to the state's

Table 8.3   Summary of Selected State Guarantee Programs

State Program	Allowable Loan Uses	Maximum Guarantee	Guarantee Percentage	Notes
Alaska Business and Export Assistance Program (www.aidea.org/ BEALG.htm)	Real and personal property Working capital Export transactions	$1 million	80%	Covers principal, interest, and liquidation costs
California Loan Guarantee Program (www.sfvfdc.org/ guarantee.htm)	Working Capital Equipment Leasehold improvements	$350,000	90%	2% fee. Made by authorized nonprofit corporations
Indiana Agricultural and Rural Development Project Guaranty (http://www. stateagfinance.org/ indiana.html)	High-growth tech firms, manufacturers, rural development projects, value-added agricultural enterprises	$300,000 for rural/ agriculture projects. Larger for high-growth tech firms	75% to 90%	
Massachusetts Mortgage Insurance and Expanded Guarantee (www. massdevelopment. com)	Real estate, equipment, and term working capital for manufacturing, real estate development, education, and cultural services	$500,000	10% to 50%	Fees range from 1% to 3%
Minnesota Working Capital Loan Guarantee Program	Export transactions	$25,000 to $250,000	90%	
Missouri Agricultural and Small Business Development Authority (www.mda.state.mo.us/ Financial/a2g.htm)	Livestock, land, facilities, equipment, and animal waste systems for independent livestock producers	$50,000	25% first loss guarantee	
Ohio Mini-Loan Guarantee Program (www.odod.state.oh.us/ DMBA/MiniLoan.htm)	Fixed assets	$100,000	45%	For firms with 25 or fewer employees
Oregon Credit Enhancement Fund (www.econ.state.or.us/ cef.htm)	Real and personal property Equipment Working capital Export transactions	$500,000	90%	Provide with 25% first loss guarantee

economy. A snapshot of several state guarantee programs suggests some differentiation from the 7(a) program but also shows considerable overlap. Among the eight state programs listed in Table 8.3, three guarantee export transactions, a financing need not directly served by the 7(a) program, whereas two serve agriculture enterprises, which are important to states with rural economies. Most states also have guarantee limits well below the SBA's $750,000 cap, with three states, Ohio, Missouri, and Minnesota, focusing on the low end of the SBA range. Concentrating on small loans may fill a gap in the SBA 7(a) program if lenders view SBA guarantees as inefficient for small loans. However, it is striking that five of the eight states provide broad-based small business loan guarantees that appear to duplicate the SBA 7(a) program.

This survey of state loan guarantee programs, despite its limited size and scope, suggests that state economic development policy makers would benefit from rethinking their economic development loan guarantee programs. Ones that duplicate guarantees available under the 7(a) program do not expand capital availability; they simply substitute state credit support for a federal guarantee. If in-state banks are not using the 7(a) program, then expanded education or loan-packaging services to increase bank use of federal guarantees is a better investment of state resources. Rather than guaranteeing general small business loans, state guarantee programs would generate greater economic development impact by targeting industries with specialized credit needs that fall outside the 7(a) program or filling 7(a) gaps by addressing larger or high-risk transactions.

Capital Access Programs

The Capital Access Program (CAP) is an innovative approach to expand bank small business lending developed by Pete Hansen when he served as California's deputy banking commissioner and first implemented by Michigan in 1986. Over the next 15 years, its use expanded to over 20 state and local government programs. CAP uses a portfolio-based guarantee rather than guaranteeing individual loans. Banks that participate in the CAP program establish a loan loss reserve for all loans made under the CAP program. The borrower pays a fee, usually 3% to 7% of the loan principal, which is matched by the state or local CAP program.[10] Both the fee and matching amount are deposited into the loan loss reserve at the participating bank to cover losses on the bank's CAP loans. The reserve fund constitutes the bank's sole cash available to address loan losses; no additional back-up guarantee is provided. Thus, the CAP fees and loan loss reserve are designed to address average losses over an entire loan portfolio. When a bank makes many CAP loans, only a small number are likely to generate losses and the CAP reserve will be adequate to cover expected losses. The availability of the loan loss reserve, however, provides a mechanism for lenders to make riskier loans outside their normal credit standards but still make loans that are likely to be repaid. Examples of such riskier lending situations are start-up businesses, firms with lower collateral coverage or weaker financial ratios than required, or loans that require extending repayment beyond the standard maturity. With cap reserves at 6% to 14% of loan principal (the sum of the borrower fee and matching amount), they exceed conventional small business loan loss rates and, thus, allow for higher-risk lending. On the other hand, CAP encourages banks to carefully manage their lending risks since guarantee levels are modest and the reserves that cover losses are limited.

A 1999 study by the U.S. Treasury Department[11] provided the first national analysis of the use and impact of the CAP program. The report identified 20 states and two cities (New York and Akron, Ohio) with CAP programs. In 1998, 315 banks were actively originating CAP loans, and over $1.2 billion in loans had been made through CAP programs since the first loan in 1986. Three states, California, Massachusetts, and Michigan, accounted for 68% of cumulative CAP loans.[12] However, when measured on a per-firm basis, Michigan and New Hampshire had the largest programs, with $725 and $694 in CAP loans per firm, respectively. CAP programs were growing when the study was undertaken with all but three states reporting growth of 10% or more in CAP loan volumes during 1998 and eight states reporting growth above 30%.

While the Treasury study did not formally evaluate the CAP program's impact on credit availability, data on loan size, loss rates, and borrower characteristics indicate that CAP loans address common capital gaps. First, CAP loans are small with the average loan nationally at $59,151 and individual state and city program averages ranging from $18,223 to $150,556. Second, the 3.2% cumulative loss rate for CAP loans indicates that banks are using the program to make higher-risk loans because standard loan loss rates are typically in the 1% to 2% range.[13] Finally, a large share of CAP loans in some states serves either low-income areas or start-up firms, both of which have historically lacked access to conventional bank credit. Almost 30% of CAP loans in California and Oregon are made in low- and moderate-income census tracts. In Massachusetts and Illinois, a sizable share of CAP loans, 18% and 15%, respectively, go to start-up businesses.

Key advantages of the CAP program are its administrative simplicity and flexibility. Participating banks make all credit decisions without review by the state or local program. Banks usually complete an application to participate in the program and then file a simple form for each new CAP loan to receive the matching fee. Borrowers deal only with their lender without filing additional paperwork or applying to a separate program. These simple procedures also make the program easy for state and local governments to administer. Governments and banks can also adapt the program to fit unique goals or market conditions. Some states increase the state match for CAP loans to minority- and/or women-owned firms or to firms located in distressed areas, providing an incentive for banks to expand lending to these target borrowers. Connecticut, for example, increases its matching reserve fee by 20% for loans in certain urban areas. Illinois, Indiana, and Pennsylvania increase matching fees for loans to minority-owned firms. Banks also decide how to best use the additional loss risk protection provided by the CAP loan loss reserve. Some banks use CAP to target a new customer base or to ensure subordinate loans made as part of overall financing packages (U.S. Department of the Treasury, 1999).

Effective practices identified by the Treasury study include active marketing to banks, providing significant program funding, and using broad eligibility criteria with incentives to target lending to specific groups or areas. Active marketing of the CAP program is critical to enrolling banks and creating a large lending network to implement the program, especially during the initial year after the program is established. Direct one-on-one contact and seminars were the more common and effective marketing tools. Large initial appropriations and a mechanism to ensure ongoing funding of state matching fees also are critical to CAP programs. Without stable and substantial funding, it is difficult to attract participating banks, and CAP programs are forced to become inactive when their initial appropriations are exhausted. West Virginia ended its CAP program, and Colorado suspended it after initial funding ran out. On the other hand, some states have dedicated funding streams to ensure the CAP matching fees endure. California and Pennsylvania, for example, fund the CAP match with fees from tax-exempt bond programs that serve larger firms. Broad eligibility criteria, without restrictive firm or loan size limits or tight geographic boundaries, work best to encourage widespread bank and business participation and to establish the program with statewide availability. Targeting objectives can then be addressed by offering higher matching fees as an incentive to serve certain areas, industries, or business owners. Some states use special tools to overcome a program start-up dynamic that occurs when the loan volume is too small to generate sufficient reserves to cover loan losses during the first year or two. Vermont and Pennsylvania provide an initial $50,000 credit line to participating banks to bridge the buildup of the loan loss reserve, and Michigan grants a two-to-one matching fee for each bank's initial $2 million in loans.

Issues in the Design and Management of Guarantee Programs

Guarantee programs pose special challenges and design issues. Before establishing a program, planners need to consider how these issues affect both a guarantee program's ability to achieve economic development goals and the capacities required to effectively implement it. This section helps development finance professionals structure this analysis by discussing the policy levers available to alter private capital allocation, challenges faced in implementing guarantee programs, and best practices in program design and management.

Guarantee Program Policy Levers

Guarantee programs have five basic policy tools to influence how private lenders extend credit to further economic development goals. Fine-tuning these tools is at the core of designing effective guarantee programs. The first policy lever is the program's *targeting policy,* which defines the type of firms and projects that are eligible to receive a guarantee. Three considerations shape targeting policy: economic development goals; capital availability gaps; and program scale. A guarantee program should focus on firms and financing needs that fit economic development goals and strategies. Strategies that seek to retain and grow manufacturing firms, for example, might use a guarantee program to finance their modernization or export expansion activities. On the other hand, a city working to attract and grow businesses in low-income neighborhoods might focus a guarantee program on small retailers and immigrant businesses. Program targets also need to avoid capital substitution by assisting firms and financing needs that are not adequately served by existing lenders, either directly or via SBA 7(a) guarantees or other programs. Consultation with lenders and target firms is needed to define this difficult, but critical, issue. Small loans, firms with specialized collateral, firms in emerging or especially risky industries, and real estate projects in weak market areas are potential financing situations in which the SBA 7(a) program does not adequately address capital availability gaps. Finally, program targets must be consistent with the program's available resources. Although limited funding and development goals favor narrowly targeted programs, it is important to maintain a broad enough focus to secure lender participation and to achieve sufficient scale to cover program costs and the clustering of losses in some years.

Financing policies are the second set of levers. These policies, which define the guarantee terms and lender risks covered, need to address the loss coverage provided, the type of losses guaranteed (principal, interest, or collection costs), the percentage of both the total project cost and private loan amounts that are guaranteed, the guarantee maturity period, and fees charged for the guarantee. Policies should be tailored to the level of financial risk that lenders face in the targeted financial transactions. Fees should reflect the transaction risk and the extent of coverage provided; guarantees that provide first loss coverage for a large share of the loan should carry much higher fees than residual loss coverage for a small loan share. Guarantee terms may need to be adjusted over time based on loss experience and lender acceptance.

The third policy area relates to *how the guarantee is secured.* In other words, what mechanism reassures lenders that the guarantor will meet its obligations? Three forms of guarantee security are typically used: (1) a general obligation pledge; (2) a cash reserve; and (3) direct cash collateral. A general obligation pledge is a promise to make guarantee payments based on the guarantor's overall financial strength. This mechanism requires a guarantor with strong credit. For example, the SBA 7(a) program, with the federal government as guarantor, uses this form of security. A cash reserve fund is a dedicated cash account established to make guarantee payments. With cash set-aside to cover guarantees, lenders have comfort that guaranteed losses will be paid. However, the quality of a guarantee backed by cash reserves depends on the ratio of reserve funds to total guarantee obligations and the likelihood of losses. Consequently, a fund guaranteeing high-risk transactions needs a larger reserve ratio than one backing loans with modest expected losses. Direct cash collateral is sometimes deposited with a bank to secure a loan guarantee. Although this approach provides strong collateral for the bank, it has drawbacks for the guarantor because the cash deposit guarantees a single loan rather than providing security for multiple loans. Despite this disadvantage, direct cash collateral might be used when lenders are risk averse, or for small programs in which the costs of establishing and administrating a reserve fund offset its benefits.

Underwriting criteria, the fourth policy tool, set the risk level that the guarantor will incur based on financial and other characteristics of the guaranteed transactions. For example, a guarantee program might accept higher collateral risk than a private lender but still require a 90% loan-to-value ratio. Alternatively, a program might accept much greater collateral risk but set strong requirements for the firm's management, competitive position, and industry outlook. Underwriting criteria need to be consistent with the economic development goals embodied in targeting criteria and the nature of the capital gaps being addressed. For example, a guarantee program designed to expand credit for immigrant and minority-owner businesses in inner city neighborhoods would need to accept significant collateral risk since the guarantee substitutes for the borrower's limited collateral. A program targeted to manufacturing firms in turnaround situations, on the other hand, might be able to have underwriting criteria with a 90% or 100% loan-to-value ratio but needs more flexible criteria for recent earnings and cash flow.

Finally, guarantee programs set policies on their *process for underwriting, monitoring, and loss collection.* One critical issue is the extent to which the guarantor relies on the lender to perform these responsibilities. At one extreme, as in the SBA Preferred Lender Program, the guarantor fully delegates responsibility to the lender. At the other extreme, a guarantor can exercise full responsibility and due diligence for these functions. A program between these two extremes gives the lender lead responsibility, but the guarantor reviews its underwriting analysis, loan monitoring, and collection performance with recourse to take over the lead role when the lender fails to perform. The delegation of responsibility between the guarantor and lender is tied to the lender's loss exposure and the incentives for strong lender care. When a program guarantees nearly all of a loan and has large first lost exposure, there is less incentive for the lender to carefully underwrite and monitor loans. Thus, the guarantor needs to either assume these responsibilities or create strong penalties for the lender's failure to exercise sufficient care.

Program Challenges and Best Practices

When designing and implementing guarantee programs, practitioners need to consider four challenges that are critical to ultimate program success and use effective practices from existing programs to address these challenges. The first challenge is building widespread lender participation in the guarantee program. Extensive lender involvement is critical to expand credit availability, but it also generates a sufficient volume and portfolio size to reduce the risk of excessive losses. Because guarantees are based on average losses over many loans, developing a large loan portfolio reduces the odds that a bunching of losses will impair the program's financial health and credibility, especially in its early life. Two practices help build lender participation. First, practitioners can consult with lenders during the initial program design to build early awareness of the program and avoid policies that may inhibit lenders' use of the guarantee. Second, programs must be actively marketed to lenders, business technical assistance providers, and target firms, especially in their initial years. Firms and technical assistance providers are a key marketing audience because they generate demand for lenders to use the guarantee. Technical assistance providers, moreover, can simplify the work for borrowers and lenders in using a guarantee.

Establishing confidence in the guarantee's quality is a second challenge. Finding the right solution to this challenge entails both legal and financial considerations. Some state constitutions prohibit the government from lending its credit to private businesses, which precludes a state general obligation pledge to back a guarantee program. In this case, the state can use a cash reserve fund, capitalized with state appropriations, federal grants, or existing assets within a quasi-public entity. When no constitution prohibition exists, states or local governments with a strong credit rating can use a general obligation pledge to provide financial backing for a guarantee program. For organizations and governments without strong credit, establishing a cash reserve fund to support the guarantee program is the best means to create financial credibility for it. Although a new program needs to be conservative in setting the size of its guarantee reserves before a loss record is established, the reserve level can be adjusted over time based on loss experience. A low loss record also may allow a program to purchase backup loss insurance from a private company to reduce its exposure to large losses.

A third challenge concerns setting guarantee terms that gain lender participation and expand credit availability while minimizing the incentives for lenders to make bad loans and/or monitor guaranteed loans poorly. Despite the need to fit guarantee terms to target transactions and local capital market conditions, some best practices emerge from studies of the SBA 7(a) program. First, programs should avoid guaranteeing all or most of a loan to ensure that the lender has a sizable loss exposure. A good rule of thumb is to limit the maximum guarantee to 75% to 80% and use a lower guarantee when appropriate. Second, programs should set market-rate fees that reflect the expected loss rate and vary fees with the level of risk. Market-rate fees also avoid credit substitution—an important goal for guarantee programs that seek to expand capital availability rather than reduce its cost. Firms that can access conventional loans will choose not to pay the fee. Setting fees based on loss rates will help programs self-insure against losses and reduce their reliance on government appropriations. Furthermore, varying fees with credit risk can provide a feasible way to finance high-risk loans because the cost of bearing greater risk can be recovered from the borrower. Because varying fees by credit risk increases administrative costs and complexity, a streamlined way to achieve this goal is desirable. One approach is to set fees based on defined credit risk situations (e.g., credit scores, financial ratios—current ratio, debt–to-equity ratio, loan–to-value ratio, etc.) or other sound loss predictors. A second option is allowing the lender to set the guarantee fee within a defined range and offering an incentive to correctly set the fee (e.g., having the lender retain a percentage of the fee to supplement its loss coverage).

The final challenge is crafting an approval process that is efficient and timely for lenders and borrowers. Since the introduction of a guarantor adds a layer of review, a third party to the transaction, and new legal issues and documents, it is important to minimize the added time and cost that can result from using guarantees. Both the SBA and CAP programs suggest effective practices to address this challenge. First, programs can maximize the lender's role in the process and minimize the duplication of effort between the lender and guarantor. One simple way is to piggyback the guarantee program's underwriting and monitoring reviews on those of the lender. Programs can use the lender's loan application and underwriting analysis in their application process and add a simple application for information needed to confirm eligibility. This approach can be extended to loan oversight by reviewing the borrower's reports to the lender and the lender's associated analysis rather than requiring separate submissions to the guarantor. Once a program is established with good lender relationships and sizable transaction volumes, managers might consider delegating the authority to issue and oversee guarantees to select lenders. By delegating this authority to lenders with a strong track record, a second layer of review is eliminated and the administrative efficiency improves for all parties. Incentives for continued sound performance should accompany this delegation (e.g., a preferred fee schedule that reflects the lower administrative costs and the power to revoke the delegated authority if loss experience and guarantee volumes deteriorate). Finally, guarantee programs should standardize documents and legal reviews to minimize these transaction costs for borrowers.

Case Study: Massachusetts Emerging Technology Fund

In March 1993, Lt. Governor Paul Cellucci signed Chapter 19 of the Acts of 1993 into law, the state's largest investment in economic development programs. Chapter 19 created a new program, the Emerging Technology Fund (ETF), with a mission to "leverage private financing for state-of-the-art manufacturing and research and development facilities for emerging technology firms." Responsibility for implementing the ETF was assigned to the Government Land Bank, a quasi-public agency that financed affordable housing, commercial development, and industrial parks but lacked experience lending to high-technology firms. The legislation set broad program objectives and parameters but left the Land Bank responsible for formulating the program's rules and regulations.

Background

The Massachusetts economy, after an extended period of job growth, low unemployment, and a real estate boom during the 1980s, crashed hard from 1989 to 1992. Job losses totaled 340,000 from December 1989 to May 1993—close to 13% of total employment—and caused the unemployment rate to rise above the national average to 9%. During this period, Massachusetts had the largest percentage job loss of the 15 major industrial states. A declining economy also reduced state tax revenue and generated large budget deficits for several years.

These economic and fiscal problems helped elect William Weld, the state's first Republican governor in 20 years. After first focusing on the state's budget problems, Weld turned his attention to economic development issues in 1992, as the state's economic recession continued and the region's troubled banking industry, faced with large losses from bad real estate loans, drastically reduced credit availability.

As state officials sought economic development strategies, they naturally turned to stimulating Massachusetts's technology-based sectors. With strong research universities, numerous high-tech firms, and a large venture capital industry, the promotion of "emerging technologies" seemed a sound strategy. The emphasis on new technologies was also fostered by the recognition that Massachusetts needed new industries to replace tens of thousands of jobs lost in the region's minicomputer industry, facing obsolescence with the rise of personal computers. One industry that gained the attention of state economic development officials was biotechnology.

Massachusetts was one of the nation's leading biotechnology centers with many research hospitals and universities and over a hundred small biotechnology firms. Through the Massachusetts Biotechnology Council (MBC), this young industry was well organized and vocal in seeking state assistance to nurture its growth. Biotechnology firms were principally engaged in developing new pharmaceuticals and medical technologies, a process that required 10 or more years to complete and secure regulatory approval. During this period, biotech companies relied on successive rounds of equity financing, first from venture capitalists and then from public stock sales, to raise the several hundred million dollars needed to complete the process. Biotechnology firms also required costly R&D laboratories to develop their products and even more expensive pilot production plants to manufacture products for clinical trials. Seeking to preserve expensive equity capital, biotech firms approached banks for loans to construct these facilities. Bankers, however, were unwilling to finance them, given the biotech firms' uncertain future cash flow. Furthermore, with large losses from real estate loans, bankers did not relish lending for very costly buildings that could easily lose value if the demand for lab and pilot production space declined.

Frustrated with their inability to secure bank loans, MBC approached state officials. After meeting with biotech firms, banks, and developers, state economic development staff formulated the idea for an Emerging Technology Fund (ETF). This fund would provide loan guarantees to reduce the banks' risks in lending for specialized real estate facilities. Through a state guarantee fund (ETF), they concluded, a dollar of state funds could leverage several dollars in bank loans and help many firms invest in new facilities and create jobs. State officials also feared that a continued absence of real estate financing might lead biotech firms to invest in other states, a fear reinforced by Rhode Island's aggressive effort to attract biotech firms. Since the financing problems faced by biotech firms might exist for other emerging industries, the ETF legislation was drafted to allow the fund to provide loan guarantees to help emerging technology firms, not just biotechnology firms, finance specialized laboratories and plants. In September 1992, Governor Weld filed legislation to establish the ETF, with $30 million in initial capital, along with bills to establish two other economic development finance programs (an export loan guarantee program and a capital access program).

Faced with skepticism in the legislature, the ETF bill was changed to reduce its $30 million price tag. Senator Lois Pines, cochair of the legislature's Joint Committee on Commerce and Labor, was strongly committed to the ETF and sought ways to craft a viable bill. Working with the Massachusetts Government Land Bank, she prepared a new version of the ETF legislation, whereby the Land Bank used its existing income and assets to borrow $15 million to capitalize the ETF. The Senate passed this plan in December 1992 and it was signed into law as part of Chapter 19 of the Acts of 1993 in March.

The ETF Legislation

The ETF legislation provided a broad and flexible framework for the new program that primarily addressed governance issues and the nature of guarantees. It included the following provisions:

- Its mission is to "leverage private financing for state-of-the-art research and development or manufacturing facilities that are necessary for the commercial development of emerging technologies that will lead to greater employment opportunities and economic well being in the Commonwealth of Massachusetts."

- The ETF is a separate fund of the Government Land Bank with broad authority to use a range of financial instruments, called "Qualified Investments," to achieve its objectives.
- The initial $15 million capitalization and all subsequent income earned by the ETF has to stay within the fund and be used only to make Qualified Investments, to make payments to honor ETF guarantees, and to pay program administrative costs.
- An ETF Advisory Committee recommends ETF investments to the Land Bank Board of Directors for approval. This five-person committee includes the secretary of administration and finance, the secretary of economic affairs, two appointees of the Land Bank Board, and a fifth member appointed by the governor.
- All ETF investments also have to be approved by the secretary of administration and finance.
- All projects or transactions in which the ETF participates require the financial participation of at least two "at-risk private parties."
- A minimum reserve level equal to the greater of 30% of total outstanding guarantees or 2 years' worth of guaranteed payments has to be maintained.
- ETF guarantees are *not* supported by a full faith and credit pledge of Massachusetts. However, the law creates a process for further legislature appropriations up to $45 million to meet ETF guarantee obligations if its reserves prove insufficient.
- The Land Bank Board of Directors is directed to adopt program rules and regulations before any Qualified Investment can be made.

Designing the New Program

With the passage of Chapter 19, the Land Bank faced the task of implementing the ETF under close scrutiny from the Weld administration, the biotechnology industry, banks, and developers who hoped to benefit from it. The Land Bank needed to design the program in far greater detail, including key policies, investment processes, and staffing. There were three key implementation issues:

- Defining the program's targeting policy and eligibility criteria
- Establishing the terms and mechanics for how ETF guarantees would work
- Defining the application, commitment, and investment monitoring process

As the Land Bank's deputy director, you have been asked to prepare a memo that defines policy options for these three issues and makes a preliminary recommendation on the best option to advance the ETF mission and generate strong interest in the program among firms, lenders, and developers.

Consider how the lessons and experience from other guarantee programs apply to the ETF.

Endnotes

1. This article can be downloaded from the Web address http://rru.worldbank.org/ Toolkits/highways/documents/pdf/86.pdf

2. An explanation of the formula and its application can be found in Brealey and Myers (2002), Chapter 21, pp. 591–615, with put options covered on pp. 594–596. Almeyda and Hinojosa (2001) discuss how to use the Black-Scholes formula to value a partial loan guarantee for an infrastructure project (pp. 23–28).

3. Almeyda and Hinojosa (2001) discuss the application of the binomial tree method to a 1-year guarantee (pp. 28–30) and cite two articles that address extending this method to longer periods.

4. Under the 7(a) Export Working Capital Loan Program, the maximum guarantee is 90%.

5. A higher $1.25 million limit exists for guarantees under the International Trade Loan Program.

6. Fixed rate loans of $50,000 or more cannot exceed prime + 2.25% when the maturity is less than 7 years, and prime + 2.75% when the maturity is 7 years or more. Loans between $25,000 and $50,000 have maximum interest rates of prime + 3.25% for maturities of less than 7 years and prime + 3.75% when the maturity is 7 years or more. Loans of $25,000 or less have an interest rate limit of prime + 4.25% if the maturity is less than 7 years and prime + 4.75% if the maturity is 7 years or more.

7. A 1989 SBA study found that the processing time for preferred loans was one third of that for the certified loan program and one quarter of that for guaranteed loans (cited in GAO report GAO/RCED-92-124). A 1992 GAO study found that the rate of failed loans was lower for preferred loans (4.5%) compared to certified loans (10.2%) and regular loans (15.8%). This difference partly reflected the younger age of preferred loans; but even for loans with the same age, the failure rate for preferred loans was less than that of certified and regular loans.

8. The U.S. Economic Development Administration receives less than $400 million in appropriations while even the large Community Development Block Program had annual appropriations of $5 billion, only a fraction of which is used for economic development purposes. SBA 7(a) guarantees also exceeded the $8.4 billion in EXIM Bank guarantees, which serves many large businesses.

9. See Haynes (1996), pp. 360–361, which reports that firms receiving SBA-guaranteed loans, with an average age of 7.3 years, were younger than those of the general small business population, at a mean age of 11.7 years. SBA-guaranteed loans were granted to a larger share of minority-owned firms (13%) than all small businesses (8%).

10. The funding for these matching fees is set by the state or local government CAP appropriation and limits the total amount of CAP loans that can receive

matching fees for the loan loss reserve. When the appropriated funds are exhausted, an additional appropriation is needed to continue providing matching fees.

11. The original study was completed in May 1998 and then updated in November 1999. See U.S. Treasury Department (1999), *Capital Access Programs: A Summary of Nationwide Performance*.

12. CAP loan volumes for these three states in 1998 were $85 million in California, $52 million in Michigan, and $35 million in Massachusetts.

13. Haynes (1996) reports a 1.2% annual net loss on all commercial loans outstanding in 1987. Parzen and Kieschnick (1994) cite loan loss rates that vary from .69 to 2.89% for commercial bank loans and .19% to 2% for a range of financial institutions (pp. 135–138).

9 Banking Regulations and Development Banks

The Critical Role of Banks in Economic Development Finance

As the primary financial intermediary serving households and small businesses, banks are a critical development finance resource. They are the largest institutional source of debt for small businesses, and with a widespread geographic presence and retail offices, banks are better positioned than other capital market intermediaries to overcome information and transaction cost barriers to capital availability. Moreover, as publicly insured depository institutions, banks have access to a large supply of low-cost deposits accompanied by public charters and regulations that shape how they deploy this capital. This regulatory oversight provides an accountability mechanism that governments, community reinvestment advocates, and development finance professionals can use to change banking practices and expand capital for economic and community development purposes. Under the Community Reinvestment Act (CRA), banks must serve the banking and credit needs of their entire service area, including low- and moderate-income households, small businesses, and small farms. Over the past 20 years, the CRA has been an important federal policy and local development tool to expand housing and community economic development investment in many communities. This chapter begins with an overview of the act followed by a discussion of how the CRA is used to expand capital availability. The growing literature on the CRA's impact on bank lending and the relative profitability of CRA loans versus conventional lending is also reviewed in the first section. Although this research focuses on home mortgage lending, it is relevant for economic development finance in two ways. First, it indicates whether CRA is effective in changing bank credit practices to remedy market failures and capital supply gaps. If CRA can address these problems in housing credit markets, then it offers promises to improve capital availability for small firms and economic development projects. Second, this research reveals lessons and effective approaches to expanding bank lending that are applicable to economic development practice. One critique of the CRA is that it does not apply to financial assets controlled by nonbanking institutions, including insurance and investment subsidiaries that banks can establish under the 1999 Graham-Leach-Bliley Act. Since Massachusetts is the first state to apply community reinvestment requirements to the insurance industry, the early experience with this policy is discussed as a precedent for new frontiers in community reinvestment practice.

Banks also have considerable flexibility to innovate and supply higher-risk loans and investments. Bank Community Development Corporation (CDC) regulations allow federally regulated banks to undertake lending, development, and investment activities that fall outside standard banking practices. Practitioners need to be familiar with these regulations and how to apply them to development finance needs in their communities. Thus, the second part of this chapter is devoted to bank CDCs.

Rather than using regulatory policies to change conventional banks, some entrepreneurs have acquired or established banks to achieve economic and community development goals. A well-known example is ShoreBank,[1] an existing commercial bank that was acquired and converted into a "community development bank" focused on revitalizing Chicago's South Shore neighborhood. In the third section, the ShoreBank model is examined along with approaches used by other community development banks. Special issues and requirements related to operating a regulated community development bank are also reviewed in this section.

The Community Reinvestment Act

History and Overview of the Community Reinvestment Act

Although the *Community Reinvestment Act* (CRA) was enacted in 1977 as an immediate response to bank "redlining" practices that withdrew credit and banking services from entire areas of cities, it was also an outgrowth of the civil rights movement and efforts to eliminate housing discrimination.[2] After the Federal Fair Housing Act of 1968 prohibited discrimination in the sale and rental of housing, courts interpreted this right to include appraisal practices and the provision of credit for housing (Squires, 1993). In response to poor enforcement of the federal fair housing laws and the limited availability of data to document discrimination in home mortgage lending, civil rights and neighborhood activists advocated for congressional passage of the *Home Mortgage Disclosure Act* (HMDA), which was enacted in 1975 (Squires, 1993). HMDA required federally chartered banks, savings banks, and credit unions to report annually on the number of home mortgage loans made by census tract in every metropolitan area. The Financial Institution Reform, Recovery and Enforcement Act (FIRREA) of 1989, passed to address severe financial problems in the savings and loan industry, extended HMDA disclosure requirements to mortgage banks, and required the reporting of mortgage loan applications along with the applicant's race, gender, and income. HMDA was a breakthrough bill for community reinvestment as it provided data that allowed civil rights and neighborhood activists to document actual home mortgage lending in each neighborhood and demonstrate that de facto "redlining" was occurring in many cities. This information helped persuade Congress that action was needed to address "redlining," which led to passage of the CRA. HMDA continues to be a key tool for monitoring home mortgage lending to identify potential redlining and other discriminatory lending practices and then to use this information to alter banking policies and practices (Belsky et al., 2000).

CRA established an affirmative requirement in federal law that banks[3] provide credit to their entire service area, including low- and moderate-income (LMI) neighborhoods and directed bank regulators to assess bank performance in meeting this requirement (Haag, 2000; Marsico, 2002). More importantly, the law authorizes and requires bank regulators[4] to use their supervisory authority to "encourage" banks to comply with the CRA requirement to meet community credit needs. Regulatory enforcement of the CRA takes two forms: (1) regular examinations of bank CRA performance; and (2) consideration of a bank's CRA record when reviewing applications for bank expansion and other regulatory actions (Haag, 2000; Marsico, 2002).[5]

CRA is also a regulatory response to market failure that promises to improve the efficiency of banking markets and expand the supply of credit and other financial services to low-income communities. Three types of market imperfections are addressed through CRA requirements. First, CRA promotes competition to serve low- and moderate-income areas, which helps ensure the supply of credit and financial services at fair prices within these communities.[6] Second, CRA seeks to overcome statistical discrimination or misinformation that can lead banks to perceive low- and moderate-income areas, small businesses, or other categories of customers as unprofitable markets. By requiring banks to serve these markets and regularly testing their performance in these markets, CRA is a countervailing influence on discriminatory behavior. Moreover, through motivating banks to gain experience and knowledge in serving these markets, CRA contributes to reducing information costs that impair the supply of financial services. Finally, CRA can be viewed as a way to address externalities that result from the failure to supply capital and banking services to certain areas;[7] in this sense CRA requires banks to internalize some of these external social costs in return for receiving a public banking charter and access to federal deposit insurance. When research on how CRA has affected bank lending is reviewed later in this chapter, we shall see evidence that CRA has helped to reverse these market imperfections.

In its first 15 years, CRA enforcement had limited impact on bank lending practices. Regulators emphasized banks' processes in identifying and responding to community credit needs[8] and did not uniformly apply CRA standards (Belsky et al., 2000). CRA gained greater import in the 1990s for several reasons. First, FIRREA required public disclosure of CRA ratings for the first time. Second, bank regulators in the Clinton administration increased attention to CRA enforcement and adopted new regulations in 1995 that established more consistent and outcome-based CRA rating standards (Belsky et al., 2000; Haag, 2000). Third, community organizations, civil rights, and advocacy groups became more active and effective in using CRA to secure community development lending and other commitments from banks (NCRC, 1999). Fourth, as industry consolidation and mergers grew, bank executives recognized that good CRA ratings reduced the chance of regulatory denials and mitigated community opposition (Belsky et al., 2000; Haag 2002).

Under CRA regulations,[9] a bank first defines an assessment area that corresponds to the geographic regions that it serves. An assessment area usually corresponds to entire metropolitan areas or political jurisdictions where the bank has its headquarters, branches, and ATMs, and where it makes a large share of it loans. Assessment areas cannot be defined in a way that excludes low- and moderate-income areas (Marsico, 2002). Bank regulators conduct periodic examinations of bank activities within their assessment areas and then issue a report and CRA rating based on the examination. One of five CRA ratings is provided: Outstanding, High Satisfactory, Low Satisfactory, Needs to Improve, and Substantial Noncompliance. CRA ratings are public and can be obtained through the Federal Financial Institutions Examination Council (FFIEC) Web site (www.ffiec.gov).[10] Under the 1995 CRA regulations, federal bank examiners use different CRA assessment criteria to rate three types of banks: small banks (assets below $250 million), large banks, and wholesale and limited purpose banks.[11] Since large banks are the primary focus for CRA enforcement, this section addresses CRA performance criteria for these banks. CRA ratings for large banks are based on three tests: (1) a lending test that assesses bank lending for home mortgages, small businesses, small farms, and community development; (2) a service test that covers retail banking and community development services; and (3) an investment test that covers grants, donations, and innovative financing for community development purposes. A specific rating and numerical score is provided for each test. The final CRA rating is based on the combined score from the three tests. Table 9.1 summarizes the specific data and measures used to conduct these tests. Banks can also prepare a strategic CRA plan, in consultation with community groups, that sets alternative standards and benchmarks for CRA rating, but few banks have used this option.

Despite improvements over the earlier assessment rules, several CRA advocates criticize the current CRA examination and rating system. Marsico cites several shortfalls that prevent CRA examinations from providing a full picture of how well a bank addresses community credit needs. These shortfalls include not evaluating race-based lending patterns, reliance on subjective examiner judgments rather than standard quantitative measures and benchmarks, not considering either the volume of applications received or application denial

Table 9.1   Performance Measures Used in CRA Ratings for Large Banks

Lending Test	Service Test	Investment Test
Number and amount of loans in AA.	**Distribution of branches** among low-, moderate-, middle-, and high-income areas.	**Dollar amount of qualified investments.**
Geography of loans: (1) % in AA; (2) dispersion in AA; and (3) number and amount by low-, moderate-, middle-, and high-income areas.	**Record of opening and closing branches,** especially ones in LMI areas or that serve LMI individuals.	**Innovative nature and complexity** of qualified investments.
Distribution by borrower characteristics: (1) number and amount of HMLs to low-, moderate-, middle-, and high-income individuals; (2) number and amount of small business and small farm loans; and (3) optional: number and amount of CLs to low-, moderate-, middle-, and high-income individuals.	**Availability and effectiveness of alternative systems** for providing retail banking services in LMI areas and to LMI individuals.	**Area of Benefit:** qualified investments must benefit the AA or a larger area (state or region) that includes the AA.
Community development loans: (1) number and amount; (2) complexity and innovation.	**Range of services provided** in each type of area and extent to which services are tailored to meet area needs.	**Fill private investment gaps:** degree to which qualified investments are not routinely provided by private investors.
Innovative or flexible practices	**Community development services:** extent of services and their degree of innovation and responsiveness.	
Optional: consideration of lending by affiliates, consortiums, or related third parties.		**Optional:** qualified investments by an affiliate bank if not claimed by other institution.

SOURCE: Federal Reserve Bank of Dallas (n.d.)

AA = assessment areas, HML= home mortgage loan, CL = consumer loans

rates across communities, letting banks decide whether to include affiliate lending activities in the examination, and using too few banks as a basis for comparing bank lending records (Marsico, 2002). A more comprehensive and objective three-part method for evaluating CRA lending is proposed by Marsico:[12] (1) comparing lending activity in four types of "subject communities" (LMI neighborhoods, minority neighborhoods, LMI households, and minority households) to a comparison control community with opposite characteristics; (2) using loan applications, originations, and denials as the quantitative performance measures; and (3) assessing CRA performance by comparing a bank's market share of applications and originations and its denial rates in subject communities to that in control communities and to the respective averages for all lenders in the metropolitan area (Marsico, 2002). Immergluck (1997), on the other hand, does not criticize the CRA assessment methodology but rather questions regulators' high rating of virtually all banks under the new CRA rating system. When he compared CRA ratings for 101 banks under the old and new CRA rating systems, Immergluck found that ratings were unchanged for 71% of the banks, improved for 14%, and downgraded for 16%.[13] Despite some downgrading, 92% of these banks received an outstanding or satisfactory rating, compared with 97% for all 1995 CRA ratings. Moreover, Immergluck found lending test ratings were particularly high and expressed concern that regulators are lenient in this evaluation since it is weighed heavily in the overall CRA ratings. Consequently, banks can receive a satisfactory CRA rating even when they receive substantial noncompliance ratings on the other tests, which creates an incentive for lenders to neglect improvements to banking services and community development investments in LMI neighborhoods.

The 1995 CRA regulations also required banks to disclose small business and small farm loans by census tract, which began in 1997. This data helps community activists and development finance professionals assess bank performance in addressing economic development credit needs and should increase attention to expanding small business credit. However, the small business and small farm data is far less comprehensive than HMDA data since it does not include loan applications or detail the race, gender, or income of the loan recipient.

Using CRA to Expand Capital Availability

Community-based coalitions[14] in the 1980s and 1990s organized around redlining and advocated for expanded banking services and lending in low-income areas and to minorities. Coalitions researched and disclosed information on bank lending, intervened in regulatory hearings over proposed bank expansions and acquisitions, and advocated for expanded bank lending, services, and other practices to address the needs of low-income and minority communities. These efforts typically led to formal CRA agreements whereby banks agreed to provide certain credit products and banking services to target areas or types of borrowers and committed to specific dollar goals for each loan type. Some CRA agreements encompass other bank practices, such as changes to loan terms, underwriting standards, expanded marketing activities, and minority employment and contracting. Most CRA agreements are negotiated between banks and community coalitions, advocacy groups, or governments, but some banks—often large regional or national ones engaged in a merger or acquisition—announce them voluntarily (NCRC, 1999). According to the National Community Reinvestment Coalition (NCRC), over 360 CRA agreements committed $1.05 trillion to community development

Table 9.2   Economic Development Commitments in Bank CRA Agreements

Bank	CRA Group	Year of Agreement	Key Provisions
Northern Trust	Chicago Reinvestment Alliance	1984	$5 million over 5 years for purchase and rehab of mixed-use properties in LMI areas.
Chicago NBD	Chicago CRA Coalition	1998	5,190 small business loans over 6 years in LMI neighborhoods.
Washington Mutual	California Reinvestment Committee/ Green-lining Institute	1991	$25 billion in small business loans over 10 years; 75% for $50,000 or less; $9 billion targeted to firms in Enterprise Zones and to minority-, women-, and disabled-owned businesses.
Union Planter National Bank	Shelby County Community Reinvestment Coalition	1990	$6 million loan pool for long-term loans to commercial real estate projects in LMI census tracts.
Wells Fargo Bank	California Reinvestment Committee/Green-lining Institute	1995	$25 billion for small business loans with most devoted to loans of $50,000 or less.
First Interstate Bank	Montana's People Action	1990	Help create small business incubator with seed grant and technical assistance.
Chemical Bank and Manufacturers Hanover Trust	New Jersey Fair Banking Initiative Coalition	1991	$7.5 million over 5 years for economic development initiatives in targeted urban areas.
Home Savings of America	California Reinvestment Committee/Green-lining Institute	1998	$3.5 million in SBA, Capital Access, and other government-guaranteed small business loans.
Shawmut Bank	Massachusetts Affordable Housing Alliance	1990	$1 million in capital and $10 million in credit to a minority business financing entity.
NBD Bank	Detroit Alliance for Fair Banking	1998	Buy $15 million over 3 years from African American vendors.

SOURCE: National Community Reinvestment Coalition (1997).

lending from 1977 to 1998. Housing, especially single family home mortgage lending, is the largest and most common focus of CRA agreements, but they address other issues that include business and economic development; consumer loans; community capacity building; banking services and branches; hiring and procurement policies; and community marketing, outreach, and accountability. Examples of economic development-related commitments in CRA agreements are presented in Table 9.2.

CRA agreements increased in number and size in the late 1990s due to stronger regulatory enforcement, more frequent and larger bank mergers, and increased effectiveness among CRA coalitions. Banks often entered into these agreements to forestall community opposition to proposed expansions, acquisitions, or mergers. In other cases, CRA agreements were a way for banks to correct documented redlining or racial disparities in mortgage lending and avoid negative publicity and public perceptions (Schwartz, 1998; Squires, 1993). With growing industry consolidation and greater experience with community development lending, banks become more proactive in their CRA activities. Instead of responding to CRA coalition proposals, several banks announced their own CRA investment programs as part of proposed mergers. For example, Bank of America announced a $350 billion 10-year CRA program as part of its merger with NationsBank, and Citigroup offered a $115 billion CRA initiative as part of the 1998 merger of Citibank and Travelers Insurance (Haag, 2000).

CRA practice has two critical components: (1) organizing an effective campaign to gain CRA commitments that address community needs; and (2) collaborating with banks to implement CRA agreements and improve ongoing credit availability and banking services. Case studies of individual CRA campaigns and comparative research on CRA practice provide insight into best practices for both activities. John T. Metzger documented several effective practices for CRA campaigns in his case study of the Pittsburgh Community Reinvestment Group (PCRG).[15] PCRG was created as a citywide coalition of almost 20 community-based organizations in 1987 in response to the proposed merger between the holding company for Union National Bank (UNB) and Pennbancorp.[16] An initial analysis of HMDA data showed that UNB made no home purchase loans to Pittsburgh's 36 majority African American census tracts during 1986 and 1987 and only two such loans in the city's 102 low- and moderate-income census tracts in 1987. One of PCRG's first steps was having member organizations assess credit needs in their neighborhood and then prepare a 5-year lending plan to address these needs. These neighborhood plans were aggregated into a $109 million citywide reinvestment plan that PCRG presented to UNB when it sought regulatory approval for its proposed merger. After originally rejecting PCRG's plan, UNB changed course and accepted the full plan in June 1998. According to Metzger, two PCRG tactics contributed to this outcome. First, PCRG kept the presiding bank regulators informed about their concerns and negotiations with UNB. Second, the coalition let UNB management know that it was prepared to file a public protest against the merger and release data on UNB's lending history to the media if the negotiations were not fruitful. UNB's hiring of a new CEO and vice president for community development was also instrumental in changing the bank's course. The final CRA agreement committed UNB to provide $55 million in home mortgage loans, $6 million in home improvement loans, $8 million in small business loans over 5 years, and $40 million in real estate loans without a time limit. The $55 million in home mortgage loans included provisions to improve access for low- and moderate-income households, including a 50-basis-point rate reduction, no origination points, loan-to-value ratios up to 95 %, and higher allowable debt-to-income ratios.

PCRG worked closely with UNB to implement the CRA agreement. A community development advisory committee with PCRG and UNB representatives met monthly to monitor progress and reported quarterly to UNB's board of directors. The committee developed marketing initiatives to generate demand for the CRA lending programs[17] and helped UNB develop a training program on community economic development attended by over 100 bank employees. The advisory committee also revised lending targets and eligible areas based on program experience, expanding the service area to include low- and moderate-income neighborhoods in greater Pittsburgh and increasing lending targets to $188 million. After two and one-half years, over 1,300 loans totaling $71.2 million were made, or 65% of the original $109 million target. The small business lending and home improvement components were particularly successful, exceeding their goals by 362% and 28%, respectively. Following the successful UNB agreement, PCRG expanded its work by forming CRA oversight committees with additional banks. Rather than pursuing large lending targets, these committees created new programs and lending products to address additional community credit needs, expanded community outreach and credit counseling services, and provided operating grants for PCRG (Metzger, 1992; Schwartz, 1998). Three new housing-related loan programs at Pittsburgh National Bank, Mellon Bank, and Equibank in 1989 and 1990 emerged from these committees. PCRG also received $100,000 in annual funds from the four banks to support its ongoing work to monitor community credit needs, advocate for new programs and services, and help banks to market and improve CRA programs.

Alex Schwartz studied the implementation of CRA agreements in Cleveland, Chicago, New Jersey, and Pittsburgh to identify their accomplishments and the factors that contributed to successful agreements (Schwartz, 1998). From interviews with community organizations, banks, and other stakeholders, he found that banks were most successful in four areas: (1) meeting CRA targets for single-family home mortgage lending; (2) investing in low-income housing development; (3) providing grants to community organizations; and (4) creating and retaining branches in low-income communities. Banks in all four places met or exceeded home mortgage lending goals in most years. In Pittsburgh, 12 banks doubled their loans to African American households from 1991 to 1994, as their approval rates grew from 28% to 62%. Community coalitions were less satisfied with the fulfillment of real estate and small business lending goals. Chicago reported the most success in reaching CRA goals in these areas, partly because their CRA agreements designated community organizations to help firms and developers assess project feasibility, provide technical assistance, and prepare the documentation required to secure loan approval. Provisions for increased bank hiring of minorities and contracting with minority-owned firms in two cities did not achieve their goals and received less attention than bank lending and branch targets. Bank officials and community advocates credited CRA agreements with realizing two key outcomes beyond their formal goals: (1) getting banks to rediscover profitable inner city markets; and

(2) fostering effective partnerships between banks, city government, and community groups to address community development and credit needs.

Successful CRA agreements require special implementation and monitoring efforts. Schwartz cited three success factors for CRA agreements: (1) community coalitions having dedicated staff to monitor and enforce CRA agreements, including ongoing analysis of HMDA data and the progress reports prepared by banks; (2) extensive marketing and community outreach by banks and community organizations to expand awareness of new lending products and services available under CRA agreements; and (3) specialized lending units with strong community development expertise to handle real estate and small business loans while training and utilizing all bank branches to provide the single-family mortgage loan products provided under CRA agreements (Schwartz, 1998). Another study cited active involvement in implementation by bank CEOs and strong working relationships between banks and community groups as critical to successful CRA agreements (Haag, 2000).

CRA's Impact on Bank Lending

Given the large effort entailed in securing and implementing CRA agreements, it is important to ask how these agreements affect banking practices. One part of this question concerns whether banks do, in fact, increase lending to low-income and minority borrowers and communities, or simply place loans that they would otherwise provide under a new CRA umbrella. Because overall home mortgage lending to low-income and minority borrowers increased at much higher rates than lending to upper-income and white households during the 1990s (Haag, 2000), this outcome may reflect national market and banking trends rather than the role of CRA regulations and agreements. A second question is whether CRA-based lending is subsidized lending that is accepted as a cost of securing regulatory approval for bank expansions, or represents a newfound profitable market. If the first situation is true, banks are more likely to reduce or abandon products and services developed under CRA agreements when regulatory scrutiny and political pressures abate. On the other hand, if CRA activities establish profitable businesses for banks, they are more likely to generate a lasting change in capital availability. Studies that address these questions conclude that CRA agreements do increase home mortgage lending to low-income and minority borrowers and that many types of CRA lending, and particularly small business lending, are as profitable as conventional lending.

Three types of evidence support the conclusion that CRA regulations and agreements have expanded lending to low-income and minority borrowers and neighborhoods. First, bankers themselves state that CRA led them to rediscover and serve the inner city market. In both case-study research on CRA agreements (Schwartz, 1998) and discussion groups on CRA lending in four cities (Belsky et al., 2000), bankers reported that the CRA process changed lending practices and ways of doing business. Important changes included establishing community development departments or units that focus on serving low- and moderate-income communities; providing more complex and innovative lending to address community development needs; forming partnerships with community groups to provide outreach, counseling and technical assistance that reduce banks' costs to serve low- and moderate-income borrowers, and funding intermediaries that provide "wholesale" financing to community development projects, organizations, and community-based financial institutions (Belsky et al., 2000; Haag, 2000). A survey of 143 large retail banks conducted by the Federal Reserve Board of Governors confirms these results (BOGFRS, 2000). Most banks reported finding new profitable business opportunities in home mortgages (63%), home improvement loans (71%), and small business lending (81%) from CRA-related lending efforts. Most banks had created at least one special CRA-lending program and established special lending units or departments to manage these CRA programs.[18] Moreover, 74% of the banks listed obtaining a "Satisfactory" or "Outstanding" CRA as a reason for establishing these programs, and 95% indicated "responding to the credit needs of the local community" (i.e., the governing CRA standard) as a reason for creating new CRA lending programs. This "testimony" from bankers indicates that CRA advanced more efficient capital supply by reversing discrimination or misperceptions that forestalled lending in low-income and minority areas and generating new practices that reduce information and transaction costs to serve these markets.

A second indicator that CRA agreements change lending behavior is found in two studies, which found that banks with CRA agreements had a greater market share in home mortgage lending to low-income and minority borrowers than banks without CRA agreements. Schwartz compared banks' market share of home mortgage loans to certain types of borrowers and census tracts within a metropolitan area to their overall market share in the region (Schwartz, 1998). For banks with CRA agreements, their market share of mortgage loans in low-income and high-minority census tracts exceeded their total regional market share by 40% and 30%, respectively. Among black and Hispanic borrowers across the metro region, their market shares were 18% and 16% above their total regional share, respectively. On the other hand, banks without CRA agreements had market shares in home mortgage loans among low-income and minority borrowers that were 20% to 30% below their overall regional level, and their market shares in high-minority and low-income tracts were also below their regional market share. In all these cases, the difference in relative market shares between banks with and without CRA agreements was statistically significant.[19] A second study[20] reached mixed conclusions on the impact of CRA agreements. Banks with CRA agreements had larger increases in home mortgage lending to low-income and minority individuals and neighborhoods than banks without agreements. However, when the author compared home mortgage lending trends from 1990 to 1995 in three cities with multiple CRA agreements to trends in cities without CRA agreements, loans to low-income and minority households and areas grew at a faster rate than overall home mortgage lending in both types of cities. The author concluded that a positive market environment and the national CRA regulatory climate, rather than specific CRA agreements, led banks to expand home mortgage lending to low-income and minority markets (Haag, 2000). A third form of evidence on the impact of CRA agreements is found in Campen's analysis (see Haag, 2000) of home mortgage lending in Boston from 1990 to 1997, which documented the share of citywide home mortgage lending made under CRA agreements. During this period, the market share of home mortgage loans in Boston received by low-income households and combined low- and moderate-income households increased from 2.8% to 10.1% and from 22.4% to 34.7%, respectively.[21] Lending under three CRA agreements accounted for a large portion of these loans, ranging from 13% in 1993 to almost 30% in 1995 to 1997 (Haag, 2000).

Several studies[22] have analyzed differences in loss rates, repayment, and returns for CRA-related lending, but this literature almost exclusively addresses home mortgage lending and uses proxies for CRA loans or definitions that do not match those in CRA regulations (BOGFRS, 2000). However, the Board of Governors of the Federal Reserve System (BOGFRS) conducted a comprehensive study of CRA-related lending, as mandated by the Graham-Leach-Bliley Act. The study, based on surveys from 143 of the 500 largest retail banks, provides data on the 1999 return on equity, delinquency rates, and charge-off rates for CRA-related lending[23] and non-CRA lending across four categories: (1) home purchases and refinancing; (2) home improvement; (3) small businesses; and (4) community development (BOGFRS, 2000). Since most banks do not separately calculate the return and performance of CRA versus non-CRA lending, the study focuses on banks' qualitative assessment of their relative profits, delinquencies, and losses from CRA-related loans. Table 9.3 summarizes the results for home mortgage, home improvement, and small business loans. The results show that CRA-related lending is profitable for over 80% of banks across all three loan types with at least half of lenders reporting that CRA-loans are at least as profitable as non-CRA ones. Small business CRA loans are profitable for a larger share of banks and have better relative profitability and performance than CRA housing loans. Almost all lenders (96%) report that CRA small business loans are profitable with 86% indicating that these loans generate equal or higher returns than non-CRA loans. CRA small business loans also perform similarly to their non-CRA counterparts with the reported differences in average delinquency and charge-off rates very small. In fact, lenders reported lower average delinquency rates for CRA small business loans. On the other hand, the greatest discrepancies between CRA and non-CRA lending profitability occurred with home mortgage lending. Almost

Table 9.3   Relative Profits and Performance of CRA-Related and Non-CRA Small Business and Housing Loans

Measure	Small Business Loans	Home Purchase/ Refinance Loans	Home Improvement Loans
Percentage of lenders stating CRA loans are profitable[a]	96%	82%	86%
Percentage of lenders stating CRA loans have equal or higher returns than non-CRA loans	86%	56%	72%
Mean difference in ROE	−.1%	−1.8%	−1.3%
Median difference in ROE	0	0	0
Mean difference in % of loans delinquent 30 to 89 days	−.03	1.02	.24
Percentage of lenders stating CRA loans had equal or lower 30–89-day delinquency rates	90%	49%	53%
Mean difference in % of loans delinquent 90 days or longer	−.05	.78	−.01
Percentage of lenders stating CRA loans had equal or lower 90-day or longer delinquency rates	92%	52%	76%
Mean difference in loan charge-off rates	.05	.08	.23
Median difference in loan charge-off rates	−.04	0	.01
Percentage of lenders stating CRA loans had equal or lower charge-off rates	84%	69%	72%

SOURCE: BOGFRS (2000, Tables 3a, 3c, 4a, 4c, 5a, 5c).

NOTE:

a. The table row sums the percentage from two responses: "Profitable" and "Marginally Profitable." The responses for "Profitable" alone are 85%, 50%, and 63%, respectively.

half (46%) of the banks responded that CRA home mortgage loans were less profitable than non-CRA loans. On average, banks cited returns on CRA loans that were 1.8% lower than for other home mortgage loans. However, this disparity in profitability does not occur for at least half of the banks since the median difference in returns was zero. Banks reported higher delinquency rates for CRA home mortgage and home improvement loans, with almost 50% indicating that CRA-related loans had higher 30- to 89-day delinquency rates. Discrepancies in loan charge-off rates are far less. Only 30% of banks stated that charge-off rates were higher for CRA-related loans, and the median difference in charge-off rates was zero for home mortgage loans and .01% higher for home improvement loans. In light of the large disparities in income and assets between low- and moderate-income households and middle- and high-income borrowers, these differences in the performance of CRA housing loans are quite small.

The Federal Reserve study shows that CRA lending is profitable for most lenders. Consequently, the housing and small business lending markets in low- and moderate-income and minority communities uncovered through the CRA process are sound business opportunities that should be sustainable without subsidies. However, ongoing advocacy and collaboration is needed to keep banks focused on and responsive to these markets. Moreover, the particularly strong profitability and performance of CRA small business lending suggests that banks have a strong market incentive to sustain and expand small business lending in low- and moderate-income neighborhoods. Economic development practitioners have a strong case both to convince banks that expanded small business lending will be profitable and to elevate the role of small business initiatives in CRA agreements.

Critiques of CRA

Although many studies report positive outcomes from the Community Reinvestment Acts, several arguments against the continued need for CRA regulations have been made. Apgar and Duda (2002), in their twenty-fifth anniversary study of the CRA, group these arguments in three categories:[24] (1) that strong competition in current credit markets will prevent discrimination and the withdrawal of credit from low-income and minority communities; (2) that CRA is neither an appropriate nor efficient remedy for addressing discriminatory practices against individual borrowers; and (3) that past market failures, if they existed at all, have now been corrected. In the first argument, lenders that practice discrimination are presumed to miss profitable market opportunities and lose market share to nondiscriminatory competitors who gain profits serving these markets. Sufficient banking competition, therefore, offers a self-correcting mechanism to eliminate discriminatory credit practices via the competitive advantage gained by not practicing discrimination. Apgar and Duda (2002) point out that discrimination may add to profits when it is less costly to gauge creditworthiness by a statistical group characteristic rather than by individually underwriting each borrower. Moreover, they find that many studies and statistical evidence used in court cases show that discriminatory lending practices still exist, notwithstanding countervailing competitive pressures. Since discrimination in providing credit is illegal under civil rights and bank laws, the second argument views existing remedies under these laws as the appropriate way to address discrimination. The relatively small number of discrimination complaints in which lenders were found guilty is also cited as evidence that discriminatory credit practices are not widespread, thus, do not warrant an additional regulatory remedy.[25] However, this argument ignores the possibility that many applicants either are unaware that they were victims of discrimination or lack confidence that available legal remedies are effective (Apgar & Duda, 2002). Since CRA seeks to proactively change bank behavior rather than remedy individual discrimination cases, it promises a more efficient policy remedy that prevents discrimination and its costs in the first place while addressing the problem at the industrywide level. A third group of authors believe that expanded competition and improved technology have removed barriers to serving low-income communities, and thus CRA is no longer necessary. This case against CRA ignores that market failures may still exist despite these improvements, overlooks that disclosures under HMDA and CRA increase information on low-income markets, and that CRA contributed to expanded competition to serve low-income markets (Apgar and Duda, 2002). There is also no guarantee that the current competition for low-income markets will continue as the banking industry and credit markets undergo far-reaching changes.

CRA has also been criticized for imposing high costs on banks. Besides the direct cost of administrative compliance, critics argue that CRA imposes two other costs. First, some argue that CRA agreements represent a "merger tax" on banks that activists can extract from banks during the regulatory process (Brannon, 2001). Second, when banks make less profitable loans to comply with CRA requirements, this represents an additional cost burden.[26] Although CRA may well impose these costs on banks, they need to be quantified and compared to the benefits generated by CRA to evaluate whether they represent a significant shortcoming of the law.

New Challenges for the Community Reinvestment Act

With profound changes in the financial services industry over the past two decades, practitioners face a new context for using the CRA. One critical change is the growing role of financial institutions that are not subject to CRA regulations in managing financial assets and supplying credit (Apgar & Duda, 2002; Haag, 2000). As savings held outside of depository institutions increase, the pool of capital accountable to CRA regulatory standards declines. Moreover, nonbank institutions make a sizable share of loans in several lending markets[27] including conventional home mortgage and home improvement loans, commercial real estate lending, and small business finance. These trends raise the issue of whether laws and regulations should be altered to establish standards for other financial institutions to address the credit and financial services needs of LMI households, rural and low-income areas, small businesses, and other underserved groups. Evidence of statistical discrimination or other market imperfections faced by these other institutions is one rationale for such amendments. A few studies have compared home mortgage lending by mortgage banks, which are not subject to CRA, to that for depository institutions subject to CRA, yielding mixed findings. Some studies reported comparable lending rates to low-income or minority neighborhoods and borrowers for depository institutions and mortgage banks, but a study of home mortgage lending in Boston during 1997 found that mortgage banks accounted for much lower shares of loans to low-income and minority borrowers than their 54% share of all home purchase loans. A second argument for extending CRA regulations to non-depository institutions is to ensure common standards and rules for all financial institutions, which are increasingly competing to supply similar products and services. Mortgage banks, insurance companies, and other nonbank lenders should compete with banks on a level playing field where they have the same responsibility to meet the credit and financial service needs of the entire community, and incur the same costs and advantages presented by CRA requirements. Massachusetts' insurance industry CRA initiative, discussed below, demonstrates one early approach to extending CRA-type requirements to additional segments of the financial services industry.

A second set of challenges concerns the consolidation and growing size of banks. Bank mergers create new opportunities to negotiate CRA agreements, but they can weaken commitments to prior agreements negotiated by the acquired banks and disrupt relationships between bank officials, local activists, and community development practitioners (Schwartz, 1998). When mergers require practitioners to build relationships with new executives, lenders, and branch managers, additional work must be undertaken simply to sustain prior CRA initiatives. Moreover, as banks grow to encompass national or multistate markets, CRA lending programs shift from the city level to a regional and national scale. In large mergers, banks define their own mega-CRA commitments, which may be neither responsive to local credit gaps nor closely allied with the agendas of local government and community coalitions. The largest banks seek products and investments that will yield a high volume of CRA lending and investments and often channel them through intermediaries that offer wholesale-level investment scale and efficiency (Belsky et al., 2000; Haag, 2000). With bank CRA initiatives operating on a national scale, CRA advocacy and partnerships also need to transcend city and state lines to be effective. There is some progress in this respect with national development finance organizations working with large banks to create new investment vehicles. National Community Capital and Citibank, for example, created an equity equivalent investment vehicle for CDFIs (Haag, 2000). Creating coalitions that can negotiate, monitor, and implement multidimensional CRA initiatives on a regional and national scale is a complex undertaking that requires local practitioners to become active in shaping the agendas of national coalitions and trade associations, while still working with bank managers in their community to implement national and regional CRA programs locally. CRA activists also need to monitor capital and financial service gaps in more communities and advocate for more far-reaching and multifaceted CRA agendas that respond to the diverse conditions and needs across large regions.

Community Reinvestment and the Insurance Industry

One response to the declining share of savings managed by banks is extending CRA-type requirements to other financial institutions. Massachusetts pioneered this approach by linking tax reform to the insurance industry's economic and community development investments. The first such initiative occurred in 1978 when the Massachusetts Capital Resource Company (MCRC) was established as part of a state law to shift industry taxes from a gross income to a profit-based formula (Osborne, 1999). In exchange for this tax change, life insurance companies had to invest $100 million over 5 years in MCRC, which was mandated by statute to make higher-risk loans and investments in Massachusetts firms. For over 25 years, MCRC has provided subordinate financing to traditional manufacturing and technology-based firms. MCRC financing serves firms with good growth prospects that are too risky for conventional lenders but do not satisfy the high return expectations of venture capitalists and provides financing in smaller amounts and with longer terms than private mezzanine funds. In 1998, following a multiyear advocacy effort, Massachusetts passed the Insurance Investment Act, extending the MCRC approach to community reinvestment (Luquetta & Thrash, 2000). Under the act,[28] two investment funds were created, one for the life insurance industry ("the Life Initiative") and one for the property and casualty industry ("the Property and Casualty Initiative") with each industry required to contribute $100 million to their respective fund over 5 years. Each fund invests its capital as loans, equity, credit enhancements, or securities in seven types of qualified investments designated by the law: (1) minority-owned firms; (2) women-owned firms; (3) small businesses with less than $5 million in revenue; (4) housing targeted to low- and moderate-income households or communities; (5) community health centers serving LMI areas; (6) job creation initiatives for LMI households; and (7) investments in two state quasi-public intermediaries. In return for investments in the initiatives, insurers received special tax benefits.[29] Organized as limited liability corporations with a 24-year life, each fund will reinvest their capital for the first 20 years and then return it to investors over the last 4 years. The state insurance commissioner oversees the act by reviewing and certifying that investments comply with the statute before insurance companies can receive reduced tax rates (Luquetta & Thrash, 2000).

In their first 4 years, the experience of each fund has differed. Life insurance companies contributed the full $80 million in capital to the Life Initiative allowing it to make $83 million in financing commitments through December 2002.[30] One early focus for the Life Initiative was loans to development finance entities, with 58% of the value of commitments in the first 3 years made to local and regional financing programs. This was especially true for economic development transactions, where 77% went to intermediaries versus direct investment in firms or projects. The Property and Casualty Initiative (PCI) has raised less capital, ($65.6 million versus the $80 million goal in its first 4 years). Consequently, its commitments have been less, at $44.7 million.[31] Moreover, the PCI has emphasized direct investment in projects and firms rather than funding intermediaries, which accounted for less than 10% of its commitments through 2002. However, both funds have expanded the total supply of capital for small businesses, housing, community development projects, and development finance institutions. Moreover, the funds provide higher-risk capital than private lenders—subordinate debt and occasionally equity—and tailor their interest rates and repayment terms to help projects achieve financial feasibility.

Bank Community Development Corporations

Two federal bank regulators, the Office of the Comptroller of the Currency (OCC) and the Board of Governors of the Federal Reserve System (BOGFRS), have established regulations that allow nationally supervised banks to undertake a wide range of investments and activities that advance the public welfare. These regulations permit banks to make a one-time investment, via grant, loan, or equity, in a specific project or entity (referred to as a Community Development Project [CDP], and to establish and capitalize ongoing entities (Community Development Corporations [CDC]) to finance and/or undertake economic development activities. Bank CDC regulations provide a tool to create partnerships with banks to deploy their large capital base to address diverse economic development finance needs. Community development investments by national banks regulated by the Office of the Comptroller totaled $2.8 billion in 1999, and their cumulative value through 1999 was $10.5 billion (OCC, 2000). With billions of dollars in potential bank capital for CDC investments and their growing use to improve CRA ratings and respond to new market opportunities, bank CDCs are a key resource to fund economic development projects and the development finance institutions discussed in the following chapters. To help practitioners apply this tool, this section summarizes bank CDC regulations and presents examples of their myriad uses.

Bank CDC Regulations

The regulations governing bank community development investments address five areas: (1) eligible banks; (2) investment standards and allowable activities; (3) investment limits; (4) community representation; and (5) the approval process. Table 9.4 summarizes the regulations issued by OCC and BOGFRS. The applicable regulations for a specific bank depend on its supervisory agency and charter: national banks establish bank CDCs under the OCC regulations; bank holding companies and state banks (that are Federal Reserve members) fall under separate BOGFRS rules. Although minor differences exist across the three regulations, they all authorize banks to invest substantial funds in a broad array of economic and community development activities with little red tape. Bank CDC or CDP investments must meet a public welfare standard tied to generating direct benefits to either low- or moderate- income (LMI) persons or target areas (based on low- or moderate-income population and/or economic distress). OCC's target area definition, however, relies on government-designated redevelopment areas, which can encompass geographies that are not predominantly LMI. Investments can include small businesses development, commercial and industrial real estate development, community services, and technical assistance. The broad set of eligible activities under all three regulations allows bank CDC investments to be used flexibly to advance local economic development initiatives, as the following examples demonstrate. Investment limits place an aggregate cap on bank CDC and CDP investment equal to 5% of total capital and surplus (i.e., the bank's equity capital). OCC allows the limit to be increased to 10% with their approval, and state member banks under BOGFRS rules are also subject to a 2% cap on individual investments. Although the BOGFRS rules for bank holding companies do not set an investment limit, they do require approval for investments above 5% of capital and surplus. Although 5% is a small share of bank equity, it often translates into a large pool of investment capital, especially for regional and national banks. FleetBoston Corporation, for example, had capital and surplus of $16.8 billion as of September 30, 2002, which allows up to $843 million in community development investments.

Two differences between the OCC and BOGFRS rules are the treatment of community involvement and the approval process. OCC requires community support for and participation in bank CDC activities whereas the Federal Reserve only encourages community involvement. Acceptable forms of community involvement for the OCC include representation on the bank CDC entity board, a community advisory board, a formal business relationship with a CBO, a contractual agreement with community partners to provide services, and joint ventures or coinvestment with a local small business, public entity, or CBO. The OCC allows banks to self-certify their investments or activities as eligible if they meet certain conditions including adequate bank capital levels and a satisfactory or outstanding CRA rating. BOGFRS also permits state member banks to make bank CDC investments in certain entities without prior approval. In both cases, banks must still file information documenting the investment. Bank holding companies, on the other hand, must get prior approval for new investments, but no further consent is needed for follow-on investments in the same bank CDC entity.

Bank CDC Experience

Under these regulations, banks have used a wide range of financing roles and organization forms to support local economic development needs. This diversity includes subordinate lending to small businesses and development projects; equity investments in firms and real estate projects; providing

Table 9.4   Comparison of OCC and BOGFRS CDC Regulations[a]

Regulatory Issue	OCC Rules for National Banks	Federal Reserve Rules for Bank Holding Companies	Federal Reserve Rules for State Member Banks
Eligible Banks	National banks with outstanding or satisfactory ratings that are well capitalized and have certain financial ratings.	Bank holding companies.	State chartered banks that are Federal Reserve System members.
Investment Limits	Total outstanding investment up to 5% of capital and surplus (can be raised to 10% with OCC approval).	No limit: total must be prudent for holding company and appropriate to the nature and scope of activities.	Individual investments up to 2% and total investments up to 5% of capital and surplus.
Investment Standards	Primarily benefit LMI low- or moderate-income persons, low- and moderate-income areas, or government-targeted redevelopment areas.	Promote community welfare, i.e., benefit LMI persons or economically disadvantaged communities.	Promote public welfare by providing jobs, housing, or services to LMI communities and persons.
Allowable Activities to Finance or Support	Affordable housing; community services or permanent jobs for LMI persons; equity or debt financing for small businesses; area revitalization or stabilization; other activities that promote the public welfare.	Rental or ownership housing for LMI families; community service facilities; small business development in distressed areas; technical assistance to community development organizations.	LMI housing; commercial development or revitalization; small business development, industrial development, job training, counseling and technical assistance, other community development services.
Community Involvement	Nonbank community support for or participation in the investment or entity.	None required: mechanisms for community outreach and consultation encouraged.	None required: mechanisms for community outreach and consultation encouraged.
Approval Procedures	Automatic approval by submitting "letter of self-certification" in most cases. Noneligible national banks submit application for prior approval to OCC.	File regulation Y notice and narrative proposal to regional reserve bank. After approval, up to 5% of consolidated capital can be invested without further notice or approval.	No prior approval (only notice within 30 days) for investments in qualifying entities.[b]

SOURCE: 12 Code of Federal Regulations, Part 24; BOGFRS (1995).

NOTES:

a. The specific regulations are 12 CFR, Part 24 for the OCC, Section 225.25 (b) (6) of Regulation Y of the Federal Reserve System for bank holding companies, and Regulation H (12 CFR Part 208) of the Federal Reserve System for state member banks.

b. These are corporations, limited partnerships, or other entities, for-profit or nonprofit, that engage solely in qualified community development activities and under which the bank's liability is limited to its investment. Qualified investments include low-income housing partnerships, federally certified community development financial institutions (CDFIs), and entities previously approved by the OCC or Federal Reserve as meeting bank CDC regulations.

deposits, loans, and equity to development finance entities; direct real estate development; and consulting, technical assistance, and training services. Bank CDC activities can be organized in many ways: a bank division or business unit; a for-profit or nonprofit subsidiary; a partnership with a community-based organization or public agency; a multibank organization; and an umbrella entity to pool bank funds with other funding sources. Although the full set of bank CDC possibilities cannot be covered in this brief section, the following examples demonstrate options to address common economic development needs and may stimulate creative thinking about new ways to apply this tool.

A common use of bank CDCs is to supply riskier debt to small businesses, as exemplified by Mellon Bank and Security Pacific Bank. Mellon Bank was established in 1986 as a specialized lending unit for small businesses and minority-owned businesses in the bank's service area (Immergluck & Bush, 1995).[32] A common role for the CDC is providing subordinate debt for small business expansions that do not meet conventional credit standards, often pairing them with a Mellon Bank senior loan. Thus, the bank CDC generates demand for conventional bank lending. Mellon Bank CDC also provides expertise and loan packaging assistance on government credit programs to other bank staff and conducts a "second-look" review on loan turndowns (Immergluck & Bush, 1995). Security Pacific Bank established the Business Development Center as a bank CDC in 1989 to provide market-rate mezzanine financing for high-growth firms through subordinate debt with warrants or an alternative "equity kicker" (NCUED, 1990). In this case, the bank CDC allowed Security Pacific to obtain returns that compensated it for providing high-risk growth capital. Banks can also pool resources and share risks in offering subordinate debt financing through a multibank CDC. In Dallas, 17 banks established a $3.7 million multibank CDC, the Southern Dallas Development Fund, to provide market-rate subordinate debt to small firms and contracted with Southern Dallas Development Corporation, a community-based economic development organization, to manage the program (Immergluck & Bush, 1995). Some bank CDCs combine lending with small business development services. The Arkansas Enterprise Group, a nonprofit subsidiary of Southern Development Bancorporation, operates a small business incubator and an entrepreneurial development program along with three business finance funds.

Another bank CDC role is expanding the supply of equity capital for businesses, real estate projects, and development finance entities. In 1997, BankBoston (now FleetBoston Corporation) created BankBoston Development Corporation (BBDC) as a bank CDC with $100 million in capital to provide equity and debt to minority- and women-owned businesses and real estate development projects and those located in LMI urban neighborhoods (OCC, 1999). BBDC financing ranged from supplying equity to a minority-owned construction and development firm in Boston to investing in the Boston Community Loan Fund. In Hartford, Wisconsin, First National

Bank used bank CDC rules to make a $165,000 equity investment to establish a small business incubator building (NCUED, 1990).

Bank CDCs can pursue a real estate, rather than finance, mission by redeveloping severely distressed properties and building the properties needed to attract new economic uses. In this case, bank CDCs fill a market void when private developers perceive an area as too risky for investment, and/or severely blighted properties entail especially difficult and complex efforts. During the 1970s and 1980s, North Carolina National Bank created NCNB CDC to address decline in the central city neighborhoods of Charlotte. This CDC helped revitalize downtown Charlotte and its surrounding neighborhoods through undertaking housing development projects that restored deteriorated historic homes and rebuilt blighted urban renewal areas (CUED, 1990). In Chicago and Cleveland, ShoreBank Corporation created for-profit bank CDC subsidiaries to undertake real estate development as part of its revitalization efforts in low-income neighborhoods.

Commercial Banks as Development Finance Institutions

With broad financing powers, access to federally insured deposits, and the ability to originate SBA-guaranteed loans, commercial banks have critical capacities to expand capital availability for a range of economic and community development needs. Moreover, bank CDC regulations allow banks to augment lending with other economic development activities, such as real estate development, equity financing, business technical assistance, and job training. In the early 1970s, Ron Grzywinski recognized this potential and acquired an existing Chicago bank, South Shore Bank, as a market-based vehicle to reverse the decline of poor urban neighborhoods.[33] ShoreBank Corporation (originally called the Illinois Neighborhood Development Corporation) tested whether a bank could be a focal point for reversing urban disinvestment and revitalizing low-income urban neighborhoods. Through experimenting with different focus areas and varied finance and development roles, the management team created a development finance model that uses a bank holding company as an umbrella organization to set up entities with separate but related missions that reinforce community development in the targeted neighborhood (Grzywinski, 1991; Taub, 1994). Exhibit 9.1 diagrams ShoreBank Corporation's structure and subsidiaries.

ShoreBank Corporation is a bank holding company that oversees activities of the subsidiary units. ShoreBank is the core entity with assets of $1.2 billion on June 30, 2002. As a commercial bank, it provides a full range of banking and credit services including home mortgage and home improvement loans, multifamily housing loans, consumer loans, and small business loans primarily to minority-owned firms and manufacturers (McCall,

Exhibit 9.1   Organization of ShoreBank Corporation

```
┌─────────────────────────────────────────────────────────────┐
│         ShoreBank Corporation (a bank holding company)        │
└─────────────────────────────────────────────────────────────┘
```

ShoreBank (full service commercial bank)	ShoreBank Development Corporation (real estate company)	ShoreBank Capital (SSBIC)	The Neighbor-hood Institute (nonprofit service agency for low-income residents)	ShoreBank Advisory Services (consulting firm)

Shore Staffing Works (employment agency) Studio Air (teenager-run art studio)

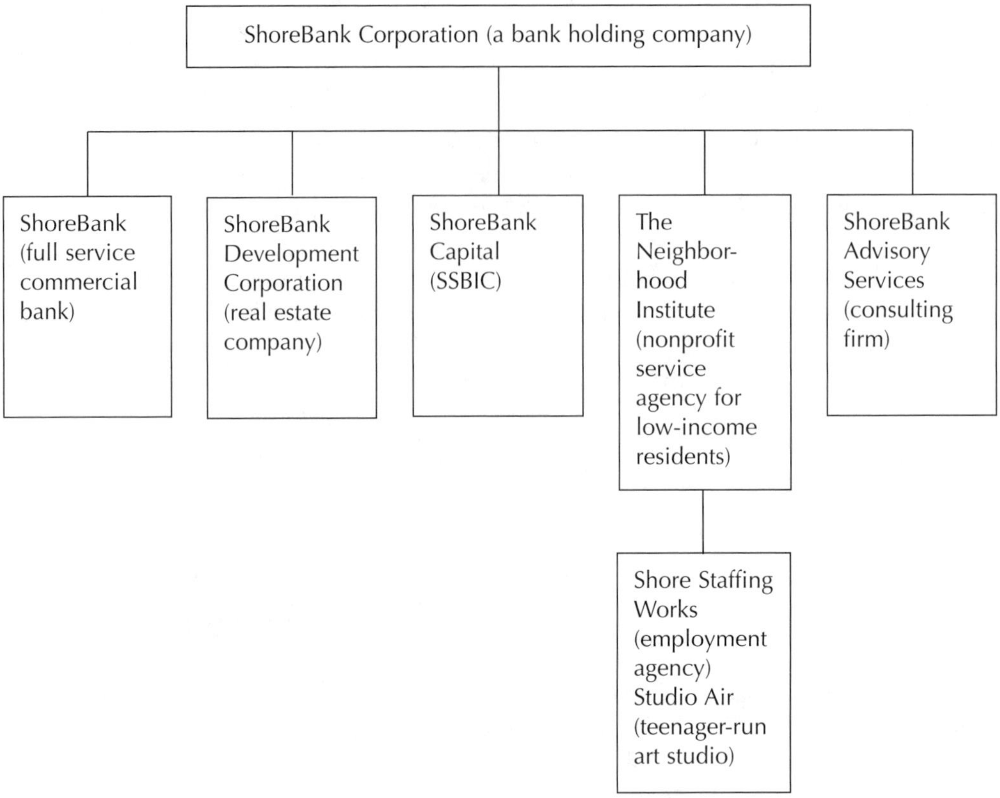

SOURCES: Grzywinski (1991, May-June); McCall (1997).

1997). ShoreBank Development Corporation (formerly City Lands Corporation) is a for-profit real estate developer that undertakes residential and commercial real estate projects. Through 2002, it developed 2,250 housing units and 129,000 square feet of commercial space.[34] ShoreBank Capital is a SBA-licensed Special Small Business Investment Corporation[35] that supplies subordinate debt and equity to minority-owned businesses. The Neighborhood Institute (TNI), a nonprofit entity, helps neighborhood residents pursue job, business, and wealth-building opportunities through job training, small business technical assistance, and other services. TNI also has two subsidiaries, an employment agency and a youth-run art design and production studio.[36] ShoreBank Advisory Services, the fifth subsidiary, is a consultancy that advises other organizations on community development issues. ShoreBank uses these five units to advance neighborhood revitalization through complimentary activities that include expanding credit to small businesses and households; completing development projects to improve blighted areas; attracting new economic uses; creating housing for different income groups; and providing services to increase the

Table 9.5   Distribution of ShoreBank Corporation Development Investment by Unit, 1974 to
1995

ShoreBank Corporation Unit	Total Development Investment	Percentage of Total
South Shore Bank	$317.1 million	64.5%
ShoreBank Development Lands Corporation	$134.4 million	27.3%
ShoreBank Capital and The Neighborhood Institute	$40.2 million	8.2%
Total	$491.7 million	

SOURCE: McCall (1997).

income and assets of low-income residents. According to their 2000 annual report, the ShoreBank Corporation has invested $1 billion to improve its target neighborhoods and to finance minority businesses outside these areas. Real estate lending by ShoreBank and real estate development through ShoreBank Development Corporation have been the main engines of development impact, accounting for 92% of development investments over the holding company's first 22 years (see Table 9.5). Small business lending, however, grew in importance after 1995, accounting for 27% of development investment from 1995 to 2000 versus 60% for real estate lending and investment (ShoreBank, 2001).

In his 1991 *Harvard Business Review* article, Grzywinski emphasized three lessons from ShoreBank's experience. First, he noted the need to import capital to finance development in LMI communities. Through its commercial bank, ShoreBank created deposit products to attract capital from a national pool of "socially oriented" investors. A below-market Rehab CD targets deposits to finance the most difficult housing rehabilitation projects. Development Deposits provide a market-rate vehicle for depositors to direct their savings toward a beneficial use. Development Deposits, which accounted for 52% of South Shore Bank's total deposits in 1990, were critical to fueling ShoreBank's growth. Beyond bank deposits, the subsidiary entities imported capital by securing and packaging funding streams to undertake real estate projects and deliver community services. A second lesson is that combining targeted large-scale development projects with bank lending to small real estate entrepreneurs accelerated and expanded revitalization impacts. These entrepreneurs acquired and rehabbed many small buildings around large publicly assisted projects. By cultivating and lending to small developers, ShoreBank identified an untapped lending market and helped improve the housing stock in large portions of the South Shore neighborhood. It also contributed to economic development by nurturing a new group of local entrepreneurs who used the neighborhood's large multifamily housing stock as a way to build their income and assets. Grzywinski's third lesson is that small business lending and commercial district revitalization is especially difficult in low-income neighborhoods, which are not large commercial centers and face stiff competition from suburban malls. Despite these difficulties, ShoreBank succeeded in developing a supermarket-anchored shopping center, becoming an active citywide SBA lender, and creating a small business incubator to support early-stage firms (Grzywinski, 1991; McCall, 1997).

While no formal evaluation that measured ShoreBank's impact exists, three studies found significant improvements in the South Shore neighborhood following the bank's entry. The most detailed study, prepared by the Woodstock Institute in 1982, found that median home sales prices increased 45% from 1975 to 1980, which reversed a 15-year trend of declining real estate prices and exceeded the citywide increase for the period (41%). Other improvements from 1975 to 1980 included a large increase in home mortgage lending, especially conventional mortgages, a decline in multifamily tax delinquencies, and an increase in building permits issued (Woodstock Institute, 1982). However, South Shore continued to experience increased housing abandonment and a declining commercial strip in the late 1970s (Woodstock Institute, 1982). Richard Taub used median single-family home sales price data and attitudinal surveys to argue that the South Shore neighborhood improved relative to four comparable Chicago neighborhoods (Taub, 1994). Prices in South Shore increased 96% from 1973 to 1978, a growth rate that exceeded three of the four neighborhoods by at least half. Resident surveys in 1979 found that the share of South Shore residents who felt their neighborhood improved for the better in the prior 2 years was twice that in two racially changing neighborhoods.[37] Moreover, South Shore residents were two to three times more likely to predict neighborhood improvements in the next 2 years than four comparable neighborhoods (Taub, 1994).[38] McCall (1997) compared and statistically tested changes in housing, community development, and economic development measures for the South Shore neighborhood and three comparable neighborhoods from 1970 to 1990. She found statistical evidence that South Shore improved relative to comparison neighborhoods for several housing and income measures, including higher population growth (1970s only) and increases over both decades in the median housing value, owner-occupied housing, people living in the same house 5 years earlier, and mean family income. However, the changes in other measures were either negative or not statistically significant.[39] ShoreBank Corporation's financial performance is another indicator of its success. While actively pursuing a community development mission, the corporation increased its assets almost 30-fold, consistently earned profits, and achieved a 12% risk-based capital ratio in June 2002, above the 10% standard for well-capitalized banks.

Despite ShoreBank's success, community development banks have not been widely replicated. Among the 615 CDFIs certified by the federal Community Development Financial Institutions Fund as of November 2002, just over 50 were community development banks,[40] well below the numbers for most other types of development finance entities. ShoreBank Corporation helped create new development banks in Arkansas, Cleveland,

Michigan, and the Pacific Northwest. In 1986, ShoreBank worked with the Winthrop Rockefeller Foundation to create a bank holding company, Southern Development Bancorportion (SDC),[41] to support rural economic development throughout Arkansas. SDC first acquired an existing bank, Elk Horn Bank & Trust Company, and then added two subsidiaries, the non-profit Arkansas Enterprise Group to focus on small business development and finance, and Opportunity Lands Corporation, a for-profit real estate developer. Over 14 years, SDC has grown to over $350 million in assets and expanded its service area to include the Arkansas and Mississippi Delta, one of the nation's poorest regions. Its structure also evolved to include (1) three subsidiary banks; (2) Southern Financial Partners, a nonprofit entity that provides loans and technical assistance to small businesses; (3) Opportunity Lands Corporation, a for-profit developer that builds housing and small business incubators in the delta region with a nonprofit affiliate focused on affordable housing; and (4) Good Faith Fund, a nonprofit organization that provides job training, entrepreneurial assistance, and special savings programs to service area residents. ShoreBank Corporation has expanded geographically creating subsidiary banks in Cleveland (ShoreBank Cleveland) and the Pacific Northwest (ShoreBank Pacific), adding a bank branch and a special purpose affiliate in Detroit and establishing two special purpose affiliates in Michigan's upper peninsula. These subsidiary institutions are smaller than the Chicago bank[42] and emphasize small business development and lending rather than housing lending and development.

Challenges to Creating and Operating a Commercial Bank

The limited replication of community development banks reflects the obstacles to their creation and management. One critical hurdle is raising initial capital to either start a new bank or acquire an existing one. According to one expert, community development banks need to reach $100 million in assets, or close to $10 million in capital, to achieve the economies of scale to serve low-income communities and generate ongoing profits (Surgeon, 2002). To raise this amount of capital with the uncertain profitability of a new bank requires substantial investments from institutional sources such as foundations, banks, or corporations. ShoreBank Cleveland, for example, raised its $10.7 million in initial capital from the Cleveland Tomorrow foundation ($5 million), Fannie Mae ($3.3 million) and the Ford Foundation ($2.4 million). A second challenge is attracting executives with strong bank management experience. Whereas conventional banks attract experienced executives with both competitive salaries and potential capital gains from stock options and share appreciation, development banks offer neither comparable salaries nor the same prospect for stock appreciation. Instead, they must attract executives who are firmly committed to the bank's community and economic development mission (Surgeon, 2002). Banks also need managers with strong community and economic development experience; these professionals are easier to recruit from a growing network of development finance and community development practitioners. Third, establishing a community development bank requires bank regulatory approval, either for a charter to establish a new bank or to acquire an existing one. In reviewing new charter applications, regulators evaluate the business plan and the bank organizers to determine if the board and management are competent to operate the bank, the initial capital is sufficient to support the bank's projected scale and operations, and the bank is likely to be operated in a profitable, safe and sound manner (OCC, 2002).[43] A special national bank charter as a community development bank is available from the OCC, which requires submitting additional information to document how the bank will benefit LMI individuals, LMI areas, or redevelopment areas, and the nature of community involvement in its activities (OCC, 2001). For nationally chartered banks, a 120-day period is usually required to review new charter applications (OCC, 2002). Given the obstacles and higher regulatory scrutiny involved in establishing a new bank, acquiring an existing bank is an alternative way to create a community development bank, as was the case for ShoreBank and Southern Development Bancorporation.

Special Operating Requirements

Once established, community development banks, as regulated depository institutions, require special management and operating capabilities compared to other development finance entities. One critical capacity is the ability to secure deposits. Potential deposit markets must be identified and sustained efforts undertaken to attract deposits. Since community development banks can import deposits from socially oriented investors outside their service area, such as religious organizations, foundations, and financial institutions, special marketing materials and cultivation efforts are needed to build this deposit base. Special back-office systems to provide the data processing and accounting capacity to manage many deposits are another important operating need. A third management issue is regulatory compliance, which requires managers and staff with expertise in banking regulations, systems to monitor compliance, and the capacity to fulfill reporting requirements and prepare for examinations. Finally, banks must carefully manage the correspondence between their assets and liabilities. Assets are the loans and investments made by banks, and liabilities are their obligations to depositors and lenders. On the one hand, bank managers must acquire assets that generate sufficient interest income to cover their interest expense and operating costs and generate a profit. On the other hand, they need sufficient liquid investments to meet the demand to redeem deposits for cash. Moreover, since regulators adjust the amount of required bank capital based on the risk level of bank assets, managers also must maintain an asset mix that complies with capital requirements. Community development bankers must balance these requirements while supplying more complex credit and development services to low-income markets. This requires a dual focus on sound financial management and development banking. As exemplified by ShoreBank, which took many years and made many mistakes before settling on its successful mix of lending and development activities, finding the right set of products, services, and practices to achieve this balance in a specific community takes time, persistence, and innovation (Surgeon, 2002; Taub, 1994). Careful research and planning, ongoing reflection and evaluation of successes and failures, and sharing experiences and gaining advice from peers at other community development and conventional banks are all valuable practices to help overcome these challenges.

Endnotes

1. ShoreBank was originally established as the Illinois Neighborhood Development Corporation before it changed its name to South Shore Bank and then ShoreBank.

2. Squires (1993) provides a good overview of how federal policies have addressed racial discrimination in housing first by fostering racial segregation under Federal Housing Administration underwriting standards and then in the 1960s establishing federal executive orders and laws to prohibit racial discrimination in housing (pp. 5–9).

3. Under the law, banks are defined as entities insured by the Federal Deposit Insurance Corporation (FDIC).

4. Four federal bank regulatory agencies are responsible for CRA enforcement over a different set of banks. The FDIC supervises state-chartered banks that are not members of the Federal Reserve System. The Office of the Comptroller of the Currency (OCC), within U.S. Department of Treasury, supervises federally chartered banks. The Federal Reserve System supervises bank holding companies and state-chartered banks that are members of the Federal Reserve System. Office of Thrift Supervision oversees savings banks and associations that are insured by the FDIC.

5. CRA performance is a consideration for five types of regulatory actions: (1) to obtain or change a bank charter; (2) FDIC insurance; (3) to establish a new domestic branch; (4) to relocate a main office or branch; and (5) to merge, consolidate, or acquire bank assets or liabilities. See Haag (2000), p. 1.

6. Brannon (2001) cites expanding competition as an original motivation for CRA's enactment.

7. These externalities might include disinvestment and declining property conditions, which can lead to lower property values and government revenues, loss of employment and income from reduced business growth, and social problems that might accompany any physical deterioration and/or property abandonment.

8. During this period, CRA ratings were based on 12 assessment factors that emphasized process over outcomes.

9. Although there are four regulatory agencies enforcing CRA, each agency has issued virtually identical CRA regulations (Marsico, p. 7).

10. The site provides a wealth of additional information on banks, including branch locations and deposits, total assets, small business loans, and home mortgage loans.

11. A wholesale bank does not provide home mortgage, small business, small farm, or consumer loans to retail customers whereas a limited purpose bank provides a narrow product line to a large market area (Marsico, p. 11).

12. A more complete explanation of this bank lending assessment method along with a detailed demonstration of its application is provided in Marsico, 2002, pp. 25 to 43.

13. These percentages do not add up to 100% due to rounding to the closest whole percentage.

14. Although community-based coalitions were the primary advocates for expanded bank services and lending in low-income and minority communities, city governments and statewide advocacy organizations also led such campaigns. City government, under Mayor Michael White, championed CRA efforts in Cleveland while New Jersey Citizens Action led CRA efforts in that state. See Schwartz (1998), pp. 637–638.

15. The following summary of PCRG's activities is based on Metzger (1992).

16. PCRG was initiated by Manchester Citizens, a community development corporation, and Stanley Lowe, its CEO, after a preliminary analysis of HMDA data indicated that UNB was not lending to Pittsburgh's low-income and minority neighborhoods based on the advice of the National Training and Information Center. See Metzger, pp. 79–84.

17. These included training sessions for CDCs and realtors, education programs for women and minority-owned small businesses, and widespread advertising in neighborhood newspapers.

18. Among the largest banks, with at least 30 billion in assets, 89% had created special CRA programs while 80% had separate CRA lending units or departments. See BOGFRS (2000) Table 9.

19. On the other hand, few differences were found in loan denial rates between banks with and without CRA agreements. One exception was African American households; banks with CRA agreements denied African American applications at 2.5 times the level for white applicants whereas banks without CRA agreements had denied African American loan applications 3.13 times more often than white applications.

20. The study by Anne B. Shlay is summarized in Haag (2000).

21. The total market share for low- and moderate-income borrowers peaked in 1993 at 40.6% and then declined through 1997 whereas for low-income borrowers, it peaked in 1995 at 11.6%. African American and Hispanic borrowers' share increased through 1996 before declining below 1990 levels in 1997. See Haag (2000), pp. 10–12, for a more complete summary of the Campen study.

22. Summaries of 12 publications on this issue are provided by Haag (2000), pp. 119–122.

23. The study defined CRA-related home mortgage loans as any mortgage loan made within a lender's CRA assessment area to either a low- or moderate-income borrower or in a low- or moderate-income neighborhood. CRA-related small business loans were defined as any small business loan made within a lender's CRA assessment area either to a business with $1 million or less in revenues or in a low- or moderate-income neighborhood (regardless of firm size). A community development loan was defined as any community development loan under CRA regulations that were considered in a firm's CRA rating evaluation.

24. These arguments are summarized and evaluated in Apgar and Duda (2002), pp. 42–45.

25. Apgar and Duda (2002) cite statistics from a 1999 study by G.J. Bentson in which more than 2,000 Fair Lending complaints received by the Department of Housing and Urban Renewal under the Fair Housing Act and other civil rights laws from 1989 through 1995 resulted in guilty findings for only 1% of the cases (23 cases) with HUD referring only 9 to the Justice Department for prosecution.

26. Although most banks in the BOGFRS (2000) Federal Reserve study reported that CRA loans were equal or more profitable than other loans, a sizable share did report that small business (14%), home purchase/refinance (44%), and home improvement loans (28%) were less profitable.

27. Apgar and Duda (2002) report that mortgage banks originated 56% of home mortgage loans in 1997, and commercial banks and thrift institutions originated 25% and 18%, respectively.

28. The following description of the Massachusetts Act and its outcomes is based on Luquetta and Thrash (2000) and additional data provided by the Massachusetts Association of Community Development Corporations.

29. Life insurers receive a decrease in their income taxes while property and casualty insurers receive lower income taxes and deductions for retaliatory taxes imposed by other states in response to Massachusetts's taxation of out-of-state firms. Firms in both industries are also eligible for a 1.5% tax credit on investments in each fund beyond the minimum requirement.

30. These commitments include $47.5 million for affordable housing intermediaries and projects, $15.5 million for community service projects or funds, and $20 million for economic development funds, projects, and firms. See Massachusetts Life Insurance Community Investment Initiative (2003) *2002 Annual Report*.

31. While the PCI did not break down its cumulative investments by type, a large majority finances housing developments. For example, 69% of the $4 million in new commitments made in 2002 were for affordable housing projects, 25% was divided equally among economic development projects and small businesses, and the remaining 6% was to a small business loan fund. See the Property and Casualty Initiative (2003) *2002 Annual Report*.

32. The bank CDC emerged out of a reorganization of the bank's Community Development Division and its response to community development organizations'

interest in creating a fund to finance community development projects. See Immergluck and Bush (1995), Vol. 2, p. 32.

33. Richard Taub (1998) documents the origins and early history of South Shore Bank in *Community Capitalism*. See pp. 17–25 for a discussion of its initial acquisition and objectives, based on the efforts of four founding managers, Ron Grzywinski, Milton Davis, Mary Houghton, and Jim Fletcher.

34. Figures are from the ShoreBank Corporation Web site www.ShoreBankcorp.

35. Special Small Business Investment Corporations are SBA-licensed entities created to provide equity and risk capital to small businesses owned by women, minorities, and economically disadvantaged groups. Chapter 11 provides an overview of the role and experience of SSBICs.

36. In the past, TNI was also active in affordable housing development.

37. The percentage for South Shore was 16.6% versus 8.5% and 8.2% for Austin and Back of the Yards, respectively.

38. In South Shore, 35.8% predicted better conditions compared to 17.3% in Austin, 14.4% in Back of the Yards, 10.1% in East Side, and 10% in Portage Park.

39. These other measures included growth in vacant units, increases in median rent, the change in self-employment income, slower rates of poverty growth, increased education levels, and improvements in housing quality.

40. The CDFI Funds lists 69 certified banks, thrift institutions, and bank holding companies, but 16 are holding companies or affiliates of the same banking group. (U.S. Department of Treasury Community Development Financial Institution Fund, 2002.)

41. This history of Southern Development Bancorporation is based on its Web site www.southerndevelopmentbancorp.com/know/history.

42. The Cleveland and Pacific banks had $57 million and $49 million in assets, respectively, as of June 30, 2002.

43. Other considerations include potential risks to the Federal Deposit Insurance Fund and whether the planned corporate powers are consistent with the Federal Deposit Insurance Act.

PART IV

Institutional
Models for Economic
Development Finance

10

Revolving Loan Funds

R evolving loan funds (RLFs) are one of the oldest and most widely used development finance models. They emerged as an important economic development tool in the 1970s as state and local governments expanded their economic development role in response to capital availability problems and the growth of federal grant programs (NCUED, 1995a). During the 1990s, the number of RLFs mushroomed as more local governments implemented economic development programs and a nonprofit development finance sector emerged. Although the exact number of RLFs is not known, several thousand probably exist across the United States.[1]

This chapter reviews the practice of RLFs as the first alternative development finance institution used to address economic development capital availability gaps. A brief explanation of the RLF and its role in addressing capital market imperfections is covered in the first section. Next, the existing literature on RLF characteristics and their performance is summarized. Although the overall industry's economic development role is significant, most RLFs are modest in size and impact. To become valuable sources of development finance, RLFs require an economic development and financial strategy that targets key market segments and allows them to grow to scale. The chapter's third section discusses the major policy issues to address in designing a highly effective RLF. The concluding section moves from policy to operations and highlights critical management challenges and best practices to implement a well-designed RLF.

The Revolving Loan Fund Model

A revolving loan fund is an unregulated pool of capital used to provide loans to small businesses and/or development projects with loan repayments recycled, or revolved, to make additional loans over time. Through this revolving mechanism, a RLF serves as an ongoing source of debt capital for a community. Even with a one-time grant of capital, a RLF can make several generations of loans. Figure 10.1 presents a simple diagram of how a revolving loan fund operates. The RLF receives capital from a combination of grant and debt sources. It then lends this capital to businesses and/or development projects that advance the RLF's economic development goals. Borrowers repay their loans to the RLF, which uses these loan repayments to make new loans. If the RLF borrowed money to partially capitalize the fund, then some of the cash flow from loan repayments will go to repay debt sources. This simple example illustrates the importance of grant sources to a RLF. Since grants are not repaid, all grant proceeds can be revolved within the RLF. Grant capital also allows greater flexibility in defining lending roles and loan terms. Since grants require no return of capital or interest payments, they allow RLFs to make higher-risk loans and set flexible repayment terms to address a wide variety of local development finance needs. Loan sources, on the other hand, must be repaid, reducing the portion of RLF capital that is recycled within the RLF. The impact of debt sources on RLF lending capacity depends on their repayment schedule. Long-term loans will allow repeated recycling of capital while a short- or medium-term loan provides a one-time infusion of funds that will not be revolved within the RLF. Moreover, borrowing constrains RLF financing polices since the interest rates and principal amortization on RLF loans must allow it to repay its own lenders.[2]

Since the last two chapters demonstrated that loan guarantees and CRA regulations are effective in expanding capital supply, it is important to consider why RLFs are needed. The crux of this issue is RLFs' capacity to respond to capital market imperfections and supply gaps that are not sufficiently addressed by guarantees and regulatory tools. Guarantees and bank regulations directly alter nonprofit-maximizing behavior of financial

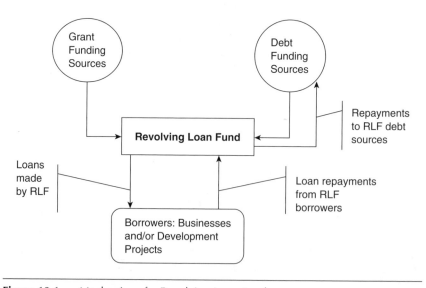

Figure 10.1   Mechanics of a Revolving Loan Fund

institutions, such as risk aversion and discrimination, while helping overcome information and transaction cost barriers to capital supply. By encouraging expanded lending to small firms, low-income areas, and minority borrowers, they help banks gain efficiencies in serving these markets through experience, new approaches and technologies, and economies of scale. Since guarantees increase the potential for a viable financing transaction from firms or projects that present high perceived risks, they also encourage lenders to underwrite loans (and incur information costs) that they might not otherwise pursue. However, important limitations exist for these interventions. First, conventional financial institutions are constrained in supplying risky debt by risk aversion among their own capital sources, regulations on asset quality, and highly leveraged balance sheets. Second, information and transaction cost barriers may still impair the pursuit of and competition within lending markets that are perceived as too small or specialized to be profitable. Such barriers are more likely to affect rural areas, small loans, young and highly specialized industries, and emerging entrepreneurial populations. Finally, loan guarantees and most regulatory policies[3] do not address externalities by supplying capital for specific economic development uses that generate significant social benefits and compensate for below-market financial returns. Due to their funding sources and nonregulated status, RLFs have the capacity and flexibility to overcome these market imperfections.

An important RLF feature is their unregulated status, which offers both advantages and drawbacks. Unlike commercial banks, thrift institutions, or credit unions, RLFs do not need a federal or state government charter to operate and are not subject to regulatory supervision. Consequently, they can be established without the time and expense of meeting regulatory hurdles. Moreover, a RLF can set financing policies based on economic development goals and organizational needs, rather than meeting safety and soundness standards. This allows RLFs to use alternative methods to evaluate and manage lending risks and to lend to riskier projects and borrowers. However, the absence of regulations reduces accountability and public oversight. Consequently, RLFs can be established and operate without sufficient expertise, policies, and systems to prudently manage their funds, which increases the potential for poor credit decisions and unwarranted losses. RLFs also are not subject to CRA standards and examinations, which allows them to target their markets and lending activities in ways that do fully address the needs of low-income and minority neighborhoods and business owners, small firms, and small farms. Instead, RLF performance is guided by the policies and oversight practices of their funding sources and local governance bodies, which are more variable than the uniform national standards for banks.

RLFs rely heavily on grants, which provide critical financial flexibility to address capital supply gaps. Without any interest and principal payments to depositors and lenders, grants allow RLFs to supply riskier debt with more flexible repayment terms than banks and other financial institutions. This permits lending to earlier stage firms, loans with less collateral and debt coverage, and debt with long repayment periods. Since grants have no cost of funds, they reduce a major operating cost and permit RLFs to bear higher information and transaction costs, and to finance firms that need more intensive technical assistance.[4] Finally, RLF funding sources support investments in projects that provide social returns that financial return-driven private market institutions do not value. Grants provide a subsidy to absorb lower financial returns that are justified by social benefits. Social return goals can also attract nongrant funding from investors that seek both a financial and social return, which will be discussed more fully in subsequent chapters on venture capital and community-based financial institutions.

Federal programs are a major source of RLF grant funds. Six federal agencies administer grants to capitalize economic development RLFs, but three agencies are the primary RLF funding sources: (1) Housing and Urban Development through the Community Development Block Grant (CDBG) Program; (2) Economic Development Administration through its Title IX Economic Adjustment Program; and (3) Department of Agriculture.[5] The Corporation for Enterprise Development (CfED), through its *Counting on Local Capital* research project, provided the first comprehensive review of federal RLF funding. CfED collected and analyzed data from six federal agencies to complete a census of all federally funded RLFs (CfED, 1997). The resulting data on RLF funding by each agency is summarized in Table 10.1. Despite data problems that prevented a complete census and comparative analysis, these results provide the best overview of both federal agency funding and national RLF characteristics. In the following section, the groundbreaking *Counting on Local Capital* research and other studies are used to profile the use, impact, and characteristics of RLF. Although these studies do not cover the entire RLF sector, they demonstrate how RLFs operate as development finance entities and inform the subsequent sections on RLF policies and best practices.

Table 10.1   Federally Funded RLFs by Agency

Federal Agency	Number of RLFs	RLF Loans Outstanding ($ Millions)	Year for Data
Appalachian Regional Commission	27	$44.70	1996
Economic Development Administration	322	298.7	1995
Health and Human Services	16	1.8	1995
Small Business Administration	103	36.5	1995
Department of Agriculture	223	305.9	1994
Total	603	$560.70	
	Number of RLF Grants	Value of RLF Grants ($ Millions)	
Housing and Urban Development	2,541	$506.1	1991–93

SOURCE: Corporation for Enterprise Development (1997)

NOTE: Columns do not sum to totals since duplicate data is subtracted for RLFs funded by multiple agencies.

Revolving Loan Funds' Characteristics and Performance

CfED undertook the most comprehensive RLF study during 1997 and 1998 through the *Counting on Local Capital* project. This study included a census of RLFs funded by six federal agencies, profiles of RLF activity in seven states, and a review of prior RLF studies and evaluations. The federal RLF census, summarized in Table 10.1, identified 603 RLFs funded by five agencies, including 92 that received funds from several agencies. HUD, the sixth agency, did not collect data on individual funds, but reported making over 2,500 CDBG entitlement grants totaling $506.1 million that were used for RLFs. Since multiple grants to one RLF are possible, the number of CDBG-funded RLFs was indeterminate. Because loan funds supported solely by the CDBG program, one of the largest RLF funders, are omitted, the 603 figure significantly underestimates total RLF activity.

RLF Characteristics

The summary data in Table 10.2 indicates that the average federally funded RLFs had modest capitalization, made few loans, and provided small loans, as of the mid-1990s. Although data on total fund capital was not collected, the

Table 10.2   Summary Statistics for RLFs Funded by Five Federal Agencies[a]

RLF Characteristic	Value	Sample Size
Number of RLFs	603	603
Number of Current Loans	10,841	603
Value of Current Loans	560.7 million	603
Number First Funded in 1975 to 1980	36	603
Number First Funded in 1981 to 1989	182	603
Number First Funded in 1990 to 1995	290	603
Cumulative Number of Loans	13,829	364
Cumulative Value of Loans	577.8 million	364
Average Loans per RLF	18	603
Average Loan Amount	51,725	603
Median Current Loans per RLF	715,663	603
Average Current Loans per RLF	965,141	603
Total Jobs Created or Retained	202,141	356
Average Jobs Created or Saved	568	356
Median Jobs Created or Saved	276	356
Average $/Job Created or Saved	$5,338	299
Median $/Job Created or Saved	$3,761	299
Aggregate Default Rate	10%	290
Median Default Rate	5.68%	290

SOURCE: Corporation for Enterprise Development (1997)

NOTE: a. Omits HUD CDBG-funded RLFs where data was not available.

amount of current loans provides a proxy for RLF size. Because current loans averaged $965,000, and probably constitute the bulk of RLF assets, the average RLF likely had total assets in the $1 to $1.5 million range. However, the median level of current loans was $715,663, indicating that half of these RLFs had assets of $1 million or less. Several RLF studies from the 1980s (see Table 10.3) reported average capitalization levels closer to $2 million, but these studies focused on a subset of federally supported RLFs. This difference also may indicate that the rapid growth of RLFs in the 1990s included the creation of many new small funds, such as SBA and Health and Human Services–funded microenterprise loan funds. With an average of 18 current loans and a median of 11, the federally funded RLFs make few loans on an annual basis.[6] One reason for these small averages may be the young age of many RLFs. Half of the identified RLFs received their first federal grant between 1990 and 1995 and were still in the start-up or early implementation stage during the study. The average loan made by federally funded RLFs, as of the mid-1990s, was small, at $51,725. This loan size suggests that RLFs are filling capital gaps by either supplying small loans that are unavailable from conventional lenders or supplementing private lenders to fill gaps for specific financing transactions. As with RLF capitalization, the average loan size in the CfED study (Table 10.2) is lower than that in most of the earlier RLF studies (Table 10.3). This change reflects the growth in microenterprise RLFs during the 1990s because the average loan among nonmicroenterprise funds in the CfED census was $77,165, close to the level in earlier studies.

Table 10.3   Comparison of Findings From Four RLF Studies

Category	McManis (1980)	Mt. Auburn Associates (1987)	Barringer and Roche (1990)	Rapoza (1993)
Study Population	U.S. EDA-funded RLFs	U.S. EDA-funded RLFs	NRC-associated RLFs	USDA-funded RLFs
Study Period	1979 to1980	1982 to1984	1984	1980 to1991
Cost per Job Created/Saved	NA	$4,726	$5,000	$4,278
Leverage Ratio	2:1 to 3:1	4:1	2.3:1	4:1
Default Rate	7% average anticipated by surveyed RLFs	22% of borrowers defaulted after 4 years	Mean rate of 13% of outstanding loan principal	NA
Average Capital Level	$250,000 to $4 million	~$2 million	$1,813,520	$1,264,822
Average Loan Size	>$100,000	$77,282	$33,500	$81,652
Average Loan Maturity	10 years	6.75 years	5.5 years (median)	7.57 years
Average Loan Interest Rate	7% to 8%	9.3%	7.5% (median)	9.3%
Technical Assistance (TA) Services	4 of 19 RLFs offered TA	30% of RLFs offered TA	NA	Over half of RLFs provided TA

SOURCE: Grossman et al. (1998)

More detail emerges from the seven state RLF profiles prepared by CfED and summarized in Table 10.4. These profiles clarify common RLF traits, such as heavy reliance on grant funds, but demonstrate important interstate differences in RLF structure and practices. The modest size and lending activity of most RLFs is confirmed by data across the seven states. The median cumulative value of loans was $1 million or less for five states; only California reported a higher level of $2.7 million. Moreover, median RLF capital ranged from $400,000 to $1.3 million for the five states that reported this data. Several state reports also emphasized the prevalence of poorly capitalized RLFs and their difficulty becoming sustainable entities. In California and Illinois, for example, half of all RLFs had capital of $500,000 or less, and over 70% had under $1 million. Beyond the sustainability challenge, small RLFs made few loans and generated little impact; the median number of loans among RLFs in three states was 12 or fewer, and the median job impact per RLF was 100 or less in five states. The expansion of the RLF sector appears to have come through the proliferation of many small RLFs with limited capital and impact. Communities may be quick to establish a RLF as a cookie-cutter development finance tool without carefully considering the requirements for a sustainable and effective development finance entity.

Across all states, RLFs consistently made small loans with medium-term maturities and provided technical assistance to borrowers. Median loan sizes ranged from $30,000 in Washington to $51,500 in North Carolina with most median loan terms in the 5- to 8-year range. Washington RLFs, however, provided the shortest term and smallest loans, with a median term and loan size of 3.5 years and $30,000, respectively. RLFs in most states reported lending at below market interest rates. Four of six states had median interest rates between 4.5% and 6% in 1997 to 1998, versus a prime rate of 8% to 8.5% at this time.

The use of below-market interest rates and medium-term lending is consistent with findings from prior RLF studies. However, RLFs appear to have expanded their provision of technical assistance during the 1990s. Although older studies of EDA-funded RLFs found that less than one third offered technical assistance,[7] a majority of RLFs across the six state surveys conducted in 1998 provided technical assistance, primarily through one-on-one counseling. In three states, over three quarters of all RLFs provided technical assistance and/or training to borrowers.

RLFs' organization and funding vary across the seven states. Governments operate the majority of RLFs in four states whereas nonprofit RLFs are the norm in Arkansas and Washington. Nonprofit RLFs are especially prevalent in Arkansas, where they accounted for 84% of the identified funds. In North Carolina, government and nonprofit entities operate roughly equal shares of RLFs at 45% and 41%, respectively. Government-operated RLFs, however, were prevalent in states with the most funds. If this pattern applies nationally, then governments are the primary RLF managers. Grants and equity accounted for over two thirds of RLF capital in all seven states, but the role of federal and private sources differed. RLFs in Washington and Illinois relied

Table 10.4   Comparison RLF Characteristics by State

Data Category	Arkansas	California	Illinois	Minnesota	North Carolina	Ohio	Washington
Number of Surveyed Organizations	28	176	302	549	88	215	56
RLFs Identified	18	110	118	124	27	81	41
Percentage Government	16%	52%	63%	68%	45%	53%	16%
Percentage Nonprofit	84%	30%	20%	31%	41%	40%	68%
Total RLF Capital	$43.7 million	$376 million	$197 million	$205 million	$90 million	$423 million	$77 million
Percentage Grant or Equity Funding	NA	70%	95%	75%	69%	76%	90%
Federal Share	48%	24%	72%	69%	44%	24%	42%
Private Share[a]	42%	20%	12%	17%	22%	2%	23%
Total Value of Loans Made	$47 million	$208 million	$95.6 million	$163 million	$102.4 million	$434 million	$59.1 million
Total Number of Loans Made	1,088	2,827	1,743	2,634	2,060	2,081	1,077
Median RLF Capital	NA	$500,000	$400,000	$500,000	$1.3 million	$1.3 million	< $500,000
Median Cumulative Loan Value per RLF	$1 million	$2.7 million	$383,000	$600,000	$1 million	NA	$270,230
Median Number of Loans per RLF	21	34	8	12	33	NA	12
Median Loan Size	$42,500	$48,000	$37,433	$37,500	$51,500	NA	$30,000
Median Loan Term	5 years	7 years	7 years	8 years	8 years	NA	3.5 years
Median Interest Rate	8%	6%	5%	6%	4.5%	NA	10%

SOURCE: Corporation for Enterprise Development (1997). State data summaries from *Counting on Local Capital* state RLF profiles. Data based on surveys conducted from December 1997 to May 1998.

NOTE: a. Includes foundations, utilities, banks, and other private sector sources.

most heavily on nondebt funding, using grant and equity to provide 90% and 95% of their capital, respectively. Federal funds supplied over two thirds of RLF capital in Illinois and Minnesota, but less than one quarter in California and Ohio. Large state funding programs in these two states explain the smaller federal role. Private funding constituted less than a quarter of RLF capital in six states, but it was critical in Arkansas where it supplied 42%, just below the federal government's 48% share.

RLF Performance

Three measures are consistently used to evaluate RLF performance: cost per job created or retained, leverage ratio, and loan default rate. The cost per job measure provides an overall indicator of RLF efficiency in achieving a key economic development goal; it compares the dollar value of RLF loans made to the reported number of jobs created or retained by these loans.[8] A leverage ratio compares the amount of RLF loans to other financing that borrowers secure in conjunction with the RLF debt. When leverage ratio is used, only the leverage of private financing is measured. It indicates the RLF's effectiveness in securing co-lenders and structuring its loan to minimize the funding gap that it must fill. Default rates document the extent of nonperforming loans and potential loan losses. However, defaults do not directly correspond to actual losses because either a borrower's fortunes may change, allowing it to repay the loan after an initial default period, or a lender may recoup some loan principal from the sale of collateral. Since definitions vary across RLFs, the reported default rates do not offer a consistent measure of problem loans. Default rates also should be evaluated in light of RLF goals. Since RLFs are designed to make riskier loans than conventional lenders, their default rates should be higher. Thus, a high default rate may reflect a high-risk lending strategy (e.g., financing start-up firms or emerging industries) rather than poor management practices. Despite these limitations, default rates indicate a RLF's ability to manage lending risks and maintain its capital base. High default rates can lead to large loan losses that reduce a RLF's capital and lending capacity.

Collectively, RLFs report a large job creation and retention impact and are a cost-effective economic development tool. However, a small share of RLFs generate substantial impacts, and, in many states, at least half of all RLFs have modest job impacts. The federal RLF census reported that 202,141 jobs were created or retained by 364 loan funds as of the mid-1990s; the average RLF job impact was 568 new or retained jobs, and the median RLF created and saved 276 jobs. Note that the median job impact was less than half the average amount. This indicates that a small percentage of RLFs create or retain the most jobs and raise the average level, but the majority of RLFs have a modest effect on local employment. State RLF profiles support both findings—large industrywide impacts but with most RLFs creating or saving a moderate number of jobs. On a statewide basis, RLFs reported aggregate job impacts that ranged from 11,091 in North Carolina to 25,135 in Minnesota. The median number of jobs created or retained per RLF, however, was small. In California, the median RLF reported creating or saving only 46 jobs. North Carolina had the highest median—226 jobs per RLF. Once again, these data indicate that most RLFs are small in size and impact. Thus, the large industrywide job creation and retention figures are attributable to a minority of highly effective RLFs. North Carolina clearly demonstrates this phenomenon, as one RLF, Self-Help Ventures Fund, accounted for 47% of all job creation and retention among the 88 RLFs in the study.[9] Although many communities can cobble together resources to create a small loan fund, the real challenge for development finance practitioners is creating an RLF (or other financing entity) with the capacity and capital base to generate impacts comparable to Self-Help Ventures Fund. In the last two sections of this chapter, we will return to the policies and effective practices that help build sustainable and high-impact economic development finance institutions.

RLFs have a strong track record as a cost-effective economic development tool. Across multiple studies, the cost-per-job created or retained through RLF loans ranged from $4,000 to $6,000. The federal RLF census, with data from 299 RLFs, reported a $5,338 average cost-per-job and a lower median of $3,761. Three other RLF studies (see Table 10.3) had comparable results in the $4,000 to $5,000 range.[10] Although the state RLF profiles found a higher cost- per-job figure across six states, three states reported costs of $5,000 to $6,500. RLFs in California and Ohio, however, lend far more per job created and retained, $14,308 and $21,188, respectively (see Table 10.5). Since most of this data is self-reported by RLFs, it probably overstates the true job impacts because no adjustment is made for jobs that would have been created or retained without RLF assistance.

Nonetheless, even when this problem is considered, most RLFs achieve a cost-per-job level well below the standards for several federal programs and outcomes reported for other economic development tools. HUD, for example, requires a maximum of $35,000 in CDBG funds per job created or retained, and the SBA uses the same standard for its 504 program. RLFs' strong cost-per-job performance may reflect their success at leveraging private sector financing. Among the few studies that measured private leverage, the average RLF secured $2 to $4 in private financing for every $1 in RLF financing (see Table 10.3).

RLFs have a mixed, but improving, default record. RLF studies from the 1980s found very high default rates. Barringer and Roche (see Grossman et al., 1998) reported that Neighborhood Reinvestment Fund-affiliated RLFs had default rates equal to 13% of total principal outstanding. Mt. Auburn Associates' (Kwass & Siegel, 1987a) analysis of EDA-funded RLFs found a 22% cumulative default rate over 4 years. At these rates, RLFs would lose a large portion of their capital if most defaults led to a substantial loan loss. However, more recent data suggest that the

Table 10.5   Performance Data From State RLF Profiles

Performance Measure	California	Illinois	Minnesota	North Carolina	Ohio	Washington
Total Jobs Created and Saved	14,537	18,570	25,135	11,091	20,483	9,877
Average Cost per Job[a]	$14,308	$5,148	$6,485	$9,233	$21,188	$5,984
Aggregate Default Rate	6.9%	7.3%	6.1%	3.5%	1.2%	<5%

SOURCE: Corporation for Enterprise Development (1997). State data summaries from *Counting on Local Capital* state RLF profiles. Data based on surveys conducted from December 1997 to May 1998.

NOTE: a. Calculated from CfED data by dividing total loans made in a state by the total jobs created and saved.

RLF industry has improved its lending skills and reduced default rates, although room for further improvement exists. The federal RLF census found an aggregate default percentage of 10% (i.e., the total value of loans in default equaled 10% of total outstanding loans). The median default rate across these 290 RLFs was much lower, at 5.68%, but this figure treats all RLF default rates equally without accounting for the size of defaulted loans. Microloan funds, which make much smaller loans than other RLFs, had lower default rates (3.85%) than other RLFs (5.91%), explaining why the median default rate is lower than the aggregate rate. State RLF profiles from 1997 to 1998 provide an even better picture of default performance (see Table 10.5). Aggregate default rates were less than 7.5% across all six states, and two states, Ohio and North Carolina, had rates of 1.2% and 3.5%, respectively. If the pattern for these six states applies nationwide, it indicates that RLFs achieved a major improvement in their management of loan defaults and losses during the 1990s, an important step toward institutional sustainability.

Design Issues for Revolving Loan Funds

Strategic design and sound policies are essential to establish a sustainable and high-impact RLF. This section reviews six policy areas that shape RLFs' capacity to achieve significant economic development impacts and achieve financial longevity: *targeting policies* define the type of businesses or projects that a RLF funds; *financial policies* set the loan products and financing terms offered; *capital policies* shape the amount and type of capital that is available to lend; *underwriting criteria* establish risk standards to evaluate potential loans; *development services* determine the technical assistance and other help provided to support business growth; and *relationship policies* focus on building key relationships to implement the RLF strategy. Beyond formulating sound policies in each area, RLF boards and managers need to formulate an overall strategy that integrates these policies in a synergistic manner. Because these six policy areas apply to all economic development finance entities, they are treated in some depth in this chapter. Later chapters will consider important variations that relate to the institutional model covered in that chapter.

Targeting Policy

Targeting policies are the key strategy lever for a RLF that defines its economic development mission. Targeting policies are the fund's economic development criteria; they determine which enterprises qualify for its services and financing, and thus, its potential economic development impact. Since RLFs have scarce resources, targeting focuses these resources to address financing gaps that maximize development impact. Two key factors shape targeting policies. First, targeting should reflect the economic development goals and strategies of the RLF and its partners. A governing economic development strategy frames a targeting policy that reinforces and benefits from other development initiatives. Second, to avoid capital substitution, the targeting strategy should focus on firms and projects that face capital availability problems, and complement, rather than duplicate, lending in private capital markets and among other alternative financial institutions. As RLFs and other development finance entities expand in size and number, it is increasingly important to consider the activities of other development finance entities when setting targeting policies. Beyond these two factors, RLF capacity and available capital inform targeting. RLFs face the challenge of setting a targeting policy that is neither too broad to dissipate impacts nor too narrow to generate insufficient demand and reach a sustainable size. Most targeting policies fall within four general categories:[11] targeting by industry or sector (e.g., manufacturers); targeting by business ownership (e.g., women-owned); geographic targeting (e.g., an enterprise zone); and targeting by firm stage (e.g., start-ups) (Kwass, Siegel, & Henze, 1987).

Financial Policies

Financial policies shape a RLF's success in avoiding capital substitution while affecting its financial sustainability and ability to revolve capital. Key financial policies include loan size, interest rate, repayment terms (both maturity and amortization schedule), and security position. Offering debt terms that are not provided by conventional lenders, such as small loans and ones with extended repayment periods, helps RLFs avoid capital substitution. Subordinate debt is a particularly effective financing policy to fill capital availability gaps. Through a subordinate collateral position, RLFs supply debt that banks and finance companies usually do not offer and increase the total capital that a firm can raise. Subordinate debt can make the difference between a firm having sufficient capital to undertake a project and being forced to delay, scale back, or not proceed with an investment. It reduces the senior lender's risk by increasing the loan-to-value ratio and provides a firm with the financial resources to implement its plans. Beyond supplying subordinate debt, a RLF's financing policies can allow for longer repayment periods, which increases the cash flow available to reinvest in the firm—an especially important need during start-up, high-growth periods, and restructuring.

Financial policies shape RLFs' cash flow and, thus, their ability to recycle capital for maximum impact, and to cover operating costs, loan losses, and any debt service. For this reason, financial policies entail trade offs between maximizing economic development goals and enhancing financial sustainability.

Although firms benefit from low-interest and long-term loans, these policies reduce RLF cash flow, slowing the pace at which RLF capital is revolved and possibly forcing the fund to dip into its capital to cover its costs. These trade-offs are demonstrated in Table 10.6, which shows how certain financial polices impact RLF annual lending capacity and financial position. The scenarios in this table assume a RLF with $2 million in capital and $75,000 in annual operating expenses that lends $1 million annually in its first 2 years and then lends at a constant annual amount in subsequent years. Changes in interest rate, repayment period, and loss rate are compared to a "base case" (loans at a 7% interest rate, 5-year amortization, and a 2% loss rate) to measure their impact on the RLF's annual lending capacity, cash account, and loan receivable balance after 10 years. By raising its interest rate to 9%, the RLF can expand annual loans from $310,000 to $400,000. Over 10 years, the higher interest rate allows it to make another $720,000 in loans while adding $344,000 to its assets. Reducing loan repayments from 5 to 3 years yields a greater impact on annual lending, raising it to $550,000. Over 10 years, the RLF can make another $1.92 million in loans—a 43% increase in total lending—and has a slight growth in assets. When annual loan losses change from 2% to 4%, perhaps from lending to riskier firms, the annual lending capacity drops to $250,000. After 10 years, the RLF lends almost $500,000 less as its assets drop by $277,000. These examples demonstrate that RLFs must balance the market need to supply riskier loans and flexible terms with their goals of improved RLF financial condition and expanded impact that result from market-rate loans with shorter repayment periods.

Table 10.6 Impact of Financial Policies on RLF Lending Capacity and Financial Position

Financial Policy or Outcome	Base Case	Increase Interest Rate to 9%	Shorten Amortization to 3 years	Loss Rate Grows to 4%
Interest Rate on Loans	7%	9%	7%	7%
Interest Rate on Cash	5%	5%	5%	5%
Annual Loss Rate on Loans	2%	2%	2%	4%
Principal Amortization Rate	5 years	5 years	3 years	5 years
Annual Lending Volume	$310,000	$400,000	$550,000	$250,00
Cumulative Loans	$4,480,000	$5,200,000	$6,400,000	$4,000,000
Initial Capital	$2,000,000	$2,000,000	$2,000,000	$2,000,000
Cash Balance in 10th Year	$358,785	$349,827	$267,826	$370,706
Loans Receivable Balance in 10th Year	$1,459,910	$1,812,950	$1,573,932	$1,171,363

Capital Policies

Capital policies set the financial structure and funding sources that ultimately determine a RLF's ability to achieve its development goals. These capital policies affect financial policies and, thus, the ability to offer financial products that fit the capital gaps and financing needs of target markets. The type of capital raised by an RLF defines what kind of financing it can provide. A RLF funded exclusively from grants has no cost of capital and no debt payments to make. Consequently, it has considerable flexibility to set interest rates and repayment periods while still preserving its capital base. However, a RLF funded substantially with debt must link its lending terms to its debt payments. The interest rate on its borrowed funds provides a floor for its interest rates while the repayment schedules on loans made by the RLF must allow it to meet its debt obligations. In development finance, you are what you eat. A RLF that borrows short-term to address long-term credit needs has a mismatch between its sources and uses of funds that is not sustainable. It must either change its loan products to fit its capital sources or find alternative funds to meet short-term debt obligations. Sound capital policies require RLF managers to define a capital structure that is consistent with their targeting strategy and then identify, cultivate, and secure funding sources to create and maintain that structure.

A second goal of capital policies is securing capital sources that allow the RLF to achieve a sustainable scale. As studies show, most RLFs have assets below $1 million, half of the minimum $2 million level needed to be sustainable.[12] Thus, as an industry, RLFs must expand their capital sources to become financially viable entities. Although grant funds allow high-risk lending and flexible financial policies, limited grant sources exist. RLFs that rely solely on grants must be extremely creative to cultivate new grant sources to expand without debt. Most RLFs will need to alter their capital policies and attract nongrant capital to become financially sustainable. In addition to borrowing funds on terms consistent with their mission, RLFs can sell loans and manage funds for private investors. These capitalization strategies, employed by many larger RLFs, are elaborated in Chapter 18.

Underwriting Criteria

These policies institute standards that formalize a RLF's capacity to make sound loans, manage lending risks, and achieve economic development objectives. Underwriting criteria define the economic development, business, and financial characteristics desired by a RLF in its loan transactions. A RLF tests how well a proposed loan meets these criteria during its underwriting analysis. Some RLFs eschew formal underwriting policies and, instead, rely on the expertise of RLF staff or loan review committees to evaluate loans. Although this nonbureaucratic approach is appealing, partly as an antithesis to large commercial bank practices, it leaves lending policies and the quality and consistency of loan decisions dependent on the skills and views of a few individuals. Consequently, staff or loan committee turnover can lead to unintended policy changes and shifts in loss risks.[13] Underwriting standards also help staff identify a borrower's weaknesses and potential problems so the business can address them.

Underwriting policies encompass three types of criteria. First, they set standards for economic development outcomes. One common example is a threshold for RLF loan dollars-per-job created or retained. However, RLFs also need economic development criteria for other important impacts, such as job quality (pay and benefit levels), hiring of targeted individuals, investment in employee training, physical improvements, and commitments to remain in a community. The Portland Development Commission, for example, required borrowers from its loan funds to use the Private Industry Council and its community hiring network[14] as a first source to fill job openings. Legislation creating the Massachusetts Community Development Finance Corporation required it to lend or invest in firms that pay at 150% of the minimum wage and provide health insurance.[15] A second set of standards addresses the firm's capacity to achieve business and financial targets—the core of its ability to repay a RLF loan. These criteria typically include the existence and quality of the firm's business plan, the management team's experience and skills, the firm's past performance, and its capacity to achieve sales and earning targets given the competitive environment. Finally, underwriting criteria set standards for financial risk through the required loan-to-value ratio, debt service coverage ratio, and guarantees.

Underwriting criteria should match a RLF's targeting and financial policies. Economic development criteria align targeting and underwriting policies, but targeting policies have additional underwriting implications. For example, a RLF that targets low-income entrepreneurs needs business capacity standards that reflect the realities of this target population. In lieu of prior business management experience, it might require work or personal experience in the industry, completion of a training course, or a mentor. Financial underwriting policies for higher-risk early-stage or turnaround businesses will differ from those for expanding established companies. Whereas a 1.10 to 1.25 debt service coverage ratio fits a RLF targeting the latter market, those serving the former may need to accept a 1:1 coverage or even earnings that do not cover debt payments for some period when equity investments or debt service reserves cover the cash flow deficits. Financial policies also have implications for underwriting standards. When financing polices include subordinate lending, the RLF will need to accept a higher loan-to-value ratio and, perhaps, a lower debt coverage ratio for these loans. To manage greater risks under their targeting and financial policies, RLFs create sound business capacity standards and offer more extensive development services.

Development Services

Development services advance RLF economic development goals by expanding the capacity of borrowers to succeed and grow. Firms targeted by RLFs often lack key business and management skills, which training and technical assistance help overcome. Moreover, small businesses must respond to considerable competition with fewer resources and smaller management teams than large businesses. Development services help level this playing field. Training and technical assistance services also increase the pool of potential borrowers and improve their performance after receiving a loan,[16] helping to lower loss rates and preserve the jobs created through RLF lending. Some development services expand the impact of RLF assistance beyond the firm, such as job placement and training services to link target populations to the jobs created by RLF borrowers. RLFs have learned the value of development services to accomplishing their mission. Although a small share of RLFs offered training and technical assistance services in the 1980s, most funds provided them in the 1990s.

The primary RLF development services are loan packaging, business technical assistance, and training. *Loan packaging* refers to helping a business structure an overall financial plan and prepare the application package to apply for financing, including loans and investment outside the RLF. Technical assistance helps a business address planning, management, and operating needs. Some assistance concerns general matters, such as business plan preparation or financial management and accounting systems while other services can be technical and firm-specific, such as improving quality control on a manufacturing line. Training educates groups of firms around specific business skills and issues.

A RLF's development services policy concerns both what services to provide and how to deliver them. Although development services vary with a RLF's mission and target markets, most loan funds will benefit from providing core services that include loan packaging assistance, one-on-one advice on general business planning issues, and referrals to specialized technical assistance providers. These core services can be supplemented with specialized assistance that is either customized to individual firm needs or focused on technical issues shared by many borrowers. To address weak financial systems, Cascadia Revolving Loan Fund hired a full-time CPA to work with their borrowers to set up sound bookkeeping and accounting systems. As firms saw the benefit of this assistance, they demanded more of the CPA's time to help them use their new financial systems to flag problems and monitor performance. This intensive assistance is an important factor in Cascadia RLF's low historic 1% loss rate (Clones, 1998). Given the specialized nature of many business issues, even large RLFs will lack the internal capacity to address all business needs and need to supplement staff assistance with external consultants and specialized technical assistance providers. Massachusetts's Economic Stabilization Trust provides matching grants for borrowers—a diverse set of manufacturers—to hire a third-party consultant to address specialized needs. Individual Development Accounts are an emerging development service for RLFs that target low-income entrepreneurs; these accounts accelerate savings growth through federal funds that match individual contributions to a savings account. Entrepreneurs can use IDA savings for either training or business investment purposes.[17]

Relationship Building

Relationships are central to most RLF activities. Referral networks help RLFs to market their programs and secure quality financing requests. Private lenders and other financial institutions collaborate to complete financing packages for firms. Partnerships with technical assistance providers and economic development programs allow RLFs to expand development services. Elected officials provide political support and help secure funding. Effective relationships with multiple funding sources allow RLFs to raise additional RLF capital and fund development services. Although RLF managers understand the importance of building these relationships, demands on their time, especially at small RLFs, often limit their attention to this work. An explicit relationship-building policy focuses staff on creating strong external relationships and defines board and staff responsibilities.

Relationship-building policies begin with an inventory of potential partners that can help the RLF advance its mission. RLFs should assess the contribution of each organization to its work and honestly assess the quality of its existing relationship. Through this "relationship mapping," RLFs can identify important relationships that were overlooked and ones that need improvement. Next, the RLF must define goals for each potential partner. Some goals may be modest (e.g., increased awareness and referrals), while others may involve a formal partnership (e.g., a collaboration to raise funds for expanded technical assistance services). Since strong relationships are built on reciprocity and mutual benefit, practitioners should consider what each potential partner could gain from the relationship. A RLF that shows how working together will advance the other organization's goals and interests will be more successful in generating collaboration.

The final relationship-building strategy has both policy and operational dimensions. The policy component defines specific relationships and their role in advancing RLF goals and implementing activities. For example, it may include a referral network with lenders and finance professionals to generate deal flow, formal partnerships with the Small Business Development Center and Manufacturing Extension Program to provide technical assistance services, strengthening funding relationships with major banks and foundations, and having board representation for the city economic development director, manufacturing association, and a commercial bank. The policy's operational component details specific actions and responsibilities to build these relationships. It may assign the board chair to recruit new board representatives, direct the RLF executive director to negotiate partnerships with technical assistance providers and explore funding opportunities with banks and foundations, and require all staff to cultivate referral relationships with specific professionals. Relationship building should also include organizing events or awards to recognize important partners and creating tools to keep stakeholders informed about the RLF's mission and programs.

Although each of the six policy areas is distinct, they clearly interact in many ways. Consequently, RLF managers must align and integrate policies to ensure they are compatible and synergistic. Figure 10.2 provides one way to view the interrelationships among the six policy areas based on a three-tier model with economic development targeting as the primary integrating policy. In this conception, targeting policies, as economic development goals, are the first tier that shapes the formulation of financial, capital, and development policies. The design of these second-tier policies is critical to advance the targeting policy and must be most carefully aligned. Thus, capital policies must raise the type and amount of funds that are consistent with the financial products offered and support the desired development services. Similarly, financing policies need to work within the goals and constraints of capital policies, and development services should be tailored to generate demand and prepare potential borrowers for the type of financing supplied by the RLF. Third-tier policies serve to implement second-tier policies. Relationship-building activities are crafted to form collaborations that are critical to effectuating the financial, capital, and development service policies. Underwriting policies primarily translate targeting and financial policies into more detailed lending standards but also need to reflect the development services and capital policies. Underwriting standards for business plans and management capacity, for example, may be adjusted based on the extent and form of development services provided. Similarly, the financial structure and risk expectations of funding sources incorporated into RLF capital policies shape underwriting policies. Underwriting standards also affect capital policies since they define the risk profile for RLF borrowers, which may preclude using certain debt sources.

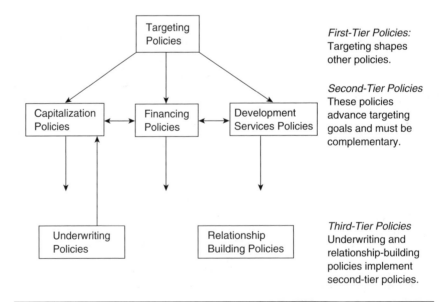

Figure 10.2 Integrating RLF Policies

_____ Management Challenges and Best Practices

Although the RLF model is simple, establishing a sustainable and effective loan fund is a complex task. This concluding section summarizes the major management challenges that RLFs confront and best practices to tackle them. Box 10.1 lists six challenges to creating a viable RLF with significant economic development impact. These challenges fall into three categories: RLF strategy, lending operations, and capitalization. Because these challenges were introduced in the overview of the RLF industry and the preceding policy discussion, this section emphasizes two issues that cut across the six challenges in Box 10.1: the importance of scale to RLF effectiveness and the need for strong and varied technical skills.

Box 10.1   RLF Management Challenges

Strategy Challenges

Formulating a Strategy to Maximize Impact With Limited Capital.

RLFs must define a financing role to advance economic development goals with limited resources. An effective strategy targets limited capital, avoids capital substitution, and links financing with development services and other economic development activities.

Balancing Economic Development Goals With Financial Objectives.

RLF strategies confront trade-offs between maximizing economic development outcomes and achieving financial sustainability. Key trade-offs include balancing risk taking with limiting losses and weighing long loan terms that enhance borrower cash flow against short-term loans to revolve capital.

Operating Challenges

Establishing an Effective Origination, Underwriting, and Approval Process.

RLFs need a sound and efficient lending process that generates demand to fully utilize capital, provides timely decisions coordinated with other lenders, and preserves capital through sound financial decisions and active portfolio management. RLFs often need to achieve these operational goals with limited staff but while serving higher-risk borrowers.

Providing Quality Technical Assistance to Client Firms.

RLFs must deliver considerable technical services to borrowers with staff and funding constraints. They need to access diverse and sometimes intensive services for borrowers without tapping into their loan capital.

Building Strong Relationships With Multiple Partners.

RLFs need the collaboration and support of many constituencies and must find the time and tools to build effective relationships with lenders, political leaders, economic development agencies, and technical assistance providers.

Capitalization Challenges

Securing Sufficient and Appropriate Capital to Achieve a Sustainable Scale.

RLFs require multiple and recurring capital sources to reach a sustainable asset base of several million dollars and offer financial products that address their economic development goals and local capital market gaps.

Scale expands resources to hire staff, deliver development services, and increase economic development impacts. It is also fundamental to achieving financial sustainability. Securing capital is critical to reaching scale, but RLF strategy is also important. RLFs must identify target markets and financing roles with sufficient demand to reach scale. Many RLFs focus on too narrow a geography or business type to achieve a significant size. In these cases, RLFs should consider serving secondary markets to generate loan demand and attract capital to become financially self-sufficient. A RLF that finances manufacturing firms in a small city faces limited demand. To expand its market and potential size, this RLF can expand its service area or serve additional sectors that advance its goals, or both. Similarly, a RLF that targets minority-owned start-up businesses in a city's low-income neighborhood could also lend to other locally owned small businesses to expand its loan volumes and raise more capital. Secondary lending markets will also improve financial performance when they reduce lending risks and allow shorter repayment periods. These secondary markets offer the greatest benefits when they are linked to the RLF's goals and draw on capabilities involved in serving the primary market. RLFs also need access to multiple technical skills to succeed. Although lending skills may seem paramount, RLFs require four types of expertise: economic development, commercial lending, financial management, and business management. Economic development skills are critical to strategy formulation, designing development services, and building relationships with other economic development organizations. Commercial lending expertise allows the RLF to run an efficient lending process, make sound lending decisions, and build credibility with private lenders. Financial management capacity ensures strong internal accounting and reporting systems and maximizes the growth and use of RLF capital. Finally, business management expertise enhances the RLF's capacity to deliver technical assistance to its borrowers. A combination of experienced staff, consultants, and partnerships help RLFs access and apply this skill set. Small and early-stage RLFs, in particular, need to use consultants and partnerships with other entities to augment their capacity. Because RLFs are strongest when they posses internal capacity in all four areas, they should work to achieve this goal as they grow.

Best Practices in RLF Management

The evaluation and practitioner literature[18] suggests several best practices that RLFs can apply to achieve scale, improve operations, and increase their impact. First, RLFs can use their *board composition* to advance strategic goals and enhance capacity. In addition to ensuring accountability to their target market and key stakeholders, RLF board members should be recruited to strengthen important relationships and provide expertise. Collectively, the board should have expertise in the four aspects of RLF operations (economic development, commercial lending, financial management, and business management). Thus, important people to invite onto the RLF board include private sector lenders, other economic development organizations, business owners, and technical assistance providers. When a RLF works with many organizations, it can create an advisory committee to communicate with this larger group and involve it in policy deliberations. Second, *staff capacity* is a critical success factor for any organization. To develop sufficient staff with skills in all the required technical areas, especially in their early years, RLFs need to subsidize staff costs, invest in staff training, and supplement staff with outside consultants. Third, RLFs should charge market interest rates and supply subordinate loans to enhance their financial sustainability and development impact. By charging *market interest rates,* RLFs increase their income and avoid capital substitution. This policy recognizes that expanding capital availability, rather than lowering its cost, is the primary development finance mission. Moreover, borrowers that can secure conventional financing have no incentive to seek a RLF loan when no interest rate subsidy is available. Subordinate debt allows RLFs to supplement private lenders by filling the funding gap left by conventional underwriting standards. It also reduces the required RLF loan per business, spreading limited capital among more firms. However, since subordinate debt carries greater risk, RLFs should charge a fair market interest rate for these loans. Forth, *sustained marketing* is important to build the RLF's profile and credibility while generating loan demand. One-on-one outreach by RLF staff is a core marketing tool that should be linked with the overall relationship-building strategy to build strong referral networks with lenders, technical assistance providers, accountants and attorneys, economic development agencies, and other parties that work with potential clients. Fifth, RLFs need *explicit underwriting standards and an efficient and transparent lending process.* These practices ensure that the RLF targeting and financial strategy are implemented and build institutional capacity to survive staff turnover. Moreover, when borrowers know what is required up front, they can avoid delays by better preparing for loan underwriting and the entire process. While RLFs should not sacrifice a thorough and well-documented lending system, they can reduce paperwork burdens and streamline their decision making and closing timelines. Loan packaging services help advance these goals, as does RLF staff coordination with other lenders to eliminate duplicative or conflicting requirements and resolve problems that arise throughout the lending process. A final RLF best practice is the creative pursuit of *capital sources* to reach a sustainable scale. Effective capitalization practices include securing grants from diverse government and foundation sources, supplementing grants with debt, originating and managing funds for other investors (e.g., bank loan pools or the SBA 504 program), and using loan sales, loan participations, and asset securitization to generate renewable sources of funds.

Although this discussion of RLF challenges and best practices focused on RLFs, it also applies to the other economic development finance entities covered in the next three chapters. By introducing these topics in this chapter, readers have a better understanding of how development finance institutions operate and a lens to view differences across institutional models. As each model is presented in the following chapters, variations in these challenges for each institution will be considered along with the unique assets and tools that each model offers to address them.

The preceding explanation of RLF policies and practices may seem too brief and raise more questions than it answers. However, a fuller treatment of management practices to tackle common challenges across development finance institutions is reserved for later chapters. Chapter 16 covers approaches to planning and designing new entities to address strategy challenges. Chapter 17 focuses on management of the lending and investment process. Chapter 18 addresses strategies and tools to manage capital and tackle capitalization challenges.

Endnotes

1. This figure is based on the census of federally funded RLFs conducted by the Corporation for Enterprise Development in its Counting on Local Capital research project, which uncovered approximately 3,000 RLFs. It is also supported by the surveys of RLFs conducted in six states where over 500 RLFs were identified. If this level of RLF use exists in other states, then there would be several thousand nationwide.

2. A RLF also may be more risk averse and set stricter underwriting standards with its own debt obligations to meet.

3. Chapter 9 did argue that CRA policies address externalities associated with the withdrawal of credit from low-income areas. RLFs can be directed toward a more diverse set of externalities, such as reducing the social costs of unemployment and helping firms reduce pollution.

4. Grants also can directly fund this cost by funding staff, systems, or other related services.

5. USDA offers long-term 1% loans to RLFs in addition to grants.

6. If the average RLF has 18 loans, they most likely accumulated this loan portfolio over several years and receive repayments over several years, so the average annual lending volumes would be less than 18, probably in the range of 4 to 6 loans.

7. From the McManus and Mt. Auburn Associates' studies cited in Grossman et al. (1998), *Counting on Local Capital: A Literature Review of Revolving Loan Funds*.

8. Several methodological issues relate to this measure. First, accurate figures are needed for the number of jobs created or retained that account for any capital substitution effects. Sometimes these figures simply report the firm's total employment or jobs added since receiving a RLF loan without assessing whether the firm could have received financing without the RLF loan or if the loan was a necessary condition for the jobs to be retained or added. An independent evaluation is the best method to get

an accurate estimate of true job impacts. A second issue relates to calculating the cost side; although using loan capital is the most common approach, some analysts prefer using the subsidy cost-per-job rather than the loan capita-per-job. The subsidy cost is a better indicator of the true cost to the RLF since the firm repays its loan principal. The subsidy cost is estimated by adding RLF interest subsidy and loan losses. If there are staff cost subsidies for technical assistance or loan packaging for private lenders, then this should also be included in the subsidy cost estimation.

9. Self-Help Ventures Fund's large job impacts reflect its long life (almost 15 years when the data was collected) and its large lending capacity, with $27.9 million in capital and 20 employees.

10. One study, by Mt. Auburn Associates, was particularly rigorous, adjusting for financial substitution effects and only counting jobs when the business would not have received financing without the RLF loan.

11. For a more detailed discussion of targeting options, see Kwass, Siegel, and Henze (1987), *The Design and Management of State and Local Revolving Loan Funds: A Handbook*, pp. 30–36.

12. CfED cites National Community Capital, the industry association for community-based loan funds, as stating that loan funds with $1 million or less cover only half of their operating costs and thus require continued external subsidies to stay in business. See Levere (1998), p. 12. A RLF with modest operating costs of $150,000, a 1% annual loan loss rate, and an 8% average interest rate needs over $2 million in capital to cover its expenses and losses and maintain a constant capital base.

13. This occurred at one state economic development corporation when a new manager shifted a fund's emphasis from debt-oriented transactions toward equity investments in firms with high growth potential. Without formalized underwriting polices set by the board, the full implications of this change were not analyzed, and the corporation suffered a significant loss of capital and cash flow.

14. This policy is discussed in the Portland Development Commission's Industrial Site Loan Fund in Kwass and Siegel, 1987b.

15. See Chapter 40F of the Massachusetts General Laws.

16. An evaluation of the federal Empowerment Zone/Enterprise Community (EZ/EC) Program found that business technical assistance services were central to the success of EZ/EC loan funds by helping entrepreneurs to qualify for loans and generate strong demand for credit. See Hebert et al., pp. 96, 99, and 116. The report states "The most common problem with access to capital programs was the inability of prospective borrowers to qualify for loans. Entrepreneurs needed technical assistance with such matters as getting financial statements in order, developing financial plans and improving their credit records." (p. 99)

17. Two examples of RLFs with IDA programs include the Women's Initiative Loan Fund (Levere, 1998, p. 25) and The Neighborhood Institute (Marcoux, 1998, pp. 35–36).

18. Two good sources for more detailed information on RLF best practices are the case studies in the Corporation for Enterprise Development's state RLF profiles and Kwass et al. (1987), *The Design and Management of State and Local Revolving Loan Funds.*

11

Venture Capital and Equity Investment Funds

Venture capital is a relatively new but fast-growing form of development finance that emerged after World War II to finance high-growth early-stage firms with the potential for large investment returns. Despite its youth, the venture capital industry has played an important role in the economic development process through financing technology-based firms, emerging industries, and high-growth businesses. Since venture capital is tied to new technologies and fast-growing firms, both key sources of new jobs, expanding the availability of venture capital is often included in state and regional economic development strategies. The co-location of large concentrations of venture capital funds and technology-based industries in Silicon Valley and the Boston region has heightened practitioner and policy maker interest in expanding the supply of venture capital to attract and nurture technology-based businesses. Venture capital is also the primary institutional source of equity for small businesses, outside the public stock markets. Just as a community without commercial banking services is disadvantaged in providing debt to finance business growth, the absence of venture capital impairs firms' ability to raise equity to finance their growth and to create the financial cushion required to raise debt. Thus, venture capital and equity funds help small firms access both equity and debt capital.

This chapter introduces the private venture capital industry and discusses the major policies and institutions used to expand the supply of business equity capital. Since venture capitalists operate quite differently from commercial banks and other private debt intermediaries, the first section summarizes the industry's key attributes, practices, and recent trends. An appreciation for how venture capital works provides insight into equity capital gaps and the appropriate interventions to address them. The next four sections address development finance practice to expand the supply of equity capital. One section reviews the federal experience licensing and funding equity investment funds under the SBA Small Business Investment Corporation (SBIC) and Special Small Business Investment Corporation (SSBIC) programs. Next, the policy options and lessons from state government efforts to expand venture capital supply are considered. Third, the emerging model of community development venture capital, which invests private funds in enterprises that promise financial and social returns, is discussed. The chapter concludes by summarizing lessons and best practices in the design and management of venture capital institutions with an economic development mission.

The Private Venture Capital Industry

Although the first venture capital firm, American Research and Development,[1] was founded in 1946, significant growth in venture capital funds did not occur until the late 1970s and early 1980s. From 1978 to 1984, the annual number of new venture funds increased sixfold from 23 to 150 while the capital invested in these funds grew from $451 million to $5.2 billion (Gompers & Lerner, 1999). Venture capital investment levels then declined in the late 1980s and early 1990s before mushrooming again in the middle 1990s. By 1997, close to 500 venture capital funds managed almost $50 billion in capital with $11.7 billion in new funds raised during 1996 alone (Gompers & Lerner, 1999). The 1990s venture capital boom peaked in 2000 when the Internet frenzy helped venture capital funds raise $92 billion in new investments (Venture Economics, 2001). With the stock market decline and the failure of many Internet-related firms, both the level of new money raised and the total size of all venture capital funds declined in 2001 and 2002. This cyclical investment pattern reveals the close link between the public stock markets and venture capital. Because venture capitalists earn the greatest profits from an initial public offering (IPO) of stock, a strong IPO market raises venture capital returns, which generates increased investor interest in funding venture capital partnerships. Thus, large inflows to venture capital funds usually follow strong IPO markets whereas new investment in venture capital declines after market downturns (Gompers & Lerner, 1999). However, other factors also influence investment in venture capital funds, including capital gains tax rates and pension fund investment regulations (Bygrave & Timmons, 1996; Gompers & Lerner, 1999).[2]

Venture capital (VC) funds fall into three categories: independent firms, financial institution subsidiaries, and corporate subsidiaries (Florida & Smith, 1993). Independent venture capital firms are the most common and seek to maximize returns for investors. VC firms linked to financial institutions may serve strategic goals beyond maximizing investment returns, such as providing a full array of financing services to customers or generating IPO transactions for a parent investment bank. Corporations may form venture capital funds to support the development of new products or technologies related to their core businesses. Most venture capital funds, with the exception of many corporate funds, are organized as private limited partnerships. Investors provide capital as limited partners, limiting liability to their investment in the partnership. A professional venture capitalist, as general partner, manages the investment of these funds on behalf of the investors. Limited partners provide almost all the investment capital and typically receive 80% of the investment returns. The general partner invests a small amount of funds (often 1%) but contributes expertise in making and managing the fund's investments. In return, the general partner receives an annual management fee, often around 2.5% of the fund's committed capital or total assets, and a share of the fund's profits, typically 20% (Gompers & Lerner, 1999). Each investment partnership has a fixed life, usually 10 to 12 years. When the partnership expires, all assets, both cash and equity investments, are distributed to the partners. This structure allows venture capital firms (i.e., management companies) to raise a large pool of funds up front and have a long time horizon to invest in companies, nurture them, and then, it is hoped, exit from them with a large capital gain. Yet the fixed life of the fund pressures venture capitalists to exit or liquidate their investments. Gompers and Lerner, however, question the importance of the limited partnership structure to successful venture capital investing. They found that corporate venture capital funds, organized as subsidiary corporations, had comparable investment returns to funds organized as limited partnerships. Moreover, companies financed by corporate funds with a strong strategic focus were more successful than firms financed by other venture capitalists. Thus, they argue that "strategy and incentives are critical to successful venture capital investing," rather than organizational form.[3]

In their detailed 1999 study, *The Venture Capital Cycle*, Gompers and Lerner describe three distinct phases of the venture capital industry: fund-raising, investing, and exiting investments. Venture capital firms need to successfully manage all three activities to generate strong investment returns and gain the track record to repeat the cycle. Since economic development-oriented venture capital funds must address this three-part cycle (and do so in a manner that overcomes supply gaps in the conventional venture capital market), it is important to review the key issues and practices in each phase of the venture capital cycle.

Fund-raising

Two aspects of venture capital fund-raising, the explosive growth in monies invested in venture capital and the cyclical nature of these investments, are documented in Table 11.1, along with the funding sources for venture capital funds from 1981 to 2000. Over these 20 years, pension funds became venture capitalists' largest investment source. Their share of new investments grew from 23% in 1981 to a high of 59% in 1993 before leveling off to around 40% in the late 1990s. This large infusion of pension investments helped fuel increases in total venture fund capital and the average fund size. From 1992 to 2000, the median venture capital partnership increased from $57.7 million to $138 million (Venture One, 2001).

Since venture capital investors, as limited partners, have no direct control over how general partners manage their funds, they establish incentives and covenants

Table 11.1   Sources of Investment Into Venture Capital Funds for Selected Years, 1981 to 2000 (in $2000 millions)

Source	1981	1984	1987	1990	1993	1997	2000
New Investment	1,964	5,553	6,171	2,876	2,920	12,552	92,000
Pension funds	23%	34%	39%	53%	59%	40%	40%
Corporations	17%	14%	10%	7%	8%	30%	4%
Individuals	23%	15%	12%	11%	7%	13%	12%
Endowments	12%	6%	10%	13%	11%	9%	21%
Insurance companies and banks	15%	13%	15%	9%	11%	1%	23%
Foreign investors and others	10%	18%	14%	7%	4%	7%	Not detailed

SOURCE: Gompers and Lerner (1999) for data on years 1981-1997, and Venture Economics (2001) for data on 2000.

in partnership agreements to align the interests of investors and managers and to limit managers' self-serving behavior. The primary incentive to align interests is the large compensation that general partners receive from fund profits. In their analysis of general partner compensation, Gompers and Lerner (1999) found that 81% of agreements provided managers with between 20% and 21% of fund profits. However, older and larger firms received a slightly higher share, as did funds focusing on high-technology and early-stage firms. Although no statistical relationship existed between incentive compensation and performance, the authors found that compensation is more closely linked to performance for older and larger venture capital firms. These findings suggest that venture capitalists that perform well can negotiate higher compensation from investors. Investors negotiate a wide array of covenants to restrict how general partners manage funds, such as the size, form, and type of investment and general partner activities. These covenants seek to control general partners' ability to invest funds in ways that increase their profits relative to the limited partners and to ensure that they devote significant time and effort to placing and managing investments. However, covenants also reflect the relative market power of general partners and investors. At times of high demand for venture capital managers (i.e., when the inflow of investment capital is large) general partners negotiate less restrictive covenants, but they must accept stronger covenants when the supply of new capital declines (Gompers & Lerner, 1999).

Investing

Venture capital funds seek high rates of return through equity investments in early stage, high-growth firms. In pursuit of this goal, VC funds concentrate their investments in certain industries and regions. Historically, investments have been heavily clustered in 4 technology-intensive sectors among the 20 major manufacturing industries: drugs, office and computing machines, communication and electronic equipment, and professional and scientific instruments. These four industries consistently accounted for 80% of venture capital investments from 1980 to 1996 (Gompers & Lerner, 1999). Since 1997, venture capitalists have focused on information technology industries, including hardware, software, and service providers. Collectively, these industries accounted for 60% of investments, in real dollars, made from 1997 to 2001 (see Table 11.2). Venture capital investments are also highly concentrated geographically, as shown in Table 11.3.[4] Throughout the 1980s and 1990s, California attracted the largest share of venture capital, usually over one third of the total number and dollar value of investment. Massachusetts was the second largest recipient, attracting 6% to 9% of venture capital investments, followed by Texas, which received 4% to 7%. Collectively, these three states have accounted for 52% of venture capital investments (in real dollars) made from 1980 to 1996. Moreover, their share increased from 32.5% in the early 1980s to 62.5% in 2001.

Table 11.2   Venture Capital Investment by Industry, 1997 to 2001 (in $2001 millions)

Industry Group	1997	1998	1999	2000	2001	Total 1997- 2001	Percent 1997- 2001
Pharmaceuticals	$1,224	$1,533	$1,847	$3,889	$2,887	$11,380	5.4%
Medical Devices	$919	$1,024	$1,451	$2,009	$1,606	$7,008	3.3%
Health Services	$848	$661	$597	$436	$307	$2,850	1.4%
Medical Information Systems	$536	$562	$1,130	$2,535	$773	$5,538	2.6%
Health Care Total	$3,529	$3,781	$5,025	$8,874	$5,574	$26,783	12.8%
Communications Hardware and Services	$2,987	$4,369	$10,025	$24,072	$8,397	$49,849	23.8%
Electronics and Computer Hardware	$634	$6,746	$1,080	$2,001	$1,242	$11,702	5.6%
Semiconductors	$667	$695	$1,468	$3,346	$2,137	$8,312	4.0%
Information Services	$930	$1,938	$6,543	$9,400	$1,917	$20,728	9.9%
Software	$2,824	$3,694	$9,159	$18,492	$7,323	$41,491	19.8%
Total Information Technology	$8,041	$11,370	$28,288	$57,496	$21,015	$126,209	60.2%
Consumer and Business Products	$375	$211	$317	$472	$165	$1,539	0.7%
Consumer and Business Services	$1,260	$2,627	$11,738	$24,795	$4,934	$45,354	21.6%
Retailers	$626	$795	$4,619	$2,157	$246	$8,442	4.0%
Total Consumer and Business Products and Services	$2,264	$3,692	$16,674	$27,423	$5,344	$55,397	26.4%
Other Companies	$262	$230	$140	$425	$196	$1,252	0.6%
Total, All Investment	$14,09	$19,072	$50,126	$94,218	$32,129	$209,640	100.0%

SOURCE: Venture One (2002).

Table 11.3   Venture Capital Investment by State, 1980 to 1996 and 2001 (in $2001 millions)

State	1980-84	1985-89	1990-96	2001
California	$8,403	$12,108	$17,032	$13,527
Massachusetts	$2,433	$3,542	$4,239	$4,018
Texas	$1,453	$2,718	$2,517	$2,523
New York	$862	$1,758	$1,746	$1,584
New Jersey	$463	$1,521	$2,143	$1,023
Colorado	$617	$1,007	$1,191	$979
Pennsylvania	$463	$1,916	$1,388	$857
Illinois	$360	$1,513	$1,769	$555
Minnesota	$338	$509	$653	$361
Connecticut	$399	$1,832	$907	$395
Total, all states	$19,108	$38,492	$46,530	$32,129

SOURCE: Gompers and Lerner (1999) for 1981-1997 data, and Venture One (2002) for 2001 data.

As venture capital funds grew in size, their average investment also increased continuously from 1970 to 2000 (see Table 11.4). Although the growth was gradual through the mid-1990s, growing 48% in real terms over 20 years, it skyrocketed by almost 250% during the 1997 to 2001 period. The massive infusion of new capital into venture capital funds during the late 1990s led managers to make much larger investments. With the pressure to make larger investments, venture capitalists shifted from financing early-stage to later-stage companies that needed more capital (Gompers & Lerner, 1999). There is also evidence of investment herding among venture capitalists, whereby many funds focus on the same industry and increase the level of investment beyond what the market and industry size warrants. This phenomenon likely creates competition that raises company values and investment levels. One possible outcome from herding is underinvestment and slower growth in industries with strong growth potential that get overlooked by venture capitalists.[5]

Venture capitalists use investment staging, active monitoring of portfolio firms, and coinvesting to address the uncertainty, information costs, and high risk of investing equity in early-stage businesses.[6] Staged investments

Table 11.4   Average Size of Venture Capital Investments, 1970 to 2000 (in $2000 millions)

	1970-74	1975-79	1980-84	1985-89	1990-96	1997-2000
Number VC Investments	847	847	5,365	8,154	9,406	14,800
Total VC Disbursements	2,356	2,750	18,579	37,427	45,243	172,512
Average Investment Size	2.78	3.25	3.46	4.59	4.81	11.65

SOURCE: Gompers and Lerner (1999) for 1970 to 1996 data, and Venture One (2001) for 1997 to 2000 data.

allow venture capitalists to limit losses and concentrate funds on firms with the greatest potential to succeed. Staging entails disbursing funds over time as firms demonstrate progress in implementing their business plan by reaching set milestones. Venture capitalists also use the decision point inherent in staging to collect and analyze more detailed information on the firm's activities and progress. When a firm is not performing well, the venture capital fund stops investing and reduces its risk of further losses. Venture capitalists also actively monitor their investments through frequent visits to firms and serving on their boards of directors. Monitoring furnishes information on the firm's progress and allows venture capitalists to deliver advice and guidance to improve performance, including intervening with company directors to change company management or strategy when it is necessary to protect their investment. Because active monitoring is costly, venture capitalists manage these costs by tailoring their level of monitoring to the investment risk and by playing a more active role in nearby and more troubled firms (Gompers & Lerner, 1999).

Venture capitalists typically coinvest in firms through forming an investment syndicate among several venture capitalists. One firm serves as the lead investor that organizes the syndicate and actively monitors the investment. Coinvestment allows funds to diversify by investing in many firms and reduce losses from failed investments, but it also serves two other purposes. Gompers and Lerner (1999) argue that syndication provides venture capitalists with a "second opinion" on the investment. Florida and Smith (1993) suggest that coinvestment networks help venture firms overcome the geographic constraints related to the active monitoring of investments while also financing firms outside their region, in effect to be both "local and highly mobile." In their analysis of the geographic pattern of venture investing in the mid-1980s, the authors found that venture capital fund offices were highly concentrated in both financial centers and high technology complexes, but that their office location was not a statistically significant factor in determining where investments were made (Florida & Smith, 1993).

Exiting Investments

To realize a profit, venture capitalists must convert their illiquid equity in a privately held firm into cash (or a marketable security) by exiting their investments. The three forms of investment exit are (1) an initial public stock offering (IPO); (2) acquisition of the firm by another company; and (3) a buyback of stock by the firm.[7] IPOs are the most profitable type of exit, which can lead some venture firms to push companies to prematurely undertake their first stock sale. Exiting strategies and returns are closely linked to the performance of IPO markets, which impacts both fund-raising and investing. Strong IPO markets allow funds to raise more capital and lead venture capitalists to focus on "hot" industries with strong prospects for completing IPOs, which creates the investment herding discussed above.

A successful exit with a high return is the exception, not the rule, for venture investing. Most investments provide only modest returns with a small share of investments generating the bulk of profits. Many others, usually one quarter to one third, fail and result in a total or partial investment loss. The difficulty of exiting from pure equity investments leads some VC funds to use debt instruments with equity kickers and equity-like features, such as deferred interest and principal payments. Although deferred debt repayment provides an alternative exit strategy, it cannot produce the high returns of successful equity investments.

Implications for Development Finance

Several development finance implications emerge from the nature of venture capital and recent industry trends. First, the growing size of private venture funds has shifted investments toward large deals and later-stage firms.[8] This trend is moving venture capital away from its historic role in supporting start-up and early-stage firms and reducing the supply of equity capital at levels below $2 to $3 million.[9] Consequently, creating funds that address equity supply gaps for early-stage firms and small investments is likely to be an important development finance need in many regions. Second, herd investing among venture firms diverts available equity from fast-growing industries and firms outside those sectors favored in IPO markets. This gap, although national in scope, is particularly important to states and regions with firms concentrated in less favored high-growth industries and creates the potential for geographic and industry-targeted venture funds. The potential to strategically target venture capital for economic development purposes is also supported by the success that Gompers and Lerner (1999) observed among strategic corporate venture capital. However, the experience with state venture capital investing discussed below indicates that narrow targeting impairs a fund's ability to reach the deal flow and scale needed to cover management costs and earn good investment returns.

Development finance interventions must recognize that creating a sustainable supply of venture capital depends on demand conditions (i.e., a sizable set of high-growth firms with real investment exit potential). Since venture capital fits a small set of companies with the potential to provide a large investment return, practitioners need to be realistic about the potential for such firms within their region's technology and entrepreneurial base. As with revolving loan funds, development services that identify and nurture high-growth businesses are an important antecedent and complement to expanding venture capital supply. Strengthening the technology and entrepreneurial platform for high-growth businesses, however, is a challenging and long-term project that requires larger and more strategic efforts than the technical assistance and training services linked to revolving loan funds. Pennsylvania's Ben Franklin Partnership program that provides sustained multimillion dollar funding to regional economic development partnerships for applied research projects, business incubators, and entrepreneurial development services exemplifies the type and scale of activities needed to change the demand-side environment (Osborne, 1999).

Venture capital interventions also need to foster local management expertise to provide the time-intensive due diligence, monitoring, and advice necessary for successful investing in early-stage firms while building relationships with national venture capital centers. Such relationships provide access to capital for coinvestment and successive funding rounds and gain the benefits of a "second look" at the investment. The discussion of state venture capital polices identifies tools and practices that help build this type of local venture capital capacity.

The SBIC and SSBIC Programs

Two long-standing federal programs seek to expand the supply of small business equity. In 1958, Congress passed the Small Business Investment Corporation (SBIC) Act, which authorized the Small Business Administration (SBA) to license and finance private investment firms to supply capital to start-up and early-stage small firms (Bygrave & Timmons, 1996). With an SBIC license, private investment firms could receive up to four dollars in low-interest government loans for every dollar of private capital contributed to the SBIC. SBA later added a participating security program that funds SBICs through preferred equity rather than loans. The availability of federal subsidies encouraged the creation of hundreds of SBICs (585 were licensed by 1962), which became a major part of the private venture capital industry in the 1960s (Bygrave & Timmons, 1996).

Although it spurred the creation of the private venture capital industry, several problems plagued the SBIC program. First, using debt to fund SBICs was fundamentally incompatible with providing patient equity capital. Faced with the need to repay SBA loans, SBICs often provided debt or hybrid financing rather than straight equity. Since this required investing in firms that could generate cash flow to service debt, it moved SBICs away from the purported mission of providing longer term risk capital to early-stage firms. Debt also made portfolio firms more susceptible to short-term financial losses from recession, industry changes, and firm-specific problems, which contributed to losses and insolvency within the SBIC industry. Second, large federal subsidies and a booming stock market attracted inexperienced and unscrupulous managers to the SBIC program. A bust followed the SBIC boom, as the SBA liquidated several hundred SBICs during the late 1960s and 1970. Problems continued into the mid-1990s when the U.S. GAO uncovered multiple problems and abuses,[10] leaving only a small share of licensed SBICs in business. The SBA issued 782 SBIC licenses from 1976 to 1997, but only 25% (or 192) remained active as of January 1997; another 564 SBICs either surrendered their licenses, had them revoked, or were liquidated.[11] After the large shake-out, the remaining SBICs are providing equity to early-stage firms. During FY1996, the most recent year for which data is published, SBICs completed 1,219 transactions totaling $1.5 billion. Straight equity accounted for 59% of these investments (in dollars), with 54% of them made to firms under 3 years old.[12] As private venture capital partnerships grew and many SBICs failed, the surviving SBICs represented a small portion of venture capital investments. From 1990 through 1996, SBIC investments were 14% of total venture capital disbursements (see Table 11.5). This share is undoubtedly far lower today, given the explosion of private venture capital investment during the late 1990s. SBIC investment returns also lag behind those of the overall venture capital industry. From 1977 to 1996, the weighted annual rate of return for SBICs averaged 10.1%, compared to a cumulative 10-year rate of return of 13.5% for all venture capital firms formed between 1969 and 1995.[13]

In 1972, Congress authorized the Special SBIC program (originally called the Minority Enterprise Small Business Investment Corporation, or MESBIC program) to finance the start-up and growth of minority-owned firms, primarily in inner city communities. MESBIC emerged, partly in response to urban unrest in the 1960s, as a way to stimulate economic development in poor and predominantly urban neighborhoods through "black capitalism," but it also addressed a perceived lack of capital availability for minority-owned firms (Bates, 1997). Under this program, the SBIC model was applied to license and fund entities that financed minority-owned businesses. Although implemented 14 years later, the SSBIC program repeated many of the problems with SBICs, including reliance on debt funding, small capital levels, and poor management, which led to high failure rates and low returns. Among the 285 SSBICs licensed between 1976 and 1996, 30%, or 88, were still active in 1997. As with SBICs, the vast majority (68%) were either liquidated or lost their licenses. Moreover, the weighted annual rate of return averaged only 1.2% for SSBICs over this 20-year period, although performance did improve from the primarily negative returns through the mid-1980s to positive levels that averaged 5% from 1986 to 1996.

Table 11.5   Investments by SBICs, SSBICs, and All Venture Capital Partnerships, 1990 to 1996

Type of Fund	Dollar Amount ($1997 Millions)	Percent of Total Dollars
SBIC	$5,976	14%
SSBIC	$943	2
All Venture Capital Disbursements	$46,169	100%

SOURCE: SBIC and SSBIC data are "SBIC Financing to Small Businesses" from SBA SBIC Financing Statistics (www.sba.gov/INV/tables/) and correspond to federal fiscal years. All venture capital disbursements are calendar year data compiled from Venture Economics and reported in Gompers and Lerner (1999).

Timothy Bates' (1997) analysis of SSBICs' financial performance emphasizes the importance of size to viable and effective entities.[14] Based on data through 1993, he found that small SSBICs with total assets of $2 million or less could not generate sufficient revenue to cover their expenses and invested a large share (35% to 40%) of their assets in cash and money-market investments to help cover their costs. Larger SBICs, with $5 million or more in assets, had greater operating efficiency and used far more of their assets to finance small businesses. The largest entities, with $10 million or more in assets, were the most likely to provide equity capital to businesses and to realize profits on their equity investments. A large capital base is critical to SSBIC equity investing because it provides the cash necessary to cover several years of operating expenses until investments can be sold and gains realized. Small SSBICs quickly deplete their capital if they do not generate short-term income to cover operating expenses, which explains their focus on money market and debt investments rather than equity. Bates concluded that thinly capitalized entities are not viable vehicles for providing equity capital. In a second article, Bates identified two types of successful SSBICs (Bates, 2000). One type focuses on asset-based lending to firms in which there are sufficient business and owner personal assets to ensure loan payments. Businesses served by these SSBICs include New York taxicab owners, restaurants, laundries, and grocery stores. The second type provides debt and equity to larger minority-owned firms serving fast-growing markets with sophisticated and experienced managers.

The failures and problems with the SBIC and SSBIC programs highlight several key venture capital policies. First, venture capital entities require the right form of capital to succeed. Debt is not appropriate to finance equity investments since it does not allow the long-term deferral of returns. Second, funds must be large enough to operate efficiently and cover operating expenses while retaining the bulk of their capital to invest. Third, private sector investment and management does not guarantee success. SBICs and SSBICs relied on private sector capital and management, yet the vast majority of them failed. Private managers need the right skills and experience to make and manage sound investments in early-stage businesses; they also must have an appropriate structure and incentives to apply these skills. When selecting private venture capitalists to manage venture capital funds, development practitioners need to choose them carefully, provide incentives that align with economic development goals, and monitor their performance. Overall, these lessons emphasize quality over quantity; creating fewer well-capitalized and effectively managed local venture capital entities is likely to yield better results than spreading limited capital and expertise over several small funds.

State Government Venture Capital Policy

State government initiatives to expand venture capital in pursuit of economic diversification and entrepreneurial development goals[15] provide a second arena for identifying sound approaches to expanding the supply of equity to small firms. Massachusetts was one of the first states to intervene in venture capital markets by creating a quasi-public state corporation, Massachusetts Technology Development Corporation (MTDC), to directly invest in firms with funds provided by federal grants and state appropriations. MTDC emerged from the recommendations of the Governor's Task Force on Capital Formation that was established in 1975 to formulate state economic development policies in the wake of a severe economic recession (Osborne, 1999). In the 1980s, other states followed Massachusetts in formulating proactive economic development strategies to rebuild economies hurt by a severe decline in manufacturing. Several states focused on growing and attracting high-technology firms, with expanded venture capital supply an important part of these strategies (Eisinger, 1993; Osborne, 1999). Other states used venture capital policies to improve their overall environment to support entrepreneurs and small businesses, increasingly viewed as the key source of new job growth (Litvak & Daniels, 1979). Although state venture capital programs declined in the early 1990s (Eisinger, 1993), a 2000 National Governors' Association report identified 45 states with policies and programs to expand venture capital supply (see Table 11.6). Many states augment venture capital initiatives with services to help entrepreneurs raise equity, including information and assistance on how to raise capital, technical assistance with business plan preparation, and brokering efforts such as holding venture capital fairs and forming angel investment networks (Heard & Sibert, 2000; Barkley et al., 1999).[16]

Table 11.6   State Government Venture Capital Programs

State	Direct Investment by State Entity	Tax Credits for Investment in Privately Managed Restricted Funds	State Investment in Restricted or Targeted Privately Managed Funds	Investment in Privately Managed Funds With Best Efforts Focus
Alaska	A		F	
Alabama				A
Arizona			F	
Arkansas	A	A		F
California	A			A
Colorado			I	A
Connecticut	A		A	
Delaware			A	
Florida				A
Georgia				A
Hawaii			A	
Idaho				
Illinois	I		A	
Indiana	A	I	F	
Iowa	I	I	F	

(Continued)

Table 11.6 (Continued)

State	Direct Investment by State Entity	Tax Credits for Investment in Privately Managed Restricted Funds	State Investment in Restricted or Targeted Privately Managed Funds	Investment in Privately Managed Funds With Best Efforts Focus
Kansas	A	F	A	I
Kentucky		A		
Louisiana	A	A	A	
Maine	A			
Maryland	A		A	A
Massachusetts		I	A	A
Nebraska	I		F	
New Hampshire			A	
New Jersey	A		A	A
New Mexico			A	A
New York	A	A	F	
Nevada			F	
Michigan			F	I
Minnesota	I			
Mississippi			I	
Missouri		A	I	
Montana	I	F	F	
North Carolina	A			F
North Dakota	A			
Ohio			I	F
Oklahoma	I	A	A	A
Oregon	A			
Pennsylvania	A		A	A
Rhode Island				
South Carolina		F		
South Dakota		F		
Tennessee				
Texas	I		A	
Utah	A			I
Vermont		F		
Virginia				
Washington				
West Virginia	A	A		
Wisconsin	A			
Wyoming				
Total Active Programs	18	7	14	11
Total Fully Invested Programs	0	5	9	3
Total Inactive Programs	7	3	4	3

SOURCE: Heard and Sibert (2000).

NOTE:

A = Active Program, F = Fully Funded Program, I = Inactive Program

States use three approaches to expand venture capital supply. One option directly invests in firms through state-controlled institutions. Second, states invest in privately managed funds to expand local venture capital. Some privately managed funds are restricted to investing within the state (or are targeted to industries or areas within the state) whereas others operate on a best-efforts basis. A third option provides incentives, usually via tax credits, to increase private investment in venture capital funds dedicated to financing firms within the state. State funding for venture capital investment has primarily come from state appropriations (31 states) and from public pension funds or other fiduciary funds (27 states) (Heard & Sibert, 2000). More states rely on privately managed funds to expand venture capital; 39 states have used either state investment in privately managed funds or tax credits, or both, whereas only 25 have invested through state entities. A second study, based on completed surveys from 40 states, had similar findings; 29 states invested in privately managed funds whereas 17 used tax credits. However, it identified only 12 states with public VC funds (Barkley et al., 1999). There also appears to be considerable attrition in state venture capital efforts since 11 of the 45 states listed in Table 11.5 no longer have an active venture capital program. Considerable variation also exists in how states have implemented the three approaches. Examples of different implementation vehicles are provided in Table 11.7.

Although no comprehensive evaluation of state venture capital programs exists, several studies provide case studies of selected programs and discuss general policy issues, impacts, and best practices. Peter Fisher's 1988 analysis of MTDC's first eight years concluded that the program generated profits and modest job impacts but was unlikely to make a large contribution to the state's technology sector or overall job development. Although MTDC was larger than most state programs at the time, the 1,200 jobs in its portfolio companies in 1984 equaled only .04% of Massachusetts' nonagricultural employment. Eisinger's 1993 review of state venture capital funds reported two outcomes from these programs: (1) filling an early-stage financing role that private venture capital firms were not addressing; and (2) helping expand private venture capital industries in some states, such as Michigan, Pennsylvania, Iowa, and Kansas, where few in-state venture capital funds had existed. By demonstrating that good deals existed within their borders, the state funds attracted private venture capital funds to their economies. However, Eisinger also found tensions between public sector values and the needs of venture capital investing that make state venture capital funds difficult to sustain. In particular, the long investment time frame and high failure rates common in venture capital investing are difficult for politicians and public sector agencies to accept.

Two other studies, one by Heard and Sibert (2000) for the National Governors' Association and a second by Bartley, Markley, and Rubin (1999) for the Rural Policy Research Institute, focus on the lessons and best practices from state venture capital policies and detail specific methods and

Table 11.7   Examples of State Venture Capital Programs

Program	Mission	Capital	Investments	Lessons/Innovations
Publicly Managed				
Maine Small Enterprise Growth Fund	Fill capital gaps for early-stage firms	$5 million	Invested in 9 firms with commitments to 4 others (1998)	Larger fund needed; adding services to build deal flow
Minnesota Technology Corporation Investment Fund	Help small and medium firms use technology to improve competitveness	$7 million; 80% targeted to non-metro areas	Invested $5.5 million in 16 firms (1997)	Converted to independent nonprofit in 1998
Privately Managed				
Colorado CVM Equity Funds	Finance start-up and early-stage firms; maximize investor return	$12.5 million in four partnerships	Invested in 54 firms, 53 in CO (1997)	State invested $4.2 million of pension and other funds in two partnerships
Pennsylvania Public School Employees' Pension Fund	Advance state economic development while achieving market returns	$193 million invested in 17 regional VC funds	$120 million invested in 117 PA firms (1997)	Set-aside targeted to regional VC firms with track record of investing in-state
Magnolia Venture Capital Corporation	Increase capital formation to stimulate formation of high growth businesses	$13.8 million from state bond proceeds	$650,000 invested in one firm with $4.5 million in expenses	Hire skilled and experienced managers; provide for strong and competent state oversight
Tax Credits				
Missouri CAPCO Program	Induce private investment in small businesses	$100 million raised from $100 million in state tax credits	$55 million in thirteen firms (1999)	State gets 25% of profits above 15% IRR; new round of credits targeted to distressed communities

SOURCE: Heard and Sibert (2000), and Barkley, Markley, and Rubin (1999).

experiences across a sample of state initiatives.[17] Both studies emphasize four best practices that advance two critical goals: (1) achieving good investment results and sustainable programs; and (2) creating a local venture capital infrastructure that builds confidence within and connections to the national venture capital industry. First, state policy makers and managers should not be involved in investment decision making; they need to leave this critical task to experienced and skilled venture capital managers. Instead, the government's role is threefold: (1) setting policy goals, broad strategy, and benchmarks for state-assisted programs; (2) selecting experienced professional managers; and (3) actively monitoring program performance. Second, programs must provide sufficient compensation to attract skilled and experienced managers. This requires operating funds outside public agency and civil service salary caps and giving managers a share of investment profits. Managers also must apply the same best practices used by private funds, namely following sound investment strategies, conducting extensive due diligence, actively monitoring and assisting portfolio companies, and staging and diversifying investments. Third, funds need a strong focus on investment returns to ensure political and financial viability, but they also need to attract private investors and coinvestment from other venture capital funds. Although Heard and Sibert (2000) argue that publicly supported funds must earn returns comparable to private investors, Barkley et al. (1999) believe that successful funds can make trade-offs between economic development goals and investment returns, when it is appropriate to their mission and is done strategically and explicitly. Fourth, special marketing and development services are necessary to generate a good stream of viable deals. States and regions without a critical mass of successful entrepreneurs and/or technology-based firms need a feasible plan to foster the creation and success of high-growth firms. Without successful demand-side initiatives, there will be insufficient business and investment opportunities to utilize the expanded venture capital supply. Moreover, because very few venture capital investments result in high financial and economic development returns, demand-side efforts must generate scores of new businesses to yield one firm as a major job generator.

Several additional issues must be addressed to create effective public sector venture capital programs. To manage the expectations of legislatures and other political stakeholders, public initiatives need to be explicit about and plan for the high risks and long-term horizon for realizing economic development and financial returns. A large fund capitalized with equity provides the financial capacity for patient high-risk investments, but practitioners also need to educate policy makers about these aspects of venture capital investing to avoid unrealistic expectations and goals for a government-sponsored fund. Another key design issue is whether to invest through a public entity or a privately managed partnership. Although public entities provide greater accountability and closer adherence to economic development strategies, investing through private funds advances a fundamental goal: developing local venture capital capacity networked to the national industry network. Using public capital to build a strong track record for local venture capitalists can create the conditions for attracting sustainable private investment into state and local venture capital funds. Colorado used public investment to expand the capacity and capital base of Colorado Venture Management (CVM) Equity Fund's initial partnerships to finance Colorado-based firms. As CVM's track record grew, it attracted over $220 million in follow-on venture capital investments from outside the state to supplement its $12.5 million in capital (Heard & Sibert 2000). Nonetheless, public entities may be appropriate in two situations: (1) when insufficient local capital and management exists and a state entity is needed to attract and build local capacity; and (2) when private venture firms, due to their investment thresholds or industry orientation, fail to invest in firms and industries with strong growth and profit potential. Finally, states should think carefully before relying on tax credits to stimulate private venture capital investment. Tax credits are a costly way to generate private venture capital and provide far less accountability than directly investing public funds in private venture capital partnerships. The inefficiency of capitalization through tax credits is demonstrated by some Certified Capital Company (CAPCO) programs that provide tax credits to insurance companies for venture capital investments. Some states provide tax credits that equal or exceed the gross capital invested in VC partnerships. Because CAPCO partnerships invest a large share of their capital in bonds to meet guaranteed investment returns sought by insurance companies, as little as 25% to 50% of every dollar of tax credits may be invested in firms.[18]

Community Development Venture Capital _____

Community Development Venture Capital (CDVC) is an emerging type of *private* venture capital that invests in firms with the potential for both high financial and social returns; these twin goals are often called a "double bottom line." According to the Community Development Venture Capital Alliance (CDVCA), 60 funds existed in early 2002 with $400 million in capital (Gaither, 2002), an average fund size of under $7 million. Since an October 2000 report identified 48 CDVC funds with almost $300 million in capital (Cherry, 2000), the CDVC sector appears to be growing steadily both in the number and size of their funds. Despite their name, only about 40% of CDVC funds focus on equity investing, with the balance providing debt capital or hybrid vehicles (Cherry, 2000; Gaither, 2002). Although some CDVC funds date to the late 1960s,[19] most were formed after 1990 (Gaither, 2002). CDVC differs from conventional venture capital by targeting investments to achieve economic development as well as financial goals and by its nonprofit organization or affiliation. CDVC funds, which are primarily financed by private investors, provide a tool for community-based and regional economic development practitioners to expand the supply of equity capital from private sector sources.[20] Although most CDVC funds operate independently of state and local government programs, they reinforce public efforts to build local and regional capacity in venture capital investing.

Industry Profile

Elyse Cherry's 2000 report to the Ford Foundation offers a profile of a young industry that is providing modest-sized investments to early-stage firms across diverse industries. The primary funding sources for the 14 funds surveyed for the report were banks and financial institutions (34% of total capital), foundations (22% of total capital), government (23% of all capital), and corporations and other investors (21% of total capital). However, banks and financial institutions are expanding their investments and emerging as the primary capital source for the CDVC industry.[21] Funds are modest in size, averaging $6 to $7 million, and target annual investment returns in the 10% to 15% range. This return target is below that sought by venture capitalists—typically 30% or higher. Along with lower financial returns, CDVC funds invest to realize social returns, typically defined as increased good quality jobs in economically distressed areas—both poor rural regions and low-income urban neighborhoods.[22] Some funds pursue other social investment goals (e.g., supporting women- and minority-owned businesses, promoting employee ownership, expanding environmentally sustainable businesses, and expanding services in poor areas).

CDVC investments are quite different from those made by private venture capitalists. The average investment made by surveyed CDVC funds was $185,000,[23] which is equivalent to that of SSBIC investments but far smaller than investments by SBICs and conventional venture capitalists (Cherry, 2000). CDVC fund managers, unlike venture capitalists, do not typically target specific industries for their investments. Instead, they seek a large pool of companies across many industries to find investments capable of providing large financial and social returns. However, CDVC funds do serve small, early-stage enterprises. Among surveyed funds, the average portfolio company had annual revenues of $3.5 million, and 46% of investments through 2000 were in either start-up or R&D-stage businesses. Another 21% were in early-stage companies. Given the industry's short life, there is little data on investment exits, returns, and economic impacts. However, the CDVCA provided an update on the performance of 25 equity-oriented funds at its March 2002 annual meeting (Gaither, 2002) based on 54 investment exits from equity investments in 162 firms. The most common exit was through a company sale (37%), and only 9% involved an IPO. The remaining exits included management buyback of stock (11%), company failure (16%), repayment of a debt-like instrument (11%), and one conversion to an employee stock ownership plan. Net investment gains from these exited investments were $9.2 million.[24] CDVCA also reported an average cumulative job impact for the 25 CDVC funds of 655 jobs.[25]

Industry Trends and Challenges

Despite the CDVC industry's youth and emerging practices, several important trends and challenges are evident. First, CDVC funds are focusing more on investment returns in response to investor expectations. For their initial funds, CDVC managers advocated a new investment model based on the double bottom line, but they had no investment track record to guide expectations. With no standard to apply, managers often did not state specific return objectives to their investors. However, when raising capital for later funds, managers had to report past and expected returns. Moreover, investors are becoming more concerned with investment returns and seeking higher returns, especially as banks become a leading CDVC investor (Gaither, 2002). Second, CDVC funds are getting larger and altering their investment strategies. In her study of three CDVC entities, Gaither found that the target capitalization for their second investment fund averaged $18.7 million compared to $5.6 million for the first fund. Each CDVC manager altered its investment strategy to accommodate the larger size of the second fund. Two funds shifted their targets to larger size investments, one expanded its geographic area and all placed less emphasis on early stage equity investing, adding either later-stage companies or near-term income generating investments, or both, to their investment targets. A hybrid approach that combined investments in later-stage and less risky firms with some riskier and more labor-intensive investments in early-stage enterprises was a common strategy. If these three funds typify the entire CDVC industry, then the continued growth in CDVC may be accompanied by a declining focus on financing start-up and early-stage firms.

CDVC funds face many of the same challenges as SSBICs and public venture capital funds. They need to attract skilled managers with the experience and expertise to make and nurture investments in high-growth firms and to build critical relationships to raise capital and secure coinvestments. However, talented managers with venture capital experience demand high salaries that many CDVC funds cannot afford (Cherry, 2000). The ability to attract professional managers is closely linked to a second challenge, reaching a sustainable scale. A large fund allows CDVC funds to draw on their capital to cover operating expenses (including manager's fees) while retaining significant funds to invest in firms. Since CDVC funds invest in early-stage firms across many industries, they incur relatively high costs for due diligence and managing portfolio investments (Cherry, 2000). The median operating budget for CDVC funds with capital of $10 million in FY1999 was $500,000, or 5% of capital. To cover these costs, funds either must consume their investment capital or raise money to subsidize these costs. Since the first option greatly reduces investment returns, small funds are compelled to raise operating subsidies to achieve returns that allow them to attract future rounds of capital. Moreover, as CDVC funds become larger, they need to carefully consider what investment strategy and development services will generate a sufficient flow of investment opportunities that promise both high investment returns and strong social benefits.

A critical challenge for the CDVC industry is finding investment exits, given their lower return objectives compared to conventional venture capital. Although CDVC funds are less likely to exit investments through IPOs,[26] they still must exit investments to realize returns and demonstrate that they are viable investment vehicles. One option is to seek firms and structure investments that allow for alternative exits through royalty-based compensation, stock buybacks, or company sales. Another option, advocated by Elyse Cherry of Boston Community Venture Fund, is to build institutions and investment vehicles that create a national market with liquidity and regular trading of investments generated by the CDVC industry. Cherry identified five options to create a market for CDVC investments: (1) a publicly traded entity that buys and sells investments that it acquires from CDVC funds, (2) a federally charted intermediary to create a secondary market for CDVC investments, (3) a closed-end mutual fund; (4) packaging and selling CDVC investments as securities, and (5) packaging and selling CDVC investments as a fixed income security like a bond. Although each option has distinct advantages and disadvantages, the next few years will determine whether a national market for CDVC investments is viable and which option, if any, will be most effective at establishing it. The outcome depends on the volume, nature, and quality of investments made by CDVC funds and the commitment of the CDVC industry and its investors to create new market-making institutions.

A final issue for the CDVC industry is codifying practices to measure, track, and realize social return objectives. Given their commitment to achieving a "double bottom line," CDVC funds must show the achievement of social returns and create effective investment strategies and practices to realize them. Gaither (2002), in her three case studies, found that some funds have rudimentary systems for addressing social returns and more attention is needed to strengthen practices in this area. The three funds achieved mixed social return outcomes: only one fund created jobs that paid average wages above the area's living wage, one third or less of each fund's investments were in minority-owned firms, and only one fund had a large share of its portfolio firms in high-poverty census tracts. Moreover, only one fund, Silicon Valley Community Ventures (SVCV), consistently monitored social return outcomes and developed specific practices to advance social return goals. SVCV created a social return measurement tool that counts portfolio firms' net hiring of "designated employees" into jobs with specific characteristics on a quarterly basis.[27] SVCV also administers an annual survey to monitor company wages and benefits, employee training, and other practices. Moreover, SVCV incorporated social objective practices (e.g., working with a local workforce development program to hire low-income employees) into its financing agreements and uses a consultant to help portfolio firms set up employee wealth-sharing programs.

Addressing Venture Capital Challenges

The survey of federal, state, and community-based venture capital initiatives identified common challenges to the effective use of this development finance model. Box 11.1 summarizes these challenges, applying the threefold framework introduced with the discussion of revolving loan funds. Lessons and effective practices to address these strategy, operating, and capitalization challenges are discussed below.

Box 11.1   Venture Capital Management Challenges

Strategy Challenges

Identifying High-Growth Business Opportunities That Can Achieve Financial and Economic Development Objectives. Venture capital initiatives need to be linked with demand-side entrepreneurial development and/or technology commercialization services to generate these businesses.

Building Strong Local Investing Capacity While Generating Investment Interest Within the National Venture Capital Industry. Investment strategies should nurture local managers while cultivating relationships and awareness among national VC managers. Local managers need to actively network within the national VC industry.

Operating Challenges

Securing Quality Professional Managers Who Employ Sound Due Diligence, Investing, and Monitoring Practices. Fund structure and capital must allow for competitive compensation. Careful scrutiny of experience, methods, and prior performance is needed. Managers also need to understand and support economic development mission.

Defining Appropriate Roles for Public and Social Investors. A strong role-setting strategy and overseeing performance is needed with contractual controls and regular reporting and meetings.

Identifying Feasible Exit Strategies for Firms Without IPO Potential. Stock buyback and royalty-based compensations are sound options. Investment strategies linked to the regional economy can generate good acquisition opportunities.

Capitalization

Securing Sufficient Capital as Equity to Permit Long-Term Equity Financing to a Diverse Portfolio of Firms. Funds must be large, at least $5 to $10 million, to cover several years of fees, attract professional managers, and allow follow-on investing.

Shaping Understanding and Expectations Among Investors to Foster a Long-Term Horizon on Returns and Cultivate Sustained Support. Funds require sound measures and tools to document social returns and need to educate investors about their social impact.

Strategy Challenges

Unlike revolving loan funds, venture capital is not easily replicated and requires special economic conditions to succeed. These conditions include (1) many entrepreneurs seeking to start high-growth businesses; (2) an innovative environment and/or technology base that generates new high-growth business on a sustained basis; (3) a skilled labor force with expertise in the key occupations needed for these enterprises; and (4) a support infrastructure or attorneys, consultants, angel investors, and the like to help young firms grow. Venture capital initiatives, especially in places lacking strong technology-based industries and entrepreneurial traditions, need demand-side programs to nurture high-growth enterprises and strengthen their local entrepreneurial environment.

Two broad approaches help strengthen a region's capacity to create high-growth businesses. One strategy focuses on cultivating and supporting entrepreneurs as the engine for new business creation. Multiple activities are undertaken to identify and attract entrepreneurs from outside the area,[28] providing intensive mentoring and technical assistance to local existing and early-stage firms with strong growth potential and building networks to provide knowledge, services, and support to entrepreneurs.[29] One organization, with an economic or small business development mission, often delivers or coordinates these services. A second option links venture capital investing to technology development and commercialization programs that foster business creation from new technologies developed at universities and/or research laboratories. These technology-based initiatives combine university policies that encourage the commercial use of new technologies, funding for applied research and seed-stage business development activities, and business development services linked to university or research laboratories (e.g., business planning, technical assistance, help raising venture capital, and small business incubators).[30]

A related issue is the appropriate targeting strategy for both demand-side services and venture capital investments. When setting targeting strategies for new venture capital funds or initiatives, economic development policy makers need to be realistic about the potential demand and define a geographic and industry focus that will generate a large flow of potential investments. Narrow geographic or industry targeting can be effective where strong research centers or industry concentrations exist, but some narrowly targeted programs, especially those serving small regions without a sizable base of entrepreneurs or technology-based firms, have had difficulty generating a sufficient flow of sound investments.[31] Consequently, a statewide or large regional program is appropriate for new funds in areas without a strong entrepreneurial tradition or history of venture investing.

Operating Challenges

Attracting fund managers with the skills and experience to successfully direct venture capital investments is one of the greatest challenges for economic development-oriented funds. Since venture capitalists are highly compensated, funds must be prepared to pay competitive management fees or staff salaries and link compensation to investment returns. When political and civil service constraints prevent hiring staff managers at these salaries, another option is to contract with a private venture capital firm to serve as fund manager. To achieve economic development goals, the private manager should be based within the region, or agree to establish a sustained regional presence, and be committed to the fund's economic development goals.

Whether a private VC firm or internal staff manages the fund, a key lesson from state VC initiatives is that strong public and community oversight of the fund's investment strategy and performance is critical to achieving the desired financial and development outcomes. Consequently, policy makers, economic development officials, and other stakeholders must take a stronger oversight role than is practiced by traditional limited partner investors. This role includes receiving regular reports on marketing, development, and investment activities and meeting periodically (e.g., quarterly) to review progress and future plans. These meetings can also serve to coordinate the activities of VC funds with related economic development programs. An oversight board with economic development policy makers and practitioners, successful entrepreneurs, attorneys, and financial community leaders can perform this role. Management contracts can also set standards for both compensation and key program and investment activities (e.g., marketing; development services; coordination with other programs; investment due diligence; and the managers' role in assisting firms).

Exiting equity investments is a challenge for all venture capitalists, but it is especially difficult for economic development funds that invest outside the industries favored in IPO markets. To compensate for limited IPO opportunities, managers need to adopt strategies and practices that maximize the use of alternative exit options: company acquisitions and stock buybacks or other "self-exiting" investments. By strategically investing in new enterprises with strong potential value to key industries and firms in their region, fund managers can expand the potential to sell their portfolio firms. This approach requires monitoring the growth and acquisition plans of major regional firms and industries and applying this knowledge to investment choices. Fund managers will also need to publicize the successes and assets presented by portfolio firms and form relationships with key firms and industry leaders to cultivate interest in acquisition candidates. Although an acquisition-oriented strategy may seem to steer investments toward the needs of large firms, it can advance important economic development goals by investing in firms that commercialize new technologies and products that diversify or strengthen the competitiveness of important industries. Alternatively, venture capital funds can rely on the cash flow of portfolio firms to exit investments either by structuring their investments with a mandatory stock buyback or call provision, or through royalty- or debt-based financial products. This form of investing depends on finding firms that can generate substantial cash flow beyond what must be reinvested to finance their continued growth. It also requires more creativity and attention to structuring investments that provide a real prospect for exit via internal cash flow and are viable for each firm's situation. One firm may be able to repay a royalty-based investment with high returns, but another may need to defer cash outflows to investors for several years and then be able to gradually buy back its stock over 5 years. Investment terms also need to carefully define the methods for valuing the company's stock for repurchases (or verifying the basis for royalty payments when applicable). This approach also necessitates that fund managers exercise close oversight and controls to accumulate cash flow in reserves to repurchase stock.

Capitalization Challenges

Venture capital funds also need sufficient capital to diversify their portfolios, cover operating costs for several years before investment returns accrue, and make follow-on investments needed to bring a firm to sustained profitability and investment exit. Whereas revolving loan funds may be sustainable with $2 to $3 million in capital, venture capital funds perform best with minimum funding of $5 to $10 million.[32] Moreover, venture capitalists need to raise successive investment funds over time to continue financing new enterprises after their capital from prior funds is committed. A major challenge for economic development-oriented venture capital programs is creating long-term relationships with investors who will finance multiple funds over time. This is especially important for entities seeded with government grants and/or appropriations that are unlikely to be a sustainable source of capital.

Institutional investors, including banks, foundations, and pension funds, are likely to be the most important long-term investors in venture capital funds with economic development missions. Banks, particularly ones that seek to improve their CRA ratings, are a prime investment source; they have been central to the early growth of community development venture capital funds. Foundations are also key investors to target since their missions are often tied to improving specific regions, and many seek *program-related investments,* in which they invest their endowment, rather than provide grants, to advance program goals. However, public pension funds are probably the most valuable tool to help expand the supply of venture capital managed for economic development goals.[33] Michigan was a pioneer in this respect, using its state pension investments in venture capital to get the major East and West Coast venture capitalists to actively investigate investment opportunities in the state during the 1980s (Osborne, 1999). Over the past 20 years, other governments have joined Michigan in using public pension funds to expand the supply of venture capital in their regions. The California Public Employees' Retirement System (CalPERS), the nation's largest public employee pension manager, was the key investor in Silicon Valley Community Ventures's second, and greatly expanded, investment fund (Gaither, 2002). Consequently, economic development practitioners who are managing or establishing venture capital funds need to understand the investment rules and processes for public pension funds in their state and work with legislators and pension fund managers to invest a portion of this large capital source in economically targeted venture funds.

Endnotes

1. American Research and Development Corporation (ARD) founded in Boston in 1946 is considered the first formal venture capital corporation created in the United States. Its creation is well documented in Etzkowitz (2002), Chapter 8.

2. Gompers and Lerner (1999) cite two authors who argue that lower capital gains tax rates increase the supply of venture capital funds. Their own research shows that tax exempt institutions increase their venture capital investing when capital gains tax rates decline, supporting the view that these lower tax rates stimulate entrepreneurial activity and demand for more venture capital, which then leads to increased supply. See pp. 21–22.

3. Quote is from p. 27. A complete discussion of their analysis of the effect of fund structure on investment outcomes is found on pp. 94 to 123.

4. State data are a proxy for investment concentration within specific metropolitan areas. Florida and Smith (1993) analyzed venture investments in the 1980s by MSA and found that the San Jose, Boston, and San Francisco MSAs received 40% of the 9,326 venture capital investments made from 1983–1987.

5. Gompers and Lerner (1999) provide evidence of investment herding and price competition among venture firms, including a study of overinvestment in the Winchester disk drive industry during the 1970s and 1980s and their own analysis that increases in company valuations by venture capitalist are associated with increased capital inflows rather than an improved environment for early-stage firms (pp. 135–136).

6. Gompers and Lerner (1999) provide a detailed discussion of these practices and their relationships to the investment challenges and risks of venture capital in Chapters 6 through 8.

7. A fourth form of exit, firm liquidation, occurs with failed investment and usually results in an investment loss.

8. The focus on Internet-related firms in the late 1990s was a countertrend in terms of firm stage because most Internet firms were early-stage, but the size of investments still grew.

9. The gap in small amounts of equity is raised in several reports. See Heard and Sibert (2000), Karl F. Seidman Consulting Services (2001b) and Weaver (1998).

10. See U.S. GAO (1995) *Small Business Administration: Prohibited Practices and Inadequate Oversight in SBIC and SSBIC Programs.*

11. Twenty-five licensees merged with other SBICs. Data is from the SBIC Financing Statistics provided on the SBA Web site (www.sba.gov/INV/tables).

12. Data from the SBIC Financing Statistics provided on the SBA Web site (www.sba.gov/INV/tables).

13. Data on venture capital returns is from Venture Economics (1996), *Investment Benchmark Report,* and covers over 400 funds.

14. This paragraph summarizes findings from Bates (1997).

15. Some regions and cities have established venture capital funds to expand their supply of venture capital, but these are less common and comparative data and studies on these substate initiatives is not readily available.

16. Angel investors are wealthy individuals who invest in small firms; in many cases they are entrepreneurs or former entrepreneurs.

17. Heard and Sibert (2000) summarize programs in Colorado, Pennsylvania, Indiana, and Oklahoma, and Barkley et al. (1999) discuss the experiences of 13 state initiatives.

18. Barkley et al. (1999) report that Louisiana's CAPCO program from 1988 to 1998 used $570 in tax credits to create investment funds with $517 in capital, of which $149 was invested in qualified companies (i.e., the targeted firms under the program).

19. Kentucky Highlands Investment Corporation, created in 1968 to attract firms and entrepreneurs to rural Kentucky, is often mentioned as the first CDVC fund (Gaither, 2002).

20. Some funds also raise investment capital from federal and state sources. The Silicon Valley Venture Fund, for example, secured a $10 million investment from the California state employees pension fund for its second investment partnership.

21. Gaither (2002) cites CDVA data that lists banks as supplying 55% of CDVA funding as of the end of 2001.

22. Gaither (2002) reports that CDVC funds are divided evenly among those serving rural regions and those targeting low-income urban areas.

23. Based on investments in 123 companies.

24. If these exited investments had the same average size as all investments made by 25 funds, then the net gain equals 52% of the original invested equity.

25. Based on 16,378 jobs (11,788 retained jobs and 4,590 newly created ones).

26. Cherry reports that less than 10% of investment exits were through an IPO.

27. A designated employee is one who was hired for an entry level or managerial position with specified earnings who was either hired through a nonprofit, job training, or welfare to work agency or resides in a low- or moderate-income zip code (Gaither, 2002, pp. 70).

28. Kentucky Highlands Investment Corporation used this approach to expand its entrepreneurial talent and capacity to operate existing and new businesses in its rural service area. See Litvak and Daniels (1979), pp. 146–147.

29. One common tool is sponsoring "enterprise forums" where entrepreneurs present their business plans or existing business strategies and get feedback from a panel of experts.

30. Pennsylvania's Ben Franklin Partnership is one of the largest and oldest technology-based economic development initiatives. Its origins and early experiences are documented in Osborne (1999), pp. 43–82.

31. The Colorado Rural Seed Fund targeted a rural portion of the state with a limited economic base and was unable to identify sufficient investment opportunities. Most of its portfolio firms failed. See Barkley et al. (1999), pp. 18 to 19.

32. This range reflects the experience of SSBICs and the experience from several cases discussed in Barkley et al. (1999). Some narrowly targeted venture capital funds may not have sufficient demand to support this size fund. Operating subsidies could address the high management costs for a small fund without eating up capital, but this still raises doubts about the impact and viability of a narrowly targeted fund that would invest only a few million dollars.

33. Union-managed pension funds are another capital source for economic development-targeted venture capital, especially to target traditional or unionized industries. Although union funds have been used less often for this purpose, there is growing interest. The Heartland Network (www.heartlandnetwork.org) is an organization devoted to using union pension capital for jobs-oriented investments. See Fung et al. (2001), *Working Capital: The Power of Labor's Pensions* for a detailed treatment of this subject.

12

Community-Based Financial Institutions

An important group of development finance entities are organized around their ties to specific communities. Their mission is to serve a defined community, often low-income, that is underserved by conventional capital markets, and be directly accountable to this community. This segment of the development finance world, often referred to as community development financial institutions[1] (CDFIs), is dominated by two organizational models: the community development loan fund (CDLF) and the community development credit union (CDCU). Despite important differences, these entities are treated together in one chapter for two reasons. First, they share a mission of using financial entities to promote community development goals in a specific place. Second, they are private sector institutions funded primarily from interest-bearing deposits rather than grants. With these shared features, both entities present common benefits and challenges to practitioners. They use private deposits to grow their institutions but must balance the terms and risk level of their credit products with the need to repay depositors. With a strong social mission, both institutions can raise capital from a growing base of social investors and need to define the right development services to achieve this mission. On the other hand, CDLFs and CDCUs have important differences. CDLFs are nonregulated financial intermediaries that largely lend to other organizations—businesses, developers and nonprofit organizations. CDCUs are federally regulated institutions that can supply diverse financial services to individuals and organizations. CDLFs are covered in the first half of the chapter, beginning with an explanation of the model's key features, followed by a consideration of the financing roles for which it is well suited, and concluding with a discussion of key management issues and challenges. Similar topics are addressed for CDCUs, but their longer history and more research allows for a richer consideration of their experience and best practices in two areas: delivering banking services to poor households and providing small business credit.

Community Development Loan Funds

Community development loan funds are locally organized and controlled nonprofit organizations that provide credit to businesses, affordable housing projects, and nonprofit organizations to advance local community development goals. In some ways, CDLFs resemble revolving loan funds. They provide debt to fill gaps in credit markets and use loan repayments to cover operating costs. CDLFs also face similar management challenges in defining sound and sufficiently large target markets, managing lending risks, and building strong partnerships. Yet CDLFs depart from RLFs in several ways. First, they are community nonprofit organizations rather than government-controlled entities, so their board and governance structure emphasizes accountability to target communities rather than to elected government officials. Nonprofit status also provides access to charitable and foundation funding sources that government RLFs do not have. Second, CDLFs are not primarily grant funded; they raise much of their funding by borrowing from social investors who invest to achieve both financial and social objectives. Social investors who lend to CDLFs include individuals, religious congregations, foundations, and financial institutions. Thus, CDLFs provide a simple institutional model to direct this growing stream of capital from "social investors" to finance community development lending. The ability to import and channel this new class of investors toward local development goals, without incurring the costs and difficulties to create a government-chartered financial institution, is the key innovation of CDLFs. Heavy reliance on borrowed funds means that CDLFs face much greater financial constraints than grant-funded RLFs. Since CDLFs pay interest to their investors, they must cover all operating costs and loan losses from the difference, or spread, between the interest rate charged borrowers and the cost of funds paid to investors. Consequently, they must operate on a larger scale to be financially self-sufficient. A fund that provides loans with an average interest rate of 8% and has annual expenses of $400,000 needs $5 million in total loans to cover its expenses when it is fully grant funded. However, if the fund borrows 75% of its funds from investors with an average cost of funds at 4%, then it needs $8 million in loans to cover $400,000 in operating costs.[2] Its assets must be 60% larger to be self-sufficient. CDLFs also must return borrowed principal to their investors, which limits the losses they can incur and requires careful management of asset and liability maturities. Consequently, CDLFs tend to be moderate-risk and medium-term lenders. They bear more risk than banks but cannot afford to incur the high risk and loss rates of many RLFs. CDLFs take their responsibility to prudently manage investors' funds very seriously because any failure to repay investors will impact both their ability to raise future funds and the credibility of other CDLFs (Swack, 1987).

CDLFs can reach greater scale than grant-based revolving loan funds while avoiding the regulatory hurdles and oversight faced by community development banks and credit unions. Debt capital from social investors combined with foundation, corporate, and government grants provide CDLFs with access to a far larger pool of capital than RLFs, allowing them to build larger institutions with more capacity to provide loans and technical assistance. Because CDLFs can build a deposit base without securing a federal banking charter, they need not raise several million dollars in investor equity, assemble a management team to fit bank regulators' expectations, and negotiate the regulatory process. CDLFs also operate without regulatory supervision, which also permits greater flexibility to address community credit needs. In short, CDLFs are easier and less costly to establish than regulated depository institutions but gain the benefits of deposit-like funds via loans from social investors.

The pool of investment capital for CDLFs, however, is much smaller than that available to depository institutions because investor loans to CDLFs often pay below-market interest rates and are not federally insured. However, the below-market financing supplied by social investors creates higher interest rate spreads to cover operating costs and permits CDLFs to offer loan products at below-market interest rates, which is important for financing projects such as affordable housing and community facilities that require subsidies to achieve their mission. A final CDLF advantage is their commitment to community accountability. Although each fund implements this commitment differently, it entails representation of community organizations and client groups on boards and advisory committees and sustained efforts to communicate with, understand, and respond to credit needs within their target markets (Lehr, 1998).

CDLF Characteristics

With few studies of CDLFs and no comprehensive directory, limited data exists on the industry's size and characteristics. One indicator of industry size is the number of loan funds certified by the federal CDFI fund. Through November 2002, 323 federally certified CDFIs were classified as business, housing, or housing/community facility loan funds. This figure may underestimate the industry's size because some CDLFs may not be federally certified. About half of these CDLFs have an economic development mission with 155 of the 323 certified funds classified as business loan funds. A second estimate of industry size is found in the Corporation for Enterprise Development 2003 study of CDFIs, which collect surveys from 235 CDLFs with $3.9 billion in total assets (CDFI Data Project, 2003).

A good source of CDLF industry data is National Community Capital (NCC), a CDFI trade association. NCC surveyed its membership in 2001 to document fund size, capital sources, lending performance, and outcomes during 2000 and published the results in *CDFIs Side by Side*. Data on over 80 CDLFs from this report provide a good proxy for understanding the entire CDLF industry. Table 12.1 summarizes survey results and compares averages

Table 12.1   Average CDLF Ratios by Fund Type

Financial Ratio	Both Types	Business Lenders	Housing Lenders
Number of Funds in Sample	82	41	41
Total Capital or Assets	$9,617,808	$6,656,294	$12,579,321
Loan Size	$57,298	$37,726	$76,870
Loan Portfolio (Number of Loans)	99	109	88
Loan Portfolio ($ of Loans)	$5,446,230	$4,118,528	$6,773,932
2000 Loan Volume (Number of Loans)	44	53	36
2000 Loan Volume ($)	3,085,696	$2,012,773	$4,158,619
Percentage of Capital in Debt	55.8%	48.0%	63.6%
Share of Capital From Financial Institutions	21.9%	11.9%	32.0%
Share of Debt From Individuals and Religious Institutions	23.3%	14.5%	32.1%
Share of Capital From Foundations	16.5%	14.1%	19.0%
Share of Capital From Government	25.9%	46.4%	5.5%
90-day Delinquency Rate	4.5%	7.4%	1.7%
Cumulative Loss Rate	4.6%	7.2%	2.0%
Loan Interest Rate	7.8%	9.3%	6.2%
Loan Maturity (Months)	76	70	81
Self-Sufficiency Percentage[a]	54.3%	52.2%	56.3%

SOURCE: National Community Capital Association (2002).

NOTE:

a. Self-generated revenues from fees, interest income, etc. divided by total expenses.

between 41 housing-oriented loan funds and an equal number of business-oriented ones.[3] Collectively, the 82 funds had total capital or assets of $789 million with 57% held in outstanding loans. The average CDLF had $9.6 million in capital, a $5.4 million loan portfolio, and made $3.1 million in 44 new loans during 2000. CDFIs made small, medium-term loans, with a mean principal of $57,298 and an average term just over 6 years (76 months). Debt capital represented just over half (55%) of CDLF capital, on average, supplied in fairly equally proportions from five sources: government; financial institutions; foundations; individuals, and religious entities. Access to a diverse funding base and the capacity to support debt contribute to CDLFs' larger size compared to conventional revolving loan funds. Despite their size, most CDLFs are not financially self-sufficient; own-source revenue from interest, fees, and contracts covers 54% of operating costs for the average fund.

These industrywide averages, however, mask important differences between housing and business loan funds. Housing-oriented funds, on average, have 95% more capital than business loan funds, and the value of their loan portfolios is 65% larger. Business funds make more loans than housing funds, originating an average of 53 loans in 2000 versus 36 for housing lenders, although their portfolios held 20% more loans. The large investment needed for housing projects, and perhaps greater funding availability for housing, probably account for the larger size of housing-oriented CDLFs.

The funding structure also differs across fund types, with business funds using less debt (48% versus 64%) and relying more heavily on government as a debt source. Business-oriented funds have much higher delinquency and loss rates than housing funds, indicating the higher risk of financing small enterprises, but they partly compensate for this greater risk by charging interest rates that are 300 basis points above that charged by housing funds.

A richer picture of business-oriented CDLFs is provided in Table 12.2, which separates fund characteristics and performance by asset size. As expected, large funds perform better than smaller funds; they generated higher loan volumes, greater job impacts, and improved financial self-sufficiency. The largest group of funds averaged $14 million in total assets, financed 26 firms in 2000 that created or retained over 1,000 jobs, and achieved a 72% financial self-sufficiency rate. Small funds, with under $2.5 million in assets, originated only six business loans in 2000 with 87 new or retained jobs, had a 24% self-sufficiency ratio, and incurred cumulative loss (11.1%) almost twice that of the largest funds. One important finding from Table 12.2 is that medium-size funds perform quite well, suggesting that economic development CDLFs may be able to become largely sustainable and generate significant impacts at a scale close to $5 million in assets. These funds averaged $4.5 million in capital, one-third the level of the largest group, but had a higher share of their capital in loans, incurred lower loss rates, utilized more debt capital, reached comparable self-sufficiency levels, and made 60% as many annual business loans. However, their job impacts were disproportionately lower—one-quarter the level of the large funds. Research on how these medium-size funds, which have strong financial results, can enhance their job impacts would benefit the CDLF industry, given the challenges to reaching a $10 to $20 million scale.

CDLF Financing Roles

Community development loan funds demonstrate how sources of capital shape the uses of capital for development finance entities. Since CDLFs rely on borrowed funds from social investors to survive and grow, their loan assets must allow them to meet interest and principal obligations to these investors. When loan losses are too high or repayments on loans made by the CDLF exceed amortization requirements on its borrowed capital, the CDLF will not be able to repay its investors. A default on borrowed capital threatens the fund's financial viability because existing investors will be less likely to roll over loans, and new investors will be difficult to find. Without sustained access to borrowed funds, the CDLF will, at best, need to greatly reduce lending and, at worst, declare bankruptcy. Given these costs, CDLFs are careful to structure financial products and make loans that ensure sufficient cash flow to meet their obligations to investors. Consequently, CDLFs tend to make loans with moderate and manageable risks and for short- to medium-term periods, as investor loans typically have terms of several years.

Table 12.2   Average CDLF Ratios for Business Loan Funds by Asset Size

Financial Ratio	Small Funds (<$2.5 million)	Medium Funds ($2.5 to $ 8 Million)	Large Funds (> $8 million)
Number of Funds in Sample	15	12	14
Total Capital or Assets	$1,376,946	$4,559,979	$14,109,581
Loan Size	$25,181	$34,694	$68,009
Loan Portfolio (No. of Loans)	43	142	152
Loan Portfolio ($ of Loans)	$771,366	$3,038,787	$8,630,265
2000 Loan Volume (No. of Loans)	19	91	57
2000 Loan Volume ($)	$350,525	$1,615,779	$4,131,034
Percentage of Capital in Debt	53.0%	51.0%	40.0%
Cost of Debt Capital	3.7%	2.6%	2.5%
Term of Debt Capital (Months)	89	169	175
Share of Debt From Financial Institutions	21.0%	11.5%	8.5%
Share of Debt From Individuals and Religious Institutions	17.9%	19.7%	6.3%
Share of Debt From Foundations	4.6%	13.5%	24.7%
Share of Debt From Government	44.9%	46.7%	47.8%
90-day Delinquency Rate	10.6%	6.2%	5.0%
Cumulative Loss Rate	11.1%	4.0%	5.9%
Loan Interest Rate	10.5%	9.1%	8.3%
Loan Maturity (Months)	47	69	95
Operating Expenses	$684,661	$1,184,570	$2,350,376
Self-Sufficiency Percentage	26.4%	61.1%	72.3%
Percentage of Minority Borrowers	53.0%	29.0%	13.0%
Percentage of Female Borrowers	54.0%	32.0%	25.0%
Number of Business Loans in 2000	6	15	26
Cumulative Job Impact	524	1462	6355
2000 Job Impact	87	235	1032

SOURCE: National Community Capital Association (2002).

CDLFs can make riskier and longer term loans, however, to the extent they secure long-term debt, equity-equivalent capital, and grants or other subsidies to cover loan losses. Since grants and long-term capital are in limited supply, the core financing provided by CDLFs fits this profile of intermediate risk and medium term maturity. CDLFs, on the other hand, can hold a larger share of their assets in loans than banks. Banks need larger holdings of cash and marketable securities (which are easily converted to cash) to satisfy demand deposits that can be withdrawn at any time. Since CDLFs borrow at predictable terms, they can operate with 70 % or more of their assets in loans, as compared to the 50% to 60% ratio that is typical for banks.

Based on these financial requirements, CDLFs are well suited to four lending products: (1) short-term predevelopment and construction loans for real estate projects; (2) medium-term financing for real estate projects (e.g., bridge financing repaid from property sales or syndication proceeds); (3) cyclical and medium-term business working capital loans; and (4) equipment financing. All four examples allow CDLFs to manage risks and be repaid within several years. With the first two products, CDLFs fill financing gaps for affordable housing, commercial real estate development, and nonprofit or community facilities that include acquisition and predevelopment financing, subordinate construction and bridge loans, and debt for tenant improvements. For the second two products, CDLFs serve business needs that conventional lenders fail to address, such as small loans, subordinate debt, and more flexible debt coverage and collateral requirements.

The Chicago Community Loan Fund (CCLF) exemplifies the first type of CDLF, serving the real estate financing needs of affordable housing developers, cooperatives, and nonprofit organizations. It offers five real estate loan products, including predevelopment, construction, and permanent financing (see Exhibit 12.1). Most products are short- or medium-term loans, but CCLF does offer long-term mortgage loans. Its lending terms are more flexible than a bank (e.g., the 100% loan-to-value maximum for most products), but repayment risk is controlled with tight collateral requirements. A first mortgage loan is preferred and additional security through guarantees, cash collateral, letters-of-credit, or the like is required when a second mortgage is granted. CCLF also manages risks with technical assistance on real estate development matters that is provided through a phone help desk service, project-readiness workshops, and customized assistance to address development capacity needs.

Cascadia Revolving Fund (CRF) exemplifies CDLFs that specialize in small business financing. CRF offers five lending programs for small firms and child care providers in Washington and Oregon (see Exhibit 12.2). Beyond its two core lending products (the Community Loan Program and lines of credit), CRF developed specialized products for microloans, equity-like financing for rural manufacturers and child care providers. All five programs supply short- to medium-term loans, with 7 years as the longest maturity. Risk-based market interest rates are standard for all but the Child Care Fund. However, CRF has flexible collateral policies that rely on detailed underwriting and extensive borrower technical assistance rather than pledged assets to reduce loan losses.

CDLF Operating Challenges and Needs

Community Development Loan Funds face special challenges partly due to their debt-based capital structure, which are summarized in Box 12.1. A central strategic challenge, as discussed above, is finding lending markets that match their capacity to provide moderate-risk short- to medium-term debt and are large enough to support CDLFs at a sustainable scale. Since CDLFs pay interest on a large share of their capital, they need relatively large

Exhibit 12.1   Chicago Community Loan Fund Financing Products

---

Predevelopment Loans
Loan Size: Up to $350,000
Term: Up to 2 years
Interest Rate: 8% to 9%
Maximum LTV: 100%
Uses: Acquisition and soft costs for affordable housing, social service, or economic development projects with benefits to LMI people or areas
Collateral: First mortgage preferred

For-Profit Predevelopment Loans
Loan Size: Up to $350,000
Term: Up to 2 years
Interest Rate: Prime + 1% to 4%
Maximum LTV: 90%
Uses: Acquisition and soft costs for affordable housing, social service, or economic development projects with benefits to LMI people or areas
Collateral: First mortgage preferred

Minipermanent Loans
Loan Size: Up to $350,000
Term: Up to 15 years
Interest Rate: 7% to 9%
Maximum LTV: 100%
Uses: Acquisition/rehab of affordable housing, social service, or economic development projects with benefits to LMI people or areas
Collateral: First mortgage preferred

Cooperative Housing Loans
Loan Size: Up to $700,000
Term: Up to 15 years
Interest Rate: 7% to 9%
Maximum LTV: 80% to 100%
Uses: Acquisition/development of limited equity of low-income housing cooperatives
Collateral: First mortgage preferred

Equipment and Working Capital Loans
Loan Size: Up to $350,000
Term: Up to 7 years
Interest Rate: 8% to 9%
Maximum LTV: 100%
Uses: Equipment for nonprofits and worker-owned firms to expand operations.
Collateral: First lien preferred

Construction Loans
Loan Size: Up to $350,000
Term: Up to 1.5 years
Interest Rate: 8% to 9%
Maximum LTV: 100%
Uses: Construction of affordable housing, social service, or economic development projects with benefits to LMI people or areas
Collateral: First mortgage preferred

SOURCE: Chicago Community Loan Fund. www.cclfchicago.org

loan volumes to cover operating costs. With $2 million in capital and a 5% spread between the interest earned on loans (and idle cash) and the rate paid to depositors, a CDLF generates only $100,000 to pay operating costs before covering loan losses. A higher spread and grants add revenue to cover operating costs, but expanding loan volume is the surest path to

Exhibit 12.2   Cascadia Revolving Fund Financing Products

Community Loan Program
Loan Size: Up to $500,000
Term: Up to 5 years
Interest Rate: Fixed rate usually above
bank rates
Borrowers: Small businesses that
don't meet bank qualifications
Uses: Equipment, inventory, working
capital, building improvements,
refinancing
Collateral: Required on flexible terms

Rural Development Investment Fund
Loan Size: Up to 10% of fund capital
Term: Up to 5 years
Interest Rate: Negotiated low rate
plus a percentage of firm revenues
Borrowers: Industries with
competitive advantages in rural areas
Uses: Equipment, inventory, working
capital, building improvements,
refinancing
Collateral: Subordinate equity-like

Lines of Credit
Loan Size: $50,000 to $500,000
Term: 1 year
Interest Rate: 15% to16%
Borrowers: Small manufacturers,
wholesalers, and service firms
Uses: Cyclical working capital

Olympia Microloan Fund
Loan Size: $1,000 to $25,000
Term: 1 to 5 years
Interest Rate: Fixed rate usually above
bank rates. Averages 10%.
Borrowers: Small businesses in nine
Washington counties that don't meet
bank qualifications
Uses: Equipment, inventory, working
capital, real estate acquisition, and
refinancing

Child Care Fund
Loan Size: Up to $500,000
Term: Up to 7 years
Interest Rate: 8% to 10%
Borrowers: Child care providers
Uses: Large and small property
improvements, equipment, and
supplies
Collateral: Required on flexible terms

SOURCE: Cascadia Revolving Fund. www.cascadiafund.org

self-sufficiency. CDLFs can grow their lending market in two ways: (1) serving a larger geographic area; and (2) diversifying their borrower base. Thus, CDLFs should consider serving a metropolitan or statewide region, and even a multistate region, when their home state is small, rather than individual neighborhoods or cities. To diversify their customers, CDLFs can extend their core lending competencies to related projects or specialized niches. CDLFs with affordable housing expertise might expand into nonprofit

Box 12.1   CDLF Management Challenges

Strategy Challenges

Defining Appropriate Target Markets and Financing Roles.

CDLFs need financing roles that fit key community development goals, are consistent with their capital sources, and are large enough for a sustainable scale. Effective strategies avoid capital substitution but manage lending risks to ensure capital repayment to investors.

Operating Challenges

Managing a Professional Origination, Underwriting, and Approval Process.

CDLFs require a sound and efficient lending process to achieve economic development goals and preserve capital but must be especially attentive to managing risks, loan terms, and losses to service their own debt.

Balancing Asset and Liabilities

With their reliance on many debt sources, CDLFs need to actively manage cash flow and liquidity to ensure their capacity to fulfill interest and principal payments on their own debt. They are closer to banks in this respect than most other development finance institutions.

Building Strong Relationships With Multiple Partners

CDLFs need the collaboration and support of multiple constituencies to succeed. Effective relationships are needed with community organizations to generate support and loan referrals, lenders to complete financings, technical assistance providers, and a diverse set of "social investors" to supply capital.

Capitalization Challenges

Cultivating a Large Core Investor Base to Achieve Sustainable Scale.

CDLFs need a large and diverse investor base to provide sufficient debt capital to reach a sustainable asset base of $5 to $10 million. Core investors committed to renewing deposits and providing long-term debt are key to predictable capital flows. Dedicated staff capacity is essential to build and manage these investor relations.

Securing Sufficient Grants and Long-Term Investments.

Grants, equity-like investments, and long-term debt are critical to lending flexibility, covering unexpected losses, and subsidizing development services.

---

facilities or commercial real estate lending. Business-oriented CDLFs can expand the range of industries served and apply their skills in financing working capital and equipment to nonprofit organizations.

As with all lenders, CDLFs need strong loan origination, underwriting, and servicing systems and the capacity to secure technical assistance for borrowers. Strong technical assistance capacity and gaining detailed knowledge of borrowers are key loss management tools that allow CDLFs to balance the risks of gap financing with the low loan losses needed to repay investors. Loan losses can also be addressed financially by raising endowment funds and grants to fund loan loss reserves and charging fees and interest rates that fully cover these costs. A second important CDLF operating need is developing the capacity to cultivate and manage a large social investor base through dedicated staff, sound information systems, and senior management leadership. This includes undertaking consistent outreach and education to attract funds and manage relationships with investors and developing financial systems to administer investor deposits and manage CDLF assets and liabilities to address liquidity needs and interest rate risks. For the latter task, CDLFs must regularly review and set both the maximum interest rate and minimum term offered for investor deposits and its lending products to balance borrower and investor demand while ensuring sufficient operating revenue.

A third set of challenges concerns capital management. CDLFs must build stable and diverse debt sources to grow (and maintain) their asset base to a minimum sustainable scale of $5 to $10 million. This requires core depositors who supply funds on a predictable basis with low turnover. The core deposit base should encompass religious organizations, socially conscious individuals, foundations, banks, and other financial institutions. Boston Community Loan Fund (BCLF) exemplifies the scale and diversity that CDLFs should seek in their deposit base. In 2002, BCLF raised $24 million in "deposits" ranging in size from $1000 to $1,000,000 from over 300 sources that included 204 loans from individuals, 25 from financial institutions, 12 from foundations, and 72 from religious organizations. Beyond their core investors, CDLFs need to raise long-term loans and grants to allow some higher risk lending, fund development services, and to have equity to cushion losses and support growth. Sources for these more flexible long-term funds include the federal CDFI Fund, foundation grants and program-related investments, bank CRA investments, intermediaries such as National Community Capital and the National Community Development Fund, and some state and local governments.

_____ Community Development Credit Unions

Credit unions are financial cooperatives that provide banking services and loans to members with a common affiliation or bond that defines the eligible "field of membership" for the credit union. Credit unions are also democratically controlled financial institutions in which members are shareholders who elect the board of directors and approve major business decisions based on one-member-one-vote governance. With democratic membership-based governance systems, credit unions provide the best institutional fit for a community-controlled financial institution. Credit unions are regulated depository institutions chartered and overseen either federally by the National Credit Union Administration (NCUA) or by state banking commissioners. Since credit unions offer insured deposits through the NCUA, they share banks' capacity to attract and recycle deposits from within their local community while importing capital via external "development deposits." Thus, credit unions can use low-cost deposits to grow to substantial scale while remaining accountable to their membership. Although they must obtain regulatory approval to secure this power, credit unions face much lower capital requirements and start-up costs to obtain a charter than do banks. The major hurdles are recruiting a sufficient membership and deposit base to start the entity, and recruiting staff members with the necessary experience and management skills.

Credit unions emerged as cooperative financial institutions during the early 1900s, often organized around religious congregations or workplaces.[4] After Massachusetts passed the first state credit union enabling law in 1909, other states followed suit and the federal government passed the Federal Credit Union Act in 1934, which provided for federal chartering and supervision of credit unions (Isbister, 1994). In 1970, federal credit union oversight was shifted to an independent agency, the National Credit Union Administration (NCUA), and federal share (i.e., deposit) insurance was introduced (Isbister, 1994). Over time, credit unions evolved into conventional financial institutions that provide deposit and credit services to a working and middle-class membership with minimal member involvement in their governance and management (Isbister, 1994). Since the 1960s, however, a new breed of credit unions, known as Community Development Credit Unions (CDCUs), emerged with a mission of serving low-income individuals and neighborhoods. In 1978, NCUA formerly acknowledged this special class of institutions by creating a low-income credit union designation and offering special rules and services for them. To obtain this designation, over half of the credit union's membership must either have an income below 80% of the national median household income or earn less than 80% of the national average wage. Several benefits come with the low-income designation: (1) authority to accept nonmember deposits;[5] (2) exceptions to aggregate limits on business loans; (3) access to low-interest loans, deposits, and technical assistance from NCUA's Community Development Revolving Loan Fund; and (4) greater flexibility in defining their field of membership (NCUA, 2002).

Many new CDCUs were formed in the late 1960s through the efforts of the credit union association (CUNA), civil rights groups, and the federal Office of Economic Opportunity. By some accounts, as many as 400 new credit unions were formed to address poverty and reduce racial and class inequities in credit availability (Isbister, 1994). Although most of these credit unions failed, a core group of over 40 survived, and the lessons from this experience contributed to a steady start-up of more successful community development credit unions in the 1970s and 1980s. By 1993, 165 low-income credit unions existed (Isbister, 1994). Over the next 8 years, the number of NCUA-designated low-income credit unions (LICU) increased almost five-fold to 789 (NCUA, 2002). Although this growth largely reflects existing credit unions obtaining designation as low-income credit unions, it also includes new CDCUs that apply the credit union model in new ways to pursue community and economic development goals.[6] Innovative CDCUs include Self-Help Credit Union, a major statewide small business and housing lender, and Vermont Development Credit Union, which uses banking and credit services to build financial literacy, self-sufficiency, and wealth among the state's low-income population. Before exploring CDCUs' effective practices in supplying small business credit needs and delivering a new brand of banking services to the poor, the next section summarizes key financial characteristics and trends among CDCUs to better understand their financial structure and challenges.

CDCU Characteristics

A good overview of CDCUs is provided in semiannual reports compiled by the National Credit Union Administration (NCUA), the federal agency that regulates and provides deposit insurance to nationally chartered credit unions. Table 12.3 summarizes several key LICU ratios for 2001, comparing them to all federally chartered credit unions and to 1991 CDCU data compiled by John Isbister. These comparisons highlight how CDCUs differ from conventional credit unions and identify key industry trends during the 1990s. This analysis uses the NCUA "low-income credit union" designation (LICU) and the industry term, "community development credit union" (CDCU), interchangeably to refer to credit unions that primarily serve low-income households and areas.[7]

The NCUA designated 789 active low-income credit unions (LICUs) with total assets of $10.9 billion at year-end 2001 and total assets averaging $13.8 million. This average asset size is large for development finance entities and indicates the value that insured deposits provide in raising capital to grow an institution. Total assets grew by $3 billion in 2001, with 43% of this growth from the designation of new LICUs.

Table 12.3   Comparison of CDCU Financial Ratios

Financial Ratio	2001 LICUs	2001 All Federal CUs	1991 LICUs
Average assets	$13.8 million	NA	NA
Average share of assets in loans	66%	64%	62%
Average share of assets in cash and investments	30%	NA	37%
Average share of loans made for auto loans	43%	NA	17%
Average share of loans made for unsecured loans and credit cards	16%	NA	29%
Average share of loans made for first mortgages, other real estate, and other purposes	41%	NA	53%
Average delinquency rate	1.84%	0.85%	5.4%
Average loan charge-off rate	.66%	.46%	1.8%
Average net worth percentage	11.1%	10.9%	9.1%
Average return on assets	0.77%	.95%	0.7%

SOURCES: 2001 data from NCUA (2002) based on Performance Reports from 780 LICUs; 1991 data is from Isbister (1994), which compiled figures from 180 CDCU Call Reports.

Two thirds (66%) of LICU assets were invested in loans as of December 2001, with auto loans the most common loan type. This ratio is slightly higher than the 64% level for all federal credit unions and shows modest growth in loans as a share of CDCU assets since 1991. Surprisingly, this ratio is above the 57% average share of assets held in loans that NCC reported for 81 CDLFs. Because credit unions need liquidity to address members' short-term cash needs, one would expect their loan-to-asset ratio to be below that of CDLFs. Moreover, loans equal 75% to 85% of member shares[8] (i.e., deposits), indicating that CDCUs deploy a large share of member funds as community credit, using retained earnings and secondary capital to provide much of their liquidity reserves. Auto loans accounted for 43% of the $7.2 billion in loan assets held by CDCUs in December 2001, with home first mortgage loans the second largest category at 20%. Over half of these auto loans are for used cars, reflecting CDCUs' low-and moderate-income membership. Twenty-one percent of loans fall in the other loan and other real estate categories where business and commercial development debt would be counted.

These data indicate that CDCUs are most active in addressing the housing, auto, and consumer credit needs of low-income households rather than financing small businesses and commercial real estate. This growth in household and consumer lending is a key trend in the 1990s; auto, unsecured, and credit card loans grew from 47% to 59% of CDCU loans from 1991 to 2001 whereas other loans, mortgages, and other real estate loans dropped from 53% to 41%. Personal credit services are an important economic development tool for low-income persons, especially when they are tied to increasing economic self-sufficiency and asset accumulation. Auto loans, for example, can help access better job opportunities, and mortgage loans help poor households build savings and wealth through home ownership. Personal loans also may function as small business loans when borrowers use them to finance self-employment or microenterprises. Average industry figures also mask variation in lending activities across credit unions and the fact that some CDCUs are active business lenders. In his study of lending practices among seven CDCUs in the early 1990s, Isbister found that four had a substantial share of small business loans in their portfolios, ranging from 28% to 48%. One rural credit union provided agricultural loans to small farmers, and the others financed locally owned small businesses (Isbister, 1994).

CDCUs demonstrated sound financial conditions and results in 2001, although their earnings, loan delinquency, and loss performance was below that of all federal credit unions. The average net worth ratio for CDCUs was 11.1% in December 2001, which was equivalent to the 10.9% level for all federal credit unions.[9] Since a 10% net worth ratio is considered sound for banking entities, the average CDCU exceeded this standard. Moreover, the financial condition of CDCUs improved during the 1990s from an average net worth of 9.1% in 1991 to 11.1% in 2001. On the other hand, CDCU loan delinquency rates, at 1.84%, were more than twice the level for all federal credit unions, and their loan charge-off rates were 43% higher. NCUA attributed the higher incidence of poorly performing loans to CDCUs' larger share of unsecured loans and weakly collateralized used auto loans and the financial pressures faced by their low-income borrowers (NCUA, 2002). Nonetheless, CDCU delinquency and loan charge-off rates are still low, in the range experienced by many banks, indicating that they are effective lenders to low-income communities. Furthermore, CDCU lending performance improved markedly, as both delinquency and loan charge-off rates declined by almost two thirds from 1991 to 2001.

CDCUs averaged a .77% return on assets in 2001, about 20% lower than the average for all federal credit unions and similar to the .7% rate in 1991. Lower earning at CDCUs result from both higher expenses for loan write-offs, as mentioned above, and higher operating costs (NCUA, 2002). Additional expenses for outreach, education, and development services to serve low-income borrowers probably contribute to higher operating costs along with lower efficiencies from their smaller size. The stable return on assets for CDCUs from 1991 to 2001 is an interesting puzzle because their loan charge-off rate dropped by 63% during this period. Perhaps increased operating costs offset their lower loan loss expenses as CDCUs invested in lending staff and systems to improve lending results. Stable earnings could also reflect a decrease in CDCU lending spreads from lower interest rates and increased competition, in which case the lower loan losses protected CDCUs from deterioration in their earnings. Recent data supports the latter explanation. CDCU's average interest rate spread on total assets declined by 120 basis points from 1988 to 2001.

CDCU Lending and Development Roles

As membership organizations and by regulation, credit unions provide banking services and credit to their members. Regulations also limit total business loans to 12.5% of a credit union's loan portfolio with lending to a single business entity capped at 15% of reserves or $75,000 (Parzen & Kieschnick, 1994). Consequently, credit unions are structured to provide financial services to households rather than businesses or development projects. Most CDCUs are also small organizations with modest staffing[10] and lack the capacity to undertake more complex lending to businesses, real estate projects, or nonprofit organizations. CDCUs, therefore, are well suited to deliver basic and affordable financial services to low-income communities that are underserved by traditional banks. These basic services typically consist of savings accounts (called share accounts), check cashing, money orders, and personal and auto loans. Core services can grow to include checking accounts, certificates of deposits, automated teller machines, and additional loan products such as home mortgage and home improvement loans, as the credit union grows in size, sophistication, and banking relationships (Tholin & Pogge, 1991). As part of their community development mission, many CDCUs also offer education, counseling, and specialized products to expand the financial literacy, capacity, and assets of their low-income members.

CDCUs are not limited to serving individuals and households. Because community development credit unions receive regulatory relief to accept nonmember deposits and exceed the limits on small business lending, they have the capacity to supply other types of development credit to small businesses, nonprofit organizations, and real estate development projects. Examples of CDCUs that provide credit to independent farmers in rural areas and small businesses in urban neighborhoods were mentioned above. Other CDCUs, most notably North Carolina's Self-Help Credit Union, have grown to become key regional or statewide small business lenders, providing a credit availability role comparable to the largest loan funds and community development banks. The next two sections summarize best practices and present examples for these two CDCU roles: banking services for the poor and small business lending.

Banking Services for the Poor

Many poor households receive financial services from nondepository entities such as check-cashing companies, payday lenders, pawnshops, and small finance companies. These financial service firms offer convenient solutions to customers' needs for check cashing, bill payment, wire transfers, and short-term loans, but they often charge high fees and interest rates that add to the financial burdens of low- and moderate-income households (Caskey & Brayman, 2002). Some lenders target low-income minority and immigrant borrowers who cannot qualify for conventional lending products and use predatory practices to generate excessive fees and interest rates among poorly informed borrowers. These high borrowing costs make loan repayment extremely difficult, placing borrowers at risk of losing the car or home that secures the loan and further damaging their credit ratings.[11] Use of these alternative financial service firms is concentrated among poor and minority households that are least likely to use conventional bank accounts. According to Federal Reserve figures, a quarter of both African American and Hispanic households and those earnings below $20,000 have no bank accounts (Stegman & Lobenhofer, 2002). Over 80% of the families without checking accounts have annual incomes under $25,000, and 60% of them are minorities (Leibsohn, 2002).

Community development credit unions can compete with these financial firms to provide low-cost services and credit products while introducing low-income customers to development services that build their financial literacy, income, and assets. To perform this role, CDCUs need to recognize that check-cashing companies, payday lenders, and the like offer products and package services that effectively address real financial needs of low-income customers (Caskey & Brayman, 2002). These firms combine check cashing, bill payments, stamps, mailing, and wire transfer services at one location, providing a convenient package of services for households with no bank account. Similarly, short-term "pay day" loans help people with no month-to-month savings and poor credit records cover cash shortfalls between paychecks to pay for essential needs such as rent, heat, and medical emergencies. Caskey and Brayman argue that credit unions must offer comparable products and services to alternative financial firms to effectively serve this "unbanked" market via operating models that allow them to do so in a cost-effective and financially sound manner. They recommend a three-part approach. First, credit unions need to add check cashing, money orders, bill payment, and related services. By requiring customers to join the credit union through opening a small share account (e.g., with a $5 minimal deposit) and then charging a moderate fee for check cashing or other services, CDCUs can meet regulatory requirements and offer lower fees. Second, CDCUs can partner with community-based organizations to expand marketing to target clients and offset the higher costs of serving low-income customers. The Cincinnati Central Credit Union used this approach to provide emergency loans to high-credit risk borrowers and raised grant funds as collateral to reduce losses (Caskey & Brayman, 2002). Third, CDCUs can partner with other credit unions to provide these services by either forming a credit union service organization or establishing a shared branch. This collaborative approach reduces the financial risk and overhead costs to expand services. Service organizations also allow credit unions to provide check cashing, money orders, and other services to nonmembers, which increase fee income and broaden their customer base (Caskey & Brayman, 2002).[12]

Some credit unions have partnered with check-cashing firms to expand their services and membership. Bethex Federal Credit Union formed a partnership with RiteCheck, a New York City check-cashing firm, which allowed credit union members to use the eleven RiteCheck branches to make withdrawals and deposits, cash Bethex checks at no cost, and cash other checks at a reduced fee (Stegman & Lobenhofer, 2002). The partnership was feasible, in part, because of RiteCheck's existing investment in point of banking (POB) terminals and Bethex's payment of check cashing and POB fees for their members at a discounted "wholesale" rate. Although this partnership was a cost-effective way for Bethex to expand its banking network, member services, and membership, it poses risks that credit unions need to consider and address (Stegman & Lobenhofer, 2002). First, the partnership was based on careful regulatory scrutiny and oversight that exists in New York[13] but is not present in many other states. Second, liability and bonding for the handling of CDCU deposits by the check-cashing firm must be provided for to protect CDCU members from theft, fraud, or errors. Third, CDCUs need to consider the business practices of their partner and how their reputation and image may be affected by affiliation with the check-cashing industry.

CDCUs are also developing alternatives to high-cost payday loans[14] to address low-income credit needs.[15] These loans are usually small (usually several hundred dollars) to allow borrowers to repay them from the next one or two paychecks over a 6- to 8-week period and carry annual interest rates in the 15% to 20% range (Woodstock Institute, 2001). To manage losses, credit unions verify the borrower's employment and pay levels and may require direct deposit of the borrower's paycheck to allow automatic account debits to repay the loan. To foster financial skills, one-on-one counseling or financial literacy workshops are often offered, and some credit unions transfer a portion of the loan proceeds into a savings account to address future emergencies (and provide collateral). The "Stretch Plan," offered by ASI Federal Credit Union in Louisiana, is one example of a credit union payday loan product. This plan provides a revolving line of credit for up to $500 at 18% interest and with a $3 weekly fee (that includes other benefits). Loans are subject to a direct deposit requirement and borrowers have access to one-on-one financial counseling. Under the Stretch Plan, a borrower would pay interest and fees of $22.15 for a $200 six-week loan, compared to $120 for the same loan from an Illinois payday lender (Woodstock Institute, 2001). ASI experienced strong demand and few losses with this product from 1999 to 2001 when 2,390 loans were closed totaling $700,000 and delinquency and loss rates were 1.1% and .56%, respectively.

Perhaps the most important element of the CDCU approach to serving the poor is the inclusion of education, counseling, and products designed to build individual financial literacy and start members on a path toward economic self-sufficiency. Vermont Development Credit Union (VDCU) exemplifies how to link financial literacy and development services with banking and credit products. VDCU combines counseling, education, and lending to help low-income members build financial knowledge and management skills, set personal goals, and secure financial services to meet their goals. This lending philosophy, reflected in their motto, "We don't say no, we say when," emphasizes helping borrowers gain the capacity to secure credit. One-on-one counseling on financial literacy, personal credit, and home ownership supports members to overcome prior credit problems and gain key financial skills. VDCU also created special loan and saving products to move members toward personal financial goals. These products include "Tracker Loans" to repair or establish a credit record, "Working Wheels" auto loans for welfare-to-work clients, loans to meet down-payment and closing costs needed to buy a home and individual development accounts to build savings for home ownership, college education, and small business creation. With counseling and customized products, VDCU has a formula for high-volume lending to low-income households that is both self-supporting and low risk. In 2001, the credit union closed over 1,500 loans totaling $16.4 million,[16] generated interest and fees to cover its operating costs, and experienced a

.5% loan loss rate, below the average federal credit union and most banks (VDCU, 2002). A recent study found that VDCU generated significant improvements in their members' lives (Kolodinsky et al., 2002). Almost two thirds of VDCU members reported improved financial skills, better debt repayment, increased savings, expanded financial goals, and greater self-confidence since joining the credit union. Moreover, VDCU was an important contributor to these outcomes because the number of services used by a member was the most consistent factor in predicting positive impacts. Finally, the study estimated that VDCU's social benefits greatly exceeded the $478,000 in external grants that it received; these grants equaled less than one cent per dollar of loans made and were less than 6% of members' interest savings on these loans.

Small Business Lending

CDCUs can be important sources of small business credit, both to serve their members and to achieve large-scale economic development outcomes. In his 1997 study, Malizia found that CDCUs were more active small business lenders than conventional credit unions. Across 12,000 regular credit unions, business loans accounted for 2.9% of the number of outstanding loans and 1.1% of their total value in 1995. Among CDCUs, business lending represented 14.7% of all loans and 5.3% of their outstanding value.[17](Since some personal and auto loans may be used for business purposes, these figures may understate the true level of small business lending by credit unions.) CDCUs pursue small business lending in three ways. First, small business loans can be an extension of personal credit services by providing capital to self-employment and business start-ups among low-income members. Alternatives Federal Credit Union in Ithaca, New York, follows this approach (Malizia, 1997). Second, small business lending can target the credit needs of independent small businesses within the CDCU service area (Isbister, 1994). This may entail serving small farmers and handicraft businesses for rural CDCUs, lending to neighborhood retail and service firms by urban CDCUs, and financing the full range of small businesses for regional or statewide CDCUs. A third CDCU commercial lending role is to finance alternative organizations, such as cooperatives, employee-owned firms, or nonprofit organizations (Malizia, 1997). In all three cases, CDCUs expand capital availability by serving different borrowers than commercial banks—entrepreneurs who need less capital and offer limited collateral, but bring strong character and business plans to the table (Malizia, 1997).

Malizia also identified ways for CDCUs to expand and improve their small business lending. Because scale predicted both the likelihood to provide commercial loans and lending performance,[18] CDCUs need to grow their membership and assets to become effective small business lenders. A larger size yields more members to seek loans and more income to support specialized business lending staff. Thus, success factors for achieving scale and financial sustainability, such as building a diverse membership base beyond low-income individuals and attracting large deposits from nonmembers to reach $5 to $10 million in assets, are also central to making CDCUs vital sources of business credit. Beyond increasing their size, CDCUs can build their business lending capacity over time through starting with small loans, gaining lending experience, and then expanding into larger loans and higher volumes. Formal credit analysis to ensure sound banking decisions and offering counseling to borrowers (mirroring an essential CDCU personal banking service) to reduce loan losses are also central to effective CDCU commercial lending. Finally, Malizia argues that CDCUs must be realistic about the size and quality of their true lending market. When servicing small low-income neighborhoods or rural areas, the number of viable small business loans may be small. CDCUs need to carefully assess the market for small business loans and how they can best address loan demand. When demand is limited, CDCUs may need to focus on smaller loans that are extensions of personal lending services rather than create dedicated small business lending staff. For example, St. Luke Credit Union, which serves African Americans in two rural North Carolina counties, does a modest volume of loans averaging $10,000 to $15,000, primarily to help individual members start or grow their enterprises. In other cases, an expanded service area may generate the demand and loan volumes needed to support a dedicated small business staff.

Self-Help Credit Union demonstrates that CDCUs can be effective vehicles for small business lending. Based in Durham, North Carolina, Self-Help is a full-service statewide business lender that provides conventional business credit products, SBA guaranteed loans, SBA 504 loans, and a microloan program. Through its statewide presence and diverse loan products, Self-Help achieves high loan volumes, providing $17.5 million in debt to 180 businesses in 2001. With a large share of its borrowers minority-owned (47%), women-owned (49%) and in rural areas (41%), and over half of loans under $35,000, Self-Help Credit Union addresses business credit needs that are often overlooked by conventional lenders (Self-Help Credit Union, 2001). A key part of Self-Help's success is its parent, the Center for Community Self-Help, and its affiliate, Self-Help Ventures Fund. The parent organization provides training and technical assistance services to small businesses, undertakes new market and product development work, and cultivates funding and other partnerships. By funding these services and development costs outside the credit union, the strong financial performance of the credit union is maintained, and additional funding, such as foundation and government grants, allows for a higher level of investment in these critical activities. Self-Help Ventures Fund, on the other hand, complements the credit union by providing higher-risk loans that do fit regulatory standards for credit unions. With these two entities, Self-Help can service most business financing needs (Immergluck & Bush, 1995). This strategy guided Self-Help to become one of the nation's largest community-based financial institutions with total assets of over \$122 million in 2002[19] and cumulative lending of \$1.78 billion over 22 years across its small businesses, nonprofits, and home mortgage products (Self-Help Credit Union, 2001).

CDCU Operating Challenges and Needs

Although the preceding discussion highlighted CDCU best practices in two areas, this section offers a broader consideration of the management challenges facing CDCUs and successful practices to address them (see summary in Box 12.2). Both the experience of highly successful credit unions and studies of CDCU practices inform this presentation.[20] Reaching scale, as with all development finance institutions, is a core challenge, but it has a different nature for CDCUs, as membership-based depository institutions serving low-income communities. Since CDCUs raise most of their funds from member deposit accounts and generate their assets by lending to members, a large membership base is critical to asset growth. Although regulators seek at least 500 members before issuing a charter, several thousand members are needed to become a self-supporting \$5 to \$10 million institution. Thus, CDCUs must build their membership strategically by establishing a field of membership that can supply thousands of members and operationally through active outreach and marketing, choice of branch locations, and partnerships with organizations that can refer members. When planning a new CDCU, organizers need to analyze and design their scope of membership, geographically and demographically, to allow for substantial growth. In most cases, CDCUs need to serve either a city or a large portion of one, a metropolitan or multicounty region, or an entire state to create the potential for a large membership. Credit unions that target a small area where the low-income population is not large enough to reach a sustainable size can expand their membership to include moderate- and middle-income persons. This change helps them reach a revenue and asset size to better serve their core low-income market. By serving more diverse income groups, CDCUs also can balance the higher costs associated with serving low-income members with serving less costly middle-income households.

Once the right membership field is set, a strong initial membership drive is needed to start the credit union on a strong footing. A highly committed sponsor is essential for starting a new CDCU. This sponsor provides the seed funds and people to undertake an effective education and organizing drive to recruit hundreds of members and create an initial management team. Subsidies are also needed after the start-up phase to underwrite operating costs until the CDCU grows to sustainable size. Even after initial organization, membership recruitment remains a critical part of CDCU operations. A membership development strategy should establish the primary means to attract members and devote the necessary management attention and resources for implementation. Options include expansion via an office or branch network; recruitment

Box 12.2 CDCU Management Challenges

Strategy Challenges

Defining a Membership Field and Service Area to Achieve Scale

CDCUs need a service base with the capacity to reach several thousand members and $5 million or more in assets. Serving mixed-income memberships and larger regions help reach this scale.

Tailoring Banking and Credit Services to Low-Income Communities

Products and services must address the financial and development needs in low-income communities. Education and counseling, bundling services for convenience, and specialized loan products to build personal credit histories and serve niche markets are often necessary.

Operating Challenges

Efficiently Delivering Counseling and Transaction-Intensive Services

CDCUs need cost-effective systems and service models to provide counseling and handle many small accounts and transactions. Good data-processing systems, cost sharing, volunteers, and staff training all contribute to greater efficiencies.

Reaching and Building a Large Membership Base

A large investment in outreach, marketing, and partnerships with organizations trusted by their target membership helps attract a customer base in communities where financial institutions may not be trusted.

Building Strong Relationships With Multiple Partners

CDCUs need strong collaborations with community organizations, social service and technical assistance providers, government, and financial institutions to expand their membership and deposit base, help members gain allied services, and subsidize some activities.

Capitalization Challenges

Building a Large Deposit Base

Since they primarily rely on deposits for funds, CDCUs must grow a large deposit base with large nonmember deposits from government, banks, and others.

Securing Secondary Capital

Grants, equity-like investments, and long-term debt help CDCUs develop and offer higher-risk loan products and expand their education, counseling, and other development services.

---

through community agencies, religious groups, and other organizations that have strong connections to the target membership; and growth through partnerships that attract new members with new services or affiliations.

Effective CDCU operations require specialized services tailored to low-income and small business members and strategies to address the costs associated with the development services, modest accounts, and small transactions entailed in serving these customers. Market research helps CDCUs understand customer needs and the obstacles they face in accessing conventional financial institutions, and thus, to design effective banking, credit, and development services. VDCU established its service model for low-income members after conducting focus groups, studying 400 loan applications, and analyzing available consumer financial education services in its area. From this study, VDCU decided that it needed to embed personally tailored education, counseling, and advocacy into its products and services to overcome the limited knowledge, guilt, and fear about financial matters among low-income persons (Kolodinsky et al., 2002). As a result, the credit union created several counseling-based lending and education services and established principles and staff awareness of the need for a supportive and accepting service culture.

CDCUs employ several practices to achieve cost-effective operations. First, several credit unions use companion nonprofit organizations to undertake research and product development, provide more costly development services, such as business technical assistance, and undertake higher-risk lending. Self-Help Credit Union pioneered this approach, with the nonprofit Center for Community Self-Help funding policy, planning and technical assistance activities, and Self-Help Ventures Fund extending business and home mortgage lending capacity. This structure is analogous to how ShoreBank employed bank holding company affiliates to tap new funding sources and add synergistic capabilities to its core commercial bank. Second, partnerships allow CDCUs to efficiently serve members in a large area and expand services. Some partnerships build referral networks with community action agencies, religious congregations, and other community-based organizations to reach and serve more members. Collaborations with other credit unions or other financial entities allow credit unions to expand member services and reduce their costs. Although the Bethex/RiteCheck partnership discussed earlier in the chapter is one option, credit union service organizations (CUSOs) are another alternative. Through pooled purchasing of key services, such as data processing and insurance, CUSOs reduce CDCU costs while expanding member services, such as access to ATM networks, credit cards, insurance, and investments. Third, as democratic membership organizations, CDCUs often use member volunteers to perform important functions. Although volunteers do not replace staff, they can augment staff capacity by assisting with many activities, such as member education and counseling, market research, planning and product development, grant writing, outreach to potential depositors, and other tasks. Special efforts should be undertaken to identify member skills, recruit and involve them in credit union activities, and acknowledge them for their service.

Since CDCUs rely heavily on deposits to raise funds but serve low-income members with limited funds to save, they face a special challenge in raising capital. Fortunately, several options exist to overcome this constraint. Nonmember deposits from financial institutions and social investors are an important source of low-cost and stable capital to grow CDCUs. Isbister found that nonmember deposits represented a higher share of assets for large CDCUs and were an important source of funds for the one third of CDCUs that used them, averaging 21% of total assets (Isbister, 1994). Several institutions provide CDCUs with long-term secondary capital through loans or equity-equivalent investments (investments that require only dividend or interest payments but no or a long-deferred return of capital); sources include the NCUA, the CDFI Fund, and National Community Capital. Lending partnerships with governments, nonprofit agencies, and secondary market institutions are important sources of CDCU lending capital. Self-Help Credit Union received two separate state appropriations of $2 million to support its small business lending and a low-down payment mortgage program. It is also an active SBA lender and partners with the Ford Foundation and Fannie Mae to package and sell affordable home mortgages.[21] VDCU has lending partnerships with the Vermont Department of Aging and Disabilities, statewide community action agencies, an electric utility, and Fannie Mae (Kolodinsky et al., 2002). Finally, foundation grants provide critical funding to support new program development, development services, and capital for higher-risk lending activities.

Endnotes

1. The U.S. Treasury Community Development Financial Institutions Fund and other analysts have a more expansive definition of CDFIs that includes community development banks and community development venture funds. This name corresponds to the name of the federal Community Development Loan Fund (CDLF). Although the CDLF encompasses a broader set of financial entities than meet its criteria for a CDFI (see Chapter 15 for more information), this chapter concentrates on the two organizational models that dominate this field and whose historic mission and focus has been community-based development finance.

2. The $400,000 in revenue comes from $160,000 earned on $2 million in equity funds without any cost of funds and $240,000 from the 4% spread on $6 million in borrowed funds.

3. Loans funds were categorized by their primary activity, although about one quarter of the funds, especially larger ones, offered both housing and business loans. About 60% of the housing funds and 30% of the business funds also financed community facilities.

4. See Isbister (1994), pp. 55–62 for a brief history of conventional credit unions in the United States.

5. Credit unions are typically not allowed to take deposits from nonmembers but NCUA allows low-income credit unions to receive up to 20% of their deposits from nonmembers, and institutions can petition for an exception to this limit (Isbister (1994), p. 114).

6. A database search by NCUA identified 79 newly established low-income credit unions between 1991 and 2003.

7. NCUA does not use or officially recognize the CDCU term. While some LICUs may focus on traditional credit union services without a self-conscious community development mission, both definitions refer to membership-controlled institutions that provide banking and credit services to a primarily low-income population or area.

8. The typical loan to member share ratio for all federal credit unions was 70 to 75% in December 2001.

9. The CDCU net worth ratio is not identical to the conventional credit union figure because it includes secondary capital, such as subordinate loans and deposits. However, secondary capital at CDCUs was $8.8 million in 2001, only .7% of their total net worth. Thus, these accounts had almost no effect on the overall CDCU net worth ratio.

10. Isbister's analysis of 1991 data for 180 community development credit unions found the average CDCU had 1.9 employees compared to 6.9 for all credit unions. Larger CDCUs, with assets over $500,000, had a higher average of 3.2 staff, which is still quite small to permit specialized business lending staff. See pp. 135 to 137.

11. See Caskey (2002) for a discussion of recent developments in the check cashing industry. Pennington-Cross (2003) provides a study of subprime lending in the home mortgage market.

12. Caskey and Brayman (2002) provide detailed financial projections showing the economics for credit unions to expand into check-cashing and related services through an existing branch and a shared branch. They estimate the cost to cash a check under the shared branch option at $1.99 to $2.46.

13. The partnership required 4 years of negotiations with regulators at the NCUA and New York State before it could be implemented.

14. Payday loans are small loans extended for a few weeks to cover the borrower's expenses until the next paycheck. Their fees and interest payments are small in dollar amounts but carry extremely high interest rates. When loan repayment is extended beyond a few weeks, the fees and interest costs can equal or exceed the original principal.

15. This discussion of credit union payday loans is based on the Woodstock Institute's March 2001 Reinvestment Alert.

16. This included 99 home mortgage loans totaling $8.8 million, 1,361 individual loans for $6.2 million, and $828,025 in 84 small business loans.

17. Malizia (1997) also found that 15.3% of all CDCUs formally offer business loans compared to 12.5% of regular credit unions.

18. CDCUs with $20 million or more in assets were over twice as likely to make commercial loans, and those with the largest lending volumes also had the lowest delinquency and loss rates. See pp. 14 to 16.

19. This includes $94.5 million for Self-Help Credit Union and $28 million for Self-Help Ventures Fund. Figures are from the NCUA credit union records.

20. Several useful studies of CDCU practices include Kolodinsky et al. (2002), Williams (1999), and Isbister (1994).

21. Information on Self-Help's partnerships is from its Web site www.self-help.org

13

Microenterprise Finance

O ver the past 15 years, programs targeted at developing and financing very small enterprises have emerged as an important area of economic development practice in the United States. Microenterprise finance programs originated in developing countries to raise incomes and reduce poverty through self-employment. As practitioners and policy makers learned of successful programs and institutions in developing countries, especially the Grameen Bank in Bangladesh and Accion International in Latin America, they transferred these models to the United States, initially as an antipoverty strategy and then to address broader community and economic development goals.[1] With foundation and federal government support[2] and strong practitioner interest, microenterprise programs (MEPs) mushroomed in the 1990s, reaching over 200 by the mid-1990s and then growing to 560 in 2002 (Black et al., 2002; Edgecomb et al., 1996).

Microenterprise programs serve both individuals seeking to start a business and existing firms with a few employees, typically five or less, by providing credit and business development assistance. These programs target populations that historically lacked access to business credit, training, and technical assistance, including low-income persons, immigrants, minorities, and women. Some MEPs help welfare recipients, refugees, or other disadvantaged groups use self-employment as a vehicle to achieve economic self-sufficiency. Two needs within these groups shape the design of microenterprise finance. First, intensive technical assistance and training is provided to help disadvantaged entrepreneurs that lack business skills plan and successfully operate an enterprise. Although technical assistance is important for most economic development finance programs, it is integral to microenterprise development. Many MEPs devote more resources to training and technical assistance and serve more people via these services than through lending. Second, microbusinesses begin small scale, often as self-employment to supplement labor market income, and require modest capital to start up and grow. Consequently, microenterprise finance programs provide very small loans, in the $500 to $25,000 range, that are too costly for conventional lenders to supply, even when a business meets their credit standards.

This chapter provides an overview of microenterprise practice in the United States, its potential economic development impact, and key program issues. The first section explains the three service models used by microenterprise programs: peer-group lending, individual lending, and training-based services. In the second section, studies and data on the operations, performance, and outcomes of microenterprise programs are summarized. This discussion concludes with different perspectives on the economic development impact of microenterprise development and its potential role in advancing economic development goals. Program design and management are addressed in the next two sections, first by elaborating the special challenges to funding and operating MEPs and second by presenting lessons and best practices gained through demonstration programs, evaluations, and case studies. The chapter concludes with a case study through which the reader can apply his or her understanding of microenterprise development to recommend ways to expand the impact of a MEP in a low-income immigrant community.

_____ Three Models of Microenterprise Finance

Microenterprise programs deliver training, technical assistance, and credit within three service models: (1) peer group lending; (2) individual-based lending; and (3) training-based programs (Edgecomb et al., 1996). These models differ in their emphasis on training and technical assistance services versus credit services and by whether credit is provided to individuals or through a peer group. Both the peer group and individual lending models are "credit-led" programs that stress helping entrepreneurs secure loans to start or expand their businesses. Training-based programs concentrate on providing training and technical assistance, with credit as an optional service (Edgecomb et al., 1996). The characteristics of each model and its unique benefits and disadvantages are summarized below.[3]

Peer Group Lending

This model is closest to successful microenterprise finance programs used in developing countries, most notably the Grameen Bank. Entrepreneurs operate as a group to extend loans to group members, collect loan payments, and repay the loans to the microfinance entity. Entrepreneurs receive initial training on basic business skills, program policies and expectations, group organization and lending and are then organized into groups (groups may be formed first and then trained). The group serves as both the credit gatekeeper that approves loans made to members and the guarantor that ensures the repayment of all members' loans. Loans are staged with short repayment periods. Borrowers graduate to larger loans after their earlier loans are repaid. New larger loans, however, are not provided until all prior loans to group members are repaid, which reinforces the group repayment obligation. Peer groups also contribute to business success through emotional support and encouragement, informal technical assistance, and access to members' social networks for customers and business relationships.

One promise of the peer group model, based on results in developing countries, is serving small start-up businesses that lack collateral with low administrative costs and few loan losses. Because the peer group performs key lending functions, including credit decisions and collections, program staffing and administrative needs should be lower than under the individualized lending approach. Furthermore, the combination of group-level guarantees, staged lending, and mutual support improves loan repayment rates; Grameen Bank, for example, reports loss rates of 2%, despite lending to poor rural business owners (Yunis, 1989). Finally, the peer group process makes starting a business and borrowing money more accessible for new entrepreneurs, people with limited financial literacy, and groups that face discrimination or social exclusion.

In practice, U.S. programs have found it difficult to realize these benefits. Organizing and sustaining effective peer groups has proven difficult and staff-intensive, limiting their cost saving and loss reduction benefits (Edgecomb et al., 1996; Taub, 1998; Varma, 2001). Programs have addressed this problem by expanding training and assistance to support group effectiveness, using existing business associations to create peer lending groups, reducing group functions, and offering alternative individual lending programs (Edgecomb et al., 1996; Taub, 1998; Varma, 2001). However, many of these changes increase costs and reduce the administrative efficiency of peer group lending.

In addition to the complexity and time involved in organizing groups, the peer lending model can have other disadvantages. Some entrepreneurs prefer to borrow funds individually without joining a group or guaranteeing other loans. The requirement to join a group may deter such a person from obtaining assistance and pursuing a business idea. In other cases, weak group dynamics or business failures within the group can stall the growth of successful businesses because they cannot borrow additional funds until the loans of all group members are repaid. Even when groups operate well and member businesses succeed, it takes considerable time for borrowers to graduate to a substantial loan. This last problem can be addressed by having fast-growing businesses graduate to an individual loan program.

Individual Lending Model

As the name applies, this model provides loans to entrepreneurs on an individual basis. Although this approach resembles conventional lending in its focus on credit and assessing the repayment capacity of the individual firm, it has important differences. First, it serves entrepreneurs who lack access to and would not qualify for traditional loans by applying less stringent credit standards, accepting more forms of collateral, and giving more weight to nonfinancial aspects of the business (e.g., the business plan and owner's commitment). Second, these programs usually offer training and technical assistance services through one-on-one staff assistance, referrals to affiliated assistance providers, and training workshops and courses. Individual lending programs typically provide loans in larger amounts and with longer terms than those made by peer group lending programs.

Key advantages of individual lending programs include their administrative simplicity relative to peer group lending and their ability to tailor credit and assistance to the borrower's needs. Since they use a well-known and accepted lending approach and forgo the time, training, and work needed to create peer groups, these programs are easier to establish and can grow to scale more readily. Another advantage is their ability to respond to individual business needs without the constraints of group lending. A large or fast-growing firm can obtain a loan that fits its business plan unconstrained by the staged borrowing process of peer group lending. Similarly, technical assistance services can be designed to address the individual and industry-specific needs of each client. These advantages make individual lending programs well suited to established businesses, those with faster growth, and firms that need larger loans.

Nonetheless, individual lending programs have important weaknesses. First, they do not offer the social support, networking potential, and problem-solving mechanism found in peer groups. Thus, they can be less effective in serving nascent entrepreneurs and those requiring strong social support to succeed. Second, they are staff intensive because each loan must be evaluated and serviced by a staff person, who also may provide technical assistance. Finally, individual lending programs require more capital to make larger loans with longer repayment terms than do peer group programs. However, since most microenterprise programs have portfolios of several hundred thousand dollars, rather than millions of dollars, raising capital has not been a problem. Instead, as discussed below, managing and funding high operating costs is a far greater challenge for the field.

Training-Led Model

Many programs use training as the primary tool to foster microbusiness development, recognizing that knowledge and skills rather than credit are the foundation for business success. Despite variation in their structure, content, and clients, most training-led programs provide an extended course[4] built around the creation of a business plan. Participants attend formal classes and complete assignments that lead to creating a final plan by the end of the course (Edgecomb et al., 1996). Business skills, such as accounting, market analysis, and marketing are acquired by applying them to the student's business concept or existing enterprise. Some training-led programs do not offer credit, and others provide credit as an optional service upon course completion, through either their own programs or partnerships with lenders. Upon completing the course, an entrepreneur may seek a loan to start a business, use his or her savings or informal credit, or choose not to start a business. In fact, an important training outcome may be preventing aspiring entrepreneurs from starting a business when they learn that the prospects for their business idea are poor and/or the demands of business ownership are not compatible with their personal goals and strengths.

This basic training format can be altered with the target client. One important variation is programs that help Temporary Assistance for Needy Family (TANF) recipients move from welfare to economic self-sufficiency. Programs serving TANF recipients need to help build self-esteem and provide life skills training while addressing clients' greater obstacles to self-employment. Consequently, these programs combine "personal effectiveness" skills training with teaching business skills and use highly structured and step-by-step learning methods (Edgecomb et al., 1996; Bonavoglia, 2001). Moreover, clients receive additional services, such as case management, mentoring, support groups, and network development, to help overcome barriers to personal and business success that extend well beyond the formal training period (Bonavoglia, 2001).[5] A second variation in training-led programs is short-term courses that either address specific business issues (e.g., taxes, market research, licensing) or train for specific industries (e.g., landscaping, day-care, or restaurants). Short courses also allow MEPs to serve existing businesses along with entrepreneurs in the prestart-up stage.

Training-based assistance is a valuable microenterprise strategy for several reasons. First, it develops core business knowledge and skills that are critical to individual business success and expands entrepreneurial capacity in economically distressed and low-income communities. It creates the foundation for profitable businesses that can effectively utilize credit and, therefore, hold promise for greater economic impact. Second, training programs reach more people than credit-led programs because they serve entrepreneurs who are not seeking credit. As with peer-group lending, training provides a wholesale approach to skill development that promises to assist more people at lower cost than the one-on-one assistance provided by individual lending programs. Third, training-led programs without credit services avoid the cost of capitalizing and staffing a loan fund and do not duplicate services that other lenders may provide. On the other hand, training-led programs have two major disadvantages. Training is costly with the small class sizes, new methods, and specialized materials to teach MEP target client groups. Additionally, loans provide an incentive that attracts some entrepreneurs to take and complete courses. Thus, programs without a lending component may find it harder to recruit students and have lower graduation rates. Partnerships with private banks and other lenders can overcome this limitation and provide graduates with credit options.

Practitioners combine and adapt these models to meet program goals and respond to the needs of different target groups. Some programs, such as the Good Faith Fund in Arkansas and the Los Angeles Coalition for Women's Economic Development, add individual lending programs to their original peer-group model to serve a broader set of entrepreneurs (Edgecomb et al.,

1996). Other agencies create new programs tailored to specific client groups, such as refugees, welfare recipients, and established businesses that incorporate appropriate elements of the three prototypes. Some organizations use innovative approaches that straddle or expand upon the three standard models. For example, the Institute for Social and Economic Development (ISED) in Iowa combines intensive technical assistance and training with assistance securing bank loans and sometimes provides a guarantee for the bank loan. Portable Practical Education Program (PPEP) supports the expansion of existing business in Arizona's border areas with technical assistance and loans that it delivers through associations of 20 to 30 businesses rather than smaller peer groups (Edgecomb et al., 1996).

An Overview of the U.S. Industry and Its Performance

Despite their short history, U.S. microenterprise programs have been well studied. The Aspen Institute has undertaken long-term studies of microenterprise development practice and funded demonstration projects to both increase industry knowledge and develop and disseminate best practices. Through these efforts, considerable data exist on the characteristics and performance of U.S. microenterprise programs. The Aspen Institute identified 560 U.S. microenterprise programs in 2002 and compiled survey data from 308 of them, which is summarized in Table 13.1. These data demonstrate the centrality of training to U.S. microenterprise practice and the programs' role in serving nontraditional entrepreneurs. Although the percentages of programs providing training services (68%) and credit (64%) are similar, far more clients receive training than loans. Since the average program served 175 clients but made 41 loans, more than four entrepreneurs received training or technical assistance for every loan recipient. With almost two thirds of their clients women and over half from low-income households, MEPs served nontraditional business owners who are often overlooked by mainstream banking and economic development programs.

In their finance capacity, MEPs primarily use the individual lending model and have small loan portfolios and capital needs. A breakdown of lending programs for 1999 shows that 77% used individual lending programs alone, 9% relied solely on peer group lending, and 14% employed both lending approaches (see Table 13.2). Most programs combined credit with training services as only 30% of programs offered only training services.[6] Although programs made an average of 41 loans in 2000, higher than many other development finance programs,[7] the total value of these loans averaged $273,496 (the mean loan size for all programs was $6,670). The average program's entire loan portfolio was only slightly larger, at $341,000. Consequently, most MEPs need to raise a modest amount of loan capital, on the order of $500,000 to $1 million. Even the program with the

Table 13.1   Summary Data for U.S. Microenterprise Programs in FY2000

Program Characteristic	Industrywide Percentage or Average
Number of Programs	308
Percentage offering credit	64% ($n = 308$)
Percentage offering training	69% ($n = 308$)
Average number of clients served	175 ($n = 285$)
Average number of loans disbursed	41 ($n = 176$)
Average value of FY2000 loans	$273,496 ($n = 176$)
Average value of loan portfolio	$341,025 ($n = 198$)
Average annual budget	$378,781 ($n = 308$)
Percentage of clients that are low income[a]	58% ($n = 154$)
Percentage of clients that are women	64% ($n = 254$)

SOURCE: Black et al. (2002).

NOTE:

a. Based on HUD's 80% of median income guideline.

largest loan portfolio, $3.4 million, had capital needs well below that of most other development finance programs. Funding operating costs, on the other hand, poses a greater challenge. The average program had an annual operating budget of $378,781 in 2000, which exceeded both the average amount of new loans ($273,496) and the average loan portfolio ($341,025). Although these figures are not directly comparable (the operating cost figure is for all programs, and the loan portfolio average applies to a subset of credit programs), they indicate that annual operating costs and loan capital are on the same scale. Whereas most development finance programs expand their capital base to increase financial self-sufficiency, MEPs cannot follow this approach. Instead, they must continually raise annual operating grants to sustain their programs. Moreover, the figures suggest that more than one dollar of training and administrative costs is used for every dollar of loans made.[8] These high costs require MEPs to document the impact of their activities to justify operating subsidies while improving their efficiency and increasing revenue to reduce subsidy levels as they expand.

Table 13.2   Distribution of U.S. Microenterprise Programs by Type in 1999

Program Type	Number of Programs	Percentage of Lending Programs	Percentage of All Programs
Peer group lending only	18	9.0%	6.4%
Individual lending only	154	77.4%	54.4%
Both lending types	27	13.6%	9.5%
Total lending programs	199	100.0%	70.3%
Training and technical assistance only	84	NA	29.7%
Total, all programs	283	NA	100.0%

SOURCE: Calculated from data in Table 1 in Varma (2001).

Program Performance

Through its MicroTest initiative, the Aspen Institute collects data from a subset of programs, which provide a detailed picture of industry performance.[9] The 56 MicroTest programs that reported data for FY2000 were larger, on average, than the entire microenterprise field, but they serve a similar clientele of primarily low-income, female, and minority entrepreneurs and operate in the same mix of urban and rural areas.[10] Table 13.3 summarizes performance data for the MicroTest sample, comparing figures for lending and training-led programs.

In addition to confirming the scale of microenterprise programs and the nature of their clients, the MicroTest data documents the industry's financial parameters and identifies key differences across programs types. Whereas the average program made 76 loans totaling $395,000 in FY2000, credit-led entities, not surprisingly, were the most active lenders. They funded $621,000

Table 13.3   FY2000 Performance Measures for MicroTest Microenterprise Programs

Performance Measure	Median for all Programs (n = 56)	Median for Training-Led Programs (n = 30)	Median for Credit-Led Programs (n = 24)
Number of clients	205	171	287
Percentage of women clients	60%	76%	53%
Percentage of low-income clients served[a]	63%	68%	50%
Percentage of pre-start-up clients	31%	55%	15%
Percentage of start-up clients	18%	15%	29%
Percentage of existing business clients	31%	18%	45%
Number of loans disbursed	28	20	41
Value of loans disbursed	$153,685	$43,011	$306,811
Value of outstanding loan portfolio	$355,359	$100,013	$592,706
Average loan size	$4,905	$2,926	$5,745
Share of start-up loans in portfolio	40%	60%	29%
Loan loss rate	5%	5%	3%
Total portfolio risk rate[b]	10%	20%	5%
Operating cost per client	$2,068	$2,304	$1,983
Operational cost rate[c]	.81	2.31	.50
Operating cost per loan[d]	$3,538	$4,346	$3,492
Short-term self-sufficiency[e]	17%	7%	33%
Percentage grant funding	71%	81%	64%

SOURCE: Black et al. (2002).

NOTES:

a. At 80% or less of HUD low-income guidelines.

b. Percentage of loans 30 days or more past due.

c. Annual credit-related costs/loan portfolio.

d. Annual credit-related costs/annual number of loans.

e. Income from lending activities/credit-related operating, financial, and loans loss expenses.

in 112 loans, on average, four times the mean for training-led programs (28). Moreover, credit-led programs, which comprised 46% of the sample, accounted for 84% of total loans and 89% of total dollars lent by all MicroTest organizations. Given their borrowers with limited business experience and personal assets, MicroTest loan portfolios performed well. The median loan loss rate in FY2000 was 5% while the median total portfolio risk rate (the percentage of loans that were 30 days or more past due) was 10%. Portfolio quality indicators were similar for credit- and training-based programs, except for total portfolio risk, which averaged 20% for training-led programs and 5% for credit-led ones. This difference may result from the larger share of loans to start-up enterprises among training-led programs (Black et al., 2002). Rural programs had the highest loan loss and overall portfolio risk rates, three times that for urban programs.[11] Although these higher loss and delinquency rates probably reflect more lending to start-up businesses by rural programs, the smaller markets and economic resources in rural economies may also be a factor. Finally, the MicroTest data shows that microenterprise portfolios can perform on par with conventional credit sources; the best performing MEPs had loan losses below 2.2% and 30-day past due loans of 3.1%. These rates fall between bank commercial loans and consumer credit card debt and are at a level that can be recouped through market interest rates.

An important finding from the MicroTest data is that training-led and credit-led programs serve different clients. Training-based programs serve a lower income population and assist more prestart businesses than do credit-oriented programs. In 2000, the median share of clients at the lowest income levels was twice as high for training-based programs compared to credit-led ones.[12] Credit-based programs also focused on businesses with the greatest capacity to repay loans; existing businesses accounted for 45% of clients for the median program in FY2000. On the other hand, training-led programs primarily served people seeking to start a business; their median share of pre-start-up firms in FY2000 was 55%. These differences in client groups influence the services provided and the concomitant operating costs and subsidies required for each program type. Training-led programs incur higher per client costs to provide more intensive services to people with little business experience. Moreover, training-based programs have less capacity to generate revenue because they have small loan portfolios and serve poorer clients. Consequently, training-led programs are far less financially self-sufficient and require higher subsidy levels than do credit-led programs.

U.S. microenterprise programs appear unlikely to become financially self-sufficient in the foreseeable future since their operating costs are several multiples of their potential interest and fee revenue. Lending costs, at a median of $3,538 per loan, far exceeded interest income from loans that averaged under $7,000. Despite lower training expenses (median of $1,459), fees from the predominantly low- and moderate-income clientele were insufficient to recoup these costs. Several measures quantify this funding situation. The total cost recovery rate (share of operating costs recouped from program income) averaged 14% for MicroTest programs in 2000, and the median rate was even lower at 7%. For lending programs, the median short-term financial self-sufficiency ratio (the share of all lending-related costs, including interest expenses and loan loss reserves, covered by revenue) was 17%; credit-led programs performed much better at 33%. With the highest ratios for total cost recovery at 75% and for short-term financial self-sufficiency at 85%, even the best performing program was not self-sufficient. The demand for training services, the more intensive assistance needed by microenterprise clients compared to more established small businesses, and far higher costs than in developing nations combine to make U.S. programs costly and in need of ongoing subsidies.

Despite this need for subsidies, the MicroTest data show that cost efficiency increases with program size and that the industry's financial performance is improving. Credit-led programs, which operate on a large scale, have lower costs and achieve higher levels of self-sufficiency than training-based ones. Credit-led programs achieved median total cost recovery rates of 23% compared to 2% for training-led programs. In addition to their scale, this outcome reflects the greater revenue generated by loans and a large client base of existing businesses that need less intensive assistance. From 1999 to 2000, the 2 years during which MicroTest collected data, the average cost per loan dropped 17%. Moreover, financial self-sufficiency improved with the average rates for both total program cost recovery and short-term financial self-sufficiency increasing.[13] However, a longer time series is needed to determine whether these trends will continue.

Program Outcomes

Several studies indicate that MEPs succeed at generating business start-up and expansions, but with modest job creation impacts. This outcome reflects the fact that microbusinesses are primarily self-employment vehicles for their owners, often generating income to supplement labor market earnings that helps raise owners' households out of poverty. The Aspen Institute Self-Employment Learning Project (SELP) undertook the most extensive outcome study of MEPs, tracking 405 program clients, including 133 who were very poor, from 1991 to 1997. SELP found that these clients started 386 enterprises with almost half (49%) surviving for 5 years. Two thirds of the businesses had no employees beyond the owner, but the remaining third created 332 jobs beyond the owner's self-employment (Servon, 1998). Among poor MEP clients, an important focus of the SELP study, 72% increased their household income, with an average gain of 61%, or $8,484, over 5 years. For just over half of the poor households, these income gains allowed them to move out of poverty (Clark & Kays, 1999). Microenterprises that stayed in business contributed 37% of the gain in household income on average—an important factor in clients' ability to escape poverty. Individuals with businesses that stayed open were more successful in getting out of poverty than clients whose business closed or who chose wage employment alone (Clark & Kays, 1999).

Other studies confirm modest job impacts from microenterprise development but document smaller income gains. Lisa Servon surveyed 63 clients as part of her analysis of six MEPs. Most enterprises were home-based businesses in the service (48%) or retail (21%) sectors, and only 29% had employees beyond the business owner. The 17 firms with employees created 41 part-time and 28 full-time jobs. Moreover, business income was small (the median monthly profit was $200) and insufficient to raise participants out of poverty (Servon, 1998). Self-reported data collected from the six programs, on the other hand, indicated that programs, over time, helped create several hundred enterprises and jobs, a cumulative impact on a par with small revolving loan funds. Based on this data, summarized in Table 13.4, the average outcome for these programs was 60 new businesses and 69 jobs created or retained per year. An earlier study of self-employment programs for welfare recipients in five states found that 31% of the 1,687 clients

Table 13.4   Self-Reported Outcomes From Six Microenterprise Programs

Program	Number of Start-up Businesses	Number of Businesses Retained or Expanded	Number of Jobs Created or Retained	Period Covered by Data
Institute for Social and Economic Development (Iowa)	139	107	94[a]	1997
Northeast Entrepreneur Fund (Minnesota)	186	56	470[b]	1993 to 1997
West Company (California)	126	49	126[a]	1993 to 1997
Women Entrepreneurs of Baltimore (Maryland)	341	Not applicable	No data reported	FY1991 to FY1996
Women's Economic Self-Sufficiency Team (New Mexico)	51	No data reported	No data reported	1997
Lawrence Working Capital (Massachusetts)	360	No data reported	450	1990 to 1996
Annual Average	60		69	

SOURCE: Servon (1998).

NOTES:

a. New jobs created only.

b. Jobs created and retained.

started or expanded a business, of which 79% survived at least two years. Job and income outcomes were small; median annual business gross income was $8,000 and employment averaged 1.5 full- or part-time jobs (Servon, 1998; Bonavoglia, 2001). However, some recent studies to test and identify effective practices found more promising outcomes. For example, the Women's Initiative for Self-Employment in San Francisco documented a 97% increase in participant's total income over 1.5 years with the percentage living at 150% or less of the poverty level declining from 63% to 18%. These outcomes were linked to strong business survival and growth rates, with 76% of enterprises still in business after one year and 70% having an expansion in which sales increased by at least 30% (Edgecomb, 2002b).

The Economic Development Role of Microenteprise Development

Although many studies have detailed program clients, operations, and outcomes, there is considerable debate about the economic development impact of microenterprise programs. In his study of the Good Faith Fund, Rich Taub argues that businesses developed by the program generated little economic development due to their scale and nature (Taub, 1998). Because most enterprises were small retail or service businesses catering to the local population, they created few jobs and generated no new income for the region. Taub believes that this outcome is inherent when providing very small loans, which cannot help firms grow to a significant size in an economy with substantial competition from large firms. Lisa Servon and Jeffrey Doshna, on the other hand, argue that microenterprise programs generate meaningful job outcomes and yield economic results that are not captured by traditional economic development measures (Servon & Doshna, 1999). The authors argue that mature microenterprise programs are cost-effective job creation tools. The average cost per job created in three such programs ranged from $4,114 to $6,115, which was comparable to job creation costs for traditional economic development activities, including industrial recruitment ($1,906 to $50,580), business incubators ($1,500 to $2,000), infrastructure development ($4,857), and revolving loan funds ($3,312 to $5,439). However, the different methods used to generate these figures and the lack of any comparative analysis of the type and quality of the jobs created across each program limits the value of this comparison.[14] Servon and Doshna also use data from Minnesota's Northeast Entrepreneur Fund (NEF) to suggest that microenterprise programs created jobs in diverse sectors with significant economic impact. Among the 462 jobs created or retained by NEF-assisted firms from 1993 to 1997, 24% were in agriculture, construction, and manufacturing. Moreover, using state-level economic multipliers, they estimate that these 462 direct jobs had a total impact of 880 jobs when indirect and induced effects are considered.[15] Finally, the authors believe that microenterprise programs generate additional benefits that include participants' education and life skills, helping individuals become productive employees, and providing supplemental and transition income that helps families and regions adjust economically. Given these outcomes and their job creation impacts, Servon and Doshna view microenterprise development as a vital part of a continuum of comprehensive business development and employment services.

Although microenterprise programs are not large-scale job generators, they can advance important economic and community development goals. Practitioners need to define appropriate goals for these programs and link microenterprise development with initiatives to extend their economic development impact. Goals for which microenterprise programs are well suited include (1) fostering self-esteem and personal skill development as part of education and economic self-sufficiency initiatives; (2) using self-employment and business ownership to raise incomes and reduce poverty, especially for populations with limited labor market options; (3) overcoming barriers to credit for entrepreneurs not served by conventional credit sources; and (4) revitalizing and strengthening commercial districts with many small independent stores.

Design Issues and Management Challenges

Microenterprise programs face distinct design and management challenges given their client base, large training and technical assistance component, and financial constraints (Box 13.1 summarizes these challenges). Although microenterprise programs, like other finance entities, must define target markets and offer appropriate products and services to assist them, they have less experience and no readily transferable model to guide them. Instead, practitioners need to select the right mix of training, technical assistance, and credit services to overcome obstacles faced by their target clients and formulate methods for delivering them in an accessible and effective manner. Since the U.S. microenterprise field is young, managers need to test new approaches and learn from the experience of other programs.[16] Nonetheless, MEPs face some common strategy issues that include deciding how narrow a client base to target, choosing between the individual- or peer-lending approaches, and defining the range of loan products and training services to provide. A limited clientele and service area, especially with service-intensive groups (e.g., welfare recipients), make it difficult to achieve scale and manage costs. Credit-based programs, in particular, need a sizable target market because a small share of their clients typically seek loans and many programs have difficulty finding sufficient demand for even modest loan capital. For example, loan portfolios averaged 40% of available capital for the seven MEPs studied in the Aspen Institute's Self-Employment Learning Projects (Edgecomb et al., 1996). Some programs mix a focused target clientele with a large service area to reach significant scale. Accion USA, for example, concentrates on providing credit to existing Latino businesses in several regions with large Latino populations. Programs need to consider both their expansion potential and

Box 13.1   Microenterprise Program Challenges

Strategy Challenges

Defining Appropriate Service Areas and Target Populations

MEPs need to target groups excluded from conventional credit and training services but with a real interest in forming and growing businesses. Target areas and clients groups must be able to produce substantial demand and recognize that a small share of participants create businesses and/or seek loans.

Choosing the Right Mix of Services and Appropriate Delivery Mechanism

Programs should reflect local conditions rather than copy models from developing countries. Intensive training and peer-based services fit pre-start-up and very low-income clients. Credit-based and individual services suit existing entrepreneurs. Offering a mix of services and delivery mechanisms helps achieve program scale.

Operating Challenges

Reaching and Involving Target Clients

Special marketing is needed to recruit potential and existing entrepreneurs who are outside the formal training and economic development systems and may distrust government or social programs.

Managing Lending and Servicing Many Small and Unconventional Loans

Programs must be able to handle many clients and small loans while adapting credit standards and lending practices to low-income clients and informal enterprises. Programs have learned the value of formal policies and processes that support new entrepreneurs and generate sound loans.

Providing Effective Training and Technical Assistance

Training needs to be tailored to target clients and supplemented with posttraining technical assistance. Specialized training and technical assistance services are critical to supporting enterprise growth and increasing program impact.

Building Strong Relationships With Funders, Other Agencies, and Lenders

MEPs need long-standing relationships with diverse funding sources to provide stable operating funds and collaborations to gain client referrals and expand training, technical assistance, and credit services for their clients.

Funding Challenges

Securing Income From Program Services

Expanding loan interest income and training fees reduces dependence on grants and improves financial sustainability.

Obtaining Core Grants and Developing Diversified Funding Sources

Stable core funding addresses the need for ongoing operating subsidies. Diverse sources hedge the risk of losing funding when priorities change.

client needs when deciding what training or credit services to provide. An important trend among MEPs is expanding services to assist entrepreneurs at different stages and with different needs (Edgecomb et al., 1996). In addition to increasing a program's scale, new services allow practitioners to help clients over time as they move from pre-start-up to established businesses and to nurture enterprises with greater potential to create more jobs and income.

Program operations are especially challenging since MEPs serve many clients, underwrite and administer numerous loans, and address diverse training and technical assistance needs. Although U.S. programs are far smaller than international ones, they still serve 200 or more clients and close at least 20 loans each year while managing portfolios of over 50 loans. Initial efforts at informal and peer-lending approaches to credit have not fared well, and programs have shifted to more formalized processes and staff-based systems to reduce loan losses (Edgecomb et al., 1996). Although more costly than expected, the efficiency of formal lending systems can be improved with experience and increased loan volumes. The recent trend in higher loan volumes and lower per loan costs among MicroTest programs supports this hypothesis. A second lending challenge is adapting credit standards and evaluation tools to the financial and business context of low- and moderate-income early-stage businesses that do not fit conventional criteria for credit history, financial ratios, and collateral (Gershick, 2002). Alternative standards focus on borrower character, business skills and plans, household finances, and bill payment history.

MEPs also need to deliver diverse training and technical assistance services to address a range of client needs. Although these services vary with each program's target entrepreneurs, they often encompass (1) self-esteem, financial literacy, and personal life skills; (2) basic business planning and management concepts; (3) specialized business or industry skills training; (4) one-on-one technical assistance and referrals; and (5) training peer groups for their lending and collection roles. Programs that begin with focused training and technical assistance services often need to increase services to address expanding client needs as entrepreneurs move from pre-start-up to established businesses and as their client base diversifies (Edgecomb et al., 1996). Since training is the modal MEP service and central to program success, considerable effort has been devoted to developing effective training and technical assistance approaches. The following section on best practices summarizes key lessons from this work.

As the discussion of program performance emphasized, the key funding challenge for MEPs is raising operating funds. Programs need ongoing subsidies to address the staff-intensive nature of their work and to compensate for the limited revenue potential from providing small loans and serving low-income clients. Raising operating funds, therefore, is a long-term need because few programs will achieve financial self-sufficiency through increasing their scale. To address this funding challenge, programs need both core grants from stable funding sources and a diversified funding base to hedge against shifting priorities among funding sources. Diversified funding is especially important because governments fund half of the operating costs for the average program, and this funding availability could easily decline or disappear with fiscal problems, changes in political leadership, and new policy priorities. Federal agencies are the largest source of government support, providing an average of 24% of microenterprise program revenue.[17] However, federal funding is particularly at risk with the shift in executive and congressional leadership and the growing emphasis on military and civil defense funding. Beyond diversifying grant sources, MEPs can increase their own-source revenue to reduce required subsidies. Charging market interest rates on loans and making larger loans increases interest earnings. Training and technical assistance fees, especially from moderate-income clients and existing businesses, represents a promising new revenue source, as many programs provide courses and technical assistance at no charge (Edgecomb et al., 1996). Finally, some programs have parlayed their expertise into program income by selling manuals and providing consulting services.

Best Practices in Microenterprise Finance and Development

Although a full discussion of domestic microenterprise practice is too lengthy for this chapter, emerging best practices can be highlighted.[18] Because most efforts to improve and document best practices focus on training and technical assistance, rather than lending, this section emphasizes effective practices in these two areas and program marketing, which is critical to attract potential clients.

Marketing

Because MEPs serve entrepreneurs who are not well connected to mainstream business development organizations and may distrust government and other institutions, special marketing and outreach activities are vital to build trust and identify new clients. Media advertisements, both paid and via free public service announcements, reach many people and build general program awareness but have not proven effective at attracting clients (Edgecomb, 2002a; Klein, 2002).[19] More effective approaches include creating marketing partnerships and referral networks with organizations that work closely with target clients and cultivating existing clients as a referral source (Edgecomb, 2002a; Klein, 2002). MEPs have worked with community organizations, immigrant associations, ESL providers, banks, and welfare offices to market programs and recruit clients. Partners are chosen strategically based on their contact and connections with target clients, commitment to MEP goals, level of client trust, and gatekeeper role in accessing services (i.e., welfare agencies for TANF clients). Effective marketing collaborations require ongoing work to educate and equip the partner organizations to make good referrals. Beyond holding information sessions and providing marketing materials, MEPs have developed videos and manuals to help staff at partner agencies understand program goals and eligibility and to screen candidates (Edgecomb, 2002a). These tools are especially important for programs serving clients with complex eligibility rules, such as welfare recipients. Accion Texas expanded some marketing relationships to include initial client intake and screening, for which the partner entity is paid a fee (Edgecomb, 2002a). A growing marketing approach involves using MEP clients to both gain referrals and build awareness of the program. Client-based marketing includes offering financial incentives to refer clients and creating marketing tie-ins with a client's business, such as placing posters and brochures at their place of business and advertising on product labels (Edgecomb, 2002a). Effective marketing is not a short-term endeavor; it requires a sustained commitment of substantial staff, resources, and agency leadership and periodic assessment of which marketing approaches, partnerships, and channels generate appropriate new clients.

Training

With increased experience and growing evidence on how training impacts business outcomes, the components of effective microenterprise training practice are emerging. These best practices include pretraining assessment of participant attributes and readiness to start a business, a strong focus on completing a business plan and building finance skills, and developing short training modules that can be combined to address the customized needs of different client groups. Research on several training programs shows that clients who complete courses and are more engaged and conscientious in their coursework are more likely to start a business or expand their existing enterprise. Moreover, these studies discovered four training practices that increase course completion rates and yield positive business outcomes: (1) using dynamic instructors; (2) requiring the completion of a business plan for graduation; (3) employing structured assignments that relate to real business circumstances; and (4) creating strong basic financial skills in bookkeeping, cash flow preparation, and breakeven analysis (Edgecomb, 2002b). MEPs that incorporate these elements into their business training courses are more likely to graduate stronger entrepreneurs and generate greater economic results.

MEPs can also apply knowledge on the factors that promote training completion and business success to assess and prepare training candidates. Practitioners have found three indicators of an individual's readiness to start a business and ultimate success: (1) the quality of the business concept; (2) the individual's experience and traits, including prior business ownership experience or exposure (e.g., via family-owned businesses), relevant work experience, clarity of goals, and commitment; and (3) situational and support resources, including personal support network, financial resources and credit, and access to housing, transportation, day care, and other basic services (Klein, 2002). By developing simple assessment tools[20] and working with clients to evaluate their strengths and weaknesses in each area, MEPs can target training to individuals whose traits and situation make business ownership a good and realistic prospect. Assessment results also allow programs to help individuals overcome personal or situational obstacles and position themselves to successfully pursue business ownership in the future. Multiple assessment tools can be used, including written intake forms, staff-client interviews, group sessions, and the first part of a training course, but the assessment process should match the program's philosophy and client needs (Klein, 2002).

MEPs have learned that businesses value short-term specialized training on key business skills and industry-specific issues. Short courses are easier for established business owners, who work long hours, to attend. Moreover, training needs vary with business maturity, industry, and location. While pre-start-up entrepreneurs need basic skills to test their concept, develop a business plan, and set up operations, once in business, they benefit from stronger skills in marketing, financial management, inventory control, and other topics, as do more established business. Thus, specialized training allows MEPs to build the skills of their successful graduates while serving other micro and small business owners (Grossman, 2002). The value and flexibility of short courses has led some MEPs to reorganize their core business skills training into modules that can be taken individually or combined to address varied training needs across heterogeneous client groups (Nelson, 2002).

Technical Assistance Services

Technical assistance has two critical roles in microenterprise development. First, it helps graduates of training courses establish their businesses. Second, it supports the success and growth of both newly established firms and existing microbusinesses. Most new entrepreneurs require several months, sometimes as long as 18 months, to convert their business plan into an operating venture. Posttraining technical assistance helps these aspiring entrepreneurs overcome obstacles to opening their enterprises while reinforcing the value and application of skills introduced during training (Edgecomb, 2002b). Regular contact with the entrepreneur for 1 to 2 years after training is important to offer direct advice, and to provide a coaching and referral role. Because many businesses do not recognize the need for assistance or wait too long to pursue it, regular contact guides the entrepreneur to identify their needs and get appropriate assistance (Edgecomb, 2002b). Thus, effective posttraining technical assistance should include regular contact with the entrepreneur for close to 2 years, a staff that can tailor assistance and advice to the needs and goals of each entrepreneur, information about assistance options, and guidance for clients in choosing appropriate high-quality help (Edgecomb, 2002b).

A second form of technical assistance focuses on expanding market access to grow larger businesses that can compete in the mainstream market and generate more substantial economic impacts. Through a Mott Foundation demonstration program, nine MEPs implemented initiatives to help low-income entrepreneurs gain more sophisticated product design, marketing, production, and distribution capacity to reach larger and more lucrative markets (Grossman, 2002). These initiatives enabled MEPs to provide multiple services[21] related to three technical assistance functions: (1) creating direct sales transactions; (2) creating new venues and channels for sales; and (3) creating capacity within firms. In her analysis of these demonstration projects, Grossman emphasized several best practices in designing and implementing effective programs to greatly expand microbusiness market access (Grossman, 2002).[22] First, a single industry or target market focus allows programs to provide more value-added services, attract clients, and develop greater expertise to move clients down the learning curve more quickly. To realize these targeting advantages, programs must allocate staff and funding to track key customer and industry trends in their target industry or markets because current market and industry information was critical to designing and providing effective services across all functions. Second, clients require extended time and assistance to develop "market-ready" products and expand production capacity necessary to access mainstream markets. Consequently, programs need to address these core capacity issues along with marketing. Third, the recruitment, retention, and continuity of skilled professional staff is a critical ingredient in program success; it provides the basis for building and sustaining relationships with industry players. Fourth, programs can expand their scale and impact by recruiting and serving firms outside their core microbusiness clientele that can benefit from the market access services.

Case Study: Lawrence Working Capital[23]

Background

Lawrence, Massachusetts, an industrial city located 26 miles north of Boston, was established in the 1840s by Boston industrialists as a textile manufacturing center. The city has served as a gateway for immigrants throughout its history, most recently attracting a large wave of Hispanic immigrants from Puerto Rico and the Dominican Republic. Over 60% of the city's residents are of Hispanic origin, according to the 2000 census. Lawrence is also Massachusetts's poorest community; 24% of all households and 31% of Hispanics lived in poverty in 1999. The city's large Hispanic population serves as a source of low-wage labor for traditional manufacturing firms and low-wage businesses, such as janitorial services and temporary employment agencies.

The large influx of Hispanic residents presents two economic development opportunities for Lawrence. First, a strong entrepreneurial culture among Dominican immigrants and the dynamic growth of new small businesses has accompanied the Hispanic population growth. These small businesses provide a base for further economic development and an engine for revitalizing traditional commercial corridors. Second, the concentration of Hispanic residents represents a significant consumer market, estimated at over $570 million, to support local businesses.

In response to civic disturbances and a growing sense of political isolation, Latino businesses and social service agencies formed the Lawrence Minority Business Council (LMBC) in 1989. Two LMBC board members, Leonora Sanchez and Cesar Camargo, worked to bring Working Capital, a microenterprise program based on the peer-group lending model, to Lawrence. After the first lending group was formed in 1992, the Lawrence Working Capital program grew rapidly to encompass 27 peer groups with 170 borrowers in its first 2 years. By 1997, it served 344 enterprises in 53 loan groups and had lent almost $1 million. By 1998, however, the program faced new challenges with a large and more diverse client base, the proliferation of many similar businesses, and new small business development programs within Lawrence. Consequently, Lawrence Working Capital is evaluating how the program can best respond to these challenges and advance the growth and economic impact of the city's Hispanic businesses.

Lawrence Working Capital Program

Working Capital is a Massachusetts-based organization that uses a peer-group lending model to promote self-employment and microbusinesses through local programs in eight states.[24] Working Capital uses local enterprise agents to organize peer groups of individuals who either want to start a business or secure credit for an existing business. Leonora Sanchez, Mildred Rodriguez, and Rosa Orellana are three enterprise agents who fostered the growth of Lawrence Working Capital (LWC) by recruiting home-based entrepreneurs and other business owners within the city's Dominican community. Once a peer group is organized, Working Capital provides training to members on running a business, business finances, and its peer-group lending system. Training is provided through an intensive daylong session prior to forming peer groups and self-paced modules conducted within peer groups. This core training is supplemented by workshops on key business topics (e.g., marketing and technical assistance from enterprise agents). After completing the training, group members can secure loans beginning at $500 and increasing in five steps to $5,000. Loans are granted and collected by the peer group. Group members graduate to larger loans after all members of the group repay earlier loans. By early 1998, LWC had over 340 participants in peer lending groups and had made 793 loans totaling $964,000. Over two thirds of these loans were below $1,000 while 3% were in the $3,000 to $5,000 range.

Most program participants are Dominican women with a home-based business. A 1996 survey found that 70% of the businesses are home-based, 23% rent storefronts, and the balance operate in flea markets or on the street. Most businesses have one employee or less (including the owner) and are concentrated in the retail and service sectors. Common retail businesses include resellers of wholesale clothes, home furnishings, cosmetics, and other products purchased in New York. Service businesses are more diverse and include restaurants, caterers, day care providers, and auto mechanics. Some entrepreneurs are small-scale manufacturers of clothing, furniture, or other wood products. One study categorized Working Capital businesses into three groups: (1) home-based businesses that supplement family income, in which the owner does not seek to create a larger formal business; (2) growth-oriented part-time enterprises in which the owner plans to build a larger established business; and (3) established full-time businesses, often in storefronts and with paid employees. Over half of LWC participants (58%) are poor, with annual household incomes of $15,000 or less.

Working Capital has contributed to the sales and income growth of entrepreneurs but on a small scale. A 1996 study determined that the average participant had a 60% increase in sales and 56% increase in profits since joining Working Capital. However, the average dollar growth in monthly sales and the owner's draw from the average business were small at $109 and $16 per month, respectively. Beyond these financial impacts, entrepreneurs credit Working Capital with increasing their self-confidence, economic opportunities, business skills, and community involvement. LWC's broader community impacts include fostering a positive image of the Hispanic community, increasing community and political involvement, and expanding goods and services for residents. However, the program has had limited impact on job creation and market growth among microbusinesses.

Lawrence Hispanic Business Community

Beyond Working Capital's clientele, Lawrence has over 250 established Hispanic-owned firms primarily located on the two main commercial streets, Broadway and Essex Street. Broadway, in particular, has become a center of Hispanic firms. Common businesses include auto repair services, hair salons, restaurants, grocery stores, and clothing stores. A 1998 survey of 63 Latino businesses found that most are established enterprises with an average age of 15 years that primarily serve Latino customers from within and outside Lawrence. A majority of owners reported stable or declining sales and 79% had three or fewer employees. Despite their historic growth, Hispanic businesses face several obstacles to future expansion and success: (1) language barriers that deter access to non-Spanish-speaking customers and technical assistance services; (2) limited business and financial management skills; (3) entrepreneurial interest concentrated on a few types of business (e.g. grocery stores, travel agencies, hair salons); (4) limited experience, knowledge, and access to capital to form higher-growth and higher-margin businesses; and (5) the informal business status of many entrepreneurs. Lawrence's image as a distressed city also makes it harder to attract new businesses and customers, as does the city's proximity to New Hampshire, which has no sales tax and a large concentration of retail stores.

New Business Development Programs

In recent years, several Lawrence agencies expanded their business development activities. Key business development programs include (1) a new City Small Business Center designed to serve as a "one-stop" assistance center to coordinate services among business assistance agencies and provide technical assistance to start-ups and existing small businesses; (2) the Lawrence Business Assistance Center (LBAC) at the local community college, which provides 7- to 8-week courses in business planning and business management. LBAC is also translating the city's business licensing documents into Spanish to make them accessible to Hispanic businesses; (3) the state's regional Small Business Development Center provides counseling on a scheduled basis at the local community college and offers NxLevel, a 13-week course that helps entrepreneurs prepare a business plan (graduates join an alumni network to provide support and advice after graduation); and (4) the Latino Merchants Association provides its members with networking opportunities, informational and educational workshops, and informal mentoring to business owners. It also advocates for Latino merchants with the city government.

These new services are a valuable resource for the Hispanic business community, but they pose a challenge for Working Capital. It now faces competition for new and existing clients and must design any new programs and services to avoid duplicating their services. On the other hand, these programs could be a valuable source of referrals and complementary services.

Assignment

Your assignment is to draw upon your knowledge of effective microenterprise practice and the current environment in Lawrence to recommend new services, programs, and activities that Lawrence Working Capital should implement to strengthen and expand Lawrence's Hispanic businesses as a source employment for city residents and wealth generation for business owners. These recommendations should build on the program's existing services and successes, address key barriers to further business growth, and consider Working Capital's relationship to other small business development programs in Lawrence.

Endnotes

1. Accion International also directly expanded into the United States, setting up programs in six states (Varma, 2001).

2. Farnan (2001) provides a summary of federal government programs that fund and support microenterprise development.

3. The program model summaries are based on the discussion in Edgecomb et al. (1996), pp. 11 to 15, but also draw on the author's knowledge and work with microenterprise programs in Massachusetts.

4. Edgecomb et al. (1996) studied seven microenterprise agencies that offered nine training programs that range in length from 7 to 17 weeks.

5. Microenterprise programs working with TANF recipients also help clients manage with welfare rules and regulations that impede their personal and business development efforts and advocate for changes in problematic regulations. See Bonavoglia (2001), pp. 14, 17–18 and 30–31.

6. This figure is slightly higher than the 2000 survey data, which shows 64% providing credit services and thus 36% offering only training or technical assistance. This difference many reflect variations in survey responses rather than a shift in industry practices. Black et al. (2002) suggest that the 2000 survey data underreports lending activities.

7. Federally funded RLFs averaged 18 loans per year, and the median number of portfolio loans for RLFs in seven states ranged from 8 to 34. SBICs and venture capital funds averaged six to seven investments per year in the late 1990s.

8. For the subset of 56 funds, the Aspen Institute calculated an operational cost rate, which measures the cost to make and manage each dollar of its loan portfolio. In 1990, the median ratio was .81 and the average was 2.75. This suggests that a majority of funds have annual operating costs for their lending activities that are close to or exceed their total loan portfolios and that a subset of these funds is spending far more than two dollars to originate and manage every dollar lent.

9. Under the MicroTest program, reported data is checked for accuracy and revised when needed to ensure accuracy and comparability. Programs also use common performance measures and definitions to report data on a comparable basis.

10. Averages for MicroTest programs were 273 clients, 76 annual loans that totaled $395,038, annual operating costs of $568,165, and clients that were 64% low-income, 63% women, and 51% minority. Forty-five percent of the MicroTest sample served urban areas compared to 42% for the entire field. Rural regions were 25% of the areas served by MicroTest programs and 26% for the entire field. Respective shares for dual areas were 30% and 32%, respectively.

11. Rural programs had FY2000 median loan loss rates of 7% and total portfolio risk of 27% compared to 2% and 8% for urban programs.

12. For credit-led programs, 13% of clients had household incomes equal to or below the HHS low-income level, whereas the share for training-led programs was 29%. At the next highest level (150% of the HHS low-income level), the median percentages were 24% and 49%, respectively.

13. The average total cost recovery rate increased from 12% to 14% and the average short-term financial self-sufficiency rate grew from 17% to 21%.

14. Some estimates are based on econometric analysis and others use a case study approach. Some count only the program's cost whereas others count both program investments and leveraged funds. Furthermore, the microenterprise program figures are based on operating costs and do not count loan capital whereas RLF studies typically measure the cost per loan dollar. In terms of job type, Servon and Doshna do not consider differences between creating a new retail job, which is supported by local spending and thus may displace another retail job, and jobs in an export-oriented business that adds net employment to an area. Finally, the figures do consider differences in wage levels and benefits among jobs created by the different economic development approaches.

15. Indirect effects reflect jobs created at supplier firms while induced effects count additional jobs from the recycling of income from direct and indirect jobs within the state economy. This analysis, however, does not consider jobs displaced at other businesses from new firms created with NEF assistance.

16. The Aspen Institute's Field Program is a valuable resource in advancing microenterprise practice through funding new approaches and disseminating lessons learned from these experiences. Many publications from their work are available at www.fieldus.org.

17. Based on the MicroTest sample. See Black et al. (2002), Appendix b.

18. More extensive information and publications on microenterprise practice are available at www.fieldus.org, the Aspen Institute's Web site for its Microenterprise Fund for Innovation, Effectiveness, Learning, and Dissemination (FIELD).

19. However, news coverage appears to help build program awareness and legitimacy because people trust news coverage more than advertisements. See Edgecomb (2002a).

20. Klein (2002) includes an assessment tool and training application form developed by the Women's Initiative for Self-Employment.

21. Grossman (2002) categorized these services into eight different roles: advocate, trainer, resource provider, product developer, market channel developer, consumer educator, sales representative, and social business operator.

22. This discussion covers five of the eight best practices reported by Grossman (2002). The omitted practices help entrepreneurs to overcome business and personal supply side barriers, help clients minimize risks from entering highly competitive mainstream markets by either planning for risks or directly bearing some or all of them, and expect and learn from failures.

23. The case study relies on studies of the Lawrence Working Capital program by Lisa Servon (1998) and Cathy Mahon (1995) and work by the author's economic development planning classes.

24. Working Capital later merged with Accion USA.

PART V

Federal and Municipal Government Finance Tools

14

Federal Economic Development Programs

ederal government programs remain an important resource for development finance practitioners despite two decades of declining federal domestic spending. This chapter provides an overview of the major federal economic programs and their application to development finance. Program information within the chapter is organized by federal agency to simplify its presentation and because programs are often linked to agency funding systems. The Economic Development Administration's (EDA) funding, for example, is linked to its process for regional comprehensive economic development strategies (CEDS). However, practitioners should view federal programs based on their capacity to serve local development finance needs and transcend agency silos. To address this concern, the chapter first provides a framework for how practitioners can apply federal programs to fill local capital market gaps and strengthen development finance institutions. Next, the programs of five federal agencies are summarized. Three agencies with the largest and most widely used programs, the Small Business Administration (SBA), Housing and Urban Development (HUD), and the U.S. Treasury Community Development Finance Institution (CDFI) Fund, are discussed first, followed by the EDA and Health and Human Service (HHS). The chapter concludes with a case study on using federal programs to fill the funding gap for a specific development project. One caution for readers is that funding levels and rules can change with each federal budget. While a program's goals and tools remain unchanged, the available funds, some rules, and new initiatives may vary from year to year. The reader should consult current program Web sites, documents, and staff for the most up-to-date information.

The Uses of Federal Economic Development Programs

Practitioners can deploy federal economic development programs in four ways to address their local development finance needs. Some programs, most notably SBA programs, provide an ongoing tool to expand capital availability to small businesses. By incorporating these SBA programs in their portfolio, development finance institutions expand their capacity to address business finance needs and can generate revenue to support program staff and overhead. Thus, many development finance entities help package SBA 7(a) guarantees to expand bank use of this key program and become SBA-certified development corporations to provide firms access to fixed asset financing through the SBA 504 program. A second use of federal programs is to capitalize development finance entities. Grants and loans through EDA, Community Development Block Grant (CDBG), and the CDFI Fund programs are a major source of loan and investment capital for state and local government revolving loan funds and community-based financial institutions. Moreover, local practitioners can use the $15 billion New Market Tax Credit program to attract private investors to establish new finance programs or expand existing ones that serve low-income areas. Third, federal programs fill funding gaps for specific firms or development projects through supplying direct grants and below-market rate and high-risk debt. EDA, HUD, and HHS programs serve this role, especially for real estate development projects. Finally, some programs can support an institution's operations by funding either specific operating costs (e.g., technical assistance services) or one-time projects that enhance program performance. Table 14.1 illustrates the use of different federal programs for each of these purposes.

Table 14.1   Four Uses of Federal Economic Development Programs

Development Finance Use	Applicable Federal Program	Examples
Ongoing tool to expand capital availability	SBA 7(a) Program SBA 504 Program	SEED Corporation organized a multilender enterprise fund for 7(a)-guaranteed loans.
Capitalize development finance entities	SBA SBIC/SSBIC Programs SBA Microloan Program EDA Economic Adjustment Grants CDFI Fund Core/Intermediary Program New Market Tax Credits HUD CDBG Program	Many entities use EDA and CDBG grants to establish RLFs. CDFIs use CDFI Fund Core Program to expand their capital.
Finance specific projects	HUD CDBG Program HUD 108 Loans and EDI Grants EDA Public Works and Economic Adjustment Grants HHS Community Economic Development Program	Use of HUD 108 loan to finance firms and real estate projects. Use of EDA public works grants for industrial park development.
Support operations	SBA 504 Program SBA Microloan Program CDFI Fund Small and Emerging CDFI Assistance Program	SBA 504 fees fund staff and overhead costs. SBA Microloan Program grants help fund technical assistance services.

_____ **Small Business Administration**

Since the SBA has many programs,[1] most of which are targeted for very specific situations (e.g., disaster relief or defense adjustment), this section summarizes the largest and most relevant programs for economic development professionals. A more detailed discussion of key programs was provided in prior chapters, including Chapter 5 for the 504 program, Chapter 8 for the 7(a) program, and Chapter 11 for the SBIC and SSBIC programs.

SBA programs use three delivery mechanisms to reach small businesses, which provide a useful way to categorize present programs. The three service delivery mechanisms are (1) programs delivered through banks or other financial institutions (e.g., the 7(a) loan guarantee program and surety guaranty programs); (2) programs delivered to businesses directly by the SBA (e.g., disaster assistance and the Service Corps of Retired Executives (SCORE) technical assistance program); and (3) programs delivered through a SBA-licensed entity (e.g., the 504 and Small Business Investment Company programs).

Programs in the first two categories provide resources to address ongoing business credit and technical assistance needs. Development finance practitioners should become familiar with them, establish good referral relationships, and work to maximize their role in serving local small businesses. The last category, on the other hand, supplies organizations with capital and tools to expand their capacity to offer direct business financing.

Programs Delivered by Banks and Financial Institutions

Loan guarantee programs are the SBA's primary means to expand credit for small businesses. The 7(a) program is the SBA's largest guarantee program and provides the authority under which the SBA has fashioned guarantees targeted to different purposes and loan sizes. A second program guarantees obligations under surety bonds made by insurance and surety companies to ensure the performance of small contractors.

SBA 7(a) Loan Guarantee Program. This program guarantees loans of up to $2 million made by private banks or finance companies to small businesses for working capital and fixed asset acquisition. Guarantees cover up to 85% of the loan principal for loans of $150,000 or less and 75% for loans above $150,000, up to a maximum guarantee of $1 million. Although the terms for loans made with 7(a) guarantees are negotiated between the borrower and lender, they are subject to SBA limits on interest rates and maturity periods. The maximum interest rate varies from prime plus 2.25% to prime plus 4.75%, based on loan size and maturity.[2] Maturities up to 10 years for working capital loans and 25 years for fixed assets loans are allowed.

Through the 7(a) program, the SBA has introduced several variations in its vanilla guarantee product to improve its use and accessibility. Through preferred and certified lender programs, the SBA seeks to streamline the approval process by delegating authority to lenders with extensive 7(a) program experience. Certified lenders receive a partial delegation of authority and a 3-day SBA turnaround on 7(a) applications. Preferred lenders are the SBA's best lenders and have full authority to issue guarantees on behalf of the SBA in exchange for a lower guarantee percentage. The SBA regularly examines preferred lenders guaranteed loan portfolios and periodically reviews them for renewal of their lending authority. Two other programs simplify the guarantee process for small loans. Under the LowDoc program, lenders submit a shortened two-page application and the bank's underwriting analysis for SBA review and approval on loans of $100,000 or less. A new SBAExpress program allows approved lenders to largely use their own documents and procedures to gain loan guarantee approvals for loans of $250,000 or less. It also provides rapid guarantee approval from a centralized SBA office for loans with a 50% guarantee rate. Collateral requirements are also simplified for smaller loans with lenders able to waive collateral for loans up to $25,000 and apply their own policies, rather than those of SBA, for loans up to $150,000. Other examples include CAPLines guarantees for short-term and cyclical working capital loans and the Export Working Capital Program that provides more flexible guarantee terms to encourage lenders to extend credit for export transactions.[3]

In federal FY2001, the SBA approved almost 43,000 guarantees for loans with a total value of $9.89 billion. Small loans of $150,000 or less represented 63% of total guaranteed loans, with the LowDoC program generating almost one third of them. The certified and preferred lender programs were also important, generating one third of all guarantees and 59% of their total value. Export and international trade programs, on the other hand, were quite small, supplying just 2% of all guarantees and 3% of the total value of guaranteed loans.[4]

Surety Bond Guarantee Program. Under this program, the SBA guarantees the bond that surety companies provide to small construction and service firms to ensure their performance on public sector construction projects. A surety bond is a contract under which a surety company takes over the obligations of a contractor when it fails to perform. Since surety bonds are required on most government contracts, this program expands access to public sector contracts for small and disadvantaged contractors. The SBA guarantees bonds of up to $2 million in value and covers 90% of the losses on bonds up to $100,000 (and for bonds to socially and economically disadvantaged contractors) and 80% of the losses for all other bonds. As with the 7(a) program, a Preferred Surety Bond (PSB) program allows participating surety companies to issue guarantees without SBA approval in exchange for lower (70%) loss guarantee coverage. Surety guarantee authority was $1.7 billion in FY2002.

Programs Delivered Through SBA-Approved Intermediaries

For several programs, the SBA relies on special purpose intermediaries, rather than conventional banks and finance companies, to deliver financing to small businesses. The SBA first approves or licenses the intermediary and then relies exclusively on the intermediary to originate loans and may provide capital to the intermediary to re-lend or invest. SBA programs that use this delivery system include the 504 program, the Microloan Program and the SBIC program. Depending on the specific program, a development finance institution can access capital at below-market interest rates, secure subsidies to provide technical assistance, and earn origination and services fees by becoming a SBA-approved intermediary.

SBA 504 Program. Under this program, the SBA uses approved Certified Development Corporations (CDCs) to provide long-term fixed-rate financing for fixed asset investments by small companies. The 504 program relies on a three-part financing structure that includes a senior mortgage by a private bank for 50% of the total project, a SBA subordinated debenture for 40% of the project investment, and a 10% equity contribution from the small business. The maximum SBA debenture amount is $1 million, but it can be raised to $1.3 million for projects that achieve certain public purpose goals, such as business district revitalization, export expansion, rural development, and minority, veteran, or women business ownership. Loan maturities can be up to 10 years for equipment and up to 20 years for fixed assets. The SBA prefers projects that create at least one job for every $35,000 in SBA 504 financing. In FY2002, the SBA had budget authority to issue $4.5 billion in 504 subordinate loans.

Certified Development Corporations (CDCs) originate 504 loans and then submit them for approval to the SBA district office. Once approved and funded, the CDC is responsible for loan servicing on the SBA debenture. As compensation for these services, CDCs receive an origination fee of up to 1.5% of the SBA debenture amount and monthly servicing fees that can range from .5% to 2% of the outstanding loan principle. A CDC is a nonprofit corporation that has a minimum of 25 members from the local small business and lending community. It can operate on a statewide, regional, citywide, or subcity basis and can be either a stand-alone organization or a subsidiary of another organization. The SBA has approved close to 270 CDCs under the 504 program.

SBA Microloan Program. Originally authorized in the FY1992 Appropriations Act, this program provides loans to nonprofit corporations to operate microenterprise loan funds and grants to provide technical assistance to microbusinesses. Each local fund establishes its own lending policies and terms but must comply with the SBA loan size limit of $35,000 and maximum loan maturity of 6 years. Loans under this program average about $10,500. Through FY2001, the SBA had approved 170 microenterprise lenders.

Department of Housing and Urban Development

HUD primarily administers housing programs, but it also funds economic development projects and financial institutions, largely through the Community Development Block Grant Program (CDBG), which provides grants to local governments for community development activities. However, HUD has created related programs, especially the Section 108 program and the Economic Development Initiative Program, through which it directly finances local economic development projects. After a short overview of the CDBG program and its potential economic development uses, the mechanics of the HUD 108 and EDI programs are explained.

Community Development Block Grants

This is the federal government's largest community development program with annual appropriations of almost $5 billion in FY2002. Authorized in the Housing and Community Development Act of 1974, which combined multiple categorical grant programs into one block grant, the CDBG program has three components: (1) entitlement grants; (2) small cities grants; and (3) Section 108 financing. *Entitlement grants* are distributed by formula to every city that either has a population of at least 50,000 or is a county seat. Cities determine the use of CDBG funds as long as funded activities meet at least one of the program's three national objectives: (1) benefiting low- or moderate-income families; (2) aiding in the prevention or elimination of blight; and (3) meeting a critical community need. Entitlement cities must submit an annual plan to HUD detailing how the CDBG grant (and other HUD program funds) will be used to address community needs and national objectives. Although cities have flexibility in how they program CDBG monies, many regulations govern how funds are expended and the achievement of national objectives is documented. *Small cities grants* provide CDBG funds to nonentitlement communities to undertake community development activities consistent with national program objectives. In all states except Hawaii, the small cities program is administered by a state government agency under a plan approved by HUD. Local communities apply for grants directly to the state agency and do not deal with HUD, which delegates program administration and oversight to the state government. Some states also set aside part of their small cities CDBG funds for categorical programs. For example, Massachusetts created the Massachusetts Community Capital Fund with small cities CDBG monies, allowing it to provide direct loans and grants to economic development projects in non-CDBG entitlement communities.

Economic Development Uses of CDBG Funds. Given their flexibility, communities have used CDBG grants for diverse economic development activities. CDBG funds are often used to provide capital for a revolving loan fund, microenterprise loan fund, or finance entity. Through a direct grant of capital, CDBG funds are a good source of core "equity" that helps an entity establish a sound financial foundation and leverage other funding. CDBG grants are also used to fund small business technical assistance and training programs provided by city agency staff, contracts with third-party vendors, such as community development corporations, or grants for firms to hire consultants. A third common use of CDBG funds is funding economic development projects. Since CDBG dollars have no cost of funds, they are a good funding source for grants to write down development costs and/or high-risk debt, in which repayment is deferred to help ensure a project's feasibility. CDBG grants also can fund staff costs for economic development finance institutions. This type of subsidy may be needed for smaller finance programs or ones that provide extensive technical assistance, loan packaging, or other staff-intensive services. Finally, CDBG funding can underwrite up front costs, such as market research and feasibility studies, to create new development finance entities, design new programs, or plan development projects.

Issues in the Economic Development Use of CDBG Funds. CDBG rules raise several complications in using these funds for economic development or business assistance activities.[5] Although a detailed discussion of these issues is beyond the purpose of this chapter, practitioners should be aware of these issues to evaluate whether CDBG funds are a viable financing source. First, projects or programs receiving CDBG funds must show that they achieve a national objective. For most economic development activities, this requires demonstrating that they generate jobs that benefit low- or moderate-income persons by documenting that either the majority of employees at an assisted firm are low- or moderate-income or that the jobs at the assisted firm are available to job-seekers in an area with a population that is at least 51% low- and moderate-income. Second, HUD has a public benefit requirement of no more than $35,000 of CDBG funds per job created or retained by the business. Third, HUD applies an "appropriate assistance" standard, which requires that CDBG funds provided to a business are necessary and appropriate for the project and do not unduly enrich the private firm. Although HUD has established rules for this standard, they are subject to different interpretations and judgments given the nature of the issue, and evaluating this standard can entail extensive underwriting by HUD. Finally, HUD requires that a direct threat of job loss to low- or moderate-income workers exist for CDBG funds to be used to finance an enterprise to retain employment. Activities or financing that helps businesses proactively invest to avoid future sales and employment decline, such as improving their competitiveness or diversifying their products, do not fit within current HUD standards.

Section 108 Program[6]

Under this third element of the CDBG program, HUD allows communities to use their CDBG allocation as a guarantee to backup federal financing for community and economic development projects, including commercial and industrial real estate projects and business financing.[7] To fund the Section 108 financing, HUD sells notes to investors that are backed with a HUD guarantee. The sale proceeds are passed on to the city, which uses them to finance the approved economic development project. Cash flow from the Section 108-funded project is used to repay the notes. However, if the project defaults and is unable to repay the notes, then HUD draws upon the city's annual CDBG allocation to make these payments. In effect, the city pledges part of its future CDBG funds as a guarantee to borrow funds needed to finance a current project. Since Section 108 notes carry a federal agency guarantee, they bear an interest rate close to the federal borrowing rate. This allows cities to lend at a below-market interest rate, if warranted, by passing on the note rate to the borrower. However, cities also can add a spread onto this rate and charge the project or business a higher interest rate. It can also charge a lower rate, in which case the city's CDBG allocation must cover the cash flow gap between the interest rate paid by the borrower and the rate paid to investors. In this case, the city subsidizes the project with future CDBG funds. Repayment periods for Section 108 loans can be up to 20 years, but HUD is required to seek additional collateral beyond CDBG funds for loans with terms of 10 years or longer. Additional collateral can be a mortgage on the project's real estate, a lien on business assets, a pledge of city CDBG program income, or other assets. A community can draw up to five times its annual CDBG funding through the Section 108 program. Thus, a city with a $10 million annual entitlement has access to $50 million in capital to finance economic development projects through the Section 108 tool.

A strong appeal of the Section 108 program is its ability to expand a city's economic development funds. When used to finance projects or programs that fully repay their loans, a city can finance additional projects but still retain its full CDBG allocation. Thus, the Section 108 program is a good tool to finance projects or businesses with strong repayment prospects so that future losses in CDBG funds are avoided. There is also flexibility in how the Section 108 program is used. It can fund direct loans to projects or firms, provide loan guarantees or credit enhancement to secure private financing, and capitalize new or existing lending programs. Boxes 14.1 and 14.2 summarize two examples of Section 108 financing.

Economic Development Initiative

To encourage greater use of the Section 108 program and reduce the financial risk to participating communities, HUD established the Economic Development Initiative (EDI) program in 1994. Under EDI, HUD receives separate appropriations to subsidize projects that use Section 108 loans.

Box 14.1   Grove Hall Mall Section 108 Project Summary

Project Description: Development of a new 50,000 square foot shopping center on a 5-acre site in Boston's Roxbury neighborhood within a HUD-designated Enhanced Enterprise Community.

Impacts: Redevelop blighted and vacant site in center of commercial district, create over 100 new full-time jobs for local residents and bring needed stores and services to community.

Total Development Costs: $10.5 million.

Section 108 Financing: $3.2 million second mortgage loan with a 15-year term and principal payments deferred for 2 years.

EDI Funds: $3.6 million direct grant. City has a claim on 50% of excess cash flow and/or property sale proceeds up to $1.5 million for 30 years.

Other Financing Sources: $3.7 million first mortgage bank loan.

Box 14.2   Worcester Biotechnology Park Section 108 Project Summary

Project Description: Development of a new 93,000 square foot multitenant research and development building for biotechnology firms in Worcester's Biotechnology Research Park.

Impacts: Providing space to attract 12 companies that create 135 new full- and part-time jobs.

Total Development Costs: $14.1 million.

Section 108 Financing: $11.7 million loan guarantee to AFL-CIO Building Trust. Guarantee declined to 20% of the loan over 60 months. Loan was repaid and guarantee ceased with the building's sale after 5½ years.

HUD awards EDI grants to communities through a competitive process. EDI grants can be used in several ways to help finance a project: providing a direct project grant; subsidizing the borrower's interest rate on the Section 108 loan; and serving as a debt service reserve or guarantee for the Section 108 loan. This last use reduces the community's risk of having to draw upon its CDBG funds to repay the Section 108 notes if the funded project incurs financing problems. However, EDI appropriations and availability have varied greatly from year to year. After reaching a high point of $225 million in FY1999, no new EDI appropriations were made in FY2002, and HUD was limited to funding new projects with $3 million in carryover funds. Since FY1999, HUD has also offered EDI grants under a Brownfields Economic Development Initiative (BEDI), which is targeted to projects that redevelop environmentally contaminated sites. The program operates similarly to the regular EDI program but is targeted to projects on Brownfield sites.

However, this is a small program with annual appropriations of $25 million in FY2002.

Community Development Financial Institution (CDFI) Fund

Congress established the CDFI Fund in 1994 to fund community-based financial institutions with a community development mission and to provide incentives for expanded community development lending by conventional banks. Since its creation, the CDFI Fund has emerged as the most important federal program for development finance entities by both certifying entities as Community Development Finance Institutions (CDFIs) and providing capital and technical assistance to support CDFI lending and investment programs.

CDFI Certification

Through certification, the CDFI Fund determines that a financial institution meets the statutory requirements to qualify for financial assistance. This certification allows a CDFI to access CDFI Fund programs, qualifies an organization as a Community Development Entity for New Market Tax Credits and also helps a CDFI secure bank and foundation funding that is targeted to CDFIs. A separate application, with supporting documentation to demonstrate compliance with the six certification criteria, is submitted to the CDFI Fund to secure certification. These criteria, summarized in Table 14.2, focus on ensuring that the applicant advances a community development mission through providing financial and development services to a distressed target area, low-income population, or other populations that face barriers to capital. Governmental entities are not eligible for certification; only community-based organizations with measures that provide accountability to the target market can be certified. As of February 15, 2002, the CDFI Fund certified 553 entities, of which over 200 were devoted to small business finance.[8] Once certified, a development finance entity can apply for financial and technical assistance under three programs: the Core/Intermediary Program, the Native American CDFI Technical Assistance Program, and the New Market Tax Credit Program. A fourth program, the Small and Emerging CDFI Assistance Program, offers capacity-building assistance to either existing early-state CDFIs or organizations seeking to become CDFIs.

Core/Intermediary Program

This is the CDFI Fund's primary program, which provides technical assistance grants and capital funds to CDFIs themselves (Core Program) and to

Table 14.2   CDFI Certification Criteria[a]

Criteria	Standard	Required Documentation or Evidence
Primary Mission	The entity's mission entails promoting community development.	Bylaws, Articles of Incorporation, Mission Statement.
Financing Entity	The entity's primary activities are providing financial products and services. At least 50% of staff and assets are devoted to financing activities.	Financial Statements, CDFI Fund Asset Information Table, CDFI Fund Staff Allocation Table.
Target Market	At least 60% of activities focus on serving either an "investment area," "low-income target population," or "other target population" fitting CDFI Fund definitions.	Description of target market and its unmet needs. CDFI Fund Activity Table with share of activities directed at target market.
Development Services	Provide development services along with financial services.	CDFI Fund Development Services Table.
Accountability	Demonstrate accountability to target market through board representation or alternative means.	CDFI Fund Accountability Chart or description of alternative mechanism(s).
Nongovernmental Entity	Applicant cannot be a government entity or be controlled by one.	Narrative description to demonstrate absence of government control.

NOTE:

a. This summary of certifications is based on the CDFI Application for Certification (August 2000) and an analysis of certification potential for the Franklin County Community Development Corporation prepared by Robert Buchanan, Paul Carney, and Lauren Sager Weinstein.

intermediary organizations that assist CDFIs (Intermediary Program). Capital funding can take several forms, including equity investment, deposits, grants, loans, credit union shares, or a combination of tools. CDFIs specify the amount and form of assistance that they are seeking in their application. Annual awards under the Core and Intermediary Program are typically up to $2 million; the fund cannot award more than $5 million to any one entity over a 3-year period. To receive funding, the applicant must submit a detailed 5-year business plan and secure matching investments from nonfederal sources on at least a dollar-for-dollar basis. The matching investment must be in a comparable form and value to the CDFI Fund investment. Thus, a grant from the CDFI Fund cannot be matched by a loan from another source. Assistance is awarded in annual competitive funding rounds based on the applicant's track record, financial soundness, management capacity, and impact in providing financial products and services to an underserved target market. Both certified CDFIs and those seeking certification can apply for assistance. Under the Clinton administration, the CDFI Fund Core and Intermediary Program was a major source of new capital for non-governmental development finance institutions. From FY1999 to FY2002, 194 awards totaling $190 million were made, largely for financial assistance. This assistance was primarily made through capital grants (69%) and equity investments (11%), which provide CDFIs the greatest financial flexibility to address capital access needs and leverage other funding. CDFIs serving small businesses represent a large share of these awardees (42%), and community development loan funds were the most common type of development finance entity funded, accounting for 73% of award recipients.

Small and Emerging CDFI Assistance (SECA) Program

This program provides technical assistance grants and financial assistance to organizations seeking to establish a new CDFI or smaller existing entities that seek to expand their capacity. To be eligible for SECA, an organization must meet CDFI Fund certification requirements, not have received prior CDFI Fund financial assistance, and must either have less than $5 million in assets (for nondepository institutions) or have been chartered within 3 years of the Notice of Funding Availability. Organizations that are not yet certified CDFIs can apply and receive funding, but they must then receive certification within a specified time period and cannot receive financial assistance until certification is secured. The maximum technical assistance grant and financial assistance award amounts are $50,000 and $200,000, respectively. As with the core program, financial assistance can take many forms, and all awards must be matched with at least an equal amount of nonfederal funds. In FY2002, the CDFI Fund awarded $6.9 million to 61 entities through this program.

Native American CDFI Technical Assistance Program

This program, newly established in FY2002, set aside funds to provide technical assistance grants to establish new entities and expand the capacity of existing ones that serve Native American or Native Alaskan populations. Three types of organizations are eligible for assistance: (1) a CDFI or an organization seeking to establish a CDFI that primarily serves Native American or Native Alaskan populations; (2) a tribe, tribal entity, or nonprofit organization that primarily serves a Native American or Native Alaskan community; and (3) technical assistance providers or other assistance providers that specialize in economic development or banking and lending in Native American or Alaskan Native communities. Grants for up to $100,000 can be used for consulting services, to acquire improved technology, to undertake board and staff training, and for nonrecurring staff expenses related to special projects or consulting work. Thirty-six entities received $2.5 million in grants under this program in FY2002.

New Market Tax Credit Program

The CDFI Fund also administers the allocation of $15 billion in New Market Tax Credits, authorized by Congress in 2000 to stimulate private investment in economically distressed areas. Under the law, private investors receive tax credits in return for making equity investments in Community Development Entities (CDEs) that invest in qualified businesses located in distressed urban, rural, and Native American communities. A for-profit entity must first be certified as a CDE, and then it may apply for an allocation of New Market Tax Credits from the CDFI Fund. The allocated tax credits are then provided to investors in return for an equity investment in the CDE. Investors receive their tax credits over 7 years; a credit for 5% of their investment is allowed in each of the first 3 years followed by an annual 6% credit for the next 4 years. Since the tax credits total 39% of the investment, private investors will expect to earn additional returns from the CDE. With tax credits providing an enhancement to attract capital rather than a substitute source of investment income, CDEs will need investment strategies that can generate a real return to their investors, albeit at a below market rate.[9] Both certified CDFIs and SSBICs automatically qualify as CDEs and can register electronically with the CDFI Fund for CDE designation. Other entities must complete a more thorough certification application to demonstrate that their primary mission is to serve or invest in low-income communities and that their board is accountable to low-income residents. As of June 30, 2002, 340 organizations were certified as CDEs. The first round of $2.5 billion in New Market Tax Credits was awarded to 66 entities in March 2003. The median allocation was $18 million, with awards ranging from $500,000 to $170 million. Seven CDEs received over $100 million in tax credits and together accounted for over $1 billion, or 40%, of the total awards.

Economic Development Administration

The Economic Development Administration (EDA) is a federal agency within the Department of Commerce charged with alleviating economic distress in communities, cities, and regions. EDA funds economic development planning and implementation by state and local governments, planning commissions and economic development districts, and nonprofit development organizations. Since EDA's mission is to assist high-distress areas, it targets its assistance to communities and regions with high unemployment or other indicators of economic distress. EDA funds economic development activities primarily through four programs:[10] (1) planning grants; (2) technical assistance grants; (3) public works grants; and (4) economic adjustment

Table 14.3   FY2002 Appropriations for EDA Programs

EDA Program	FY2002 Funding Level
Public Works Grants	$268 million
Planning Grants	$24 million
Technical Assistance and University Center Grants[a]	$9 million
Economic Adjustment Grants	$41 million
Total EDA Appropriation	$353 million

NOTE:

a. Close to 71% of this appropriation funds university centers.

assistance grants. A brief summary of eligible activities and funding requirements under each program follows.[11] Table 14.3 summarizes FY2002 appropriations for each program.

Planning Grants

This program assists Economic Development Districts, Indian tribes, state governments, and other economic development planning organizations to prepare and implement a comprehensive economic development strategy (CEDS).

EDA's primary goal under this program is enhancing local economic development capacity by supporting the formulation of sound strategies and policies and building local institutional capabilities. Eligible activities include preparing a strategy, implementing elements of a strategy, and providing technical assistance to communities or local governments located within the grantee's jurisdiction. Planning grants can also be used for program development planning. Priority is given to funding activities of current EDA grantees. Grants can cover up to 75% of the activity's cost with a minimum 25% local match. In FY2001, the average planning grant to Economic Development Districts, Indian tribes, and state governments was $56,500, $46,000, and $68,800, respectively.

Local Technical Assistance Grants

Through this program, EDA funds activities that fill information gaps to help practitioners make sound decisions on economic development projects and programs. Grants often fund feasibility studies or other detailed technical planning for real estate-based projects such as industrial parks or business incubators. However, studies also support research and planning to establish a new program, pursue an innovative economic development idea, or expand local capacity (e.g., creating a geographic information system). Grants fund up to 75% of the costs for the technical assistance study or activity. The average grant amount in FY2001 was $31,000.

Public Works and Economic Development Program

EDA's largest program (76% of its FY2002 appropriation) funds projects that expand and upgrade physical infrastructure to help attract and grow long-term private sector investment and jobs in distressed areas. An infrastructure project is defined broadly to include both standard facilities (e.g., water and sewer systems, access roads, port improvements), and buildings owned by public or nonprofit economic development entities that are linked to economic development strategies (e.g., skills training centers, small business incubators, and leased commercial or industrial real estate). Grants cover up to 50% of total project costs. In FY2001, the average grant was $1,007,000.

Economic Adjustment Assistance Program

Grants from the Economic Adjustment Program assist areas facing serious structural changes to their economy by supporting the design and implementation of strategies and activities to achieve economic diversification or other changes necessary to adjust to the structural impacts. Eligible activities are very diverse, reflecting the range of potential local responses, and can include industry research and analysis, infrastructure projects, organizational development, business development, and business financing. This program is often used to create or expand revolving loan funds that finance local business expansion to compensate for job losses in other industries. Periodically this program distributes special EDA appropriations to help communities recover from specific industry decline, federal policies, or natural disasters.[12] Grants fund up to 75% of project costs; the average economic adjustment grant was $281,000 in FY2001.

EDA funding priorities are also influenced by other federal policies and initiatives. Following numerous military base closures and defense procurement cutbacks in the early 1990s, EDA became the primary federal funding agency for implementing base reuse plans and defense contractor adjustment activities. Consequently, a large portion of EDA appropriations during the mid- to late-1990s was dedicated to defense conversion projects, which reduced available grants to distressed regions without large defense adjustment impacts.

Funding Process

Grants are awarded through a three-step process. Because grant applications originate through a state economic development representative (EDR), the first step is to contact the EDR to gain his or her support for the project. The EDR considers whether the applicant's community or region meets eligibility criteria for economic distress and if the specific project or program to be funded is a priority under the local comprehensive economic development strategy (CEDS). After the EDR determines that the community is eligible and the project is consistent with local priorities, a preapplication is submitted to a regional office and reviewed for compliance with EDA general funding criteria (detailed in 13 CR 304.1) and funding priorities (detailed in EDA's annual Notice of Funding Availability). Once the regional office decides that the application fits EDA criteria and is competitive with other applications, the sponsor is invited to submit a final application with supporting documentation. The EDA grant award follows its approval of the final application.

Health and Human Services

This agency operates a program that provides grants to nonprofit community development corporations for economic development projects that generate jobs or business opportunities that advance the economic self-sufficiency of low-income persons. Although the Office of Community Services (OCS) Community Economic Development Program is quite small (FY2002 appropriation of $27 million) and there is substantial competition for awards, it is the only federal program specifically targeted to support CDC-based economic development projects in low-income communities. Grants can be used to finance physical or commercial development projects, provide debt or equity financing for a business start-up or expansion, or support the development of new service industries. However, grants cannot be used to establish an SBIC or SSBIC or for projects that focus on education and job training, although a grantee can use funds for training that is directly linked to jobs for low-income persons created by a grant-funded business or development project. The maximum grant amount is $700,000 and the ratio of grant funds to jobs created must be $15,000 or less. OCS awards grants through an annual funding competition.

Case Study: Financing an Inner-City Supermarket

Charles Quintera, community development director for the city of Nolton, has contacted you to help with the financing of a difficult project. Nolton Community Corporation (NCC) is developing a supermarket in a vacant building in the city's Northside neighborhood. Although the project is worthwhile, its feasibility depends on filling a large financing gap. Your assignment is to devise a financing plan for the project. This plan needs to delineate the required amount of debt, private investment, and grants for the project to be feasible and to identify the specific sources for each part of the financing plan. He is particularly concerned about the amount and type of financing that the city of Nolton may need to provide to make the project feasible. As the CD director, Charles wants to have a realistic plan to propose to the mayor when NCC approaches the city for help. Since it is an election year, he knows the mayor will be responsive, but the city already faces budget cuts due to level tax collections and declining state aid. Although the city has Community Development Block

Grant (CDBG) funds to fund the project, the demand for these dollars far exceeds available funding. He wants a plan that maximizes other resources, in a realistic manner, to reduce the city's financial contribution.

Northside

Northside is a low-income neighborhood that faces the multiple problems of crime, disinvestment, housing abandonment, and limited jobs that confront many inner-city communities. With a growing population (the core neighborhood population grew by 17% to 2,997 persons from 1980 to 1990) and a rapidly increasing minority population (the share of minority residents grew from 15% to 43% from 1980 to 1990), the neighborhood is undergoing considerable change. These changes have been accompanied by housing abandonment and loss from arson, foreclosure, and crime. Approximately 50 buildings are vacant, representing over 10% of the neighborhood's housing units. Disinvestment also encompasses commercial properties, with a supermarket and a discount store closed in recent years. Drug trafficking has hurt the neighborhood by increasing gang activity and related crimes.

Local Response

To address these problems, local residents, the city housing authority, and city officials established the "Reclaim Our Community" (ROC) demonstration program. ROC organized residents to address neighborhood safety and physical deterioration while expanding youth services. It established a neighborhood crime watch, secured improved street lighting, and sponsored several neighborhood cleanups. It also converted an abandoned lot into a garden, secured the reopening of several city parks, and organized youth activities such as field trips, dances, and talent shows. Nolton Community Corporation (NCC) was started 3 years ago as a community development corporation to address affordable housing and economic development needs. NCC started a microloan program to support home-based and start-up businesses and rehabilitated several abandoned three-family properties for sale to low-income residents.

Supermarket Project

In addition to addressing crime and housing abandonment, ROC and NCC are pursuing additional projects to stem disinvestment and improve the neighborhood. Both organizations have focused on a vacant former discount store on the neighborhood's main commercial street, which they believe is a potential supermarket site. The site is a former Ames discount store that was used as a flea market before the current owner, an office furniture store, used it for storage. The current owner is offering the property for sale with a $400,000 asking price. Since the Northside neighborhood has no supermarket, this use appears to be an appropriate reuse option. A supermarket will benefit residents by reducing their reliance on high-cost convenience stores and decrease their need to travel to stores on the outskirts of the city for groceries while creating jobs for local residents. NCC obtained a $15,000 Economic Development Administration technical assistance grant to study the supermarket's feasibility.

Market Analysis

A market analysis was completed as a first step in assessing the supermarket's feasibility by determining whether a sufficient market remained in the Northside neighborhood to support a supermarket, given other supermarkets in the city. Based on the number of households and income levels within the 1.5-mile primary trade area for the Ames site, the market analysis concluded that almost $57 million in spending potential existed for a new supermarket. However, with competition from four supermarkets located in or adjacent to the primary trade area, the market analysis concluded that a new supermarket would not generate sufficient sales to support the minimum 35,000-square foot store size required to attract a major chain supermarket. Therefore, an independent grocery store operator represented a more probable candidate for the site. Based on capturing 10% of trade area spending plus additional sales from catering to the citywide minority population and a sales level of $350 per square foot, the study concluded that the market could support a 16,000- to 18,000-square foot independent grocery store.

Development Plan

Based on the market analysis, NCC decided to focus on attracting an independent grocery store and include additional retail space for other neighborhood-based stores that could benefit from being located next to the grocery store. Potential stores for this space include a hairdresser, small restaurant, or laundromat. With another 2,000 to 4,000 square feet of retail space and a grocery store, the project would be developed as a 20,000-square foot neighborhood shopping center. With this development plan, NCC next focused on determining the project's development costs and operating income.

Development Budget

The project's development budget is presented in Exhibit 14.1. Total development costs are estimated at $1,965,291. Although the current asking price is $400,000, a lower $200,000 acquisition is included as a more realistic estimate of fair market value. Construction costs reflect the proposed uses and a phased approach to the 60,000-square foot building. It includes site and shell building repairs, roof repairs for the entire building, rehabilitation for the 20,000 square feet of leased space, new HVAC and electric systems for the improved space, and costs to finish space for the grocery store and retail tenants.

Soft costs were estimated based on figures from comparable projects, an estimated construction period of 7 months, current real estate taxes, and insurance estimates from an insurance agent. A 5% soft-cost contingency is included along with a $28,000 debt service reserve and an operating reserve close to 20% of the first year's operating budget. No provision is made for tenant equipment because equipment is generally the tenant's responsibility.

Operating Budget

A 10-year projected operating budget is presented in Exhibit 14.2. Income projections assume 5-year leases with tenants responsible for common area costs and increases in taxes and operating expenses above the first-year costs. Tenants also would pay all their own utility costs. Rents are projected at $7 per square foot for retail space and $10 per square foot for the grocery store. A 10% allowance for vacancy and bad debts is included. Rental income is almost $170,000 in the first 5 years and increases to over $215,000 for the second 5 years. Common area charges and escalators range from just above $10,000 in the first year to a maximum of $37,000 in year five. When new or renewed leases take effect in year six, the base operating costs are once again fully assumed by the landlord, as is typical in commercial leases. Operating and tax escalators are zero for this year and then grow relative to the base costs in year six over the following four years.

Operating expenses are based on expenses for comparable neighborhood shopping centers. Real estate tax estimates use the current commercial tax rate of $25.78 per thousand and an estimated final assessed value of $1 million. Total operating expenses begin at $88,300 and grow to $101,689 in year five. This increase reflects a 4% inflation rate and increases in real estate taxes.

Exhibit 14.1   Supermarket Development Budget

Uses of Funds	Amount
Acquisition	$200,000
Construction Hard Costs	$1,059,093
Contractor's Overhead, Profit, and Contingency	$211,819
Design, Engineering, and Project Management	$190,637
Legal Fee	$75,000
Financing Fee	$3,000
Accounting	$2,500
Insurance	$8,000
Appraisal	$5,000
Construction Interest	$36,000
Taxes During Construction	$10,200
Developer's Overhead and Profit	$100,000
Miscellaneous Fees	$500
Debt Service Reserve	$28,000
Operating Reserve	$14,000
Soft-Cost Contingency @ 5%	$21,542
Total Uses	$1,965,291

Exhibit 14.2   Nolton Supermarket\Retail Center 10-Year Operating Pro Forma

Category	Year 1	Year 2	Year 3	Year 4	Year 5	Year 6	Year 7	Year 8	Year 9	Year 10
Revenue										
Rent—Retail Space	$28,00	$28,000	$28,000	$28,000	$28,000	$33,600	$33,600	$33,600	$33,600	$33,600
Rent—Grocery Store	$160,000	$160,000	$160,000	$160,000	$160,000	$192,000	$192,000	$192,000	$192,000	$192,000
Less Vacancy (at 10%)	($18,800)	($18,800)	($18,800)	($18,800)	($18,800)	($22,560)	($22,560)	($22,560)	($22,560)	($22,560)
Net Rent	$169,200	$169,200	$169,200	$169,200	$169,200	$203,040	$203,040	$203,040	$203,040	$203,040
Common Area Charges	$10,440	$10,858	$11,292	$11,744	$12,213	$12,702	$13,210	$13,738	$14,288	$14,859
Tax Escalator	$0	$580	$1,175	$1,784	$2,409	$0	$656	$1,329	$2,018	$2,725
Operating Cost Escalator	$0	$1,386	$2,827	$4,327	$5,886	$0	$4,980	$6,734	$8,558	$10,455
Total Revenue	$179,640	$182,024	$184,494	$187,054	$189,708	$215,742	$221,886	$224,841	$227,904	$231,079
Expenses										
Management Expense	$13,000	$13,520	$14,061	$14,623	$15,208	$15,816	$16,449	$17,107	$17,791	$18,503
Maintenance and Repairs	$10,000	$10,400	$10,816	$11,249	$11,699	$12,167	$12,653	$13,159	$13,686	$14,233
Common Area Maintenance	$9,000	$9,360	$9,734	$10,124	$10,529	$10,950	$11,388	$11,843	$12,317	$12,810
Common Area Utilities	$2,600	$2,704	$2,812	$2,925	$3,042	$3,163	$3,290	$3,421	$3,558	$3,701
Insurance	$10,000	$10,400	$10,816	$11,249	$11,699	$12,167	$12,653	$13,159	$13,686	$14,233
Real Estate Taxes	$25,780	$26,425	$27,085	$27,762	$28,456	$29,168	$29,897	$30,644	$31,410	$32,196
Marketing and Brokerage	$500	$520	$541	$562	$585	$11,888	$633	$658	$684	$712
Legal and Accounting	$5,000	$5,200	$5,408	$5,624	$5,849	$6,083	$6,327	$6,580	$6,843	$7,117
Replacement Reserve	$10,000	$10,400	$10,816	$11,249	$11,699	$12,167	$12,653	$13,159	$13,686	$14,233
Operating Reserve	$2,500	$2,600	$2,704	$2,812	$2,925	$3,042	$3,163	$3,290	$3,421	$3,558
Total Expenses	$88,380	$91,529	$94,793	$98,179	$101,689	$116,610	$109,106	$113,022	$117,083	$121,295
Net Income	$91,260	$90,495	$89,701	$88,875	$88,018	$99,132	$112,781	$111,820	$110,821	$109,784

Financing Plan

Using the projected development and operating budgets, prepare a financing plan for the project that minimizes the amount of city funds needed. This plan needs to encompass

- The achievable level of debt financing for the development and the proposed debt source(s) (e.g. private lender, state development agency, etc.)
- The potential to attract private equity investment and the amount, if any, of such equity
- The amount of required grant funds and sources from federal economic development programs
- The amount of city funding needed and the recommended form of the city's financing
- An explanation of why each source was selected

Table 14.4 lists several potential debt and equity sources and their financing terms and requirements.

Table 14.4   Summary of Potential Debt and Equity Sources

Funding Source	Interest Rate or Investment Return	Term	Amortization Period	Required Debt Service Coverage	Required Loan to Value
Private Bank	Prime + 2%, floating rate (9.25%) Treasury + 3% (9.5%) fixed rate	10 years	Up to 20 years	1.20 to 1.25 minimum	.70 to .80 maximum
Equity Investor	20 to 30% with at least 15% from annual cash flow. Additional return from property appreciation within 5–7 years	NA	NA	NA	NA
State Economic Develop. Agency	9%	10 years	Up to 25 years	1.10 minimum	.90 maximum
Local Initiative Support Corporation Equity Fund	10%	10 years	10% annual cash return. Initial investment repaid at year 10	1.00	NA
HUD 108 Loan	Treasury + .5% (7%) floor; city can add spread	Up to 20 years	Up to 20 years	Determined by city	Determined by city

Endnotes

1. The SBA publication, *SBA Programs and Services,* offers a good overview of all SBA programs. SBA program summaries are based on this publication and descriptions on the SBA Web site (www.sba.gov).

2. Fixed rate loans of $50,000 or more cannot exceed prime plus 2.25% when the maturity is less than 7 years, and prime plus 2.75% when the maturity is 7 years or more. Loans between $25,000 and $50,000 have maximum interest rates of prime plus 3.25% for maturities of less than 7 years and prime plus 3.75% when the maturity is 7 years or more. Loans of $25,000 or less have interest rate limits of prime plus 4.25% if the maturity is less than 7 years and prime plus 4.75% if the maturity is 7 years or more.

3. Under this program, the maximum guarantee percentage is 90%, instead of 75% to 85% under the standard 7(a) product, and no caps are placed on lender fees and interest rates.

4. Figures are from the SBA's Web site (www.sba.gov/cgi-bin/loan-approvals 4.pl).

5. The CDBG regulations related to these issues include CFR 570.203, 507.208, and 507.209.

6. For more detailed information on the Section 108 program, consult the HUD Web site and the applicable regulations in 24 CFR 540, Subpart M, "Loan Guarantees."

7. As with other CDBG-funded activities, the project must fit the CDBG national objectives and regulations to receive Section 108 financing.

8. A list of certified entities by organizational type and state is on the CDFI Fund Web site (www.treas.gov/cdfi).

9. This is different than low-income housing tax credits, in which investors received their full return from tax credits.

10. EDA also has a university center program that funds university-based information and technical assistance services that support economic development entities, funds several Trade Adjustment Centers to assist firms impacted by imports, and funds research and evaluation studies.

11. Program descriptions are based upon the EDA Program Guide and March 1, 2002, Federal Register Notice of Funding Availability, both posted on the EDA Web site (www.doc.gov/eda).

12. For example, the FY2002 Economic Adjustment Assistance Program included $13.5 million for communities affected by downsizing in the coal mining and timber industries.

15

Municipal
Finance Tools

S tate and local governments have long been active in economic
development finance and have introduced many innovations to the
field.[1] As shown in prior chapters, governments influence capital availability
for small firms and development projects through their regulation of the
financial services industry, providing incentives and guarantees to expand
private lending and investment and by establishing alternative institutions to
fill capital market gaps. This chapter considers how two financial tools available to state and local governments, the power to tax and the tax-exempt
status of state and local government debt, can be used to achieve economic
development ends. Together, they provide powerful and prevalent tools
that practitioners can apply to finance firms, real estate projects, and other
economic development activities. The chapter's first focus is the use of
municipal debt for economic development, with special attention to industrial development bonds (IDBs)—a widely utilized, and frequently abused,
instrument to finance business facilities. Tax-increment financing and assessment districts, which target tax revenues to finance economic development,
are considered in the second half of the chapter.

An Overview of Municipal Debt

Although the term municipal debt suggests the borrowing undertaken by
local governments to support their financial needs, it has a larger meaning
tied to federal tax law and the operation of debt markets. Under the U.S.
Internal Revenue code, the interest payments on most debt issued by state
and local governments, including authorities and quasi-public entities, is
exempt from federal income taxes. Consequently, investors accept a lower
interest rate on tax-exempt municipal debt than on taxable debt. The
recipients of these borrowed funds benefit from the lower interest rate
subsidized by the federal tax exemption. Thus, state and local governments
can pass along this interest rate subsidy to certain firms, organizations, and
developments, with the cost borne by the federal government.

As one might expect, the federal government has limited the use of this interest rate subsidy to reduce forgone federal tax revenue. From the 1960s through the 1980s, the U.S. Congress placed new limits on the use of tax-exempt bonds for "private activity" purposes. A bond is labeled a *private activity bond* when it finances facilities either owned or used by private, for-profit parties and there is a revenue flow from the private users that serves to repay the bonds. These limits prohibit the use of tax-exempt bonds for certain purposes (e.g., financing shopping centers and commercial buildings), place restrictions on the remaining allowed uses, and set an annual volume cap on the total amount of private activity bonds that can be issued in each state.[2] Despite these limitations, state and local governments can still issue tax-exempt bonds for several purposes. No cap exists on tax-exempt debt used to finance the general activities and facilities of governments. Similarly, tax-exempt debt used for 501 (c) (3) charitable organizations is not subject to a volume cap. Tax-exempt bonds can also be used for the following purposes, subject to IRS rules and within a state's annual volume caps: (1) industrial development bonds for manufacturing facilities; (2) exempt facilities, which include wastewater, solid waste treatment and pollution control facilities, water facilities, local district heating and cooling installations, and government-owned transportation facilities; (3) multifamily and single-family housing for low-income households; and (4) bonds to finance qualifying businesses and projects in federally designated Empowerment Zones.

Municipal debt is also categorized by the revenue sources pledged to repay bonds. *General obligation (GO) bonds* are backed by a full faith and credit pledge from the issuing government entity. Under GO bonds, the issuing government or authority promises to use all of its available revenue and assets to repay bondholders. With this broad repayment commitment, general obligation bonds are the highest quality debt offered by an issuer. *Revenue bonds,* on the other hand, are backed by the pledge of a specific and limited revenue source. For example, the fees from airport operations may be the sole revenue pledged to repay bonds issued by an airport authority to fund airport expansion. Similarly, a public parking garage may be financed by revenue bonds backed solely by the parking fees collected at the garage. In these cases, bondholders face the risk that the actual revenues may be insufficient to fully repay the debt if airport use or parking demand is below the projected levels. With limited sources of repayment, revenue bonds are riskier and carry a higher interest rate than general obligation debt issued by the same government or public authority. *Industrial development bonds* are a type of revenue bond backed by the cash flow and credit of the business using the bond proceeds. There is no pledge of revenues or credit by the government body that issues an IDB.

Although municipal debt usually carries a below-market interest rate due to its federal tax exemption, it entails larger transaction costs than direct borrowing from a commercial bank or other financial institution. Higher transaction costs result from two factors: (1) the special legal opinions needed to verify the tax-exempt status for investors; and (2) the costs associated with selling debt on public credit markets, including credit ratings, printing, trustee fees and investment banking fees. These higher transaction fees offset the savings from tax-exempt interest rates such that a minimum debt sale of several million dollars is often necessary for tax-exempt bonds to be financially beneficial.

Economic Development Uses of Municipal Debt

Despite federal tax code restrictions and higher transaction costs, municipal debt serves several important economic development finance functions. First, state and local governments can issue debt to raise capital for development finance programs. Although annual appropriations fund most government programs, debt has several advantages for funding economic development finance programs. Because development finance programs need a large capital base to be sustainable, it is frequently more feasible for governments to supply the $10 million or more needed to establish a new finance program through a debt sale than through an annual appropriation. Moreover, providing substantial initial capital frees the program from having to rely on uncertain annual appropriations and reduces an avenue for political interference in lending and investment decisions. Because economic development finance programs make sustained investments in the economy, funding them with debt is good finance practice; a long-term liability is used to fund a long-term public asset. Second, municipal revenue bonds are used frequently to finance infrastructure projects that are critical to supporting economic activity and local quality of life. Roads, water and sewer systems, port facilities, airports, and parking garages all use revenue bonds supported by user fees to finance their construction. Beyond financing the infrastructure platform for regional economic development, municipal debt can also fund improvements that are needed to bring new development and private investment to blighted areas with outdated or deteriorated infrastructure. Because infrastructure projects are long-term assets with a large up front investment that provide a return from expanded economic activity over time, they are well matched to debt financing, which allows a large current investment to be amortized over many years. Tax-increment financing, discussed below, is typically used for this purpose. A third use of tax-exempt debt, specifically IDBs, is supplying capital at below-market interest rates to support the growth of small manufacturing firms. With the pooling of smaller loans and providing credit enhancement, IDB programs can address market gaps and expand capital availability for small manufacturers.

Industrial Development Bonds

Industrial development bonds are a form of tax-exempt debt used to finance manufacturing plants. Mississippi initiated the use of IDBs in 1938 when it passed a law authorizing local governments to use bonds to finance private industrial facilities. IDB use grew exponentially in the 1960s as forty states established programs and annual issuance increased from $46 million in 1960 to $1.59 billion in 1968 (CUED, 1995b). This growth was fueled by the expanded use of IDBs to finance all types of private facilities, including discount stores, restaurants, and sports facilities (Litvak & Daniels, 1979). IDBs are now offered in all fifty states subject to strict limitations in the IRS code. Consequently, the primary users of IDBs are now small- to medium-size manufacturers seeking to borrow several million dollars to build a new plant or expand an existing one.

Under current tax law, industrial development bonds are subject to restrictions on the use of bond proceeds, the size of a bond issue, a firm's lifetime use of IDBs, and a cap on each state's annual issuance of IDBs and other private activity bonds.[3] IDBs can only be used to finance costs (called capital expenditures) related to manufacturing facilities. Allowable capital expenditures include land acquisition (capped at 25% of the bond proceeds); construction of a new plant; expansion of an existing one; leasehold improvements; equipment used in the plant; and building access roads, parking lots, utilities, and other accessory facilities directly related to the manufacturing plant. Proceeds also can be used to acquire an existing plant as long as renovations that equal at least 15% of the purchase price are undertaken within 2 years. IRS rules also limit a firm's capital expenditures financed with IDBs to $10 million over a 6-year period that begins 3 years prior to IDB issuance and extends forward for 3 years. If a company received $4 million in IDB financing for a plant expansion 3 years ago, then the maximum allowable IDB available to the firm would be $6 million. Once a firm reaches the $10 million cap within a 6-year period, it is limited to a maximum of $1 million in new IDB proceeds. Firms also face a $40 million lifetime limit on the amount of IDB proceeds that they can receive. Finally, each state has an annual cap on the total private activity bonds issued (under all private activity categories including IDBs, low-income housing bonds, and exempt facility bonds) equal to the lesser of $150 million or $50 per capita. Even with these restrictions, new IDB issues averaged $3 billion annually from 1993 to 1999.[4]

Although IDBs provide a capital subsidy that enhances project cash flow and feasibility, they typically do not expand access to capital for small manufacturers. IDBs are sold to private investors or mutual funds that seek bonds with an investment grade credit rating or borrowers with strong credit. When a credit rating is needed, a bank letter of credit (LOC) typically provides the strong guarantee needed to secure an investment grade credit rating. Because a firm that can secure a bank letter of credit can also qualify for a conventional mortgage loan, IDBs substitute one source of financing for another. To finance riskier borrowers and use IDBs to expand access to more affordable long-term financing, an alternative source of credit enhancement must be provided. Two options exist for this credit enhancement: (1) guaranteeing bond repayment; and (2) creating a bond insurance fund. In the first case, the credit of the parent government or the issuing agency is lent to the company to secure the needed credit rating. The issuing agency can provide the guarantee as long as its financial position is strong enough to receive an investment grade credit rating. Although a guarantee from the parent state or local government provides the strongest credit support, many states have constitutional prohibitions against using their credit to benefit private parties.[5] Under the second option, a cash reserve fund is established at the issuing agency that insures against losses to bondholders if a business cannot repay the IDB. Capital for the reserve fund can be appropriated, transferred from the agency's accumulated reserves, or can come from a dedicated revenue source. Several states use credit enhancement to expand small firms' access to IDB financing. Arkansas has two bond guaranty programs for this purpose; one operated by the Arkansas Development Finance Authority, the state's primary IDB issuer, and the second run by the state's Economic Development Department.[6] The ADFA Bond Guarantee Program guarantees IDB principal and interest payments for amounts up to 80% of total project costs (70% for start-ups). A reserve fund secures the guarantee, with a back-up guarantee from pledged interest earned on the state's daily treasury balances.[7] Through August 2001, ADFA had over $88 million in outstanding bond guarantees. MassDevelopment does not directly guarantee IDBs but instead uses its mortgage insurance program to help firms secure a bank LOC by providing a partial guarantee to the LOC bank. This helps firms with repayment or collateral risks outside the LOC bank's underwriting standards to gain access to IDB financing.

A second way to expand small firms' access to capital markets with IDBs is to pool small loans into one large bond issue. A pooled bond program spreads transaction costs over several borrowers and allows businesses with small projects to utilize IDB financing. Pooled bonds may also be advantageous to investors because they have a more diversified source of repayment revenues that can reduce default and loss risks. Although pooled IDBs are not widely used, some state and local governments do offer them. Timing is a major obstacle to pooled financing because several firms must qualify for and need IDB financing at the same time for a pool to be feasible. Thus, pooled bond programs are most feasible in large states and municipalities where a high volume of deals exists. One of the most active pooled bond programs is the Pennsylvania Economic Development Financing Authority (PEDFA)'s Composite Bond Program, which had $350 million in pooled bonds outstanding as of June 2002.[8] This program uses a master LOC from PNC Bank to secure an investment grade credit rating independent of each individual firm's credit. PEDFA also uses standard documentation and the same working group of attorneys, underwriters, LOC bank, and trustee bank to reduce transaction costs. Through the Composite Bond Program, PEDFA can finance projects as small as $400,000 and reduce issuance costs to 2% to 2.5% of the bond principal, a very low level for tax-exempt bonds. PEDFA addresses the timing issue by assembling three to four pooled bonds each year and sticking to a set schedule. This ensures predictability about when companies receive debt proceeds and allows firms to complete their financing within 3 to 4 months.

Finally, several agencies have developed "mini-IDB" programs that reduce transaction costs to expand access to IDB financing for smaller firms and projects. These programs use standard documentation to reduce legal costs and private placement of bonds with banks or other investors to lower underwriter and credit rating fees. In typical transactions, bonds are offered and sold to multiple investors and require a credit rating from a bond rating agency such as Fitch, Moody's, or Standard and Poor's. Direct placement of bonds to institutional investors can avoid the cost of securing a credit rating, reduce investment banking fees, and in some cases, eliminate the need for a LOC. Indiana's Small Bond Program issues bonds of $1 million or less through placing them with banks and using standard documents. The bank must agree up front to purchase the bonds, and they typically use the program to serve good customers needing a $300,000 to $1 million loan. Bonds as small as $300,000 can be issued under this program with the average interest rate at 85% of prime. St. Louis County's Mini-Bond Program uses a streamlined application and standard documents that are preapproved by the IDA, the bond counsel, and the bond trustee to reduce costs and accelerate decisions to finance small projects. Projects ranging from $500,000 to $2 million are funded under this program through bonds that are privately placed with banks. To use the program, a business must first locate a bank that is willing to purchase the bonds. Total transaction costs are about 2.5% for a $1 million issue and 3.25% for a $500,000 bond.[9]

IDB Case Study: New Boston Seafood Center

In January 1997, the City of Boston Industrial Development Finance Authority issued an IDB to finance the New Boston Seafood Center project. This project involved the construction of a modern fish processing facility divided into four separate condominium units for four firms. Each firm contributes funds to pay bond interest and principal. The shared facility, in effect, provided a mechanism for pooled financing by aggregating the small space and finance needs of each firm into one larger project financed with a single bond.

Exhibit 15.1 displays the cover page for the official statement used to detail the bond transaction for potential investors. This cover page summarizes several important aspects of the financing. It indicates that the principal amount is $4.425 million and the maturity date is January 1, 2022 (a 25-year term). It also states that First National Bank of Boston (FNBB) is providing a "direct pay" LOC for the bonds, which means that FNBB promises to pay scheduled interest and principal payments directly to the bondholders if New Boston Seafood fails to make any required debt service payments. This letter of credit provides the repayment guarantee needed to attract investors, who can then make their investment decision based on FNBB's credit without having to understand the underlying project risks. New Boston Seafood pays FNBB an annual fee for the LOC. No interest rate is listed on this statement because these are variable rate bonds in which the interest rate is reset weekly. This arrangement provides a low short-term interest rate but subjects borrowers to the risk of increased interest rates over time. At the top of the statement, the first sentence provides a legal opinion that the bonds are tax-exempt under the IRS code. This opinion provided by a law firm hired by the issuer to

Exhibit 15.1   New Boston Seafood Bond Offering Memorandum

NEW ISSUE - BOOK-ENTRY ONLY

Unrated

In the opinion of Davis, Malm & D'Agostine, P.C., Bond Counsel, under present law, interest on the Bonds is excluded from gross income of the owners of the Bonds for federal income tax purposes assuming continued compliance by the Issuer and the Borrower with the Internal Revenue Code of 1986 (the "Code"), except for interest on any Bond for any period during which such Bond is held by a person who is a "substantial user" of the Project financed by the Bonds or a "related person" within the meaning of Section 147(a) of the Code. Interest on the Bonds will be included, however, as an item of tax preference in computing the federal alternative minimum tax for individuals and corporations. In the opinion of Bond Counsel, under existing law, interest on the Bonds and any profit on the sale thereof are exempt from Massachusetts personal income taxes and the Bonds are exempt from Massachusetts personal property taxes. See "Tax Exemption" herein for further details.

$4,425,000
CITY OF BOSTON
INDUSTRIAL REVENUE BONDS
(New Boston Seafood Center Project - 1997 Series)

PRICE 100%

Dated: Date of Initial Delivery

Due: January 1, 2022

The Bonds are being issued by the City of Boston, Massachusetts, acting by and through its Industrial Development Financing Authority (the "Issuer") pursuant to, and payable solely from and secured by the payments to be made by New Boston Seafood Center, Inc. (the "Borrower") in accordance with the Loan and Trust Agreement (the "Agreement") dated as of January 1, 1997 among the Issuer, the Borrower and Fleet National Bank, Boston, Massachusetts, as Trustee (the "Trustee"), as well as certain funds to be held thereunder.

While the Bonds are in the initial Weekly Mode an irrevocable direct pay letter of credit (the "Letter of Credit") issued by

THE FIRST NATIONAL BANK OF BOSTON

will entitle Fleet National Bank, Boston Massachusetts, as Paying Agent (the "Paying Agent") to draw an amount equal to (a) the principal of the Bonds when due, whether upon maturity, redemption or acceleration, (b) up to 49 days of interest on the Bonds when due, and (c) the Purchase Price of Bonds tendered for purchase pursuant to the mandatory or optional tender provisions of the Agreement. The Letter of Credit will expire on October 31, 1997 (or upon the earlier occurrence of certain events), unless extended or renewed. The Bonds shall be subject to mandatory tender as described herein on such date, unless the Letter of Credit is extended or renewed. The Agreement provides that a substitute credit facility may be delivered to the Trustee under certain conditions.

The Bonds will be issued initially under a Book-Entry Only System, registered in the name of Cede & Co., as registered owner and nominee for the Depository Trust Company ("DTC"), which will act as securities depository for the Bonds. Individual purchases of beneficial interests in the Bonds will be made in book-entry form. Purchasers of beneficial interests in the Bonds will not receive certificates representing interests in the Bonds that they purchase. See "Book-Entry Only System". Details as to payments on the Bonds are set forth in this Private Placement Memorandum.

The Bonds will be issued in fully registered form initially in denominations of $100,000 and integral multiples of $5,000 in excess thereof and in the Weekly Mode as described herein. The Bonds will bear interest while Bonds are in the Weekly Mode at the Variable Rate to be determined not later than the Business Day preceding the Effective Date, as described herein. Interest on Bonds in the Weekly Mode will be payable on the first Business Day of each month, beginning February 3, 1997 by check or draft mailed to the registered owners or by wire or bank transfer as provided in the Agreement.

While the Bonds are in the Weekly Mode and subject to certain conditions described herein, the Bonds may be tendered to the Paying Agent in multiples of $100,000 and integral multiples of $5,000 in excess thereof for purchase at a price equal to the principal amount thereof plus accrued interest, if any, to the Purchase Date, as defined herein upon seven days' written notice of tender from the Bondowner and upon delivery of the Bonds to the Paying Agent.

At the option of the Borrower and upon certain conditions as described herein, the Bonds may be converted or reconverted from time to time to or from any of the Variable Rate Modes or may be converted to the Fixed Rate Mode. On the date of conversion from one mode to another, or the conversion to a longer or shorter maturity within Multiannual Mode, or upon the expiration or substitution of the Credit Facility providing security for the Bonds, the Bonds will be subject to mandatory tender for purchase at a price equal to the principal amount thereof, plus accrued interest to the Purchase Date, unless a Non-Tender Election has been filed as described herein.

The Bonds are subject to redemption prior to maturity, including mandatory and optional redemption at par in certain circumstances, as set forth in this Private Placement Memorandum.

THE BONDS DO NOT CONSTITUTE A GENERAL OBLIGATION OF THE ISSUER OR A PLEDGE OF THE FAITH AND CREDIT OF THE ISSUER OR A DEBT OR PLEDGE OF THE FAITH AND CREDIT OF THE COMMONWEALTH OF MASSACHUSETTS; THE PRINCIPAL AND PURCHASE PRICE OF, PREMIUM, IF ANY, AND INTEREST ON THE BONDS ARE PAYABLE SOLELY FROM THE REVENUES AND FUNDS PLEDGED FOR THEIR PAYMENT UNDER AND PURSUANT TO THE AGREEMENT.

The Bonds are offered when, as and if issued, subject to approval of legality by Davis, Malm & D'Agostine, P.C., Boston Massachusetts, Bond Counsel, and certain other conditions. Certain legal matters will be passed upon for The First National Bank of Boston by its special counsel, Bingham, Dana & Gould LLP, Boston, Massachusetts and for the Borrower by its special counsel, Davis, Malm & D'Agostine, P.C., Boston, Massachusetts. It is expected that the Bonds will be available for delivery in definitive form to DTC in New York, New York on or about January 13, 1997.

Tucker Anthony

INCORPORATED
PLACEMENT AGENT

Dated: January 9, 1997

---

prepare legal documents needed for the bond transaction (bond counsel) is essential to attract investors. The last paragraph identifies two other law firms involved in the financing, one representing FNBB and a second representing the borrower. Other parties to the financing include

Bond issuer (Boston Industrial Development Finance Authority) is the entity with legal authority to offer the bonds for sale. The issuer is not responsible for repayment of the bonds—a fact emphasized in capitalized text near the bottom of the page.

Trustee (Fleet National Bank) collects funds from the New Boston Seafood firms and makes payments to bondholders. The trustee acts on behalf of the bondholders if a financial or other default occurs.

Placement Agent (Tucker Anthony) finds investors to purchase the bonds. Some bond sales use an *underwriter* who buys the bonds from the issuer and then resells them to investors instead of a placement agent.

As this example shows, there are many parties involved in municipal bond transactions. The fees paid to all these entities result in the high transaction costs associated with most IDB financings.

Tax-Increment Financing

Forty-eight states allow a special form of financing entitled tax-increment financing, or TIF (Klacik & Nunn, 2001).[10] Under TIF, incremental tax revenues generated in a designated area are set aside to fund specific projects or activities rather than paid to the normal taxing jurisdictions. TIF often finances infrastructure improvements in a deteriorated or blighted area that are critical to attracting new investment, development, and business activity. In this application, TIF provides a way to use the development generated by new public improvements to directly finance their cost. Although TIF is usually based on property taxes, some states allow TIF that is based on sales taxes (Mikesel, 2001).[11]

With TIF, the tax revenue collected in the designated TIF district is divided into two parts: the base-year tax amount and the tax increment. Base-year taxes are the taxes collected on the property assessments in the year when the TIF district is established. They continue to be paid to all the normal taxing jurisdictions, but the assessments upon which these base-year taxes are collected are frozen for the life of the TIF district.[12] Incremental tax revenues are the taxes collected on any increases in the assessed property values. This increment includes taxes from three sources: (1) growth in existing property assessments from higher market values over time; (2) assessment increases from new investment in existing properties; and (3) new property development. Incremental tax revenue is diverted from the normal taxing jurisdictions and instead paid to either a redevelopment agency (or other public entity) that oversees improvements to the TIF district or for alternative purposes allowed by law.

Communities use three approaches to finance infrastructure (or other district improvements) with TIF revenue. The first approach is "pay as you go" financing in which TIF revenue is invested as it is collected. For example, a community that collects $100,000 in annual TIF revenue would either undertake a small project that costs $100,000 or accumulate annual TIF collections until it had enough funds to support a larger project. Although the "pay-as-you-go" approach is simple and straightforward, improvements occur slowly because investment in any year is limited to current or accumulated TIF revenue. Under the second approach, TIF revenue is used to borrow funds, usually through a municipal note or bond sale, to make large up-front investments. TIF debt financing is more complicated and costly to execute than "pay-as-you-go" financing, but it permits more rapid and larger scale infrastructure investments, helping to accelerate new private development. A third option is for a private developer or company to fund the new infrastructure and then be repaid with TIF revenue.

Although TIF debt is widely used, many communities still rely on "pay-as-you-go" financing. From 1990 to 1995, governments in 27 states issued 819 TIF-backed debt securities that totaled $10.9 billion (Johnson, 2001). California is by far the most active state for TIF debt, accounting for 80% of the total dollar amount of TIF securities sold in this 6-year period (Johnson, 2001). A 1996 survey of 85 TIF districts in Indiana found that 61% used TIF debt to finance improvements, but 24 districts, or 28%, planned to rely solely on pay-as-you-go funding (Klacik, 2001). A study of 20 TIF projects in Texas found that "pay-as-you-go" financing was the most common funding method. Nine projects relied solely on pay-as-you-go financing and four used it in combination with either debt or developer financing (Arvidson, Hissong, & Cole, 2001).

The Tax-Increment Financing Process

Although the requirements to create a TIF district vary by state,[13] a similar process is used in most states. This section presents a generalized TIF process that includes the steps required in most states (see Figure 15.1).[14] First, the geographic area for the TIF district is established. When defining the district boundaries, communities need to consider local economic development goals, the area's development potential, and its fit with legal requirements. Second, an entity to oversee the TIF district must be established that is responsible for approving the overall district redevelopment plan and individual projects and authorizing any TIF-backed debt. Third, a survey of conditions in the area is conducted to document blight and slum conditions that are required to qualify as a TIF district and for redevelopment planning. Fourth, a district redevelopment plan is prepared that defines the expected new private investment, required infrastructure improvements, and the use of TIF revenues. A key part of the TIF plan is determining viable private development opportunities and identifying the necessary infrastructure projects to realize this new investment. Once the TIF plan is approved, more detailed feasibility and financial evaluations of specific development projects and infrastructure improvements are completed. This analysis includes an assessment of the likely new development and whether it will generate enough TIF revenue to cover infrastructure costs, including any planned debt. Once feasibility is established, the TIF governing board approves infrastructure projects, the expenditure of TIF revenues, and borrowing (if applicable). When pay-as-you-go or developer financing is used, the infrastructure improvements are completed and are then followed by new private development and investment. When debt financing is used, the loan transaction must be completed before infrastructure improvements are made. Finally, tax increment revenues are collected over time and used to repay any debt holders or developers who funded the infrastructure.

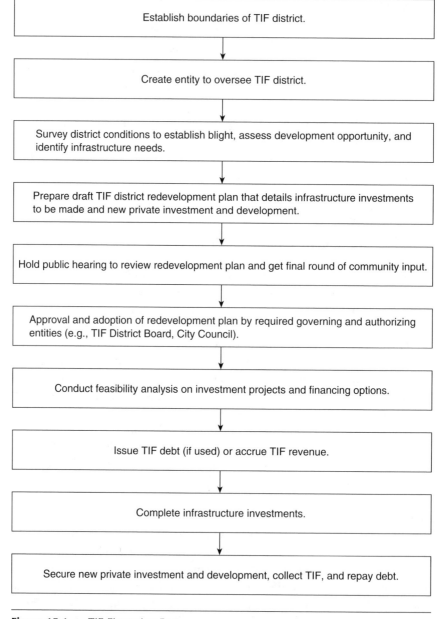

Figure 15.1   TIF Financing Process

Economic Development Uses of TIF

TIF can be applied in several ways to finance infrastructure improvements and generate new development. One option is to fund improvements that address site and infrastructure problems for a specific project. For example, a city may need to upgrade water, sewers, and roads serving a site to address the needs of a major manufacturer seeking to locate a new plant in the community. Alternatively, a downtown parking garage may be needed to support a new shopping center or other project, but its costs may exceed what the potential parking fees can finance. A second use of TIF is to address districtwide conditions and infrastructure problems that impair new development. For example, former military bases often need to reconfigure and upgrade roads, water and sewer systems, storm drainage, and utilities to make the base suitable for business use. Older downtown districts may need site assembly, parking, and widespread infrastructure improvements to attract and support new private development. A third TIF use is targeting the investment of tax revenues to an area that experienced disinvestment from both the private and public sectors. In this case, TIF provides a mechanism to ensure that tax revenue growth in the target area is reinvested there to address historic neglect and stimulate private reinvestment. A TIF district also might be drawn to include both areas with strong investment demand and surrounding blighted areas; tax revenues from development in the high-demand locations could then be used to finance improvements, and stimulate investment, in the deteriorated area.

TIF financing has been criticized for subsidizing development that would occur anyway rather than removing barriers to growth.[15] Some states have allowed the use of TIF financing in any area for general economic development purposes without targeting its use to redevelop blighted and deteriorated areas (Johnson & Kriz, 2001). In these states, communities can use TIF to finance road and infrastructure improvements near major highway interchanges or vital commercial areas, locations that are likely to attract new private development without TIF funding.[16] Consequently, tax revenue from development that will ordinarily occur is diverted from general government purposes to benefit a specific company or developer. TIF, in effect, functions as a tax incentive rather than as a redevelopment tool. Some communities prefer to use TIF to finance infrastructure because it is exempt from debt limits or voter referendums that are required for general obligation borrowing. Using TIF to bypass these requirements diverts communities from using TIF to address development barriers, and thus, generate new economic development.

Several studies on the economic impact of tax-increment financing evaluate whether TIF serves to generate new development or simply redistributes tax burdens. Joyce Man summarized several of these studies in her 2001 article.[17] In the Detroit area, one study concluded that TIF was the only one of four local economic development programs that had a positive effect on retail sales. A study of pre- and post-TIF adoption property values in Indiana cities found a positive and statistically significant relationship between TIF adoption and property values. In this study, the TIF impact did not occur until after 2 years and affected both the TIF district and surrounding communities. A third study of the Chicago metropolitan area did not find a statistically significant impact of TIF adoption on the cities' annual property value growth rate and concluded that TIF stimulated growth in targeted blighted areas at the expense of other areas.[18] Finally, two studies on TIF's net fiscal impact on both the TIF district host city and surrounding communities suggested that taxpayers in the surrounding communities initially subsidized development in the TIF district but gained benefits in the long run. Although most of these studies indicated that TIF had a positive impact on economic growth, methodological problems make them inconclusive. Most studies used a crude measure of TIF use—the adoption of a TIF district. By simply comparing growth between communities that adopted a TIF district and those without a TIF district, they neither measured the actual use of TIF financing nor related the extent of TIF use to increases in property values or employment. The TIF indicator may serve as a proxy for other factors correlated with TIF adoption that are generating the higher observed employment and property growth rates, such as more activist economic development leadership and programs or more land zoned for commercial and industrial use.

Issues in TIF Debt Financing

TIF revenue is often tied to debt sales that raise capital for infrastructure projects. Indeed, one of TIF's strongest appeals is its capacity to accelerate infrastructure investment needed to spur new private development. Despite their widespread use, TIF bond transactions are difficult to complete due to the uncertainty of future TIF revenue and the complexities of matching TIF revenue to debt service. Incremental property tax revenue depends on growth in real estate values and the level and pace of new real estate investment. However, these drivers of TIF revenue are very uncertain and hard to accurately forecast. New real estate investment is particularly tricky to predict because delays in government permitting decisions and financial market conditions can postpone it, along with changed economic and market conditions. Although incremental taxes on existing properties are more predictable, and typically grow as values increase over time, they can decline when prices fall due to economic recession, population decline, overbuilding, and speculative bubbles. Consequently, investors are cautious about relying solely on TIF revenue to repay bonds and seek credit enhancements to protect them from shortfalls in TIF revenue. A second challenge in structuring TIF-backed debt is that TIF revenue growth lags district improvements by several years because the growth in property values from appreciation and new development occurs gradually. (One exception is a sales tax TIF in which TIF-funded improvements are linked to a large retail development.) Debt service payments, however, must be made on time and cannot wait for property assessments to accrue. If TIF revenues are not large enough to make interest payments in the initial years, then an alternative source of cash flow is needed to cover bond payments.

Several options exist to overcome each problem. To address TIF revenue uncertainty, TIF entities often commission an independent analysis of projected property assessment growth and TIF revenues to verify the cash flow projected to repay bondholders. A second option is using a high debt service coverage ratio for the financing to ensure payments will be made even with significant shortfalls in TIF revenue. Although this option reassures investors, it reduces the amount that can be raised from a given TIF revenue stream. A third option is setting aside part of the debt proceeds to fund reserves to make interest and principal payments if TIF revenue falls short of the required debt service. Finally, many TIF debt issues use third-party credit enhancement through bond insurance or a bank LOC. This credit enhancement helps secure a good bond rating and reduces the interest rate needed to attract investors. Institutions that provide credit enhancement require some of the other risk reduction measures to mitigate their exposure in guaranteeing the bonds. When private credit enhancement is unavailable or too costly, the government that created the TIF district can provide a guarantee. However, once guaranteed by the government, the debt is a general obligation borrowing, and the rationale for using TIF is gone. To compensate for initial TIF revenues that are too small to meet interest payments, capitalized interest reserves are used. Similar to a debt service reserve, the capitalized interest reserve sets aside a portion of the bond proceeds to cover interest payments until the TIF revenue is large enough to fully pay scheduled payments. When a capitalized interest reserve is needed, principal payments also must be deferred until the TIF revenue is sufficient to pay both interest and principal.

The Inland Valley Development Agency's (IVDA) 1997 TIF bond issue, summarized in Box 15.1, demonstrates how these financing issues were resolved in one transaction. IVDA is an authority created by three cities and a county to undertake the redevelopment of Norton Air Force Base. A 14,000-acre TIF district that encompasses the 2,000-acre base and a large surrounding area was established to provide IVDA with TIF revenue to fund redevelopment costs. In 1997, IVDA issued $44.485 million in long-term bonds to refinance two medium-term notes sold in 1993. IVDA used several credit enhancement and debt-structuring tools to address repayment risk and make the bonds more marketable to investors. First, IVDA deferred principal payments for 5 years until 2002. By only paying interest, debt service payments were reduced by $1 million for 5 years, which provided IVDA an extended period to secure new development, increase property values, and expand tax increment revenue. Second, capitalized interest and debt service reserves of $3.67 million were created to cover debt payments if tax increment revenues did not meet projections. This reserve was 1.67 times annual debt service in the first 5 years and 1.15 times the bond's highest annual debt payment. Third, IVDA secured a letter of credit from Sumitomo Trust & Banking Company to guarantee interest and principal payments to bond-holders if IVDA fails to make these payments. This letter of credit allowed IVDA to secure an investment grade bond rating, which lowered its interest rate and made the bonds more marketable.

Box 15.1   Summary of Inland Valley Development Agency Tax
Allocation Bond, Series 1997

Issuance Date:	March 1, 1997.
Total Principal Amount:	$44,485,000.
Interest Rate:	Variable rate set weekly, initial rate of 4.2%.
Final Maturity Date:	March 1, 2027.
Purpose of Debt Issue:	Refinancing of two previous notes used to fund the redevelopment of Norton Air Force Base in San Bernardino County, California.
Source of Repayment:	Tax increment revenue in the project area.
Additional Security:	Letter of Credit from Sumitomo Trust & Banking Company.

Sources of Funds:

Bond Proceeds	$44,485,000
Transfers from Prior Notes	1,432,576
Total	$45,917,576

Uses of Funds:

Repayment of Prior Notes	$41,335,815
Capitalized Interest Reserve	820,544
Debt Service Reserve	2,848,370
Cost of Issuance	912,847
Total	$45,917.576

First Principal Payment Date: March 1, 2002.

Assessment District Financing and Business Improvement Districts

Assessment district financing collects a special charge from property owners or businesses in a geographic area to fund needed infrastructure or services. It resembles TIF financing in its focus on defined development areas but creates a revenue stream from a new fee rather than garnering cash from tax increases. Consequently, assessment district financing does not depend on tax base growth to be a feasible financing tool—an important advantage over TIF. Assessment financing also requires that the beneficiaries of new services or improvements pay for their cost, necessitating a linkage between the assessment fee and benefits received (Snyder & Stegman, 1986). Thus, assessment district fees are usually based on property value, property square footage, street frontage, or another formula that is tied to the benefits generated by the district's funded activities. Assessment districts, like TIF, are frequently used to finance infrastructure. However, although TIF emphasizes the redevelopment of blighted areas, developers and local governments commonly use assessment districts to finance infrastructure needed to open up new areas for development (Snyder & Stegman, 1986). A second application of assessment districts, more relevant to economic development practitioners, is the business improvement district (BID) through which assessment district fees fund special services and activities to revitalize commercial districts.

Assessment districts are one of the oldest and most common municipal finance tools, dating back to 1691 when they financed street and drain construction in New York (State of California, 1997). Assessment districts are widely used to finance services, facilities, and infrastructure within a defined geography. Libraries, parks and recreational facilities, roads, water and sanitary facilities, and utilities are examples of facilities that can be financed through assessment districts. The prevalence of assessment districts is indicated by data from the 1997 U.S. Census of Governments, which counted 34,683 special districts. Although this figure includes special districts that are not used for assessment financing, including TIF districts, it provides a good proxy for them and shows their extensive use.[19] The growing number of assessment districts also suggests their increasing importance as a financing vehicle. Special districts increased in number by 17% from 1987 to 1997 while other local government units showed little change. California and Illinois were the most active users of these districts, each having over 3,000 (U.S. Census Bureau, 2000).

Despite variations in state law, most assessment districts employ a common financing process. A special district is first established that defines the geographic area and beneficiaries of the infrastructure or services to be provided. Next, a district plan is formulated that addresses the improvements or services to be provided, their cost, and the required assessments to be charged. Third, the affected property owners, businesses, or other beneficiaries petition the local government for authorization to create the district and must be granted approval by the governing authority. Once the assessment district is established, it collects the assessment and uses the resulting revenue to fund services or to repay debt issued by the district to fund infrastructure, or both. In some cases, the district is created purely as a financing entity to raise revenue for the infrastructure or services that are delivered by existing entities. In other cases, the assessment district constitutes a separate organization that constructs and maintains the infrastructure and/or provides services.

Assessment districts offer some advantages over conventional municipal debt financing and TIF.[20] First, because fees are tied to direct beneficiaries, it can be a fairer and more efficient way to finance improvements. For example, a new sewer treatment plant needed for an expanding industrial park could be financed by an assessment on the firms in that park rather than by all taxpayers in the community. Because these firms are paying for the plant through an assessment, they also have an incentive to reduce their discharge and minimize the plant's required size and cost. In this manner, assessment financing can promote more efficient service delivery. Second, assessment districts allow the level of services to vary with different demands for public goods within a community. Thus, a business district that wants more security services or a group of homeowners that wants more recreation facilities can fund them without imposing costs on other taxpayers. Third, it provides a mechanism to fund projects and services when budgetary constraints or tax limitations prevent general government funding, but specific groups are willing to pay for them. Thus, it can reduce political conflict over a project because local users and beneficiaries will pay for it. Finally, assessment districts provide a more stable and predictable financing stream than TIF or user fees because a new assessment is set and collected based on the revenues needed to finance the desired project or service.

On the other hand, there are disadvantages to assessment district financing. It is a more complex and expensive form of financing than general obligation or conventional revenue bonds. The time and expense to create a special district add to transaction costs, and the higher credit risk from the district's limited geographic revenue base increases borrowing costs. Second, unfair and inefficient fiscal practices can occur when an assessment district is manipulated for political expediency. For example, the assessment district and contribution formula can shift costs unfairly either from existing property owners to new residents and property owners or from current to future generations of users. Because new and future generations of property owners have little political representation, a strong potential exists for this type of cost shifting with assessment districts. A third problem is that assessment districts can fragment service delivery and create coordination problems when multiple districts that provide similar or overlapping services exist in an area. This fragmentation can also create disparities in important services between wealthier and less well-off sections within a city or region. Finally, assessment districts facilitate overbuilding, speculative development, and sprawl when a developer or municipality uses them to fund infrastructure in new development areas, especially when the assessments are paid by future residents. Because current taxpayers do not incur the costs of expanding developed land, there is less political scrutiny and countervailing pressure to finance the growth in developed land.

Business Improvement Districts

Business improvement districts (BIDs) are a type of assessment financing used to improve a defined business area, typically a downtown commercial district. Through a BID, local businesses and/or property owners agree to assess themselves to fund services, projects, and activities that address pressing problems and enhance their district's attractiveness. State laws authorize BIDs, set the specific process and requirements for their creation, and create their funding mechanisms and powers. In most states, private parties that include at least a majority of district property owners petition the local government to create a BID. Once established, the local government collects an assessment for the BID, providing it a steady funding stream. BID activities are usually defined through a planning process with downtown property owners, businesses and institutions, and negotiations with the local government (Houston, 1997; Mitchell, 2001).[21] Unlike most special districts and TIF districts, BIDs finance and undertake more diverse improvements than infrastructure. These include "soft" services such as public safety, cleaning, beautification, special events, promotion, and marketing that improve the environment for businesses, shoppers, and employees and attract more shoppers and businesses to the district. Thus, BIDs provide a tool for downtown and neighborhood commercial districts to fund amenities and market themselves to compete more effectively with suburban shopping centers.

According to a study by Jerry Mitchell (2001), over 404 BIDs existed in the United States in 1999, encompassing 43 states and most large cities. BID use mushroomed in the 1990s, with 60% created after 1990. California, New York, and Wisconsin, with 73, 63, and 54 districts, respectively, accounted for almost half of all U.S. BIDs. Through a survey of 264 BIDs, Mitchell collected data on their budgets, staffing, and services. The median BID had a budget of $200,000, employed 2 full-time staff, and operated in a city with a population of 104,445. However, BIDs varied by budget and community size; the smallest BID had an $8,000 budget whereas the largest spent $15 million. BID communities ranged in size from 1,000 to over 7 million (Mitchell, 2001).

Marketing and district maintenance (cleaning, graffiti and snow removal, etc.) were the most common BID activities, but Mitchell found that BID services varied with city size. Overall, 78% of BIDs were very involved in marketing, and 58% were active in maintenance activities. Public advocacy work and capital improvement projects were also common activities with half of surveyed BIDs undertaking them. However, BIDs in large cities[22] provided the broadest range of services and were more likely to conduct maintenance and public safety activities. Small city BIDs, on the other hand, focused primarily on marketing and capital improvement projects (Mitchell, 2001). Philadelphia's Center City BID, one of the nation's largest BIDs with an $11.9 budget and 2,100 property owners, demonstrates BIDs' potential role in downtown improvement. Center City BID's activities include extensive cleaning and maintenance services (daily sidewalk sweeping and cleaning, graffiti removal, and landscape maintenance); public safety and crime prevention through supplemental security, outreach, education, and crime mapping; streetscape installation and maintenance; and active downtown promotion with advertising and special events. An important focus for Center City BID is attracting more suburban shoppers by creating a safer, more attractive and easily navigated environment

(Ryan, 2000). BIDs, however, also operate on a smaller scale to strengthen neighborhood commercial centers. In Oklahoma City, the Stockyards City BID generates $88,000 from 75 property owners to support a nonprofit Main Street program, which promotes the district through direct marketing and special events, advocates for city services and improvements, helps firms secure city permits and technical assistance, and facilitates new business recruitment.

BIDs are an effective funding mechanism for commercial district revitalization, but their benefits and effective practices transcend financing. They organize property owners, merchants, and local governments to define common goals and agendas, formulate improvement plans, and work together to implement them. By formulating a shared agenda and expanding the commitment of property owners and businesses to improvement efforts, BIDs also generate individual actions that reinforce their collectively funded activities. In response to the BID, businesses and property owners often improve their buildings, increase their own cleaning and crime prevention efforts, and expand their marketing. Thus, BIDs need to provide ongoing communication, encouragement, and assistance to leverage these private actions and sustain commitment to the overall revitalization plan. Because most BIDs are established for a fixed period, regular outreach and communication also builds stakeholder support for BID reauthorization. BIDs also motivate increased public sector support for commercial district improvements. When the private sector commits funds to improve an area, it has greater political and moral authority to seek government action. Government support may involve direct funding,[23] a commitment to improve city services, establishing more consistent zoning and design regulations, or expanded city investment in infrastructure and key development projects. Thus, BIDs have an important advocacy role to coordinate public and private action to advance a shared revitalization vision for their business districts.

Case Study: Downtown Orlando TIF District[24]

It is late 1982 and the head of the Orlando Community Redevelopment Agency (CRA) has called you into his office. The city is proceeding with its planned Tax-Increment Financing (TIF) district and you have the task of thinking through how to complete the required tax-increment financing.

Orlando has undergone an economic transformation in the past 10 years. Prior to 1967, the economy of the Orlando Metropolitan Statistical Area (MSA) was based on agriculture and citrus products, tourism, light manufacturing, and industries tied to the nearby Kennedy Space Center. Recently, Orlando has become home to Walt Disney World, other tourist attractions, and growing convention activity that expanded Orlando's trade and service sectors. Orlando also experienced growth in its high-technology industries. These economic changes are matched by rapid population growth, with the MSA population projected to increase by 90% from 1970 to 1985 to 862,000.

Within Orlando, two agencies address downtown revitalization: the Downtown Development District and the Community Redevelopment Agency (CRA). The Orlando Downtown Development District encompasses 1,000 acres in the heart of the city's downtown and is governed by a five-member board that is appointed by the mayor for 3-year terms. Through powers granted by state law, the city council created a 569-acre TIF district within the larger Downtown Development District in 1980 and established the CRA to foster redevelopment of this subdistrict. The CRA is authorized to collect incremental tax revenues within its 569-acre area and to issue tax-exempt revenue bonds backed by these tax increments to finance capital improvements based on a redevelopment plan approved by the city council. The annual tax increment available to repay bonds is a function of increases in the district's assessed property value above the assessed value when the redevelopment plan was adopted (the base year) and the tax rate adopted by the respective taxing jurisdictions (city, county, and school district).

The Downtown Orlando Redevelopment Plan was adopted by the city council in July 1982.[25] This plan set the base-year tax assessment for all property in the TIF district as the FY1981 amount of $136.56 million, which will be used to determine incremental tax revenues. Capital improvements under the plan will be implemented over 10 years and include upgrading of infrastructure systems (water, sewer, and storm drainage), improved traffic circulation, enhancement of the pedestrian environment, and new parking.

Developers have expressed interest in the area with several projects close to development, others in the financing stages, and others in the planning phase. A consultant was hired by the CRA to evaluate the planned development projects and forecast increases in TIF district assessed tax values from new development projects and increases in existing property values. The consultant classified projects into three categories by their likelihood of development (most probable projects, probable projects, and uncertain projects) and estimated the incremental tax assessment for each project in total over the next 10 years (detailed in Tables 15.1 and 15.2). Note that the tax increment has two components: increases from new development projects and overall appreciation of all property values. Anticipated new construction includes 1.23 million square feet of office space to be completed by 1989, a 119,000-square foot retail marketplace slated to open in 1988, five new hotels planned to open between 1985 and 1989, 125 new residential units to open in 1985, and a large three-phase, mixed-use development with over 1 million square feet of office space, 550 hotel rooms, 100,000 square feet of retail space, and a 200,000-square foot trade mart.

Incremental taxes from taxing authorities, including the city, Orange County, and the Downtown Development Board, will be diverted to the TIF district trust fund to support the financing of capital projects. For each property within the TIF district, 95% of the tax increment (the difference between property taxes in a given year and those based on the 1981 assessment) is contributed to the trust fund. Thus, projected TIF revenues equal

Table 15.1 Projected Assessed Values for Projects by Probability, FY1983 to FY1992

Fiscal Year	Most Probable Projects ($000)	Probable Projects ($000)	Uncertain Probability Projects ($000)	Total Assessment for All Projects ($000)
1983	40,000	18,555	—	58,555
1984	7,426	—	—	7,426
1985	10,000	—	—	10,000
1986	60,000	—	5,296	65,296
1987	34,094	—	—	34,094
1988	33,073	3,868	85	37,026
1989	5,345	46,883	1,024	53,252
1990	75,061	79,292	9,427	163,780
1991	12,240	13,513	6,183	31,936
1992	30,000	10,296	—	40,296

Table 15.2 Projected Tax Assessment and Tax Increment Revenue

Fiscal Year	Prior Year Assessed Value ($000)	Appreciation in Assessed Value at 10% ($000)	Assessed Value From New Projects ($000)	Total Assessed Value ($000)	Assessed Value Increment[a] ($000)	Tax Rate Per $000 of Value	Projected Tax Increment ($000)
1983	136,557	13,656	58,555	208,768	72,211	10.9474	791
1984	208,768	20,877	7,426	237,071	100,514	9.8473	990
1985	237,071	23,707	10,000	270,778	134,221	9.2925	1,247
1986	270,778	27,078	65,296	383,152	226,595	10.5466	2,390
1987	363,152	36,315	34,094	433,561	297,004	10.1093	3,003
1988	433,561	43,356	37,026	513,943	377,386	9.6935	3,658
1989	513,943	51,394	53,252	618,589	482,032	9.3002	4,483
1990	618,589	61,859	163,780	844,228	707,671	8.9302	6,320
1991	844,228	84,423	31,936	960,587	824,030	8.6302	7,112
1992	960,587	96,059	40,296	1,096,942	960,385	8.3302	8,000

NOTE:

a. Using base-year assessment of $136,557,000.

95% of the consultant's estimated tax increment. The CRA plans a first phase of capital improvement projects to be undertaken at a cost of $19 million. Your task is to evaluate how much debt the projected TIF revenues can support and recommend how to structure the bond financing to raise the required funds and provide sufficient credit quality to attract investors. The analysis needs to address the following questions:

1. Is the TIF revenue sufficient to borrow the required $19 million dollars, assuming a 10-year serial bond issue with a 10% interest rate on each maturity and required debt service coverage of 1.40? If there

is not enough revenue, how can the structure and terms of the bond financing be changed to raise $19 million?

2. What are the major credit issues and risks that investors will have with a TIF bond financing? Is there sufficient credit strength to support the financing based on the TIF revenues alone?

3. How can the CRA strengthen the credit quality of the TIF bonds?

Endnotes

1. Litvak and Daniels (1979), *Innovations and Development Finance*, discuss many of the early innovations in state development finance during the 1970s as well as provide an excellent framework for thinking about state development finance policy.

2. For a concise history of the legislative restrictions placed on industrial development bonds, see National Council for Urban Economic Development (1995b), *Small Issue Industrial Development Bonds: A Finance Tool for Economic Development,* pp. 1–9.

3. The discussion of IDB restrictions is based on National Council for Urban Economic Development (1995b), *Small Issue Industrial Development Bonds: A Finance Tool for Economic Development,* pp. 13–14, 22–25.

4. See U.S. Census Bureau (2000), Statistical Abstract of the United States: 2000, Table 506.

5. A state or local government guarantee may be politically difficult to obtain, given the precedent that it establishes. Government guarantees should be used carefully when there is a clear public interest served and the public benefit generated is commensurate with the financial costs entailed.

6. Information on the Arkansas programs is based on e-mail correspondence with ADFA staff.

7. This state guarantee is available to pay debt service on ADFA bonds issued to capitalize the guarantee reserve fund if its reserves are inadequate.

8. This summary of the PEDFA Composite bond program is based on an interview with Kim Kaufman, PEDFA executive director and a June 2002 presentation by Kim Kaufman and Tim Frenz.

9. Typical costs are $10,000 to $11,000 in legal fees, issuance fees of .25% to .375% and a bank commitment fee between 0% and 1%.

10. TIF was first used in California in 1952 to provide matching funds for federal grants and then grew to be allowed in 28 states by 1984, 44 in 1992, and 48 today. See J. Drew Klacik and Samuel Nunn (2001), "A Primer on Tax Increment Financing," in Johnson and Man, editors, *Tax Increment Financing and Economic Development: Uses, Structures and Impacts* for a history and overview of its use.

11. John L. Mikesel (2001) discusses the use of sales tax-based TIF in 10 states and the District of Columbia in "Nonproperty Tax Increment Programs for Economic Development: A Review of Alternative Programs," in Johnson and Man, editors, *Tax Increment Financing and Economic Development: Uses, Structures and Impact.*

12. Some state laws provide for adjustments to the base year assessment and tax revenue.

13. See Johnson and Kriz (2001), "A Review of State Tax Increment Financing Laws" in Johnson and Man, editors, *Tax Increment Financing and Economic Development: Uses, Structures and Impact.*

14. The process summarized in this section draws upon the discussion in Klacik and Nunn (2001) and Paetsch and Dahlstrom (1990).

15. See Haulk and Montarti (2000) for a critique of TIF practices in Pittsburgh.

16. Mikesel (2001) cites a study of sales tax increment financing that found that most TIF districts were designed for specific retail strip or mall developments and did not contribute to redeveloping blighted center city commercial areas.

17. This summary is found on pages 102 to 106.

18. Man (2001) found methodological problems with the Chicago study that include the variable used to measure property tax growth and the authors' interpretation of their results.

19. This figure does not include school districts, which numbered 13,726 in 1997.

20. This discussion of the advantages and disadvantages of assessment districts draws upon Snyder and Stegman (1986), Chapter 6.

21. Although the time period to create a BID varies with state requirements and the preexisting organization, an average period to complete the planning, petitioning, and approval process for a BID is 18 months.

22. Mitchell's (2001) large city classification had a population range of 736,015 to 7 million.

23. For example, Dayton's downtown BID receives one third of its funds from business assessments, one third from city funding, and one third from the county government.

24. This case study is adapted from one originally written by Theo Selzer based on consulting reports prepared by Hammer Siler George Associates for the City of Orlando.

25. This plan has been amended several times since its adoption in 1982.

PART VI

Managing Development Finance Institutions

16

Program Planning
and Design

Defining a targeting and financing strategy is the first and central
management issue for development finance programs, as stressed in
the discussion of management challenges for each institution. Up to this
point, however, the issue has been flagged without considering how to
prepare an effective strategy. This chapter, the first of three addressing
the management of development finance institutions, presents a framework for the research and planning needed to set strategy and to design a
new institution, program, or financial product to implement the strategy.
Although program planning is especially critical to design a new entity or
program, it is an important ongoing function for all development finance
organizations. Faced with dynamic economies and capital markets,
practitioners need to periodically assess how demographic and economic
trends alter their development goals and opportunities, the nature of
capital supply gaps, and how to adapt their products and services
in response to new conditions (Lehr, 1998). The program planning
approaches presented in this chapter are part of a management tool kit
for effective development finance institutions; they address core capacities
to monitor the economic and capital market environment and apply this
information to updating, improving, and expanding financial products
and development services.

Program planning integrates four factors into program strategy and
design (see Figure 16.1). First, economic development goals are set, which
are critical to defining customers and setting the targeting strategy. This
step is particularly important because it sets the framework and constraints
for other planning tasks. A program aimed at creating wealth in a rural
region through new business creation targets different customers than an
entity whose goal is retaining and expanding high-wage jobs by supporting
the competitiveness and growth of manufacturers. Consequently, each program will pursue different questions to understand the supply, demand, and
capacity factors that will shape its development finance strategy. Market
demand is the second element, which should be analyzed to inform targeting decisions and the appropriate products and services to provide. Demand

side information may alter program targeting; for example, a shift in sector targeting and/or geographic focus may be necessary when fewer than expected targeted firms are found within a community. This analysis also identifies unmet demand for financial products and development services to incorporate into the program design. Capital market conditions, the third factor, determine what financial products and services other capital sources supply and indicate potential financing gaps for the program to fill. This supply-side analysis helps practitioners avoid capital substitution by defining financial products that will expand capital availability and understand what related services will strengthen firms' capacity to productively use financing. For the fourth factor, the capacities needed to serve target markets, realize development goals, and achieve sustainable scale are considered. Finally, the findings related to these four design elements are integrated into the overall program strategy and design. The chapter's organization follows this five-part planning framework. Key issues and research methods are elaborated for each factor and illustrated with planning conducted to design the Massachusetts Growth Fund. To help readers apply this framework to a specific program, the chapter concludes with a case study on evaluating expansion opportunities for a microenterprise loan fund.

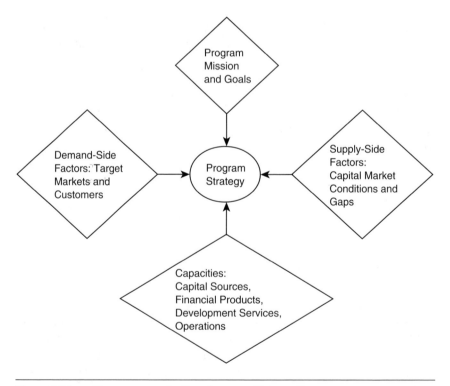

Figure 16.1   Components of a Development Finance Strategy

Defining Development
Goals and Targeting Strategy

Clear goals are the foundation of development finance planning because they frame the potential markets and customers. Goals include desired development outcomes and the geographic area for those outcomes. For development finance planning, broad goals should be refined into measurable and operational goals that provide strategic focus. Operational goals typically fall within four categories: business outcomes, employment outcomes, group outcomes, and place outcomes. Business outcome goals concern the level, type, and location of firms (e.g., increasing the number of new businesses and their success rate or retaining expanding firms within the city). Employment outcomes address the number and type of jobs created and who receives them (e.g., increasing living-wage jobs for low-income workers or expanding entry-level opportunities for youth). Group goals focus on outcomes for specific populations (e.g., increasing employment and earnings for displaced workers or reducing poverty rates among welfare recipients). Place-based goals relate to development outcome in specific areas, such as revitalizing a downtown or neighborhood commercial district or redeveloping a closed military base. The geography for realizing goals can range in scope from multistate regions to subcity areas, such as neighborhoods, enterprise zones, or business districts. In some cases, geographic targets may include a set of smaller areas within a region (e.g., enterprise zones within a state or a city's commercial districts).

Once goals are set, targeting strategies are identified by considering what type of enterprises, projects, and investments are most capable of realizing these goals and which ones are likely to face capital availability problems. Several potential targets may be identified at this stage and then refined by the demand and supply analyses. It is also helpful to formulate ideas about the financing products and development services that are needed to serve these markets and reach economic development goals, which can then be evaluated as part of the demand and supply analyses.

Analysis of secondary demographic and economic data is a valuable input to formulate goals and preliminary targeting strategies. This analysis provides baseline information on (1) the size and geographic distribution of potential customers; (2) indicators of finance and development service needs; and (3) occupations and earnings within industries to assess their potential to meet employment and income goals. In addition to statistical analysis, mapping data with geographic information system (GIS) software may unveil geographic patterns that influence decisions on the appropriate service area and target customers. In lieu of an extended discussion on secondary data analysis and program planning, Table 16.1 summarizes the major secondary data sources and links them to program planning information needs.[1]

Table 16.1   Secondary Data Sources Used to Plan Targeting Strategies

Data Series Source and Name	Data Provider and Web Site	Description and Type of Data Available	Development Finance Program Planning Uses
Census of Population and Housing	Bureau of the Census (www.census.gov)	Detailed household-based information on population and housing characteristics for geographic areas at 10-year intervals.	Identify size, geographic concentration, and development needs of target populations. Identify development needs within geographic areas.
Population Estimates Program	Bureau of the Census (www.census.gov)	Annual data on population size for states, metro areas, counties, and places.	Update data and track trends for target populations.
Small Area Income and Poverty Estimates Program	Bureau of the Census (www.census.gov)	Median household income and poverty rates for states and counties. Produced every 2 to 3 years.	Identify development needs within geographic areas.
Economic Census	Bureau of the Census (www.census.gov)	Establishments, employment, payroll, and output for detailed industries by state, county, city, and town. Produced every 5 years.	Analyze economic trends, major job sources by industry. Identify development needs within geographic areas. Identify target industries.
Current Employment Statistics	Bureau of Labor Statistics (www.bls.gov)	Employment and average wages for major industries in states and metro areas. Monthly and annual data.	Analyze economic trends, major jobs sources by industry. Identify development needs within geographic areas. Identify target industries.
Covered Employment ES-2002 Data	Bureau of Labor Statistics (www.bls.gov) State labor market agencies	Establishments, employment, payroll and average wages for detailed industries by state, county, city and town. Monthly and annual data.	Analyze economic trends, major jobs sources by industry. Identify development needs within geographic areas. Identify target industries.
County Business Patterns	Bureau of the Census (www.census.gov)	Establishments, employment, payroll by business size class for detailed industries by state and county. Some zip code data. Produced annually.	Analyze economic trends, major jobs sources by industry. Identify development needs within geographic areas. Identify target industries.
Occupational Employment Statistics	Bureau of Labor Statistics (www.bls.gov)	Employment and earnings data by occupation for states and metro areas. National data on occupations and earnings by industry.	Analyze job structure and wages by industry and area. Identify development needs within geographic areas. Identify target industries.
Local Area Unemployment Statistics	Bureau of Labor Statistics (www.bls.gov)	Labor force, employment, and unemployment for states, metro areas, counties, and cities of 25,000 or more.	Identify employment needs and unemployment trends within geographic areas.
Multiple data series	(www.econdata.net)	Web portal with descriptions and links to many data sources.	All of the above.

Growth Fund Example

A target industry analysis for the Massachusetts Growth Fund also shows how secondary data analysis can be used to identify potential customers.[2] The Economic Stabilization Trust, a Massachusetts quasi-public fund that provides management assistance and financing to traditional manufacturers, was interested in expanding its financing programs to high-growth manufacturing and technology-based firms. It commissioned a study to identify the state's high-growth manufacturing and value-added industries, assess capital gaps, and design financial products to address any identified gaps. Secondary data analysis was an important first step that identified candidate industries to assess for capital gaps. Table 16.2 summarizes the results from this analysis, which used the ES-2002 data series to identify industries with high job growth, above average wages, and a critical mass of firms. County business patterns supplied figures for the share of small firms in each

Table 16.2   Secondary Data Analysis Results From Massachusetts Growth Fund Study

SIC Code	Industry Description	MA Job Growth 1995 to 1999	U.S.Job Growth 1995 to 1999	Average Annual Wage 1999	Number of Establishments 1999	Percentage of Firms With <50 Employees 1997
282	Plastics Materials and Synthetic Resins	31.9%	−2%	$59,000	38	67%
283	Drugs	31.6%	15%	$95,000	85	65%
289	Miscellaneous Chemical Products	7.7%	−1%	$64,000	65	80%
308	Miscellaneous Plastic Products	4.5%	4%	$39,000	399	72%
345	Screw Machine Products	14.1%	7%	$41,000	82	83%
347	Coating, Engraving, and Allied Services	4.4%	11%	$34,000	206	90%
358	Refrigeration and Service Industry Machinery	8.7%	5%	$45,000	42	80%
361	Electric Transmission and Distribution Equipment	22.9%	−1%	$55,000	39	69%
366	Communications Equipment	4.2%	−1%	$83,000	94	60%
384	Surgical, Medical, and Dental Instruments	17.4%	7%	$67,000	189	73%
7372	Prepackaged Software	15.4%	51%	$86,000	964	87%
7373	Computer Integrated Systems Design	72.2%	59%	$87,000	582	91%
	Massachusetts, All Industries			$40,331		
	Massachusetts, All Manufacturers			$51,742		

SOURCES: Karl F. Seidman Consulting Services (2001b, Table 2) © 2001 by CommCorp and the Commonwealth of Massachusetts.

industry that are the most likely enterprises to face capital availability problems. From the secondary data analysis, five industries surfaced as potential targets based on having (1) state job growth above the national rate; (2) average annual wages above the statewide manufacturing average; and (3) at least 50 firms with 50 or fewer employees. These five industries were drugs; miscellaneous chemical products; communications equipment; surgical, medical, and dental instruments; and computer-integrated systems design. Prepackaged software was added as a sixth target, despite having a state job growth rate below the national average due to its large size and high wages.

Assessing Demand

Once preliminary target markets are identified, a more thorough analysis is needed to evaluate unmet demand for capital and design-appropriate financing roles and development services. Demand analysis also provides initial estimates of the expected financing volumes and required program scale. Six questions are addressed in this analysis: (1) What is the size of the target market and its key characteristics and trends? (2) What are firms' financing needs and how are they currently addressed? (3) What are the primary obstacles to firms' access to capital? (4) What development services and financing interventions best address these obstacles? (5) What specific financing products do firms need and seek? (6) What is the expected demand (i.e., the likely number and amount of loans and other services provided per year)? In conducting this analysis, it is important to distinguish between perceived need and actual demand. Potential customers may think that they need capital but lack the capacity to qualify for financing or productively use it. Other firms may be able to use financing but prefer to rely on internal funds, even at the price of slower growth and lower profits. Moreover, technical assistance and other development services will likely increase the pool of enterprises (or other customers) that seek financing and meet investment standards. Both influences must be considered in projecting actual demand among enterprises that will seek and qualify for financing.

Demand analysis relies on multifaceted information sources that include secondary data, surveys, key informant interviews, focus groups, and knowledge from existing experience. Secondary data helps determine the size and characteristics of potential customer groups and provides some demand indicators, but more detailed information is needed to gauge likely demand and evaluate specific financial products and services. Through surveys, practitioners learn directly from customers and gain more detailed information on their demand for capital and experience securing it. Surveys are especially helpful in three areas: (1) detailing firms' financing needs and the current capital sources used to address them; (2) uncovering firms' experience with existing capital providers and its implications for likely capital gaps; and (3) assessing target customers' interest in specific products and services. Surveys, however, require significant time and effort to gain a good response rate, tabulate data, and analyze results. Given the time commitment and technical issues involved, hiring a professional survey firm or consultant is often the most effective way to complete a survey. Key informant interviews provide an efficient way to gain information on target markets by drawing on the knowledge of experts. These interviews test findings from secondary data and survey analyses, generate ideas for new products and services, and build support and buy-in from key stakeholders for a new program. Key informants are chosen based on their knowledge and breadth of experience with financing and development assistance for target markets and to represent a diverse range of institutions. They can include trade association leaders, economic development practitioners, lenders at conventional and alternative financial institutions, technical assistance providers, and private advisors (i.e., accountants, consultants, and lawyers). A standard set of questions is used for each interview, although it may vary by type of informant. Interviews should be documented so that notes can be analyzed to identify consistent themes and responses.

Focus groups are another option to gain nuanced information on capital market gaps and demand for specific products and services. By bringing together six to twelve participants, they allow for more dialogue and exploration of key issues among similar stakeholders whose opinions are critical to program success. Therefore, separate focus groups might be organized with technical assistance providers, other financing entities, and target firms to gain each group's view of capital availability problems and their ideas for and likely participation in proposed solutions. By exploring the later issues, focus groups are especially useful to develop and test ideas for new financial products and services. Moreover, they may identify implementation obstacles and promising partners by uncovering differing values, priorities, and biases across stakeholders. To undertake this research, the specific types of focus groups to conduct must be delineated (e.g., clients, lenders, government agencies, etc.). Next, a discussion guide is developed that tailors questions to each group based on the information that it can provide. A focus group with lenders might concentrate on their view of capital gaps and how to address constraints on their ability to extend capital whereas one with firms would emphasize their views on specific products and services to address unmet financing needs. One of the most difficult tasks is recruiting focus group participants. Although incentives, such as meals and cash payments, help attract attendees, it is wise to recruit twice the desired number of participants because a high percentage of no-shows is common. To properly facilitate and document the focus group, a separate moderator is needed to guide the discussion while another person records and takes notes on the conversation. Finally, the results should be summarized and analyzed to identify common issues and themes and their implications for program design and implementation.

For existing development finance institutions, valuable demand-side information is also gained from compiling and reviewing data from field experience. Both changing needs among existing customers and expansion opportunities in new markets can emerge from analyzing trends in inquiries, applications, and loan denials and by querying marketing and lending staff about their observations on changed practices among other lenders, emerging sources of demand, and altered conditions or challenges among core clients.

Growth Fund Example[3]

For the Massachusetts Growth Fund study, key informant interviews and a telephone survey of firms were conducted to evaluate financing gaps and the potential demand for mezzanine debt products in the six candidate industries. Interview subjects included economic development professionals, industry association staff, private and quasi-public lenders, and venture capitalists. The survey sample was selected randomly from state directories of manufacturing and technology firms. This research produced critical information on capital supply gaps and the required characteristics of financial products to address these gaps. It found that firms in these high-growth industries relied heavily on equity financing from founders, angel investors, and venture capitalists but that debt still supplied 50% or more of the capital in all but one industry. Second, firms were facing more difficulty securing debt and equity as lenders and equity investors tightened their standards and reduced their supply in response to an economic downturn and bear stock market. Third, the relative use of debt and equity varied by industry, with drug and software firms primarily financed with equity. This suggested that these industries would be less promising targets for any new debt-based financing program. Finally, several implications for specific financial products emerged from the research. Compared with the Trust's core clientele of traditional manufacturers, the firms in high-growth industries required more capital to fund rapid expansion and longer repayment periods to reinvest cash flow to finance growth and to address the extended time frame needed to achieve stable profitability. Consequently, a new loan program targeted to these industries would need substantial initial capitalization to supply this larger size and long-term debt.

Analyzing Capital Market
Supply and Identifying Financing Gaps _____

Understanding capital supply conditions is central to program planning. A study of the institutions that provide capital to firms, projects, and households in the target region addresses three key design issues: (1) defining the financing gaps faced by target customers; (2) identifying the obstacles to filling these gaps that a new product, program, or institution must tackle; and (3) assessing the potential competition and capital substitution risk for the proposed financing roles. The research process for supply-side analysis begins by identifying the capital sources that serve target customers in the geographic area being studied, including both private and public organizations and formal and informal sources. Formal institutions consist of depository institutions (commercial banks, savings banks, and credit unions), nonbank finance companies, venture capital firms, and public and nonprofit entities. Informal sources include angel investors, family members, suppliers, and rotating credit associations. Although data on formal institutions is far easier to come by, it is important to understand the contribution of informal capital sources and their problems and limitations. Once the major capital sources are inventoried, information on their market environment, available capital and financial products, and investment policies is collected and analyzed. This analysis focuses on capital availability problems and their causes (e.g., limited competition, regulatory barriers, high transaction and information costs, and potential discrimination). One indicator of competition is the number and type of financial institutions serving the community and the distribution of capital among them. A small number of institutions serving an area or the concentration of deposits and other capital among a few institutions indicates limited competition and the potential for supply gaps in high-risk or complex financing. With deregulation, remote banking, and a growing number of nontraditional financial institutions, households and firms are increasingly likely to obtain financing outside of banks, and the capital supply analysis needs to encompass this expanded and more complex marketplace. The study should assess how these other capital sources affect competition, even if the available information is qualitative. A second focus is to understand what financial products are supplied to target customers and any resulting capital gaps. This analysis begins with the stated products and services supplied by each capital source but must also consider how market trends and the culture and policies of key institutions affect the actual financing extended and the type of borrowers that can meet investment standards. Insight into capital supply gaps often emerges from these details of lending and investment practices, such as high loan or investment thresholds, risk-averse or overly rigid credit standards, or biases toward or against certain industries. A third issue is the availability and use of public, quasi-public, and nonprofit finance programs that address common capital gaps. Because SBA programs are the largest and most widely available ones, it is especially important to analyze data on their utilization. When firms and banks are not utilizing SBA, nonprofit, and government programs that address capital gaps, then expanded marketing and training to help lenders use these programs and/or technical assistance and loan packaging services to address demand-side constraints may be a more appropriate response than creating a new program or financial institution.

Although capital supply analysis uses the same research methods as demand-side research, data sources and analytical questions are different. Extensive secondary data is available via the Internet to assist with a capital supply analysis. Key data sources for federally insured and regulated depository institutions are the Federal Deposit Insurance Corporation (FDIC) and the Federal Financial Institution Examination Council (FFIEC). The SBA supplies some data on its loans and loan guarantees via the Web with more detailed information available through regional offices. Several private firms compile directories and data for the banking and venture capital industries.[4] Table 16.3 summarizes valuable secondary data sources for capital market supply analysis. EconData.net is a useful Internet portal with links to most capital market and economic data sources (www.econdata.net).[5]

Table 16.3   Secondary Data Sources for Capital Supply Analysis

Data Provider	Web Site	Type of Information	Uses
FDIC	www3.fdic.gov/idasp//main.asp	Identifies current bank offices and branches in an area.	Identify banks and number of offices in area. Assess bank competition.
FDIC	www3.fdic.gov/sod/index.asp	Deposit data by banks and geographic areas down to zip code level.	Analyze level and trends in bank deposits. Assess bank competition. Identify banks with the largest deposit base.
FDIC	www.fdic.gov/bank/index.html	Financial data on individual banks.	Assess financial performance and lending for key banks.
NCUA	www.ncua.gov	Directory of credit unions. Financial data on individual credit unions.	Identify credit unions in area and their deposits. Assess financial performance and loans for key credit unions.
FFIEC	www.ffiec.gov	HMDA Data CRA Ratings Data on Small Business and Small Farm Loans Call Reports	Identify major small business lenders. Analyze market share and trends in home mortgage and small business lending. Assess CRA performance and loans for key banks. Assess home lending and denial rates for low-income area and minorities.
Venture Economics	www.ventureeconomics.com	Data on venture capital investment for state and metro region.	Assess venture capital supply and trends for different industries and firm stages.
National Venture Capital Association	www.nvca.org	Data and reports on VC industry trends and issues.	Analysis of the impact of VC industry trends on the supply of equity capital.

Comparative and trend analysis are especially important for assessing capital supply issues. Through comparison with other areas, significant differences are identified in total capital supply, market structure (both the extent of competition and what types of financial institutions manage local capital), and how capital is being invested. Comparison areas depend on the size and location of the region being studied, but the metropolitan area and state are important reference areas to use. Counties and cities also provide useful comparisons for city-level or neighborhood-level studies. Comparisons with similar areas both within and outside the subject state and region are also valuable, especially when gauging capital market conditions relative to economic competitors. Thus, a capital supply analysis for technology-based firms in Portland, Oregon, might compare city-level data with the state and metropolitan region but also with city-level data for Seattle, San Francisco, San Jose, and Oakland. Trend analysis indicates how regional capital markets are changing and responding to new economic and demographic conditions. A key trend to study is the overall growth in capital supply—indicated by the number and type of financial institutions, bank deposits, small business loans, and venture capital investments—and how supply growth compares to changes in demand indicators, including population and household growth (overall and for target groups) and firm and employment growth (overall and for target industries). As with the other data items, trends for the study region should be contrasted with comparison areas.

Secondary data analysis should be supplemented with key informant interviews, surveys, and focus groups conducted with financial institutions, technical assistance providers, and other experts to understand the detailed lending policies and practices of key capital sources. Critical issues to address in this research include the business strategies and target markets that inform financing activities, loan and investment terms offered (including the minimum and maximum sizes), investment and lending criteria, key trends affecting capital availability, and the perceived financing gaps and obstacles faced by target customers. Individual firms should also be queried on their experience raising capital from different institutions. The greatest challenge to gaining this information is convincing busy managers to participate. For surveys, sponsorship by a business or banking association can increase response rates whereas a personal relationship or referral is helpful to secure a key informant interview. Focus groups are particularly hard to organize among private entities when the subject concerns business strategies and policies that may be considered confidential. Individual interviews and surveys, which promise to keep answers confidential, will be more effective.

To conclude the analysis, the demand- and supply-side research is synthesized to determine specific capital gaps, their causes, and the appropriate programmatic response to address them. Conclusions on capital availability that emerge from analyzing capital sources are compared with the demand-side information on firms' need for capital and their experience securing it from different capital sources. A convergence of findings from both parts of the market provides strong evidence that the identified capital gap exists. The reasons behind these supply gaps also need to be understood because they affect decisions on the best way to address the problem. Gaps in the supply of low- to moderate-risk capital within a banking market with many competitors favor interventions to expand supply through existing financial institutions without creating a new institution or program. On the other hand, when financial institutions are ignoring a significant market due to limited competition or core business strategies, then the creation of a new financial institution to address the supply gap is warranted. Similarly, the limited supply of high-risk capital, and/or limited local capacity to manage these investments, also supports establishing new entities or programs that will build the capacity to raise and manage such capital. These conclusions also need to detail the specific terms of financial products and development services that will address the capital supply gap. The next section uses the example of the Massachusetts Growth Fund to show how the supply-side and demand-side results were integrated to design a new financing product.

Because capital markets are dynamic and cyclical, supply conditions should be reevaluated periodically to uncover emerging capital availability problems and reassess how well existing programs match the new market environment. Although the development finance entity's ongoing experience serving its customers uncovers new problems and opportunities, a formal analysis provides a more rigorous assessment of capital market changes and formulates specific proposals to translate this knowledge into program changes. By incorporating capital market analysis into their regular strategic planning process, development finance institutions can bring this critical information to bear in updating their goals, near-term plans, and long-term initiatives.

Growth Fund Supply Analysis

The analysis of capital availability for the targeted industries was based on key informant interviews with lenders, venture capitalists, and economic development professionals, supplemented with data on trends in private and public equity markets. Both sources indicated a shift toward large investments for both venture capitalists and banks that limited the availability of private equity financing below several million dollars and bank loans that required detailed underwriting below $250,000 to $500,000. A tightening of bank credit standards and two recent mergers also reduced the supply of bank debt, in part, because banks reduced their loan-to-value ratios and valued collateral more conservatively. These trends posed problems for high-growth firms with large working capital needs and collateral that was perceived as high-risk, such as foreign receivables and/or specialized inventory. Most high-technology lenders also focused on serving venture capital-backed companies, which limited debt sources for privately held firms and companies out of favor with venture capitalists. A declining stock market also reduced capital availability by diminishing the wealth and capacity of angel investors to provide informal debt and equity. A final supply issue was the potential for two active quasi-public corporations, which supplied patient subordinate debt, to finance growth firms. Because one lender focused on large transactions ($1 million or more) and the other served venture-backed companies, funding gaps remained for smaller loans to non-venture capital-funded enterprises. These findings were confirmed by the experience of surveyed firms in five industries who reported difficulties securing financing, especially for working capital purposes, due to their specialized inventory, low valuation of accounts receivables, changes in personnel and policies following bank mergers, and an inability to raise small amounts of equity.

From this analysis, a new investment fund was proposed to supply flexible subordinate debt to finance the expansion of high-growth manufacturing and value-added firms. This fund would provide a subordinate loan product with a 48-month term and a target return of 15% for two purposes: (1) permanent working capital to finance the growth of firms with strong prospects for significant sales growth; and (2) turnaround capital for firms with good growth prospects that are recovering from a cyclical downturn, consolidation, or restructuring. Loans from $100,000 to $1 million would be offered with the greatest demand expected between $500,000 and $1 million. When needed, flexible terms would be available, including a longer repayment term and interest rate step-ups to reduce the loan's near-term cash flow impact. In return for these risks, financing fees and interest rate kickers would be charged to achieve the 15% target return.

Implementation Needs and Resources

Once the appropriate financial products and development services are defined, the resources required for implementation are considered. This evaluation helps practitioners formulate more effective institutional and resource development initiatives to achieve their development goals. An evaluation of implementation needs is best framed around three central challenges faced by development finance entities: (1) securing the scale and form of capital to address the target financing role and achieve sustainability; (2) establishing the operating policies and capabilities to professionally manage the investment process and deliver development services; and (3) building strong relationships with important allies and constituencies. Implementation planning requires detailed thinking about the financial and operational aspects of fulfilling the targeted development finance role, evaluating the feasible institutional options, and considering the available resources and partnerships to implement each option.

On the financial side, key planning issues include (1) the expected annual demand for each financial product and service to be delivered; (2) the amount of capital required to meet demand and generate sufficient revenue to cover operating costs; (3) the liability structure and type of capital necessary to supply the planned financial products and reach the desired scale; and (4) the potential funding sources and investors that can supply this capital. Financial planning also includes forecasting the amount and sources of start-up funds and operating subsidies needed until the new program is sustainable. The demand-side analysis informs the first and third issues, but additional analysis is needed to understand the long-term impact of different liability structures and capital sources. A financial model of the planned program is a valuable tool to both understand the financial requirements to meet demand and cover operating expenses under different scenarios and financial structures. Chapter 18 discusses how to prepare a financial model for a development finance institution that demonstrates how capital sources, financing volumes, loss rates, and operating costs interact to affect a program's capacity to meet demand and operate on sustainable basis. Key outputs from financial modeling analysis include the minimum asset size needed to be sustainable and targets for raising different forms of capital. Financial models also help practitioners refine the design of financial products by assessing the impact of different fee schedules, interest rates or investment returns, and repayment periods on lending (or investment) capacity and financial performance.

Planning for program operations involves anticipating the capabilities needed to implement and sustain an effective development finance institution and how they interact with institutional choice and capitalization. Operating requirements that need to be addressed include (1) the program's governance structure; (2) staff levels and expertise; (3) policies and systems to align operating results with the program's mission and achieve sound financial results; (4) outside professional advisors and services; (5) regulatory approval and compliance for depository institutions; and (5) facilities and equipment. Operating needs will vary with the program's goals, target markets, and local environment, but practitioners should incorporate the experience and lessons from other development finance institutions into their planning. Several critical lessons are summarized here, but readers should refer to Chapters 8 to 14 for a more detailed discussion of operating lessons for specific program models.[6] First, practitioners should develop and use their governance board strategically to provide strong leadership and accountability and to strengthen relationships with key partners. This requires careful planning in three areas: (1) recruiting board members that provide the necessary representation, expertise, and relationships; (2) formulating policies on the board roles, responsibilities, and conflicts of interest; and (3) incorporating board orientation, training, and strategic planning into operating plans (Lehr, 1998). Recruiting a board chair with the standing and relationships to be effective at raising capital is especially important. Second, a long-term and substantial investment in development services probably will be needed to reach the projected levels of demand, especially for historically underserved markets, less developed regions, and emerging industries. Similarly, new programs should plan to establish sound management and lending/investment systems up front to support good decision making and manage losses. These systems are critical to avoiding large losses that can undermine a program's capital base and credibility. (Effective policies and practices for managing the lending and investment process are discussed in Chapter 17.) Because these investments in development services and internal systems require extra staff, consulting services, and collaborations in a program's early years, operating plans need to identify the funding resources and partnerships to implement them. A final lesson is the importance of planning for and developing capacity in marketing and financial management along with the core lending and technical assistance functions (Lehr, 1998). Thus, program plans should address the staffing, professional advisors, and policies needed to implement sound financial management and information systems, manage legal and regulatory issues, undertake ongoing marketing and public relations, and oversee fund-raising and capital management. Although in-house capacity is critical and should be developed as the organization grows, a heavy reliance on pro bono services and consultants will probably be needed in the start-up years.

To guide their implementation planning, practitioners can draw on operating data for the relevant program models that are assembled by trade associations and some researchers. These data provide a good starting point for estimating staffing needs and operating costs. Discussions with trade association staff and managers at institutions that provide comparable services to similar markets are another useful information source for implementation planning.

A final implementation planning issue is identifying relationships and partnerships that are vital to program success and including activities to cultivate them in the program's business plan. Potential collaborators include providers of development services and technical assistance, co-lenders and investors, trade associations, related economic development agencies, elected officials, and community or service organizations that have strong relationships with the target customers. Partnership relationships can and should take many forms, such as board membership, cross and joint marketing initiatives, formal agreements to provide complementary services, periodic meetings to review potential and pending deals, and informal communications. Specific roles should be identified for key partners, tested, and refined through discussions with them, and built into implementation plans. Essential partnerships and ones that will shape important aspects of the program need to be worked out in the early planning stages. Funding sources and providers of key development services fit this category.

Implementation Needs for the Growth Fund

Three implementation needs were identified for the Massachusetts Growth Fund. The first and most critical requirement was raising $6 to $10 million in new capital. New funding was needed to protect the Economic Stabilization Trust in serving its core mission of preserving traditional manufacturing and to attract long-term capital consistent with the Growth Fund's financial products. A minimum capital level of $6 million was chosen to allow the new fund to complete at least 10 deals at an average investment of $600,000, a scale with the potential to generate economic development impacts and establish its presence in this new market. State government appropriations and private community development investment funds were identified as the likely capital sources. Hiring a new fund manger with experience in financing high-growth industries was a second implementation requirement. Existing Trust staff would support this manager by providing credit analysis and overhead functions and assisting with marketing and investment oversight. Staff and other overhead costs would be funded through the 3% financing fee paid by borrowers. The third implementation challenge was to build awareness for the new fund to generate the required deal flow. Strong partnerships with the target industry trade associations and an early marketing program to reach lenders, venture capitalists, economic development professionals, and key business advisors were planned to address this need.

Finalizing Program Strategy and Design

The last step in program planning is integrating the results from all four analytical tasks into an overall strategy. Preparing a written business plan that presents the program strategy and operating plan is a good way to consolidate research into the final program design and demonstrate how the research findings support its feasibility. Moreover, a persuasive business plan advances implementation by convincing others to support the plan through funding, joining the board, providing pro bono services, or other means. Key elements of the plan include (1) the program's mission and development goals (and broad strategy to achieve them); (2) target customers and evidence of their demand for financing and other services; (3) a summary of the financial market environment, capital gaps, and potential competition; (4) specific products and services to be supplied, how they address development needs and market gaps, and their expected levels over time; (5) the program's governance structure, management, and operating plan; (6) background information on the key principals and managers; (7) the implementation calendar and plan; (8) the financial plan with proposed capital sources; and (9) financial projections that demonstrate the program's feasibility and ability to provide any promised return to investors. Box 16.1 shows the content of one such business plan from the outline of an investment prospectus for the Massachusetts Growth Fund.

Two especially important issues in formulating the final program strategy are choosing the appropriate institutional model and designing the specific products and services to supply. The first, and primary, consideration in selecting an institutional model is its capacity to supply the desired type of financing; the selected institution must possess the necessary powers and allow for raising the right type of capital to serve the targeted financing role and customers. A second decision factor is the amount and type of capital

Box 16.1 ｜ Outline for Massachusetts Growth Fund Prospectus

---

1. Executive Summary

2. Purpose and Role of the Fund
   a. Combining economic development and investment objectives through working capital financing for high-growth firms
   b. Support economic and job growth in Massachusetts
   c. Earn a market return for investors

3. Background and Market Environment
   a. Background on Commonwealth Corporation and the Economic Stabilization Trust ("Trust")
   b. Track record and capabilities of the Trust
   c. Analysis of market opportunities and capital gaps

4. The Investment Opportunity and Focus
   a. Targeted industries and firms
   b. Financing role and investment vehicles
   c. Management assistance services
   d. Sample financing transaction
   e. Projected investment returns

5. Fund Structure, Governance, and Management
   a. Legal form of the fund
   b. Fund manager
   c. Relationship to other entities
   d. Board and staff composition with brief bios
   e. Underwriting process
   f. Investment decision making

6. The Investment Offering
   a. Total fund size
   b. Commonwealth Corporation contribution
   c. Minimum investment
   d. Investment closings
   e. Benefits to investors
   f. Return of investment and earnings
   g. Expenses
   h. Accounting

7. Risk Factors for Investors

8. Appendices
   a. Annual report of the Trust
   b. Resumes of Trust management and lending staff
   c. Financial projections

© 2001 by CommCorp and the Commonwealth of Massachusetts

needed to fund the program. Programs that need to reach a very large scale either require the use of a depository institution model (bank or credit union) or must have access to large sums of institutional capital that will invest under an alternative model. The desired level of accountability also affects institutional choice. When direct accountability to customers is a critical goal, then a community development credit union is the logical choice. Revolving loan funds and community development loan funds offer the ability to customize accountability to specific groups of stakeholders. Depository institutions provide broad accountability to the public and applicable laws, including the Community Reinvestment Act, through government regulation. The choice of institutional model is simpler for an existing organization, which can always add new products, programs, or services within its existing institution. However, even a well-established organization should consider whether a different model, implemented through a new subsidiary or affiliate, provides a better vehicle to achieve the goals of a new program.

The decision on which products and services to supply is based on the needs of target customers and the identified capital gaps, but it still entails some important nuances. First, a new financial product should be defined as completely as possible to encompass key financial policies (debt or equity, pricing, term, security, etc.), allowable uses of the financing, and its relationship to customers' overall financing needs. This expansive product description minimizes confusion or inappropriate expectations among both program staff and customers after the produce is rolled out and enhances an organization's understanding of implementation needs. Second, its financial terms must be balanced with the available sources of capital and the program's operating costs. In other words, the product must address the needs of investors and the management entity, along with those of target customers. Some refinement to the pricing, sources of investment return, and repayment periods may be needed to balance all three needs. The Growth Fund, for example, included an up-front 3% fee in the pricing of its financial product to ensure that sufficient revenue was generated to cover the program's operating costs. Finally, the type and timing of development services should be planned carefully. Because these services are often critical to generate demand and realize the expected returns, they should be designed as diligently as the financial products. Moreover, development services may need to be implemented earlier than financial products and be available for some time to generate substantial demand for financing. When this situation exists, it may be appropriate to raise capital in phases that match the pace of new demand and avoid having a large pool of idle funds for several years.

Case Study: Expanding an Urban Microloan Program[7]

Dorchester Bay Economic Development Corporation (DBEDC) is a community development corporation founded in 1979 to reverse economic decline in the Dorchester section of Boston. The CDC has been an active developer of 650 affordable rental and home ownership units and 150,000 square feet of industrial and commercial space and led efforts over many years to revitalize the Upham's Corner and Bowdoin-Geneva commercial districts. DBEDC also established a small business assistance program in 1992 to provide technical assistance and loan packaging to local small firms and Dorchester residents seeking to create a new enterprise. To address a limited supply of small loans and start-up capital for microenterprises, DBEDC founded the Small Business Loan Fund (SBLF) in 1995. After operating the SBLF on a modest scale for several years, DBEDC is seeking to expand the fund to serve more businesses and provide more diverse loan products. The capital for this expansion will come from the SBA Microloan Program, and possibly the SBA 504 program. DBEDC has applied to become a lender under the Microloan Program and is confident that it will secure approval based on feedback from SBA staff. With access to $750,000 in funding, this program will more than double DBEDC's capital base. To fully utilize this program, DBEDC needs a better understanding of the potential demand for microloans and the specific loan products that should be supplied. Some preliminary market data has been collected, but DBEDC wants to undertake a thorough market study to advise it on which customers to target, specific loan products and terms to offer, and how to market the new program.

Loan Fund Background

The SBLF provides loans between $500 and $25,000 to entrepreneurs who either live or work in Dorchester and the adjacent lower Roxbury neighborhood. Businesses must have less than $500,000 in sales to qualify. The maximum loan term is 5 years. Over the past 4 years, the fund has made five to six loans per year that averaged $14,365. Total fund capital is $576,000 with $357,000 in outstanding loans, or 62% of total capital. A two-person staff manages the loan fund and provides business technical assistance. All loans are approved by a board that includes area business owners, bankers, and economic and community development professionals.

The SBLF is one of four alternative lenders serving Boston small businesses. These other lenders include (1) Accion USA, which had 108 borrowers and a $572,000 loan portfolio as of FY2002; (2) Boston Loan and Equity Fund, a $2 million fund created by several CDCs to finance commercial real estate and small business projects; and (3) the Urban Initiatives Fund administered by a state quasi-public corporation.

DBEDC also belongs to the Community Business Network (CBN), a collaboration of 12 CDCs that provide technical assistance and loan packaging to neighborhood small businesses. As a lead CBN member, DBEDC works with two affiliate entities, CDC of Boston in lower Roxbury and Viet-Aid in the Fields Corner section of Dorchester, to identify clients for both technical assistance and loans.

Dorchester Business Base

An analysis of information from a private database identified the scale and composition of Dorchester's small business base. Almost 1,300 businesses were identified with sales below $500,000 and fewer than 10 employees. These businesses are concentrated geographically, with three commercial areas—each with over 200 enterprises—accounting for 53% of all businesses (see Table 16.4). However, firms are quite diversified by industry. The 16 largest business types, each with at least 15 firms, together equal 34.6% of all microenterprises. Two of the largest concentrations are restaurants and hair/nail care. The former category includes 90 enterprises (7% of the total) and the latter has 144 businesses (11.2% of the total) (see Table 16.5).

The Assignment

Your assignment is to recommend a research plan to help DBEDC identify the target markets and financing strategy to maximize the use of its lending capacity under the SBA Microloan Program to advance the economic revitalization of Dorchester. Because DBEDC wants to be ready to implement the SBA program upon approval, the study must be completed within 4 months. It plans to undertake the study with a small consulting budget ($10,000) and assistance from three graduate students completing a project for an economic development course. The research plan should present the detailed steps to (1) complete both demand-side and supply-side analyses; (2) address implementation needs related to adding this SBA program; and (3) develop final recommendations. For each part of the research plan, explain the key questions or issues that need to be addressed, based on the study's goals and background information provided, and the specific research methods, tools, and data sources that will be used within the budget and time constraints.

Table 16.4   Distribution of Dorchester Small Businesses by Neighborhood

Commercial Area	Number of Businesses	Percentage of Total
Bowdoin-Geneva	90	7.0%
Codman Square	237	18.5%
Fields Corner	185	14.4%
Four Corners	121	9.4%
St. Mark's	223	17.4%
Upham's Corner	216	16.8%
Other Areas	209	16.3%
Total	1,282	100%

SOURCE: Collins, Neel, and Smith-Frances (2003).

Table 16.5   Largest Business Types Among Dorchester Small Businesses

Business Type	Number of Businesses	Percent of Total
Beauty salons	93	7.3%
Limited-service eating places	69	5.4%
General automotive repair	47	3.7%
Law offices	39	3.0%
Child day care services	38	3.0%
Barbershops	32	2.5%
Insurance agencies and brokerages	29	2.3%
Dry cleaning and laundry services	27	2.1%
Dentist offices	26	2.0%
Grocery stores	25	2.0%
Full-service restaurants	21	1.6%
Flooring contractors	19	1.4%
Nail salons	19	1.4%
General merchandise stores	18	1.4%
Physical/occupational/speech therapists offices	18	1.4%
Auto body and interior repair shops	17	1.3%
Total listed businesses	444	34.6%
Total all Dorchester businesses	1282	100.0%

SOURCE: Collins, Neel, and Smith-Frances (2003).

Endnotes

1. A detailed discussion of data sources and their economic development uses can be found in Cortright and Reamer (1998), *Using Socioeconomic Data to Understand Your Regional Economy* available on the Economic Development Administration Web site (www.doc.gov/eda).

2. This discussion is based on an unpublished consulting report to the Commonwealth Corporation by Karl F. Seidman Consulting Services (2001b) entitled *Massachusetts Growth Industry Analysis*.

3. Information related to the Massachusetts Growth Fund in this and subsequent sections is based on an unpublished consulting report to the Commonwealth Corporation by Karl F. Seidman Consulting Services (2001a) entitled *Financing Gaps and Recommended Financing Roles for the Trust to Serve Targeted Massachusetts Growth Industries*.

4. Two key banking directories include the *Polk Financial Institutions Directory* and *Moody's Bank and Finance Manual*. Venture Economics and Venture One are the primary private sources of data on the venture capital industry.

5. Financial market and banking data are listed under the economic asset subject category.

6. A good summary of best practices for managing development finance institutions can be found in Lehr (1998), *Best Practices for CDFIs: Key Principles for Performance*.

7. This case study draws upon summary information on the DBEDC Small Business Loan Fund and data on the Dorchester small business base from Collins, Neel, and Smith-Frances (2003).

17

Managing the Lending and Investment Process

Development finance institutions supply capital to firms and projects through completing financing transactions. Consequently, effective management of the financing process is the core competency for development finance institutions to master. A sound investment process (in this chapter the investment process refers to both lending and equity financing) advances economic development goals while protecting the income and capital needed for long-term sustainability. This chapter addresses key operating issues and effective practices for managing the investment of capital. The chapter begins with an overview of the stages in the investment process and a discussion of core elements of an effective and well-managed system. In the next four sections, the goals, issues, and best practices for each stage of the process are reviewed. A case study of the Portland Development Commission's Industrial Site Revolving Loan Fund concludes the chapter, giving readers the opportunity to evaluate and identify ways to improve the lending process for an economic development finance entity.

The Investment Process and Key Management Principles

Investing development capital in enterprises and projects entails a four-stage process that is summarized in Figure 17.1. The process begins with the marketing stage, which builds program awareness and understanding to generate inquiries and identify potential projects for investment. In the second stage, project inquiries are screened to ensure that they fit economic development criteria and are ready for a formal evaluation of their financing application. During this stage, the first decisions are made about whether and how to proceed with a transaction based on its potential to generate the desired economic development benefits. After the screening stage, firms submit an application package, which triggers the third phase—investment underwriting and commitment. The underwriting stage determines whether financing is provided and on what terms. By selecting which projects will receive capital, decisions at this stage largely shape an entity's economic development and financial outcomes. Consequently, considerable staff time and board attention should be devoted to the underwriting and commitment decision. The commitment process continues until the firm satisfies all the conditions required to close the financing transaction (i.e., signing the legal documents that govern the financing and receiving investment proceeds). After the closing, the loan-servicing and monitoring stage begins. In this phase, the development finance institution collects loan payments (for debt investments), administers provisions of the investment contract, monitors the financial and business performance of its investments, and works to resolve problems and improve client success. This phase is the longest, typically continuing for years until the loan is fully repaid, equity investment is exited, or the investment is liquidated and written off.

Principles for Sound Investment Management

Before attending to each stage, it is important to consider several unifying principles that ensure an effective overall investment process. The first essential ingredient is *well-defined policies and procedures* that align investment decisions with the development finance strategy. These policies and procedures establish the systems and structure to translate financing strategies into day-to-day operating practices, and integrate each stage into a well-coordinated process. Because development finance institutions pursue economic development and financial goals, policies and operations must address and balance both agendas. Accordingly, investment criteria and monitoring systems should include economic development and financial measures, and operating procedures and services need to support the realization of development goals along with the recovery of investment returns. The critical policies and procedures to establish include (1) an overall statement of the institution's mission, goals, and investment philosophy; (2) a summary and diagram of the entire investment process with a description of each party's role; (3) eligibility and economic development criteria for investments; (4) a description of available technical assistance and development services and how they are delivered within the investment process; (5) investment underwriting standards and how satisfaction of standards is determined; (6) application forms and requirements; (7) closing processes and requirements; and (8) servicing and monitoring requirements. Policies and procedures must be carefully crafted to reflect an entity's development strategy and to be internally consistent. Investment criteria for a fund fostering living wage jobs by targeting high-growth start-up firms, for example, would emphasize the enterprise's market potential, business plan, and entrepreneurial and management capacity rather than historic financial performance and collateral levels. Moreover, this strategy needs to be embedded in the entire investment

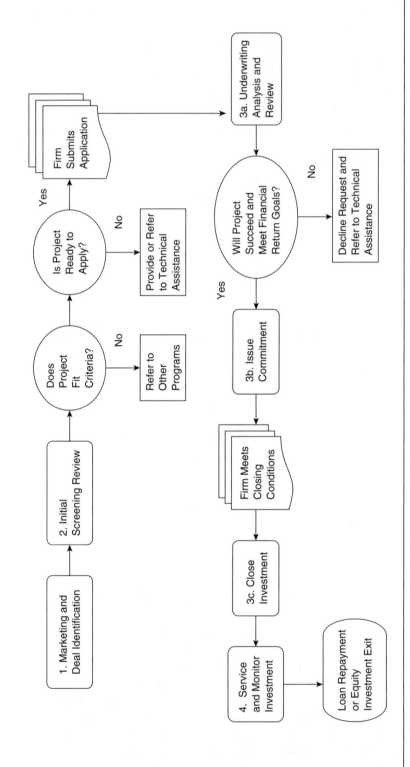

Figure 17.1   Stages and Decisions in the Investment Process

process, including eligibility criteria, technical and management assistance to support business planning and execution, application requirements based on the business plan and management team qualifications, and an active and extensive investment monitoring role. Investment policies and procedures also should be well documented in two formats. One format is a concise and plain English overview for external audiences, including potential applicants and their advisors, economic development professionals, and other lenders. A second version details policies and operating procedures for employees that administer the investment process. This internal policy manual covers topics like the analytical and research tasks to be completed in investment underwriting, the format for an investment analysis memo, and collection and accounting procedures for new investments.

A well-documented process advances a second principle for effective investment management—transparency. Through a *transparent investment process,* decision making is more efficient and accountable. Key requirements and steps in the investment process are revealed up front, which helps applicants understand what is needed to secure a financing commitment. When firms know the details of application requirements and underwriting standards, they can assemble a complete information package and reach critical thresholds before engaging in the underwriting process. They can also self-assess their capacity to qualify for financing and decide whether they should resolve certain issues and strengthen aspects of their enterprise before seeking capital. In this manner, transparency promotes more complete and appropriate financing applications, which avoids delays and frustrations in investment screening, underwriting, and closing. A transparent system also promotes accountability by informing stakeholders about how investment standards and processes relate to the institution's goals and strategy, and commits the entity to follow stated procedures. Finally, a transparent system creates a foundation for communication and trust that is essential to establishing a mutually beneficial long-term relationship between the firm and development finance entity.

A sufficient and skilled staff is the third pillar for effective investment management. Staff implement strategies and policies and exercise their judgment on applications, which ultimately determines the effectiveness of even the best-designed systems. Because development finance is mission-driven, people-oriented, and multifaceted, the investment staff needs diverse talents and skills. Good communication and people skills are essential to manage the many relationships involved in development finance transactions. Experience and technical knowledge in economic development, the business and financial aspects of an institution's target market, and structuring financial products for customers also are key qualifications when hiring investment personnel. Finally, employee commitment to the development mission is important to ensure an organizational culture that focuses on realizing economic development goals, not just completing financial transactions.

Beyond hiring people with the right values, skills, and talents, strong management accountability and appropriate staffing levels are vital. To reach their full potential, development finance entities need sufficient staffing to professionally operate all aspects of the investment process. Besides staff responsible for investment underwriting, strong capacity is needed for sustained marketing and active investment servicing and monitoring. These functions can be undertaken by separate staff dedicated to marketing and servicing, respectively, or through having investment staff responsible for all three roles (the relative merits of each option are discussed below). In either case, establishing clear management responsibility, performance measures, and incentives for each activity is critical to ensure that sufficient attention and resources are devoted to all three areas: marketing, managing investment transactions, and overseeing the investment portfolio.

Treating investments as *a relationship with shared goals and mutual benefit* for the provider and user of capital is a fourth principle. A successful relationship with positive outcomes for both parties requires good communication, clear documentation, understanding of each party's responsibilities, and mutual trust (Kwass, Siegel, & Henze, 1987). This is especially true for development finance programs, in which practitioners often work closely with applicants to assess weaknesses and secure services to strengthen their capacity, on the one hand, and to achieve specific development outcomes through hiring, project design, subcontracting, and other business practices, on the other hand. Development finance programs, therefore, need a culture that fosters respect, open communication, and a commitment to shared goals with their customers. Practices that foster such a culture include a transparent investment process, understanding and responding to the customer's objectives in seeking financing, and providing honest information on the customer's prospect for receiving financing and the associated obligations. Although practitioners should help customers address weaknesses and gain the capacity to successfully use financing, they must also be candid about the institution's financial goals and ensure that customers understand the responsibilities and risks associated with the financing contract.

The fifth principle is establishing an investment process with *strong accountability at both the policy and transaction level*. Oversight by the board of directors is the primary accountability mechanism, and thus, board representation for all key stakeholder groups is a precondition for accountability. For effective policy oversight, the board must be active in setting the overall strategy and investment policies, approve all large transactions, and review new financing activities on a frequent basis. To have the knowledge and skills to be sound stewards, board members need to be well educated about the institution's strategy, target markets, finances, and program activities and collectively possess expertise in key subject areas, such as economic development, business management, and financial management. Policy accountability is also enhanced through advisory committees that allow diverse customers and stakeholders to provide feedback on financial products, development services, and the investment process. Formal vetting of staff underwriting analysis and investment recommendations with a loan or investment review committee provides accountability at the individual transaction level. This committee approves all investments, except routine small transactions, before a commitment is issued or the project proceeds to final board action. For large organizations with sufficient executive depth, the committee's membership can be drawn from senior managers. Small organizations, however, need board members and outside volunteers to make the review committee a strong oversight vehicle.

A final principle is *continuous improvement* of programs and processes. This reflects the ongoing need to adjust to a dynamic environment and the value of applying new learning to both reconsidering core values, goals, and strategies and improving operational effectiveness. Continuous improvement is pursued through formal mechanisms to critically assess assumptions, goals, and strategies; collect and analyze information on the external environment; elicit customer and stakeholder feedback; and evaluate the development outcomes from products and services.

Marketing and Project Identification

This first stage of the investment process builds demand for financial and development services by identifying investment opportunities in the short term and building knowledge of the development finance institution to increase financing requests over time. Marketing, however, should be managed to accomplish broader strategic benefits. Expanding other organizations' understanding of one's program lays the foundation for building partnerships to achieve long-term objectives. Marketing also generates valuable information on target market trends, evolving clients' needs, and the efforts of other capital market entities. To gain these benefits, marketing plans should target outreach to organizations based on strategic considerations that include the organization's knowledge and relationships with customer groups and its capacity to provide complementary financing and services. Capital market research conducted for program planning will identify good prospects for strategic marketing. Outreach with these organizations should begin a two-way conversation that surfaces opportunities for collaboration and mutual benefit. When the initial contact is promising, regular follow-up should occur to strengthen the relationship and act on opportunities for collaboration. Senior executives need to be active in these marketing and relationship-building efforts to signal a strong commitment to collaboration with external organizations and to provide leadership for an institutionwide commitment to the marketing plan. By encouraging all staff to view marketing and relationship building as part of their responsibilities, a marketing culture can be embedded in the entire organization. This includes training and empowering all employees to promote the organization's mission and services, giving marketing assignments to all staff, and encouraging staff to generate new marketing ideas. Finally, information gained from marketing activities needs to be culled for strategic planning purposes. For example, the summaries of marketing visits that staff complete can include questions on broader planning issues along with information on short-term deal prospects. Staff discussions to explore important trends and issues that emerge from marketing activities (and other work) are another way to generate insights and uncover new opportunities to inform future plans.

Marketing Approaches and Audiences

Effective marketing plans use multiple tools to reach different audiences, reinforce key messages, and build a strong network of referral relationships. The advantages and disadvantages of major marketing tools are summarized in Table 17.1. Although some experimenting with different tools is warranted, marketing planners need to consider which approaches will be most effective in reaching their target markets, generating actual demand for services (as opposed to simply inquiries), and advancing other organizational goals. Based on this analysis, marketing tools can be customized to distinct customers. For example, an entity that finances small businesses and nonprofit organizations needs to vary its media outlets and outreach effort to reflect the unique information sources and professional networks used by small firms versus non-profit agencies. Similarly, credit unions and community development banks that serve both individuals and businesses should supplement communitywide advertising with marketing initiatives targeted to each customer segment.

Marketing plans also require a balance between wholesale and retail approaches. Wholesale marketing, through advertising, targeted mailing, and media coverage, is cost effective because it reaches a large audience and fosters broader community awareness. However, because wholesale tools are not well targeted and communicate limited information, their results can be unpredictable and of poor quality.[1] Retail marketing, via one-on-one visits, group presentations, and referral network development, reaches fewer people and is more time and staff-intensive but is more likely to generate new customers because it delivers better quality information to a carefully targeted audience.

Choosing audiences is the second main element in marketing plans. Both relationship-building goals and the capacity to generate new clients drive this decision. Besides potential customers themselves, individuals and organizations with regular contact and knowledge of customer groups, especially around financing and development, are the prime marketing audiences. Leading candidates include (1) lenders and other financing sources; (2) technical assistance entities; (3) private attorneys, accountants, and consultants; (4) business and trade associations; and (5) active civic and community organizations. With their potential to pass on many customers, these organizations are strong candidates to include in a referral network. Creating a strong referral relationship begins with a persuasive one-on-one appeal and regular follow-up. Practitioners should also enhance their partners' capacity to make good referrals through preparing customized brochures, providing staff training, and giving feedback

Table 17.1   Marketing Tools

Tool	Advantages	Disadvantages
Advertising	Reaches a large audience. Can reach new audiences. Builds recognition and awareness.	Costly. Scattershot approach that may not reach target customers. Can generate many inappropriate inquiries.
Targeted mailings	Reaches target customers and audiences. Moderate cost.	May be discarded without information being read.
Press coverage	Low cost. Establishes recognition and credibility. Reaches a large audience. Can reach new audiences.	Unpredictable since coverage not certain. Scattershot approach that may not reach target customers. Can generate many inappropriate inquiries.
One-on-one visits	Reaches target customers and audiences. Builds personal relationships. Provides direct information on deal prospects. Two-way communication and information gathering.	Costly and staff-intensive. Reaches a small number of people.
Presentations	Reaches target customers and audiences. Wholesale approach. Personal contact. Allows some two-way communication.	Unpredictable—depends on available groups and events. Attendance may be poor. Can be staff-intensive to plan and prepare.
Referral networks	Reaches target customers. Low-cost. Wholesale approach. Extends network of contacts. Can reach new audiences. Can lead to partnerships around other activities.	Staff-intensive to develop and maintain. Unpredictable—depends on commitment of referral source.

on referrals. Incentives also help motivate referrals. A financial reward for referring new clients is one option, but reciprocity (in making referrals or providing other support to the organization) and recognition (via printed materials, thank-you letters and events, and reporting back on referral outcomes) also motivate others to make new referrals.

Effective Marketing Practices

Despite the need to customize marketing activities to each institution's context, several practices are central to effective marketing. First, organizations need a marketing strategy and annual plan that is strongly endorsed by the institution's chief executive and senior management. Second, cultivating and sustaining a strong referral network should be central to the marketing strategy. Consequently, sufficient management and professional staff time must be devoted to the personal outreach and meetings needed to build such a network. Third, practitioners can foster awareness of their organization and its services by being active in their communities and professional networks and generating free media coverage[2] in outlets that reach target customers, key stakeholders, and important professional and community networks. Finally, programs should track where new clients learn about their services, which referral sources generate new customers, and what wholesale marketing approaches lead to successful inquiries. This information allows organizations to evaluate and improve different marketing approaches. To gain this capacity, organizations need to query new customers on where they learned about their programs and maintain a database to track which referral and information sources yield customers that use specific products and services.

Project Screening

Project screening constitutes the initial conversation with potential customers on two issues: (1) the fit between their plans and the program's economic development goals; and (2) the availability of services that fit their needs. The first issue is a threshold for further engagement; it ensures that resources assist projects with the potential to advance development goals. In this screening, the proposed project is compared to the eligibility and economic development criteria for specific programs. Projects that fail to meet these criteria do not warrant further review because they will not advance economic development goals. The second screening determines whether an organization's services and financial products match the prospective applicant's needs and assesses their readiness to submit a financing application. Three possible decisions result from this screening. The prospective applicant is referred to another program when the institution does not offer appropriate financing or development services. Secondly, when a firm needs financing offered by the organization and is ready to proceed, it is advised to submit an application. In the third case, when the financing request has weaknesses or when the applicant must complete critical tasks before an underwriting review is warranted, staff help the entrepreneur obtain services to improve her or his plans and qualify for financing. Thus, the second screening step should put the project or entrepreneur on a path to secure financing.

Best Practices for Investment Screening

Two practices ensure an effective screening process. The first one is establishing explicit screening criteria that reflect both economic development goals and financial standards. These criteria foster consistency in the staff's application of goals and policies to screening projects and their advice on how potential customers can qualify for financing. Good screening criteria also facilitate efficient investment underwriting by helping entrepreneurs or project proponents prepare a sound financing application. One useful screening tool is an application standard that defines the project status and application materials required to undergo investment underwriting. By clearly stating what an applicant must have accomplished to be seriously reviewed for financing, this standard helps finance programs avoid either a drawn out underwriting process for applicants that did not address key business issues, or turning down financing requests due to incomplete plans. Table 17.2 illustrates an application standard for supplying permanent debt to real estate projects.

A second effective practice is helping potential applicants create strong investment proposals. To foster local entrepreneurial and financial capacity, development finance professionals need to provide helpful responses to firms that don't initially meet development criteria and investment standards. For ineligible requests, this means connecting the sponsor to appropriate services and financing sources through referrals and introductions. For *incomplete or weak proposals*, practitioners should diagnose the project's shortfalls, define what changes or steps are needed to create a sound project, and work with the proponent to secure development services to improve their plans. Finally, when confronted with an *infeasible or poorly conceived enterprise*, a staff person needs to explain the flaws in the business concept and plan to the proponent. Because supplying valuable assistance is critical to this role, development finance institutions need to either create internal technical assistance capacity or establish strong partnerships with technical assistance

Table 17.2   Application Standard for Permanent Real Estate Loan

Application Standard	*Supporting Materials*
Project Site Control Secured	Evidence of site control.
Capable Development Team Assembled	Summary of qualifications and prior experience of development team members.
Sound Development Concept and Plan in Place	Description of the development concept, plan, and preliminary design.
Environmental Risks Identified	Initial environmental site assessment and remedial plan (if needed).
Financing Plan Developed	Detailed development budget with sources and uses of funds.
Evidence of Operating Feasibility	Detailed multiyear revenue and expense operating pro forma, market study or data to support projected revenue.
Required Permitting, Zoning, and Public Approvals Identified	List and status of all required permits, zoning decisions, and other public approvals.

providers. In either case, the staff responsible for screening proposals should keep in touch with these prospective applicants to track their progress and help navigate them toward a solid financing application.

The Underwriting and Commitment Process

In this stage, a thorough evaluation of the proposed financing is conducted and a decision is made on whether to supply the requested financing. To generate good investment decisions, the underwriting and commitment process must be structured to achieve several objectives. First, it must provide a thorough assessment of whether the proposed firm or project is viable in the marketplace and has the ability to repay the requested loan (or provide the target return for an equity investment). Second, a good underwriting analysis clarifies the applicant's business and financial risks. Practitioners use this understanding to secure appropriate technical and management assistance, decide on the right financing terms, and set conditions for the receipt of financing. An economic development professional's mission is not simply to accept or reject a financing application but to structure and assemble financing that builds successful firms and development projects. Consequently, a third objective is to produce a financing plan that addresses the applicant's needs while meeting the financial objectives of the development finance entity. A fourth goal is to establish checks and balances that minimize bad decisions from errors, omissions, or unexplored options in staff underwriting. Finally, the process should document key decisions and the final financial transaction to give all parties a clear understanding of their obligations and provide full legal rights and protections to the financial institution.

Best Practices in Investment Decision Making

Managing the underwriting and commitment process involves the integration of three tasks: (1) setting sound underwriting standards; (2) defining the evaluation/due diligence process, and (3) organizing a well-structured and efficient decision-making process. *Underwriting standards* are the business and financial parameters that a firm or project must meet to present an acceptable risk for investment. Explicit underwriting standards promote transparency and guide applicants in preparing strong investment proposals, but they also have a critical strategic function—aligning investment decisions with an institution's financing strategy. Underwriting criteria translate the risk and financial components of an investment strategy into operating policies. Because the success and financial returns of an enterprise are shaped by many factors, underwriting standards must be multifaceted, encompassing financial, management, and market/business criteria. They need to transcend financial criteria, such as loan-to-value and debt service coverage ratios, to address the management and business attributes that are critical to success. Table 17.3 summarizes the type of underwriting standards that apply to business debt and equity products and to real estate loans. Explicit underwriting standards, however, are not inherently conservative or overly strict but should reflect an entity's economic development goals, target customers, and investment philosophy. Institutions established to supply high-risk subordinate debt, for example, require standards with a high loan-to-value ratio and low debt service coverage. Alternatively, programs that finance business start-ups among nontraditional entrepreneurs need standards based on business plan quality, completion of entrepreneurial training, and access to technical assistance.

Due diligence refers to the collection and analysis of information needed to assess whether the project meets underwriting standards. The first step in due diligence is reviewing the financing application to ensure that it is

Table 17.3 Sample Underwriting Standards for Business Debt, Business Equity, and Real Estate Debt Financing

Type of Standard	Business Debt	Business Equity	Real Estate Debt
Financial	1. Loan-to-value ratio 2. Valuation of collateral 3. Debt service coverage ratio 4. Historic financial ratios 5. Credit history of firm and principals	1. Existing and future company valuation 2. Expected rate of return 3. Principal's investment in firm 4. Credit history of principals 5. Investment exit potential	1. Loan-to-value ratio 2. Debt service coverage ratio 3. Developer's credit history 4. Tenant credit quality
Management	1. Depth and experience of firm management 2. Strong financial and key management systems	1. Depth and experience of firm management 2. Strong financial and key management systems	1. Developer experience and prior projects 2. Development team breadth and experience 3. Strong financial, construction, and property management systems
Business/Market	1. Quality of business plan 2. Sustainable cost structure 3. Marketing and distribution channels 4. Sales contracts/orders 5. Production capacity	1. Quality of business plan 2. Market size and growth potential 3. Gross margins 4. Proprietary technology 5. Regulatory status	1. Quality of development/ management plan 2. Pre-leasing 3. Project location and amenities 4. Permitting status and issues

complete and provides sufficient information to complete a thorough evaluation. A thorough "completeness" review and requests for missing information should be completed early to quickly assemble the materials needed for the investment evaluation.

Underwriting staff then analyzes this information and conducts additional research to evaluate whether the firm or project fulfills underwriting criteria, and determines what weaknesses and major risks exist. The due diligence evaluation typically includes (1) a review of the business plan; (2) research on industry trends and competitive factors affecting the firm or project; (3) a review of key manager's experience, references, and credit history; (4) an evaluation of historic financial results, the accuracy and realism of financial projections, and a sensitivity analysis for downside risks; (5) a site visit to the firm's main facilities and/or the project site; (6) interviews with the firm's customers, suppliers, main competitors, and industry experts; and (7) an assessment of whether the proposed financial plan is appropriate and meets key financial investment criteria. The expected scope of analysis and tasks to be completed as part of the due diligence process should be documented in an institution's investment policies and procedures, both to ensure that sufficient analysis has been conducted and to promote comparable due diligence practices across staff. The extent of due diligence should be tailored to the type of financing, loan size, and level of investment risk. For small loans with good collateral, a review of the business plan, management experience, credit history, and historic financial statements may be sufficient without a detailed analysis of industry factors, customer and supplier references, and sensitivity analysis. On the other hand, a large equity investment in a start-up firm requires a thorough analysis of the business plan, management team, market size and trends, competitive factors, and the timing and potential for an investment exit. Staff expertise in target markets and industries is a valuable asset for high-quality and efficient underwriting analysis. Deep knowledge of industry conditions, regulatory factors, and management and competitive requirements allows staff to thoroughly evaluate an applicant's business and financing plan and better identify potential problems and investment risks. Because hiring staff with this knowledge of target industries is not always feasible, institutions must develop this expertise among existing staff via training and self-learning. This is especially true for entities that expand into new markets or that serve several target industries with a small staff. By assigning specific industries to different employees and encouraging them to gain expertise through research, specialized training, and developing a network of experts and key informants, small development finance institutions can cultivate greater industry knowledge when hiring new staff is not feasible.

Investment underwriting involves considerable personal judgment that cannot be eliminated through underwriting and due diligence standards (Lehr, 1998). The emphasis on developing comprehensive underwriting standards and a well-documented due diligence protocol neither denies the importance of personal judgment nor suggests that systems will eliminate the risk of judgment errors. Instead, they help ensure that personal judgments are informed by sound analysis and operate within a policy structure that aligns investment decisions with an institution's economic development and financial goals. Even highly experienced professionals with sound underwriting skills and judgment can create unexpected investment risks and outcomes when they operate outside strong policy and underwriting guidance. One state quasi-public corporation incurred this problem when an experienced investment professional assumed management of its primary business investment fund. The new manager emphasized debt and equity in investments in high-growth firms that promised substantial job growth and long-term returns. However, these investments reduced current interest income and slowed the return of capital to reinvest, which created serious financial problems for the corporation. By relying on its staff to define appropriate investments, rather than establishing explicit standards and policies, investment staff altered the risk profile and cash flow structure of its investment portfolio.

Beyond formal standards and due diligence procedures, proactive management of the underwriting and commitment process is critical to achieving positive development outcomes. Economic development entities should direct the underwriting and commitment process to resolve issues and problems that arise and move all parties to a viable financing plan. When staff identify weaknesses in an application or determine that a proposed financing plan is not viable, they need to work with the applicant and other lenders or investors to find ways to overcome these problems and get to a feasible business and financial plan. This requires staff to think through what actions, changes, and resources are needed to sufficiently strengthen the proposed venture and then convince the applicant and other investors to adopt this modified plan. Moreover, practitioners need to *provide leadership in financial packaging* through understanding the constraints and requirements of other financing sources, visualizing a viable financial plan that can meet all parties' objectives, and convening them to negotiate and coordinate the details of the financial plan. In this way, development finance professionals are advocates for entrepreneurs and development projects that are fundamentally sound and will advance key development goals. This advocacy role, however, can be hazardous for a financial institution when it leads staff to overlook or downplay important risks or push the envelope too far in structuring debt or equity transactions. Designing an effective decision-making process helps mitigate this problem.

Structuring *the investment decision-making process* is the third critical element in managing the underwriting and commitment process. This process must balance the need for timely decisions with ensuring strong accountability and oversight. An effective system makes decisions within a predictable schedule that is responsive to the time constraints and needs of applicants, while providing a thorough review of the staff underwriting analysis and proposed investment. Figure 17.2 illustrates three options for organizing the decision-making process. All alternatives begin with staff preparation of an investment proposal but vary in the subsequent steps for review and authorization. Option A uses internal management to review and authorize investments. This process is appropriate for small loans and/or routine transactions that don't deviate from established policies. Institutions with large loan volumes also use an internal committee to review most transactions, reserving board review for particularly large, complex, or atypical investments. For internal decision-making processes, managers with the ultimate decision-making authority should have extensive experience and expertise to provide a sound check on the staff analysis and recommendation. Small entities with one professional staff or organizations where senior managers lack investment expertise cannot rely on an internal staff decision-making process but need to employ one of the other options.

Under Option B, investments are first reviewed internally with final decision-making authority resting with the governance body. This process ensures a valuable "outside" review by people who are not enmeshed in day-to-day issues and can bring a fresh perspective to raise questions and propose options that the staff may have overlooked. Review by board members also provides a check on improper staff actions and accountability to important stakeholders. Board members often bring special expertise that expands the capacity to analyze and address key issues, especially for organizations with a small staff. For these reasons, all development finance organizations should utilize Option B to some extent. Institutions with a large staff, strong internal management controls, and many routine loans can reserve this process for large or complex transactions, investments that fall outside standard policies, or when first implementing a new financial product. Other organizations may decide to use Option B for all decisions either to provide board oversight for a small staff, supply critical expertise, or strengthen accountability.

Option C, which adds a review layer between the staff and board, is valuable when a board lacks broad expertise in critical areas needed for investment review. For example, boards that largely include political representatives or economic development practitioners may lack the business and financial expertise to provide a strong review of staff underwriting and structuring. A loan committee with board members and additional experts could be established to provide the necessary technical review. Alternatively, a board may delegate the detailed review of investment proposals to a loan committee to provide a more thorough review than is possible at board meetings. Loan committees are also helpful in sorting out complex transactions, handling deals that pose new policy issues, and surfacing and resolving internal controversies prior to formal board action. This approach can minimize delays, political problems, or embarrassment that can occur when unexpected issues arise at formal board meetings.

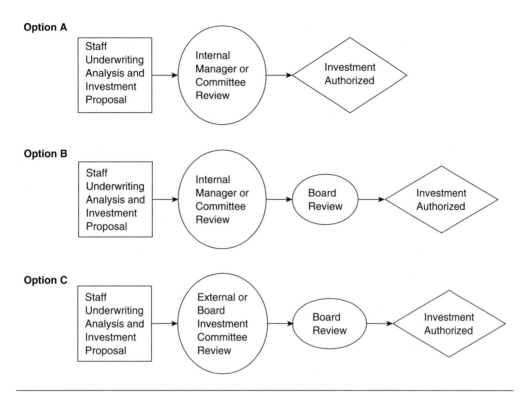

Figure 17.2   Options for the Investment Decision Process

An investment commitment is the first of several steps in completing the financing transaction. This decision defines the terms of the final investment and sets conditions that must be satisfied before funds are disbursed. It is critical to document both aspects of the investment in a well-crafted letter that covers standard policies and the specific investment terms negotiated with the applicant. Organizations should work with their legal advisors to create a standard commitment letter for each financial product that can be easily customized to reflect the terms of each transaction. A good commitment letter facilitates a smooth closing of the transaction and provides legal protections to prevent unsound investments if conditions at the loan closing either differ significantly from those at the time of commitment or do not conform to sound legal and financial practices. Thus, it is important to fully document financing terms and closing conditions in the commitment letter and make sure the applicant understands and accepts them. This minimizes problems and surprises at the closing by establishing a shared recognition of what is needed to close the final investment contract.

After the commitment letter is executed, practitioners need to track the applicant's progress in meeting conditions and work with other parties to prepare for a smooth closing. Closing a financial transaction can be difficult, time-consuming, and expensive when multiple financing sources (and their attorneys) are involved, but several practices simplify the process. First, *standard closing requirements and documents* reduce the preparatory work for the closing and help applicants to prepare the necessary documents. These requirements should be communicated to firms when they apply for financing and receive their commitment letter. Second, *a coordinated closing agenda,* which lists all the required documents and details which party is responsible for preparing or providing each one, provides a road map to the closing and avoids duplicative efforts, omissions, or confusion among attorneys and investors. Third, designating a lead attorney, typically counsel for the senior lender or lead equity investor, to coordinate the preparation of financing documents and the resolution of legal issues also saves time and costs through clarifying responsibilities and decision making for technical legal matters. Finally, practitioners should not leave the closing to attorneys; they should coordinate the process and resolve problems to conclude the investment without undue costs and delays.

Investment Servicing and Monitoring

In this stage, development financiers supervise the repayment of investments after they are closed—an activity that usually continues for several years. Although the underwriting and commitment process sets the stage for successful investments, servicing and monitoring activities help fulfill their financial and development promise. From a financial perspective, these efforts facilitate timely repayment of the loan or investment and protect the collateral securing an investment. However, their broader mission is to track each firm's progress, identify problems, and provide guidance to help the enterprise overcome these problems and realize its potential. This latter focus recognizes that development and financial outcomes depend on a venture's overall business performance, not simply on compliance with the formal terms of an investment contract. When efforts to work out a problem investment fail, the goal shifts to managing the collection process to minimize financial losses.

Servicing refers to administering the financial and contractual side of investments and largely applies to loans. Key servicing functions, summarized in Table 17.4, address routine loan repayment and compliance matters. The effective handling of these mundane tasks, however, is central to the sound management of any development finance institution. Servicing generates prompt and predictable cash flow to the organization and provides early warning signs of borrower problems, which facilitates an early, and hopefully effective, response.

Monitoring involves overseeing investments and working with firms to resolve problems and achieve expected outcomes. Equity investors, as discussed in Chapter 11, are far more active monitors than are lenders. This difference partly reflects the legal status of owners, who have the right to appoint managers and vote on major business decisions. Lenders, however, supply funds under specific contractual terms and are not involved in a firm's management.

Table 17.4   Loan Servicing and Monitoring Functions and Activities

Function	Activity
Establish complete and accurate records	Complete initial loan servicing set-up after closing. Maintain database of loans, their terms, and history. Provide written documentation of compliance and collection problems.
Ensure timely repayment	Set up payments "tickler" system and notices. Track and respond quickly to late payments.
Protect collateral and security interest	Maintain escrows to pay taxes and insurance or require evidence of payment. Regularly inspect condition of collateral. Track expiration dates and file renewal notices under uniform commercial code.
Track borrower performance	Maintain regular personal contact with borrowers. Collect and analyze financial reports and development outcome information. Conduct periodic site visits.
Identify and resolve problems	Develop and track early warning indicators. Analyze business trends and conditions from financial statements and other reports. Review payment and loan compliance history. Meet with firms to review and discuss concerns. Develop risk reduction plan to address problems with firm and co-lenders/investors.

Moreover, lenders can be legally liable for financial losses that result from their direct involvement in management decisions. The line between protecting a lender's collateral and influencing management is not always cut and dried, as loan covenants often establish affirmative requirements on borrowers and prohibit certain actions. Nonetheless, equity investors, particularly venture capitalists, are more likely to monitor firms through frequent contact with senior managers, serving on a firm's board of directors, and implementing management changes and other actions to address problems. Lenders, on the other hand, are less familiar with day-to-day operations and rely on reviewing financial statements, tracking loan compliance, and site visits to monitor borrowers. They also use the leverage provided by loan covenants to convince management to address problems rather than propose specific actions. Development lenders, however, are more proactive than conventional lenders; they use more attentive monitoring to identify problems and try to resolve them with technical assistance and restructuring loan repayment terms.

Servicing and Monitoring Options

Three options exist for organizing the servicing and monitoring function. One option is having the staff responsible for investment underwriting oversee loan servicing and monitoring. A second approach uses separate staff to perform these functions. The third option is contracting with another financial institution or specialized company to perform servicing activities. Although the first approach carries over the knowledge and relationships cultivated during the underwriting stage to loan monitoring, it has potential pitfalls. Because underwriting new investments is more interesting and challenging than routine servicing and monitoring tasks, staff may focus on the former activity and devote too little time to their postclosing responsibilities. Underwriting staff also may fail to confront problems that arise in later years, either out of a need to shield earlier mistakes or from their familiarity and personal relationship with the borrower. For these reasons, creating a dedicated investment servicing/portfolio management staff is often a more effective organizational choice. A dedicated servicing unit also may improve efficiency because investment underwriting and servicing/monitoring require different competencies. Staff and managers that specialize in each function can handle more transactions and develop greater expertise than when staff must master skills in both areas.

Choosing between these options depends on an organization's level of investment activity and size. Programs with a small staff and modest transaction volumes lack the resources for a dedicated servicing staff and will gain few efficiency benefits. However, as institutions grow and manage a large investment portfolio, a specialized servicing/monitoring unit offers increasing advantages. The third option can help small- and medium-size organizations that lack the scale to support an internal servicing unit obtain the economies of scale that exist for loan servicing. In this case, it may be less costly to contract with a local financial institution or specialized loan-servicing company for routine servicing functions such as collections, internal accounting reports, tax and insurance oversight, escrow payments, and financial report collection. A large economic development lender or intermediary that shares an organization's mission and values is a good candidate to perform this servicing role. This option also allows scarce staff to concentrate on the key marketing and underwriting functions needed to grow to scale. However, when a third party handles servicing, development lenders still must review the financial and business performance of each borrower to stay informed about their loan portfolio and be prepared to address problems.[3] Given this need to understand the status of their portfolio and directly manage problem investments, development lenders should use third-party contractors for administrative servicing functions and retain an active investment monitoring role.

Best Practices For Servicing and Monitoring

Because servicing involves careful tracking and follow-up on many items, good administrative systems and attention to detail are critical practices.

Effective systems begin with establishing explicit policies on servicing and monitoring requirements and incorporating them into standard legal documents. Key policy issues to address include late payment periods and penalties, financial and development outcome reporting, insurance coverage levels and documentation, evidence of tax payments, escrow requirements for key expenses (e.g., taxes, insurance), and regular visits and inspections. Once these policies are in place, implementation depends on clear and consistent procedures in four areas: (1) the transition from closing to servicing; (2) tracking payments and compliance with other requirements; (3) quick follow-up to remedy late action or problems; and (4) internal accountability for servicing and monitoring functions.

The transition from closing to servicing involves the proper setup of new loans or investments by entering key terms, requirements, and dates into a comprehensive database and creating files with key documents and correspondence. A second part of the transition is communicating servicing policies and procedures to each new portfolio firm[4] and establishing a personal contact between the company and servicing staff. These actions create the information platform to administer and monitor investments and help establish communication and trust with portfolio firms.

After the transition, servicing staff need to closely administer and track these requirements and follow up promptly with firms to resolve any problems. One way to simplify loan collections and minimize late payments is to use an automatic debit of the borrower's checking account to receive scheduled debt service. Automatic payments eliminate the borrower's need to issue a check each month, reduce manual bank deposits, and ensure that timely loan payments are made (as long as the firm's bank balance is sufficient to cover the required amount). Computer databases are another valuable servicing tool. They help staff maintain records needed to track borrower compliance with various requirements such as report submissions, insurance renewals, tax payments, and loan payment history and also produce portfoliowide reports that identify delinquencies that require follow-up action. Software products exist that can perform this and related loan-servicing tasks. Some organizations, however, may prefer to create their own customized database, especially when special items must be tracked to document development impacts and address compliance issues for funding sources. To effectively use this database, records must be frequently updated and regular reports prepared to identify late payments and submissions. When loan payments and/or other submissions are late, prompt contact with the portfolio firm should be made, as a phone call or e-mail message often will remedy the situation. However, written communication is appropriate when a problem recurs or to communicate a serious breach of loan requirements; this documents the problem's history if it becomes necessary to declare a default and collect on the loan. Good documentation also minimizes the risk of lender liability claims if a firm believes it was treated unfairly.

When responding to a firm's tardiness or failure to meet its obligations, it is important to identify the source of the problem. Because these performance issues may indicate more serious difficulties, servicing staff should speak with the firm and use information from recent financial statements, past conversations, and site inspections to assess whether more fundamental troubles exist. When a serious problem is uncovered, practitioners need to encourage the firm to confront it and help the company obtain any technical assistance needed to do so. In some cases, the solution may require modifying loan or investment terms and, possibly, supplying new capital. However, new funds should only be invested when the firm has demonstrated a sound plan and progress in remedying its underlying difficulties.

Several practices help development finance institutions take a proactive approach to managing their portfolios and avoid having important tasks fall through the cracks. Strong management oversight and accountability for servicing and monitoring activities is at the core of these practices; it is achieved through holding regular meetings with the portfolio management staff to review the status of investments and decide on follow-up actions and reporting regularly to senior management and the board. Portfolio reports should be submitted biweekly or monthly to senior managers and on a monthly or quarterly basis to the board and need to document gross performance measures (e.g., the number and percent of loans that are 30, 60, and 90 days delinquent), along with the status of problem loans or investments. Development finance institutions also need to conduct a formal portfolio-wide risk analysis that identifies potential problem investments and formulates action plans to address them. Risk analysis applies uniform criteria to evaluate and classify the loss risk for every loan and/or investment. Each asset is assigned risk points based on a set of factors, such as payment and compliance history, financial condition, and loan-to-value ratio, and then placed in a loss risk category based on its total point score. An action plan is then formulated to reduce the loss potential for portfolio firms in higher risk categories. This systematic assessment of all loans and investments provides a check to ensure that problems with some assets are not overlooked. It also can uncover deteriorating credit among firms early, which allows a more effective response to help the firm reverse its situation.

Case Study: Portland Development Commission Industrial Site Loan Fund[5]

The Industrial Site Revolving Loan Fund (ISRLF) was established in the early 1980s with a $1.3 million grant from the U.S. Economic Development Administration (EDA) to grow and retain manufacturing firms within Portland, Oregon, and to target jobs within these firms to low- and moderate-income residents. ISRLF has provided below-market rate loans to

Portland area manufacturers to expand or develop an industrial site within two industrial areas, the Central Eastside and the Northside. Loans have supplemented private financing for firms that cannot secure all of the capital needed for a facility due to high interest rates and/or bank underwriting standards. Consequently, a minimum 3:1 leverage ratio for private to public investment applies to all projects. ISRLF also has required borrowers to sign a First Source Employment Agreement with the Portland Private Industry Council (PIC) to foster the hiring of low- and moderate-income residents for job openings.

Financial Products

ISRLF supplies long-term fixed rate loans at 5% with terms ranging from 5 to 20 years, and amortization periods of up to 30 years. A financing fee of 2% is also collected. Loans are made on a shared first position basis with private lenders, but the fund will subordinate when strong collateral exists. The low interest rate was established to address the very high interest rates in the early 1980s that prevented many firms from expanding or robbed them of needed working capital funds when they did expand. The long amortization period was also designed to enhance firms' cash flow to reinvest in the business. ISRLF applies five criteria to screen and approve projects for financing. First, projects must be located in one of the target areas and must be developed exclusively for private firms to use for manufacturing, assembly, or distribution purposes. Second, loan proceeds can only be used for real estate acquisition and improvement. Third, the applicant must show that ISRLF financing is needed either to make the project feasible in light of insufficient funding or to prevent relocation to a suburban site. Fourth, projects must meet job standards that include (1) at least 50% of the retained or created jobs need to be blue-collar, (2) firms agree to use the PIC to screen and hire employees for new job openings, and (3) at least one job must be created or retained per $20,000 of ISRLF loan capital. Finally, projects must demonstrate economic viability and the ability to repay all debt and invested capital.

Organization and Staffing

The Portland Development Commission's (PDC) Economic Development Division manages the ISRLF. PDC oversees the city's downtown development, housing, and economic development programs and projects and is governed by five commissioners appointed by the mayor. These commissioners are from the private sector, including two from small businesses, one from a large corporation, and two from financial firms. The Economic Development Division manages multiple programs and projects, including eight separate loan funds. One professional, a former vice president of a real estate construction and development firm with both public and private sector experience, oversees these eight loan funds with one assistant. Together they handle all ISRLF activities including marketing, screening, underwriting, loan servicing and monitoring, and staff support to the PDC board and loan committee.

Operations and the Lending Process

ISRLF is marketed through PDC promotional literature, local press coverage, PDC business assistance staff, and a private sector referral network cultivated through one-on-one staff visits. Local realtors are a key referral source because they serve firms seeking new facilities and have an incentive to use ISRLF to make property sales feasible. When a firm contacts PDC about an ISRLF loan, it receives a complete list of policies, lending procedures, and loan conditions; this lets potential applicants understand what is required before they decide to apply.

Next, the staff reviews loan applications based on the five criteria cited above and prepares a loan approval sheet with their recommendation. Loans below $50,000 are then reviewed and authorized by the five-member PDC's Investor Rehabilitation Loan (IRL) Committee, which includes four senior staff members and one PDC commissioner, who is executive vice president of a prominent Portland bank. Loans above $50,000 are first reviewed by IRL and then go to the full PDC Commission for approval. Because IRL was established to review housing loans, staff has worked to educate committee members about the underwriting issues involved in business lending. All loan applications are presented to the IRL, even when the staff does not recommend loan approval. When the IRL approves an application, it is forwarded to the PDC Commission for final approval. PDC commissioners typically do not reconsider the financial and underwriting analysis but instead focus on whether the loan's job benefits support making a loan.

An important issue for PDC staff in the underwriting and approval process is negotiating its relationships with the private lender. From prior commercial lending experience, the staff seeks a shared first position and proportional repayment of principal with private lenders. This policy helps to reduce losses and minimizes the incentive for banks to shift loss risk and collection costs onto PDC. Consequently, a second mortgage position is only considered when strong collateral from other pledged assets or guarantees exists.

Loan-servicing responsibilities are divided between PDC's central loan-servicing department and ISRLF program staff. The servicing department handles routine matters such as payment processing, late payment notices, and verification of real estate tax payment and property insurance. Program staff monitor the borrowers' financial condition and job outcomes and resolve problem loans. They maintain contact with borrowers through regular phone contact, semiannual meetings, and a review of annual financial statements. Periodic portfolio status reports are provided to the PDC Board along with semiannual reports to the EDA. When problem loans require a restructuring of loan terms or a foreclosure, the staff submits the recommended workout plan to the IRL for review. PDC does not typically provide technical assistance to ISRLF borrowers because most firms are established and well run. Occasionally, PDC requires a detailed business plan when an applicant does not have a well-formulated strategy, or it may request more frequent financial statements when it believes the firm's financial management or internal accounting systems need improvement.

A primary PDC focus during the application process is coordinating the negotiation of a First Source Employer Agreement between the applicant firm and the PIC as a condition for securing an ISRLF loan. These agreements detail which positions the firm will fill through the PIC and states that the "employer will select its employees from among qualified persons referred by the PIC." Firms must then list job openings exclusively with the PIC, which uses its own programs and a job referral network of community-based organizations to identify qualified low- and moderate-income city residents for the listed job. If the PIC cannot find a qualified applicant within a fixed period of time, the firm can then advertise and fill job openings through other means. PDC provides space and support for a PIC employee who negotiates and monitors these agreements with firms. When PDC receives an application, it refers the firm to PIC staff, who explain how the agreement and process works and its benefits. If a company does not want to sign an agreement, then the loan application process stops. For other cases, the PIC employee and the firm identify the specific clerical and blue-collar jobs that will be covered by the agreement, develop a 3-year projection with specific employment targets, and negotiate other details of the agreement. Because the PIC emphasizes a cooperative rather than regulatory approach to implementation, there are no enforcement or penalty provisions. When a firm acts in bad faith and does not comply with the agreement, the PIC stops providing services and instead focuses on assisting cooperative firms. PIC staff maintain frequent contact with borrowers to check on job openings, confirm hiring decisions, and monitor the success of new employees in their jobs.

Lending Activities and Outcomes

During its first 4 years, the ISRLF made 11 loans totaling almost $1 million to 10 firms. Because these loans contributed to a total investment of $5.2 million, $4 in private funds matched every dollar of ISRLF loan capital. Seven companies are manufacturers, one is a wholesaler and two are business repair operations. All but one firm is locally owned. ISRLF's major impact has been to retain firms and jobs in Portland that might otherwise have moved to the suburbs. A survey of five borrowers found that these firms had added 29 jobs but retained another 110 jobs within the city as a result of the ISRLF-financed projects. The average cost per job created or retained was $15,065 for these five firms.

After 4 years of stable loan demand, interest in ISRLF loans declined by late 1986 as interest rates declined. Lower interest rates allowed more projects to be feasible without below-market interest rates and reduced the value of ISRLF's subsidy. Moreover, high development costs in the Central Eastside area made it difficult to achieve the 3:1 private-to-public leverage ratio. PDC responded by lowering this requirement to 2:1.

Assignment

As part of a strategic review of the ISRLF, PDC has hired you to evaluate its lending process and make recommendations to improve it. To begin the project, an initial analysis of the lending process is needed to identify areas of concern and prepare a plan for a more detailed evaluation. Based on the ISRLF description above, address the following questions:

1. What are the strengths of the ISRLF lending process? What parts of the process are well designed and appear to function well?

2. What are potential problems or areas for improvement, either for the overall process or within specific stages?

3. Prepare a flowchart of the process with annotations that summarize your answers to the above two questions.

4. What data is needed to complete a thorough evaluation of the ISRLF lending process? Describe your plan to obtain this information and analyze it to complete the evaluation and prepare recommendations for PDC.

5. What recommendations would you make to PDC based on your current knowledge and analysis?

Endnotes

1. For example, Accion Texas invested heavily in wholesale marketing via radio advertisements and public service announcements (PSA). The former generated few inquiries, and the latter generated inquiries but only a few new clients. See Edgecomb (2002a) for more information.

2. This free media can include public service announcements, news articles, and special features.

3. The development finance organization also needs to oversee the servicing agent to ensure that they are performing all their responsibilities well.

4. A concise document that summarizes servicing policies and procedures in plain language and lists contact persons facilitates this communication, making matters that can be lost in the fine print of loan or investment documents accessible to firms.

5. This section is based on a detailed case study of this program from Kwass and Siegel (1987b), *Factors Influencing the Performance of U.S. Economic Development Administration Sponsored Revolving Loan Funds* (Vol. 2, Case Studies), pp. B1–20.

18

Raising and Managing Capital

For all development finance institutions, financial strategy is critical to reaching sustainable scale and fulfilling their economic development mission. This chapter addresses the core financial strategy issue—raising and managing the capital needed to supply financial products. The discussion begins by considering how capital management shapes development finance institutions and presenting the three management areas that practitioners can use to preserve and grow development capital. The following three sections then address effective policies and practices in each area, concentrating on the critical challenge of expanding capital sources. To make sound capital management decisions, practitioners must understand their long-term consequences. Thus, the fifth section explains how to prepare a financial model to evaluate how policies, products, and capital sources impact an institution's financial capacity and position over time. The chapter concludes with a case study that involves developing a financial model and using it to evaluate options to raise new capital for a loan fund that serves manufacturers.

Capital Management and Development Finance

In development finance, you are what you eat. The way capital is raised and managed defines the type of financing that an institution can supply in three ways. First, the form of capital raised and its repayment provisions constrain the type of financing that can be supplied to customers. An entity financed with short- to medium-term market-rate debt must meet the interest and principal payments on its capital. Consequently, it cannot supply equity capital or long-term debt without facing a high likelihood of financial failure. This constraint is illustrated by the experience of SBA-licensed SBICs and SSBICs that did not raise a large base of equity capital and relied heavily on SBA debentures.[1] They were forced to become lenders or cash management funds, rather than the intended suppliers of equity, to cover their debt payments. An institution primarily funded with equity, on the other hand, has the flexibility to supply long-term debt or equity because it has few short- and medium-term payment obligations. The form and cost of capital also influences the capacity to deliver technical assistance and development services because either dedicated grants funds or a large spread between investment earnings and their cost of funds is needed to fund these activities. Second, an institution's financial products and policies shape its access to capital and capacity to grow and present practitioners with trade-offs between achieving scale and addressing key capital gaps. Although many entities provide long-term and higher-risk financing that is undersupplied in conventional capital markets, these products require funding through grant and equity capital that allow sufficient financial flexibility. However, the availability of this type of capital is limited whereas market-rate and short- to medium-term debt is more abundant. To grow to significant scale, development finance institutions must find ways to deploy more abundant market-rate debt while cultivating sources of flexible equity-like capital. Finally, an entity's ability to bear risk (i.e., serve high-risk customers or supply risky financial products) is shaped by the risk preferences of its capital sources and its risk management policies. Institutions financed largely with insured deposits must limit their lending risks to meet regulatory standards and maintain a base of risk-averse depositors. However, entities can expand the envelope of lending risks through development services and other risk management policies. SBA guarantees, for example, allow regulated banks to supply riskier business loans. Vermont Development Credit Union used a counseling-based lending approach (see Chapter 13) to supply credit to low-income borrowers with poor credit histories that conventional banks and credit unions, which operate under the same regulatory constraints, will not serve.

Capital management, as the above discussion demonstrates, transcends raising new funds. It covers the set of policies and practices that shape an institution's available funds to supply financing to its customers. This chapter focuses on three critical areas of capital management practice: (1) setting the price and repayment terms for financial products; (2) managing and funding loan and investment losses; and (3) securing new and ongoing sources of capital. The first two topics concern preserving capital whereas the last one addresses expanding the capital base to achieve institutional growth. However, capital preservation directly affects an organization's ability to expand its capital base. Without sound loan pricing and loss management policies, an institution that raises new capital will see these resources (and its credibility) dissipate as operating and loan losses deplete their funds. These policies also contribute to capital growth through generating retained earnings and by demonstrating effective management—a critical threshold to attract funds from capital sources.

Pricing Loans and Investments

The interest rates (or investment returns) and repayment terms established by development finance entities affect their capacity to preserve and grow capital. Pricing policies determine whether income is sufficient to cover expenses and investment losses, and thus, avoid operating losses that reduce capital. Moreover, pricing affects the type of capital that an institution can attract. Market-rate pricing allows an organization to fully compensate investors for their investment risk and, thus, allows for capital to be raised from a broad pool of potential sources. Below-market pricing, on the other hand, limits potential investors to those willing to accept a below-market return. Finally, the ability to manage potential losses from fluctuating interest rates is also affected by pricing policies. When interest rates increase, financial assets with a fixed interest rate decline in value because other investments will provide a higher return. Development finance institutions, like all owners of financial assets, will see the value of their fixed rate loans decline. If an entity needs to sell these assets to generate new funds, then it will receive proceeds below the book value (i.e., the outstanding principal) and incur a capital loss.[2] Even when assets are not sold, rising interest rates will reduce future income because new funds must be borrowed at the higher interest rate, but the entity must cover this increased cost with a fixed revenue stream. When interest rates are volatile or during periods of high inflation, interest rate risk can produce large losses that threaten an institution's viability. This occurred in the late 1970s and early 1980s when many thrift institutions with large portfolios of long-term fixed rate home mortgage loans failed after inflation and interest rates exploded. Because economic development lenders face this same danger, they must monitor and manage their interest rate risk, especially when they rely heavily on borrowed funds for capital. Loan maturity is a second, closely related, capital management issue. Because interest rate risk increases with a loan's term, the amortization schedule and maturity for fixed interest loans is central to managing interest rate risk. Repayment terms also influence the pace at which an entity can recycle its capital to serve more firms. Thus, short- and medium-term loans are preferable to lower interest rate risk and increase lending volumes. However, practitioners need to balance these benefits with their mission to fill capital market gaps. Many institutions must supply long-term financing to achieve their goals and apply creative policies to limit the associated risks and constraints.

Managers can use several policies to preserve capital while advancing economic development goals and serving the financing needs of target customers. The first and foremost way to protect capital is to charge a market interest rate (or return on equity) that reflects the real risks of a transaction. Because the primary economic development finance goal is expanding capital availability, rather than subsidizing the cost of capital, market-rate pricing is consistent with most financing strategies. Moreover, market-rate pricing expands economic impact by minimizing the opportunities for capital substitution. When no subsidy exists, firms lack an incentive to seek financing from an economic development entity when they can secure conventional financing in private capital markets.

When a below market rate is warranted (e.g., real estate financing in weak market areas), a floor rate should be set that recovers all costs based on the following formula:

$$\text{Floor rate} = \text{cost of capital} + \\ \text{expected loss rate} + \text{operating cost percentage}$$

The cost of capital is the interest rate (or the return to equity investors) paid on funds raised either to supply that financial product or the institution's most recent transaction to raise capital for general purposes. The expected loss rate is the average annual loss percentage on the total outstanding loans for comparable products. Finally, the operating cost percentage is the ratio of operating costs to total income-generating assets.

Variable interest rates are the best way to manage interest rate risk. This policy, however, conflicts with development goals when it shifts interest rate risk to borrowers that can ill afford to bear it (e.g., small businesses, public purpose projects, and low-income individuals). For those financial products and situations in which borrowers can afford to bear interest rate risk, development lenders should use variable rate loan products. Examples include short-term line of credit loans, medium-term loans of modest size, loans to well-established firms that face capital supply gaps due to collateral risk, and real estate loans in which the tenants can absorb the interest rate risk. Lenders can also set interest rate caps on variable rate loans to limit their impact on borrowers, in effect, sharing the risk with customers. When development goals mandate the provision of fixed rate financing, two tools help development finance entities manage their loss exposure to rising interest rates. One option is to sell fixed rate loans to investors. Because some investors desire a fixed rate return or seek assets with a specific maturity, it is often possible to shift the interest risk to these investors.[3] The home mortgage finance market operates in this manner with lenders selling their fixed loans to large intermediaries that package them into mortgage-backed securities, which are sold to investors. This practice is discussed further in the section on capital sources. The second tool for managing interest rate risk is match funding whereby loan interest rates are matched to capital sources with the same term. Under match funding, a specific investor is located that will supply capital at a fixed rate for the same term as the loan being made. The loan interest rate is set based on the cost of the "matched funds." Loan repayments retire this funding source, and the financial institution avoids bearing the interest rate risk. Match funding can be practiced on a transaction basis for large loans and on a program basis for smaller loan products. In the latter case, an entity borrows fixed rate funds to capitalize a new program and then sets its interest rates based on this cost of funds. Depository institutions can match-fund through a "development deposit" account in which deposits are dedicated for specific loan programs. Development deposits can also support below-market rate loan products by attracting depositors that will trade some return for achieving a social goal. Institutions can also cultivate a broad range of depositors with different investment horizons to develop funding sources for matched funding. For Federal Home Loan Bank members, primarily banks,[4] their Community Investment Program is a good option to match fund transactions. This program allows members to borrow fixed rate funds at a slightly discounted rate to finance economic and community development projects that benefit low- or moderate-income individuals or areas. A more costly alternative for depository institutions is to secure matched funds through deposit brokers, who link organizations with surplus funds to insured banks and credit unions willing to pay the highest rate. This tool should be used cautiously because the cost of funds is high and deposits are not stable, with depositors often moving their funds to gain a higher interest rate. Although match funding reduces risks from rising interest rates, it can yield losses if loans are prepaid after interest rates decline. Because the prepaid funds must be reinvested at a lower interest rate while the matched funding source is repaid at the original higher rate, a negative spread and losses result. Because borrowers have an incentive to refinance when interest rates decline, this loss risk can be significant. This risk can be addressed by either charging borrowers a prepayment penalty that covers the lost interest income or raising matched funds that have a prepayment option.

Loan maturity and amortization policies are a critical tool to expand lending capacity and development outcomes. Shorter repayment periods return capital more quickly, allowing higher lending volumes. As shown in Chapter 10, reducing loan amortization has a far greater impact on lending capacity than raising interest rates or lowering loss rates. However, long-term economic development capital is scarce, and practitioners should not scale back long-term loans or rush to shorten repayment periods. Instead they need to consider how repayment policies can both advance development goals and recycle capital more quickly. One option is combining long-term amortization with medium-term maturity. This approach lowers the borrower's debt service costs to make a project feasible but returns capital in a shorter period. It is appropriate for borrowers or projects that are expected to qualify for conventional debt within a few years so that refinancing is a feasible way to satisfy the large balloon payment at maturity. A second option is to trigger refinancing when a borrower's financial situation improves. Although somewhat difficult to administer, it can be achieved by including a call provision that allows the lender to require full repayment under certain circumstances (e.g., when net income or the debt service coverage ratio reaches a set level). Alternatively, interest rate kickers can be built into the loan over time, which will provide a monetary incentive to refinance. Table 18.1 summarizes interest rate, loan maturity, and loss management policies that help development finance institutions preserve their capital.

Table 18.1 Loan Pricing and Risk Management Policies to Preserve Capital

Policy Issue or Risk	*Effective Policy or Practice*
Generating Income to Cover All Costs	1. Set market-rate interest rates and/or investment returns. 2. Set floor interest rates that cover the cost of funds, losses, and operating costs.
Reduce Interest Rate Risk	1. Use variable interest rates. 2. Sell fixed rate loans. 3. Match fund fixed rate loans.
Avoid Prepayment Losses	1. Borrow funds with prepayment/call option. 2. Include prepayment penalty in match-funded loans.
Shorten Repayment Period While Advancing Development Goals	1. Medium-term loans with long-term amortization. 2. Call options or interest rate kickers to accelerate repayment by borrowers that become "bankable".
Minimize Loan/Investment Losses	1. Annually fund loss reserves at average loss rate. 2. Charge interest rates and fees that cover the true cost of losses. 3. Raise funds for a dedicated loss reserve. 4. Diversify lending activities.

Managing and Funding Losses

The foundation for managing losses is an effective investment process with sound underwriting standards, thorough due diligence, and active monitoring systems, as elaborated in Chapter 17. However, several additional loss management policies warrant discussion here. Because losses are inevitable, even with highly effective investment methods and strong technical assistance services, institutions need to consistently fund adequate loss reserves. Because actual losses are not evenly distributed but concentrate in particular years (e.g., during recessions), they pose a significant risk when financial institutions do not plan for them (Parzen & Kieschnick, 1994). When large investment losses occur in one year, they generate a large income loss that reduces an institution's equity capital. This result is most problematic for highly leveraged banks and credit unions because it can lead regulators to close the entity. In less extreme cases, investment losses undercut the short-term cash flow needed to cover operating costs and repay investors and reduce the asset base to support financing activities over the long-term. Finally, large losses undermine an institution's credibility and capacity to raise new capital. To avoid the impact of large losses, and their uneven timing, development finance entities should reserve for losses annually based on their average loss rate over an economic cycle, rather than the expected level for the year. This practice allows institutions to build up reserves (i.e., reduce the book value of investment assets) in good years so that when large losses occur in bad years, their effect on the income statement and the balance sheet will be minimal. Although the loss reserve on an entity's financial statement is an accounting convention that is "funded" with noncash loan (or investment) loss expense items, its cash analog is the loss of income and capital that occurs when actual loans or equity investments are written off. Therefore, development finance entities need to collect cash flow to cover these losses and preserve their capital. One option, as discussed above, is to charge interest/investment income that will compensate for expected losses. A second option is collecting a fee that "self insures" against losses, especially for high-risk transactions. The Capital Access Program (CAP), discussed in Chapter 8, which uses a special fee to fund a portfolio loan loss reserve, exemplifies this approach. A third approach is to raise grants earmarked to fund a loan/investment loss reserve, essentially finding a financial partner to underwrite losses for special purpose financing. This option is appropriate for small entities that lack a sizable capital cushion to absorb losses or for organizations that are entering new and potentially risky markets for which the loss experience is not known. Some credit unions, for example, raise grants to underwrite losses that may result from an expansion into small business lending. Start-up and early-stage financial institutions, which lack the history to determine their average loss rate and build-up reserves, should look to secure grants for an initial loan loss reserve (along with raising sufficient start-up equity) as a prudent way to manage their greater loan loss risk. Finally, lenders should utilize the SBA and other loan guarantees to reduce their exposure to loan losses. This option is most relevant for community development banks and credit unions that qualify for the SBA 7(a) and CAP programs.

Raising New Capital

Securing funds to operate on a sustainable scale is the primary capital management focus for development finance institutions. This section reviews the four components of a comprehensive funding strategy: (1) raising core grant and equity capital; (2) cultivating stable sources of debt; (3) managing capital for other investors; and (4) selling loan and investment assets. Each entity needs to tailor these approaches to its capital structure, financial products, and target markets. Venture capital and equity investment funds focus on the first and fourth components, whereas elements two and four are especially important for community development banks and credit unions. On the other hand, securing grants is most critical for microenterprise funds. Revolving loan funds and community development loan funds have diversified funding needs that encompass all four. Table 18.2 presents an overview of the primary sources and issues for each approach elaborated below.

Table 18.2   Options for Raising New Capital

Capital Funding Option	Sources/Tools	Comments/Issues
Grants and Equity	1. Federal grants: EDA, CDBG, CDFI Fund 2. State and municipal grants/appropriations 3. Foundation grants and PRIs 4. Financial institution equity and equity equivalent investments 5. Intermediaries: NCC, NCIF, CRF	1. Grant sources are scarce 2. Equity sources growing 3. May limit borrowers or areas served 4. May restrict form of financing offered, operating costs, manager compensation
Debt Sources	1. Insured deposits: households, businesses, foundations, financial institutions, congregations, and governments. 2. Uninsured deposits: same as above 3. Intermediary loans: FHLB, NCC, CRF, NCIF, etc. 4. Government Loans: SBA Microloan Program, RDA 5. Bank/Financial Institution Loans	1. More plentiful than grants and equity 2. Insured deposits offer access to a large market 3. Time new debt to match demand 4. Pricing and repayment: set target rates and maturities for borrowed funds to match product and customer needs 5. Loan covenants: assess impact and negotiate changes 6. Security: minimize assets pledged; avoid full recourse debt.
Managing Funds	1. Loan origination for financial intermediaries: SBA 504 program 2. Organizing loan pools and investment partnerships: New Market Tax Credits, venture capital fund, mezzanine funds 3. Loan/investment participations	1. Key source of new capital with New Market Tax Credit Program 2. Reduces and diversifies financial risks 3. Source of fee revenue
Asset Sales and Asset Securitization	1. Loan or portfolio sales to private intermediaries (CRF) 2. Loan sales to financial institutions 3. Direct issue of asset-backed securities	1. Continuous source of new capital 2. May result in discount to book asset value 3. Most feasible for large portfolios 4. Investors: intermediaries, financial institutions and foundations

Grants and Equity Capital

Grants and equity are the financial foundation for development finance institutions and constitute a priority during start-up and major expansions. Grants and equity provide the long-term and flexible funding to address initial operating losses, absorb unexpected investment losses, and provide a cushion to raise debt. The amount of equity and/or grants needed varies by institutional model and the riskiness of financial products offered. Venture capital funds that supply only equity are financed with 100% equity. Banks and credit unions, on the other hand, operate with equity equal to 8% to 10% of assets. Scale also shapes relative reliance on equity. Because small entities generate less income to cover their fixed costs and loss reserves than do large institutions, they require a larger share of grant or equity capital to fund these expenses.

Although grants and equity capital are difficult to raise, their supply is growing through new federal programs, CRA investments, and emerging financial intermediaries. Governments and foundations are the major grant sources. Federal programs,[5] such as Community Development Block Grants (CDBG), the Economic Development Administration (EDA) Title IX program, and the Rural Development Administration have been long-standing grants providers while the CDFI Fund grew in importance during the 1990s to become the key federal funding program for development finance institutions. However, declining federal appropriations for these programs and a shift toward tax credit-based funding via New Market Tax Credits will make federal grants less important in the future. State and local government appropriations and categorical programs are a second important grant source. Some states (e.g., Pennsylvania) established dedicated grant programs to support local development finance programs,[6] but most governmental and quasi-public development finance institutions gain state or local government funding through budget or capital outlay appropriations. However, community-based and other private nonprofit finance entities can also secure government appropriations, either to capitalize general programs or create new programs in response to key policy issues. Self-Help Credit Union, for example, received a $2 million state appropriation to fund its small business lending programs (Immergluck & Bush, 1995). For nonprofit entities, foundations are a third grant source with growing importance. National foundations, such as the Ford, Mott, and Calvert Foundations, are important investors in development finance institutions, as are many foundations associated with banks and other financial institutions. Foundations also invest part of their endowments to support program goals, a practice referred to as program-related investments (PRIs). These PRIs include direct equity and equity-equivalent investments, such as long-term or nonamortizing subordinate debt.

Financial institutions, including banks, insurance companies, and pension funds, are a growing source of equity and equity-equivalent investments, spurred by CRA investment programs and growing state government and union interest in using pension funds to advance economic development goals. Several banks, such as Bank One, have created national investment programs. The growth of bank funding for CDFIs is demonstrated by the Community Development Venture Fund sector, which has relied heavily on bank equity investments for its capital.[7] State public pension funds, as detailed in Chapter 11, have been an important funding source for economically targeted venture capital funds. The supply of equity capital is likely to increase this decade as the New Market Tax Credit incentives attract private sector investment to institutions that serve low-income areas.

Several intermediaries have emerged to pool and manage these growing funding streams from foundations, financial institutions, and governments. Some are associated with trade associations (e.g., National Community Capital), whereas others (e.g., the Community Reinvestment Fund and the National Community Development Investment Fund) are stand-alone entities with a mission to expand the capital supply to development finance institutions. These intermediaries supply equity or equity-equivalent financing, but, more importantly, promise to centralize and simplify how entities raise capital by offering multiple products and services, including debt and equity-equivalent financing, loan purchases, and structuring third-party financing.

Debt Sources

Debt is the primary capital source for most development finance institutions. It typically supplies the largest amount of funding and is critical to fuel growth. Consequently, practitioners need to cultivate diverse and stable sources to ensure access to an adequate supply of debt. Stable suppliers will renew and expand funding over time while diversified sources reduce the cost of losing a key debt provider from changes in government budgets, foundation priorities, or bank mergers. Because the terms on borrowed funds constrain the financial products that an entity can supply, sources that understand economic development financing, and will alter their terms to fit its special needs, are most valuable. Through long-term amortization, below-market interest rates, and limited or subordinate security, these sources facilitate flexibility in the financial products and terms that institutions can offer to their customers. Foundations, government programs, and social investors are the primary suppliers of flexible mission-oriented debt.

As with grants and equity, debt sources vary by institution. Banks and credits unions use insured deposits to borrow from a large potential market that includes households, businesses, financial institutions, congregations, nonprofit organizations, and governments. ShoreBank demonstrates the power of insured deposits as a development capital source. Its nationally marketed Rehab CD and Development Deposits supply half of the bank's deposit base (Grzywinski, 1991) and helped it grow to a $1.3 billion institution. Many community development loan funds have copied this approach by cultivating a stable depositor base of individuals, foundations, financial institutions, and religious congregations that supply noninsured deposit-style loans. Financial intermediaries are a third and growing debt source. Federally charted entities that provide capital and liquidity to the banking system, such as the Federal Home Loan Bank, are an attractive borrowing source for banks and credit unions that can benefit from their access to low cost funds. Development finance intermediaries, such as National Community Capital and the Community Reinvestment Fund (CRF) on the other hand, supply flexible debt designed to support development finance entities. CRF, for example, created a loan product tailored to economic and community development lenders that is secured by a senior interest in their loan portfolio. The Massachusetts Life Initiative, an insurance industry community development finance intermediary, provides below-market-rate debt to state government, local government, and community-based revolving loan funds. Banks and other financial institutions represent a fourth debt source, but they must alter their conventional credit standards and gain sophistication and experience in structuring financing for development finance entities to become viable lenders. Nonetheless, some examples of innovative transactions exist. MassDevelopment,[8] a quasi-public state economic development lender, used part of its real estate loan portfolio to raise $15 million from BankBoston in 1994. Finally, government programs supply debt to economic development lenders with the USDA's Rural Economic Development Program and the SBA Microenterprise Program notable examples.

Debt financing presents a more complex set of issues for managers than do grants and equity. First, debt proceeds must be converted into loan assets fairly quickly to avoid losses from holding large cash balances that earn less interest than must be paid on the borrowed funds. Consequently, it is best to raise new debt when strong loan demand is evident. These losses can be avoided by borrowing at interest rates equal to or lower than the rate earned on cash, a policy followed by some CDLFs (Swack, 1987). However, this approach limits the pool of potential debt sources, especially when money market interest rates are low. Second, the cost and repayment period for debt capital should be structured to support an entity's development finance products. Practitioners must know the limits on interest rates that they can charge borrowers and their required spread to cover operating and loan loss costs to define the feasible interest rate at which they can borrow. When available rates exceed this level, borrowing should be deferred and alternative capitalization utilized. Similarly, a target average maturity and amortization period on debt should be set and periodically updated as the investment portfolio changes. This target should exceed the average repayment period on the entity's loan portfolio to allow room to restructure "problem" loans to viable firms and projects as they incur the inevitable setbacks on the road to success.

Institutional lenders to development finance institutions, like business lenders, manage their financial risks by placing covenants and restrictions on borrowers. Covenants typically set minimum ratios for an entity's financial performance and condition but they also can address lending policies and practices. In one case, an intermediary required prior approval of new loans made with its capital as a condition for supplying debt to a state quasi-public corporation. Managers need to assess the potential impact of proposed loan covenants on their operations, lending capacity, and the ability to serve target markets and then negotiate changes that eliminate or minimize possible negative consequences. A final issue is the recourse nature of any borrowing. New debt that requires a corporate guarantee or full faith credit pledge poses bankruptcy or liquidation risk. A more narrow pledge of specific assets is preferable, yet managers still need to consider the risks and costs associated with offering particular assets as collateral. In either case, they should negotiate, in an assertive but realistic manner, to minimize the assets pledged to secure new capital.

Managing Capital

Originating loans or managing funds for others is an effective way to expand the capital supply to serve customers. It provides an avenue for development finance entities to overcome a key capital market imperfection by reducing information and transaction costs to expand private investment in local enterprises and projects. This approach, in which a development finance institution uses its relationships and expertise to link capital providers to its customers, has two advantages. First, no new debt and equity is secured and, thus, no direct financial obligations are incurred. In effect, third-party investors incur the lending or investment risk. Second, significant fees can be generated to support staff overhead costs, and possibly other activities. Moreover, managing funds for investors will likely dominate economic development finance over the next decade with several billion dollars of New Market Tax Credits available to attract private investment capital.

Three types of relationships fall within this category. One option is to originate loans for another financial institution. Becoming a certified development corporation (CDC) under the SBA 504 program is a common and highly effective use of this method. As a CDC, economic development lenders can supply their customers with long-term, fixed rate subordinate debt at competitive interest rates while earning origination and servicing fees. A similar relationship with the major housing finance intermediaries, such as Fannie Mae, Freddie Mac, and the Neighborhood Reinvestment Corporation, is used by community development banks, credit unions, and others to expand home mortgage and home improvement financing to underserved areas and groups. A second method is organizing and managing a fund for investors. Here, the development finance entity operates as an investment management company rather than as direct financial intermediary. One common example of this approach is organizing a loan pool or multibank CDC among local banks to address a specific capital gap and then managing these funds for the local banks. Venture capitalists also apply this method by channeling investor funds into an investment partnership or limited liability corporation and then managing the invested capital. When this capital management role becomes significant, organizations have created a subsidiary management firm to isolate the legal liabilities and revenue streams connected to this function. The third alternative is using loan or investment participation from private banks, venture capital funds, or other entities to cofinance transactions. In this instance, an entity originates and oversees the financing for a firm or project but funds the transaction by raising money from several sources. Through participations, development finance institutions conserve scarce capital by leveraging financing from other sources and diversify their portfolios to lower loss risks. Because participation financing is a retail approach that operates on a deal-by-deal basis, it is time- and staff-intensive. However, developing long-standing participation relationships with a few financiers will reduce these costs.

Asset Sales and Securitization

This last way to raise new capital entails converting loan assets to cash by either selling them directly or selling a security backed by their cash flows, referred to as securitization.[9] Loans generate predictable cash flows that have a monetary value. Because investors will pay up front for this cash flow stream, development finance institutions can raise funds to make new loans by selling their old loans to investors. Although simple in theory, two obstacles exist in practice: (1) finding the investors to purchase loans or loan-based securities; and (2) generating transactions that are large enough to interest investors and cover the associated transaction costs. Some development financial institutions, especially large ones, can overcome these obstacles by cultivating direct purchasers for their loans among banks, insurance companies, and other financial institutions or by directly securitizing them. Direct sales and securitization are most feasible for entities that have at least several million dollars in loans with similar risk and collateral features. The larger scale and similarity in loans assets helps to evaluate loss risks and structure the loan sale or security to mitigate the risks to investors.

The more common way to address these obstacles is through a financial intermediary that aggregates individual loans into large pools that can be sold to investors and develops relationships with potential investors and the many parties needed to complete a securitization transaction. In the home mortgage market, many intermediaries exist, including government-sponsored enterprises (e.g., Fannie Mae and Freddie Mac) and large financial firms (e.g., Bank of America and GE Capital). Because economic development loans are complex, nonstandardized and represent a relatively small market, few intermediaries buy and securitize them. Minneapolis-based Community Reinvestment Fund (CRF)[10] is the primary intermediary that buys community and economic development loans and packages them into securities sold to investors. Through August 2003, CRF had purchased over $309 million in loans from 103 lending organizations in 24 states and the District of Columbia. These purchases generated $283.4 million in cash proceeds to the sellers, with the sale of $208.7 in bonds and notes to investors supplying the bulk of funds returned to local organizations.[11] Although CRF usually aggregates loans from multiple entities into one security, it also can structure a transaction based on the loan portfolio from a single development finance entity as when it raised over \$4 million for the Philadelphia Industrial Development Corporation based on a portfolio of 56 loans.[12]

Two issues largely shape the benefits and risks from loan sales: (1) the proceeds received from the transaction; and (2) risk sharing between the seller and buyer. Loan sales involve a discount (or premium) to the outstanding principal based on the loan's interest rate, repayment schedule, and loss risk. Loans with below market interest rates will be discounted more than market-rate loans, and this discount will grow with longer amortization and maturity periods. Discounts also occur when interest rates increase after the original loans are made, even if the original loans were not below market, because higher current rates make these loans' cash flow less valuable.[13] Loans also face discounts based on their expected losses due to collateral, security position, borrower credit, and historic loss performance. When documentation of loss experience is limited, purchasers (or rating agencies for asset-backed securities) are likely to be conservative and steeply discount cash flows and loan values. Consequently, loan sales or securitization may yield insufficient cash proceeds to be worthwhile for entities with high-risk or low-interest rate loan portfolios. The allocation of losses is a second key issue in structuring securitization or loan sale transactions. Although the term "loan sale" suggests that the seller transfers all risks to the new owner, this is not always the case. Some sales retain recourse to seller for losses. For example, the seller may have to absorb the first losses up to a fixed percentage of the loan principal or share losses on an agreed upon percentage. Some buyers retain the option to put the loan back to the seller or request a substitute loan under certain conditions. Any liability for losses retained by the seller, however, should be reflected in a higher sale price. Practitioners need to pay attention to the details of loan sale terms and ensure they are both comfortable with and compensated for any loss risk that they retain.

When an entity directly securitizes its loans, the transaction operates differently than when loans are sold to an intermediary. Under asset securitization, loan assets are transferred to a new legal entity, a trust, and the right to loan cash flow is divided into a senior claim and a subordinate one. A security is then created and sold to investors, which is backed by the senior claim on loan cash flow. The financial institution that transferred its loans to the trust often holds the subordinate interest. Proceeds from the sale of the security are a function of the loan cash flow and the debt service coverage ratio required to gain an investment grade credit rating and generate investor interest in buying the security. As with loan sales, smaller loan payments translate into lower proceeds, but this is mediated by the required coverage ratio. A high coverage ratio (e.g., 2.0) will yield modest securitization proceeds relative to loan principal, even for loans with high interest rates and fast amortization (see Table 18.4 at the end of this chapter for an example of how this works in practice). When the lender retains a subordinate interest in the loan cash flow, it has a right to this income stream after the investors are paid. If no losses occur, all excess cash flow above that paid to the security holders will return to the development financial institution. Consequently, securitization can yield more cash for the asset owner than loan sales, especially when buyers heavily discount loans for expected losses. On the other hand, the lender retains all risk of loan losses because any loss of principal and interest payments will come out of payments to the subordinate interest. Figure 18.1 diagrams how these relationships and cash flows work for a securitization transaction.

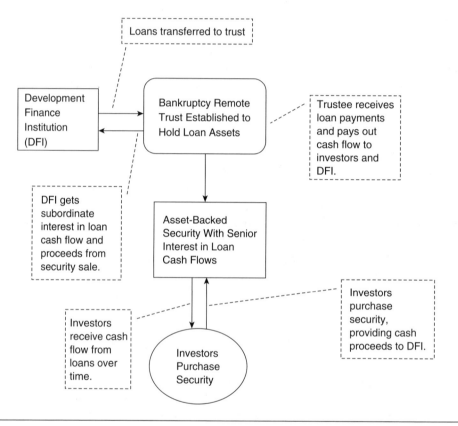

Figure 18.1   Diagram of a Loan-Backed Securitization

To expand their impact and grow to a sustainable scale, development finance entities need to diversify both their funding sources and methods. Most organizations can find opportunities to use several of the approaches discussed in this section. Practitioners need to be proactive and entrepreneurial in identifying, preparing for, and seizing these opportunities. A first step is to research potential federal, state, and local capital sources across different investor groups and the potential to utilize each of the four approaches discussed above. With this information, senior managers can expand discussions with the most promising sources and craft both short-term (2-year) and long-term (5-year) plans for securing new capital.

Financial Modeling of
Development Finance Institutions

Financial modeling is a valuable planning and management tool for development finance practitioners. On one level, it helps managers understand and plan for short-term cash flow and long-term capital needs. Moreover, models empower managers to evaluate the impact of policy and funding options on their institution's investment capacity and financial position. Although development finance entities need to maximize their capacity to finance firms and projects, managers may focus on other performance measures without quantifying their financing capacity and finding ways to expand it. The Government Land Bank, a state quasi-public corporation established to finance and undertake development projects on blighted and surplus government lands, illustrates this point. When the agency had used almost $35 million of its $40 million in state-authorized bond funds, it scaled back marketing and lending efforts because the agency believed it was running out of capital. A financial model of its cash flow, however, revealed an annual lending capacity of $5 to $6 million—well above its historic lending levels! A financial model allows managers to quantify their lending or equity investment capacity and to evaluate how it will change under different policies, capital sources, and scenarios. Moreover, a model reveals how several factors interact over time to shape an entity's development capacity and financial position. Large dynamic institutions with multiple programs, funding sources, and policy considerations, especially, need a well-crafted financial model to support sound planning and decision making.

Components of the Financial Model

Exhibits 18.1 and 18.2 present a financial model that includes a cash flow statement, balance sheet, and income statement for a simple development finance entity with one loan product and two sources of capital. It demonstrates the basic mechanics of forecasting financial statements that practitioners can adapt to their own institution. It also provides a framework that complex organizations with multiple financial products and funding sources can use through nesting submodels within the basic model structure. The components of each financial statement are presented below; the next section explains how to construct the model. The *cash flow statement* combines all major sources of cash inflows (e.g., interest on cash deposits and loans, capital gains from investments, principal repayments, fee income, etc.) and cash outflows (e.g., interest paid on borrowed funds, equity/debt repayments, operating expenses, new loans and investments made, etc.) to determine net cash flow. The *income statement* projects major revenue sources and expense items to forecast net income. Some items from the cash flow statement (e.g., interest and fee income, operating expenses and interest

Exhibit 18.1 Projected 5-Year Cash Flow Statement

Line No.	Category	Start-Up	Year 1	Year 2	Year 3	Year 4	Year 5	Explanation of Calculation
1	*Cash Inflow*							
2	Interest on cash		$57,500	$108,625	$119,516	$151,053	$99,791	Prior year cash (line 18) times the interest rate on cash
3	Interest on loans\investments		$45,000	$88,200	$245,549	$368,910	$465,626	Prior year net loans (line 21) times interest rate on loans
4	Principal Repayments		$0	$196,000	$545,664	$819,801	$1,034,724	Prior year net loans (line 21) times principal repayment rate
5	New Deposits		$2,000,000	$2,000,000	$2,000,000	$2,000,000	$2,000,00	Assumption
6	Fees		$10,000	$20,000	$20,000	$20,000	$10,000	Prior year new loans (line 10) times fee rate
7	Other income	$1,250,000	$0	$0	$0	$0	$0	
8	Total Cash In		$2,112,500	$2,412,825	$2,930,729	$3,359,764	$3,610,140	Sum of lines 1 thru 6
9	*Cash Outflow*							
10	Interest Expense		($40,000)	($120,000)	($200,000)	($280,000)	($280,000)	Prior year deposits (line 24) + new deposits (line 4) divided by 2 times the interest rate paid on deposits
11	New Loans		($1,000,000)	($2,000,000)	($2,000,000)	($2,000,000)	($1,000,000)	Assumed
12	Operating Expenses	($100,00)	($50,000)	($75,000)	($100,000)	($105,000)	($110,250)	Assumed through year 3 then inflated by assumed expense growth rate
13	Repayment of Deposits		$0	$0	$0	($2,000,000)	($2,000,000)	Assumed
14	Total Cash Outflows		($1,090,000)	($2,195,000)	($2,300,000)	($4,385,000)	($3,390,250)	Sum of lines 9 to 12
15	Net Cash Flow	$1,150,000	$1,022,500	$217,825	$630,729	$1,025,236	$219,890	Line 7 minus line 13

Exhibit 18.2 Projected 5-Year Balance Sheet and Income Statement

Line No.	Category	Start-Up	Year 1	Year 2	Year 3	Year 4	Year 5	Explanation of Calculation
16	Balance Sheet							
17	Assets							
18	Cash	$1,150,000	$2,172,500	$2,390,325	$3,021,054	$1,995,818	$2,215,708	Prior year cash (line 18) plus net cash flow (line 14)
19	Loans	$0	$1,000,000	$2,784,000	$4,182,656	$5,279,202	$5,138,895	Prior year net loans (line 21) + new loans (line 10) – principal repayments (line 3)
20	Loan\Investment Loss	$0	($20,000)	($55,680)	($83,653)	($105,584)	($102,778)	Current year net loans (line 21) times loss rate
21	Net Loans	$0	$980,000	$2,728,320	$4,099,003	$5,173,618	$5,036,117	Line 19 – Line 20
22	Total Assets	$1,150,000	$3,152,500	$5,118,645	$7,120,057	$7,169,436	$7,251,824	Line 18 + Line 21
23	Liabilities & Equity							
24	Deposits	$0	$2,000,000	$4,000,000	$6,000,000	$6,000,000	$6,000,000	Prior year deposits (line 24) + new deposits (line 4) – repaid deposits (line 12)
25	Surplus, Beginning	$1,250,000	$1,150,000	$1,152,500	$1,118,645	$1,120,057	$1,169,436	Prior year ending surplus (line 27)
26	Retained Net Income	($100,000)	$2,500	($33,855)	$1,412	$49,379	$82,389	Current year net income (Line 38)
27	Surplus, Ending	$1,150,000	$1,152,500	$1,118,645	$1,120,057	$1,169,436	$1,251,824	Line 25 + line 26
28	Total Liabilities and Equity	$1,150,000	$3,152,500	$5,118,645	$7,120,057	$7,169,436	$7,251,824	Line 24 + line 27
29	Income Statement							
30	Revenue							
31	Interest Income		$102,500	$196,825	$365,065	$519,963	$565,417	Current year interest on cash (line 1) + interest on loans (line 2)
32	Less Interest Expense		($40,000)	($120,000)	($200,000)	($280,000)	($280,000)	Current year line 9
33	Net Interest Income		$62,500	$76,825	$165,065	$239,963	$285,417	Line 31 – line 32
34	Fees		$10,000	$20,000	$20,000	$20,000	$10,000	Current year line 5
35	Total Revenue		$72,500	$96,825	$185,065	$259,963	$295,417	Line 33 + line 34
36	Less Operating Expenses		($50,000)	($75,000)	($100,000)	($105,000)	($110,250)	Current year line 14
37	Less Loan Expense		($20,000)	($55,680)	($83,653)	($105,584)	($102,778)	Current year line 20
38	New Income		$2,500	($33,855)	$1,412	$49,379	$82,389	Line 35 – line 36 – line 37

429

payments) are included in the income statement, but it also includes noncash expenses such as depreciation and a loan loss expense. Moreover, cash flow items that relate to the balance sheet (e.g., principal repayments or new capital raised) are not part of the income statement. The forecasted *balance sheet* incorporates parts of the cash flow and income statements to update asset, liability, and surplus/equity accounts. For example, the loans receivable balance is calculated by adding new loans made during the period (from the cash flow statement) to the loans receivable amount from the prior year's balance sheet and subtracting loan repayments (from the cash flow statement) and the loan loss expense (from the income statement).

Creating the Model

This section walks through the steps to build the financial model summarized in Exhibits 18.1 and 18.2. Explanations for how each item is calculated are found in the far right column of each table. The first step is to *decide on the key assumptions used in the model.* Because these assumptions drive the model's output, they need to be carefully chosen to accurately represent the entity's operating experience, policies and practices, applicable market interest rates, and other external factors. Key assumptions to address include (a) the expected interest rates earned on the fund's loans and idle cash; (b) the realized returns on equity investments (if applicable); (c) the interest rates paid on deposits, debt, and other capital; (d) the expected annual losses on loans and/or investments; (e) the rate of principal repayment on loans; (f) the growth rate for operating expenses; (g) fee income; (h) the amount of new deposits, borrowings, grants or other capital raised each year; (i) the repayment of deposits, debt principal, and other capital investments; and (j) the annual volume of new loans and investments. Some parameters may combine actual data with assumptions. For example, principal repayments from existing loans can be calculated based on their terms and combined with assumptions about the amortization of new loans to forecast total principal repayments. Table 18.3 lists the assumptions used in the model. Although the last item (new loans and investments) can be assumed, it is useful to "solve" for this variable by allowing it to be the residual value determined by the other assumptions and operating goals, such as a minimal required cash balance.

Next, *determine key operating results* that must be achieved and which serve to constrain possible outcomes under the model. These might include a minimum cash balance, minimum net cash flow or net income, or financial covenants from debt or funding sources. These constraints need to be incorporated into the model to ensure that the projected results are consistent with them.[14]

After assumptions and constraints are defined, the *annual cash flow statement is prepared.* The first step is to determine the initial balances for asset and liability accounts based on either start-up conditions or the prior year's ending balance sheet. Because Exhibit 18.2 represents a new entity created

Table 18.3   Assumptions Used in Financial Model

Assumption Description	Assumed Value
Interest Rate Earned on Cash	5%
Interest Rate Earned on Loans/Investments	9%
Annual Principal Repayment Rate	20%
Interest Rate Paid on Deposits	4%
Operating Expense Inflation Rate	5%
Annual Loan Loss Rate	2%
Fee Rate on Loan Principal	1%
Average Term on Deposits	3 years
Annual Level of New Deposits	$2,000,000

with a $1.25 million grant, cash and surplus are the sole beginning balance sheet accounts. The next step is to apply the assumptions to project cash inflows for the first period. For example, interest on cash is the product of the beginning cash balance times the assumed interest rate on idle cash whereas interest on loans is calculated by multiplying the beginning loan receivable balance times the assumed interest rate on loans, and so on. Cash outflows are calculated in a similar manner (e.g., interest paid on deposits is the beginning deposit balance times the assumed interest rate on deposits). Cash inflows and outflows are each summed; total cash outflows are subtracted from total inflows to calculate net cash flow. These steps are then repeated to forecast cash flow for subsequent years. When a spreadsheet program is used, formulas can be copied to quickly execute these calculations.

The *income statement* is prepared next, first by calculating revenue items and then expense lines. In this simple model, accruals are ignored with revenue and expense items derived from the cash flow statement. Interest income is the sum of interest on cash and interest on loans taken from the cash flow statement for the same period. Similarly, interest expense is the figure for interest paid on deposits from the cash flow projection statement during the same period. Net interest income is the difference between the interest income and interest expense amounts. Fee income and other income are also carried down from the cash flow statement and added to net interest income to compute total revenue. Expenses include the interest and operating expense line items on the cash flow statement plus a loan loss expense that is determined by multiplying the assumed loan loss rate times the loans receivable balance. Total expenses are subtracted from total revenue to yield net income. These calculations are then repeated for subsequent periods.

The *balance sheet* is the last financial statement prepared by adjusting the beginning account balances by items that increase and decrease them each period. Asset accounts are calculated as follows. Loans receivable, for example, equal the ending balance from the prior balance sheet plus new loans made during period less principal repayments for period. Cash is calculated by adding net cash flow for a period to the ending cash balance from the prior period. Liability accounts are computed next in the same manner. The deposit balance (or debt payable line item) equals the ending deposit balance for the prior period plus new deposits received (or debt borrowed) during the period less any deposit/principal repayments for the period. Surplus, the nonprofit or governmental equivalent to shareholders' equity, is determined by adding the retained earnings (or loss) for the period, obtained from the income statement, to the ending surplus from the prior period.

Two refinements to these simple calculations should be considered to correct potential errors. One refinement is changing the projection period. Although annual periods are used in the model, quarterly or semiannual projections are more accurate, especially for a growing organization in which account balances are changing significantly over each year. Calculations based on the prior period ending balance will be inaccurate in this situation. For example, when an RLF increases its loan portfolio from $5 million to $10 million in a year, a projected interest income figure based on the $5 million ending balance from the prior year will greatly underestimate the true income. A quarterly period for calculations allows each account balance to be adjusted more often to reflect changes over the year. An alternative method to incorporate changing account balances into the flow calculations is using the average account balances over the period as the basis for the computations. For example, the interest income on loans would be projected based on the average loans receivable balance for the beginning and end of the year. A second adjustment corrects for accrual versus cash accounting. Because this model treats cash flows and revenues/expenses as identical for some items, it does not accurately capture real differences between the cash flow statement and the income statement. For example, accrued interest income is usually higher than cash interest collections because interest payments are typically made in the month after interest is earned.[15] To reflect this situation, interest income on an annual cash flow statement could be calculated as 1 month's worth of interest revenue from the prior year plus 11 months' interest revenue from the current year. Similar adjustments for other items in which a large difference exists between the accrual and cash flow figure can be made.

Once all three financial statements are created, they should be reviewed for errors, inconsistencies, and implausible results. Beyond scrutinizing specific calculations and formulas, computational errors are revealed when the balance sheet total assets do not equal the sum of liabilities and equity/surplus or if an item that should be identical on multiple statements is different. Implausible results or ones that vary greatly from past experience, on the other hand, may reflect unrealistic or inconsistent assumptions, such as projecting declining interest rates on cash while loan interest rates rise or assuming that investments will earn a high return but have a small loss rate.

A last exercise is to conduct sensitivity analysis to test the impact of changed assumptions, policies, and economic scenarios on financial results. Sensitivity analysis helps refine the model and its assumptions but also provides insight into potential risks that need to be managed and policy changes to consider. Once developed and tested, the completed model is ready to use for financial planning and evaluating the impact of key strategy, policy, and capital management decisions.

Case Study: Raising New
Capital for the Manufacturer's Fund

The Manufacturers' Fund is a quasi-public state agency created in 1984 to help retain manufacturing jobs. Through diagnostic advice, technical assistance, and working capital financing, the Fund helps manufacturers manage business transitions and regain profitability. In the past 3 years, the Fund made 60 loans totaling $11 million, matched by $20 million in private financing, and stabilized 2,600 jobs. Faced with strong demand but limited capital, the Fund is actively exploring ways to expand its lending capacity. Although it closes $3 to $4 million in loans each year, the Fund is confident that demand can support twice this volume. With funding from its historic sources (the U.S. Economic Development Administration and the state legislature) unreliable, management hopes to use its existing loan assets and cash flow to secure new capital to expand its lending volume. Four options to raise additional capital have been identified, and the Fund needs to decide which ones to use.

Loan Products and Portfolio

The Manufacturers' Fund provides subordinate debt to small manufacturers that experienced a decline in sales and/or profits but are positioned for a turnaround. In underwriting loans, the Fund looks for firms that were historically profitable but had a temporary downturn that can be addressed through a combination of cost cutting, improved operations, or new market opportunities. It seeks strong management capacity to address the recent problems and execute turnaround plans. Portfolio firms have annual sales ranging from $700,000 to $50 million, with the average at $5 million. Financial criteria for loans include projected 1.0 debt service coverage, based on earnings before interest, depreciation, and taxes, and a minimum of 3 months' profitability before funding the loan. Four-fifths of its loans are secured by a blanket second position claim on all assets with the remaining 20% split equally between loans in which the Fund is the sole lender and has a senior security interest and loans in which it has a third or lesser position on assets.

Loans average $190,000 but range from $50,000 to $400,000. Repayment periods are 3 or 4 years (the average term is 40 months) with equal monthly principal payments. Interest rates average prime plus 2%, or 10.25% based on current rates, but all new loans are being originated at prime plus 3%. The Fund also collects a one-time fee equal to 3% of principal at loan closing. With historic annual loan losses (i.e., write-offs of uncollected principal and interest) between 1.6% and 7.7% of outstanding principal, the Fund budgets 4% to 5% annually for these losses.

Capitalization and Financial Position

The Fund's assets totaled $9.94 million on 6/30/99, with $2.3 million in cash, $7.56 million in loan receivables, and $84,000 in interest and fees receivable. Its fund balance was $9.91 million, and liabilities totaled $32,000 in accounts payable.

Despite aggressive efforts, the Fund has not secured new capital from the EDA, which is reducing its funding of revolving loan funds and targeting grants to new RLFs. The state legislature has appropriated $600,000 annually to the Fund over the past several years, but these monies largely offset loan write-offs and did not expand its capital base and lending capacity. After 3 years of effort, the legislature appropriated $2.45 million to the Fund for FY2000 and, therefore, is unlikely to supply another large capital appropriation in the next few years.

New Funding Options

Four funding options emerged from staff efforts to use the Fund's existing loan portfolio to raise new capital.

Community Reinvestment Fund. This nonprofit organization purchases loans from governmental and nonprofit lenders and then packages the loans into securities that are sold to investors. CRF reviewed the Fund's loan portfolio and identified 24 loans for purchase. CRF will pay $2.9 million for these 24 loans, which have outstanding principal of $3.2 million. This transaction would yield $2.9 million in cash for the Fund while CRF would receive all future interest and principal payments from the purchased loans. The Fund could continue to service these loans for a .25% fee or allow CRF to service them. Advantages of the CRF option include the nonrecourse nature of the sale and the small discount to face value. This relationship could create an ongoing market for the Fund's loans, potentially allowing it to sell part of its portfolio to CRF each year. One concern with this option is the low interest earnings on the sale proceeds before they are disbursed for new loans. Interest on cash is 5.5% compared to the 10.25% rate on loans. Delays in closing new loans after the sale would reduce income and possibly generate an operating loss.

Bank Loan. The Fund approached four banks to secure a line of credit backed by its loan portfolio. A line of credit would allow the Fund to draw down funds when loans were ready to close and avoid the lower income from holding large cash balances. A large line of credit at an interest rate below its lending rate would expand the Fund's lending capacity with a neutral or even positive impact on net income. Banks, however, were reluctant to lend to the Fund without a state government guarantee, which the Fund could not provide. Without this guarantee, the only line of credit offered was for $700,000 at prime plus .5% secured by a senior position on the Fund's entire loan portfolio. The Fund could draw down the line of credit for a year during which time it would only pay interest. After this year, the outstanding principal would be repaid over 4 years. The Fund did not pursue this option, as it provided little new capital but required pledging the Fund's entire loan assets as security.

BDC Loan Sales. The Business Development Corporation (BDC), a consortium of commercial banks, offered to purchase up to $2 million in loans at face value and receive interest payments equal to the prime rate. The loans would be purchased on a nonrecourse basis with the fund continuing to service the loans for BDC. This arrangement allows the Fund to keep a spread of two to three percentage points on each loan that is sold, which would increase the Funds' earnings and help offset any lost income if the sale proceeds were not quickly loaned to new companies. BDC identified $1 million in loans to purchase immediately with another $1 million to be purchased at a later date. Despite its attractive pricing, this option has two drawbacks. First, the timing of the second million in new capital is uncertain. Second, BDC is cherry picking the Fund's strongest loans, which may increase loss rates for the retained loans.

Securitization. Under a fourth option, the Fund would securitize its loans to raise funds. This option involves transferring loans to a separate trust that would issue debt secured by the loans and their cash flow. The cash flow would be divided into two parts: a senior investment grade senior security to be sold to investors; and a subordinate interest that would be held by the Fund. Investment bankers and rating agencies indicated that the senior security needs debt service coverage of at least 1.50 to be marketable. Thus, the Fund can raise new capital equal to the principal amount that can be serviced with a 1.50 debt coverage ratio by the loans transferred to the Trust. As the subordinate security holder, the Fund would receive only the excess loan cash flow remaining after interest and principal payments are paid to the senior debt holders semiannually. In practice, monthly interest and principal payments from loans would be paid to a trustee who would make payments to debt holders every 6 months, first paying the owners of the senior securities and then transferring the residual cash flow, after any required reserves, to the Fund. Based on a conservative estimate of $10.5 million in loans receivable at the end of FY2000 and assuming that the senior security would have 3-year maturity, 8% interest rate, and semiannual principal and interest payments, the Fund could raise $7 million from a securitization transaction. Table 18.4 summarizes this transaction, including the cash flow from the $10.5 million loan portfolio, principal and interest payments on the senior notes, and excess cash flow before any loan losses.

Table 18.4   Securitization Transaction

MMF Loan Cash Flow	Year 1	Year 2	Year 3	Total
Principal Payments	$4,200,000	$4,200,000	$2,100,000	$10,500,000
Interest Payments	$924,000	$462,000	$115,500	$1,501,500
Total Loan Cash Flow	$5,124,000	$4,662,000	$2,215,500	$12,001,500
Available for Debt Service	$3,416,000	$3,108,000	$1,477,000	$8,001,000

Debt Service on Senior Debt	Year 1	Year 2	Year 3	Total
Interest	$560,000	$331,360	$109,040	$1,000,400
Principal	$2,858,000	$2,779,000	$1,363,000	$7,000,000
Total Debt Service Payments	$3,418,000	$3,110,360	$1,472,040	$8,000,400
Debt Coverage Ratio	1.50	1.50	1.50	1.50
Excess Trust Cash Flow	$1,706,000	$1,561,640	$743,460	$4,001,100

Goals and Constraints

The Fund's goal is to increase its annual lending capacity to $6 to $7 million. Because current cash flow supports $3 to $4 million in new loans each year, the Fund recognizes that multiple transactions and capital sources developed over several years may be necessary to achieve this goal. Nonetheless, it must decide which options to pursue in the near term because it already has loans ready to close that exceed its available funds. The Fund is open to all options and is willing to offer its own guarantee to help make a transaction viable. However, any transaction must leave it with sufficient interest and fee income to cover its operating expenses and maintain a minimum cash balance of $650,000. Given the time and costs required to complete a transaction, the Fund would prefer a larger transaction and has set a $1 million floor.

Recommendation

Your assignment is to recommend which option or combination of options the Fund should use to expand its lending capacity. To support your recommendation, project each option's impact on the Fund's lending capacity and cash flow. Prepare a 3-year cash flow statement, balance sheet, and income statement for FY2001 through FY2003 using the FY2000 cash flow projection, the June 30, 2000, projected balance sheet (see Exhibits 18.3 and 18.4), the summary of each option, and the following assumptions. Base your recommendation on which option allows the Fund to maximize its lending capacity while funding its required operating expenses and minimum cash balance. However, other factors also should be considered, such as which transaction leaves the Fund in the best financial condition, downside risks to the Fund, and the impact on the Fund's capacity to raise additional capital in the future. To simplify the analysis, assume that the Fund receives the full proceeds of each transaction without paying legal fees or other transaction costs.

Use the following assumptions to first prepare a baseline projection without new capital and then to present a scenario for each alternative:

- Legislative appropriations continue at $600,000 annually
- The Fund's loans have an 11% average interest rate (prime plus 2.5%)
- The average interest earned on cash balances is 5.5%
- Loan repayments are made with equal principal payments and an average amortization period of 30 months (i.e., 1/30 of the loan principal is repaid each month)
- A 3% fee is paid for each new loan at closing
- Operating expenses grow by 4% annually
- The fund maintains a minimum cash balance of $650,000
- Annual loan losses equal 5% of loans receivable
- The fund has a $1 million backlog of loans to fund; new capital raised above $1 million will be disbursed for new loans at a maximum rate of $1.5 million per quarter
- Any funding transaction will occur at the end of FY 2000

Prepare a brief memo that presents your recommendation and explain why it is the Fund's best option. Attach pro forma financial statements that show the impact of each option on the Fund's cash flow and lending capacity.

Exhibit 18.3   Manufacturers' Fund FY2000 Cash Flow Projection

Cash Inflow	Annual Total
Regular Loan Principal Payments	$2,546,285
Early Loan Repayments	$450,000
Loan Interest Income	$1,021,046
Interest on Cash	$71,559
Fee Income	$213,900
State Appropriations	$2,450,000
Total Cash In	$6,752,790
Cash Outflow	
Operating Expenses	$1,301,520
Loan Closing Disbursements	$7,130,000
Total Cash Outflow	$8,431,520
Net Cash Flow	$(1,678,730)
Beginning Loan Receivables	$7,555,659
Principal Payments	$(2,996,285)
Loan Closing Disbursements	$7,130,000
Loan Write-offs	$(500,000)
Ending Loans Receivable	$11,189,374

Exhibit 18.4   Projected Balance Sheet, June 30, 2000

Assets

Cash and Cash Equivalents	$625,832
Interest and Fees Receivable	$60,000
Loans Receivable	$11,189,374
Total Assets	$11,875,206

Liabilities and Fund Balance

Accounts Payable	$60,000
Fund Balance	$11,815,206
Total Liabilities and Fund Balance	$ 11,875,206

Endnotes

1. This experience is summarized in Chapter 11, pp. 423 to 429, and analyzed in much greater depth in two articles by Timothy Bates (Bates, 1997; Bates, 2000).

2. This loss will be even larger if the loans sold carry a below-market interest rate. Investors will now doubly discount the asset's value—once for the below-market subsidy and second for the increase in market interest rates.

3. Loan sales have a second benefit because they generate funds to support a new round of lending.

4. FHLB members include federal- and state-chartered thrift institutions, commercial banks, credit unions, and insurance companies. For information on CIP and other economic development financing programs, see www.fhfb.gov/FHLB/ FHLBP_economic_types.htm

5. See Chapter 14 for a more complete overview of federal government funding programs.

6. Pennsylvania's Community Development Bank provides loans, grants, and technical assistance to CDFIs in the state.

7. Banks supply 55% of CDVC capital. See Gaither (2002), p. 26.

8. This transaction was undertaken by the Government Land Bank, which later merged with the Massachusetts Industrial Finance Agency to form MassDevelopment.

9. A good introduction to securitization and its history is found in articles by Kendall (1996) and Ranieri (1996).

10. CRF initially focused on securitizing loans but now offers other financial products to development finance institutions, including direct financing backed by a senior interest in a set of loans, loans structured based on overall entity cash flow, and forward loan purchase commitments.

11. CRF also provided over $54 million in loan participations to local lending organizations, funded through other sources of capital. Data provided directly by CRF.

12. This transaction was described in the Community Reinvestment Fund's 1997 Annual Report.

13. A loan will sell at a premium to its outstanding principal when it carries an interest rate above market rates, assuming it is fairly priced to reflect its repayment risks.

14. For models developed with Excel software, the goal-seek and solver functions can be used for this purpose.

15. This point is true when the loan receivable balance is increasing. When loans receivable are declining each month, accrued interest will be lower than cash interest paid.

PART VII

Conclusions

19 Economic Development Finance Practice and Its Future

Economic development finance is a diverse and growing field in which practitioners face a broad array of financial and policy tools and program models. With knowledge of these mechanisms and models, economic development professionals are equipped to design and implement effective strategies and programs for their communities. Economic development finance, as emphasized throughout this book, concerns ensuring the supply of capital to communities, business enterprises, and development projects in a strategic and sustainable manner. This involves a mode of practice that is institutional rather than transactional; a practice that transcends assembling funds for the latest project or creating a new program to focus on altering the way capital markets and financial institutions operate. Most practitioners will pursue this mission in one of two roles. The first role is as a generalist—the economic development manager or policy maker for a community, region, or state. This position offers the broadest vantage and opportunity to shape capital supply. Generalists are situated to comprehensively uncover capital gaps and address them through working with private financial institutions and regulators, on the one hand, and leveraging the resources of federal and state programs, development finance intermediaries, and existing alternative financial institutions, on the other. They can push existing financial institutions to respond to supply gaps, and convene key leaders to launch new programs that are necessary to expand development services and address the most challenging market imperfections. The second role is as an institution builder—the practitioners who create, manage, and operate development finance institutions. Their mission is to establish highly effective organizations that direct capital to underserved enterprises and communities. They establish and manage the critical relationships, financial resources, and capabilities to deliver financial products and related development services. Both roles are vital to ensuring capital availability, as is good communication and collaboration between these two types of practitioners.

Ten Principles for Economic Development Finance Practice

Effective economic development practice is guided by several principles embedded in the work of successful practitioners and high-impact organizations. These principles were highlighted in previous chapters and are repeated here for clarity and emphasis.

Define a strategy that links financing activities to broader economic development goals, opportunities, and conditions. Financial market interventions have the greatest impact when they are coordinated with other initiatives and are targeted to overcome local constraints and leverage key industries and opportunities. Strategies maximize program impact by adapting models and tools to local circumstances and targeting limited resources. Sound strategies also develop synergistic relationships with nonfinancial initiatives, recognizing that capital is only one input into the economic development process.

Understand your market. Detailed market knowledge is essential to identify capital gaps, uncover their causes, and formulate appropriate products and services. In-depth market research on both the demand and supply sides is a precondition for the effective design of new organizations, programs, and products. Regular market research also should be used by established programs to identify and respond to changing capital market conditions and customer needs, emerging customer groups, and new opportunities.

Avoid capital substitution. Nothing is gained when public or nonprofit resources supply financing that occurs under the standard operation of private markets. Practitioners must focus on filling capital market gaps and financing viable firms and projects that cannot secure sufficient conventional capital. This principle applies to all economic development finance tools, not only to direct financing programs. Loan guarantees should induce lenders to bear more risk rather than reduce their risk on credit that they already supply. Similarly, tax-increment financing must be targeted to areas and projects for which infrastructure improvements are essential to gain new development, not to subsidize costs in prime locations or as a politically expedient alternative to general obligation bonds.

Collaborate with private market institutions. Strong relationships with private financial intermediaries expand capital availability and facilitate deeper market knowledge. Private financial institutions allocate much of the capital supplied to small firms and development projects; the most direct path to expanded capital availability is through changing their policies and practices. Practitioners have many tools and incentives to pursue this outcome, including strong evidence that economic development finance is a good market opportunity with competitive returns. Banks and other private financial institutions are also an important funding source for economic development finance organizations; strong working relationships help access their capital to fuel growth. Because private institutions monitor markets and understand how industry trends shape which customers and products they supply, collaborations help unlock important information on the capital gaps and development services that economic development practitioners need to address.

Integrate financial and development services. Demand-side factors are often the most critical constraint to unlocking financing opportunities and achieving positive financial and development outcomes. Numerous programs and institutions have demonstrated how training, counseling, and technical assistance unlock new sources of demand, expand entrepreneurs' capacity to productively use capital, and reduce loan and investment losses. Practitioners need to understand the nonfinancial obstacles to economic development, design activities to overcome these impediments, and integrate them into their services and products. Moreover, a development ethos should be incorporated into the core values of economic development finance organizations.

Institutionalize accountability to stakeholders. Organizations need accountability to ensure responsiveness to their customers and partners but also to marshal resources to advance their agenda. Because economic development finance programs have diverse stakeholders with varied interests, they should use several mechanisms to ensure accountability. A strong accountability system includes formal stakeholder representation on governing boards, regular outreach and two-way communication with customers and allies, transparent decision-making and financing processes, explicit performance standards with periodic reporting on results, and independent evaluation of program outcomes and performance.

Use market-rate pricing. With the exception of some real estate development projects, subsidized financing does not help expand capital availability. A primary goal of economic development finance programs is to ensure that capital is supplied to entrepreneurs, firms, and projects that can productively use it, despite capital market imperfections. This means extending capital to users who can pay a fair market price, and not supplying below-market financing. Pricing capital fairly has many advantages for development finance entities. It increases their revenue, maximizes potential funding sources, and minimizes losses from asset sales. Moreover, it also reduces the opportunity for capital substitution by not serving firms that seek subsidies. This principle also applies to lowering the cost of capital for customers that face predatory pricing or for whom markets inaccurately assess investment risk.

Understand and manage risk. Economic development finance programs are in the business of bearing risks, especially those eschewed by mainstream financial institutions. Consequently, practitioners need a deep understanding of these risks and effective ways to manage and mitigate them. The most recognized form of risk is from investments in firms and projects; it is managed through effective development services, sound investment standards and polices, a thorough due-diligence and underwriting process, strong postinvestment monitoring, and industry knowledge. However, managers also need to understand and focus on the loss exposure from interest rate volatility and investment maturity. Conventional financial institutions use tools to manage these risks, such as variable rate loans, match funding, and asset sales, that economic development practitioners can replicate and adapt to their needs.

Raise capital that matches the financing strategy. An institution's capital shapes the type and terms of financing that it can supply. To fulfill their mission, therefore, organizations must raise capital that fits their financial products and services. This requires creativity and persistence to identify new sources that can supply the desired form of capital and to cultivate them as steady and repeat investors.

Assemble staff with the right skills, experience, and values. As with any organization, people determine the effectiveness of economic development entities. However, they require a special staff that combines expertise in economic development with both the financial skills needed to make and manage investments and the business experience to deliver development services. Moreover, a workforce that is committed to public and community service and thrives on learning and innovation is equally important. Such employees supply the drive and creativity that is essential to overcome the challenges faced in building sustainable and high-impact economic development finance programs.

An Agenda for the Future

Effective economic development finance practice clearly depends on the work of individual practitioners, but it is also the result of supportive laws, institutions, and knowledge. Important advances have occurred in all three areas over the past quarter century. Noteworthy legal changes include the Community Reinvestment Act, bank CDC regulations, and the expansion of state tax increment financing and assessment districts laws. Important support institutions include federal agencies (e.g., EDA, SBA, and the CDFI Fund), trade associations (e.g., IEDC and NCC), financial intermediaries (e.g., CRF), foundations (e.g., the Ford and Mott Foundations), and research centers (e.g., the Aspen Institute and CfED). An expanded knowledge base also has emerged from the work of leading development finance institutions, scholars, research centers, and the efforts of trade associations to document and disseminate best practices. The strengthening and expansion of this multifaceted support system is essential to overcome key challenges faced by the economic development finance field: adapting to new capital market conditions, building more sustainable and high-impact institutions, cultivating new sources of capital, and achieving long-term economic development outcomes. The following pages outline an agenda to help address these challenges and advance the scale and impact of the economic development finance field.

Expand the Community Reinvestment Act's coverage and disclosure requirements.[1] The affirmative requirement that financial institutions serve the credit and financial service needs of the entire community should be extended beyond federally chartered depository institutions to commercial finance companies, insurance companies, mortgage banks, and investment banks. These large and important sources of capital need to be held to the same standards as banks. Disclosure requirements also need to be expanded to provide more complete information on economic development lending activities. More complete disclosure of small business and small farm loans, including data on loan applications and their disposition by the race, gender, census tract, and business size would help identify business credit gaps and potential discriminatory practices. Similar disclosures are also needed for multifamily and commercial/industrial real estate loans, which are not now subject to public reporting requirements.

Create strong secondary market institutions. Access to secondary markets is critical to expanding the supply of capital to economic development finance institutions. An active secondary market will allow programs to sell their existing loan and investment assets to raise new capital while helping to manage financial risks. Moreover, it will establish a track record on the investment returns from economic development loans and equity investments, a precondition to further expand the market for these assets. Strong financial intermediaries with the expertise, relationships, and capital to buy loans and package them into securities are essential to this agenda. The Community Reinvestment Fund exemplifies this type of institution, and practitioners, policy makers, and trade associations need to support its growth. Additional intermediaries, however, are needed to add capacity, test new approaches, develop additional investor relationships, and introduce competition. The success of these secondary market intermediaries depends on cultivating new investors interested in buying their securities. More dialogue with potential investors, both mainstream and socially oriented ones, is needed to understand their investment objectives, uncover any misconceptions, and educate them on the risk, return, and other characteristics of securities backed by economic development assets. Finally, practitioners also need to be educated on the benefits of selling their assets and the mechanisms and skills involved.

Develop good data on the financial performance and impact of economic development finance institutions and investments. Good performance data helps organizations and their stakeholders evaluate program effectiveness. This data tracks the organization-level performance for specific types of institutions (e.g., revolving loan funds, community development credit unions, and microenterprise programs). Considerable progress has occurred in this arena through the work of industry associations and research centers that establish standard definitions and protocols for reporting data and analyze this information for a large sample of programs. The Aspen Institute and the Corporation for Enterprise Development have been leaders in this effort, and their work needs to be continued and expanded. One area for additional work is to develop more rigorous and complete impact measures that account for capital substitution, address broader outcomes (beyond jobs), and use consistent and sound cost measures. A second form of data tracks the financial performance of individual investments in similar asset classes. Although this data is more difficult to collect and analyze, it would demonstrate the actual risk and returns of different types of economic development debt and equity, which is necessary to cultivate new sources of capital. A collaborative initiative to study, design, and implement an asset-level performance database should be undertaken through key industry associations, federal agencies, foundations, and other stakeholders.

Increase and improve practitioner education and training. As the economic development and community development finance fields grow, the demand for practitioners with appropriate skills will increase. Ensuring the supply of skilled professionals to meet this demand is vital to the field's growth and to building and sustaining high-impact programs. These practitioners need strong financial and economic development skills along with an understanding of and commitment to the field. A second need is for senior managers with the right mix of leadership, organizational, and technical skills to build and sustain large and more complex institutions. Although some advance degree programs, short courses, and workshop exist, a more sophisticated and complete educational system is needed to support the field. This system should be rooted in a sound articulation of the skills, knowledge, and experience required to become an effective practitioner and the continuing education necessary to retain and update these competencies over time. The elements of this system include new professional degree programs (or concentrations within existing business, planning, and public policy programs); more comprehensive courses and skills training for existing practitioners; and establishing a certification program based on standards for the training, experience, and expertise that qualifies someone to be recognized as a development finance professional.

Foster dialogue and collaboration between the economic development profession and the CDFI industry. Economic development finance practice has emerged from and is organized into two distinct professional identities: economic development and community development. The former is rooted in the work of governmental and nonprofit organizations that focus on business development and job creation goals. The latter emerged out of antipoverty and neighborhood development practice and has spurred the growth of the CDFI industry. Each field possesses considerable knowledge, expertise, and resources that could benefit the other. Moreover, they face common challenges; and their capacity to secure new funding sources, build key support institutions, and develop knowledge will be greater when they work together. More dialogue between the leadership and practitioners in both fields is needed to identify common interests and formulate a shared agenda around legislation, funding, training, and knowledge development. Two avenues for promoting this dialogue include regular meetings between the leadership of key trade associations and holding one or more summits among practitioners in both fields.

Establish and fund an industrywide applied research agenda. Innovation and continuous improvement are critical to all fields, and economic development finance is no exception. Applied research supports both processes by developing new knowledge and techniques and by evaluating and codifying best practices. Applied research activities for the economic development field are quite fragmented and often not aligned to the needs of practitioners and organizations. Through formulating an industrywide applied research agenda and raising funds to implement this agenda, significant momentum would be gained in developing and disseminating critical knowledge to improve the impact of economic development finance programs. The Aspen Institute's FIELD initiative for the microenterprise field is an excellent example of such an applied research program; this type and scale of research is needed for the entire economic development field. A periodic research-oriented conference of practitioners, major funding organizations, and scholars could provide the basis for developing and implementing this applied research agenda, and help disseminate its results.

Endnote

1. Many of these proposals were included in the CRA Modernization Act of 2001 (H.R. 865) sponsored by Representatives Tom Barrett and Luis Gutierrez and described in Squires (2003).

Glossary

Accounts payable.   Unpaid bills to suppliers for goods and services used by a business.

Accounts receivable loan.   A loan with accounts receivables as collateral.

Accounts receivables.   Uncollected bills from customers for goods and services that a business has supplied.

Accrual accounting.   A financial record keeping system in which transactions are recorded to represent a firm's earned income, or economic results, over a period rather than its cash flow.

Accrued expenses.   Business costs that a firm has recognized for accounting purposes prior to receiving a bill for them or having paid for them.

Accumulated deficit.   The sum of net losses that a business has incurred over its lifetime.

Additional paid-in capital.   The difference between the actual funds raised from the sale of shareholder equity and the par value listed on the balance sheet.

Amortization.   The noncash expense item used to record the diminution of a large nonfixed asset investment over time.

Amortization period.   The time period over which the regular repayment of loan principal is determined.

Assessment district financing.   A financing mechanism that collects a special charge from property owners or businesses in a geographic area to fund infrastructure or services within that area.

Asset-based lending.   A financing approach in which a lender evaluates and lends against asset collateral value and places less emphasis on the firm's overall balance sheet and financial ratios.

Balance sheet.   A financial statement that summarizes what a firm owns (its assets) and the claims against the assets (liabilities and shareholders' equity) on a specific date.

Bank community development corporation.   A one-time investment or ongoing activity undertaken by a bank to advance the public welfare that falls outside of normal banking activities but is allowed under special regulations.

Bonds.   A form of debt used to raise funds in public capital markets and through private placements to institutional investors in which a three-way legal arrangement exists between the borrower, the bondholders (the suppliers of capital), and a trust company.

Break-even sales level. The amount of sales that a firm must obtain to begin earning a profit.

Bridge loan. A short- to medium-term loan that provides temporary funds until the permanent source of financing is available, often used in financing real estate projects.

Business improvement district (BID). A type of assessment district used to improve a defined business area, typically a downtown commercial district.

Business plan. A document that details a business's market potential, strategy, planned operations, and financing needs that is used to raise debt or equity financing.

Capital access program (CAP). A state and local government loan guarantee program that uses a portfolio-based guarantee rather than guaranteeing individual loans.

Capital market gap. The failure to supply specific types of capital to a class of firms or projects that can use it most productively due to market imperfections.

Capital policies. The forms and sources of capital that an economic development finance institution uses to fund its programs and services.

Capitalized interest reserve. A reserve fund set aside from the proceeds of a loan to cover future interest payments.

Cash basis accounting. A financial record-keeping system in which transactions are recorded and reported based on the receipt and expenditure of cash.

Cash flow statement. A financial statement that documents a firm's actual cash flow during a period, as opposed to accrual accounting results.

Certified development corporation. A SBA-licensed private corporation that originates subordinate SBA debentures for the SBA 504 program.

Closing. The signing and submission of the necessary contracts and related documents to complete a financing transaction.

Closing agenda. A list of the required documents to complete and settle a financing transaction and the party responsible for preparing or providing each one.

Collateral. In return for providing debt, lenders typically require the borrower to make available, or pledge, specific assets as collateral that provide an additional source of loan repayment if the borrower's cash flow is insufficient. When assets are pledged as loan collateral, also referred to as security for the loan, the debt holder has a legal right to sell the collateral and apply the sale proceeds to unpaid interest, principal, and collection costs.

Commercial bank. A government-chartered financial institution with broad lending powers that has access to government deposit insurance.

Commercial finance company. A financial institution that is not government-chartered and does not raise capital through deposits, and thus, has more flexibility to supply higher risk debt to households and businesses.

Common stock. The security that provides the holder with an ownership interest in a corporation.

Community development bank. Federally or state-chartered banks that are created with the mission of advancing the economic and social well-being of a specific service area and its low- and moderate-income population.

Community development block grant (CDBG) program. A federal grant program that provides city governments with entitlement grants by formula and discretionary small city grants administered by state governments to benefit low- and moderate-income individuals and advance other national objectives.

Community development credit union (CDCU). Credit unions with a mission of serving low-income individuals and neighborhoods.

Community development financial institution (CDFI). A nongovernmental organization that provides financial and related development services to population groups or areas that are underserved by mainstream capital markets, and are often low- and moderate-income.

Community Development Financial Institution (CDFI) Fund. A federal program established by Congress in 1994 to certify organizations as Community Development Finance Institutions and provide capital and technical assistance to support their programs.

Community development loan fund. A locally organized and controlled nonprofit organization that provides credit to businesses, affordable housing projects, and nonprofit organizations to advance local community development goals.

Community development venture capital fund. A type of private venture capital fund that invests in firms to achieve both high financial and social returns.

Community Reinvestment Act (CRA). A federal law enacted in 1977 that requires federally chartered depository institutions to provide credit to their entire service area, including low- and moderate-income (LMI) neighborhoods, and directs bank regulators to assess CRA performance and use their supervisory authority to "encourage" banks to comply with the CRA requirements.

Company valuation. The value placed on a company, which is used in private equity financing to determine what share of the company new investors receive for their investment.

Construction loan. A short-term loan used to finance the construction and development phase of a real estate project.

Convertible debt. A type of debt in which the debt holder has the option to convert its debt into firm equity, usually common stock, according to specified terms.

Costs of goods sold. The direct expenses incurred by a business to make its products, including materials, labor, energy, and other items.

Credit union. A cooperative financial organization that provides banking services and credit to members with a common affiliation or bond.

Current portion of long-term debt. The portion of a firm's total outstanding debt that must be repaid over the next year.

Current ratio. A ratio that measures the proportion of current assets to current liabilities that indicates its capacity to convert assets into the cash needed to meet obligations over the next year.

Debt. A contract whereby funds are provided by a lender (the debt holder) to another party (the borrower) who must repay the funds based on a specified interest rate and repayment schedule.

Debt service coverage ratio. A measure of a firm's capacity to repay debt calculated by dividing the required principal and interest payments (debt service payments) for a period, usually a year, by the projected cash flow for the same period.

Debt service reserve. A reserve set aside from loan proceeds to make future principal and interest payments.

Debt-to-equity ratio. The ratio of a firm's total liabilities to total shareholders' equity that measures its reliance on debt versus equity financing.

Debt with warrants. A loan provided to a firm partly in exchange for the right to purchase an amount of stock at a preset price for a specified period of time.

Default rate. The percentage of a financial institution's loans that have been declared in default of their loan agreement.

Deferred income. An obligation to provide goods or services for which a business has received advance payment.

Delinquency rate. The percentage of a financial institution's loans for which payments are late beyond a specified period (e.g., a 30-day or 90-day delinquency rate).

Depreciation. The noncash expense that accounts for the diminution in an asset's value over time.

Development budget. A financial statement for real estate projects that presents the uses and sources of funds to develop the project.

Development services. Nonfinancial services that an economic development finance institution provides to increase the pool of potential customers, improve the performance of its customers, or achieve other development outcomes.

Dual aspect concept. An accounting principle represented by the equation, Assets = Equities, which indicates that everything that is owned by a firm (its assets) is claimed by someone, either its creditors or owners.

Due diligence. The collection and analysis of information needed to assess whether a firm or project meets investment underwriting standards.

Equity. The owners' investment in a business.

Factoring. The sale of accounts receivable to another firm, called the factor, which then collects payment from the customer.

Financial policies. The loan or investment products and financing terms offered by an economic development finance program.

Financial projections. The forecast of a company's or a project's future cash flow and financial statements, typically to demonstrate its capacity to support a certain level of debt and/or equity financing.

Fixed assets. The land, buildings, and equipment owned by the business.

General obligation (GO) bond. A form of debt issued by a government that is backed by a full faith and credit pledge from the issuing governmental jurisdiction.

Goodwill. An accounting concept used to value the excess of the acquisition price of a company or its assets over the book value.

Gross margin. The difference between revenue and the direct costs involved in producing goods or delivering services.

Home Mortgage Disclosure Act (HMDA). A federal law enacted in 1975 that requires federally chartered banks, savings banks, credit unions, and mortgage banks to report annually on the number of home mortgage loans and applications made by census tract in every metropolitan area along with the applicant's race, gender, and income.

Income statement. A financial statement that summarizes the financial results from a business's activities over a specified period of time.

Individual lending model. The type of microenterprise program that provides loans to entrepreneurs on an individual basis rather than through peer-group lending.

Industrial development bonds. A type of tax-exempt bond used to finance manufacturing facilities and backed by the cash flow and credit of the business using the bond proceeds.

Initial public offering (IPO). The first sale of stock by a firm on public equity markets.

Insurance companies. A financial institution that provides insurance products and manages the assets and liabilities associated with these products.

Interest rate. The price charged to a borrower for the use of loaned funds that is usually indicated and calculated by an annual percentage rate.

Inventory. The goods held by the firm in one of three forms: (1) raw materials and supplies that are used in the firm's business; (2) unfinished goods-in-progress that the firm is still in the process of manufacturing; and (3) finished products.

Inventory financing or debt. A loan with inventory as collateral.

Lease. An alternative way to finance fixed assets in which another party (the lessor) owns the assets and the firm (the lessee) rents it for a specified period of time and under specific conditions in exchange for regular lease payments.

Leasehold improvement loan. A loan used to finance building improvements for rented building space.

Letter of credit. A form of guarantee made by a bank that promises to make payments on behalf of another party.

Line of credit. An open-ended loan with a borrowing limit that the business can draw against or repay at any time during the loan period.

Loan guarantee. A contract under which one party (the guarantor) agrees to compensate a lender for uncollected loan payments when the borrower fails to make payment.

Loan packaging.   Technical assistance provided to help a business structure an overall financial plan and prepare the application package to apply for financing.

Loan participation.   The partial funding by one lender of a loan that is underwritten and administered by another lender.

Loan term.   *See* **maturity period.**

Loan-to-value ratio.   The ratio of the loan principal to the market value of the loan collateral.

Market imperfection.   A way in which a market is organized or operates that violates the conditions of perfect competition and results in the inefficient allocation of resources or the undersupply of a good or service to consumers that can most productively use it.

Matching concept.   An accounting principal in which expenses are recognized in the same period when the revenues associated with those costs are recorded.

Maturity period.   The amount of time from the original date of the loan (i.e., the day when the borrower signed the debt contract and received the loan proceeds) to when the loan must be fully repaid.

Microenterprise.   A small business with five or fewer employees and including self-employed individuals engaged in a part-time or full-time business activity.

Microenterprise program (MEP).   An economic development program that provides some combination of training, technical assistance, and credit to microenterprises or individuals seeking to start a business, or both.

Mini-perm loan.   A medium-term loan used to finance real estate projects, which is often provided by banks that do not want to hold a long-term real estate loan.

Mortgage loan.   A loan secured by real estate.

Net working capital.   A firm's current assets minus its current liabilities, which indicates the amount by which short-term (one-year) assets exceed short-term (one-year) liabilities.

New market tax credit.   A type of U.S. federal tax credit provided to private investors to stimulate investment in economically distressed areas. Investors receive the tax credits in return for funding Community Development Entities (CDEs) that invest in qualified businesses located in distressed urban, rural, and Native American communities.

Operating pro forma.   A financial statement for a real estate project that presents the expected revenues, operating expenses, debt service, and net cash flow for the project over multiple years.

Order of loss.   The order in which losses are incurred between a lender and guarantor. A first loss guarantee pays for losses from the first dollar of loss incurred until the maximum guarantee amount is exhausted, whereas a second loss guarantee pays for losses that exceed the nonguaranteed portion of the loan.

Par value. The stated or face value of one share of stock in a business.

Peer-group lending. A type of microenterprise lending in which entrepreneurs operate as a group to extend loans to group members, collect loan payments, and repay the microenterprise program.

Personal guarantee. A pledge of personal assets to repay a loan made to a business.

Predevelopment financing. Funding that covers the up-front costs that real estate development projects incur before construction.

Preferred stock. A type of equity in which the shareholder has a preferred claim to the firm's dividend payments that typically must be paid on a cumulative basis before common stockholders can be paid dividends.

Prepaid expenses. Costs that a business has paid for but which are treated as expenses in a future period based on the matching concept.

Principal. The amount of loan funds borrowed.

Private activity bond. A category of tax-exempt bonds that finances facilities either owned or used by private for-profit parties and in which a revenue flow from the private users serves to repay the bonds.

Private capital markets. The set of financial institutions in which an intermediary organization manages funds for investors and directly negotiates financing transactions with the capital user.

Program-related investments. An investment of endowment funds by a foundation to directly advance its program goals.

Public capital markets. The type of financial markets in which financing is raised through the sale of standardized financial instruments and in which investors have access to widely available public information on the securities being sold. Public capital markets include the stock markets for equity investments in businesses, the bond markets for debt financing to governments, businesses, and nonprofit organizations, and the money markets that supply short-term debt.

Realization concept. An accounting principal in which revenue is recognized and credited to a firm's accounts when goods are shipped or services are rendered.

Recourse loan. A loan in which the debt holder has recourse to the personal assets of the borrower to satisfy repayment.

Retained earnings. The portion of net income reinvested in a business and which increases the book value of the firm's equity.

Revenue bonds. Bonds that are backed by the pledge of a specific and limited revenue source.

Revolving loan fund (RLF). An unregulated pool of capital used to provide loans to small businesses and/or development projects with loan repayments recycled, or revolved, to make additional loans over time.

SBA 504 program. A federal SBA program that uses approved Certified Development Corporations (CDCs) to provide long-term financing for fixed asset investments by small companies under a financing structure in which a private bank funds 50% of the investment project, a SBA-subordinated debenture funds 40%, and the small business contributes 10% as equity.

SBA 7(a) program. A federal government loan guarantee program administered by the Small Business Administration (SBA) that guarantees loans made by private banks, credit unions, or finance companies to small businesses for working capital, fixed asset acquisition, or both.

Section 108 program. A federal program through which communities can use their CDBG allocation as a guarantee to back up federal financing for community and economic development projects.

Securitization. The aggregation and structuring of the cash flow from many individual loans or financial assets into a security that is sold to investors.

Security position. The order of claims on assets that are pledged as loan collateral. A senior or first position is paid before lenders with a second or lower position (referred to as a junior position).

Selling, general, and administrative costs. The accounting category on the income statement that represents the indirect expenses of a firm.

Senior loan. A loan with a first security position that is repaid before subordinate loans.

Small business investment corporation. A SBA-licensed private investment firm that supplies capital to start-up and early-stage small firms and has access to SBA loans and securities at below-market rates.

Special small business investment corporation. A SBA-licensed private investment firm that supplies capital to small firms owned by women, minorities, and economically disadvantaged populations and has access to SBA loans and securities at below-market rates.

Subordinate loan. A loan with a second or lower security position that is repaid after senior loans.

Targeting policies. The economic development criteria for a development finance program that determine which enterprises, individuals, or projects qualify for its services and financing.

Tax increment financing (TIF). A form of financing in which the increased tax revenues generated in a designated area are set aside to fund specific projects or activities.

Term loan. A form of medium-term debt in which principal is repaid over several years, typically in 3 to 7 years.

Thrift institution. A government-chartered financial institution with access to government deposit insurance and more limited lending powers than a commercial bank that often focuses on home mortgage and real estate lending. Savings banks and savings and loan institutions are thrift institutions.

Training-led model.   A type of microenterprise program that focuses on providing training in business skills to existing and potential entrepreneurs.

Underwriting standards or criteria.   The business and financial parameters that a financial institution establishes for firms or projects in order to evaluate whether they are an acceptable investment risk.

Warrant.   An option to purchase a company's stock at a specified price.

Venture capital funds.   Private investment entities that primarily supply equity to firms with the potential for very high returns.

References

Almeyda, M., & Hinojosa, S. (2001). *Revision of state of the art contingent liability management.* Washington, DC: World Bank.

Anthony, R. N., Hawkins, D. F., & Merchant, K. A. (1999). *Accounting: Text and cases.* Boston: McGraw-Hill/Irwin.

Apgar, W. C., & Duda, M. (2002). The twenty-fifth anniversary of the Community Reinvestment Act: Past accomplishments and future regulatory challenges. In *Federal Reserve Bank Policy Review* (June 2003) (http://www.newyorkfed.org/rmaghome/econ_pol/2002/ 902apga.pdf). Federal Reserve Bank of New York, NY.

Arvidson, E., Hissong, R., & Cole, R. L. (2001). Tax increment financing in Texas: Survey and assessment. In C. L. Johnson & J. Y. Man (Eds.), *Tax increment financing and economic development: Uses, structures and impact.* Albany: State University of New York Press.

Barkley, D. L., Markley, D. M, & Rubin, J. S. (1999). *Public involvement in venture capital funds: Lessons from three program alternatives.* Columbia, MO: Rural Public Policy Institute.

Bartik, T. J. (1990). The market failure approach to regional economic development policy. *Economic Development Quarterly, 4*(4), 361–370.

Bates, T. (1997). The minority enterprise small business investment program: Institutionalizing a nonviable minority business assistance infrastructure. *Urban Affairs Review, 32*(5), 683–703.

Bates, T. (2000). Financing the development of urban minority communities: Lesson of history. *Economic Development Quarterly, 14*(3), 227–241.

Baum, S. P. (1996). The securitization of commercial property debt. In L. T. Kendall & M. J. Fishman (Eds.), *A primer on securitization.* Cambridge: MIT Press.

Belsky, E., Lambert, M., & van Hoffman, A. (2000). *Insights into the practice of community reinvestment act lending: A synthesis of CRA discussion groups.* Cambridge, MA: Harvard University Joint Center for Housing Studies.

Berger, A. N., & Udell, G. F. (1998). The economics of small business finance: The roles of private equity and debt markets in the financial growth cycle. *Journal of Banking & Finance, 22,* 613–673.

Black, J., Thetford, T., Edgecomb, E., & Klein, J. (2002). *For good measure: Performance of the U.S. microenterprise industry.* Washington, DC: Aspen Institute.

Board of Governors of the Federal Reserve System (BOGFRS). (1995). *Community development investments: A guide for state member banks and bank holding companies.* Washington, DC: Board of Governors of the Federal Reserve System.

Board of Governors of the Federal Reserve System (BOGFRS). (2000). *The performance and profitability of CRA-related lending.* Washington, DC: Board of Governors of the Federal Reserve System.

Bonavoglia, A. (2001). *Building businesses, rebuilding lives: Microenterprise and welfare reform.* New York: The Ms. Foundation for Women.

Boston Community Capital. (2003). *2002 annual report.* Boston, MA: Boston Community Capital.

Brannon, J. I. (2001). Renovating the CRA. *Regulation, 24*(2), 1–4.

Brealey, R. & Myers, S. (2002). *Principles of corporate finance.* Boston, MA: McGraw-Hill/Irwin.

Buchanan, R., Carney, P., & Weinstein, L. S. (2001). *FCCDC readiness for CDFI certification* (Unpublished memorandum). Greenfield, MA: Franklin County Community Development Corporation.

Bygrave, W. D., & Timmons, J. A. (1996). *Venture capital at the crossroads.* New York: McGraw-Hill.

Caskey, J. P. (2002). *Check cashing outlets in a changing financial system* (Working Paper 02–04). Philadelphia: Federal Reserve Bank of Philadelphia.

Caskey, J. P., & Brayman, S. J. (2002). *How credit unions can serve the "underserved."* Madison, WI: Filene Research Institute.

CDFI Data Project. (2003). *CDFIs: Providing capital, bridging communities, creating impact.* Washington, DC: Corporation for Enterprise Development.

Cherry, E. (2000). *No exit: The challenge of realizing return on community development venture capital investment.* Unpublished report to Ford Foundation. Boston Community Capital (http://www.bostoncommunitycapital.org), 56 Warren Street, Boston, MA.

Chien, D., Fenandes, D., Markel, D., Pipik, R., & Turner, M. (1996). *From despair to development: An evaluation of the Lithgow block residential and commercial projects.* Unpublished manuscript, Harvard University, Cambridge, MA.

Clark, P., & Kays, A. (1999). *Microenterprise and the poor.* Washington, DC: The Aspen Institute.

Clones, D. (1998). *The Washington RLF profile.* Washington, DC: Corporation for Enterprise Development.

Collaton, E., & Bartsch, C. (1996). Industrial site reuse and urban development: An overview. *Cityscape: A Journal of Policy Development and Research, 2*(3): 17–61.

Collins, A., Neel, E., & Smith-Frances, A. (2003). *Market assessment and marketing analysis for Dorchester Bay loan fund.* Unpublished manuscript, MIT, Cambridge, MA.

Coopers & Lybrand. (1993). *Venture capital: The price of growth* (1993 Update). Boston: Coopers & Lybrand.

Corporation for Enterprise Development. (1997). *Counting on local capital: A research project on revolving loan funds.* Washington, DC: Corporation for Enterprise Development.

Cortright, J., & Reamer, A. (1998). *Using socioeconomic data to understand your regional economy.* Washington, DC: U.S. Economic Development Administration.

Edgecomb, E. (2002a). *Field Forum Issue #13: Marketing strategies for scale-up FIELD's grantees share their experiences.* Washington, DC: Aspen Institute.

Edgecomb, E. (2002b). *Improving training and technical assistance: Findings from program managers.* Washington, DC: Aspen Institute.

Edgecomb, E., Klein, J., & Clark, P. (1996). *The practice of microenterprise in the United States.* Washington, DC: Aspen Institute.

Eisinger, P. K. (1993) State venture capitalism, state policies, and the world of high-risk investment. *Economic Development Quarterly, 7*(2), 131–139.

Elliehausen, G. E. & Wolken, J. D. (1990). *Banking markets and the use of financial services by small and medium-sized businesses* (Staff Studies # 160). Washington DC: Board of Governors of the Federal Reserve System.

Etzkowitz, H. (2002). *MIT and the rise of entrepreneurial science.* New York: Routledge.

Farnan, M. L. (2001). *Crossing the bridge to self-employment: A federal micro-enterprise resource guide.* Washington, DC: Interagency Workgroup on Microenterprise Development.

Federal Reserve Bank of Dallas. (n.d.). *A banker's quick reference guide to CRA.* Dallas, TX: Federal Reserve Bank of Dallas Community Affairs Office.

Ferguson, B. W., Miller, M. M., & Liston, C. (1996). Retail revitalization. *Economic Development Commentary, 19*(4), 4–13.

Fisher, P. S. (1988). State venture capital funds as an economic development strategy. *Journal of the American Planning Association, 54*(2), 166–177.

Florida, R., & Smith, D. F. (1993). Venture capital formation, investment and regional industrialization. *Annals of the Association of American Geographers, 83*(3), 434–451.

Frey Foundation. (1993). *Taking care of civic business.* Grand Rapids, MI: Frey Foundation.

Frieden, B. J., & Sagalyn, L. B. (1989) *Downtown, Inc.: How America rebuilds cities.* Cambridge: MIT Press.

Fung, A., Hebb, T., & Rogers, J. (Eds.). (2001). *Working capital: The power of labor's pensions.* Ithaca, NY: Cornell University Press.

Gaither, M. (2002). *New opportunities for equity: A critical examination of community development venture capital.* Unpublished master's thesis, MIT, Cambridge, MA.

Gershick, J. A. (2002). *Credit evaluation grids for microlenders: A tool for enhancing scale and efficiency.* Washington, DC: Aspen Institute.

Gillen, T. (1998). *The Minnesota RLF profile.* Washington, DC: Corporation for Enterprise Development.

Gilligan, P. (2000, Spring). The role of OTS thrifts in New England. *New England Banking Trends.* 1–6.

Gompers, P., & Lerner, J. (1999). *The venture capital cycle.* Cambridge: MIT Press.

Griffen, C. E. (1998, March). Breaking the bank: Non-bank lenders are pulling ahead in small business financing. *Entrepreneur.*

Grossman, B., Levere, A., & Marcoux, K. (1998). *Counting on local capital: A literature review of revolving loan funds.* Washington, DC: Corporation for Enterprise Development.

Grossman, K. D. (2002). *Connectors and conduits: Reaching competitive markets from the ground up.* Washington, DC: Aspen Institute.

Grzywinski, R. (1991, May-June). The new old-fashioned banking. *Harvard Business Review,* 87–98.

Haag, S. W. (2000). *Community reinvestment and cities: A literature review of CRA's impact and future.* Washington, DC: Brookings Institution.

Haulk, J. & Montarti, E. (2000). Tax increment financing: Assessing its use in Pittsburgh. *Economic Development Commentary, 24*(1), 33-37.

Haynes, G. W. (1996). Credit access for high-risk borrowers in financially concentrated markets: Do SBA loan guarantees help? *Small Business Economics, 8,* 449–461.

Heard, R. G., & Sibert, J. (2000). *Growing new businesses with seed and venture capital: State experiences and options.* Washington, DC: National Governors' Association.

Hebert, S., Vidal, A., Mills, G., James, F., & Gruenstein, D. (2001). *Interim assessment of the Empowerment Zone and Enterprise Communities (EZ/EC) program: A progress report.* Washington, DC: US Department of Housing and Urban Development.

Houston, L. O., Jr. (1997). *BIDS: Business improvement districts.* Washington, DC: Urban Land Institute and International Downtown Association.

Hunter, W. C. (1984). *Insurance, incentives, and efficiency in small business lending, Southern Economics Journal 50*(4), 1171–1184.

Immergluck, D. (1997). *Is CRA reform real? Analyzing the ratings of large banks opting for evaluation under the new CRA regulations* Chicago: Woodstock Institute.

Immergluck, D., & Bush, M. (1995). *Small business lending for economic development.* Chicago: Woodstock Institute.

Isbister, J. (1994). *Thin cats: The community development credit union movement in the United States.* Davis, CA: Center for Cooperatives, University of California.

Johnson, C. L. (2001). The use of debt in tax increment financing. In C. L. Johnson & J. Y. Man (Eds.), *Tax increment financing and economic development: Uses, structures and impact.* Albany: State University of New York Press.

Johnson, C. L., & Kriz, K. A. (2001). A review of state tax increment financing laws. In C. L. Johnson & J. Y. Man (Eds.), *Tax increment financing and economic development: Uses, structures and impact.* Albany: State University of New York Press.

Karl F. Seidman Consulting Services. (2001a). *Financing gaps and recommended financing roles for the trust to serve targeted Massachusetts growth industries.* Unpublished consulting report to the Commonwealth Corporation, Schrafft Center, Suite 110, 521 Main Street, Boston, MA 02129.

Karl F. Seidman Consulting Services. (2001b). *Massachusetts growth industry analysis.* Unpublished consulting report to the Commonwealth Corporation, Schrafft Center, Suite 110, 521 Main Street, Boston, MA 02129.

Kaufman, K., & Frenz, T. (2002, June). *Pennsylvania Economic Development Financing Authority composite bond program.* Unpublished presentation. Council of Development Finance Agencies, 2002 Annual Conference, Burlington, VT.

Kendall, L. T. (1996). Securitization: A new era in American finance. In L. T. Kendall & M. J. Fishman (Eds.), *A primer on securitization.* Cambridge: MIT Press.

Klacik, J. D. (2001). Tax increment financing in Indiana. In C. L. Johnson & J. Y. Man (Eds.), *Tax increment financing and economic development: Uses, structures and impacts.* Albany: State University of New York Press.

Klacik, J. D., & Nunn, S. (2001). A primer on tax increment financing. In C. L. Johnson & J. Y. Man (Eds.), *Tax increment financing and economic development: Uses, structures and impacts.* Albany: State University of New York Press.

Klein, J. (2002). *Entering the relationship: Finding and assessing microenterprise training clients* (FIELD Best Practices Guide: Vol. 1). Washington, DC: Aspen Institute.

Kolodinsky, J., Holmberg, S., Stewart, C., & Bullard, A. (2002). *Vermont Community Development Credit Union: A community program that works.* Burlington: Vermont Development Credit Union.

Kwass, P., & Siegel, B. (1987a). *Factors influencing the performance of U.S. Economic Development Administration sponsored revolving loan funds* (Vol. 1, Research Methodology and Findings) (prepared for the United States Economic Development Administration). Somerville, MA: Mt. Auburn Associates.

Kwass, P., & Siegel, B. (1987b). *Factors influencing the performance of U.S. Economic Development Administration sponsored revolving loan funds* (Vol. 2, Case Studies) (prepared for the United States Economic Development Administration). Somerville, MA: Mt. Auburn Associates.

Kwass, P., Siegel, B., & Henze, L. (1987). *The design and management of state and local revolving loan funds: A handbook* (prepared for the United States Economic Development Administration). Somerville, MA: Mt. Auburn Associates.

Lehr, M. B. (1998). *Best practices for CDFIs: Key principles for performance.* Philadelphia: National Community Capital Association.

Leibsohn, D. M. (2002). *Financial services programs; Case studies from a business model perspective* (http://www.finir.org/finan_serv/background2.htm). Southern New Hampshire University School of Community Economic Development Financial Innovations Roundtable, 2500 North River Rd., Manchester, NH 03106.

Levere, A. (1998). *The California RLF profile,* Washington, DC: Corporation for Enterprise Development.

Li, W. (1998). Government loan, guarantee, and grant programs: An evaluation. *Economic Quarterly, 84*(4), 25–51.

Litvak, L., & Daniels, B. (1979). *Innovations in development finance.* Washington, DC: Council of State Planning Agencies.

Luquetta, A. C., & Thrash, T. (2000). *Insuring the future of our communities: The first progress report on the Massachusetts insurance industry investment initiatives.* Boston: Massachusetts Association of Community Development Corporations.

Magaziner, I. C., & Reich, R. B. (1982). *Minding America's business: The decline and rise of the American economy.* New York: Harcourt Brace Jovanovich.

Mahon, C. (1995). *Building an enclave: The experience of microlending in Lawrence.* Unpublished master's thesis, Massachusetts Institute of Technology, Cambridge.

Malizia, E. (1997). *Development banking in low-wealth and minority communities: The roles of community development credit unions with emphasis on commercial lending.* Chapel Hill: University of North Carolina Center for Urban and Regional Studies.

Man, J. Y. (2001). Effects of tax increment financing on economic development. In C. L. Johnson & J. Y. Man (Eds.), *Tax increment financing and economic development: Uses, structures and impact.* Albany: State University of New York Press.

Marcoux, K. (1998). *The Illinois RLF profile.* Washington, DC: Corporation for Enterprise Development.

Marsico, R. D. (2002). *Enforcing the Community Reinvestment Act: An advocate's guide to making the CRA work for communities* (New York Law School Public Law and Legal Theory Research Paper Series Number 02–08). New York: New York Law School.

Massachusetts Life Insurance Community Investment Initiative. (2003). *2002 annual report and statement of financial condition.* Boston: Massachusetts Life Initiative.

Mayer, V., Sampanes, M., & Carras, J. (1991). *Local officials' guide to the Community Reinvestment Act.* Washington: DC: National League of Cities.

Metzger, J. T. (1992). The community reinvestment act and neighborhood revitalization in Pittsburgh. In G. D. Squires (Ed.), *From redlining to reinvestment: Community responses to urban disinvestment.* Philadelphia: Temple University Press.

McCall, M. J. (1997). *Chicago's ShoreBank Corporation: Is it a model community development corporation, or a farce?* Unpublished master's thesis, Department of Economics, University of Illinois at Chicago.

Mikesel, J. L. (2001). Nonproperty tax increment programs for economic development: A review of alternative programs. In C. L. Johnson & J. Y. Man (Eds.), *Tax increment financing and economic development: Uses, structures and impact.* Albany: State University of New York Press.

Mitchell, J. (2001). Business improvement districts and the new revitalization of downtown. *Economic Development Quarterly, 15*(2), 115–123.

Moser, T., & Moukanas, H. (2002). Finding the right drivers of value growth. *Mercer Management Journal, 13* (www.mercermc.com/perspectives/journal/valuegrowth/home.asp).

Mt. Auburn Associates. (2002). *The impact of CDC-sponsored commercial redevelopment projects on commercial revitalization in four Boston neighborhood commercial districts.* Somerville, MA: Mt. Auburn Associates.

National Community Capital Association. (2002). *CDFIs side by side: A comparative guide.* Philadelphia: National Community Capital Association.

National Community Reinvestment Coalition (NCRC). (1997). *Models of community lending: Neighborhood revitalization through community lender partnerships.* Washington, DC.

National Community Reinvestment Coalition (NCRC). (1999). *CRA commitments 1987–1998.* Washington, DC: National Community Reinvestment Coalition.

National Council for Urban Economic Development (NCUED). (1990). *Bank CDCs: Instruments for community investment.* Washington, DC: National Council for Urban Economic Development.

National Council for Urban Economic Development (NCUED). (1995a). *Revolving loan funds: Recycling capital for business development.* Washington, DC: National Council for Urban Economic Development.

National Council for Urban Economic Development (NCUED). (1995b). *Small issue industrial development bonds: A finance tool for economic development.* Washington, DC: National Council for Urban Economic Development.

National Credit Union Administration (NCUA). (2002). *Credit union development program and activity report.* Alexandria, VA: National Credit Union Administration.

Nelson, C. (2002). *Building skills for self-employment: Basic training for microentreprenurs* (FIELD Best Practices Guide, Vol. 2). Washington, DC: Aspen Institute.

Nicholson, W. (2002). *Microeconomic theory: Basic principles and extensions.* Cincinnati, OH: South-Western/Thomson Learning.

Office of the Comptroller of the Currency (OCC). (1999). *Small business banking issues: A national forum sponsored by the Office of the Comptroller of the Currency.* Washington, DC: Office of the Comptroller of the Currency.

Office of the Comptroller of the Currency (OCC). (2000) *National bank community development investments: 1999 Directory.* Washington, DC: Office of the Comptroller of the Currency.

Office of the Comptroller of the Currency (OCC). (2001). *Community development banks* (Memo dated October 3, 2001, from Chief Counsel to prospective organizers of community development banks). Office of the Comptroller of the Currency, Washington, DC.

Office of the Comptroller of the Currency (OCC). (2002). *Comptroller's licensing manual: Charters.* Washington, DC: Office of the Comptroller of the Currency.

Osborne, D. (1999). *Laboratories of democracy A new breed of governor creates models for national growth.* New York: McGraw-Hill.

Owen, R. R., Garner, D. R., & Bunder, D. S. (1986). *The Arthur T. Young guide to financing for growth: Ten alternatives for raising capital.* New York: John Wiley & Sons.

Paetsch, J. R., & Dahlstrom, R. K. (1990). Tax increment financing: What it is and how it works. In R. D. Bingham, E. Hill, & S. B. White (Eds.), *Financing economic development: An institutional response.* Thousand Oaks, CA: Sage.

Pagano, M. A., & Bowman, A. O'm. (1997). *Cityscapes and capital: The politics of urban development.* Baltimore: Johns Hopkins University Press.

Parzen, J. A., & Kieschnick, M. H. (1994). *Credit where it's due: Development banking for communities.* Philadelphia: Temple University Press.

Peek, J., & Rosengren, E. S. (1995). *Banks and the availability of small business loans* (Working Paper 95–1). Boston: Federal Reserve Bank of Boston.

Pennington-Cross, A. (2003). Subprime lending in the primary and secondary markets. *Journal of Housing Research, 13*(1), 31–50.

Price Waterhouse. (1992). *Evaluation of the SBA's 7(a) guaranteed business loan program.* Washington, DC: Price Waterhouse.

The Property and Casualty Initiative. (2003). *2002 annual report.* Boston: The Property and Casualty Initiative.

Raiman, L. (1999). *The new world order of the REIT business* (HG5095.R25 1999). Jack Brause Library, The Real Estate Institute (http://www.nyu.edu/library/rei/reit.htm), New York University.

Ranieri, L. S. (1996) The origins of securitization, its sources of growth and its future potential. In L. T. Kendall & M. J. Fishman (Eds.), *A primer on securitization.* Cambridge: MIT Press.

Reed, E. W., & Woodland, D. L. (1970). *Cases in commercial banking.* Norwalk, CT: Appleton-Century-Crofts.

Richards, J. W. (1983). *Fundamentals of development finance: A practitioner's guide.* Westport, CT: Praeger.

Rist, C. (1998). *The North Carolina RLF profile.* Washington, DC: Corporation for Enterprise Development.

Robert Morris Associates (2002). *RMA annual statement studies.* Philadelphia: Robert Morris Associates.

Ryan, B. D. (2000). Philadelphia's center city district and the privatization of public space. *Projections MIT Student Journal of Planning, 1*(1), 58–79.

Schwartz, A. (1998). From confrontation to collaboration? Banks, community groups, and the implementation of the community reinvestment agreements. *Housing Policy Debate, 9*(3), 631–662.

Seidman, K. F. (1987). A new role for government: Supporting a democratic economy. In S. T. Bruyn Jr. & J. Meehan (Eds.), *Beyond the market and state: New directions in community development.* Philadelphia: Temple University Press.

Self-Help Credit Union. (2001). *2001 annual report*. Durham, NC: Self Help Credit Union.

Servon, L. (1998). *Microenterprise development as an economic adjustment strategy*. Washington, DC: U.S. Economic Development Administration.

Servon, L., & Doshna, J. P. (1999). *Making microenterprise development a part of the economic development toolkit*. Washington, DC: U.S. Economic Development Administration.

Shapero, A. (1984). Entrepreneurship in economic development. In C. A. Farr (Ed.), *Shaping the local economy: Current perspective on economic development*. Washington, DC: International City Management Association.

ShoreBank Corporation. (2001). *2000 annual report*. (www.shorebankcorp.com/main/sar2001/development). ShoreBank Corporation, 7054 S. Jeffery Boulevard, Chicago, IL 60649.

Snyder, T. P., & Stegman, M. A. (1986). *Paying for growth: Using development fees to finance infrastructure*. Washington, DC: Urban Land Institute.

Sohl, J. E. (2003). *The U.S. angel and venture capital market: Recent trends and developments*. Journal of Private Equity 6(2), 7–17.

Squires, G. D. (1993). Community reinvestment: An emerging social movement. In G. D. Squires (Ed.), *From redlining to reinvestment: Community responses to urban disinvestment*, Philadelphia: Temple University Press.

Squires, G. D. (2003). Epilogue: Where do we go from here? In G. D. Squires (Ed.), *Organizing access to capital: Advocacy and the democratization of financial institutions*. Philadelphia: Temple University Press.

State of California, Governor's Office of Planning and Research. (1997). *A planner's guide to financing public improvements* (http://ceres.ca.gov/planning/). State of California, Sacramento, CA.

Stegman, M. A., & Lobenhofer, J. S. (2002). Bringing more affordable financial services to the inner city: The Bethex Federal Credit Union/Ritecheck Check Cashing Inc. partnership (www.fanniemaefoundation.org/programs/bb/v3i3-index.shtml), *Building Blocks 3(3)*.

Surgeon, G. (2002, Summer). Useful lesson for CD banks. *Community Affairs OnLine News Articles* (www.occ.treas.gov/cdd/Summer-10.pdf). Office of the Controller of the Currency, Washington, DC.

Swack, M. (1987). Community finance institutions. In S. T. Bruyn Jr. & J. Meehan (Eds.), *Beyond the market and the state: New directions in community development*. Philadelphia: Temple University Press.

Tansey, C. D. (2001). *Community development credit unions: An emerging player in low-income communities*. Washington, DC: Brookings Institution Center on Urban and Metropolitan Policy.

Taub, R. P. (1994). *Community capitalism: The South Shore Bank's strategy for neighborhood revitalization*. Cambridge, MA: Harvard Business School Press.

Taub, R. P. (1998). Making the adaptation across cultures and societies: A report on an attempt to clone the Grammen Bank in southern Arkansas. *Journal of Development Entrepreneurship, 3(1)*, 53–69.

Tholin, K., & Pogge, J. (1991). *Banking services for the poor: Community development credit unions*. Chicago: Woodstock Institute.

U.S. Census Bureau. (2002). *Quarterly financial report for manufacturing, mining and trade corporations 2001*. Washington, DC: U.S. Government Printing Office.

U.S. Census Bureau. (2000). *Statistical abstract of the United States: 2000.* Washington, DC: U.S. Government Printing Office.

U.S. Comptroller of the Currency Community Development Division. (2000). *National bank community development investments 1999 directory.* Washington, DC: Comptroller of the Currency (OCC).

U.S. Department of the Treasury. (1999). *Capital access programs: A summary of nationwide performance.* Washington, DC: U. S. Department of the Treasury.

U.S. Department of the Treasury Community Development Financial Institutions Fund (CDFI Fund). (2002). *Certified community development financial institutions—by organization type.* Washington, DC: CDFI Fund.

U.S. General Accounting Office (GAO). (1983). *SBA's 7(a) loan guarantee program: An assessment of its role in the financial market* (Report GAO/RCED-83–96). Washington, DC: General Accounting Office.

U.S. General Accounting Office (GAO). (1992). *Small business: Preferred Lenders Program would have been deprived of credit in the absence of the program* (Report GAO/RCED-92–124). Washington, DC: General Accounting Office.

U.S. General Accounting Office (GAO). (1995). *Small business administration: Prohibited practices and inadequate oversight in SBIC and SSBIC programs* (Report GAO/T-OSI-95–16). Washington, DC: General Accounting Office.

U.S. General Accounting Office (GAO). (1996a). *A comparison of SBA's 7(a) loans and borrowers with other loans and borrowers* (Letter Report, 09.20.96, GAO/RCED-96–222). Washington, DC: General Accounting Office.

U.S. General Accounting Office (GAO). (1996b). *Trends in SBA's 7(a) program* (Report GAO/RCED-96–158R). Washington, DC: General Accounting Office.

U.S. General Accounting Office (GAO). (2000). *Efforts to facilitate equity capital formation* (Report GAO/GGD-00–190). Washington, DC: General Accounting Office.

U.S. Small Business Administration Office of Marketing & Customer Service. (1999). *SBA programs and services.* Washington, DC: Small Business Administration.

Varma, S. (2001). Micro-loans, peer-lending, social support and business development: A case study of a U.S.-based microenterprise program and its members. Unpublished Ph.D. dissertation, School of Social Work, University of North Carolina, Chapel Hill, NC.

Venture Economics. (1996). *Investment benchmarks report: Venture capital.* New York: Venture Economics.

Venture Economics. (2001). *Private equity market update 2001.* (www.venture economics.com).

Venture One Corporation. (2001). *The venture capital industry report 2000.* Venture One Corporation (http://www.ventureone.com/), 201 Spear Street, 4th Floor, San Francisco, CA 94105.

Venture One Corporation. (2002). *The venture capital industry report 2001.* Venture One Corporation (http://www.ventureone.com/), 201 Spear Street, 4th Floor, San Francisco, CA 94105.

Vermont Development Credit Union (VDCU). (2002). *2001 Annual Report.* 18 Pearl Street, Burlington, VT 05401.

Weaver, A. (1998). *Venture capital investment patterns: Implications for regional economic development.* Unpublished master's thesis, Department of Urban Studies Planning, MIT, Cambridge, MA.

Williams, M. (1999). Building the savings and assets of lower-income consumers: Examples from community development credit unions. Chicago: Woodstock Institute.

Woodstock Institute. (1982). *Evaluation of the Illinois Neighborhood Development Corporation* (http://www.woodstockinst.org/institute.php). Woodstock Institute, 407 S. Dearborn, Suite 550, Chicago, IL 60605.

Woodstock Institute. (2001). Affordable alternatives to payday loans: Examples from CDCUs (Reinvestment Alert, No. 16) (http://www.woodstockinst.org/institute.php). Woodstock Institute, 407 S. Dearborn, Suite 550, Chicago, IL 60605.

Yunis, M. (1989). Grameen Bank: Organization and operations. In J. Levitsky (Ed.), *Microenterprises in developing countries*. London: Intermedia Technology.

Index

Accion Texas, 308, 410

Accion USA, 304

Accountability, 381–382, 390–391, 445

Accounting principles, 41–44, 59
 accrual versus cash basis reporting, 42–43
 dual aspect concept, 41–42, 454
 matching concept, 42, 456
 realization concept, 42, 457
 See also Financial statement

Accounts payable:
 balance sheet, 48, 69
 cash flow management, 69
 defined, 451

Accounts receivable loans, 30, 97–98, 451

Accounts receivables:
 balance sheet, 46, 53, 68–69
 cash flow analysis, 54, 57
 cash flow management, 68–69, 83
 days receivable, 68, 76, 88
 defined, 451

Accrual accounting, 41–44

Accrued expenses, 48, 451

Accumulated deficit, 53, 451

Additional paid-in capital, 49, 451

AFL-CIO Real Estate Investment Trust, 152

Air quality, 5

Almeyda, Miguel, 165

Alternatives Federal Credit Union, 285

Aluminum windows, 106–107

American Biotechnology Company (ABC), 45–53

American Research and Development, 241

Amortization, 28–29, 451

Angel investors, defined, 265

Anthony, Robert N., 41

Apgar, W. C., 197

Applied research agenda, 449

Appraisal, 150

Arkansas Development Finance Authority, 345

ASI Federal Credit Union, 284

Asian and Pacific Island borrowers, SBA 7(a) loan guarantees, 168

Aspen Institute, 297, 299, 301, 304, 448, 449

Assessment district financing, 354–356
 business improvement districts, 355, 356–358
 defined, 451

Asset-based lending, 101, 451

Assets, fixed. *See* Fixed asset financing

Assets, securitization, 425–426

Assets and liabilities, 46–49, 66–68, 91–92
 days receivable, 76

Auto loans, 280, 281

Automatic payments, 405

Balance sheet, 44–50
 accounts payable and accounts receivable, 46, 48, 53, 68–69
 assets and liabilities, 46–49, 66–68
 cash flow management issues, 68
 cash flow statement and, 54, 55, 84
 common size financial statement, 78–81
 connecting income statement, 53–54
 defined, 451
 financial model, 429, 430, 431–432
 firm evaluation insights, 65–69
 interpretations, 46
 shareholders' equity, 49–50, 53

Balloon loans, 28–29, 416
    construction loans, 148
    predevelopment loans, 147
Balloon payment, defined, 416
Bank Community Development
        Corporations, 201–205, 451.
        See also Community
        Development Corporations
Bank mergers, CRA agreements and,
        191, 199
Bank of America, 191, 424
Bank One, 420
Bank regulatory agencies, 211
BankBoston, 422
BankBoston Development
        Corporation (BBDC), 204
Banks, 12, 419–420
    CDFI Fund, 328–331
    critical role for economic
            development finance, 184–185
    debt sources, 421, 422
    equity investments, 420
    legal definition, 211
    regulatory policies, 14, 17
    venture capital investment
            sources, 263
    See also Commercial banks;
        specific types
Banks, Community Reinvestment Act
    agreements. *See* Community
    Reinvestment Act
Barkley, D. L., 253, 254
Bates, Timothy, 250
Ben Franklin Partnership, 248
Berger, Allen N., 34
Bethex Federal Credit Union, 283
Binomial tree analysis, 166
Black capitalism, 249
Black-Scholes formula, 166
Board member recruitment, 378
Board of directors, stakeholder
        representation in, 390, 445
Board of Governors of the Federal
        Reserve System (BOGFRS),
        201–202
Bonds:
    defined, 451
    fixed asset financing, 115
    general obligation, 342

    guarantee programs, 345
    industrial development (IDBs), 121,
            342–348, 455
    infrastructure funding, 343
    markets, 10
    mini-IDB programs,
            345–346
    pooling, 345
    private activity, 342
    rating, 166
    revenue, 342
    tax exempt, 342
Break-even sales level, 69–71, 452
Bridge loan, 147, 149
    defined, 452
    predevelopment funding, 136
Brownfields Economic Development
        Initiative (BEDI), 327
Building rehabilitation, 137, 141
Business Development Consortium
        (BDC), 435
Business development corporations
        (BDCs), working capital
        loans, 102
Business development
        stages, 33–34
Business improvement district (BID)
        financing, 355, 356–358, 452
Business or project financial analysis.
        See Financial analysis
Business ownership forms, 39
Business plan, 380
    defined, 452
    due diligence evaluation, 398
    evaluation for economic
            development
            financing, 61, 63–64
    microenterprise training
            program, 295
    Phoenix Forge case study,
            124–129

California Public Employees'
        Retirement System
        (CalPERS), 263
Camargo, Cesar, 311
CAPCO partnerships, 256
Capital Access Program (CAP), 161,
        172–174, 418, 452

Capital availability, 6–7
 capital market imperfections and,
  7–15. *See also*
  Community Reinvestment Act
  and, 189–193
 framework for expanding, 17–18
 real estate financing problems,
  152–153
 regional differences, 12–13, 15
 supply-side analysis, 372–377
 See also Capital management;
  Capital market imperfections;
  Capital sources
Capital gains, 53
Capital lease, 119
Capital loss, 53
Capital management, 412
 case study and assignment, 433–438
 community development loan
  funds, 277
 development finance and, 412–413
 financial modeling, 427–433
 growth to scale, 413
 interest risk, 413–416, 422
 loan maturity and amortization
  policies, 414, 416
 loss management, 417–418
 pricing loans and investments,
  413–417, 445
 raising new capital, 418–426
 relationship building, 444–445
 See also Financial modeling;
  See also Investment
  management
Capital market gaps, 7–15, 452.
  See also Capital market
  imperfections
Capital market imperfections, 7–15
 Community Reinvestment Act
  and, 186
 definitions, 9, 456
 development finance implications,
  7, 15–17
 fixed asset financing, 122–123
 information costs, 14
 institutional structure and, 9–15
 perfect competition theory, 8–9
 private capital markets, 11–15
 public capital markets, 9–11

 regional factors, 12–13
 regulatory issues, 14
 statistical discrimination, 15
 summary (table), 16
 transaction costs and, 13
Capital policies, defined, 452
Capital sources, 418–426
 asset sales, 424–425, 434–435, 447
 data for small businesses, 34–36
 fixed asset financing, 120–123
 impact on development finance
  process, 412–413
 informal sources, 12
 institutional performance data, 448
 loan or fund management
  services, 423–424
 participation financing, 423–424
 private capital markets, 11–15
 public capital markets, 9–11
 revolving loan fund policies, 227,
  230–231, 233–234
 securitization, 425–426, 435
 small business working capital,
  101–102
 venture capital fund challenges, 263
 See also Capital availability;
  Capital management; Credit
  unions; Debt financing;
  Equity financing; Federal
  programs; Grants; State and
  local government programs;
  Venture capital funds; *specific
  institutions, funding programs
  or tools*
Capital substitution,
  avoiding, 7, 414, 444
 loan guarantees and, 175, 178
 revolving loan fund policies, 228
 supply-side analysis and, 366
Capitalized interest reserve,
  defined, 452
Cascadia Revolving Fund
  (CRF), 232, 273
Cash, balance sheet, 46
Cash basis accounting, 42–43, 452
Cash flow:
 debt service coverage ratio, 31
 forecasting, 65
 short-term, ratio measures, 76–77

Cash flow projection. *See* Financial
  projection
Cash flow statement, 44, 54–58
  case study, 84–86
  defined, 452
  financial model, 427, 428,
    430–431
  firm evaluation insights, 65, 72–74
  operating pro forma, 138,
    142–144, 155, 456
  true debt service coverage ratio, 72
Cash reserve fund, 176
CDFI. *See* Community Development
  Financial Institution (CDFI) Fund
Center City Business Improvement
  District, 357
Certified Capital Company (CAPCO)
  programs, 256
Certified Development Corporations
  (CDCs), 121, 323, 423
  bank experiences, 202–205
  bank regulations, 201–202
  defined, 452
  real estate finance and, 205
  ShoreBank model, 205–211
Certified lenders, 322
Charitable organizations, 342
Check-cashing services, 281,
    282–283
Cherry, Elyse, 259
Cincinnati Credit Union, 283
Citibank, 191
Citigroup, 191
City Plaza, 153–156
Civil rights movement, 185
Cleveland Tomorrow, 209
Closing:
  defined, 452
  facilitating, 402
Closing agenda, defined, 452
Collateral, 30, 32
  appraisal, 151
  assignment of contracts, 117
  defined, 452
  effect on future debt capacity, 81
  equipment, 116
  inventory financing, 99–100
  loan guarantee security, 176
College Books, 43–44

Colorado Venture Management
  (CVM) Equity Fund, 255–256
Commercial banks, 12
  community development
    institutions, 185, 205–211
  data on small business capital
    sources, 35
  defined, 452
  fixed asset lending, 120
  real estate financing, 151–152
  working capital sources, 101
  See also Banks
Commercial banks, Community
  Reinvestment Act
    agreements. *See* Community
    Reinvestment Act
Commercial finance companies, 12
  defined, 452
  working capital lenders, 101
Common size financial
  statement, 78–81
Common stock, defined, 452
Community Business Network
  (CBN), 383
Community development banks:
  capital supply problem, 209–210
  defined, 453
  regulatory requirements, 210
  special operating requirements,
    210–211
  See also Community Development
    Corporations; Communty
    development financial
    institutions
Community Development Block
  Grant (CDBG), 220, 221,
    324–325, 420
  case study, 334–339
  defined, 453
  Section 108 program,
    326, 458
Community Development
  Corporations (CDCs), 185,
    201–205
Community development credit unions
  (CDCUs), 267, 277–290. *See also*
  Credit unions
Community Development Entities
  (CDEs), 331

Community Development Financial
    Institution (CDFI) Fund, 290,
    319, 328–331, 453
Community development financial
    institutions (CDFIs), 3, 18, 185,
    205–211, 267–291, 420
    Core and Intermediary Program,
        328–330
    defined, 453
    economic development/community
        development sector
        collaboration, 448–449
    federal funding, 320
    Native American technical
        assistance program, 330–331
    ShoreBank model, 185, 205–211
    Small and Emerging CDFI
        Assistance (SECA)
        program, 330
    See also Community development
        banks; Community
        Development Corporations
Community development loan funds
    (CDLFs), 267–277
    capital management, 277
    capital sources, 268
    defined, 453
    financing roles, 271–273
    housing and business loan funds,
        270–271
    industry size and characteristics
        data, 269–271
    interest rates, 269
    loan risk and terms, 271–273
    loss management, 276
    real estate financing sources, 152
    scale and growth issues, 268,
        273–277
    See also Community Development
        Financial Institution
        (CDFI) Fund
Community Development Venture
    Capital (CDVC), 256–259
    definition, 453
    industry profile, 257
    investment exits, 258–259
    staff requirements, 258
    trends and challenges, 257–259
Community Investment Program, 416

Community Reinvestment Act (CRA),
    184–201
    assessment areas, 187
    bank mergers and, 191, 199
    capital availability expansion,
        189–193
    critique, 185, 187–189, 197–198
    defined, 453
    examination and rating system,
        187–189
    extension of coverage and
        disclosure requirements, 447
    features of successful agreements,
        192–193
    history, 185–186
    home mortgage and small business
        definitions, 213
    impact on bank lending practices,
        186–187, 193–197
    impact on minority and low-
        income financing, 197–199
    insurance industry and, 200–201
    lending profitability, 195–197
    loss rates, repayments and returns,
        195–197
    nonbank institutions and, 185,
        198–199
    overview, 186–189
    performance measures, 188
    regulatory agencies, 211
    regulatory enforcement, 186
Community Reinvestment Fund
    (CRF), 421–422, 424–425,
    434, 447
Company valuation, defined, 453
Compensating balance, 96–97
Competitive markets theory, 8–9
Construction loan, 137–138, 147, 148
    defined, 453
    interest payments, 140
Consumer banking and credit services,
    280–285
Contingent or unfunded
    liabilities, 82
Continuous improvement, 391
Convertible debt, 33, 453
Corporate bonds, fixed asset
    financing, 115. See also Bonds
Corporate stock, 24–25

Corporation for Economic
      Development, 220–221
Corporation for Enterprise
      Development, 448
Cost escalators, 142
Cost of goods sold, 51, 453
Costs, expenses versus, 59
Counting on Local Capital
      project, 220–221
Credit card debt, 32
   working capital finance, 102
Credit unions, 277–278
   capital sources, 289–290
   characteristics and trends, 279–281
   debt sources, 421
   defined, 453
   earnings and delinquency
         data, 280–281
   financial education
         and counseling, 284
   household and consumer
         lending, 280
   low-income designation, 278
   management challenges, 287–290
   market research, 288–289
   partnerships, 283, 289
   regulation and oversight,
         277–278
   scale and growth
         issues, 285–286, 287
   services and development
         roles, 281–285
   short-term loans, 284
   small-business lending, 285–287
   target membership, 287–288
   Vermont Development Credit
         Union (VDCU), 278,
         284–285, 288–289, 413
Crystal Clear Window Company,
      84–89, 103–110
Current assets and liabilities, 46–47,
      66–68, 91–92
   days receivable, 76
   See also Working capital
         finance
Current portion of long-term debt,
      48–49, 71, 453
Current ratio, 68, 76, 454
Cyclical working capital, 94

Days receivable, 68, 76, 88
Debenture, 121, 323, 412
Debt, defined, 27, 78, 454
Debt, short-term working capital. See
      Working capital finance
Debt, collateral for. See Collateral
Debt finance, mortgages. See
      Mortgage loans
Debt finance, long-term or permanent
      fixed assets. See Fixed asset
      financing
Debt financing, 23, 27–33, 421–423
   advantages and disadvantages,
         32–33
   asset sales and securitization,
         424–426
   asset-based lending, 101
   case studies (hypothetical
         firms), 37–39
   contracts or covenants, 81, 422
   data on small business capital
         sources, 34–36
   differences from equity, 27
   equity-debt hybrid financing, 33
   information costs, 14
   loan participation, 114
   market rate versus below-market
         rate pricing, 177–178, 237,
         414–415, 445
   minimum loan amounts, 14
   private capital markets, 12
   ratios, 31–32
   real estate instruments, 146–149
   recourse loans, 33
   senior and subordinate lenders, 30
   term loans, 100–101,
         115–116, 458
   terms and issues, 27–32
   working capital sources,
         101–102
   See also Mortgage loans; specific
         lending institutions, tools
Debt guarantees. See Loan guarantee
      programs
Debt-related cash flow, 58
Debt service coverage ratio, 31,
      71–72, 78
   case study, 87
   defined, 454

projecting, 65
real estate development
budget, 144–145
Debt service reserve, 140, 454
Debt-to-equity ratio, 66, 77–78, 454
Debt-to-total-assets ratio, 77
Debt underwriting.
See Underwriting issues
Debt with warrants, 33, 454
Default, 405–406
defined, 454
revolving loan funds, 225, 226–227
Deferred income, 48, 123
cash flow analysis, 57
defined, 454
predevelopment funding, 136
venture capital investment exit
strategy, 247
Delinquency rate, defined, 454
Demand analysis, 370–372
Department of Housing and Urban
Development. *See* U.S.
Department of Housing and
Urban Development
Depreciation, 47
defined, 454
income statement expense, 52
Design fees, 139
Development budget, 138–141,
154–155, 454
Development services, defined, 454.
See also Technical assistance;
Training and education
Discounted cash flow, 151
Discriminatory practices, 15
Community Reinvestment Act and,
186, 197–198
Home Mortgage Disclosure Act
and, 185–186
Dividends, 49
Dorchester Bay Economic
Development Corporation
(DBEDC), 382–385
Doshna, Jeffrey, 303
Dual aspect concept of accounting,
41–42, 454
Duda, M., 197
Due diligence evaluation,
397–398, 417

defined, 454
fixed asset financing risk
management, 114
loan guarantees, 176
Dun & Bradstreet, 81

Economic Adjustment Assistance
Program, 333
Economic development,
defined, 5
Economic development, role of
finance in, 5–7
Economic Development
Administration (EDA), 182, 319,
331–334
Economic Adjustment Assistance
Program, 333
funding process, 333–334
local technical assistance
grants, 332
planning grants, 332
public works and economic
development programs, 333
Title IX Program, 220, 420
Economic development finance
capital. *See* Capital availability;
Capital sources
Economic development finance
practice, 3–4, 443–444
applied research agenda, 449
avoiding capital substitution, 7,
175, 178, 228, 366, 414
capital market imperfections and
funding gaps, 7, 15–17
capital market intervention
model, 7, 17–18
data sources, 269
economic development/community
development sector
collaboration, 448–449
firm development stages
and, 33–34
framework for expanding capital
availability, 17–18
recommendations, 446–448
role of banks, 184–185
ten principles for, 444–446
venture capital implications
for, 247–248

Economic development finance
    practice, management issues. *See*
    Capital management; Investment
    management
Economic development finance
    practitioners:
    generalist and
        institution-builder, 443
    necessary skills and
        knowledge, 3–4
    training and education of, 448
    See also Staff
Economic development financing
    programs, planning and design
    issues, 365–385
    accountability, 381–382
    avoiding capital substitution, 366
    business plan preparation, 380
    case study and assignment,
        382–385
    defining goals and targeting
        strategy, 367–370
    demand assessment, 370–372
    financial modeling, 377–378
    identifying relationships and
        partnerships, 379
    implementation needs and
        resources, 377–380
    institutional model selection,
        380–382
    market analysis, 365–366
    products and services, 382
    supply-side analysis, 372–377
    synthesizing demand and supply-
        side research, 375–376
    See also Financial modeling;
        Financial projection
Economic development goals, 5
    development financing planning
        issues, 365, 367–370
    framework for firm evaluation,
        60–63
    investment management issues, 394
    revolving loan fund performance
        standards, 224–227, 231
    venture capital's "double bottom
        line," 256, 257, 258, 259
Economic Development Initiative
    (EDI), 326–328

Economic development program
    growth. *See* Scale
    or growth issues
Economic Stabilization
    Trust, 232, 369
Educational services. *See* Technical
    assistance; Training and
    education
Employee-operated corporation,
    123–132
Empowerment Zone (EZ), 3, 239
Enterprise Communities (EC), 3, 239
Enterprise development stages, 33–34
Enterprise or project financial analysis.
    See Financial analysis
Entitlement grants, 324
Entrepreneur microenterprise
    programs. *See* Microenterprise
    finance
Environmental indemnification, 117
Equipment as collateral, 116
Equipment financing, 30, 111.
    See also Fixed asset financing
Equipment leasing, 118–120
Equity financing, 23, 24–27, 419–421
    advantages and
        disadvantages, 26–27
    bank CDCs as capital
        sources, 204–205
    case studies, 37–39
    company valuation, 25
    corporate stock, 24–25
    data on small business capital
        sources, 34–36
    debt-to-equity ratio, 66, 77–78
    definition, 24, 454
    development financing implications
        for, 412–413
    differences from debt, 27
    equity-debt hybrid financing, 33
    forms of returns for investors, 24
    governance rights and investment
        terms, 25–26
    public capital markets, 10–11
    terms and issues, 24–27
    transaction costs, 10–11
Equity investment, venture capital. *See*
    Venture capital funds
Exercise price, 166

Expenditure, 43
Expenses, 43
    accrued, 48
    costs versus, 59

Factoring, 98, 454
Fannie Mae, 423, 424
Federal Deposit Insurance Corporation
        (FDIC), 211, 373
Federal Fair Housing Act, 185
Federal Financial Institution
        Examination Council (FFIEC),
        187, 373
Federal Home Loan Bank, 416, 421
Federal Housing Authority (FHA), 106
Federal programs, 420
    case study, 334–339
    CDFI Fund, 328–331
    Community Economic
        Development Program, 334
    debt sources, 422
    Economic Development
        Administration, 331–334
    fixed asset financing, 121
    industrial development bonds
        (IDBs), 121
    predevelopment funding, 147
    real estate financing sources, 152
    revolving loan fund funding
        sources, 220
    Small Business Investment
        Corporations, 248–250
    uses, 319–320
    See also Loan guarantee programs;
        Small Business Administration;
        U.S. Department of Housing
        and Urban Development;
        specific agencies, programs
Federal Reserve Bank, 14
Fees. See Transaction costs
Finance fees, 139–140. See also
    Transaction costs
Financial analysis, 60–90
    assessing economic development
        benefits, 60–63
    balance sheet, 65–69
    business plan evaluation, 61, 63–64
    case study, 84–89
    cash flow statement, 65, 72–74

common size financial
        statement, 78–81
    contingent or unfunded
        liabilities, 82
    debt contract evaluation, 81–82
    framework for firm
        evaluation, 60–65
    income statement, 65, 69–72
    interest and principal payment
        requirements, 81–82
    ratio analysis, 74–81
    short-term liabilities, 88–89
    See also Ratio analysis
Financial institutions. See Banks; other
        specific institutions
Financial institutions, alternatives for
        expanding capital availability,
        18. See Community development
        financial institutions;
        Microenterprise finance;
        Revolving loan funds; Venture
        capital funds
Financial literacy education, credit
        union services, 284
Financial modeling, 377–378,
        427–433
    changing projection period, 432
    components, 427–430
    financial statement preparation,
        430–432
    key assumptions, 430
    key operating results, 430
    sensitivity analysis, 432
Financial planning, 377–378. See also
        Economic development financing
        programs, planning and design
        issues; Financial modeling
Financial policies, defined, 454
Financial projection, 65, 82–83
    defined, 454
    Phoenix Forge case study, 130
    ratio analysis, 81
    tax impacts, 83
    working capital loan
        underwriting, 103
Financial Reform, Recovery and
        Enforcement Act (FIRREA), 185
Financial statement, 41
    accrual accounting concepts, 41–44

capital gains and losses, 53
connecting balance sheet and
    income statement, 53–54
development budget, 138–141
financial models, 427–433
lease obligations, 119
loss reserves and, 418
operating pro forma, 138, 142–144
real estate projects, operating pro
    forma, 138, 142–144
uses of, 44, 58–59
See also Balance sheet; Cash flow
    statement; Income statement
Financial statement, analyzing, 60
balance sheets, 65–69
case study, 84–86
cash flow statement, 65, 72–74
income statement, 65, 69–72
See also Financial analysis; Ratio
    analysis
Financing, debt and equity. *See* Debt
    financing; Equity financing
Financing process, management of.
    See Investment management
Firm development stages, 33–34
First National Bank of Boston
    (FNBB), 346
Fisher, Peter, 253
Fixed asset financing, 111–132
balance sheet, 47
case study and assignment,
    123–132
corporate bonds, 115
debt instruments, 115–120
equipment leasing, 118–120
financing gaps, 122–123
financing sources, 120–123
implications for underwriters,
    113–114
industrial development
    bonds, 121
leasehold improvement loans,
    117–118
legal documents used in, 117
net present value analysis, 113
real estate mortgage loans,
    116–117
SBA 504 program, 323
term loans, 115–116

working capital finance
    versus, 112–114
See also Real estate finance
Fixed assets:
business operations and, 111
defined, 455
depreciation, 47
Fixed costs, break-even sales
    level and, 69–71
Fixed rate loans, 28, 116,
    148, 414, 415
FleetBoston Corporation, 202
Floating (variable rate)
    loans, 28, 116, 148, 415
Focus groups, 371, 375
Ford Foundation, 209
Forecasting. *See* Financial projection
Foreclosure, 116
Foundation grants, 209, 420.
    See also Grants
Freddie Mac, 423, 424
Fully amortizing loan, 29
Fund-raising, and capital management,
    412, 418–426. *See also* Capital
    availability; Capital management;
    Capital sources; *specific funding
    sources*

GE Capital, 424
General obligation (GO)
    bonds, 342, 455
General obligation pledge,
    175–176, 177
General partner, 39, 242, 243
Geographic information
    system (GIS), 367
Glossary, 451–459
Good Faith Fund, 296, 303
Goodwill, 47, 455
Governance rights, 25–26
Government Land Bank, 427
Government programs. *See* Federal
    programs; State and local
    government programs
Graham-Leach-Bliley Act, 185
Grameen Bank, 292, 293
Grants, 290, 419–420
community development bank
    capital sources, 209

EDA, 332–333
initial loan loss reserves, 418
predevelopment funding, 136
revolving loan funds and, 218,
  219–220, 230
small cities program, 324
See also Community Development
  Block Grant
Gross margin:
  break-even sales level, 69–71
  income statement, 51–52
  defined, 455
  percentage, 52, 74–75
Grzywinski, Ron, 205, 206
Guarantee programs. *See* Loan
  guarantee programs

Hansen, Pete, 172
Hawkins, David F., 41
Haynes, George, 168
Heard, R. G., 253, 254
Heartland Network, 266
Herd investing, 245, 247
Hinojosa, Sergio, 165
Hispanic business community,
  310–313
Historic preservation tax
  credit, 141, 146
Home loans. *See* Mortgage loans
Home Mortgage Disclosure Act
  (HMDA), 185–186, 455
Housing and Community
  Development Act of 1974, 324
Housing discrimination, 15, 185–186
Hunter, William, 169–170
Hybrid financing, 33

Income before interest
  and taxes (IBIT):
  cash flow statement, 56–57
  income statement, 50–51
Income statement, 44, 50–53
  cash flow statement and, 54, 55, 84
  common size financial statement,
    78–81
  connecting balance sheet, 53–54
  defined, 455
  estimated debt service coverage
    ratio, 71–72

financial model, 427, 429,
  430, 431
financial performance trends
  and, 72
firm evaluation insights, 65, 69–72
profitability information, 69–71
Income taxes payable, 48
Individual lending model, defined, 455
Industrial development bonds (IDBs),
  121, 342, 343–348
  allowable capital expenditures, 344
  case study, 346–348
  defined, 455
  mini-IDB programs, 345–346
Industrial Site Revolving Loan Fund
  (ISRLF), 406–410
Informal capital sources, 12
Information costs, 14, 17
Infrastructure development
  finance, 6
  assessment district financing,
    354–356
  EDA funding, 333
  municipal revenue bonds, 343
  tax-increment financing, 348–354
Initial public offerings (IPOs), 10,
  14–15, 241, 246–247, 262, 455
Inland Valley Development Agency
  (IVDA), 353–354
Inner city supermarket development,
  334–339
Institute for Social and Economic
  Development (ISED), 297
Insurance, mortgage, 31
Insurance companies, 12
  Community Reinvestment Act-type
    agreements, 200–201
  community reinvestment
    requirements, 185
  debt sources, 152, 422
  defined, 455
Interest and interest rates:
  accrued expenses, 48
  capital management issues,
    413–416, 422
  caps, 100, 415
  community development loan
    funds, 269
  construction loans, 148

definition and terminology, 28, 455
discounts for loan sales, 425
financial model, 430
fixed rate loans, 28, 116, 148,
    414, 415
HUD Section 108 program, 326
kickers, 416
market rate versus below-market
    rate pricing, 177–178, 237,
    414–415, 445
match funding, 415–416
mini-perm loans, 149
mortgage loans, 116, 148
predevelopment funding, 147
prime rate, 28, 148
revolving loan fund loans, 223, 237
SBA 7(a) loan guarantees, 167
state and local government
    subsidies, 341–342
step-ups, 123
term loans, 100
variable or floating rate loans, 28,
    100, 116, 148, 415
Interest only loan, 29
Internet stock boom (late 1990s),
    11, 241
Inventory:
    balance sheet, 47
    defined, 455
    financing or debt, 99–100, 455
    turnover, 76, 77, 88
Investment banks, 10–11
Investment fads, 11, 14–15, 241
Investment herding, 245, 247
Investment management,
    386–411
    accountability, 390–391, 445
    case study and assignment,
        406–410
    continuous improvement, 391
    investment process
        transparency, 389
    loan-servicing and monitoring, 387,
        402–406
    marketing, 386, 391–394 444
    policies and procedures, 387, 389
    project screening, 386, 394–396
    relationship building, 390,
        391, 392

responding to repayment problems,
    405–406
staffing, 389–390, 446
technical assistance, 395–396
understanding and managing risk,
    445–446
underwriting and commitment,
    386–387, 396–402
See also Capital management
Investment staging, 245–246
Investment turnover ratio, 75
IPOs. See Initial public offerings

Jacobs, Jane, 5
Job creation impacts:
    Community Development Block
        Grant program, 325
    community development loan
        funds, 271
    microenterprise programs, 301,
        302, 303
    revolving loan fund performance,
        224–226, 231
Just-in-time system, 128

Key informant interviews,
    371, 372, 375

Lawrence Working Capital, 310–313
Lease, defined, 118, 455
Leasehold improvement loans,
    117–118, 455
Leasing, 118–120
    advantages, 119–120
    disadvantages, 120
    operating and capital leases, 119
Legal fees, 139
Lending. See Debt financing
Letter of credit, defined, 455
Leverage, 26, 66
Li, Wenli, 165
Liabilities:
    balance sheet, 46, 47–49, 66–68
    cash flow analysis, 54, 57
    contingent or unfunded, 82
    debt defined as, 78
    debt-to-equity ratio, 66
    financial model, 431–432
    short-term, 88–89

Limited partnerships, 39, 241–242
Lines of credit, 95–97
    compensating balance, 96–97
    defined, 455
    transaction fees, 96
    working capital finance, 108
Liquidity, 92–93, 103
Lithgow Block, 153
Loan guarantee programs, 30–31,
        161–183, 444
    advantages and disadvantages,
            164–165
    approval process, 178
    avoiding capital
            substitution, 175, 178
    building lender participation, 177
    Capital Access Program, 161,
            172–174
    case study, 178–182
    defined, 455
    design and management issues,
            174–178
    due diligence, 176
    financing policies, 175
    fixed asset financing, 114, 122
    forms of security, 175–176
    government programs, 31
    guarantee forms, 162–163
    loss coverage, 162–163, 418
    market-rate fees, 177–178
    policy levers, 175–176
    SBA 7(a), 161, 166–170, 321–322
    small business working capital
            debt, 101–102
    state programs, 170–172
    targeting policy, 175
    underwriting criteria, 176
    valuing, 165–166
Loan management, third-party
        services, 423–424
Loan maturity, 28, 414, 416, 456
Loan note, 117
Loan packaging, 232, 456
Loan participation, 114, 456
Loan pricing policies. See Interest and
        interest rates
Loan sales, 424–425, 434–435, 447
Loan-servicing and monitoring, 387,
        402–406, 408–409

Loan-to-value ratio, 31–32, 456
Local capital market conditions,
        12–13, 15
Local government. See State and local
        government programs
Local Initiative Support Corporation
        (LISC), 152
Los Angeles Coalition for Women's
        Economic Development, 296
Loss management, 417–418
Loss reserves, 417–418
Low-income credit unions (LICUs),
        278. See also Credit unions
LowDoc program, 167, 168

Man, Joyce, 351
Management of capital. See Capital
        management
Management of investment.
        See Investment management
Manchester Citizens, 212
Manufacturers' Fund, 433–437
Manufacturing firms:
    fixed asset financing, case study,
            123–132
    industrial development bonds
            (IDBs), 121
Market imperfection, defined, 456.
        See also Capital market
        imperfections
Market research, 365–366,
        391–392, 444
    business plan evaluation, 63–64
    community development credit
            unions and, 288–289
    demand assessment, 370–372
    focus groups, 371
    key informant interviews, 371, 372
    Phoenix forge case study, 124–125
    supermarket case study, 336
    surveys, 370–371
Marketable securities, 46, 59
Marketing, 386, 391–394, 444
    identifying target
            audiences, 392, 394
    Industrial Site Revolving
            Loan Fund, 408
    microenterprise programs,
            307–308

relationship-building, 391, 392
revolving loan fund, 237
staff, 390
tools, 392, 393
venture capital services, 255
wholesale and retail
    approaches, 392
Markley, D. M., 253, 254
Massachusetts Capital Resource
    Company (MCRC), 200
Massachusetts Community Capital
    Fund, 324
Massachusetts Emerging Technology
    Fund, 178–182
Massachusetts Growth Fund, 369
    implementation needs, 379–380
    supply analysis, 376–377
Massachusetts Life Initiative, 422
Massachusetts Technology
    Development Corporation
    (MTDC), 251
MassDevelopment, 422
Match funding, 415–416
Matching concept
    of accounting, 42, 456
Maturity, 28, 414, 416, 456
Mellon Bank, 204
Merchant, Kenneth A., 41
Metzger, John T., 191
Microenterprise, defined, 456
Microenterprise finance, 18, 292–315
    applied research program, 449
    capital needs, 297–298, 306–307
    case studies and assignments,
        310–313, 382–385
    default rates, 227
    defined, 456
    economic development role,
        303–304
    individual lending models, 294–295
    industry characteristics, 297–298
    management challenges, 304–307
    marketing and outreach, 307–308
    operating costs, 298, 300
    peer group lending model,
        293–294, 311
    program outcomes, 301–303
    program performance, 299–301
    SBA programs, 323, 383, 422

    target clients, 304
    training-based programs, 292, 293,
        295–297, 306, 308–310
    welfare-to-work programs, 295
MicroTest, 299–300
Military base conversion
    development, 333
Mini-perm loan, 147, 149, 456
Minority-owned businesses:
    Capital Access Program loans, 173
    CDFI technical assistance program,
        330–331
    SBA 7(a) loan guarantees, 168
Minority Enterprise Small Business
    Investment Corporation
    (MESBIC), 249
Mission statement, 387
Modeling. See Financial modeling
Monitoring and servicing, 387,
    402–406
Mortgage and security agreement, 117
Mortgage insurance, 31
Mortgage loans, 30, 116–117, 147,
    148–149
    community development loan
        funds, 273
    Community Reinvestment Act,
        191–197, 213
    defined, 456
    foreclosure, 116
    Home Mortgage Disclosure Act
        (HMDA), 185–186
    interest rates, 28, 116, 148,
        414–415
    mini-perm loans, 149
    racial discrimination, 15
    SBA 504 and Certified
        Development
        Corporations, 323
    second or third mortgages, 149
    sources of, 151
    working capital finance, 102
Municipal finance, 6, 341–32
    assessment districts, 354–356
    business improvement districts,
        355, 356–358
    case study and assignment,
        358–361
    economic development uses, 343

overview, 341–342
transaction costs, 342–343
See also Bonds; State and local
    government programs;
    Tax-increment financing

National Community Capital (NCC),
    269, 421
National Community Reinvestment
    Coalition (NCRC), 189
National Credit Union Administration
    (NCUA), 277, 278, 279
NationsBank, 191
Native American technical assistance
    program, 330–331
The Neighborhood
    Institute (TNI), 206
Neighborhood Reinvestment
    Corporation, 423
Neighborhood Reinvestment
    Fund, 226
Net cash flow, 58
Net profit on sales ratio, 74–75
Net working capital, 68, 91, 456
New Boston Seafood Center,
    346–348
New Market Tax Credit program,
    320, 331, 420, 423, 456
North Carolina National Bank, 205
Northeast Entrepreneur
    Fund (NEF), 303
Norton Air Force Base, 353

Office of Community Services (OCS)
    Community Economic
    Development Program, 334
Office of the Comptroller of the
    Currency (OCC), 201–202, 211
Office of Thrift Supervision, 211
Operating cost escalator, 142
Operating lease, 119
Operating pro forma, 138, 142–144,
    155, 456. *See also* Cash flow
    statement
Operating profits, 52
Operating reserve, 140, 144
Option pricing theory, 166
Order of loss, 456
Orellana, Rosa, 311

Orlando Community Development
    Agency, 358–361
Ownership forms, 39

Par value, 49, 457
Partially amortizing loan, 29
Participation financing, 423–424
Partnerships, 39, 379
    CAPCO partnerships, 256
    credit unions, 283, 289
    general, 39, 242, 243
    limited, 39, 241–242
Peer-group lending model, 293–294,
    311, 457
Pennsylvania Economic Development
    Financing Authority (PEDFA)
    Composite Bond Program, 345
Pension funds:
    real estate financing, 152
    union management, 266
    venture capital investment, 243,
        253, 263
Personal banking and credit
    services, 280–285
Personal guarantee, defined, 457
Philadelphia Center City Business
    Improvement District, 357
Philadelphia Industrial Development
    Corporation, 425
Phoenix Forge, 123–132
    business plan, 124–129
    financial plan, 129–130
Pittsburgh Community Reinvestment
    Group (PCRG), 191–192, 212
Portable Practical Education Program
    (PPEP), 297
Portland Development Commission
    Industrial Site Revolving Loan
    Fund, 406–410
Predevelopment financing, 134–136,
    138, 147, 457
Preferred lenders, 167, 322
Preferred stock, 25, 457
Preleasing, 137
Prepaid expenses, 47, 457
Price Waterhouse, 169
Pricing policies. *See* Interest and
    interest rates
Prime rate, 28

Principal, defined, 28, 457
Private activity bond, 342, 457
Private capital markets, 11–15
    defined, 457
    minimum loan amounts, 14
Pro rata guarantee, 163
Profit and loss statement, 44, 50.
    See Income statement
Profitability:
    Community Reinvestment Act
        loans, 195–197
    income statement information,
        69–71
    ratio measures, 74–75
Program growth issues. *See* Scale or
    growth issues
Program planning and design. *See*
    Economic development
    financing programs, planning
    and design issues
Program-related investments
    (PRIs), 420, 457
Project proposal financial analysis.
    See Financial analysis
Projection. *See* Financial projection
Property, plant, and equipment, 47,
    111. *See also* Fixed assets
Property and Casualty Initiative (PCI),
    200–201
Property taxes, incremental revenue.
    See Tax-increment financing
Public capital markets, 9–11, 457.
    See also specific institutions
Put option, 166

Quality-of-life goals, 5
Quick ratio, 76

Racial discrimination, 15, 185
Ratio analysis, 74–81
    capital structure and debt capacity,
        77–78
    case study, 87–89
    common size financial statement,
        78–81
    current assets and liabilities
        (current ratio), 68
    data sources, 81
    days receivable, 68

debt-to-equity ratio, 66, 77–78
gross margin percentage, 74–75
loan-to-value ratio, 31–32
net profit on sales, 74–75
return on investment, 75
short-term liquidity, 76–77
See also Debt service coverage ratio
Real estate appraisal, 150
Real estate finance, 6, 111, 133–157
    bank CDCs as capital sources, 205
    bridge loan, 147, 149
    capital availability issues, 15,
        152–153
    capital sources, 151–152
    case study, 153–156
    cash flow risk evaluation, 150
    collateral appraisal, 150
    community development bank
        model, 207
    community development loan
        funds, 273
    construction and development
        phase, 136–137
    construction loan, 147, 148
    debt instruments, 146–151
    determining supportable debt and
        equity, 144–146
    development budget, 138–141,
        154–155
    development stages, 134–137
    development team capacity, 150
    finance process, 138
    financial statement, 138–146
    Lithgow Block, 153
    mini-perm loan, 147, 149
    occupancy and management
        phase, 137
    operating pro forma, 138,
        142–144, 155
    predevelopment, 134–136, 138,
        146–147
    tenant credit evaluation, 150
    underwriting issues, 149–151
    See also Fixed asset financing;
        Mortgage loans
Real estate investment trusts
    (REITs), 157
Real estate mortgage loans.
    See Mortgage loans

Realization concept
of accounting, 42, 457
Receipt, 43
Recourse loans, 33, 457
Recycling, Inc., 37
Redlining, 186
Regional capital market
conditions, 12–13, 15
Rehab CD and Development
Deposits, 421
Rehabilitation projects, 137, 141
Relationship building, 233–234, 390,
391, 392
Rental income, real estate cash
flow budget, 142
Rented building improvements,
leasehold improvement
loans for, 117
Replacement cost, 151
Replacement reserve, 144
Retail marketing, 392
Retained earnings, 49, 52–53, 58, 457
Return on assets ratio, 75
Return on equity ratio, 75
Return on investment, ratio
measures, 74–75
Revenue, 43
Revenue bonds, 342, 457
Revolving loan funds (RLFs), 18,
217–239
capital policies, 227, 230
capital sources, 237
capital substitution avoidance, 228
community development loan
funds, 268
debt sources, 218, 219–220
default rates, 225, 226–227
defined, 217, 457
design issues, 227–232
economic development performance
measures, 224–227, 231
federal capital sources, 320
financial policies, 227, 228–229
funding sources, 230
grants and, 230
Industrial Site Revolving Loan
Fund, 406–410
interest rates, 223, 237
limitations, 219

management challenges, 235–236
marketing, 237
microloan funds, 227
relationship policies, 227, 233–234
scale issues, 236
staff and board members, 236–237
studies and comparative data,
221–224
targeting policies, 227–228
technical assistance services, 223,
227, 231–232
underwriting issues, 227, 230–231,
234, 237
working capital finance, 102
Risk analysis, 406. *See also* Financial
analysis
Risk-sharing tools and policies, 17.
See also Loan guarantee
programs
RiteCheck, 283
Robert Morris Associates, 81
Rodriguez, Mildred, 311
Rubin, J. S., 253, 254
Rural Development
Administration, 420
Rural economic development
capital availability, 13
community development bank
investment, 209
Rural Economic Development
Program, 422

St. Luke Credit Union, 286
Sales forecasting. *See* Financial
projection
Sales to inventory ratio, 88
Sanchez, Leonora, 311
Savings banks, working capital
sources, 101
Scale or growth issues:
community development credit
unions, 285–286, 287
community development loan
funds, 268, 273–276
Community Development Venture
Capital, 256–259
impact of capital sources, 413
revolving loan funds, 236
Schwartz, Alex, 192

SCORE, 321
Seasonal working capital, 94
SECA, 330
Section 108 program, 326, 458
Secured line of credit, 96
Securities brokers or
    dealers, 10
Securitization, 425–426, 435, 458
Security agreement, 117
Security Pacific Bank, 204
Security position, 458
Self-Employment Learning Project
    (SELP), 301, 304
Self-Help Credit Union, 278, 282,
    286, 289, 420
Self-Help Venture Fund, 237, 286
Selling, general, and administrative
    costs (SGA expense), 52,
    70–71, 458
Senior lenders, 30, 458
Service Corps of Retired Executives
    (SCORE), 321
Servicing and monitoring, 387,
    402–406
Servon, Lisa, 303
Shapero, Albert, 5
Shareholder's equity, 46,
    49–50, 53
    return on equity ratio, 75
ShoreBank, 185, 205–211, 421
    subsidiary structure, 205–206
Short-term liquidity, 88–89, 94
    credit union sources, 284
    ratio measures, 76–77
    Working capital finance
Sibert, J., 253, 254
Silicon Valley Community Ventures
    (SVCV), 259, 263
Small and Emerging CDFI Assistance
    (SECA) program, 330
Small Business
    Administration (SBA), 319
    capital supply analysis, 373
    debenture, 121, 323, 412
    microloan program, 323, 383, 422
    preferred and certified
        lenders, 167, 322
    SBA 504 program, 121, 122, 320,
        323, 383, 423, 458

SBA 7(a) loan guarantee program,
    101–102, 161, 167–170,
    321–322, 458
service delivery mechanisms, 321
Small Business Investment
    Corporations (SBICs),
    248–250, 412, 458
Special Small Business
    Investment Corporation
    (SSBIC), 412, 458
Surety Bond Guarantee
    Program, 322
Small business finance:
    bank CDCs as capital sources, 204
    capital availability problems, 15
    community development bank
        investment, 207
    CRA definitions, 213
    credit union sources, 285–287
    data on capital sources, 34–36
    information costs, 14
    short-term debt reliance, 94
    working capital sources, 101–102
    See also Microenterprise finance;
        specific financing programs or
        resources
Small Business Investment
    Corporations (SBICs), 248–250,
    412, 458
Small cities grants, 324
Sole proprietorship, 39
South Shore Bank, 205
Southern Development
    Bancorporation (SDC), 209
Special Small Business Investment
    Corporation (SSBIC),
    249–250, 458
Staff, 389–390, 446
    Community Development Venture
        Capital program, 258
    education and training, 448
    revolving loan fund personnel,
        236–237
    venture capital operational
        challenges, 261
State and local government
    programs, 3
    assessment district
        financing, 354–356

bond guarantee programs, 345
business improvement districts,
        355, 356–358
Capital Access Program, 172–174
case studies, 346–348, 358–361
CRA initiatives, 212
economic development uses, 343
Emerging Technology Fund,
        178–182
grants, 420
industrial development
        bonds, 343–348
interest rate subsidy, 341–342
loan guarantee programs, 170–174
real estate financing sources, 152
tax-increment financing, 348–354
transaction costs, 342–343
venture capital policy, 250–256
See also Bonds; Revolving loan
        funds; Tax incentives;
        Tax-increment financing
Stock market, 10
venture capital funds and, 241
Stock ownership, 24–25
par value, 49
See also Equity financing
Stockholder governance rights, 25–26
Subordinate debt, 30, 146, 458
bank CDCs as capital sources, 204
certified development
        corporations, 423
growth fund loan product, 377
Manufacturers' Fund, 433
mortgage loans, 148
revolving loan funds, 228, 237
SBA 504 program, 121, 122
See also Debt financing;
        specific types
Supermarket development case
        study, 334–339
Supply-side analysis, 372–377, 391
secondary data sources (table), 374
See also Capital management;
        Financial analysis
Surety Bond Guarantee Program, 322
Survey analysis, 370–371

Talking Systems, 37–38
Tax incentives, 341–342

bonds, 342–348
historic preservation, 141, 146
New Market program, 320, 331,
        420, 423, 456
venture capital
        investment, 253, 256
See also Bonds
Tax-increment financing, 348–354,
        458, 444, 458
case study, 358–361
debt financing issues,
        352–354
economic development uses,
        351–352
financing process, 349–350
Inland Valley Development
        Agency, 353–354
"pay as you go" financing,
        348–349
Tax liabilities, balance
        sheet, 48
Technical assistance, 445
best practices, 309–310
Economic Development
        Administration grants,
        331–334
Empowerment Zone/Enterprise
        Community (EZ/EC)
        Program, 239
investment management and,
        395–396
marketing loan guarantee
        programs, 177
microenterprise programs, 292,
        293, 295–297, 306, 309–310
Native American CDFI program,
        330–331
revolving loan fund services, 223,
        227, 231–232
SCORE, 321
See also Training and education
Technology sector:
Emerging Technology Fund,
        178–182
financial statement case study
        (fictional company), 45–53
venture capital management
        issues, 261
Term loans, 100–101, 115–116, 458

Thrift institutions, 12, 458
  fixed asset lending, 120
  real estate financing, 151–152
Times interest earned ratio, 78
Title IX Program, 220, 420
Town Market, 38–39
Trade credit, 32, 33, 101
  data on small business capital
    sources, 35
Training and education, 445
  costs, 298, 300
  credit union services, 284
  economic development financing
    practitioners, 448
  Lawrence Working Capital
    program, 311
  microenterprise programs, 292,
    293, 295–297, 306,
    308–309, 459
  revolving loan fund
    services, 232
  See also Technical assistance
Training-led microenterprise program
    model, 292, 293, 295–297, 306,
    308–310, 459
Transaction costs:
  capital market imperfections, 13
  capital market intervention
    model, 17
  lines of credit, 96
  loss protection, 418
  municipal debt, 342–343
  public capital market
    transactions, 10–11
  real estate development
    budget, 139–140
Travelers Insurance, 191
Troy, Leo, 81

Udell, Gregory F., 34
Underwriting issues:
  closing facilitation, 402
  criteria for loan guarantees, 176
  decision-making process
    structuring, 399–402
  due diligence evaluation, 397–398
  fixed asset financing, 114
  Industrial Site Revolving Loan
    Fund, 408

investment management issues,
    386–387, 396–402
  personal judgments, 399
  real estate finance, 149–151
  revolving loan fund loans, 227,
    230–231, 234, 237
  standards, 396–397, 459
  working capital finance, 102–103
Union-managed pension funds, 266
Union National Bank (UNB), 191
U.S. Department of Agriculture
    (USDA):
  revolving loan fund, 220
  Rural Economic Development
    Program, 422
U.S. Department of Health and
    Human Services (HHS), 319, 334
U.S. Department of Housing and
    Urban Development (HUD), 319,
    324–328
  Community Development Block
    Grant (CDBG), 220, 221,
    324–326, 334–339, 420, 453
  Economic Development Initiative,
    326–328
  Empowerment Zones/Enterprise
    Communities
    programs, 3, 239
  Section 108 program, 326, 458
U.S. Economic Development
    Administration (EDA). *See*
    Economic Development
    Administration
U.S. Small Business Administration
    (SBA). *See* Small Business
    Administration
U.S. Treasury Community
    Development Finance Institution
    (CDFI) Fund, 290, 319,
    328–331, 453

Variable rate loans, 28, 116, 148, 415
Venture capital funds, 12, 18,
    240–248, 419
  capitalization challenges, 263
  coinvestment and syndication, 246
  Community Development
    Venture Capital (CDVC),
    256–259, 453

data on small business capital sources, 35
defined, 459
development finance implications, 247–248
entrepreneur support services, 261
exiting investments, 246–247
fundraising, 242–243
growth trend, 241
incentive compensation, 243
independent firms, 241
investment, 243–246
investment exiting, 258–259, 262
investment fads, 14–15
IPOs and, 241, 246–247, 262
limited partnerships, 241–242
marketing and development services, 255
monitoring, 246
operating challenges, 261–263
pension fund investment, 243, 253
preferred stock, 25
public and community oversight, 262
regional capital availability differences, 12–13
Small Business Investment Corporations (SBICs), 248–250
social investment goals, 256, 257, 258, 259
Special SBIC (SSBIC) program, 249–250
staff needs, 258, 261
state policy, 250–256
stock market and, 241
strategy challenges, 260–261
subsidiary corporations, 242
tax incentives, 253, 256

technology development, 261
working capital sources, 101
See also Community Development Venture Capital
Vermont Development Credit Union (VDCU), 278, 284–285, 288–289, 413

Warrant, defined, 459
Wholesale marketing, 392
Women-owned businesses:
    Capital Access Program loans, 173
    SBA 7(a) loan guarantees, 168
Women's Initiative for Self-Employment, 303
Working capital finance, 91–110
    accounts receivable financing, 97–98
    business growth and, 93
    business uses, 92–93
    case study and assignment, 103–110
    factoring (third party collection), 98
    fixed asset finance versus, 112–114
    inventory financing, 99–100
    lines of credit, 95–97, 108
    permanent investment. 94
    providing liquidity, 92–93
    SBA 7(a) loan guarantees, 101–102
    seasonal or cyclical financing, 92, 94
    sources for small businesses, 101–102
    term loan, 100–101
    terms and definitions, 91–92
    underwriting issues, 102–103

Youngstown, Ohio, 123

About the Author

Karl F. Seidman is Senior Lecturer at MIT's Department of Urban Studies and Planning and an experienced economic development practitioner. His MIT courses have completed over 40 technical assistance projects for development finance organizations and prepared 12 economic development plans, including award-winning revitalization plans for Boston's Hyde Park and Egleston Square commercial districts. His professional experience includes the design, management, and evaluation of economic development finance programs, the financing and supervision of complex development projects, and the preparation of economic development plans and strategies. Mr. Seidman's accomplishments include

- Authoring laws that established two Massachusetts business finance agencies
- Building a $120 million state real estate finance and development authority
- Preparing over 15 local and regional economic development plans
- Participating in national evaluations of federal and foundation economic and community development programs

Mr. Seidman holds a master's degree in public policy from Harvard's Kennedy School of Government and a bachelor's degree in political science from Amherst College. He is the author of over 35 consulting reports, articles in professional journals, and a guide to urban commercial revitalization practice as well as the editor of a practitioner's guide to defense conversion.